This was a scene on March 14, 1942 with families and well wishers on hand to witness the departure of loved ones called to serve their country in World War II. Those standing by the bus and preparing to leave are: Alfred Gallaher, Harris Fielder, Farris Crowe, Eugene Cole, Russ Brewer, Ernest Devasure, Clint Rippy, Paul Moore, Paul Adkins, Ananias Lay, Taylor Brown, Herman Harris, Obie Lee Mathis, Ted Wilson, Emmett Skelton, Grady Wright, W.B. Miller, Jr., Reuben Odle, Jay Morris, and Malcolm Devers. Spectators seen in the lower part of the picture are: T.J. Old, Fred Moore, Martin Lawson, Charlie Norman, Joe Shaw, Ethridge Dugger, Jim Kelly, Roy Morris, Sr., Mitchell Edwards, Eldridge Kelley, Walter Helton and others.

WORLD WAR II
VETERANS

WAYNE COUNTY, TENNESSEE

TURNER PUBLISHNG COMPANY
Paducah, Kentucky

TURNER PUBLISHING COMPANY
412 Broadway • P.O. Box 3101
Paducah, KY 42002-3101
(270) 443-0121

Copyright © 2001 Wayne County, TN Historical Society.
Publishing Rights: Turner Publishing Company.

Designer/Coordinator: Herbert C. Banks II

Library of Congress Control Number: 00-110586
ISBN: 1-56311-621-9

Additional copies may be purchased directly from the
Wayne County, TN Historical Society
P.O. Box 866
Waynesboro, TN 38485

Crew members of the 330th Bomb Squadron in England.

TABLE OF CONTENTS

INTRODUCTION

We are able to say at last, "It is finished." To see Wayne County's World War II records culminate into this valuable volume is to have a long awaited dream become a reality.

It was at the Wayne County Historical Society's Annual Homecoming on Sunday, December 1, 1991, that the idea was formed to publish this material. The program was in honor of Veterans of World War II's 50th Anniversary and decendants of War Between The States veterans.

There was a great number of World War II's Veterans attending. Five Pearl Harbour Survivors were there. Two of the veterans came in original uniforms, one Navy and one Army. Period Dress of the War Between the States era was worn. The veterans had previously been asked to bring a story or short biography about themselves. Many responded to this call. A display table was soon filled with all sorts of memorabilia along with personal biographies. The information helped to make this book possible and we are most appreciative for this good response.

With drifting music of the Glenn Miller Band the reception furnished the opportunity to meet, mingle and reminisce with old comrades bonded in friendship with memories held deep in the heart, some to share with others, and some locked tightly to share no more. It was truly their day of honor.

A list of over 1,400 veterans was formed using the following sources: Wayne County's Service Officer, James Grady McGee's list furnished by Tennessee Library and Archives, a list by Carlton Estes, found in the Wayne County Public Library, Wayne County Registrar of Deeds, Ruth Butler and her staff photocopied all registered discharges, The Wayne County News, names supplied by Veterans, friends, and families, American Legion, V.F.W. Community Programs, Picture album belonging to Ernest and Ruth Bevis. After the list was completed, each name was put into alphabetical order. Calls and interviews were made to obtain stories and biographies. We wanted desperately to have information on each veteran before trying to finish or lay the work down, however no information was found in many cases.

We regret that some veterans will have no information listed, but felt it was time to complete the work. Many veterans who enthusiastically responded have since died. This has been deeply felt, and more than ever we realized we must push forward with the information at hand, and finish the book.

Errors may inadvertently appear, for which we take responsibility. Things ommitted, things reported to us in error.

We would like to see a copy of this book placed in the home of each of our veterans. They are so deserving of a printed copy of this generous heritage that belongs to them.

Imogene Rasbury Parsley has had a keen interest in helping the county in placing its pieces together in genealogy for many years. Likewise she has shared our interest in getting World War II completed. She volunteered to computerize the finished pages at her home in Knoxville Tennessee. This has been a major step in finalizing work for the publisher. We are indeed grateful for her many hours of work and dedication.

Edgar D. Byler III, expressed so well feelings shared by all of us in his notable speech given on Homecoming Day December 1, 1991, entitled "A Tribute to the Veterans of World War II" we quote:

Today we pay homage to those men and women who valiantly fought for freedom and their own way of life. Those men and women who left the hills and hollows of Wayne County, Tennessee for places in far off lands, with names that most could not at first pronounce, but which would be forever etched in their memories. The men and women of Wayne County represented their home in each and every battle of the war; from the North Africa campaign to Anzio Beach, from Normandy to the Baffle of the Bulge, along the countless small islands of the South Pacific, and on the waves of the ocean itself, in the Battle of Midway, and the Battle of the Coral Sea, in the Gilbert Islands, the Marshall Islands, Iwo Jimo, Okinawa, in France, Italy, and finally Germany itself. They and their comrades in arms marched, crawled, and pushed always onward, always forward, never failing in their resolve to finish the fight and destroy that which had sought so viciously to destroy them.

We are here today because of that valiant effort. Their victory has been celebrated joyously then and through the forty-six years since the final end to the war, with Japan's unconditional surrender on 2 September, 1945. Let us never forget them and their courage and determination. Let us never forget that we are here today to celebrate their accomplishment and their memory, because they stayed the course and emerged victorious. And let us never forget those who did not return. They are the ones who paid the supreme sacrifice for the freedom of their fellow countrymen. May the memory of their sacrifice never fade. Let us never forget!" (End quote)

Project Directors:

Ermadine Turnbo Riley   Rita Edwards Duncan

SPECIAL ACKNOWLEDGMENTS

Ermadine Turnbo Riley

Imogene Rasbury Parsley

Rita Edwards Duncan

This book is dedicated to the men and women of Wayne County, TN, who served their country in World War II and it is a small token of our appreciation, our gratitude and our thanks for their sacrifices and suffering. No "thank you" can ever be enough.

The Project directors for the volume were Rita Edwards Duncan and Ermadine Tumbo Riley. They have worked on the project since 1993 collecting the hundreds of biographies included in this book. Many time they only had the original discharge papers to construct a biography. Their tireless efforts included contacting the many veteran's families to obtain information. No ready list of veterans from ANY war are available to the public. Therefore, Rita and rmadine had to seek out as many veterans as they could by whatever means available to them. Imogene Rasbury Parsley provided the very necessary typing of the articles and committing them to computer disk for the publisher. Katherine Rasbury Fancher did the tedious job of proof reading the articles.

Thanks are also in order for Frances Smith and Mary Katherine Mathis for their invaluable help in gathering the last several articles and assisting in the construction of this publication. Paula "Sunny" Barnhart and Phyllis Rich provided very necessary proof reading. Bob Rains assisted in the project by staying in touch with the publisher and various other jobs. We would like to express our thanks and appreciation to the veterans and their families for submitting the articles. They will help us to remember that war is not just dates and places, but people!

The Wayne County Historical Society is proud to add their thanks to these dedicated preservers of history for a work well done.

WAYNE COUNTY RESIDENT IS FIRST INDIVIDUAL IN NATION SELECTED FOR DRAFT NOTICE DURING PEACETIME

Turner Smith

President Franklin D. Roosevelt instituted the Selective Service System in 1940. On September 29 of that year the first lottery of the first draft ever held in the United States during peacetime took place. Individuals drafted would serve a year's military service under conscription. Roosevelt's Secretary of War, Henry L. Stimson, drew the first number and strange as it may appear it belonged to Wayne County resident Turner Smith of Cypress Inn. At that time Mr. Smith was age 28, had been married for almost three years and was living with his family in the Cypress Inn Community. Mr. Smith passed away on September 29, 1969, (the 29th anniversary of his draft selection) at the age of 57 years of age. His widow, the former Hattie Pigg, continues to live at Cypress Inn near their three children, Elzo, Imogene and Carvil Smith.

In an interview with the family to gather information for this article Mr. Smith's daughter Imogene stated that she remembers as a child hearing her dad talk about his draft notice and the trip to be examined. He had to travel by bus from Waynesboro to the induction center at Fort Oglethorpe, Georgia for the physical examination. The trip took several days. Imogene said that she was totally unaware that her dad was the first person in the nation to receive a draft notice.

Other individuals from Wayne County who were drafted along with Mr. Smith included William Frank Martin also from Cypress Inn. Clyde Odie Pevahouse, Clifton; Pugh Henson, Cypress Inn; Dumont Hanback, Cypress Inn; James Pleas Vines, Iron City; John Richard Berry, Cypress Inn; George Donald Jones, Waynesboro; Osbie Lee Stooksberry, Cypress Inn; Clifford Irley Shepard, Cypress Inn; Gordon Jenkins, Waynesboro; Willie Raymon Sims, Waynesboro; Floyd G. Pigg, Lutts; James Bartley Craig, Cypress Inn; Emory Lopp, Waynesboro; Willie Oscar Bums, Cypress Inn; Alfred Isaac Anderson, Clifton; James Hershell Patterson, Lutts; Guilford Warrington Berry, Cypress Inn; Clarence Edward Heard, Cypress Inn; Daniel Richard Harris, Waynesboro; Roy Howard Brewer, Collinwood; Floyd Walter Gallaher, Waynesboro; Arlie Warren Holt, Cypress Inn; Bert Walker, Waynesboro; Russ Maxwell Turman, Waynesboro; Roy Harvel Long, Waynesboro; Edward McDonald, Clifton; John Monroe Goode, Lutts; William Cranston Moore, Waynesboro; Henry Allen Pevahouse, Clifton; Bannie Long, Waynesboro; Nicholas Beaumont Warren, Clifton; Clyde H. Brown, Lutts; and Joe Weeks, Cypress Inn.

The above listed names were among the first one thousand numbers drawn at Washington.

Article submitted by J. Allen Berry, 1598 Big Cypress Road, Cypress Inn, Tennessee

THE HISTORY OF A U.S. NAVAL SHIP
USS *ROBERT BRAZIER*

Robert Boyd Brazier, born at Tooele, Utah, 13 June 1916 enlisted in the Navy 6 October 1939 and served continuously until killed in action during the Battle of Midway, 4 June 1942. Gunner of a Torpedo- Squadron-3 airplane during that battle, Aviation Radioman Second Class Brazier "defended his plane by continuous gunfire against overwhelming fighter opposition until mortally wounded. "After reporting his condition, he courageously performed essential radio operations which enabled the pilot to return to his own force. For his actions, Aviation Radioman Brazier was awarded, posthumously, the Distinguished Flying Cross.

(DE-345: dp. 1745; l. 306"; b. 36'7"; dr. 13'4"; s. 24 k.; cpl. 217, a. 25"; 4 40mm., 10 20mm., 2 dct., 8 dcp., 1 dcp. (hh.), 3 21" tt.; cl. John C. Butler)

Robert Brazier (DE-345) was laid down 16 November 1943 by the Consolidated Steel Corp., Ltd., Orange, Tex.; launched 22 January 1944, sponsored by Mrs. Celia Brazier, mother of Aviation Radioman Brazier, and commissioned 18 May 1944, Lt. Comdr. Donald D. Snyder, Jr., USNR, in command.

Following shakedown off Bermuda, Robert Brazier arrived at New York, 19 August 1944, and the next day commenced escort work with a convoy run to Norfolk. There for a week, she served as a schoolship for the Destroyer Training School, conducted tests for the Bureau of Ordnance, and assumed duties as flagship, Cort Div 76 which she kept throughout World War II. Between 27 August and 7 September, she participated in a hunt for a German submarine reported off the coast Later that month, she joined TF 69 to escort a fast convoy of tankers and transports to Italy. Completing that run at New York 23 October, she sailed again 10 November, heading south, then west

Forty-one days later she anchored in Seeadler Harbor, Manus. On 26 December she sailed for Hollandia, whence she escorted tankers to Leyte, arriving 6 January 1945. Continuing escort duty, she plied the sealanes between Leyte, Kossol Roads, and Hollandia until 19 February when she sailed for Mindoro and duty with the local defense force there. For the next 2 weeks she patrolled the approaches to Mangarin Bay and the convoy lanes to Subic Bay. Then, on 6 March, the destroyer resumed duties as an ocean escort.

Assigned to the 7th Amphibious Force in late April, Robert Brazier departed Leyte for Panay on the 29th and remained at Iloilo until 4 May. Then ordered back to Leyte, she prepared for the invasion of Mindanao. On the 10th, she screened to the seaward of the landing forces in Maeajalar Bay. From the 11th through the 13th, she patrolled in the Bay. On the 14th, she departed Mindanao for Cebu, whence she escorted supply ships back to the beachhead and from then, with few interruptions, she remained anchored in Maeajalar Bay until 9 August. Six days later, at Subic Bay, she received news of the Japanese acceptance of surrender terms.

For the remainder of August and into September, she escorted ships between Subic Bay and Okinawa. Then, toward the end of the month, the destroyer extended her escort duty to Tokyo Bay. There on the 21st and 22nd, she returned to Luzon on the 27th and for the next month operated in Philippine waters. On 28 November she got underway for the United States, arriving at San Pedro, Calif., 17 December Later shifted to San Diego, she joined the 19th Fleet and commenced inactivation. Decommissioned 16 September 1946, she remained in the Pacific Reserve Fleet, berthed initially at San Diego, then at Bremerton, until struck from the Navy list, 1 January 1968. She was subsequently destroyed as a target

Robert Brazier (DE-345) earned one battle star during World War II.

WAYNE COUNTY, TENNESSEE
CASUALITIES

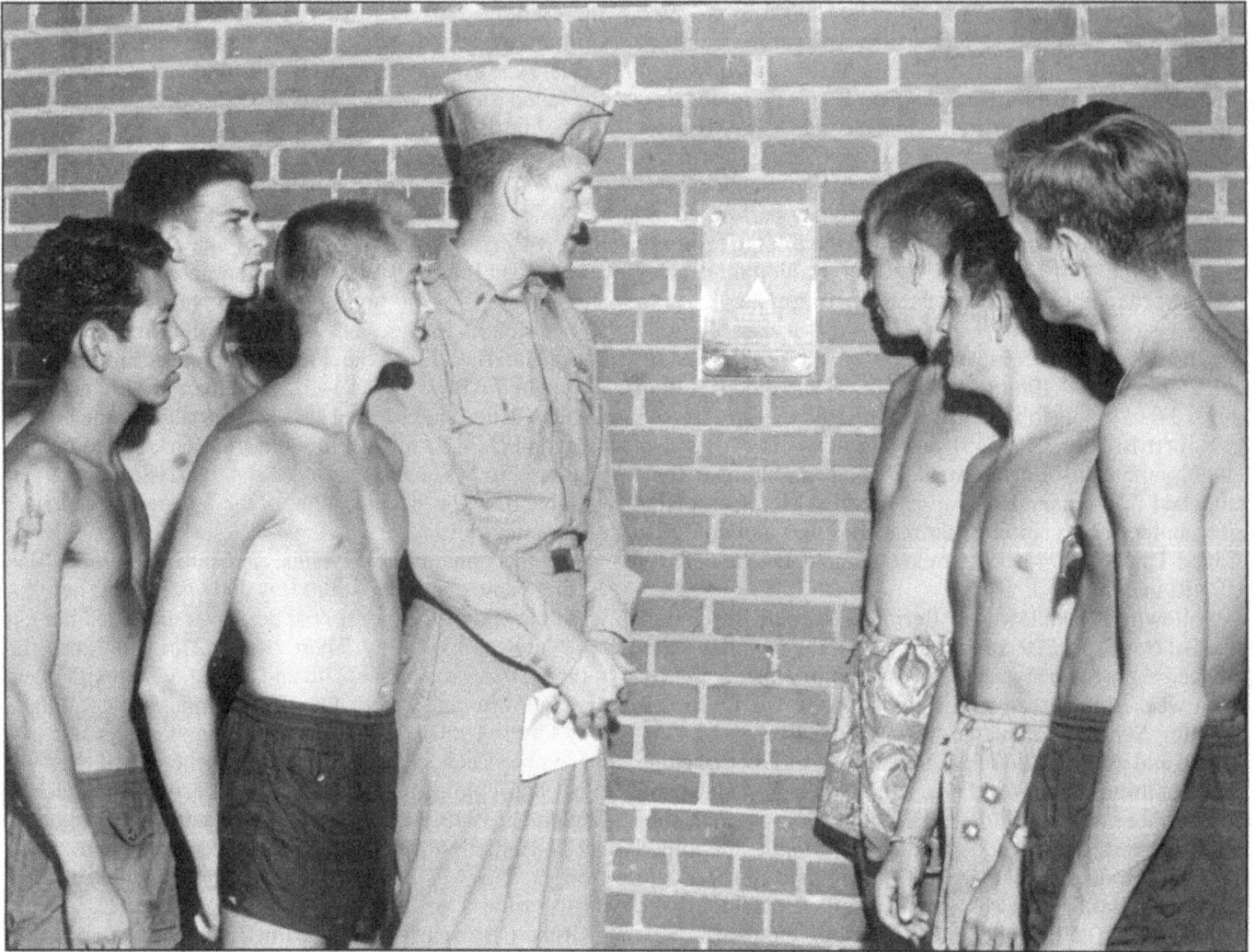

Fort Knox, KY - 1st Lt. Duryea Wilkinson, athletic officer of The Armored School, is shown with six of the lifeguards at Davis Pool here after he installed a plaque dedicating the pool in memory of Tec. 5 Jessie V. Davis, RFD 3, Waynesboro, TN. who was killed in World War II. (US Army photo)

ADAMS, HOMER FARRIS, was killed in Action in France, 4 December 1944 - Serial Number 34 986 995, was a

Private in the Infantry of the Army of the United States. He was inducted into service in the spring 1944 and served in the European Theater Operations. His home address was Route 1, Clifton, Tennessee. He was the son of Dock and Ollie Julian Adams. His siblings were Elsie Adams Kiddy and Lonnie Adams. He married Elvie Prater, daughter of William and Lou Griffin Prater. Their three children are, Marylin Joyce, Millard Leon and Dewey Adams. Source: World War II Honor List of Dead and Missing June 1946

ALLEY, OLIVER EARL, JR., was killed in Action in Germany 10 April 1945. He was inducted into service in October

1943 and received his basic training in Fort Eustis, Virginia. Then, he went to Camp Cook, California and in December 1944 was sent to served in the European Theater Operations. His body was shipped to Clifton in the summer of 1947 for burial in the Clifton Cemetery as PFC Alley, 385th Infantry, 76th Division in the Army of the United States Earl, Jr., son of Oliver Earl and Myrtle Moore Alley, was born 12

May 1925 near Clifton. His siblings were J. W., Charles and Sue Alley, Katherine Pleasant, Margaret Wheat, and Mary Ann Riddell. He attended school at Frank Hughes in Clifton.

BOYD, ALVIN WAYNE, was killed in Action or died in Germany December 1944. He was a Private with the 414th In-

fantry, 104th Division in the Army of the United States. Alvin, son of Thomas Jefferson and Emma C. Ray Boyd, was born November 1913. His brothers are: Clinton, Roscoe, and Willard Boyd. His sisters are: Clara McDonald, Mary Turnbo, Verna Conway and Genna Bruce. He married Monetta Hill and their children are: Joe Wayne, Gerald, Jerri Nell and Janice Boyd.

BOYD, WILLARD, died and was buried close to a military camp in Georgia. He volunteered for service in the Army of

the United States. Willard was the son of Thomas Jefferson and Emma C. Ray Boyd. His brothers are: Clinton, Roscoe, and Alvin Wayne Boyd. His sisters are: Clara McDonald, Mary Turnbo, Verna Conway and Genna Bruce. He married and had one daughter.

BUNCH, ROBERT "BOB" LEE, He was wounded 9 September 1944 in Nancy, France. He was placed in a hospital and

died from an infection on 19 September 1944. He was buried sometime later in 1945 in the Prater Cemetery. He was a Private First Class in the 318th Infantry, 80th Division in the Army of the United States. Bob's father, John William Bunch was born in 1890 and his mother, Nancy Catherine Inman Bunch, was born in 1893, both in Perry County. Bob was born 7 July 1919 in Perry County, Tennessee. His brothers are Carnie M, Barney, Hollie Earl and Roland Bunch. His sisters are Ida Mae McWilliams, Alma Lou Giles and Mildred Berry.

CARTER, HARVEL C., was killed in action 29 March 1945 and was permanently laid to rest in the U.S. Military Cem-

etery in St. Avold , France, plot J- row 21 grave 7, headstone is a cross. He attended school in Wayne County and worked at various jobs before volunteering for service in the Army of the United States in 1940. He was stationed at Fort Oglethorpe, Georgia, Fort Jackson, South Carolina, then to Ireland before going to Germany. There, he was with the 28th Cavalry, Troop

C, RCN Squadron (MECZ) with the Third Army under the command of General Patton. While with the 28th Cavalry and the sixth Cavalry unit, he was killed in action. He was awarded the Purple heart. He was a Technician Fifth Grade with serial number was 7 008 595. Harvel, son of Henry Clay and Susan Nutt Carter, was born 12 November 1916 in Wayne County. His siblings are Nell Martin, Marjorie Watson, Mattie Lou Purdue, Joyce Flowers, Melba Clay and Leonard Carter. He married Aileen Martin.

COLLINS, MARVIN B., was a Staff Sergeant in 358th Bomb Squadron in the Army Air Force of the United States. He

enlisted 18 January 1943 and was killed in action in England 22 February 1944. They were going on a mission in foggy weather and two planes collided. All but the tail-gunner was killed on Marvin's plane. A total of nineteen men were killed from both planes. Marvin, son of John A. and Nora Coffman Collins, was born 11 November 1922 and was buried in Anderson Bunch Cemetery on Cedar Creek in Perry County. He has a government marker. His siblings were: Sid, Hollis, Loyd Carlton, Eula and Mildred Moore.

CONAWAY, W.H., Staff Sergeant Conaway enlisted December 1942 and served his country in 184th Infantry, 7th Division in the Army of the United States. He took his basic training in California and then was sent to the Aleutian Islands in the early part of 1943, where he was wounded and received a Purple Heart. He also fought in the Marshall Islands, the Philippines and was killed in Okinawa 25 May 1945. He was buried temporarily at Okinawa and later returned to the Mt. Carmel Cemetery in Hardin County, near Clifton to be laid to his final rest on home grounds in March 1949. W.H.'s mother received a letter from one of his buddies saying that W.H. was in the hospital at the time of his death. He

also told her that W.H. was like a brother to him, and that he was a brave soldier and fought a good fight. He visited W.H.'s grave too, according to Ora Belle Graham. W. H., son of Turner and Martha Julian Conaway, was born 7 August 1922. He was one of eleven children. His three sisters are: Anna Conaway, Fleeta Foster, and Ora Belle Graham. His seven brothers are: Willie, Richard, Oscar, Barney, Harlie, Marvin D.C. and Elmer Cleo Conaway. The following letter and picture was sent to Mrs. Conaway. HEADQUARTERS SEVENTH INFANTRY DIVISION Office of the Commanding General APO 7, % Postmaster, San Francisco, California. 11 January 1946 Dear Friend, Knowing how bereaved you have been over the loss of your love one, I hesitate to reawaken your sorrow. However, feeling that you may wish a picture of the Seventh Division Cemetery in Okinawa, I am sending this to show you where the last rites were held. As a parent myself, may I say I have some understanding of your sorrow, although I realize your own deep sadness can never be fully measured by mere outsiders. For all the other officers and soldiers who shared your loved one's friendship may I offer my heartfelt condolences. Most sincerely, A.V. Arnold, Major General, Commanding

COOPER, CHARLES ELLIS, was a Private First Class in Company K, 8th Infantry in the Army of the United States. He was born 14 December 1916. He was registered with the Selective Service Board in Wayne County, Tennessee. His Civilian Occupation was Natchez Trace Construction Worker. He entered into active service at Fort Oglethorpe, Georgia. He was shipped from a camp in South Carolina to Germany. He was wounded in action in Germany and died a few months later on 19 November 1944. A Purple Heart Medal was sent to his wife. He attended Scott's Chapel Grammar School and Baptist Church. Ellis was the son of James and

Jane Pigg Cooper of Cypress Inn, Tennessee. His siblings are Russ, J.P., and Ray Cooper, and Gertrude Cooper who married Tom Ayers. Ellis was married 16 October 16 1943 in Alabama to Eva Wright who is now Mrs. Coleman Roberson.

CORLEW, WOODROW BELL, Woodrow died 24 July 1942, following an accident while on duty at Kessler Field,

Mississippi and buried in Bell Cemetery in Wayne County. He was a Private in the Army Air Force of the United States. His Civilian Occupation was Clerk in the Waynesboro Post Office and later Postmaster until he volunteered in 1941. He attended the public schools in Wayne and Perry Counties and graduated from the Wayne County High School. Woodrow, son of William Claude (1883-1964) and Nannie (Bell) Corlew, was born 17 August 1912 in Wayne County. His brothers were Robert Ross (deceased) and Lee Burns Corlew of Georgia.

CRAIG, JAMES JULIAN, Killed in Florence, Italy in a jeep accident 26 April 1945 and is buried in Swiss Cemetery in Hohenwald. He was a Corporal in the 68th Air Service Squadron in the Army Air Force of the United States. Julian, son of

J. Frank and Flora (Rasbury) Craig, was born 12 July 1912 in Wayne County, Tennessee. His siblings are: Amos, Clara, Lee, John, Stanford, and Ann Craig Sanders.

DARBY, CARL ERNEST, Private First Class, Serial Number 34 723 016, Infantry, was killed instantaneously in action by enemy machine gun fire 9 December 1944 in France and was properly buried in a military cemetery in eastern France with a Protestant Chaplain officiating at the burial. The Purple Heart Medal was awarded posthumously to PFC Darby. His remains were returned home 9 December 1948. After Carl graduated from Collinwood High School in 1942, he went to Detroit to find work where a brother was employed. Men were needed to prepare for the war, so on 31 December 1942, Carl was called back to Waynesboro by the draft board for a physical exam. He was notified that he was classified as 1-A and was ordered to report for induction 5 February 1943. He took his training at Camp Haan, California. He had several passes home, the last one was 24 July 1944 just before he reported to Camp Kelner, New Jersey for overseas duty. Mail was slow and very few letters were coming back. The night of 26 December 1944, a friend, Dr. Ander-

son, delivered a telegram to the home that their son was killed on duty. Private First Class Carl E. Darby, Serial Number 34 723 016, Infantry, was killed in action 9 December 1944 in France. The Purple Heart Medal was awarded posthumously to Pfc Darby. Carl's parents, William A. and Elizabeth House Johnson Darby, were married 2 January 1918. Carl was born 4 December 1922. His siblings are Marvin Grady and Pauline (Darby) Lutts and a half-brother William Glynn House, son of Floyd House. "We three couples, Grady and Eva, Pauline and Elmer and Glynn and Faye, witnessed the train coming to a stop in Lawrenceburg, carrying the remains of our brother Carl home. The flag draped casket was removed from the train and placed in the hearse waiting nearby that would take Carl home where mama and daddy were anxiously waiting for the return of their sons remains. The casket was opened at mama's request. Glynn and Grady witnessed this and assured her that the remains were Carl's. On the 9th of December 1948 he had a full military burial in the McGlamery Cemetery." - Pauline Lutts.

DAVIS, JESSIE VIRGIL, Killed in Action 1 December 1944 in the Battle of the Bulge, He is buried in Shiloh National

Park in Hardin County, Tennessee. He served in the European Operation under Gen. Patton. Jessie, son of George and Bessie Davis of Beech Creek, was born 13 February 1917. His sisters are: Gladys Stricklin, and Hazel Morrow. His brothers are: Elmer, Shelb, Edward, Robert, Fay, and Bluford Davis.

DIXON, EARL LEE, PFC, 34501374, US Army, son of Edgar T. and Odie M. Hanback Dixon, was born September 18, 1923. He was killed in action on June 23, 1944.

He was in Company B, 236th Combat Engineers. He received his basic training at Camp McCoy, Wisconsin. He left America for Asia and became a member of the 236" Combat Engineers, a part of the 5307th Infantry and a member of the renowned Merrill's Marauders. Combat Engineers are unique among ground fighting forces. They have the almost civilian duty of construction jobs while at the same time being fully armed and ready to do combat at any time.

The 236th Combat Engineers, under General Joe Stilwell, had the job of building and maintaining the Ledo and Burma Roads right through Japanese infested jungles. Between the Burma Road and the Ledo Road lay a strategically vital Burmese City, Myikyina. When the battle of Myikyina began in late May of 1944, the summer monsoon rains were reaching their potential. Just a few days after the fighting began, the 236th Combat Engineers were moved into Myikyina as replacements to the main fighting forces of Merrill's Marauders. For the next 60 days while the battle raged the engineering battalion was now a front line combat force. The allied forces at a terrible cost won this battle of Myikyina. It was here in this battle the Earl Lee Dixon made the supreme sacrifice. Falling in defense of freedom. Reports indicated that he was killed by an enemy hand grenade while he was in a foxhole.

In 1947, which was three years after he was killed, his body was sent to the US for burial in the Shawnette United Methodist Church Cemetery, Wayne County, TN. His mother had the following epitaph on his tombstone;

It was bard to give him up
But, O God, Thy will be done.

Earl's brother is John Otis Dixon. His sisters are; Alva M. Dixon Brison, Nina B. Dixon Kilburn and Mattie (died young.) He was engaged to be married to Octalee Brewer.

DODD, JAMES EARL, Killed in Action 13 May 1945. Dodd was a Private First

Class in 383rd Infantry 96th Infantry Division. After basic training at Camp Shelby, Mississippi and Camp Robinson, Arkansas, Dodd was sent to Okinawa, 1 May 1945 and he lost his life there a few days later in service for his country. Three years later the body was sent back to Wayne County to lay entombed in the Cromwell Crossroads Cemetery. James, son of Alonzo and Jessie Oliver Dodd, was born 31 October 1923. When he left for service, the family lived in the Piney Grove Community in Wayne County. His sisters are Vivian Heard, Gladys Bevis, Lawtell Price, Etta Mae Pefpeller, Pauline Hayes, Eunice Heard, Calley Mauveline Dodd and Sue Maxwell - Source: Family Records.

EATON, HOBART JACKSON, Killed in Action 11 June 1944. He volunteered for service and was placed in the

Cemetery in the Village of Sainte Mere Eguse, France.

82nd Airborne Glider and Paratrooper Division. He received basic training at Fort Benning, Georgia and was sent to the European Theater where he was participated in the Normandy Invasion. His parachute was hit and he fell to his death serving his country. He received the Purple Heart for his valor. Hobart, son of Elisha and Ocie Brewer Eaton, was born 25 November 1917 on Indian Creek in Wayne County, Tennessee. His sister is Lucille Eaton and

his brothers are: Clarence Edward and William Brewer Eaton. His remains were sent back 11 June 1949 for his final resting place in the McGlamery Cemetery in Wayne County.

GILLIS, JAMES CARVEL, Killed in Action in the English Channel 25 December 1944. The ship transporting his com-

pany across the English Channel from Southampton, England to Cherbourg, France was torpedoed and sank before it reached its destination. J. C. Gillis, Serial Number 34 987 515, was a Private First Class with Company H 262nd Infantry in the Army of the United States. His permanent mailing address was Cypress Inn, Tennessee. He entered the service 11 April 1944 and was stationed at Camp Shelby, Mississippi, Fort McCellan, and Camp Rucker, Alabama. Private First Class Gillis went overseas in October 1944. Before induction he was a farmer. James, son of James Thomas Gillis (1893-1967) and Susan Artie Rich Gillis (1895-1975) of Route 1, Cypress Inn, Tennessee, was born 23 November 1925 in Wayne County, Tennessee and was 19 years old when he was killed Christmas Day 1944. He had two brothers: Ira and Coy Gillis and five sisters: Lora Bevis, Iva Nora Bratten, Laveda Murphy and Elvesta Murphy. Another sister, Irene Gillis, died young. James was never married and had no children.

HAMILTON, J.W., Killed in Belgium 4 January 1945. Private First Class Hamilton served in the Infantry in the Army of the United States. He volunteered and entered the service in 1942. His body was brought to the States and buried in the Clifton City Cemetery. J.W., son of Clyde Hamilton (1885-1960) and Mattie Bell Hamilton (1889-1956), was born 24 August 1925. His brother, Leonard Hamilton, served in Germany in World War II. His other brothers were Edgar and Ernest Hamilton. His sisters were: Etta Woody,

Irene Franks, Kathleen McAlpine, and Ruth Floyd.

HELTON, LEON, Killed in action 8 September 1943. Serial Number 14 047 956, had a TSG Grade in the Army of the

United States. A newspaper clipping dated 15 April 1941 stated that Leon Helton signed for a three-year term with the 13th Bombing Squadron in Orlando, Florida. His plane went down in the English Channel 8 September 1943. His body was not recovered. He was the son of Wilson B. And Lucy Flippo Helton. His brothers were Tolbert and John A. Helton. He had one sister, Dorothy, who died young. Source: World War II - 1946 List of Dead and Missing. His personal album was left at the home of the parents of Pat Taylor. The snapshots he had sent them and evidently the V-mail letters were the last they heard from him as his plane went down in the English Channel on 8 September 1943. His body was not recovered. (See biography of Tolbert Maxey Helton.)

HENDRIX, CLYDE, Serial Number 34 584 413, was a Private and a machine gunner in 180th Infantry 45th Division in the Army of the United States. He was sent

to North Africa, then to Italy. He was killed in action 31 December 1943 in Italy and was buried in the United States Military cemetery in Fratelle, Italy (a temporary cemetery) 18 miles from Cassina, Italy. Later, the body was moved to a cemetery near Florence, Italy. His Civilian Occupation was Farming and Shipyard Worker. He attended Whitten School in Wayne County. He was inducted 10 July 1943. Clyde, son of James (Jim) and Della Keeton Hendrix, was born in 1922. His brother, Roland V. (R.V.) Hendrix, was in the Navy and brothers, Oval (twin to Lester) and Lester were in the Army. His other brothers were J.T. and Vernon Hendrix. His sisters were Lela, Earline, Bernice twin to Vernon, and Ethel twin to Clyde. Oval and Lester were also twins.
Source: Family Records.

HOLT, WILLIAM HAROLD, was a TMC Fire Control 3rd Class in the United States Navy, William Harold Holt, 19, died at a Naval Hospital at Long Beach, California, May 8, 1945. He entered the service on his 17th birthday and served both in the States and abroad. He spent 17 months overseas. William was born 30 June 1925 in Wayne County, killed in action and was buried in McGlamery Cemetery in Collinwood, Tennessee. He was the son of Marvin Leland Holt (30 January 1904-6 August 1989) and Mae Belle Bratcher (2 May 1907-26 February 1977). He had one sister, Nancy Elizabeth Holt, born 21 September 1934. He enlisted 30 June 1942 in the U.S. Navy, and had the rank of Seaman 3rd Class. He took his training in San Diego and spent seventeen months in the South Pacific. Just two weeks before his death, he spent part of his leave in Florence, Alabama. At the time of his death, he was returning to his station on a battle cruiser and to active sea duty. *Source: C. Horton*

HORTON, FRED ALOMZO, was Killed in Action June 1944. Captain Horton

of the 916 F.A. Battalion was a volunteer in the United States Army The last letter received from him was dated 17 May 1944. He mentioned that he was somewhere in North Africa and that he had visited Oran, a city and port in Northwest Algeria. He was born 24 November 1921, the son of Lon and Melissa Southerland Horton. He was killed in North Africa in June 1944. His body was returned and buried in Cromwell Cross-roads, Southwest of Collinwood on the Bear Creek Road in Wayne County. His brothers are: Roy, Robert, Wayne, Claude, Arch and Paul Horton. His sisters are Clara Victory, Lora Victory, and Dola Rich.

JACKSON, LAWRENCE A., Serial Number 34 723 015, Lawrence was a Private in the Army of the United States He

was killed in action in Italy. He was the son of Daniel A. and Lola J. Jackson. His brothers were: Ulis M., Ezra called ED, and Lawrence Jackson. His sisters were: Grace Bridges, Edna Matney, Erlene Whitehead, Bertha Runions and Jerry Lou Whitehead.

KELLY, FREELON, He was killed in Action in the Battle of the Bulge in 1944. He joined the Reserves before the war. He

was home on vacation when World War II broke out. He was inducted into the Army and went overseas and was killed. His body was returned to the states and buried in the Tom Kelly Cemetery on Factory Creek. Freelan, son of Tom and Emily Carrington Kelly, was born 2 May 1911 in Lawrence County, Tennessee. His siblings were: Burbin, Cecil Kilburn, Opal Franklin and Lois Tinin. His half brothers and sisters are: Mamie Nutt, Anna Ruth Bullard, Garnet and C. F. Kelly.

KELSO, JOHN D., Killed in Action, 4 January 1945. Sergeant Kelso served in the 327th Glider Infantry, 101st Division

of the Army of the United States. His basic training was at Fort Bragg, North Carolina. He was stationed in England before D-Day. He was engaged in the Battle of the Bulge where he lost his life. His death was reported to be 4 January 1945. His body was returned to Wayne County and buried in Memorial Gardens in Waynesboro. John D., son of Elbert R. and Mable Minnie Belle Clayton Kelso, was born 18 February 1922. His brothers are; Orvall, Dillard B., and Glenn Elbert Kelso. His sisters are: Dura Lucelle Daniels, Mary Maxine Ayers, Carolyn Sue Kelso and Janice Rene Brewer.

LYNCH, HUGHES ANDREW, was a Staff Sergeant in HD & HD Company, 3rd Armored Division in the Army of the United States. He was stationed at Fort Hood, Texas, for his basic training. He was also stationed in Sassysiua, Japan in 1945, Fort Rucker, Alabama and Fort Knox, Kentucky. Hughes, son of Charles Wesley and Bell Young Lynch, was born 27 December 1919, died 6 September 1947. He was home on leave, waiting for a discharge when he died. His children are Reba Lynch Speakman and Thomas Hughes Lynch.

(See page 14 for photo, top.)

LYNN, HERSHEL DOTSON, Serial

Hughes A. Lynch

Number 34 494 859, was a Staff Sergeant in the Army of the United States. In 1942, he took his basic training at Camp

Claiborne, Louisiana and Camp Howze, Texas. He went overseas in October 1944 as part of the 103rd Infantry Division of General Alexander Patch's 7th Army. He was killed in action 22 April 1945 by artillery fire in Germany and he is buried in France in the St. Avold Military Cemetery. S\Sgt Lynn was posthumously awarded the Purple Heart 14 July 1944. Memorial Services were held at the University of Tennessee Alumnus in Knoxville for Herschel and all the brave serviceman who gave their life. Attending these services were his wife, Frankie Lynn, a sister Martha Lynn Owens and his brother John Andrew Lynn. Herschel, son of George and Emily Cole Lynn, was born 10 April 1917 in Wayne County. He had one brother, John Andrew Lynn and three sisters, Mary Cole Meador Cross, Martha Owens and Katherine Davis. He was married 2 October 1941 to Frankie Norman Duren. He graduated from Wayne County High School in 1939 and attended UT, Martin in 1940.

MATHIS, OBIE LEE, was drafted into the Army 14 March 1942. He was stationed in Camp Lee, Virginia, Fort George

Meade, Maryland, Fort Dix, New Jersey. and many different countries overseas. While Sergeant Mathis was in the North Africa area, he stepped on a mine that took his life 26 May 1944. He received a Purple Heart. Obie Lee, son of Rubie and Eva Mathis, was born 1 December 1919. His siblings are Herbert Mathis and Dorothy Skelton.

MATHNEY, ELVIN, was one of the first volunteers from Collinwood, Tennessee. He was a Fire Man Second Class (FM2C) in the Navy of the United States. He was killed as a result of operational movements in a War Zone. Elvin is the son of Walter Matheny (18 December 1866-30 November 1931) and Cordie Pennington Matheny (8 April 1881 -). His siblings are: Dicie Kephart, Bertha died young, Walter Jr., of Washington and a World War II Veteran, and Vera Jane Sandy of Florence, Alabama.

MOORE, CLAUDE, Serial Number 20 730 580, was a Sergeant in the United States Army. He was killed in action.

MORROW, EDWARD C., son of Cicero L. and Mattie Lee Morrow, was born 7 July 1920 in Waynesboro, Tennessee. He was Valedictorian of the Wayne County High School Class of 1934. He graduated from UT, Martin in 1940 and received a Bachelor of Science Degree in Agriculture from UT, Knoxville in June 1942, specializing in soils and erosion control. He volunteered and was accepted in the United States Army Air Corps 18 August 1942. His serial number was 14 13 422. He received his basic training at Miami Air Base, Florida and was later stationed at Maxwell Field, Alabama, Denver, Colorado, and Salina and Victoria, Kansas. He was assigned to the 20th Air

Force as Senior Gunner on a B-29 operating from "an air base somewhere in India". He had been overseas six months when he was reported missing in action over Japan. S/Sgt Morrow, at this time had completed sixteen missions over Japanese territory, though in a recent letter to his parents he stated that his plane was first over the target and he had participated in the B-29 raid which carried the heaviest bomb load the longest distance of any raid in history of aerial bombardment. The Air Medal was posthumously awarded to Staff Sergeant Morrow. He was with the 770 Bomb Squadron, 462 Bomb Group. Citation for the medal : "For Meritorious achievement from 11 May - 4 November 1944 while participating in operational and/or combat flights from bases in India to bases in China and return, and from bases in China on missions over enemy territory where enemy fire was probable and expected. This individual accomplished his mission with distinction above and beyond that normally expected. This enlisted man has participated in operations and/or combat flights totaling more than 100 hours. The flights were made over extremely rugged terrain where unfavorable weather made flying hazardous. This individual exhibited untiring energy and meticulous care while flying. Undaunted by the many hazards faced regularly and continuously, this enlisted man performed his duties in such a manner as to reflect great credit to his command and to the Army Air Force." Signed Edward F. Whitsell, Major General. The following is an account in which S/Sgt Morrow is thought to have participated: "Two Superfortresses, first ever lost to enemy interceptors, were shot down by Japanese fighter planes in the 20th Air Force attack on Japan and occupied China yesterday, but the giant bombers destroyed or damaged 61 enemy planes in addition to the ruin they visited on the great Omura aircraft works and other targets." (21 November 1944). In a letter to Mr. and Mrs. Morrow: "After a lengthy investigation that had been conducted by the American Graves Registration Service for the identification of your son's remains has been concluded. The following is a brief resume of the information on record in your son's file maintained by this office. The records of the Department of the Army indicate that your son was one of a crew of eleven aboard a B-29 type airplane number 42-6278, which was attacked by enemy fighter planes while on a mission to Omura, Japan on 21 November 1944. These records also indicate that the remains of eleven deceased crew members, including your son, were recovered and taken to the cemetery for foreigners at Mezame-Machi, Nagasaki-shi. After the occupation of Japan, personnel American Graves Registration Service investigated the scene of the plane crash, searched the police records and interrogated the cemetery officials and authorities of Nagasaki. This investigation disclosed that the wreckage of your son's plane was salvaged by the Japanese 22 November 1944 and the remains of seven crew members recovered. Several weeks later the bodied of the other four washed ashore, three at Kagoshima and one at Nagasato. A list of the names of the entire crew was found in local records. This revealed that all remains were cremated by the Japanese individually, urned and stored in a cemetery vault at Nagasaki. During the atomic bombing of Nagasaki 9 August 1945, the vault was damaged and a considerable number of urns broken and destroyed. Personnel of the Marine Corps who occupied Nagasaki after the Japanese surrendered recovered six individual urns, tentatively associated as the ashes of your son and five other crew members of his plane. In the course of the investigation the urn established as those of your son was marked with the first letter of his surname and his first name, namely M., Edward. These cremated remains are now being held in the ground storage pending disposition instructions from the next of kin either for return to the United States or for permanent burial in an overseas cemetery. Signed James B. Clearwater, Colonel, QMC, Chief, Memorial Division

NANCE, BILLY R., was born March 30, 1926. He was the son of Hugh and Esther Nance. Billy enlisted in the Army in 1944. He was killed in action on July 15, 1945 in the Philippine Islands outside Manila in the mountains. He was said to have been killed in hand-to-hand combat. He was brought back home and buried at Shiloh National Park. Tennessee River Bridge at Clifton Opens, 1997. This two-lane bridge connects Tennessee 114 and Tennessee 128, linking Wayne and Hardin Counties, a cost of $9.9 million dollars. The road leading to the new bridge is named in memory of Billy Nance, who was killed in World War II. Billy R Nance, newspaper article. January 24, 1996 newspaper article: Thanks! I would like to express my sincere appreciation to County Executive Coy Anderson and the Wayne County Commission for unanimously passing the resolution renaming Highway 114 the "Billy R. Nance Highway." Also my thanks to Hubert Tinin, who was serving with my bother during the time he was killed, and who was seriously wounded about the same time. My thanks also go out to the Clifton City Commission and the Hardin County Commission, who also passed resolutions on this matter. Also thanks to Lt. Gov. John Wilder, Rep. James Peach and Rep. Steve McDaniel for their support in this effort and to everyone who signed petitions and supported this resolution. Thanks Again, Hugh L. Nance and the Nance Family.

PEVAHOUSE, JOSEPH RICHARD MARVIN, Sergeant, son of Mr. and Mrs. Oscar Lee Pevahouse of Clifton. Tennessee, was born 7 November 1918 in Clifton. He attended Little Beech Elementary School and Frank Hughes High School. He spent 1941-42 as a group leader in the Civilian Conservation Corps in Oregon. He then returned home and farmed until he was drafted into the Army. Joseph's military service consisted of basic training in Camp Claiborne, Louisiana, where he attained the rank of Corporal. He was transferred to Fort Knox, Kentucky and assigned to the 82nd Airborne Division, Glider Division of the United States Army. It was at Fort Campbell he was promoted to Sergeant. With his unit, he saw active duty in North Africa, Italy and Eastern Europe. His company took part in the invasion of Europe with the landing of troops on the beaches of Normandy from England. During the invasion he was slightly wounded and returned to England to recuperate. When he returned to duty with his company in Easter Europe, he became a Supply Sergeant. They were engaged in the Battle of the Bulge. On 24 December 1944 the supply truck and his crew struck a mine at a street intersection in Hamburg, Germany killing everyone in the truck. He was awarded two Purple hearts. After the war, Sgt Pevahouse's remains were returned to the States and were buried in Shiloh National Park in Shiloh, Tennessee with full military honors.

PITTS, WALLACE JAMES, JR., entered the United States Army Air Corps 9 March 1943. He was a member of the 873rd Bombardment Squadron, 498th Bombardment Group. All of his overseas time was spent in the Pacific Area aboard B-29's. Wallace, Jr., son of Wallace James and Lydia Burns Pitts, was born 17 December 1921. He had one brother, Billy Joe and one sister, Nettie Marie Pitts. He graduated from Frank Hughes High School in Clifton in 1941. S/Sgt Pitts died 2 April 1945 aboard a B-29 Superfortress Bomber when it was shot down and burst into flames over Tokyo, Japan. His plane was flying from Siapan, Mariana Islands to Tokyo on a bombing raid when it was shot down with eleven airmen on board. The

family received word in 1945 that Wallace was missing in action. There was not any other information until Easter weekend 1979 when a friend handed Billy Joe Pitts the Memphis Parade Magazine's article about the search for the family of Wallace Pitts, Jr. Billy immediately called the called the reporter who wrote the article. The burial site of Wallace, Jr., had been found. This is the article describing the incident: OMATA STORY by Wes Curtis In 1966 while vacationing in Japan and staying at a Golf Club about 80 miles from Tokyo, I played a round of golf with Mitsuaki Omata. I was struggling with the Japanese language and Mr. Omata was trying to tell me about a World War II incident which I was unable to fully comprehend, but I gathered that a B-29 was involved in a crash on his property. Later with the aid of an interpreter he described his experience 2 April 1944. About 0200 he and his father, Gonjiro Omata and family were trying to protect themselves from B-29 raid on the suburbs of Tokyo. They had counted nineteen B-29's and the twentieth had been hit by antiaircraft fire and was on fire and was making a wide circle which was placing the aircraft on a heading with the Omata property. Omata could see it was going to crash so everyone threw themselves to the ground and braced for it. The plane hit about 50 to 75 yards from the house and some bombs exploded with the impact. A hole about 100 feet in diameter appear when the smoke and dust cleared. Only small bits of metal and human tissue remained Gonjiro Omata was a very religious man and his concern for the souls of the crew overcame any other emotion he may have experienced. Yes, the neighbors and government would surely not be pleased with what he had in mind. He decided to bury the crew at the site of the crash and later, when he could erect a monument to the memory of the brave crew. After the war was over, Mr. Omata commissioned Professor K. Akaish of Nippon University to carve the Kannon monument and a religious ceremony was conducted at the monument 27 November 1955, with military attendance. It was always Conjiro Omata's wish to somehow contact the crew's next of kin to convey his feelings and to let them know how sorry he was. Before dying in 1955, his son, Mitsuaki, assured him his wish would be accomplished no matter how long it took. I first started working on the project in 1967 without any progress until 1970 when I was visiting with the Commander of Hamilton Air Force Base near San Francisco, and he agreed to help through his friend, who was in charge of the Archives in Washington, D.C. He gave me eleven 30-year old addresses, but progress was

slow- people moved - remarried- names had changed, etc. In 1973 Mr. Omata came to San Francisco and wanted to visit each family. I informed him the task was impossible, but I arranged for an interview with George Golding of the San Mateo Times. Golding's story was picked up by AP and UPI and we received calls from two families. Mr. Omata presented ceramic plates which commemorated the initial event to the families of Marion Birdwell and Norman Dubb and returned to Japan During the next four years, I continued my telephone and letters. The most interesting find resulted from a "Dear Occupant" letter sent to a home address in Reading, Pennsylvania. The address was now that of an office building. A secretary didn't even open the envelope, discarding it as "junk" mail. For some still unknown reason, she retrieved the letter and opened it to discover she knew the twin sister of the B-29 pilot, William Philbert. Mr. Omata returned to San Francisco 16 August 1977 and visited several cities. I met him in Philadelphia and drove him to Reading where the Mayor gave him the key to the city. A memorial service for the crew was also conducted and the twin sister attended. The pilot's widow met them in San Francisco where another memorial service was conducted. Nine of the eleven families have been found. Every family that I contacted said that they were grateful to know what actually happened since the only word received initially was "Missing in Action", then one year later, "Presumed Dead". Nothing else had ever been passed on to them. There are still two missing pieces of the puzzle - Lt. Edward Rudofsky, last known address 309 E. 34th Street, Savannah, Georgia and S/Sgt. Wallace J. Pitts, last known address Memphis, Tennessee. I spent two days in Memphis in the old neighborhood without success, so the file remains open, but without much hope of further discovery. The search has been long and at times discouraging, but very rewarding.' Signed W. E. Curtis. As a result of the above article, Mr. Omata visited the Bill J. Pitts family in Peoria the weekend of October 13 and 14, 1979 and presented him a ceramic plates which commemorated the initial event. Bill is Wallace' brother.

PRINCE, SAMUEL J., Serial Number 34 494 880, was inducted into the United States Army 29 November 1942. He took his basic training at Fort Ord, California and was transferred overseas July 1943. Private First Class Prince received fatal wounds 5 February 1944 during the Marshall Islands Campaign and was moved to a base hospital where he died 14 February 1944. The Purple Heart was awarded posthumously to Pfc. Prince and

was sent to his wife. Survivors were his parents, Mr. and Mrs. Harvey Prince of Iron City, Tennessee.; his wife, Viola and their son, Sammie Joe. His sisters: Mrs. Johnny Wayne Daniel and Mrs. Alex Lawson, both of Iron City.

PUGH, JAMES EDWARD, Entered the United States Navy and was killed in the service for his country at sea in the Pacific early during the war. His remains was returned to the states to be buried in the Benton City Cemetery in Benton, Kentucky where his mother lived. James Edward, the only child of Roy Pickney and Marie DeBerry Pugh of Clifton, Tennessee, was born on February 26, 1927. He grew up around Clifton, attended Frank Hughes School and had many friends, young and old, in the area.

PULLEY, GAVIN, was Quartermaster in the United States Regular Army. He left his Beech Creek home in Wayne County on a bright 7 November morning, whistling as he said good-bye, going to the Army Induction Center. He signed up to go to Cuba, however when his family heard from him he was in Northern Ireland. He spent quite a bit of time here and met a girl, Betty Wilson, that he planned to marry but he was sent to North Africa. He was in Sicily when he was killed in an accident. He was not engaged in combat at the time. He was buried in Shiloh National Park in Hardin County, Tennessee. His family believed he was the first Wayne County boy to be killed during the war. Gavin, son of Johnny Bell and Susan Sanderson Pulley, was born 23 September 1916 and died 23 April 1943. His siblings were: Iona Pulley Denton, Paul, Reuben, Starling "Red", and Leonard Pulley.

RAINEY, LEONARD LEE, was a Private in the Engineers Corps in the United States Army. He was in London, England when he was killed 18 October 1944. He was buried in England for two years be-

fore he was brought back and buried in Prater's Chapel Cemetery in Wayne County. Leonard was born 22 August 1924. He married Maude Staggs, who died 30 September 1976. They had a daughter, Glenda Jane Rainey Hickman, who lives in Savannah, Tennessee. She has two daughters, Lyndie Cummings and Kimberly Hickman, and one grandson, Johnathan Tyler Cummings.

RAY, BEN H., was sent to Fort Eustis, Virginia, for his basic training. He died there in 1942 from acute appendicitis and

was buried in Culp Cemetery on Beech Creel in Wayne County, Tennessee. He was a teacher in the Wayne County School System before induction into the Army. He was also a carpenter. Private Ray, son of William M. and Eldora Culp Ray, was born about 1910. His sisters were: Melven Ray and Nannie Ray Anderson, His brothers were: Wesley, Frank, Lee and Clyde. Another brother, Jim Ray was killed in World War I.

REEVES, JOHN EARL, SR., Seaman First Class, entered the United States Navy in October 1941. His base station was in the Grand Cayman Islands. He was wounded at sea in August 1943 and returned to the states 1 September 1943 and

was stationed in Fort Lauderdale, Florida. He returned to sea duty 1 December 1943 and was killed at sea 16 December 1943. He attend Frank Hughes School in Clifton. He is the son of Earl C. and Martha Rose Reeves and was born 2 February 1922 at Route 1, Waynesboro, Tennessee. His grandparents were Elvin and Ida Devers Reeves and George and Hanna Prater Rose. His sisters are : Pauline Cookson and Geneva Taylor. He was married 17 May 1941 to Tina Martin. Their children are: Tina Ramona Scothern and John Earl Reeves, Jr.

SHANN, PAUL, was inducted into the United States Army 9 September 1943 and served with the 82nd Infantry Division.

Sergeant Shann was declared Missing in Action 11 January 1945 while escorting prisoners of war to the rear lines. Paul was born 30 July 1920 in Lewis County, Tennessee. His parents were James Walter William and Bessie Galloway Shann. Paul had two sisters, Carminelle Shann and Theo Kelly, and one brother, Ostien Shann. He married Ruby Turnbow in August 1944.

STEVENS, ISAAC BLACK, JR., Serial Number 34 494 884, He was among the first Wayne County men to be drafted

in World War II. Taking his basic training in California, he was assigned to 7th Infantry Division. Private First Class Stevens served from 29 October 1942 until he was killed in action 1 February 1945. His remains were first interred in the U.S. Armed Forces Cemetery, Leyte, #1, grave 4504. The cemetery was on Leyte Island in the Philippine Islands. He is now buried in Bethel Cemetery in Perry County, Tennessee. Stevens' parents received the Bronze Star Medal that was awarded to their son posthumously for bravery and the Purple Heart Medal for his wound that caused his death. The following Citation was enclosed: "Bronze Star Medal (awarded) For heroic achievement with military operations against the enemy on 1 February 1945, during the Operation. During the attack on a hill, the assault platoon of which Pfc. Stevens was a member received a heavy volume of enemy small arms and automatic rifle fire causing the platoon to seek cover. Pfc Stevens, without regard for his own safety, moved forward, trying to locate the concealed position. He succeeded in showing his platoon the enemy emplacement so that it could be neutralized. During this action Private First Class Stevens was killed. His heroic action reflected great credit upon himself and was an inspiration to the men in his platoon." Isaac, Jr., son of Isaac Black, Sr., and Bertha Harder Stevens, was born 21 January 1922. His brothers were: Thomas, Gerald, James, Robert and Willie Stevens and sister, Ramona Farris.

TEMPLETON, WILLARD, spent most of his brief life in the Clifton area. He was the second child and oldest son of John and Pearl Templeton. His surviving family members remember Willard as a fun loving young man who loved to play jokes. Willard wasn't quite 18 when he volunteered for the army in early 1944. His parents had to sign for him to enlist. Willard was sent to Europe after his training. He participated in the fight to liberate France

following D-Day. While he was away, he and his family frequently wrote each other. In his letters, Willard express confidence that the war would soon end and he tried to reassure his family that there was nothing for them to worry about. He also remarked that he was following in the footsteps of his father, a veteran of World War I who had fought in France 25 years before. Willard Templeton was killed in action in Metz, France on 19 November 1944. He was only 18 years old. He was temporarily buried in Luxembourg. In 1948 his body was returned to Clifton and reburied in Mount Carmel Cemetery. He was awarded the Purple Heart and several other medals. His surviving family members include a brother, Glenn Templeton and a sister, Maxine Ray, both of the Clifton area.

VICKERY, DURAL O., Private, was in the 142nd Infantry Division. He was sent to Europe after completing his basic training. Dural, son of James F. and Ada Hanley Vickery, was born 2 November 1923 and was killed in action in Italy 25 February 1944. His body was returned to the United States and laid to rest in the Lindsey Chapel Cemetery in Alabama. He was married to Myrtle Peppers and they had one son, Jacky. His sisters were: Ruby Moore and Dellie Vickery. His brother were: Alver, and James Franklin, Jr.

VICKERY, JAMES FRANKLIN, JR., was a Private in 142th Infantry in the Army of the United States. James Franklin, Jr., son of James F. Sr., and Ada Hanley Vickery, was born 4 November 1921 and was killed in action in Europe 7 December 1943. His body was returned to the United States and laid to rest in the Lindsey Chapel Cemetery in Alabama. His sisters were: Ruby Moore and Dellie Vickery. His brother were: Alver, and Dural O. Vickery.

WILLIAMS, DUMONT G., 1st. Lt. We find in the January 8, 1943 edition of the Wayne County News the following notation; 1st. Lt. Dumont G, Williams , is a Jap. prisoner, a native Wayne Countian, son of J.B. (Benie) Williams and Millie William. His mothers Parents are Rev. and Mrs. John L. Morrison, all residents of Wayne County for many Years, then moved to Florida. He is the 2nd Jap. prisoner.

WOODS, WILLIAM FLOYD Private First Class, had been overseas for several months, and had satisfactorily completed

parachute packing, ground training and jumping from a plane in flight. He was killed in action in Holland 13 October 1944. He was in the Tennessee 508 Parachute Infantry 82 A.B. Division. Floyd, son of William Albert and Rosa Dicus Woods, was born 4 January 1922. He had one brother, Claude Albert Woods. He is buried in the Friendship Cemetery located on Eagle Creek in Wayne County, Tennessee.

WAYNE COUNTY, TENNESSEE
PRISONERS OF WAR

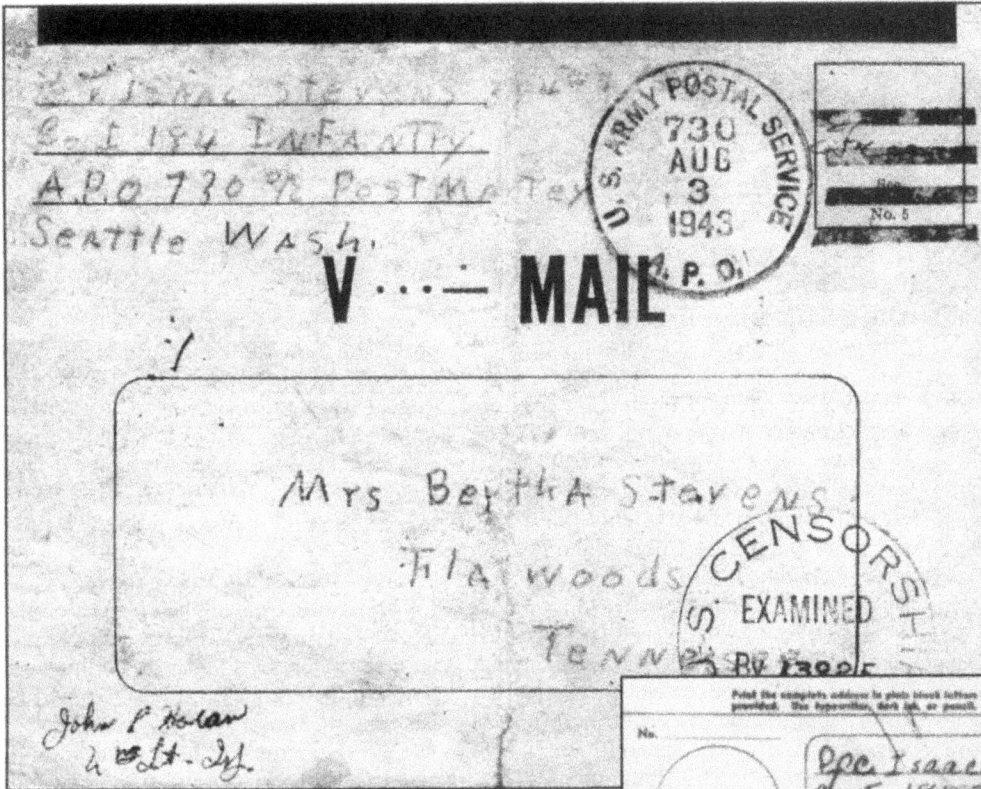

Military personnel were furnished V-Mail to correspond with family and friends. The mail the G.I.'s received was reduced in size and often censored by cutting out portions that be helpful to the enemy.

BRADY, HOWARD "POP", was inducted into service in Waynesboro in November 1943 and was discharged 5 September 1945. He fought in battles and campaigns in Rhineland and Ardennes. He was awarded the European-African Middle Eastern Theater Medal. He was a Private First Class in the 106th Division and was captured at the Battle of the Bulge. He was a Prisoner of War in the German Camp Stalag IX-B, at Bad-Orb, Germany. He was released along with 3,364 other American soldiers when a Seventh Army task force fought its way to the camp. All of the prisoners were suffering from malnutrition. Their daily ration had been a slice of bread and a cup of watery soup with occasional horse meat.

Howard, son of John Wesley and Sallie Briley Queen Brady, was born 18 April 1907 in Waynesboro, Tennessee, died 21 January 1984 and was buried in Waynesboro Memory Garden. He had two sisters, Monetta and Nannie and one brother, Charles Brady. His half brothers were: John, Jim and Walter Brady and Briley Queen. He was married 1 October 1937 to Robbie Brewer and they had one daughter, Vivian Gayle Brady. She married Clay Sherrill, Jr. Howard has three grandchildren: Jeffery, Jennifer and Earnie Sherrill and one great-grandchild, Nicle Skelton.

BUTLER, JOE W., "I was born on 2 March 1912 and I have lived in Wayne County all of my life. My father was P.A. Butler and my mother was Mary Butler. I graduated from Wayne County High School and married Mary Norman, daughter of Dr. F. H. Norman, in 1931. We had two children, Joe W., Jr., and Sandra Butler Nutt.

I was employed as an agent for Norman and Butler Insurance Agency, which is still in the family. I was employed by First Federal Savings and Loan Association of Waynesboro as a teller, then secretary-treasurer and then, as president for about fifty-six years all together. I was appointed as one of the first trustees of Wayne County General Hospital and Wayne County Nursing Home. I was a member of Wayne County Court (Magistrate) for twelve years. I also served as chairman of Jury Commission for about twenty-five years. I was an elder in the Cumberland Presbyterian Church.

After working in the office of First Federal for about twelve years, I was drafted into the U.S. Army in 1943. I took my basic training for seventeen weeks at Fort McCellan, Alabama. From there I went overseas and was assigned to the 2nd Infantry Division, 23rd Battalion as a rifleman. I was in combat for several months before I was captured as a prisoner of war during the Battle of the Bulge. I remained a prisoner for about six months. My Sergeant was captured with me and we still keep in touch. I received five Battle Stars, several commendations and the Bronze Star and had the rank of Corporal. I was asked to write about my experience as a prisoner of war. We were treated so badly as prisoners that I have tried to forget. Therefore, I cannot possibly describe the experiences as bad as they truly were. I was discharged after the war was over in 1945. I thank the Lord that I was able to return home to my family and friends.' - Joe W. Butler.

DEVASURE, ERNEST H., Serial Number 34 193 025, was a Private First Class in Company C, 168th Engineer Combat Battalion in the Army of the United States. He was registered with the Selective Service Board in Wayne County, Tennessee. His Civilian Occupation was Light Truck Driver. He was inducted into active service 15 March 1942 at Fort Oglethorpe, Georgia. His Military Occupational Specialty was Light Truck Driver. He was in the Battles of Normandy, Northern France, Rhineland, and Ardennes. The following decorations were awarded to Devasure: Purple Heart, European-African Middle Eastern Theater Ribbon with 4 Bronze Stars, Good Conduct Medal and a Lapel Button. He left the USA 2 May 1944 for the European Theater Operation, and returned to USA 21 May 1945. He was wounded in action on 21 December 1944 near St. Vith. He was discharged 12 August 1945 at Fort McPherson, Georgia.

Ernest's mother received a telegram from Secretary of War on 16 January 1945, stating that her son had been reported missing in action in Belgium since 21 December 1944. Then, on 11 May 1945 she received another telegram that Ernest had returned to Military control 15 April 1945.

According to his niece, Linda McAnally, Ernest talked very little about his Prisoner of War life. He did say that he had only raw Irish potatoes to eat the whole time he was a prisoner. He mentioned two of his German guards, one was very cruel and took their Red Cross Packages. The other guard tried to help them in a small way by slipping items of the package to them.

Ernest is the son of Henry and Sue Jackson DeVasure. Both of his parents are buried at Salem. His siblings are Nancy Gallaher, Pearl Gobble, Sherman Blassingim and Gladys Voorhies Blassingim. Ernest was born 13 October 1913 in Hohenwald, Tennessee, died 4 March 1968 and is buried in Salem Cemetery in Wayne County. He married Etah Carroll (1913-1989). They have one daughter, Helen Joyce (1936-1969)

HOBBS, HEWEY, joined the army in Giles County, came back and lived his life in Wayne County. He joined the Army December 1942 and was a private First Class. He was sent overseas in April 1944. He went to England and was in Company A, 44th Battalion. He was captured in Europe, December 1944 and was in prison about five months. He was discharged November 1945.

He married Bertie Lee Donovant and they had two daughters, Linda Faye and Mildred Hobbs. He owned a print shop and was a printer by trade. Later, he worked for the Wayne County News in Waynesboro. Hewey died in 1972 and is buried in the 48 Bridge Free Will Baptist Church Cemetery in Wayne County.

LYNCH, ROY ELMOND, was born 21 January 1916 on Indian Creek near Waynesboro, Tennessee. He was the fourth

of eleven children born to Hardy B. and Mary Clay Lynch. Roy's siblings are: Carrye, Katherine, Virginia, Geneva, Walter, Rex, Edward, Clyde, Paul and Lester. His grandparents were Jim and Irene Franklin Lynch and Carrie and Nancy McMullin Clay. His great-grandparents were William and Katherine Evans Lynch and Thomas N. and Sarah Clay.

Roy attended school through the eleventh grade in Wayne County and graduated from Frankfort Community High School in Frankfort, Illinois on 30 May 1936 in the top ten of his class of 192 seniors. Shortly after graduation, he went to work for Ragland and Potter Wholesale in Nashville.

In 1938, Roy decided to hitchhike to California. It was cold, raining and sleeting in some town in Texas when the truck driver said, "Little Buddy, this is as far as I'm going tonight. Where do you want me to take you?' Roy told him to just drop him off at the jail. He told the sheriff he was on his way to San Diego to join the Navy, but he did not have any money for food or shelter. The officer gave him food and a bed. He decided to stay there and work until he had bus fare to California. He enlisted in the Navy 8 April 1938 in San Diego.

Roy took his boot training and completed a 16 week course in the Hospital Corps in San Diego, worked in U.S. Naval Hospitals in Pensacola, Florida, Canaco in the Philippines, and duty with the Fourth Marines until he was captured by the Japa-

nese on Corregidor 6 May 1942. From the time of his capture until 13 December 1944, Roy was taken to Headquarters for Military Prison Camps of Philippine Islands. Then he was sent to Bilibid Prison, Manilla. On 31 January 1945, he was transferred to operating room and surgical duty in Camp Hospital, Fuknoker Prison Camp #17, Omuta, Japan.

The following events are a summary of what happened to Roy Lynch, one of 1600 prisoners of war, who were transferred to Japan in what is termed "Hell Ships'

On the evening of 13 September 1944, they boarded the prison ship Oryokuo Maru where they were stuffed into cramped spaces without enough room to sit or stand comfortably. With no ventilation, the heat was overpowering and dehydration and suffocation was rampant among the men. Fifty prisoners suffocated the first night. First night rations consisted of a small keg of steamed rice to be divided among every forty men and a cup of water per individual. Only rice, no water, was given the next day and to make bad matters worse, American planes attacked the convoy, bombing them throughout the day. The steering gear on the Oryokuo was shattered and the ship drifted toward the Bataan shoreline where it ran aground that evening. Prisoners received no food or water that night and again many suffered death from suffocation.

On the next day, 15 September 1944, American planes returned to finish the attack on the Oryokuo Maru. The Japanese fled the sinking ship and the remaining prisoners began to jump overboard and swim for Olongapo Shore - the old U.S. Navy Ship Yard. The Japanese on the beach ordered the prisoners to remain in the chilling water for several hours. They were marched to the old Navy Yard and held inside the tennis court for five days with no food until the third day when they were given two tablespoons of rice per man. The next day they were served dry rice in the morning and steamed rice that evening. A single hydrant with running water was available for drinking purposes. With the rotation of prisoners they were fortunate if they got a drink of water more than once every 18 hours. The Navy medical personnel set up a "hospital" at one end of the court and worked day and night to serve the prisoners.

20 & 21 December 1944 - Prisoners were taken by truck to San Fernando, Pampanga over the mountains where they often had to take refuge in the roadside ditches from the American bomber planes.

23 December 1944 - A single truck was provide for the evacuation of the sickest and most seriously wounded, about 8 to 10 men. They were taken to the nearest

cemetery where the Japs beheaded and bayoneted these poor sick men.

24 September 1944 - Nearly 1350 men were loaded into railroad cars - jam packed- standing room only, poorly ventilated, and with some of the prisoners having to ride on top of the cars. They were heading north to the China Sea.

25 December 1944- Christmas Day - The men marched from rail cars four miles through town of San Fernando la Union to a school building. Food and water were sparse and the men were exhausted and starved. The medical personnel set up a sick bay but they had very little medicine with which to treat the dehydration and diarrhea. Just after sunset when almost everyone had bedded down, the guards made them get up and march over a coral road, punishing them every time someone hesitated because their feet had been cut by coral. At nine that evening they stopped and rested their swollen bleeding feet. They had arrived in a port area.

26 December 1944 - The men waited on a sandy peninsula without food or water while the Japanese prepared their ships.

27 December 1944- Prisoners were loaded into two ships which had been used to haul cattle and horses. The sanitation conditions were even worse than before. They went without food or water for four days. On New Years Day 1945 they received four pieces of hard tack and one fourth canteen cupful of water per man. Then again rations were cut off. The ships were attacked by American Submarines off the southern tip of Formosa. Only the two prison ships made it to Takao, Formosa, out of a convoy of six ship and a destroyer escort. After docking, the American prisoners received daily a half canteen cupful of rice and one fourth cup of water.

8 January 1945- All prisoners who had survived thus fore were transferred to a larger vessel. The next day the ship was attacked by dive bombers which resulted in several hundred deaths and injuries.

13 January 1945 - The men were transferred to a small freighter which had been converted to a troop transport. There were only 800 "half-dead' Americans now. The journey across the East China Sea began with nearly 50 prisoners dying the first night from the bitter cold air.

31 January 1945 - The voyage ended as the ship dropped anchor in Moji Harbor at the northern tip of Kyusha with 425 men still alive. Approximately 235 men died within six weeks after their arrival and under conditions almost as bad as they had been on the "Hell Ships'.

13 September 1945 - Roy E. Lynch was LIBERATED from Camp #17, Omuta, Japan. Mr. and Mrs. Lynch heard this great news from Trester Nutt, their rural mail

carrier. Trester had passed the Lynch residence when he heard on his radio that Roy E. Lynch was alive and had been liberated. He turn around and drove back to tell them.

While Roy was a prisoner, he suffered from dysentery, dengue fever, beri-beri and otitia media following a rupture of the right eardrum by concussion in 1942. He was evacuated to the hospital on Guam where he spent several days for a complete work up. He arrived at the Naval Hospital, Oakland, California, on the 20th October 1945. He was released to the Naval Hospital in Great Lakes, Illinois, where he returned to duty and was immediately given a 90 day leave.

Roy was awarded the following medals: a Purple Heart with 1 Gold Star, the Bronze Star, Army Distinguished Unit Badge, American Defense, Philippine Defense with 1 Star, Philippine Liberation, Good Conduct with 2 Stars in World War II and two medals for his service in the Korean Conflict.

Roy received the Bronze Star Medal and permanent citation for "Meritorious Service as a hospital corpsman. He made every effort possible to alleviate the suffering of his fellow prisoners and sustain their morale, despite his own intense suffering.'

Roy and Edith Griggs were married 14 January 1946 in Florence, Alabama. Their children are: Patricia Joan, born 15 February 1947 in Riverside, California; Linda Faye, born 19 October 1949 National Naval Medical Center Hospital, Bethesda, Maryland; and Gary Evan, born 22 July 1956 in U.S. Naval Hospital, Agana, Guam. Patricia married Gary Burns and they live in Newberry, South Carolina with daughter Kelly and son Gary. Linda married Richard Martin and they live in Maryville, Tennessee with son Jason Evan. Gary Evan and wife Kay live in Hernando, Mississippi with their sons, Joshua, Adam and Noah.

Roy was career Navy and his job took the family to many interesting places around the world. He died 14 June 1982 and is buried in Shiloh National Military Park Cemetery.

PRATER, JAMES KURT, entered the Army in 1942. His training took him to several different stations including: California, Texas and Hawaii. Up to the time while he was in Hawaii he had been able to enjoy the company of J.C. Graham who was also from Wayne County.

James was shipped to the South Pacific Theater of War and saw combat at Luzon, New Guinea and Manila. During the worst fighting he was taken prisoner by the Japanese and endured the hardships as a Prisoner of War. He was beaten, denied food

and on several occasions singled out to be killed. He survived by eating scraps and potato peelings. He died February 2, 1997.

James was born on April 3, 1922 to Tom and Nancy Parker Prater. His siblings were: Myrtle Prater Warren, Bonnie Prater Love, Robert Earl and Herbert Prater. His grandparents were: Robert B. and Eliza Ann Crossnoe Parker; Jim and Mimie Smith Prater. All four of his grandparents are buried in the Prater Cemetery near Clifton, TN. Robert Parker's parents were Samuel and Sina Caroline Watts Parker. Samuel was about 27 years of age when he died of exposure to the weather. He served in the Civil War with Company B, of the 9th Calvary Battalion. Samuel is buried in an unkempt cemetery in Flatwoods, TN. Sina Caroline is buried in the Culp Cemetery in Perry County, TN, in an unmarked grave. She had been a teacher.

RAMSEY, ROBERT J., entered into active service in the Army of the United States 5 October 1943 at Fort Oglethorpe,

Georgia and took his basic training at Camp Wheeler, Georgia. He was sent to Europe and participated in the invasion of France on Omaha Beach 6 June 1944. He was a machine gunner in the Third Army, 9th Division attached to General Patton's

Tank Corps. After D-Day Robert's group preceded toward Berlin, Germany. Two hundred and ten were captured 5 September 1944, just after they crossed the Meuse River in Belgium. While Robert was a POW, he worked two months on the railroads in Munich, Germany. Then, twenty Pow's including Robert from Stalag 7-A in Menseburg, Germany, were sent out to a farm to work. They were there seven months before they were liberated with the help of the American Army.

As a POW he received one meal a day at noon. It was a tin cup of cabbage soup with one slice of black bread, half of it being "sawdust" and a cup of what they called coffee "yuk." Robert had stomach problems as a result of this food.

Robert, son of Albert M. and Artie S. Ramsey, was born 31 July 1924 in Fort Meyers, Florida. In late 1927 the family moved to a farm at Shawnette, about seven miles from Collinwood. Three more children were born to his parents while they lived here. They are Ira M., Ruby Mae and Boyd M. His parents moved back to Fort Meyers in 1967 and Ira passed away in 1979. Ira and Robert attended the Shawnette elementary school where Robert finished the 8th grade with Mrs. Lola (Martin) Dixon, as teacher; another teacher was Raymond Bryant.

After the war, Robert moved to Kingsport, Tennessee, where his grandfather, Rev. P. E. Ramsey was living. (Rev. Ramsey was a former pastor of the Collinwood Methodist Church in the late 1930's.) Robert owned and operated an Exxon Service Station until he sold it and moved to Fort Meyers, Florida in 1974. He worked for Morrison's cafeteria there and in West Palm Beach until the doctor found a bone tumor in his left leg in October 1979 After several months of radiation at the VA Hospital in Miami, his left leg was amputated above the knee in February 1979. He had heart attacks in 1986 and 87, and congestive heart failure in 1989. He and his wife are retired and live in High Springs, Florida since 1990. They have a daughter and three grandchildren who live in Covington, Virginia where she is a Veterinary Surgeon.

SKILLERN, PAUL WOODY, Serial Number 34 140 923, was a Private First Class in 2nd Battalion, 131st Field Artillery Regiment in the Army of the United States. His permanent mailing address was P.O. Box 51, Collinwood, Tennessee. He was born 3 July 1914 and graduated from Collinwood High School in 1935. His Civilian Occupation was Carpenter and Cabinet Work. He entered into active service 12 June 1941.

"Paul was sent to Fort Sill, Oklahoma

for basic training. In October 1941 he was sent to Hawaii for final training fitting him for service in the Philippines, for which they were assigned. While enroute to their destination, word was flashed that Pearl Harbor had been bombed thereby causing them to change their course and sail for Australia. From here his outfit was sent to Java in the East Indies. When Java capitulated, Pvt. Skillern was taken prisoner by Imperial Japanese Government and has been according to the mail received by his parent from him, held in Camp No. 3 in Thailand.' Wayne County News clipping.

His Military Occupational Specialty was Field Telephone Operator. He operated field telephone, receiving firing data from command post and relayed information to chief of section. He also laid wires between guns and command post. The following decorations were awarded to Skillern: American Defense Service Medal with 1 Bronze Star, Asiatic-Pacific Service Medal with 1 Bronze Stars, World War II Victory Medal, Distinguished Unit Badge with one Bronze Cluster and Good Conduct Medal. He left the USA 21 November 1941 for the Philippines, and returned to USA 8 March 1946. He was taken prisoner by the Japanese around 25 April 1942 and held for 42 months. He was discharged 7 March 1946 at Fort McPherson, Georgia.

It was twenty two months after Paul was taken prisoner before his mother received this notice on 23 December: "I am interned at the War Prisoners Camp in Moulein, Burma. My health is good. I have not had any sickness. I am with friends. Let me know how all the folks are.' The card came from the Imperial Japanese Army, but undated. It was signed by Pvt. Skillern, his handwriting being easily recognized by his parents and friends.

Paul, son of Thomas Andrew and Lizzie Fowler Skillern, was born 3 July 1914, died 6 July 1979 and was buried at McGlamery Cemetery in Collinwood, but later moved to Memorial Gardens in Waynesboro. Paul had two sisters, Mary Nell, born 27 Dec 1901, died 12 June 1902 and Bonnie, born 28 August 1904, married Harrison Nuszbaum. He also had four brothers: Allen, born 22 May 1906, never married. Will Ray, born 22 May 1908, married Maymaud Lawson, Clarence C., born 2 May 1903, married Christine Bryan, and Claud Y., born 28 August 1912, died 20 October 1918. Paul was married 10 January 1946 at the First Methodist Church in Florence, Alabama to Ruby D. Weaver. Ruby, daughter of Willie H. and Lennie Hanback Weaver, was born 17 November 1911 in Cloverdale, Alabama. Paul and Ruby had one child, Paul Woody Skillern, Jr., born 19 November 1947. He married Freda Coffett in Florence, Alabama on 22 June 1967. Freda, daughter of Virgie Louis and Winifred Greene Coffett, was born 6 May 1946 in Sewanee, Tennessee. There are four grandchildren: twins, Stephen Paul and Sean Louis born 28 August 1968, Sandy Christine born 26 January 1970 and Scott Woody born 3 March 197?. The Skillerns descend from William and Elizabeth Skillern who came from North Ireland to Orange County, Virginia where he received land 5 May 1738. Paul served as Trustee for Wayne County, worked for Hassell and Hughes for many years and worked at Murray of Ohio in Lawrenceburg.

STAGGS, MELVIN B. Serial Number 34 378 560, was a Private First Class in Detachment, Medical Department, 1489th Service Command Unit in the Army of the United States. His permanent mailing address was Box 27, Collinwood, Tennessee. He was born 26 August 1921 in Collinwood. He was registered with the Selective Service Board in Wayne County, Tennessee. His Civilian Occupation was Automobile Service Man. He was married with one dependent when he was inducted 21 October 1942 and entered into active service 4 November 1942 at Fort Oglethorpe, Georgia. His Military Occupational Specialty was Medical Aid Man. He was in the Battles of North Africa and the Italian Campaign. The following decorations were awarded to Staggs: European-African Middle Eastern Campaign Medal with 2 Bronze Battle Stars, Good Conduct Medal and A Purple Heart. He was shipped overseas 17 April 1943 and served with the 5th Army in Europe. He was wounded in action 15 July 1944 in the European Theater. He left 1 April 1944 for North Africa, left there 24 May 1944 for Italy and returned to USA 3 June 1945. He was a German POW, captured 8 October 1944 at Munich, and liberated 10 April 1945. He was discharged 10 October 1945 at Kennedy General Hospital, Memphis, Tennessee.

He died 7 September 1987 and was buried in McGlamery Cemetery in Collinwood. Melvin was the son of John Allen and Mary Lue Davis Staggs. He was married 1 September 1941 to Vergie Etta Overton. He was the father of three sons: Emory C., Tony E. and Charles M. Staggs. At the time of this writing, his widow is still living. In telling of this information, she smiled and told about him being a good man, and his hard work in the timber business and as a garage mechanic. He had four brothers: Frank, Lester, Wilson and Jimmy Staggs. He had three sisters: Ola Mae Staggs Hood, Gertie Staggs Jones and Christine Staggs Perry.

The American's Creed

*I believe in the United States of
America as a government of
the people, by the people, for
the people; whose just powers
are derived from the consent of
the governed; a democracy in a
republic, a sovereign Nation of
many sovereign States; a perfect
union, one and inseparable;
established upon those
principles of freedom, equality,
justice, and humanity for
which American patriots
sacrificed their lives and
fortunes. I therefore believe it
is my duty to my country to
love it; to support its
Constitution; to obey its Laws;
to respect its Flag; and to
defend it against all enemies.
William Tyler Page*

ANDERSON, MARY ALICE BEARD, "I was born 2 November 1912 in the historic Russ Hotel overlooking the

Tennessee River in Clifton, Tennessee. My parents were Captain Charles Russell Beard, a highly respected Tennessee, Ohio and Mississippi River steamboat Captain and my mother was Carrie Lee Russ, the daughter of John Goodman and Jimmie Hughes who built the hotel. I have one sister, Dorothy Beard Norman. We attended Frank Hughes High School in Clifton and I graduated in 1931. The next two years I was a student at Middle Tennessee State College in Murfreesboro, Tennessee and after that, I taught an eight grade country school for two years in Wayne County. After a marriage that ended in divorce, I worked as chief clerk in the WPA offices in Waynesboro, until I joined the WAAC; hence my name appears on all my official orders as Mary A. Miller. On 14 November 1942, I took the bus from Waynesboro to Chattanooga, then to Fort Oglethorpe, Georgia, and was officially sworn in as Auxiliary Mary A. Miller scheduled to report for active duty in two weeks - the first WAC in Wayne County! On 25 January 1943, I was chosen to report for Officers Candidate Training, Fort Des Moines, Iowa, and successfully graduated as 2nd Lieutenant on 8 March 1943. Now that I was an "officer", I had visions of being sent out "to see the world"; but alas! My orders came to report to Headquarters AAF Pilot School, Selma, Alabama, and my assignment was Company Commander to take a WAC detachment to Craig Field, Selma, with supervision over 125 enlisted women. My duties included billeting, messing and other personal and domestic services. We were the first WACs they had ever seen and we tried very hard to be good soldiers. To help me in this effort, I had a Personnel and a WAC mess officer to accompany me. Later I was eager to leave Company Commander duties and go overseas. At last I received orders to reported

on 6 May 1944 to Camp Shanks, New York. Then it was "top secret", but we were taken by harbor boat to the QUEEN ELIZABETH then traveling without convoy to Europe. There were thousands of us aboard packed in like sardines, but we made it safely across the Atlantic. I was, by that time, attached to the U.S. Strategic 8th Air Force and had no idea where I was being sent. It turned out to be Warrington in Lancashire, England, not far from London. My duties were Administrative Assistant, Chief Stock Control Division at a nearby Supply Depot. This meant that I directed operation of an administrative unit in Supply Depot handling Air Force Corps supplies in England, prepared work schedules and maintained liaison with staff sections and with the R.A.F. I received promotion to 1st Lieutenant after arriving in England in January 1945. Then came the critical illness of my father. I was informed that he had only a short time to live, so I applied for emergency leave to the U.S. I was fortunate to be granted leave by General Eisenhower in February 1945. My orders sent me to Southampton, England to await transportation to the States. I was assigned to the next convoy and my ship was the JOHN ERICSSON. The master of this ship was Captain John William Anderson and our convoy was two weeks in reaching New York. I met the Captain and married him 21 July 1946 and came to New York to live after my discharge. Our son Charles Beard Anderson was born 23 June 1947. After commanding the SS WASHINGTON, SS AMERICA and the pride of our country, the famous SS UNITED STATES, my husband was made Commodore of the United States Lines. But let me return to my Army duties . . . First after coming back to the states, I was sent to Camp Kilmer, then to Miami Beach, Florida for rest and Recuperation (R&R) and finally I reach my home in Clifton. My father died while I was home. After the funeral I reported to Colorado Springs, Colorado, for further adjustment. The final assignment proved to be Sioux Falls, South Dakota, 2 June 1945, where I was detailed to do Processing and Distribution as a Personal Affairs Officer. I continued to do this until I left the service. The separation center that I reported to was Fort Bragg, North Carolina, and on 23 December 1945, I was honorably discharged from active service in the Army of the United States."- Mary Alice Beard Anderson.

BISKUP, MARY LOU OLD, Serial Number N-763374, was a First Lieutenant in the U.S. Army Nurses Corps. Mary Lou, daughter of William Pryce and Nona Belle Meredith Old, was born 24 September on Moccasin Creek, Wayne County,

Tennessee. Her maternal grandparents were Leeden Rankin and Margaret Evaline Pollock Meredith. Her paternal grandparents were Sofina Elizabeth Morrison and Henry William Thomas Old. Mary Lou has two sisters, Mont Fling and Ruby Mae Armstrong. She married (1) Louis Biskup on 19 June 1943 in Shelbyville, Tennessee, Lois died 18 November 1963 and she married (2) Jim Graf on 12 December 1966 in Miami, Florida. Louis and Mary Lou had two daughters, Mary Lynn and Charlotte Biskup. Mary Lou attended elementary school in the Topsy Community and high school in Waynesboro. She enrolled in Union University in Jackson and graduated from Baptist Memorial Hospital School of Nursing in Memphis, Tennessee. After graduation from nursing school, Mary Lou enrolled in the American Red Cross, 1st Reserve, volunteering her service for duty in the U.S. Army Nurses Corps. She reported for duty in Memphis, on 1 February 1942, and was placed at the Kennedy General Hospital in Memphis for three months training. She was then sent to the Middle Tennessee maneuver area and later stationed at Camp Gordon, Georgia, until she was sent overseas in the fall of 1943. She was stationed in England, Belgium, France and Germany, serving in the 45th Evacuation Hospital on the front lines much of the time. She returned to the states after the war ended and was discharged 24 January 1946 in Memphis, Tennessee. Mary Lou was a housewife, private duty nurse, worked as a nurse in hospitals in Quantico, Virginia, Miami, Florida and Waynesboro, Tennessee, owned and operated an antique shop in West Palm Beach, Florida and was director of the Senior Citizen Center in Waynesboro. Mary Lou died 7 December 1980 in the VA Hospital in Nashville, the result of Amyotropic Lateral Sclerosis (Lou Gehrig's disease).

BOAZ, MARY SCOTT, served her country in World War II in a W.A.C. Unit in Romulus, Michigan where she enlisted.

Mary Scott was the daughter of John Harrison and Flora Bryant Scott of Wayne County, Tennessee. She married Dencil Boaz and they had two daughters, Patricia and Pamela Boaz. They live in Sebring, Florida. Three of Mary's brothers, Alf, Roy and John Harrison, Jr. also served their country during World War II.

BYLER, LAURA JANE, was a Lieutenant in the Army Nurse Corps, and was stationed in England, India and Germany.

She was the daughter of Edgar Byler who served in the Medical Corps in World War I and served on the Wayne County Draft board for the duration of World War II. She was made a Lieutenant in 1943. Laura's mother was Sara Jane Dunn Walsh Byler. Two of Laura's brothers served in the military during WWII: Robert Emmett Walsh in the Navy and Edgar D. Byler in the Army Air Force. They all served honorably.

LANGSTON, HAZEL TURNBO, enlisted AS V-10, 16 October 1943 at Memphis, Tennessee. She had ratings of AS, S2C and S1C. She served in the U.S. Naval Training Station (WR), Bronx, New York; U.S. Naval Air Station, Memphis, Tennessee; and U.S. Naval Hospital in Memphis. She had the rank of S1C, V-10

USNR when she was honorably discharged in Memphis. She was born 5 March 1921 in Peters Landing, Perry County, Tennessee, but moved to Wayne County at the age of 2 years. Her parents are George Allen and Flora Day Pevahouse Turnbo. Hazel has seven siblings: Tim Ed Turnbo and Myrtle Aslee Warren, both of Clifton, Della Christine Pulley, Florence Alabama, Ardes Marie Pierce, Horn Lake, Mississippi, W.B. Turnbo, Waynesboro, G.A. Turnbo, Linden, Walton D. Turnbo, Stantionville, Tennessee and Alton Brown Turnbo died in 1937 and Rubenia Carrie died in 1932. Hazel married J. T. Langston. There was no issue.

MARTIN, MARGARET LOIS, Serial Number A-403232, enrolled in the Women's Army Auxiliary Corps in De-

cember 1942 at Fort Oglethorpe. I reported for training 11 December 1942 to 1st W.A.A.C. Training Center in Fort Des Moines, Iowa. I attended Cooks and Bakers School and graduated with the Specialty, 1st Cook. I reported for duty to the 601st W.A.A.C. Filter Company AWS - Fort Brady, Sault Marie, Michigan. I was appointed Technician 4th Grade (Sergeant) on 4 June 1943. I did not reenlist when the Women's Army Auxiliary Corps was made

into the regular army (Women's Army Corps) therefore I received my Honorable Discharge from the Women's Army Auxiliary Corps 24 August 1943 at Fort Des Moines, Iowa, after having served 7 months and 15 days. Margaret was the 18th child of Henry David Martin. His first wife had ten children before she died and my mother, Margaret Lousetta Blair Martin had eight children. I was born 13 June 1914 in Lutts, Tennessee. At the time of service my home address was Collinwood, Tennessee. I graduated from Collinwood High School and Martin College, Pulaski, Tennessee. I was by profession an elementary school teacher and resumed teaching after my W.A.A.C. service. All of my brothers and sisters have passed away. I have only nieces, nephews and cousins left. On 26 December 1947 I was married to Samuel J. Prohart and our address is 1301 W. North Street, Ajo, Arizona. We have one son Timothy Blair Prohart who lives with us. One point of interest is the fact that we have a sister-in-law who is 109 years old. She is Roxie Nowlin Martin, my late brother Henry Martin's wife, and she lives in Milan, Tennessee.

McGEE, LILLIAN FLORA MAY, daughter of David Monroe and Catherine Broadfoot May. She spent four years in the

field of Nursing while serving her country during WWII from May 1942 to June 1946. During those years she served at Norfolk, VA, Camp Perry, VA, Mary Island, CA, and Pearl Harbor, Hawaii.

After receiving an honorable discharge, she attended college. She enrolled at Florence State College (now UNA) and earned her Bachelor's Degree. She later attended the University of Kentucky earning her Master's Degree in Public Health Administration. For a time she worked for the TVA but left their employment. She received the opportunity to teach Nursing at the University of North Alabama, which she did for four years. She is now retired.

OLD, MARY RUTH, - World War II Volunteer - United States Women's Marine Corps Mary Ruth Old, was born 20 April

1915 in Watertown, Wilson County, and died 1 September 1981. She was the first of four children born to Talmage Old, Sr., (1891-1942) and Grace Leo Ricketts (1890-1972). Her siblings are Martha Adeline Hassel, Talmage Old, Jr., (1920-1985) and Margaret Old Rains (1928 - 1998). Mary's paternal grandparents were Hugh Shields and Martha Adeline Morrison Old of Wayne County Her maternal grandparents are Charles Samuel Ricketts of Clifton, and Willie Shannon Hawkins, a native of Louisiana. The Old family moved from Nashville to Wayne County when Mary was thirteen years old, and in Waynesboro she completed her public school education, graduating as valedictorian of the class of 1933 at Wayne County High School. Mary attended Milligan College in Johnson City, Tennessee, where she studied for a secretarial and/or bookkeeping career. Returning to Waynesboro, Mary served efficiently as bookkeeper for the Dave Anderson Lumber Mill; she was later employed as Office Manager at the Holthouse & Hardup Lumber Mfg. Co. Her pre-WMC employment also included a year as secretary in Washington, D.C. (U.S. Civil Service). Mary volunteered for service in the United States Women's Marine Corps in 1945, completing her "boot" training in July at Camp LeJeune, North Carolina. Pvt. Old was then assigned as a clerk-typist at the Marine Base at Parris Island, South Carolina. She was promoted to the rank of Sergeant and completed her one-year enlistment tour of duty at Parris Island. Mary was honorably discharged in 1946 and returned to Waynesboro to work in the Cullen C. Woods Memorial Hospital as bookkeeper. Mary married William J. Baird, a U.S. Marine veteran from Dubuque, Iowa, in 1946. and her business career included several years as Civil Service secretary in Memphis and Oakland, California. When she retired she was secretary to the Admiral-in Charge of the Oakland Naval Yards, only a few months before her fatal heart attack. Bill and Mary were the parents of three children: Pamela Cheryl, Richard Jeffery, and Penelope Margaret. The Baird family lived in Walnut Creek, California. Currently, Pamelia and husband Mark Peterson live in Little Rock, Arkansas; they have two daughters, Rebecca Baird and Rachel Catherine Peterson. Richard lives in the San Francisco area as a business man, and Penny is a lawyer in San Francisco. Bill continues his work in Oakland (Newspaper) and lives in the family home in Walnut Creek. Mary's main interests were centered around her children and her work. Her hobbies included reading and knitting. Her home library was enviable, and her knit garments were classic in design and beauty. She was a thinker, and she delighted in taking part in discussions on stimulating topics. Efficient, dignified, and gracious was this rather enigmatic lady, and she welcomed any task which challenged her intellect. Mary Ruth died 1 September 1981, the victim of a heart attack (Cardiac Arrest) at age 66. She had been a devoted daughter to her widowed mother, a competent Lady Marine, a superior secretary, a dedicated mother, a lifelong friend to many, a Christian who tried daily to live by the "Golden Rule," and - the most loyal and loving of sisters."- Margaret Old Rains, sister of Mary Baird., November 1991 .

WAYNE COUNTY, TENNESSEE
VETERANS

Fred E. Gillham, 35, carpenter's mate, first class, USNR, and his brother Finley E. Gillham, 31, electrician's mate, second class, USNR, both of Clifton, TN operating laundry machines on Okinawa where they are helping to build thousands of homes for the natives of the island before winter arrives. (Official U.S. Navy photograph.)

ABRAMS, JAMES L., was born March 6, 1920 in Wayne County, Tennessee, to Edd and Fannie Eaton Abrams. His

grandparents were George and Sally Harbor Eaton and William Fletcher and Sarah Ann Mathis Abrams. He had four brothers. They are Edwin who lives in Savannah, Tennessee; Billy who died as a young child; T. R. who lives in Lutts; and Warren "Buck" Abrams who died in 1980. His youth was spent growing up in the Lutts community. He was a member of the Lutts Methodist Church. Daddy attended elementary school at Pinhook and graduated from Collinwood High School in 1940. He enjoyed school and always hated to miss a day. He decided to continue his education at Draughn's Business College in Nashville, Tennessee. He attended about a year, and then was called into the service. He went directly from Basic Training into the Navy at the beginning of WW II. He served from 27 October 1941 to 28 September 1945. Dad served in the South Pacific and was on several different islands. He operated radar equipment and the large guns on the ship. He once told my Uncle T. R. that their ship was hit by one of the Japanese suicide planes and thirty (30) of their men were killed. The ship had to go in for repairs and this was the first furlough that daddy had gotten since the war began. When the U. S. invaded Okinawa, his ship was hit again, and over seventy (70) men were killed. Everyone waited for the ship to sink, but it didn't! Another time a suicide plane hit the ship and the pilot survived. He was taken as a POW. My Dad spent 44 months on the U. S. S. New Mexico and went through the total war. He was honorably discharged on September 28, 1945.

James L. came back to Wayne County and farmed a while. On September 13, 1947, he married Annie Stricklin. They had one child born on July 28, 1948. They named her Judy Diane - that's me! When I was about a year old my parents moved to Mishawaka, Indiana. Daddy worked at

Oliver's and Bendix. He died 16 September 1957 at the young age of 37.

People have told me what a good person my Dad was. He was the kind of person who stood by his friends through good and bad times. I was only nine (9) years old when daddy died and it was a very traumatic time in my life. I still miss him a lot, and there are times when I would love to be able to have him to talk to and ask for advice. I've been married to Bill Steele for twenty five (25) years, and we have three sons - Kevin, Kerry, and Jamie. My mother has said one of her goals in life was to raise me so that my daddy would be proud of me. I think she did a pretty good job and I think he would be proud of all of us. I feel honored to write this brief story of his life and the contribution he made in the service to his country.

Submitted by Judy Diane Abrams Steele.

ABRAMS, WARREN G. HARDING, was born January 15, 1923 in Wayne County, Tennessee to Edd and Fannie Eaton Abrams. His grandparents were George and Sally Harbor Eaton and William Fletcher and Sarah Ann Mathis Abrams. He had four brothers. They are Edwin who lives in Savannah, Tennessee; Billy who died as a young child; T. R. who lives in Lutts; and James L. Abrams who died in 1957. Warren spent his youth in the Lutts community and attended Pinhook School. He belonged to the Lutts Methodist Church. Warren, or Buck, as he was often called, entered the U. S. Navy on April 10, 1944 and served until WW II was over in 1945.

Warren came home to Tennessee and then later moved to Jonesboro, AR. He worked as a salesman for the Tastee Bread Co. for several years. He also worked with Guaranty Mortgage and Real Estate Co. He married Bobbie Watkins on July 3, 1959. They had one son, Mark Harding, born January 1, 1962. Warren had a good personality and was liked by many people. He died in Lutts on September 15, 1980 at the age of 57.

ADAMS, RICHARD HENRY, 76, of 49 Holly Creek Road, Iron City, died 16 June 1997 and was buried in Hollis Cemetery in Wayne County. A native of Lauderdale County, Alabama, he was the son of Walter and Callie Brewer Adams. He was a retired mechanic, a Methodist and served in the Army during World War II. Survivors include his wife, Dellie Bishop Adams; five sons, Roman of St. Joseph, Frank and Marcus of Lawrenceburg, Junior and Michael both of Iron City; three daughters, Jonell Kelly of Loretto, and Jean Cozart Beardin and Ellen Wayland both of

Lawrenceburg; thirty grandchildren; forty-seven great-grandchildren and two great-great-grandchildren.

Source: Obit in The Wayne County News, 18 June 1997.

ADAMS, WILLIAM J., Army Serial Number 44 121 853, was a Private in Company C, 207th Infantry Training Battalion,

U. S. Army when he was discharged 6 December 1945 at Camp Blanding, Florida. His description was given as: blue eyes, brown hair, 5' 8" tall, 140 lbs, a farmer, and single with three dependents. He was born 27 February 1927 in Collinwood, Tennessee. His education consisted of 8 years of grammar school. He was inducted 20 June 1945 into active service at Ft. Oglethorpe, Georgia. He received the following decorations: World War II Victory Medal and a Lapel Button was issued. His total length of Service was 5 months, 16 days. He did not have any foreign service. His permanent Address was Route 1, Collinwood, Tennessee.

ADCOCK, JAMES FRANKLIN, was a Private in the Infantry of the United States Army. He was inducted May 1945 and discharged March 1946. He finished high school in Morehouse, Missouri. His Overseas Duties were in the European Theater of War, Italy and Germany. He worked in an aircraft factory in Baltimore, Maryland before entering service. After his discharge, he worked for Ford Motor Co. until his retirement.

His parents are John and Elizabeth Adcock. His sisters are Beatrice Adcock Stanfill, Aliene Adcock Hill, and Marillion Adcock Stanford. His brothers are William Henry and John Adcock, Jr. He married Iva Dell Pulley. His children are Lillian, Elizabeth, Jimmy, and Michael Adcock.

ADKINS, PAUL, Army Serial Number 34 193 022, was inducted into active service 15 March 1942 at Fort Oglethorpe, Georgia. His description was gray eyes, brown hair, 6' 1/2" tall, weight 130, and married with 3 dependents. His education consisted of 5 years in elementary school. His Civilian Occupation was dry lumber grader. His grade was Technician 4th Grade in Co K, 194th GLI Infantry, Army of the United States. His Military Occupational Specialty was Cook. His Military Qualification was Combat Infantryman Badge, Glider Badge*. His battles and campaigns were in Central Europe, Ardennes, and Rhineland. His decorations and citations were: Good Conduct Ribbon; European-African Middle Eastern Theater Ribbon with 3 Bronze Stars and with Bronze Service Arrowhead; *Rifle Sharpshooter; Button Lapel issued. He departed the USA on the 20 August '44 to go to European Theater Operation and returned to USA 14 September '45. He was discharged 19 September 1945 at Camp Atterburg, Indiana.

He was born 1 August 1919, Wayne County, Tennessee. He married Junaga Kelley of Wayne County, Tennessee.

ADKINSON, THOMAS ALLEN, was 31 years old when World War II broke out December 7, 1941. He was born May

15, 1910, in Iron City, Tennessee to Thomas Allen and Mollie Willis Adkinson. He moved with his family to Collinwood, when he was three years old. Collinwood was still in its infancy as a town.

He graduated from Collinwood High School in 1928, and for the next few years he did some carpentry work with his older brother Leonard; worked in West Virginia on various construction projects; and worked in the dismantling of the old chemical plant in Collinwood. In the middle 1930's, he purchased the ESSO service station in Collinwood.

In June 1939, he married Dona McWilliams of Waynesboro, and in March of 1941, their first child Mollie Ruth was born. After the war started, he continued

to operate the service station in Collinwood, and in November 1942, their son Thomas Leonard was born.

Thomas was inducted into the Army in January 1944. He sold the service station at that time on the condition that he could buy it back if he wanted to upon his return from the service. His basic training was in Fort Polk, Louisiana, and his advanced training was at Fort Snelling, Minneapolis, Minnesota. The transfer from Louisiana to Minnesota occurred in March, by way of train. The troops had already been issued summer uniforms and then the uniforms going to Minnesota were transferred back to winter time in about two days. They almost froze to death, or so it seemed.

While he was stationed at Fort Snelling in Minneapolis, his wife and children were able to join him for about three months before he was sent overseas in the summer of 1944.

His company crossed the Atlantic from New York to England in a convoy of "Liberty Ships. " Their ship was a small English troop ship and the American soldiers had a difficult time with the different food, while at the same time having to get their "sea legs" under them.

After a short time in England, his unit, Company A, 735th Railway Operations Battalion, was shipped to France. Their main duty was the repair and/or reconstruction of railroad track and bridges which had been destroyed during the fighting by either the retreating Germans or the advancing allies. The main hazards they encountered were unexploded shells or bombs and "booby traps" intentionally left by the Germans. Once a building next door to where they were sleeping was destroyed by a German "buzz bomb" rocket.

From France, they advanced into Belgium and were there in December and January, when the Germans counterattack known as the "Battle of the Bulge" took place. It appeared for some time as though his unit might be pressed into front line combat, but this did not happen as the Germans were driven back in the niche of time. They were, however, close enough to get shelled by German artillery. From Belgium, they advanced into Germany and were in Germany on VE Day, May 8, 1945.

Following the German surrender, the 735th continued its reconstruction duties using a large number of civilian workers in addition to their own troops. Thomas liked his German workers and often commented in later years on their willingness to work and seeming lack of bitterness.

He was able to use his prewar construction experience during this time and was offered a number of inducements to stay over in Germany, but he refused. His unit was sent home to be discharged, hopefully

in time for Christmas, but their ship was delayed about two weeks by a storm at sea. They finally arrived in the United States, and Thomas was honorably discharged with the rank of Sergeant T-4, January 29, 1946, having spent almost exactly twenty-four months in service, with almost eighteen months of that time having been overseas. He earned the World War II Victory Medal, the European-African-Mid Eastern Ribbon with two Bronze Service Stars, and the Good Conduct Metal.

Upon returning to Collinwood, he repurchased the ESSO station and ran it for about three years before selling it again. He was in the coal hauling and selling business with J. F. Farris for a short time and drove an oil truck for Ed Yeiser for a few months before becoming Parts and Service manager of Hassell and Hughes Ford dealership in Waynesboro, in the fall of 1949. He moved his family to Waynesboro in November 1949. In 1954, he ran for and was elected County Court Clerk, an office he held until his retirement in September 1974.

Thomas and Dona continued to live in Waynesboro in retirement until his death from complications due to lung cancer on June 14, 1990. He died quietly at Wayne County Hospital with his family at his bedside. He was the grandfather of five: Suzanne Duren Diercks, Keith Thomas Duren, Steven Gregory Duren, Thomas Leonard Adkinson, II, and Andrew Sidney Adkinson; and the great-grandfather of two: Kara Ann Duren and Thomas Jeffrey Diercks.

ALLEN, BUFORD CLINTON, son of John and Pearlie Martin Allen, was born September 8, 1921 in Clifton, Tennessee. He served in the United States Army. He was married to Louise Schubert and had two sons: Don and Eddie Allen; two daughters, Linda Allen Cowart and Pattie Allen Cantrell. His brothers were John Franklin, and Wayne Allen. His sisters were Pauline Allen Byrum, Ruth Allen Hime and Lucille Allen Hime.

He was a retired heavy equipment operator in Limestone County, Alabama. His home was in Athens, Alabama. at the time of his death on 20 March 1994. He was a member of the Baptist Church.

ALLEN, JOHN FRANKLIN, was born in 1928, the son of John Edwin Allen and Perlie Martin Allen. He volunteered for the United States Army at the age of 17. He was sent to Germany to stay for two years. At the end of four years in the service, he came out but remained in the Army Reserve.

He married Ledena Lineberry, daughter of Edward (Babe) Lineberry and Claytie Wheat Lineberry. They married in December 1949. John Franklin was called back into service for the Korean Conflict. He stayed two years before becoming ill. He was then given a medical discharge. When in the service, he received a certificate of engineering.

When he came out of the service, he and Ledena moved to Detroit, Michigan, to live, however they did not stay too long in Michigan. They returned to the Clifton area to live and rear their four children: Rhonda Sharon, Shelia Elaine, and twins: Johnny Barry and Jeffrey Larry. John Franklin worked in janitorial services in the factory. He held membership in the D. A. V. He was of the Baptist faith.

He died in July 1996 and was buried in the Clifton City Cemetery.

ALLEY, JAMES E., Serial Number 34 501 373, was inducted into active service 27 December 1942 at Fort Oglethorpe,

Georgia. His description was: blue eyes, brown hair, 5', 6" tall, weight 138 lbs, and no dependents. His Civilian Occupation was Circular Ripsaw Operator. He was a Saw Mill Machine Operator in the service. He was registered with Local Selective Service Board No. 1, Waynesboro, Tennessee. His home address at time of entry into service was 1200 Ross St., Corinth, Mississippi. His education consisted of 6 years in Grammar school.

He was a Technician, Fourth Grade in the Army of the United States, with the 236th Engineers Combat Battalion. His battles and campaigns were in India and Burma. His decorations and citations: Asiatic Pacific Theater Ribbon with one Bronze Service Star; Good Conduct Medal; World War II Victory Medal, Distinguished Unit Badge and a Lapel Button. He left the USA 18 November 1943 and returned 1 January 1946. Under Remarks: He was discharged 6 January 1946 at Fort Knox, Kentucky as Sgt. His permanent address was Route 1, Waynesboro, Wayne County, Tennessee

James, son of Lynn and Elizabeth Elliote Alley, was born 27 September 1922 in Waynesboro, Tennessee. His brothers are Bill, Freeman and Ray Alley. His wife is Thelma Jean Martin and his children are Jeffrey Alley, and Janie Alley Shouse.

James Alley Honored After 43 Years For Service World War II. Many Nations around the world have first-hand reason to appreciate the American fighting man. Veteran's laid down their lives on the doorsteps of friends from many foreign lands, defending those people's very lives. The gratitude of these nations has been expressed in part by heaping upon American veteran's their highest decorations for courage and valor.

In the last month of 1987, just prior to Christmas, a Wayne County veteran of World War II received just such a decoration, awarded for his contribution to the Chinese people forty-three years ago. James Alley, now an employee of the City of Waynesboro, was awarded the China War Memorial Medal by the government of the Republic of China for his combat service in Burma, when he and a few thousand nearly forgotten American G. I.'s fought side by side with Chinese troops to halt the Japanese invasion of mainland Asia.

James Alley left America for Asia accompanied by a friend from Collinwood. Alley and Earl Dixon both would become members of the 236th Combat Engineers, a part of the 5307th Infantry and members of the renowned Merrill's Marauders. Another Wayne Countian, James Thelbert Phillips of Waynesboro, would bring the Wayne County presence of this branch of the Army to three, only two could return to Wayne County when the war ended.

When Alley and Dixon arrived in India, they saw sights which were shocking even to men who had grown up in the hard times of the Great Depression. Famine was rampant in India. In that country, death came more often by hunger and its related diseases than by warfare.

The ride into Burma was equally depressing. Loaded into crowded cattle car type trains, American soldiers lived on Spam and "dog biscuits" as their main fare and endured the ever present wet and humid conditions of the jungle. When the engineers stopped to begin construction, they had to exist in the most primitive conditions.

In March 1944, a special shock force of nearly 12,000 British and Gurka Indian troops were flown into northern Burma by gliders. Alley described the Gurka's as "one of the best fighting forces in the world. " These troops would link up with Stillwell's three American trained Chinese divisions and Merrill's Marauders in the march toward Myikyina.

The battle of Myikyina was won by the Allied forces at a terrible cost. Hundreds of Allies were killed or wounded by the Japanese and hundreds more were victims of disease and fungal infections.

Alley fought with A Company, Dixon fought with B Company and Phillips fought with C Company, all in the 236th Combat Engineers. Before the fighting was over, Earl Dixon made the supreme sacrifice, falling at Myikyina in defense of freedom. Alley and Phillips survived, but not without permanent reminders of their role in history. The jungle fungus that covered the bodied of soldiers as they lay sweltering in their muddy fox holes was next to impossible to get rid of. Alley suffered from the fungus until the mid 1970's, when it was finally cured in a Veteran's Hospital in New Orleans.

The Japanese were expelled from Burma. When the war ended, James Alley and the 236th Combat Engineers were in India, serving as a maintenance force. Alley was 23 years old when the war was over.

Each second Sunday in July, the 236th Combat Engineers hold their annual reunion in Shelby Park in Nashville, a location considered central for veterans of the proud fighting force to reach. James Alley has not missed a reunion in 30 years.

When the 236th gathers each year, men who spent one of the most significant periods of history together, completely dependent on each other, rekindle deep friendships and remember lost comrades. We join the Chinese government in offering our thanks and appreciation to all of these men, living and dead, who journeyed so far from home for all of us.

Source: Wayne County News, p. 5, January 13, 1988.

ANDERSON, ALFRED ISAAC, Serial Number 967 13 46, enlisted as apprentice Seaman on 4 October 1944 in Nashville, Tennessee for two years. His descrip-

tion was: blue eyes, brown hair, ruddy complexion, height 5', 10", weight 175 lbs. He was born 12 February 1907 in Flatwoods, Tennessee. His Grade was Seaman Second Class V6 when he was discharged at the U S Naval Convalescent Hospital, under Honorable conditions, dated 24 October 1944 at Santa Cruz, California with a physical disability. His Monthly rate of pay when discharged was $54. 00. The amount paid in full on date of discharge was $141. 68.

His parents were Rufus and Bashey Briley Anderson. His married Nannie Ray and his children are James H., Edward, Sue Nelle, and Betty Anderson. Under Remarks it said that James H. Anderson, his son, was also in World War II. Alfred died 27 August 1976, and was buried in Culp Cemetery, Beech Creek, Wayne County, Tennessee. He was a farmer near Clifton, Tennessee and a member of the American Legion.

ANDERSON, JAMES H., Serial Number 34 738 880, was inducted 2 July 1943 and entered active service 16 July

1943 at Fort Oglethorpe, Georgia. His description was: blue eyes, brown hair, 5' 7" tall, weight 165 lbs, and was single. His date of birth was 16 April 1925. James H. Anderson received six months of training in Camp Ellis, Illinois. His Military Qualification was Marksman Rifle -6 September 1943. His Rank was Tec 5 with QMC 539th QM Salvage Repair Co. Army of the United States when he was discharge 21 January 1946 at Camp Chaffee, Arkansas. His home Address was Route 1, Clifton, Tennessee. His service citations: World War II Victory Ribbon, Good Conduct Ribbon, Asiatic Pacific Theater Ribbon, two Bronze Stars, Philippine Liberation Ribbon, plus one Bronze Star.

James remembers: "We had spent Christmas 1943 in New York City, seeing the Empire State Building, Statue of Liberty, and Paramount Theater. Frank Sinatra

was singing there. We left Camp Kilmer, New Jersey on January 5, 1944 and went down the East Coast to Panama Canal. They informed us there that we would go through the Canal and on to the South Pacific. We were twenty-three days getting to the first stop which was New Caledonia, a French Island in the Pacific. We spent the next twenty-one days resting, then we began working on a building for the Red Cross. Mostly we worked pouring concrete.

Our next stop was the Figi Islands to pick up Figi troops, on to Guadalcanal for supplies, then to Bongainville, an island in the Solomon chain. Our company spent one year in Bongainville attached to the 37th Infantry Division. I met Hubert Tinin, a boy from Clifton, Tennessee, there. In February 1945 we landed in Luzon, the largest island of the Philippines. We stayed there until January 1946. I met Edd Jeter and Edgar Steele in Manila, who also, were Clifton boys. I returned to San Francisco on the Aircraft carrier U. S. S. Yorktown and spent two days at Fort Orr, then on to Camp Chaffee, Arkansas to be discharged.

I am the son of a World War II Navy veteran, Alfred Anderson and Nannie Ray Anderson. I am married to Joycelyn Smith Anderson. My children are Jimmy, Douglas and Delores. I am a member of the Christian Church, a member of the Lions Club, Boy Scouts, Rotary Club, V. F. W and the American Legion. I am retired from 33 years with Northern National Gas Company, Omaha, Nebraska. I own a farm and reside outside Clifton, Tennessee. I have a high school education and had agriculture courses. "

ANDERSON, JAMES RICHARD, entered the United States Navy in May 1945, went to camp at Great Lakes, Illi-

nois, and later to Camp Parks, California. He served in South Pacific, Mariana Islands, Guam. His rank was Seaman First Class when he was discharged April 29,

1946, U. S. Naval Personnel Separation Center, Memphis, Tennessee.

James, son of Herbert T. and Ruby Y. Anderson, was born February 13, 1923. His brother is Howard Anderson. His sisters are Veanilea, Mary Jean and June Anderson. His wife is Ruby Brewer Anderson and his children are Marilyn, James Thomas and Martha Nell Anderson.

ANDERSON, RICHARD, JR., was born on April 27, 1925, the son of Richard Sr. and Eddith Stricklin Anderson near

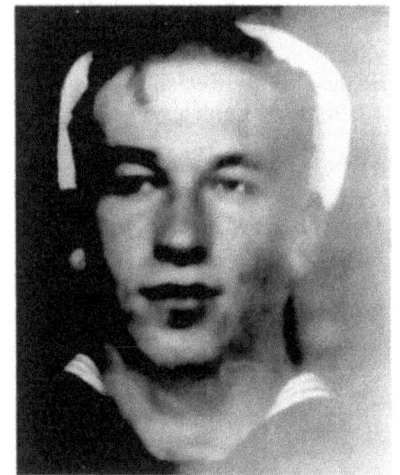

Clifton, Tennessee. I grew up there and went to church and school, completing my junior year in at Frank Hughes High School.

I was inducted into the United States Navy on August 11, 1943, in Fort Oglethorpe, Georgia, and entered into active service in Chattanooga, Tennessee. I was sent to USNTS Bain Bridge, Maryland Boot Camp for six weeks, on to NTS NOB Norfolk, Virginia, for a short time, and then to Charleston, South Carolina, to board the ship U. S. S. Albert W. Grant DD649, which I stayed on until my discharge. From Charleston, we were carried to Bermuda for a "Shake down crew" (a new aircraft carrier) and picked up. We were escorted through the Panama Canal back to San Diego, and then out to the Pacific by the Hawaiian Islands on through the Japanese joining with Task Force 58. We operated with them on the 7th fleet with Admiral Halsey. At this point, we went into the invasion of Si Pan Pinnian into the remaining islands of the South Pacific and Philippines. I received the Asiatic Pacific Medal, five stars, American Theater Medal, Philippine Operations Medal, Navy 845-93-71 N. Om 3/c V-6, SV USNR. I was in six invasions. When Peace was declared, we were sent into Japan for three months where the work carried us into two different towns. This work was taking the Japanese tugboats filled with ammunition seven miles out to sea and dumping it over board.

I remember the Japanese dirt streets and the homes zbeing very clean. I remember also seeing fish canneries. We watched the women as they held a position alongside a very long rope, feet spread like a duck clutching for a hold in the sand. In a rhythmic swaying motion, they would pull the 100-pound or more fish from the sea to the cannery.

I obtained a Japanese rifle and two Japanese kimonos to bring home. From Japan we landed in Seattle, Washington. It was here I said farewell to the USS Albert W. Grant and hurried to my place of separatism, PSC Memphis, Tennessee with an honorable discharge on March 12, 1946.

Since then I have spent maybe 18 years in Oklahoma City working as a butcher in IGA and Safe Way Grocery Stores. Then, I went on to work on boats, spending time on the Ohio, Missouri, Mississippi and Tennessee Rivers.

I married Edith Collie. We have one son, Andrew (Andy) Anderson.

I am a mason, a Shriner and a member of the VFW.

My siblings are Wanda, Rufus, Jerry and Bobby.

Submitted by Richard Anderson Jr.

ANDREWS, DOYLE, Seaman/2nd Class (Cee Bee) U. S. Navy, was inducted July 1945, and discharged October 1945. He trained at Great Lakes, Illinois, then was sent to California where he received a back injury. He worked as a farmer and truck driver before entering service. After service, he owned a garage in West Point, Tennessee until he retired.

Doyle, son of Charles and Bonnie Lee Andrews, was born 16 July 1927 in Lawrence County, died 18 December 1995 in St. Thomas Hospital in Nashville and was buried in Bethlehem Baptist Church Cemetery. He married Dorothy Stewart. His children are Doyle Ray Andrews of West Point, Sue Andrews Hanback of Florence, Linda Andrews Luker, and Janice Andrews Creecy both of West Point. His surviving siblings were Harry Andrews of Waynesboro, Howard Andrews of Florence, Alabama, Etah Todd of Hayti, Missouri, Margie Stooksberry of Lawrenceburg. He also had nine grandchildren and two great-grandchildren.

Source: Obit in Wayne County News 27 December 1995.

ANDREWS, JAMES "JACK", Serial Number 34 366 669, was inducted 26 August 1942 at Fort Oglethorpe, Georgia. His description was: blue eyes, brown hair, 5' 6" tall, weight 171 lbs., single with 4 dependents, and a farmer. He was born 22 September 1921 in West Point, Tennessee. His rank was Technician Fifth Grade with

the Battery B, 222nd Antiaircraft Artillery, Searchlight Battalion U. S. Army, CAC (AA) when he was discharged 27 December 1945 in Fort Chaffee, Arkansas. His Address was Route 1, West Point, Lawrence County, Tennessee but he was Registered with Local Draft Board No. 1, Wayne County, Tennessee. He was a Truck Driver while he was in service and drove a two and one-half ton truck for an antiaircraft battery. He hauled ammunition, food, clothing and personnel. Battles and campaigns that he was in were: Twenty-one Months in New Guinea, Dutch Indies and Southern Philippines Islands. Decorations and citations: World War II Victory Ribbon, Good Conduct Medal, American Theater Ribbon, Asiatic Pacific Theater Ribbon with two Bronze Service Stars, Philippines Liberation Ribbon, One Bronze Star, and Lapel Button. He departed the USA 16 Mar 1944 for Asiatic Pacific Theater and returned 16 December 1945.

He married Lou Ella Stockard. His children: Randall James Andrews, and Angela Andrews Pevahouse. Grandchildren: Jeremy Scott Andrews, Crystal and Jessica Pevahouse. His parents are John Thomas Andrews from Alabama and Minnie Myrtle Yarboro Andrews.

ANDREWS, JOHN EDWARD, son of Daniel and Nancy Jane Andrews, was born on December 18, 1915, and grew up in the California Branch community in Wayne County. He served several months in the United States Army during World War II, but he was discharged for health reasons when he took his physical for overseas duty.

He married Geneva Russ of Lawrence County, and they continue living in West Point. John Edward is now suffering from emphysema. They have five children: Jerry Wayne, Carolyn, Johnny, Kathie and Malcolm Henry.

ANDREWS, MELVIN, son of Daniel and Nancy Jane Andrews, was born on

May 1, 1912, in the California Branch community in Wayne County and grew up there. He served four years in the United States Army during World War II and several months of that time was spent in the European Theater.

He never married and is deceased.

ARNETT, CHARLES "CHARLIE" MARSHALL, was inducted 21 January 1944 in the United States Navy. The following ratings were held: AAS, S2C, SIC, *COX(T) in the South Pacific service. He spent fourteen months in the South and Central Pacific and was a veteran of the battles of Saipan, Philippines, Leyte Gulf and Iwo Jima. The Vessels and Stations that he served on: USNTS, Great Lakes, Illinois- USS LST 223, Com Ser RPM 7, R/S Navy 3149. His rank was Coxswain in the United States Navy when he was discharged 14 November 1945 at U S Naval Personnel Separation Center, Memphis, Tennessee. He was employed by Vultee Aircraft Corp in Nashville before entering the service

Charlie, the son of Lonnie and Ida Berry Arnett, was born 5 September 1914 in Wayne County, Tennessee. He married Gertie Rich and his children are Hazel Arlene Pigg, Charles Arnett, Jr., James Edward, and Tim Arnett.

ARNETT, JOHN HENRY, JR., resides in Lauderdale County, Alabama. He is the son of John Henry Arnett, Sr., and Leona Darby Arnett.

ARNOLD, CLARK, served in the United States Army. He was assigned to his unit as an instructor, teaching service men to operate heavy machinery. He served in limited service because of back problems. He served in camps in Virginia, North Carolina and El Paso, Texas and was discharged about 1945. Before he entered service, he was employed by TVA. After he returned home he worked as a mechanic in Florence, Alabama.

Clark, son of Bill and Eva Tucker Arnold, was born 6 June 1908 and died 1976 in Iron City, Tennessee. He married Carolyn Cofield and they had one son, Malcolm Arnold. He was a member of the Baptist Church.

ARNOLD, LEONARD W., of Waynesboro, son of C. F. Arnold of Parsons, Tn., served as Sgt. with the fourth ferrying group. He was associated with Hassell and Hughes in Wayne County prior to entering the service, October 1, 1942.

AYERS, ARCHIE, Serial Number 34 373 137, was inducted 24 September 1942 at Fort Oglethorpe, Georgia, at the age of

36 years. He was born in Lutts, Tennessee. His description was: brown eyes, brown hair, ruddy complexion, 5', 5" tall, and a farmer. His Army Specialty was Laborer. His Grade was Private, with the Quartermaster Section, Enlisted Detachment, 101st Unit, United States Army. His period of Active Duty was from 8 October 1942 to 21 August 1943 inclusive. He was discharged 21 August 1943 at Camp Gruber, Oklahoma.

AYERS, ARTHUR (Auther on discharge papers), Serial Number 34 194 552, was inducted into active service 4 April 1942 at Fort Oglethorpe, Georgia. His description was: blue eyes, brown hair 5', 6" tall, weight 130 lbs, no dependents, divorced, and a farmer. He was born 16 January 1917 Wayne County, Tennessee. His Military Occupational Specialty was Seaman. His battles and campaigns were in New Guinea, Southern Philippines, and Luzon. The decorations and citations received were: World War II Victory Ribbon, Good Conduct Medal, American Theater Ribbon, Asiatic-Pacific Theater Ribbon, Three Bronze Service Stars, Philippine Liberation Ribbon, One Bronze Star. He left the USA 21 September 1944 to go to Asiatic-Pacific and returned 21 December 1945. His Grade was Technician Fifth, with 368th TC Harbor Craft Company, Army of the United States when he was discharged 28 December 1945 at Camp Chaffee, Arkansas. His permanent mailing address was Route 2, Lutts, Tennessee.

AYERS, ERNEST L., Private in the U. S. Army, was born 17 December 1926, died March 1989, and is buried in Memorial Gardens, Collinwood, Tennessee. He served overseas in the European Theater of War. His parents are William and Sarah Ayers Harper. His brothers are William, Howard, Herman, and Hardin Ayers. He married Betty Jean Holt. His children are Lanny, Billy, Joan Ayers Risner, Kathy Ayers McCurry and Rita Ayers Staggs.

AYERS, JESSIE, Certificate In Lieu Of Lost Or Destroyed Discharge-Department of the Army:

This is to certify that <u>Jessie Ayers</u> Number 34 194 549, Pvt., 209TH General Hospital, was separated from the military service of the United States of America.

By Honorable Discharge on 21 May 1943 at Fort George G. Meade, Maryland

Given by the Department of the Army, Washington, DC on 28 September 1950.

By order of the Secretary of the Army: Edward F Witsell, Major General USA, The Adjutant General.

AYERS, LESTER JAMES, was born

on April 29, 1915, the son of Noah and Nannie Casteel Ayers. H grew up on Chalk Creek where he farmed with his father and brothers. He was a farmer and a factory worker in Indiana.

He was third of six children: Walter (born December 20, 1911) married Georgia Martin; Fred (born in 1913) lived in South Carolina; Emma (born in 1917) died on February 21, 1946, and is buried in Shields Cemetery in Wayne County; Pearl (1920-1953) married Paul McWilliams; and Ruby Irene (November 20, 1921-October or November 1999) was married to Dalton Swift and lived in Bruceton and is buried there.

Lester James married Lena Beckham in Wayne County. They had two sons: James of Foley, Alabama, and Harold of Osceola, Indiana. They also had one daughter, Stella Ayers Perry of Foley, Alabama. They have eight grandchildren and nine great-grandchildren.

Lester James Ayers, a Seaman 1st Class in the United States Navy, was honorably discharged at the United States Naval Personnel Separation Center in Memphis, Tennessee on the October 24, 1945.

He died at Eastern Shore Nursing Home in Fairhope, Alabama. He was buried in Mt. Hermon Cemetery in Wayne County, Tennessee. He was a Baptist.

AYERS, RALPH C., Serial Number 34 735 448, was inducted 2 June 1943, and entered into active service 16 June 1943 in Ft. Oglethorpe, Georgia. His description was: blue eyes, brown hair, 6' 1/2" tall, 154 lbs, weight, two dependents, and single. His education consisted of 8 years of grammar and 4 years of high school. He was born 10 August 1923 in Lutts, Tennessee and was a civilian student. His Military Occupational Specialty was Radio Operator, low speed 776. His Military Qualification: Marksman Carbine. The battles and campaigns that he served in were: Normandy, Northern France, Rhineland, Central Europe. Deco-

rations and citations received were: European African Middle Eastern Theater Ribbon, Four Bronze Service Stars, Good Conduct Medal, Lapel Button and World War II Victory Medal. He left the USA 1 Mar 1944 to European-Africa Middle Eastern Theater and returned 27 December 1945. He was Technician Fourth (Grade), Troop A, 15th Calvary Squadron, Army of the United States when he was discharged 3 January 1946 at Ft. Knox, Kentucky. His address was Route 2, Lutts, Tennessee.

He is the son of Charlie and Madgie (Horton) Ayers. After he returned home from the service, he married Maxine Kelso and lived at Lutts a few years. They moved to Lawrence County, TN and worked in soil conservation. Their four children are Benny, Pamela, Ivan and Barry; his siblings are Brice, SLesbie, Lorene, Hazel, Ross, Faye and Susie.

BAILEY, EMERALD N., son of Joe and Ollie Roberson Bailey, was born 1 July 1926. Emerald entered the United States Army 13 March 1945. He received his training at Ft. Oglethorpe, Georgia; Fort Knox, Kentucky; Camp Pickett, Virginia; and Camp Hood, Texas. He received an early discharge because the war ended. He was a Private First Class in the Armored Tank Division.

He is a member of the Free Will Baptist Church. He was married 8 May 1948 to Beatrice McFall. His children are Ronnie Rainey, Donnie Bailey, Stanley Bailey and Katie Sue Bailey Balentine. He also has seven grandchildren and two great-grandchildren. His siblings are Roy Gene married Anita Dicky, Deloyd married Eva Schelske, Billy Joe married Shirley Montgomery, Ruth married Larry Dickson and Judy married Charles Coffman.

BAILEY, JAMES H., Corporal (USMC) received major surgery in the Marine Hospital on 3 January 1946. He was to receive his discharge. He had entered the service sometime in 1943.

Source: Wayne County News, 18 January 1946.

BAIRD, WILLIAM J., born Dubuque, Iowa, married Mary Ruth Old from Wayne County, TN in 1946, She was the daughter of Talmage J. Old, Sr. and Grace Leo Ricketts Old who volunteered for service in the U.S. Women's Marine Corps in 1945.

BAKER, LEONARD N., Serial Number 34 888 804. Leonard Baker was a Private attached unassigned to Reception Center, Camp Shelby, Mississippi, United Stated Army. He was honorably discharged 30 June 1944. When inducted on 13 November 1943 in Fort Oglethorpe, he was 19 years, one month of age, a farmer, had blue eyes, brown hair, ruddy complexion, and was 5 ft, 9 in tall. He was single.

BAKER, ROBERT MORRIS, Serial Number 34 886 106. Robert Morris Baker was a Private First Class. He was born 3 December 1924. He entered into active service 27 October 1943 and was discharged 30 January 1946 in Fort McPherson, Georgia.

As a heavy machine gunner, Robert served with the 110th Infantry, 28th Division in the European Theater of Operations, participating in the Ardennes, Rhineland and Central Europe Campaigns. As a machine gun crew member, he aimed, loaded and fired the 30 caliber machine gun, estimated the range and set sights. He camouflaged the gun if a cover wasn't available, and field stripped the gun to clean or replace worn parts. Upon entering the service, Robert was sent to Fort Eustis, Virginia; Camp Cook, California; Camp McCoy, Wisconsin; Camp Chaffee, Arkansas; and to Fort Meade, Maryland.

Robert remembers the following account: His unit boarded a Dutch Ship with

an English crew. They sailed from New York harbor, going by the Statue of Liberty. In viewing the statue, they felt a desolation in leaving this last view of anything for 16 days. The Dutch ship with its English crew fed the boys very sparingly. They got so hungry that some of the unit took the food and changed the rations.

After a week or 10 days, the ship began kicking off depth charges into the ocean. The ship would tremble or vibrate as this took place. Abe Self was on another ship traveling with the same envoy. The ship pulled up into the English Channel to let the air craft men off. That night Robert's unit moved across to LeHarve, France. They got off on landing craft to get to the bank. They boarded a train to be transferred to a separation center. He went from here to the 28th Infantry Division, 110th Regiment in Company D, Heavy Weapons. They started moving in the direction where things were really moving in action; this was in January. Skirmishes were happening here and there. Before reaching Calmar, we relieved a unit. Robert found later that a close friend and neighbor back home, Glenn Davis, who was a member of the unit they relieved. They went on to the Rhine River, dug in and stayed about a week, moved slowly by Achen, through heavy fighting and joined General Patton's 3rd Army at this point. Heavy fighting continued from there to Fondorf. The Germans had blown up a large bridge here to keep us back. We stayed here until the Army of Engineers put in a pontoon bridge. We watched the 29th Division go across and saw the Germans running in another direction. That was the last combat that we saw. We went on to Lahr and to Dudweiler. Here we were split into the Army of Occupation. We spent time here, then back to LeHarve, France and then to Boston, Massachusetts, and on to Fort McPherson, Georgia, to receive a 30-day furlough, before we were to go to the Pacific Area of War. But while we were on furlough, the war ended. Robert's unit returned to Camp Shelby, Mississippi, and were divided, and he went back to Pennsylvania, then to 2nd Infantry Division in Camp Swift, Texas, and from there to Fort McPherson to be discharged. (The 28th Infantry Division had 109, 110 and 112 Regiments.)

Robert received a Combat Rifle Badge, three Battle Stars with ribbons for Ardennes, Rhineland and Central Europe, also a ribbon for Germany Occupation. The French gave each soldier or serviceman an honorary ribbon Decoration.

Robert remembers the sound of the shells, mortar fire, the sound of the German rocket as it hissed through the air. He remembers in Hurricane Forrest one cloudy day at Camp Headquarters, a German plane was flying over, then machine gun fire. A few minutes later, a German came floating to the ground, Buzz Bombs, German rockets, going to England.

Robert is the son of James Robert Baker (15 September 1889- 2 April 1981) and Ammous Borrough, (23 November 1891- 8 October 1928). His siblings are T. J. Baker and Mary Baker Conaway. Robert married Gladys Burns. They have two children: Patsy, born 21 September 1954, and David, born 3 September 1960.

Robert worked as a farmer before he entered service. After returning home he grew corn, cotton, hay and peanuts and raised hogs and cattle. He was familiar with crop rotation and hay baling, repairing barns, fences and farm equipment. Later he became a pilot and captain on towboats, from which he retired. His home address is Route 1, Clifton, Tennessee.

BAKER, T.J., Serial Number 34 189 103. T. J. was a S/Sergeant in the Air Corp with the 852nd Squadron, 491 Bombardment, AAF. His eyes are blue, hair is light, weights 160 lbs and is 5'9" tall. He has eight years of education in grammar school. He was a farmer before he entered service. His address is Route 1, Clifton. He entered into active service on 18 February 1942 in Waynesboro, Tennessee, and was discharged 11 September 1945 at Fort McPherson, Georgia.

He was assigned the job of munitions worker. He saw the following battles and campaigns: Tunisia, Egypt, Libya, Sicily, Air Offensive Europe, Naples-Foggia, Normandy, Northern France, Air Combat Central Europe, Rhineland and Ardennes. He received the following decorations and citations: European African Middle Eastern Service Medal with two Silver Stars and one Bronze Star, Distinguished Unit Badge, Good Conduct Medal. He departed 31 August 1942 for European Theater and arrived in the United States 22 June 1945.

Source: The above information was

taken from T. J. Baker's Enlisted Record and Report of Separation Honorable Discharge.

T. J. was born 13 March 1920 in Clifton, Tennessee and is the son of James Robert Baker (5 September 1889-2 April 1981) and Ammous Borrough (23 November 1891 - 8 October 1928). His siblings are Robert Morris Baker and Mary Baker Conaway.

BALENTINE, EDWARD R., Serial Number 34 495 106. Edward R. Balentine was a Private in 1885th Unit in the United States Army. He was born in Lutts, Tennessee. He has blue eyes, brown hair, ruddy complexion and was 6' tall. His Civilian Occupation was Saw Mill Laborer. He was 20 years old when he was inducted into service 22 November 1942 at Waynesboro, Tennessee, and he was discharged 16 August 1943 at Camp Howse, Texas. His Army Specialty was Rifleman.

BALENTINE,   HERMAN WILLARD, was in the United States Army in the European Theater Operations of World War II. The son of Charles Pugh and Melissa Jane Wright Balentine, he was born 22 December 1910 in Wayne County, Tennessee, and died 3 June 1983 in Mishawaka, Indiana. He was married 17 October 1930 to Helia Hoataja (Finnish). They were the parents of four children: Betty Ruth Balentine Beckham, Anna Balentine, Ralph Balentine and Johnny Balentine.

Source: Grace Carver.

BALENTINE, JAMES E., son of John Thomas and Virgie Lee Holt Balentine, was born 25 May 1925. His six siblings are: Era Phillips, Florence, Alabama; Audrey Balentine, who died at age 3; Norman Eugene Balentine, deceased from Iron City; Arnold Glenn Balentine of Florence; Irma Ruth Butler of Florence; and John L. Balentine of Athens, Georgia.

He enlisted in the United States Army 3 August 1943 at the age of 18. He did his basic training at Fort Oglethorpe, Georgia. He was sent to California where he served with the military police. He contacted typhus fever and almost died. He was discharged 16 April 1946 from Fort McPherson, Georgia. He worked for many years with the Tennessee Valley Authority. He was self-employed the last 15 years of his life. He died 24 June 1974 at the age of 49 and is buried in Green View Memorial Park in Florence, Alabama.

On 26 April 1948, he was married to Kathleen Linville, the daughter of R. G. and Mary Aileen Stults Linville of Iron City, Tennessee. They have two children: Janice Balentine Henry of Killen, Ala-

bama, and Charles Edwin Balentine of Atlanta, Georgia. James E. has two grandsons: Christopher Edwin Balentine of Florence, Alabama, and Alexander Dan Henry of Killen, Alabama. James E. has one great grandson, Christopher Edwin "Bo" Balentine of Florence, Alabama.

BARBER, ORVILLE A. "SONNY", Serial Number 44 069 586. Sonny was a Private, First Class in Company M, 3430

Infantry Regiment, 86th Division Army of the United States. He was inducted 31 January 1945 at Fort Oglethorpe, Georgia. He was honorably discharged 21 July 1946 at Camp McCoy, Wisconsin. He received his basic training at Camp Blanding, Florida. His overseas duty was in the Philippines. He received Expert Infantryman Badge, Army of Occupation Medal, Japan, Asiatic- Pacific Theater Service Medal, Good Conduct Medal, one Overseas Service Bar, and Lapel Button. His Military specialty was Barber.

Orville A. Barber, son of Braden and Ruth Pitts Edwards Barber, was born 7 November 1916, died 29 August 1987 and is buried in Clifton Cemetery. His siblings were Stewart Barber, Thelma Peeler, Lillian Hinson and Alta Bradley. His half-brothers and sisters were Jack Edwards and Nona Hendrix. "Sonny" was a barber and the Clifton Church of Christ Minister for many years. His hobby was growing roses and all kinds of flowers. He graduated from high school in Brazil, Tennessee.

BARBER, ROBERT, son of "Boss" and Lois (Bates) Barber. He lived on the Bell Farm on Tucker Branch in northern Wayne County when he was inducted. Later the family moved to Hohenwald. His siblings were Jesse, Andrew (Snooks), Arthur (Ott), Martha (Sissie) Breece and Edith Lyell.

BARBER, STEWART A., left Clifton to enter the United States Navy. He retired

from the Navy. He attended school at Frank Hughes in Clifton before entering the service. He is the son of Braden and Ruth Pitts Edwards Barber. His siblings were Orville A. "Sonny" Barber, Thelma Barber Peeler, Lillian Barber Hinson and Alta Barber Bradley. His half-brothers and sisters were Jack Edwards and Nona Edwards Hendrixs.

BARKLEY, ALLEN, grew up in Wayne County and like all able bodied boys was drafted into the service for his

country in December 1942. He went into the Antiaircraft, taking his basic training at Fort Churden, Illinois, and was sent to Dust Bowl, Texas, for more training, then to Camp Carson, Colorado. At this time, he learned the Infantry was running short in recruits and that he would continue his training in Camp Carson with the Infantry. Later on he was transferred to Camp Walter, Texas, and then to Camp Cocom, California. It was from here that he was shipped to New Guinea, then to Louistade for about two weeks, 16 days in Mindora, then on to the Philippines. Sometime after being on the front line for 29 days, they would be given a three-day rest period. Another unit would relieve them. During this three-day rest, they thought they would see the Red Cross or someone else to help them lighten the load, but they never saw them. About this time the war ended, and Allen was sent to Japan for three months.

Allen remembers: "One of my first duties in Japan was to drive a Lieutenant and a First Sergeant around in a jeep. We did not have a lot to do. We were sent back to California after a three-month period. We were unloaded during the night. Our meal for the night was a cup of coffee and a doughnut fed by the American Red Cross. After rations we boarded a train for Camp Chaffee, Arkansas. During this time I began searching faces to see if I could find someone that I knew. I found Clyde Bevis, a Wayne County soldier. We talked quite a bit, and you can imagine how happy we were to see each other. The next morning I woke with a case of malaria fever, which I had contacted in the Philippine Islands. I went to the hospital near Camp Chaffee, Arkansas, and stayed 13 days before being sent home on February 17, 1946. My rank was T/5th. I received various medals and citations during the time spent in service.

I worked in Florida that winter after coming back home. Then I went to work in Florence, Alabama, in the Electric Department and retired from there. "

Allen was born on April 4, 1922, the son of John Rich and Mary Katherine Patterson Barkley. He died on July 10, 1998, in Eliza Coffee Memorial Hospital in Florence and was buried in Memorial Gardens in Collinwood. His siblings are Alta Barkley Hammack, Alpha Barkley Franks, Gertie Barkley Dodd, Bertie Barkley Wright, Alvin and Willie Barkley. He married Earline Whitten on December 21, 1947. They have three children: Linda Kay Morgan of Iron City, Katherine Miller of Collinwood and Mary Ann Smith of Waynesboro.

Submitted by Allen Barkley.

BARNETT, ALBERT ANDREW, Serial Number 14 156, 534. Albert was a Dodge-Plymouth dealer when he volunteered to be in the United States Army Air Force on 22 September 1942. He did his basic training in Camp Luna, New Mexico. The next two years were spent in Memphis, Tennessee, then on 16 December 1944, he went to North Africa, Cairo, Egypt and Alidan, Iran. He was responsible for buying and issuing two million gallons of gasoline per month for the Air Force. He was assigned to a "Special Services" aircraft maintenance unit, where he wore the olive drab uniform. The members of this unit were flown to different air bases to repair damaged aircraft. Albert worked with sheet metal. Others from Wayne County in his unit were Jalmer Pigg, Ross Berry, Rankin Edwards, Bluford Edwards Sr., Fat Arnold and Vernon Barnett. Albert was discharged in 1946. Albert remembers that the temperature in Iran was as high as 172 degrees. They were not allowed out of their barracks between the hours of 10-2. He helped to close the base there and came home 14 February 1946. He was a Staff Sergeant and received the following awards: Sharp Shooter and Good Conduct Medal. After returning to Wayne County, he went into partnership with his brother, Vernon Barnett, forming the Barnett Motor Company in Waynesboro.

Albert was born February 1913 in Wayne County, died 23 February 1996 in Tullahoma, Tennessee, and was buried in Wayne County Memorial Gardens in Waynesboro. He is the son of Jessie Andrew and Rosie Lily Morgan Barnett. His grandparents are Jessie Andrew and Sara Sellers Barnett and George and Malinda J. Kimbrell Morgan. He married 4 April 1947 Alberta Clay, a local Wayne County girl. They have two sons, Philip Clay, born 5 March 1949 and Russell Andrew, born 10 April 1953. Philip married 7 September 1969 Pamela Faye Wyatt and their children are: Philip Clay, II, born 6 July 1971, Keith Wyatt, born 25 May 1974, and Andrea Gail Barnett, born 23 April 1976. Russell married February 5, 1982 Debra Ann Alexander and their children are: Alex Andrew, born 7 June 1986, and Adam Russell, born 28 February 1989. His siblings are John Oliver, James Frank, Vernon Lee, Willie Mae Edmond and Lily Leona Barnett. Albert is a member of the Baptist Church and is retired, living in Tullahoma, Tennessee.

BARNETT, HAROULD E., Serial Number 34 727 111, was a Private First Class in the 1521st AAF Base Unit, CPW, PD, Air Transport Command, United States Army. He was born 13 July 1924 in Waynesboro, Tennessee. His education consisted of 6 years in grammar school. He was single, had blue eyes, brown hair, was 5'8" tall and weighed 139 lbs, when inducted into active service 27 March 1943 in Fort Oglethorpe, Georgia. His Civilian Occupation was Farmer and his Military Occupation was Duty Soldier. His decorations and citations were: Good Conduct Medal, American Campaign Medal, Asiatic-Pacific Medal, and World War II Victory Medal. He left the U. S. 11 June 1945 and arrived in Hawaii 20 June 1945. He was discharged 20 November 1945 at Hickman Field, Oahu, T. H. and reenlisted 21 November 1945 at Hickman Field. This time he was assigned to 64th AAF Base unit, Squadron "Z", Andrews Field, Washington, DC. This time he was an auto equipment operator. He left Hawaii 29 November 1945 for U. S. and arrived 12 December 1945. He was discharge the second time on 14 May 1947 at Andrews Field, Washington, D. C.

BARNETT, VERNON LEE, volunteered for service in September 1942 and served in the Army Air Transport Command during World War II. He was medically discharged in September 1943.

Vernon, son of Jessie Andrew and Rosie Lee Morgan Barnett, was born on August 10, 1920, died on June 7, 1998 in Waynesboro, and was buried in Memorial Gardens in Waynesboro.

Vernon was a retired businessman and a member of the First Baptist Church in Waynesboro where he served as a deacon. He was a member of the Kiwanas Club, the Masonic Lodge and the Lion's Club.

His siblings are J. Oliver, Frank and Albert Barnett, Willie Mae Edmond and Leona Barnett Horton. Vernon married Kathryn Kilburn and they have four children: Garrett Lee, Vernon Edwin, Charles Jeffery and Susan Kathryn Barnett Raper. He has eight grandchildren and two great-grandchildren.

BARNETTE, CLAUD J., Serial Number 34 189 092, was a Pvt in Quartermaster Corp, United States Army. Born in Wayne County, he was 30 years and 2 months of age and single when he was inducted 13 February 1942 at Fort Oglethorpe, Georgia. He had blue eyes, dark brown hair ruddy complexion and was 5' 6 1/2" tall. His character was excellent and his physical condition was good when he was discharged 19 August 1942 at Clifton, Tennessee. His civilian job was boiler fireman.

BATES, CLARENCE, enlisted in the United States Army in 1942 and was sent to the European Theater of War. His feet were frozen during this time. He was sent back to a hospital in the U. S. for treatment and was later given training to be an army nurse. He was given a medical discharge in 1946. After returning home he owned and operated a grocery store in Cypress Inn.

Clarence, son of Thomas Allen and Ida Weaver Bates, was born 25 October 1925 in Wayne County, died 8 January 1991 in Wayne County and was buried in Mt. Pleasant Methodist Church Cemetery near Cypress Inn, Tennessee. His siblings are Wesley Bates, Myrtle Hanback, Cleo Bates, Mollie Fowler, Ollie Stricklin, and Joyce Dodd. He married Velvie Burgess. They had three children: Larry, Garry and Judy Bates.

BATES, JOHN WESLEY, Serial Number 34 189 153, was born in Wayne County and was 29 years and 9 months of age and single when he was inducted 18 February 1942 at Fort Oglethorpe, Georgia. He had blue eyes, brown hair ruddy complexion and was 5' 9 1/2" tall. His Military Qualifications was Marksman and his Army Specialty was Cook When he was honorably discharged 10 September 1943 at Greenville AAB, Greenville, South Carolina, he was a SGT with 342 Base Hq and AB Sq, United States Army. His physical condition was fair.

John, son of Thomas Allen and Ida Paralee Weaver Bates, died 8 July 1983 in E. C. M. Hospital, Florence, Alabama and was buried in Mt. Pleasant Methodist Church Cemetery near Cypress Inn, Tennessee. His siblings are: Clarence Bates, Myrtle Hanback, Cleo Bates, Mollie Fowler, Ollie Stricklin, and Joyce Dodd. He married Thelma Cleo _____. He had one son: Jeffery Bates and two stepsons and one grandchild.

Before entering service, he was a farmer. Later he was a shoe store owner. He was a member of the Mt. Pleasant Methodist Church.

Source: Obit in Wayne County News, July 14, 1983 and Discharge papers.

BATTLES, A.C. "ANDREW CHAPEL", was called into the service of the United States Navy on 31 December 1943 and took his basic training at Great Lakes, Illinois, then went to the Philippines. He was ship cook 3/C T. He was discharged 22 December 1945 at Memphis, Tennessee. After he was discharged, he began learning carpenter work, at which he became an expert.

A. C., son of Andy and Viola Pulley Battles, was born 22 November 1918 in Wayne County, died 4 November 1989 and was entombed in the Highland Cemetery located on Highway 64 East in Wayne County. His father died 24 July 1919 and

his mother died 14 September 1921. A. C.'s grandmother, Mary Ann Battles, raised the orphan, A. C and three sisters and one brother. They were: Edd Battles, Elise Bunch, Eva Ray and Emma Devers. A. C. was married 18 December 1937 to Elva Blasingim. They had four children: Mary Lou Hardin, Billy Joe, Jerry Lynn and Ronald Dale Battles.

BATTLES, CHARLES EDWARD, enlisted in the United States Army 18 April 1944 and was discharged 1 November 1944. Edd, son of Andy and Viola Pulley Battles, was born 8 May 1917 in Wayne Country, died 25 March 1968 and was buried in Praters Chapel Cemetery near Clifton, Tennessee. His father died 24 July 1919 and his mother died 14 September 1921. Edd's grandmother, Mary Ann Battles, raised the orphan, Edd and three sisters and one brother. They were: A. C. Battles, Elise Bunch, Eva Ray and Emma Devers. He married Wilton Fraley and they had four children: Franklin, Mary Linda, Edward and Judy Battles.

BAYS, JAMES HARVEY, age 76, of Clifton died 8 January 1998 at the Wayne Medical Center in Waynesboro and was buried in Clifton Cemetery. A native of Benton, Illinois, he was the son of Everett and Emma Martens Bays, Survivors include two daughters, Cathy Lavonda Pevahouse and Lisa Michelle Adams both of Clifton; two sisters Pauline Baburnich of Benton, Illinois and Louise Sisk of Kentucky; six grandchildren and several nieces and nephews.

BEATTY, BILLY THOMAS, son of Albert Sidney and Willie Bell Beatty, was born 10 April 1918 in Cornersville, Marshall County, Tennessee. His brothers are Albert Sidney, Jr., and Ralph David Beatty. His sisters are Mary Cliff, Bessie Joe Pruitt, Josephine Bell Barnett and Doris A. Horton. He married Kathleen Haislip and they had two daughters: Billy Kaye

Latimore and Rose Marie Cole. There are four grandchildren: Joel, Jason, Josh and Christina, and three great granddaughters. He was married secondly, 12 November 1981 to Thelma Jeter. They live in Waynesboro.

Billy was a S/Sgt in Motor Transportation. He was inducted 12 June 1941 and discharged 20 December 1945. He was active in the battles and campaigns in the Southern Philippines. After he was discharge, he returned to Wayne County to work for the telephone company. Later, he continued working for the phone company in Georgia and Mississippi. Retiring in January 1980, he came back to Wayne County to live.

BECKHAM, HOOPER, Serial Number 34 189 213, Private in Buy "A" 268th CA Sep BN (HD), received an Honorable Discharge from Darnall General Hospital, Danville, Kentucky on the 6th day of November 1942. He was inducted 18 February 1940 in Fort Oglethorpe, Georgia. He qualified as marksman April 6. 1940. His mustering out pay was $200. 00.

BECKHAM, JACK, Serial Number 34 366 691, was a Pvt in United States Army. He enlisted 25 August 1942 and was discharged 21 May 1943 in Fort Slooun, New York. He received training at Fort Gordon, Georgia. The overseas duty was in Trindad and then he was sent back to New York and was transferred to the Enlisted Reserve Corps. He remembers working in the Fire Department while in service and handling the fire hoses, sometimes it would take five or six men to hold them. Fires occurred in the barrack and in the "mess halls. "

Jack, the son of William Isom and Mary Ellen Shull Beckham, was born 8 September 1900 in Beckham Hollow, died 26 March 1985 and was buried in Mt. Hebron Cemetery on Rayburn's Creek. He married Lydia Pearl Brown. They had 9 Children: Jack, Mary Lois Bowling, Larry, Clara

Belle Snodgrass, Peggy, William Tommy, Joseph Edward, Oma Ellen, and Vickie Deniece Petty. His siblings are: Milo, Richard, Joe, Mae Beckham Melson, Sue Beckham Hooper, Alvin, Hugh, Tom Frank, Mark, Ervie, Mack and Marvin Beckham.

He was a farmer on his return home from the war. He attended school at Houston. He attended Pinhook Methodist Church.

BECKHAM, JAMES MELSON, I enlisted in the Air Corps on September 31, 1942, at the Greenville Army Flying

School, Greenville, MS. I was sworn in late one afternoon and immediately sent to Camp Shelby, MS for the necessary physical examination and clothing. I stayed there for about a week, then was sent back to Greenville where I was assigned as a crew chief on the flight line. I liked this job, but had decided to put in for the cadet program and become a pilot. I was sent to Colorado. After several months training the final day came due to lack of coordination I was eliminated from the cadet program and immediately received orders fro overseas duty. I was sent to Camp Patrick Henry where I was given all the equipment and medical examination we would need until we reached our destination which at this time unknown to all our next stop, Norfolk, the William S Young was waiting for us. The Captain told us to make ourselves as comfortable as possible as this would be our home for the next three weeks. We carried all our bags below deck and were assigned to our bunks. There were 225 of us and our quarters were in the number two hole and the rest of the ship was loaded with supplies. We were told to stay below deck until the ship was underway, but we realized that this would probably be the last time some of us would see the United States, so we all went up on deck. We watched the shore line slowly fade away and when the last trace of land was gone

we all went back into the hole to cry and sleep. The next stop was Oran, North America, where we stayed for 30 days before resuming our journey, which we had been told our destination was China. I was to spend 15 months in combat with the 14th Air Force in China where I was the flight Engineer on a B-24, flying 29 missions before being sent back to the United States. While in China, I was awarded the Distinguished Flying Cross, Air Medal, Good Conduct Medal and the Asiatic Pacific Theater Ribbon with Six Battle Stars. I was discharged from the service on October 18, 1945 at maxwell Field, AL having served three years and five days in the Air Corps.

I am the oldest son of the late Lynn and Karen Beckham have one brother, Thomas who lives in Florence, AL. I am married to Mary Jo Swafford Beckham and we were blessed with three children; Mary Lynn, James Jr., and John Franklin. We have five grandchildren and two great grandchildren.

BECKHAM, McKINLEY "PETE", JR., On January 27, 1943 he volunteered for the United States Navy. His basic training was at Great Lakes, Illinois. After a short furlough home, he was assigned to the destroyer "Young" at Orange, Texas. Immediately, they sailed for action in the South Pacific, near the Mariana Islands and the Philippines. This destroyer was engaged in fierce battles with the Japanese. They saw combat near the Solomon Islands, Guam, Midway, and a chain of smaller islands.

McKinley says, "We were at sea for two whole years. After the Enola Gay, an American plane, dropped the atomic bomb on Hiroshima and Nagasaki, the Japanese surrendered unconditionally to the American Forces. Our ship, the "Young", was in Japan's Harbor and we witnessed the surrender of Japan on the Battleship Missouri, to General MacArthur. This was a great moment in History!

Besides being a Navy Veteran of World War II with rank of MM2 Class, Pete was a retired Merchant Marine. He attended school in Collinwood.

McKinley, Jr., son of McKinley, Sr. and Shelby Miller Beckham, was born 24 December 1922 in Collinwood, Tennessee, died 26 December 1994, and was buried in Memorial Gardens in Collinwood. Survivors were sisters: Imogene Ragow, Carol S Rich, Betty Melson and Glenda Stults. He was a member of the Baptist Church.

BECKHAM, PRESTON L., is the son of A.L. and Texie McMullen Beckham, he was born 4 March 1914, died 13 July 1984 and was buried in New Jersey. He was a Military Policeman in the United States Army in the European Theater of War. He married Mary Stoveken. They had one daughter, Patricia Beckham Ronco.

BECKHAM, RAY, was born on October 17, 1925, in Lauderdale County, Alabama, but spent most of his early life in Wayne County, Tennessee.

He was the son of Herschel and Jewel (Shelby) Beckham. His paternal grandparents were Abraham Lincoln and Texie Anna (McMillan) Beckham of the Lutts community. Maternal grandparents were Lewis and Lillie (Brooks) Shelby, who lived in Lauderdale County, Alabama, and the latter part of their lives in Hardin County, Tennessee.

Ray had a brother and a sister. Bobby died when he was about 20 years of age. Virginia lives today in southern Florida. Ray also has two half-sisters and two half-brothers, most of who live in Flint, Michigan.

Ray grew up in and around the Lutts community during the 1930's and 1840's assisting his father on the farm. He attended the Pinhook School. He was drafted into the Army in 1943-44, and he was placed in the infantry where he won metals as a sharpshooter. He was honorably discharged from the Army during the mass exit of soldiers in 1946-47.

Ray died a few years ago (1980's) in Phoenix, Arizona, and is buried there.

Submitted by John Beckham and Ray Beckham.

BECKHAM, ROBERT EUGENE,

Serial Number 34 884 583, Staff Sergeant Beckham served in the U. S. Army Air

Force from 24 September 1943 to 30 March 1946. I was born on Indian Creek in Wayne County, Tennessee to Noah and Mattie Jane (Eaton) Beckham on January 1, 1923, was raised as a farm boy and attended Three Church Community and the Memorial Community Schools. I graduated from the 8th grade on 24 March 1939 and from Collinwood High School on April 2, 1943.

Before being inducted into service, I had a great desire to fly, and requested my father to go to Nashville, Tennessee, with me to take a test to enlist in the USAAF. Failing this test, I came home very dejected and asked the local draft board to send me for induction. They sent me through the Induction Center in Fort Oglethorpe, Georgia. While at Fort Oglethorpe, I was given a second test to get into the Air Force and passed. I was sent to Keesler Field, Mississippi for basic training as an aviation Cadet.

After basic training, I was sent to Minnesota State Teacher's College, Moorhead, Minnesota for a basic engineering course. This course, which included 10 hours of logged flying time and instruction in an Interstate Cadet plane, was finished 1 March 1944. I was then sent to Santa Ana, California, where for the convenience of the Government I was reclassified and sent to a specialized B-17 school to train as an aircraft Armorer and Bombardier at Lowery Field, Denver, Colorado. This course was completed July 6, 1944. Next, I was sent to the Nevada Army Air Field, Las Vegas, Nevada, where on 6 October

1944, I completed a course in flexible gunnery, camera and gun and camera maintenance and usage, The camera course later was used extensively.

Then I was sent to Lincoln, Nebraska for orientation and practice camera operation and maintenance. Afterwards, I was sent to New York for embarkation to England on a nine-man crew of a B-17, Flying Fortress on 7 March 1945. I entered the European Theater of operations on 20 March 1945 and was assigned to the 8th Air Force, 306th Bomb Group, 423rd Squadron (Heavy) at Thurleigh Air Force Base, Bedfordshire (Bedford), England. I spent approximately eight months there as K-26 camera operator, flying and making pictures of Europe from 20,000 feet altitude in a B-17 plane, mapping much of the European Continent.

After this, I was sent to Geiblestat, Germany and around Paris, France as assignee of the army of occupation. I left the European Theater of Operations and arrived in New York harbor on 26 March 1946. I was immediately sent to Camp Atterbury, Indiana, and was discharged on 30 March 1946.

I married Dorothy Jean Fowler on 9 August 1949. Three children were born of this union: Robert Steven, Richard Lowell and Melody Jan, who all seem healthy and happily married at this time. Dorothy and I were divorced on 19 May 1973, by order of Judge Jerry Scott. Neither of us has remarried. I have five grandchildren and two great-grandchildren.

Upon returning home from active service, I held several jobs around Waynesboro. As an assistant Agriculture teacher, I taught a G. I. Farming class of WW II veterans for approximately six years. I worked approximately two years as secretary for the Wayne County Superintendent of schools and approximately six months as shop foreman for Hassell and Hughes Ford dealership in Waynesboro.

Before I go further, I feel compelled to state here and now the greatest thing that ever happened in and to my life. It has been my driving force since August of 1960 and I know now that it must have been even from the day my mother gave me birth. I had known long before that someone (spirit or otherwise) was giving me instruction and guidance outside of my control. On 6 August 1960, while on a fishing trip with my dear friend Doc Anderson, (Dr. W. G), a pharmacist in Waynesboro, we were caught in a terrible thunderstorm on Pickwick Lake. The wind blew, the thunder was fierce and the lighting awesome. We pulled to an island, removed our clothing and turned the boat upside down, placing everything we had under it for protection. Not knowing that water is a con-

ductor for electricity, we waded as far out in the water as possible. The lighting was flashing so fierce I became very scared. I ask for help where it seemed no help existed. Then I began to feel the fear subsiding and a peace came over and into me that I know was from the One that had been convicting me many years for my failures to Him. There and then before God and man I gave my soul, life and being to God. I immediately told Doc and he became so happy! This I could not fully understand at that time. The next day, 7 August 1960, I went forward during worship service and confessed Christ before our congregation. I have tried to follow his teachings from that day on. I was baptized on 21 August 1960 by Rev. J. O. Smothers into the congregation of Green River Missionary Baptist Church and in the doorway to Heaven.

I began work as a Fieldman in Wayne County for Columbia Production Credit Association in Columbia, Tennessee on 1 November 1954 at a monthly salary of $225. 00. This work did not fully keep me employed and I was given permission by the company to accept a second job with Tennessee Farmers Mutual Insurance Company as an agent under district supervisor Bobby Hudson of Ethridge, Tennessee. These two jobs grew until each of them would support a full time employee. On 31 December 1971, I resigned from Production Credit Association. but continued to work with the insurance company until I retired 31 December 1987.

Upon retiring I came to the farm on Indian Creek where I raised cattle and have three catfish ponds where the general public can fish for a fee. At the time of this writing, I have been blessed in each of my endeavors back through the years. I find myself at peace with our Creator and very happy and thankful to now live comfortably this 30 November 1991. " - Robert E Beckham

Robert died 3 July 1996 in the Wayne County Medical Center and was buried in Memorial Gardens in Waynesboro. He was also survived by one brother, Billy Gene Beckham of Clifton and one half brother, Marvin Hoyt Johnson of Waynesboro. (Obit in *Wayne County News* 3 July 1996)) .

BECKHAM, THOMAS E., son of Mr.

and Mrs. J. L. Beckham of Waynesboro, Tennessee was promoted to Sergeant. He is a tail gunner on a B-24 Liberator Bomber. He is a member of a Liberator Bombardment group commanded by Lt. Col. Joseph G. Russell. This group has over 100 missions to its credit. Sgt Beckham was a student at Wayne County High School before entering the service on 13

November 1943. He attended the Air Force Flexible Gunnery School in Laredo, Texas. *Source: Wayne County News.*

BELL, COLUMBUS WILSON "LUM", Serial Number 34 922 067, was a Private in Battery C, 789th Field Artil-

lery Battalion, United States Army. At age 37 years and three months, he was inducted 30 December 1943 in Fort Oglethorpe, Georgia. He had blue eyes, brown hair, ruddy complexion, and was 5'8" tall. He received training at Fort Jackson, South Carolina. He was honorably discharge on 18 August 1944 in Fort Leonard, Wood, Missouri.

Lum, son of Henry and Dona Walker Bell, was born 12 October 1906 in Clifton, Tennessee. He married Roxie Lee Stegall and they had two children: Elizabeth and Carolyn Bell Powers. His siblings are Jesse, Earl, Robert, Adley, Richard, Cecil, Mary Bell Haggard, Maudie Bell Casner, Marie Bell Crews, Myrtle Bell Owens and Opal Bell. He died 16 March 1982 and is buried in the Culp Cemetery on Beech Creek in Wayne County. His Civilian Occupation was Edgeman.

BELL, JOSEPH EDWARD, son of Anthony and Emily Ocealis Belavich, died

22 March 1996 at the Wayne County Medical Center and is buried in Memorial Gardens in Collinwood. He was a native of Cumbala, Pennsylvania, a retired Physical Education Teacher and a member of the New Jersey Retired Teachers Association. He was a member of the Catholic Church, the American Legion, the US Coast Guard Auxiliary, a former Military Police, and Ham Radio operator. He received the European African Middle Eastern Service Medal, Air Medal, American Service Medal, Good Conduct Medal, World War II Victory Medal and the Purple Heart.

He was survived by his wife, Elizabeth O'Rourke Bell of Iron City; one son, Joseph E. Bell, II of Iron City; one brother, Anthony Belavich of Sarasota, Florida; two sisters, Ann Marut of Thomas River, New Jersey and Helen Stack of South Orange, New Jersey; and five grandchildren. (*The Wayne County News*, 27 March 1996.)

BELL, DWIGHT, was the son of Walter and Sarah Pearl (Logan) Bell. His siblings: Gladys, Mary, Marguerite, Raymond, Robert, James White and Gaston Bell. Dwight and brothers: Raymond, James, and Gaston Bell all served in the U. S. Navy during World War II.

BELL, JAMES WHITE, was the son of Walter and Sarah Pearl (Logan) Bell. His siblings: Gladys, Mary, Marguerite, Raymond, Robert, Dwight and Gaston Bell. James and brothers: Raymond, Dwight and Gaston Bell all served in the U. S. Navy during World War II.

BELL, RAYMOND TYLER, Serial Number 966 79 24. Raymond had the rank of Seaman First Class in the United States

Navy. Other ratings were AS, S2C, S1C. He was married when he entered active service on May 8, 1944, in Waynesboro. He left for the war in February 1945. Service vessels and ships that Raymond served

on were USNTS, Bainbridge, Maryland, USS Zarauk, and the repair ship USS Gunston Hall. He was discharged on November 20, 1945, in Memphis, Tennessee.

His education consisted of eight years of grammar school. His permanent mailing address is P. O. Box 42, Collinwood, Tennessee. His main civilian job before entering service was produce hand for F. B. Todd in Collinwood.

In 1929, he moved to Collinwood, Tennessee, where he met and married Louise Todd. They had three children: Margaret Virginia, David Tyler and Valerie Kay.

Raymond, son of Walter and Sarah Pearl (Logan) Bell, was born on November 20, 1908, in Moulton, Alabama. His siblings are Gladys, Mary, Marguerite, Raymond, Robert, James White, Dwight Bell and Gaston. Raymond and his brothers, Gaston, James and Dwight Bell, all served in the United States Navy during World War II. He died November 26, 1967 at the age of 59.

Submitted by Raymond and Louise Bell.

BELL, WALTER GASTON, was a son of George Walter and Sarah Pearl (Logan) Bell. He was born on April 24, 1906, in Moulton, Alabama. He died on June 15, 1998, in the Wayne County Nursing Home and was buried in Memorial Gardens in Collinwood. His siblings are Gladys, Mary, Marguerite, Raymond, Robert, James White and Dwight Bell. Gaston, at age 37, was drafted into the Navy on June 24, 1943, and served in World War II. He received a medical disability discharge on November 15, 1943. Gaston and his brothers, Raymond, James and Dwight Bell, all served in the United States Navy during World War II. The obituary says that he was survived by one sister, Mamie Rusk, of Birmingham; and one brother, Dwight Bell, of Coral Gables, Florida; five nieces; and five nephews. He was retired from the automotive industry and a member of the Collinwood Church of Christ, American Legion and Veterans of Foreign Wars.

BERRY, ARLIE - See Cecil J. Berry.

BERRY, ATHEL G. Serial Number 34 904 579, was born 4 April 1920 in Iron City, Tennessee, entered into service 1 July 1944 at Camp Forrest, Tennessee, as a divorced man with three dependents. He had gray eyes, brown hair, was 5' 11" tall and weight of 141 lbs. His education consisted of 8 years grammar school and two years in high school. He attained the rank of Private First Class in Company A, 128 Infantry, United States Army. His Military Specialty was Rifle Man. His battles and campaigns included Southern Philippine Campaign, Luzon Campaign. Awards were: Philippine Liberation Ribbon with a Bronze Star, Good Conduct Medal, Purple Heart, Asiatic-Pacific Theater Medal with two Bronze Service Stars. He was wounded in action 27 March 1945 in the Western Pacific Theater. He received an Honorable Discharge at McCloskey General Hospital, Temple, Texas. Permanent mailing address was given as Route 3, Iron City, Tennessee.

BERRY, BONNIE EARL, son of Henry and Elsie Horton Berry, he was born 25 May 1922, died 23 September 1963 and is buried in McGlamery Cemetery in Wayne County. His siblings are: James and Johnny (Jab) Berry, Roxie Berry, Ada Stricklin, Annie Holt, Mable Cameron, and Willodean Fite, He married Jewel Murphy. They were the parents of three boys: David Earl, Danny and Ronnie Berry.

Bonnie Earl was a PFC, 24th LUG CPT BN, United States Army during World War II. He was in the army, stationed in Pearl Harbor on 7 December 1941 when the Japanese bombing occurred.

BERRY, CECIL J., Serial Number 44 120 526, was inducted 29 May 1945 at Fort Oglethorpe, Georgia as a married man with three dependents. The description given was blue eyes, blonde hair, 5', 9" tall and weight 156 lbs. He attained the rank of Private First Class in the 1456th Army Service Unit, United States Disciplinary Barracks, Army of the United States. Guard Patrol was his military job. He received the World War II Victory Medal and a Lapel Pin. He was discharged 3 September 1946 in Fort Bragg, North Carolina. Permanent address given was Route 2, Collinwood, Tennessee. His civilian job was farmer. His education - 8 years grammar school and one year high school.

Cecil, son of James Oscar and Lillie Earl Rich Berry, was born 9 April 1917 in Wayne County, Tennessee and grew up on Cypress Creek. He was married on 17 April 1938 to Maggie Lou Ellen Keeton. They had three children: Wanda Elaine Berry Johnson, Jerry Boyce, and James Albert Berry, and five brothers: Athel, Arlie, Grady, Raymond and Nola E. Berry. The two sisters are: Mary Cathleen Berry Hays and Frankie Ivadean Berry Roberts. Cecil and four brothers, Athel, Arlie, Grady and Raymond were in the military service.

BERRY, EUGENE ALLEN, was born 18 September 1919 in Wayne County, entered the United States Navy 17 December 1940 and was Ships Cook 1st Class. He served on the following: USS LESLIE L. B. KNOX (D. E.) Com Ser Div 101, USS HANNIBAL, Inshore Patrol 5-N. D.

NOB, Norfolk, Virginia, COMM SCH, Phibs TRA PAC, AMP Training Base, Oceanside, California. Service medals awarded to Berry were: Asiatic-Pacific Area, American Area, Philippine Liberation, American Defense - 1 Star, World War II Victory Medal, Good Conduct Medal.

Eugene was the son of George W. and Grace Warrington Berry, grandson of James E. and Essie Amanda Davis Berry, and John Young and Catherine Cheatham King Warrington. He was married 7 January 1942 to Nellie Jones of Lutts, daughter of Marshall and Flora Copeland Jones. Eugene and Nellie have two daughters: Joyce Alexander of Daytona, Florida and Joan Hart of Florence, Alabama. The five grandchildren are: Robert James and Cary Beth Alexander, Danasa Jean Moore, Derek Glenn Pierce and Jimmy Lee Dean. Eugene died 12 July 1996 in Florence and was buried in Memorial Gardens in Collinwood. He was also survived by two brothers, Lorton and Charles Berry both of Collinwood and four sisters, Audrey Sowden of Daytona Beach, Florida, Kate Hamilton of Waynesboro, Joyce McQuarrie of Nashville and Petty Grandinetti of Florence, Alabama.

BERRY, GEORGE LORTON, Serial Number 272 50 07 entered the United States Navy 17 December 1940 and was a Signalman First Class. The Vessels and Stations served on: NRS, Birmingham, Alabama. ; NTS, Norfolk, Virginia; USS HANNIBAL; R/S San Diego, California; USS CRESCENT CITY; R/S Seattle, Washington. ; R/S Nashville, Tennessee; R/S Shoemaker, California; USS OBERON; CTU 70 4. 4 Taingato, China; COM SCH Phib Train PSC; and NATTC, Memphis, Tennessee. Service medals include: Victory Ribbon, American Theater, Good Conduct, Asiatic Pacific American Defense, and Presidential Unit Citation. George was discharge 5 November 1946 in Memphis, Tennessee.

George, born 13 October 1923 in Cy-

press Inn, was son of George W. and Grace Warrington Berry, grandson of James E. and Essie Amanda Davis Berry, and John Young and Catherine Cheatham King Warrington. He was married 24 December 1946 to Ida Pearl Montgomery. They have five children: Stanley Lorton b. 24 February 1949, Brenda Joan b. 26 November 1947, Debra Delite b. 26 January 1952, Steven Curtis b. 13 August 1955 and George Lee b. 4 May 1959.

"George L. Berry served as crewman on the USS CRESCENT CITY. George lived in Cypress Inn before entering service. The USS CRESCENT CITY was an attack transport, and was assigned to "Magic Carpet" duty in the Pacific. Ships of this fleet are assigned to bringing veterans home from overseas bases. " *Wayne County News*, January 18, 1946.

BERRY, GRADY G., Serial Number 34 936 454, born 10 February 1926 in Collinwood, Tennessee, was inducted 28 July 1944 at Camp Forrest, Tennessee and attained the rank of PFC. in Company C, 802nd Engineer Aviation Battalion, United States Army. His permanent address was Route 3, Iron City, Tennessee. His description: brown eyes, brown hair, 5' 8" tall, weight-162 lbs, and single with five dependents. His civilian job was farm hand, military was Special Vehicle Operator. His military qualification was Expert Rifleman. He left the United States on 13 February 1945 for the Pacific Theater and returned 16 November 1945. He was in the Battle at Ryukyus.

"Pvt. Berry, son of Mr. and Mrs. Oscar Berry of Little Cypress Creek, Tennessee, was separated from the service with an Honorable Discharge through the Fort McPherson, Georgia Center.

He received his basic training for military duty at Sheppard Field, Texas, Lamarre, California, and Griger Field, Washington. He was working in the ground Force of the Air Corps, and transferred to the Asiatic Pacific Theater of Operations for actual participation against the enemy. He remained overseas for ten months. Berry received the Good Conduct Medal, World War II Victory Medal and the Asiatic-Pacific Ribbon with one Bronze Star."

Source: Wayne County News, 14 December 1945.

BERRY, GUILFORD WARRINGTON, Serial Number 34 043 838, was inducted 15 May 1941 at Fort Oglethorpe, Georgia. His description was given as blue eyes, brown hair, 5' 11 1/4" tall and weighing 159 lbs. He was married with two dependents. He attained the rank of Tec 3 in the Medical Det., 767th TK BN, United States Army. He drove a trailer truck. His battles and campaigns and decorations included Eastern Mandates, South Philippines (Liberation), Ryukyus Liberation Ribbon with two Bronze Battle Stars, Asiatic- Pacific Theater Ribbon, with three Bronze Stars, Philippines Bronze Arrowhead, Good Conduct and American Defense Ribbon, He was given an Honorable Discharge on 31 July 1945 at Fort Sheridan, Illinois.

Guilford, son of George W. and Grace Warrington Berry, was born 18 September 1917 in Lutts, and died 29 July 1991. He married Ruby Montgomery of Cypress Inn. and they had four children: Guilford W., Larry G., Robert E. Berry and Beverly Berry Brown. His brothers are: Eugene, George L., and John C. Berry. His sisters are: Audrey Sowden, Essa Kate Hamilton. Joyce MacQuarrie, and Peggy Grandinetti. Guilford was a retired welder with General Motors, Flint, Michigan, a member of the UAW Local and a member of Scott's Chapel Freewill Baptist Church.

BERRY, HERSCHEL, Serial Number 94 33 24 - was a PVT in the Third Casual Company, Training Regiment, United States Marines. He was inducted 24 January 1944 to serve for the duration of the emergency in Nashville, Tennessee. His description was: blue eyes, brown hair, ruddy complexion, 69" tall and single. He was honorably discharged 24 April 1944 at Recruit Depot, Marine Corps Base, San Diego, California.

BERRY, IVAN QUINTIN, Serial Number 34 713 899, entered into active service 30 April 1943 at Camp Forest, Tennessee. His home address at that time was 4474 St. Jean, Detroit, Michigan. His description was: blue eyes, brown hair, 5' 8" tall and weighted 133 lbs. He was married and claimed one dependent. He had a seventh grade education. He earned the rank of Corporal in the 806th Army Air Force Base Unit, United States Army. His Military Occupation was Airplane and Engine Mechanic. His Military Qualifications:

AAF Technician Badge SO 97, Baer Field, 7 April 1945. He attended airplane mechanic's school in Gulfport, Mississippi and Long Beach, California. He earned the Good Conduct Medal. He was discharged 4 October 1945 at Baer Field, Fort Wayne, Indiana. His permanent mailing address was Cypress Inn, Tennessee. His civilian occupation was farmer.

Ivan, son of Richard Thomas and Nannie Wilson Berry, was born 30 December 1908 in Cypress Inn, Tennessee, died Sunday, 4 April 1993 in Wayne County Hospital in Waynesboro and was buried in Mt. Hope Cemetery in Cypress Inn. Mr. Berry was a retired machine operator with Chrysler Corporation, and a member of Scott's Chapel Freewill Baptist Church and the Masonic Lodge. His siblings: Ross Berry of Lutts, Ada Phillips of Iron City, and Christine Davis of Detroit.

BERRY, JAMES W., Serial Number 44 069 643, was inducted 31 January 1945 at Fort Oglethorpe, Georgia. His home ad-

dress at that time was Route 1, Lutts, Tennessee. His description was given as blue eyes, brown hair, 5' 7" tall, and weighed 137 lbs., a farmer, and married with three dependents. His grade was Technician 5 in the 62nd CW Gen SV CO, United States Army. Decoration received were: Asiatic - Pacific Theater Ribbon, Victory Medal, Good Conduct Medal, and Army of Occupation Medal (Japan), Lapel Button issued and two Overseas Service Bars. He departed the United Stated 6 August 1945 - destination Pacific Theater Operation and returned 6 September 1946. Some of his time was spent in Okinawa. He received his discharge on 24 October 1946 in Fort Sheridan, Illinois.

J. W., son of Elihue and Bertha Johnson Berry, was born 28 March 1919 in Lutts, Tennessee and died 19 November 1983 in Troy, Michigan. He married Gladys Southerland. His children are: Gladys

Marie Buck, Jeannette Brusseau, James Wade Berry, Garry Neal Berry and Julia Berry.

Source: Julia Berry, Cleo Mitchell and discharge papers.

BERRY, LEONARD, entered the United States Army in 1942 and was discharged 1945. He operated an Antiaircraft Gun. He was one of seven men in his group who operated this gun.

Leonard, son of John and Mary Pigg Berry, was reared in the South part of Wayne County. He had one brother, Clyde Berry and three sisters: Ada Heard, Ida Arnett, and Bessie Thrasher. He never married.

BERRY, ROSS B., Serial Number 14 156 536, was inducted 22 September 1942 at Camp Forest, Tennessee. His home ad-

dress at that time was Route 1, Cypress Inn, Tennessee. His description was given as blue eyes, brown hair, 5' 10 1/2" tall, and weighed 177 lbs., and single. Medals received were: American Theater Ribbon, Good Conduct Medal, Victory Medal World War II, and Meritorious Unit Award. For Overseas duty, he left the USA on 12 July 1945 for ATO and returned 4 April 1946. His grade was Sgt in Army Transport Command, 4th Ferrying Group, United States Army, when he received his discharge on 11 April 1946 at Camp Atterbury, Indiana. His Civilian Occupation was Skin Man; His Military Occupation was Cook and Carbine Expert. He had an eighth grade education.

Ross, son of Richard and Nancy Wilson Berry, was born 11 December 1919 in Cypress Inn, Tennessee. He was grandson of Isaac and Amanda Josephine (Blackwood) Berry and William Henry and Susan Hayes Wilson. He was the great grandson of David and Elizabeth Shipman Berry and Phillip and Nancy Willson Wilson. Ross married Juanita Robbins and they have three children: David Ross b.

December 1947, Nannie Ruth b. 23 January 1950, Jeffery Lee b. 18 February 1956 and William Jasper "Billy" b. 20 July 1962.

BERRY, WILLIAM MAYNARD, Serial Number 44 072 737, born 31 October 1923 in Collinwood, was inducted into the

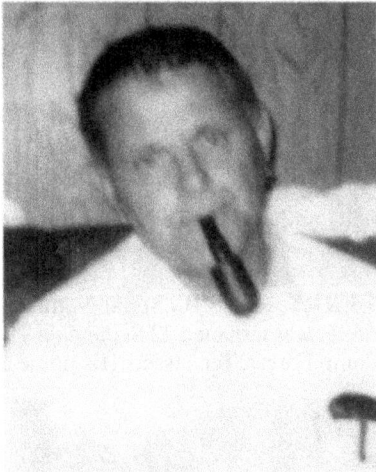

United States Army on 10 April 1945 at Fort McPherson, Georgia. His home address at this time was Route 2, Collinwood, Tennessee. His description was given as blue eyes, brown hair, height 6' 1", and weight 162 lbs., married with three dependents. He was a Private in the Infantry Replacement Center. He was discharged 20 November 1945 at Camp Craft, South Carolina so that he could reenlist.

He reenlisted the next day on 21 November 1945 at Camp Craft and attained the rank of Pfc. in Headquarters 2nd BN 31st INF, U S Army. Under description, his weight had changed to 208 lbs. His Civilian Occupation was Farmer, Military Occupation was Carpenter. Decorations were: Army of Occupation Medal (Japan) and Victory Medal. He departed the USA on 2 March 1946 for the Asiatic Pacific Theater and returned 3 January 1947. He was discharged 21 January 1947 in Fort Lewis Washington.

BEVIS, CLYDE CHARLIE, Serial Number 34 189 059 - was born 7 June 1913 at Route 1, Lutts in Wayne County. He was the son of Charlie Albert Bevis born 9 November 1887 and died 22 November 1981 and America Elizabeth Balentine Bevis born 28 June 1889 and died 7 March 1978. His paternal grandparents were Daniel Hunter Bevis born 1858, died 1932 and Josephine Victory Bevis born 1860, died 1929. His maternal grandparents were John Stephen Balentine born 26 June 1848, died 25 January 1926 and Nancy Ann Hayes Balentine born 4 February 1851, died 9 December 1930. Clyde has three sisters: Cora Victory and Geneva Reeves of Florence, Alabama and Bertha Balentine

who died 18 March 1974. He had one brother, John Daniel Bevis, born and died 10 July 1924.

Clyde attended Bevis Elementary School in Wayne County, finished eight grade in 1931. He spent his young days working on the family farm, raising crops and livestock.

He was inducted into the United States Army Air Force 18 February 1942 and was discharged 4 February 1946 in Camp Chaffee, Arkansas, with the rank of S/SGT. He served with the 80th Depot Repair Squadron for twenty months in China, Burma, India Theater of Operations as an airplane and engine mechanic. His duties included general overhauling and repairing of aircraft; assisting in preforming prescribed inspections and maintenance of aircraft; examining portions of aircraft, such as wings, fuselage, stabilizers, flight control surface, propellers, and landing gear for evidence of damage or wear, such as cracks, bent or broken members and looseness, which might cause dangerous vibrations; assisting in inspection and maintenance of engines and changing engines. He used mechanic tools, equipment and technical orders as a guide to maintenance procedures.

Clyde attended Aerial Torpedo School at the Naval Training Station in Newport, Rhode Island for 16 weeks in 1942. He received instruction in the repairing and overhauling of torpedoes in the classroom and practical work.

During the China, Burma, India Theater of Operations, he was stationed in Karachi, Pakistan and from there as transferred to Panaghar, India, where he was serving when the Japanese surrendered in September 1945. In coming back to the USA, he left India 29 December 1945 and arrived in San Pedro, California, on 28 January 1946, making a voyage of 31 days at sea on THE GENERAL PATRICK.

On October 15, 1949, he married Hazel Ruth McClanahan, daughter of James Reuben McClanahan, born 7 February

1867, died 10 February 1954 and Addie Ayers McClanahan, born 8 June 1892, died 6 September 1969. Ruth's brother, Monte, volunteered for the US Air Force and served for 21 years.

Clyde and Ruth have one daughter, Martha Carol Bevis, born 24 July 1950. She married Paul Dodd 25 June 1977. They have one daughter, April Ruth Dodd, born 14 August 1987 in Lauderdale County, Alabama.

Clyde and his wife are both retired. Ruth taught school in Wayne County for 41 years and Clyde worked at the Wayne County Farmers Co-op and farmed.
Source: Ruth Bevis.

BEVIS, HENRY F., Serial Number 34 501 394, was a Technician Fifth Grade in Headquarters Company 808th T D Battalion in the Army of the United States. His permanent mailing address was Waynesboro, Tennessee. He was born 30 September 1922 in Lutts, Tennessee. He was registered with the Selective Service Board in Wayne County, Tennessee. His Civilian Occupation was Farmer. He was single when he was inducted 20 December 1942 and entered into active service 27 December 1942 at Fort Oglethorpe, Georgia. His home address at time of entry was Route 2, Waterloo, Lauderdale, Alabama. His Military Occupational Specialty was Light Truck Driver. His Military Qualifications included MM - R. He was in the battles of Ardennes, Rhineland, and Central Europe. The following decorations were awarded to Bevis: American Theater Operations Medal, European-African Middle Eastern Theater Medal with 3 Bronze Service Stars, and Good Conduct Medal. He left the USA 11 Aug 1944 for the European-African Middle Eastern Theater Operation, and returned to USA 3 August 1945. He was discharged 11 November 1945 at Camp Rucker, Alabama.

BIFFLE, HAROLD FRANCIS, is the son of Jacob Elijah "Lige" and Anna Walker Biffle. He was a member of the 33rd Class of Aviation Cadets to graduate from the Columbus Army Air Field near Columbus, Mississippi on 15 Apr 1945. He received the Silver Wings of a Flying Officer and appointment as a Flight officer in the Army Air Force. F/O Biffle entered Pilot Training April 1944, and attended flying schools in Albany, Georgia, and Montgomery, Alabama, before his graduation at the advanced flying school near Columbus. Before he entered pilot training, he attended Frank Hughes High School in Clifton. Harold has two brothers: Everette and Olin Biffle.

Harold was born 2 Apr 1925 in Clifton, was married 16 Jul 1946 in St Louis, Mis-

souri to Marcella "Sally" Elizabeth Morff, daughter of John Jacob and Theresa Ann (Loethen) Morff.

She was born 29 October 1923. Their children:

(1) James Harold Biffle, born 3 July 1948 at Scott Air Force Base, Belleville, Illinois, married 23 May 1970 at Andrews Air Force Base, Md to Barbara Jean McLain, daughter of Jesse Edward and Velma Pearl (Newton) McLain. She was born 3 June 1949 at U S Army Hospital, Nuremberg, Germany. Their children:

a. Eric Blain Biffle born 12 December 1972 Portsmouth Naval Shipyard Hospital, Kittery, Maine.

b. Joshua Scott Biffle, born 3 December 1977 Greater Southeast Community Hospital, Washington, D. C.

(2) Donna Kaye Biffle, born 21 April 1951 at Keesler Air Force Base, Biloxi, Mississippi, married 6 January 1973 at Andrews Air Force Base to Martin Thomas Brumback, son of Eldon Herbert and Joyce (Nelson) Brumback. He was born 30 July 1951.

(3) Linda Ann Biffle, born 21 February 1954 at Johnson Air Force Base, Tokyo, Japan. She was married 7 October 1978 at Andrews Air Force Base to Michael George Weissmueller, son of Frederick George and Mabel Virginia (Maddox) Weissmueller. He was born 3 Apr 1951 in Washington, D. C. and is a Fireman with the Washington Fire Department.

(4) Karen Sue Biffle, born 18 January 1956 Chennault Air Force Base, Lake Charles, Louisiana. She is a Registered Nurse graduated from Prince George's Community College, Largo, Maryland.

(5) Diane Gale Biffle, born 24 October 1958 at Chennault AFB, Lake Charles, Louisiana. She is a Commercial Art Undergraduate at Prince George's Community College.

(6) Nancy Jean Biffle, born 17 November 1962 at Tachikawa AFB, Tokyo, Japan.

BIFFLE, OLIN ANDREW, Master Sergeant, USAF Retired, Air Force 34 189 138, Olin, is the son of Jacob Elijah "Lige" Biffle and Anna Walker Biffle. He has two brothers: Harold Francis of Clinton, Maryland and Everette Walker Biffle, deceased. He was married 18 December 1947 at Corinth, MS to Billie Jean Lynch, daughter of Charles Wesley and Maybell Elizabeth (Young) Lynch. She was born 30 September 1926 on Eagle Creek. They have two children: Deborah Jean Biffle Petty, born 13 February 1951 in Aurora, Co, and Steven Lige Biffle, born 25 October 1953 at Selma, Alabama, and two grandchildren: Heather Marie Biffle and Allen Biffle Petty.

"I was born in Clifton Tennessee on 13 November 1919 and attended Frank Hughes Elementary School until I finished the fifth grade. I then moved to Lawrenceburg, Tennessee for five years, and then moved to a farm on Hardin's Creek where I was living when World War II was declared. I was drafted for one year and a day and didn't get back to Wayne County to live until some twenty years later.

I was inducted into the U. S. Air Force at Fort Oglethorpe, Georgia and took my basic training at Keesler Field, Mississippi. I was assigned to the 93rd Bomb Group. 330th Bomb Squadron at Fort Myers, Florida, where we flew submarine patrol off the coast of Florida. Several subs were sighted and we got credit for sinking one sub. The Flight Crews flew to Alconberry Hill, England; the Ground Crews crossed the Atlantic on the ship, Queen Elizabeth, to do in the rest of the group, to form the first B-24 Liberator Outfit in European Theater Of Operations.

The 93rd Bomb Group flew 391 missions over enemy territory between August 1942 and June 1945. Probably the two most important missions the 93rd Bomb Group participated in was the Oil Refinery at Ploesti, Romania, and the Hard Water Plant in Norway. Germany was ahead of the U. S. A. at this time in the develop-

ment of the A-Bomb. The Norway mission probably gave Oak Ridge time to develop the A-Bomb used on Japan. The 93rd Bomb Group participated in the first daylight bombing raid over Europe and was the first to hit targets deep inside Germany, flying on to Russia territory to refuel.

The 93rd Bomb Group participated in the following campaigns: Rhineland, Ardennes - Normandy, Northern France - Central Europe, Egypt, Libya - Tunisia, Sicily, and Naples- Foggis and received the Presidential Unit Citation. We were returned to the USA early for preparation to reform and be sent to the Pacific Theater of Operations.

After the war, I reenlisted in the USAF at Scott Field, Illinois and was stationed at Lowry AFB in Denver, Colorado; Selma AFB in Selma, Alabama; Webb AFB in Big Spring, Texas; McGee Tyson AFB in Alcoa, Tennessee; and Tyndall AFB in Florida from which I retired in June 1963 with 20 years, 6 months active service.

During his military service, Master Sergeant Biffle received the following decorations and awards: Presidential Unit Citation, Good Conduct Medal with 1 Silver Loop, American Campaign Medal, European-African-Middle Eastern Campaign Medal with 2 Silver Service Stars and 1 Bronze Service Star, National Defense Service Medal, Air Force Longevity Service Award Ribbon with 4 Bronze Oak Leaf Clusters. He also served overseas in Iceland from 5 October 1956 to 28 September 1957. - Olin Biffle.

BLACK, RICHARD HAGGARD, I was born on 28 September, 1921 in Waynesboro, Tennessee, to Richard

Hannah and Nona Haggard Black. I attended the local school through the eighth grade, and upon completion entered high school at Columbia Military Academy, where I graduated in 1940. While attending the University of Tennessee in Knoxville, I entered active duty in May 1942

45

for service in World War II. My overseas duty was with the 25th Infantry Division. We were engaged in combat with the Japanese on the South Pacific Island of Luzon, Philippine Islands, and our occupation duty in and around Nagoya, Japan. I was with the initial occupying forces to Japan shortly after the atomic bomb was dropped on Japan. Awards include: Liasion Pilot Wings, Army Aviator Wings, Combat Infantry Badge and the Bronze Star.

Upon release from active duty in 1946, and while attending Middle Tennessee State College, I applied for, was accepted, and completed pilot training in the Army Air Corp, with ratings in fixed wing and rotary wing aircraft. After two years of service as pilot in the 82nd Airborne Division at Fort Bragg, North Carolina, I was released from active duty and found employment with the Military Department in the state of Tennessee with the duties of airplane and helicopter pilot, flight operations officer, flight standardization officer and test pilot. Retired after 30 years of service with 15 years of active service and 15 years of service with the Tennessee Army National Guard with the grade of Lieutenant Colonel.

After a long courtship, I married Joyce Sue Turman, a devoted wife for 28 years until her death in December of 1990. Our family consists of two sons, Robert Cole Turman and Richard T. Black; two grandsons, Cole and Drew Turman; and two granddaughters, Sarah Beth Turman and Caroline Black. We continue to reside in Waynesboro among our friends and neighbors.

BLALOCK, LUTHER S., Serial Number 34 375 250, was a Private First Class with the 192 General Hospital Unit, United States Army. He was born 23 October 1906 in Wayne County. When he was inducted in the Service, his description was given as blue eyes, brown hair, height 5'5" and weight 111 lbs. He was married with two dependents and was a farmer. The decorations received were: European Africa Middle Eastern Theater Ribbon, and Good Conduct Medal. His permanent mailing address was Collinwood, Tennessee.

"Blalock is the son of Mr. and Mrs. A. H. Blalock of Collinwood. He was inducted in the Service 17 October 1942. He took his basic training at Fort Sam Houston, Texas, Fort Ringold, Texas, Camp Gruber, Oklahoma, and Camp Barkley and was sent overseas in April 1944. He was stationed in England with a General Hospital Unit.

Blalock was employed by Hassell and Hughes Lumber Co. before induction. His wife was the former Willie Mae Fowler. They had a son at this reported time."

Source: Wayne County News owned by Clyde Bevis.

BLASINGIM, JAMES HENRY, son of Marvin and Ida Spann Blasingim, was born in Wayne County in 1927 and got his earlier years of schooling there. He moved to Lawrence County and lived there at the time he was inducted into the United States Army. After the army he was a truck driver and had retired a few years before his death, December 7, 1999, at Columbia Crockett Hospital in Lawrenceburg, Tennessee; he was cremated.

He has three children: Douglas, Jamey and Joyce Sue, all of Ohio. He has four siblings: Billy and Larry Gene of Ohio, Eddie of Kentucky, and a sister, Jackie, of Florida.

BLASINGIM, JOHN, JR., Private First Class Blasingim is the son of Mr. and Mrs. John Blasingim of Waynesboro. His wife is Ellamae. He entered the service June 1944. He took his training at Shephard Field, San Antonio, Big Spring and Camp Maxey, all in Texas. Later, he was sent to Fort Meade, Maryland where he was assigned to overseas duty. He has served in Holland and Germany.

Source: Wayne County News.

BOWLING, BOB TAYLOR, was the son of Joe and Rebecca Bowling. He was drafted into the United States Navy on 3 September 1943. He served on the USS Tangier for 25 months in the Pacific Theater of War. His rank was Seaman 3rd Class when discharged in 1945. He was one of the first married men with children to be called from Wayne County.

He was born in Hardin County. He came to Wayne County and married Audrey Phillips. His children were: Norman Taylor, Debra and Sherry. His siblings were: Fred, Frank, Burgess, Dexter, Joe, Jr., Tommy, Earl, Pearl, Ethel and Frances. He worked for T. S. Hassell as a clerk for many years. He attended the Church of Christ.

BOWLING, GUS, Cpl. Gus Bowling, son of William Perry "Bud" and Margaret Sizemore Bowling, received his training at Fort Oglethorpe, Georgia, Fort Knox, Kentucky, Camp Bowie, Texas and Columbus, Georgia. From there he was transferred to the European Theater of War. He was a gunner on a tank No. 13 in the 760th Tank Division. He believed thirteen to be his lucky number because he survived. His No. 13 tank was the first to enter Rome, Italy before it fell. The battles he saw action in were: Rome Arno, Naples Foggia, PO Valley, and Northern Appinnes. He received the Good Conduct Medal, The European African Medal, Eastern Theater

Ribbon and four Bronze Stars. He was discharged in May 1945.

Prior to entering the service, he was employed in the timber industry. After his Honorable Discharge, he was a farmer. He married Carmie Phillips. They have three children: Jimmy, Jerry and Marion Free.

BOWLING, LINCOLN, was a World War II veteran with the Third Infantry Division of the Seventh Army in France. His

company was the Third Division's 30th Infantry. Private Bowling's marksmanship kept his company from getting shot up by enfilade fire. Halfway up a hill when two enemy machine guns began to pump out lead, Bowling moved over farther than his original position on the extreme right of the company and continued his advance up the hill. After crawling about 100 yards under the constant machine gun pounding, Bowling stopped and patiently sweated out the Germans. His patience was rewarded later when eight of them paraded down with their extra machine gun. Bowling drew a bead. He fired twice and two Germans fell dead. Then Bowling jumped up and charged forward firing from the hip. The rest of the crew did not hesitate to give up. His heroic action not only saved his company, but it also earned him the purple heart, the silver star and other distinguished metals of honor.

Lincoln's father was the late William Perry (Bud) Bowling. His mother was the late Mary Sizemore Bowling, who died in 1925. He was married to Mildred Hardin, the daughter of the late Gipson G. and Della Hardin. They were the parents of five children, Martha Hime of Savannah, James Bowling of Union City, Janice Love of Clifton, Linda Worley of Savannah, and Randy Bowling of Clifton. Lincoln had five brothers and three sisters, as well as, several half brothers and sisters.

BOYD, CLAUDE T., Serial Number 976 82 18, of Route 2, Clifton, Tennessee, was born 19 September 1926 in Clifton.

He entered into active service in February 1945 at Chattanooga, Tennessee and received his Honorable Discharge from the United States Navy on 23 April 1946 in Memphis, Tennessee with a rank of Seaman, Second Class. At that time he was single. He was awarded the Victory Medal. His education consisted of 7 years in grammar school. The Stations/Vessels that he served on were USNTADC, Williamsburg, Virginia, USS Mattole, and USS PORTSMOUTH.
Source: Copy of his Separation from U. S. Naval Service. The copy was not very clear.

BOYD, JESSIE W., served in World War II in the 83rd Infantry Division in the United States Army. He was a private in Company L, 331st Infantry, 83rd Infantry Division during World War II.

J. W. was born on June 1, 1921, the son of Will and Ruby Wilson Boyd. They lived near Clifton.

J. W. married Maxine Conway, daughter of George and Loubell Conway.

He was a farmer. He attended school at Frank Hughes in Clifton, Tennessee.

J. W. died on March 1, 1958, and is buried in the Lone Chestnut Cemetery in Decatur County, Tennessee, about one mile across the Tennessee River in Clifton, Tennessee.

His siblings are James, Douglas Eugene, Jeronda Jean, Billy Joe, Willard, Loyd D. and Jessie.

BOYD, WILLIAM R., was born on August 29, 1924, in Cypress Inn, Tennessee, and worked as a farmhand until he was inducted into the United States Army on April 23, 1943, at Fort Oglethorpe, Georgia. He served as a medical technician and was discharged on December 24, 1945, at Camp Atterberry, Indiana. He received the following citations: Meritorious Unit Award, Victory Medal, Asiatic-Pacific Theater Ribbon with one Bronze Star and Good Conduct Ribbon.

BRADLEY, HOMER, JR., was a Corporal with the Combat Engineers Group in the United States Army. He was inducted

11 April 1944 and received his basic training at Fort Bragg, North Carolina. He was in the South Pacific for one year and spent six months in occupied Japan, was discharged 14 May 1946. He worked many years for Sealtest Milk Company until his retirement. Waynesboro, Tennessee is home to him now.

Homer, Jr., son of Homer Floyd and Beulah Morgan Bradley, was born 16 November 1925. His brothers are: Orvel, Bernie, and Jettie Bradley. His sisters are: Rachel Byrd, Lexie Ray, Ailene Fisher, Shirley Ray, Dexter Sides, Pharlea Ray and Nora Faye Searle. Homer, Jr., married Betty Byrd and they have two children: Terry and Cathy Bradley.

BRATTON, CLAUDE L., was drafted into the United States Navy in 1943. He was sent to Great Lakes, Illinois, for basic training. About three months later, he was given a medical discharge due to health problems. He returned home to Lutts, Tennessee. He became engaged in farming and

remained a farmer until his death in 1971. He is buried in the Piney Grove Cemetery in Cypress Inn, Tennessee.

Claude L. and his twin, Clara, were born 20 May 1924 in Hardin County, Tennessee. They were the children of Robert L. and Nancy Stricklin Bratton. Claude was married 1 Mar 1943 to Golina Moadlan. They had six children- three boys and three girls: James Owen, Shirley Joan, Lennie, Shelby, Sandra and Randy Bratton. His siblings are: Marshal, Margaret, Myrtle, Walter, Etta, Clara, Gladys and Evelyn Sue Bratton.

BRAY, LEWIS CRAFFORD, was a T/Sgt in the Anti-Tank Platoon in the 33rd Infantry Division in the United States

Army. He was inducted 23 May 1942 and discharged 5 June 1946 from Convalescent Hospital in Daytona Beach, Florida. He had a high school education. He received his basic training at Camp Wheeler, Georgia, Camp Forrest, Tullahoma, Tennessee, and Fort Lewis, Tacoma, Washington. Desert training was received in California and he also had Jungle training. He served in New Guinea, then on to Luzon in the Philippines. He was in this area when peace was declared. He spent several weeks in Saint Angeles. L. C. mentioned that this was a Catholic run town. Saint Angelo was a very large cathedral. He attended the small Baptist church there. He received the following citations: Asiatic Pacific Service Medal, American Service Medal, Good Conduct Medal, Philippines Liberation Medal, Bronze Star, WW II Victory Medal, Combat Infantry Badge, and Expert Infantry Badge. After L. C. returned from service, he worked as a painter, for the Alabama Power Company, Daniels Construction and then spent thirty years with TVA before he retired.

L. C., son of William Riley and Carrie Mae Yearby Bray, was born 11 Mar 1920. He married Reba Pope, Wayne County, Tennessee. Their children are: Nancy

Marie Bray Franklin, and Norman Lewis Bray. His brothers are Ralph, Robert Riley, and Thomas Edward Bray. His sisters: Ruby Beckham, Alma Keene, Mary Emma Rash, Helen Thomas, Sue Sherrick, and Peggy Pierce.

BRAY, ROBERT RILEY, Serial Number 34 495 062, was a Sergeant in the 7th Division, 32nd Infantry of the United

States Army. When inducted 29 September 1942 in Fort Oglethorpe, Georgia, his permanent address was Route 1, Waynesboro, Tennessee. His description was: brown eyes, black hair, 5'10 1/2" height, weight 165 lbs, married, 1 dependent. Civilian Occupation was farm hand. His education was 8 years in grammar school. His Military Occupation Specialty was Rifleman. Military Qualifications - Combat Infantry Badge, January 1944. His battles and campaigns included Marshall Islands Campaign, Alaskan Campaign, and Philippine Islands Campaign. His decorations included Asiatic Pacific Theater Medal, Good Conduct Medal, Bronze Star, and Purple Heart Medal. Shell fragments wounded his left knee 24 November 1944 during action in the Asiatic Pacific Theater He left the USA 22 April for the Asiatic Pacific Theater and returned 4 February 1945. He was discharge on 25 April 1945 at Welch Convalescent Hospital in Daytona Beach, Florida.

Robert, son of William Riley and Carrie Mae Yearby Bray, was born 8 Mar 1922 in Cerro Gordo, Tennessee. He married Frankie Bryant and they have six children: Robert, Jr., (Bobby), Betty Ruth, Ronnie, Mike, Anthony, and Tracy Bray. His brothers are Ralph, Lewis Crafford (L. C.), and Thomas Edward Bray. His sisters: Ruby Beckham, Alma Keene, Mary Emma Rash, Helen Thomas, Sue Sherrick, and Peggy Pierce.

BREWER, ALLEN B., Serial Number 44 120 530, was a Private in Special Training Unit SOU 1449, United States

Army. He was inducted 29 May 1945 at Fort Oglethorpe, Georgia. At that time his description was grey eyes, black hair, 5'5" height, weight 125 lbs, married with one dependent. He was born 9 February 1916 in Collinwood, Tennessee. His Civilian Occupation was General Hand. His Military Occupational Specialty was STU trainee. He served 29 days and was honorably discharged 27 August 1945 at Fort McPherson, Georgia. His permanent mailing address was Collinwood, Tennessee.

BREWER, ANDY RAY, was born, Oct. 19, 1923, at Cypress Inn and entered the U. S. Navy, March 24, 1943, at Chattanooga, Tn. He was listed as a water tender first class. He served at NRS Chattanooga, TN.; USNTS Bainbridge, Md., NTS Norfolk, VA.: USS G. W. Ingram; USNH St. Alban, L. 1. , N. Y.; USN Persedis Cen.; Lido Beach, L. I., N. Y. He was discharged at Lido Beach, Long Island, N. Y., July 26, 1945.

BREWER, ARLEN, son of Rich and Elsie (Smith) Brewer, was born, July 22, 1920, in Wayne County. He grew up in the

Forty-Eight Community and attended Wayne County High School at Waynesboro, TN. Arlen worked on his dad's farm until he was inducted into the U. S. Army, August 26, 1942, at Ft. Oglethorpe, GA. He was assigned to the infantry as a light truck driver and received his training in several different camps in the states.

March 5, 1943, six months after he entered the service, his unit left for North Africa. Arlen participated in the battles of Sicily, Normandy, Northern France, Rhineland and Central Europe. His unit, 116th Infantry, fought courageously on D Day to establish one of the main beachheads which lead to Normandy. During this encounter, August 1, 1944, Arlen received wounds which confined him to a hospital in England for several weeks.

More than two and a half years had passed since he landed on foreign soil, but the fighting was over and they were heading home. October 20, 1945, Arlen was discharged at Camp Atterbury, In. He had received the following citations; Purple Heart, Distinguished Unit Badge, Bronze Arrowhead, Good Conduct Medal and EAME Theater with five Bronze Stars.

June 27, 1946, Arlen and Margaret Yarbrough were married and lived near Waynesboro, where he worked at a Button Factory until 1947. He then worked at Genesco, Inc. until 1952, when he went to Michigan and worked at General Motors in Willow Run from, July 8, 1952 until December 31, 1985. He then retired after thirty-three years. They lived at Taylor, MI and have four children, Gerald, Gloria, Vickie Princilla; they have eight grandchildren. His six brothers are Harry, Rex, James, Robert, Donald and Herbert (all deceased except Herbert); four sisters, Edna, Ophelia, Willodean and Jewell (all living).

Arlen died from heart problems June 6, 1991 at the age of seventy-one and is buried at Michigan Memorial Garden at Taylor, Michigan.

BREWER, ARTHUR "BUDDIE" COLLIN, age 74, of North Little Rock, Arkansas, died 31 January 1994 in Fort Root Veterans Hospital. and was buried in Shawnette Methodist Church Cemetery near Collinwood. He was a native of Wayne County but had resided in Fort Root Veterans Hospital in North Little Rock since World War II. He served in the army in Fort. Benning, Georgia.

He was the son of Lynn Franklin and Lou Isabelle Smith Brewer. Survivors included five sisters: Mazie B. Calton of Collinwood, Allene B. Tomerlin and Christine B Moran both of St. Louis, Missouri, Octalee B. Dixon of Nashville and Lynell B. Jones of Houston Texas, and a host of nieces and nephews.

BREWER, CHESTER LEON, Serial Number 8 459 370, was a Seaman First Class in the United States Navy. He was inducted 4 August 1943 and entered active duty 11 August 1943 in Waynesboro. He held the following ratings: AS, S1/C, S2/C. He served on the following vessels: US NTS, Bainbridge, Maryland; NTS NOB Norfolk, Virginia; USS CATES and USS FANSHAW. His main civilian occupation was farming for Floyd Prince in Lawrenceburg. He had a 7th grade education. He was discharge 31 December 1945 in Memphis, Tennessee. He was born 16 May 1925 in Waynesboro, Tennessee. His home address was Route 6, Lawrenceburg, Tennessee.

BREWER, CREVICE D., Serial Number 37 520 116, had the rank of Technician Fifth Grade, 3162d Signal Service

Company of the United States Army. He entered active service 9 April 1943 in Ft. Leavenworth, Kansas. His description: brown eyes, brown hair, 5' 3" height, 180 lbs, married, two dependents. His foreign service was in the Rhineland. He left the USA for European-African Middle Eastern Theater 30 November 1944 and returned 28 January 1946. His decorations and Medals: World War II Victory Ribbon, Good Conduct Medal, American Theater Ribbon, European-African Middle Eastern Theater Ribbon, and one Bronze Service Star. He was discharged 4 February 1946 in Camp Chaffee, Arkansas. His mailing address was 212 West 7th Street, Lawrence, Douglas County, Kansas.

Mr. Brewer, son of Frank and Jimmie Nutt Brewer, was born 19 December 1921 in Waynesboro, Tennessee and died February 1980. His brothers are: Carmack, Russ, Frank, Jr., G. W., Lester and Herbert Gene Brewer. His sisters are: Rubye Anderson and Hester York. His wife was Dorris Lee Jackson and they had one child, Jimmie Gale.

"Two Wayne County brothers, Technical Sergeant Russ Brewer and Corporal Crevice Brewer, sons of Mr. and Mrs. Frank Brewer of Route 4, Waynesboro, met recently in Metz, France.

BREWER, EUNIS BEAUMONT, Serial Number 641 37 96, enlisted as Seaman, First class, 27 October 1942 in Nashville, Tennessee for four years. He was discharged from the U S Naval Training Center, Great Lakes, Illinois 11 November 1942. He was born 13 Mar 1905 in Wayne County. He served on the USNRS Nashville, Tennessee and USNTS Great Lakes, Illinois. His description: brown eyes, brown hair, ruddy complexion, 5'6" height and 170 weight.

Source: United States Naval Reserve Certificate of Discharge.

BREWER, GRADY GLEN, Serial Number 44 020 044, was a Private in Company C Special Training Unit, United States Army. He was only 17 1/2 years old when he enlisted 17 August 1944 at Camp Forrest, Tennessee. His description at that time: gray eyes, brown hair, ruddy complexion. 5'9" height. He was honorably discharged 3 December 1944 Fort McPherson, Georgia. He was born in Wayne County and was a general farm hand.

Funeral services for Grady Glen Brewer, 65, of Route 10, Benton, Kentucky, were conducted February 21, 1993 in Benton. Burial was in Edwards Cemetery. Mr. Brewer died 18 February 1993 at Marshall County Hospital. He was the son of the late Harrison and Ester Whitehead Brewer, a Veteran of World War II and a member of Lakeview Baptist Church and Disabled American Veterans, Benton Chapter, No. 118.

Survivors include his wife, Virginia Cummings Brewer; six daughters, Hazel Price, Denise Brewer, Veronica Galloway, Becky Rhodes, Donna Brewer and Carolyn Johnson; two sons, Glen and David Brewer; four sisters, Rachel Byron, Hazel Weaver, Alma Lee Bromley, Iva Dean Brewer,; six brothers, Grayford, Charles, James, Howard, Johnny and Ray Brewer.

Source: Wayne County News obit 24 February 1993.

BREWER, GUY, enlisted in the United States Army Air Force 15 October 1941 in Nashville, Tennessee, went to Fort

Oglethorpe, Georgia, then to Biloxi, Mississippi. He was stationed in Presque Isle Air Force Base in Presque Isle, Maine, in the 15th Ferrying Command and was then transferred to Harmon Field, Newfoundland. He was discharged 11 November 1945 with rank of Sergeant.

Guy, son of Buck and Mamie Brewer, was born 31 January 1920 in Wayne County, Tennessee His wife is Norma

Clark Brewer and his children: Gary, Robert and Jay Brewer. His siblings are: Vivian Brewer, Robbie Brewer Brady, Hazel Brewer Lutz, and Ralph Brewer.

BREWER, HARLON D., son of Leonard and Ora (Moore) Brewer, was born, June 9, 1924, in Wayne County where he grew up. He was enrolled in Lawrence County High School when he decided to join CC Camp. When his time at the camp there ended, he enlisted in the United States Navy and served until the end of the war. He married Pauline Wells of Florence, Alabama and moved to Toledo, Ohio, where he remained until his death in February 1991. He is buried at Highland Cemetery near the Lawrence County line. Harlon has two sons, Larry and Gary of Toledo. His siblings are Jean (Brewer) Haddock of Waynesboro and Sammy Brewer of Nashville.

BREWER, HARRY CLAY, son of Rich and Elsie (Smith) Brewer, was born, March 25, 1916, in Wayne County. He

grew up in the Forty-Eight Creek Community and attended school there and at Wayne County High School in Waynesboro.

He was working on highway construction operating heavy machines, when he received his notice to report to the selective service office. October 3, 1942, he reported to Ft. Oglethorpe, GA and received his training at several different camps for the next twenty-three months. He was assigned to his unit as a light truck driver and promoted to T/5. August 20, 1944, they departed for the European Theater for the next year. He participated in the battles of the Rhineland, Central Europe and Ardennes, headquartered with the 3rd Army. He returned to the states, September 27, 1945, with the following citations; Distinguished Unit Badge, Good Conduct Ribbon and EAME Theater with three Bronze Stars. October 12, 1945, Harry was discharged at Camp Atterbury, In.

After three years, he returned home and was employed at Reynolds Metal Co. at Sheffield, AL. He worked there for the next thirty-three years and retired in October 1977.

Harry and Reba McAnally were married, October 12, 1946, and made their home at Florence, AL. They have two sons, Stephen Clay born November 28, 1951 and Michael Alan born January 30, 1955. They have four granddaughters, two grandsons and two great-grandchildren. Harry has two other children-by a previous, marriage, .a daughter, Pat and-a-son, Ronnie. Reba died in 197 1.

March 19, 1972, Harry married Olene Davis in Wayne County and lived at R#2, Iron City, TN. He had been retired eighteen years when he died from heart problems, July 30, 1995, at the age of seventy-nine years. He and Olene were married twenty-three years. He is buried at Greenview memorial Cemetery at Florence, AL.

Harry's siblings are Rex, James, Robert, Arlen, Herbert, Edna, OPhelia, Willodean and Jewell.

BREWER, IRIE, Non-Registrant, Serial Number 34 366 738, was inducted 26 August 1942 at Fort Oglethorpe, Georgia. He was a Private with Headquarters Detachment, Fourth Service Command, United State Army. He was discharged 31 March 1943 at Camp Forrest, Tennessee.

BREWER, JOHN C., Serial Number 44 040 717, was inducted 31 August 1944 at Fort Oglethorpe, Georgia. His description was as follows: blue eyes, brown hair, ruddy complexion, 5' 7" height, age 23 years and 2/12, married and was born in Waynesboro, Tennessee. His Civilian Occupation was Farmer. He was a Private in Company C, 151st Infantry Training Btn., United States Army. He was honorably discharge 22 September 1944 at Fort McPherson, Georgia. His military qualifications were Marksman Rifle.

BREWER, JOHN V., Serial Number 34 140 793, was a PFC in the Second Battalion Field Artillery, School Detachment, United States Army. His description was: blue eyes, black hair, 5' 5" height, 155 lbs weight, married with 3 Dependents. He was born 7 February 1915 in Wayne County, Tennessee and had a 7th grade education. His Civilian Occupation was Truck Driver. His Military Occupation was Foreman of Labor. He departed the USA on 18 February 1942 for Peru and returned 19 February 1944. He was discharged 23 September 1945 in Fort Sill, Oklahoma. Permanent mailing address was General Delivery, Collinwood, Tennessee.

BREWER, LINCOLN, Serial Number 34 713 879, was a Private in Battery B 565th Anti-Aircraft Artillery in the United States Army. He was born 16 Aug 1924 in Iron City, Tennessee. His permanent mailing address was Collinwood, Tennessee. His description: Blue eyes, black hair, height 5'10", weight 147 lbs, and married with 7 dependents. His civilian job was farm hand. He was inducted 23 April 1943 and entered active service 30 May 1943 at Camp Forrest, Tennessee. His military speciality was cook. His military qualifications were marksman (rifle). He was in the following battles and campaigns: Ardennes, Rhineland and Central Europe. He received the following decorations and citations: American Theater Ribbon, European African Middle Eastern Ribbon, and World War II Victory Medal. He departed the USA for European Theater Operation on 6 Oct 1944 and returned 12 Oct 1945. His education consisted of 6 years in grammar school. He was discharged 20 Dec 1945 in Camp Bliss, Texas.

BREWER, LUCAS EARL, Serial Number 639 026, volunteered and was sworn in to the United States Coast Guard

on December 1, 1942, and went on active duty January 19, 1943. He was stationed in the following places: U. S. Coast Guard Training Station, Manhattan Beach, Brooklyn, New York; Coast Guard Barracks, Providence, Rhode. Island; Coast Guard K-9 Station, Fort Robinson, Nebraska; Coast Guard Detachment, U. S. Naval Ammunition Depot, Hastings, Nebraska; and U. S. Coast Guard District Office, St Louis, Missouri. He received the Good Conduct Medal. He was discharged 13 February 1946 in St. Louis, Missouri, with the rank of Coxswain (3rd Class Petty Officer). Most of his service time was spent in clerical duties. He was born 10 December 1923 in Collinwood, Tennessee. He was awarded: Honorable Discharge Button, Service Lapel Button, and Discharge Emblem.

BREWER, TOM, JR., Serial Number 34 373 131, was a Technician 4th Grade in Battery D, 491st AAA Aw Battalion. when he was honorably discharged in Camp Stewart, Georgia on 11 October 1943. Tom (NMI), Jr., was inducted 24 September 1943 at Waynesboro, Tennessee. He was 20 and 10/12 years of age and a farmer. He had blue eyes, brown hair, ruddy complexion, 6' 0" height. His army specialty was Cook. He received the Good Conduct Ribbon.

BREWER, WASH, Serial Number 34 884 584, was a Private in Hq 6855th American University Overhead Detachment, United States Army. He was inducted 3 September 1943 at Fort Oglethorpe, Georgia. His description was: blue eyes, brown hair, 5' 9" height, weight 144 lbs, married with four dependents. His Civilian Occupation was Laborer. His Military Occupation was Cook. He was born 11 November 1922 in Iron City, Tennessee. His battles and campaigns were: Northern France and Rhineland. He receive the following decorations: European-African Middle Eastern Theater Ribbon, and Bronze Service Star. He was discharged 12 December 1945 at Shrivenham American University, APO 756, U. S. Army, with excellent character. His permanent mailing address was Collinwood, Tennessee.

BREWER, WILLARD, Serial number 34 375 240, was a Private First Class, Co II 378th Infantry, United States Army. He entered service 7 October 1942 at Fort Oglethorpe, Georgia. He received the following decorations: Purple Heart, American Service Medal, Good Conduct Medal, European-African-Middle Easter Service Medal with 3 Bronze Stars, and World War II Victory Medal. He was wounded in Maselle, France on 16 November 1944 and was discharged 20 November 1945 in Fort McPherson, Georgia

Willard, son of William R. "Hoss" and Mattie Kelley Brewer, was born 7 July 1921 in Wayne County, died 26 April 1980 in the Veterans Hospital, Nashville, Tennessee and is buried in Memorial Gardens, Waynesboro, Tennessee. He attended school in Wayne County and was of Baptist faith. He married Betty Ford. There were no children. His siblings are: Dolph, Bud, Roy, Marvin, and William Brewer, Pamsey Martin, Nona Dugger, and Mattie Eva Rochelle.

BREWER, WILLIAM R., was inducted into the United States Army on 29 May 1945 at Fort McPherson, Georgia. His service was with Company B 38th Engineers Training Battalion. His description: blue eyes, brown hair, 5' 6" height, 158 lbs weight, married with 4 dependents. His Civilian Occupation was Telephone Lineman. His Military Occupation Specialty was Training. He received the Good Conduct Medal. He was discharged 29 October 1945 at Separation Center, Fort Leonard, Wood, Missouri. His permanent mailing address, Route 5, Waynesboro, Tennessee. William R. was born 29 July 1917 in Waynesboro, Tennessee .

BREWER, WILLIAM RUSS, Serial Number 20 457 398, volunteered 20 September 1940 and entered the United States

Army at Fort Oglethorpe, Georgia. He served at Fort Jackson, South Carolina He was drafted for active duty in the U. S. Army 15 March 1942 and served until 23 September 1945. This time his serial number was 34 193 001 and he was stationed at Fort Bragg, North Carolina with the 101st Airborne Division. He served in Glider Troops and as clerk in Headquarters of the 101st. From here he went overseas and was stationed in Germany, England and France. His rank was Tech Sgt., then promoted to Staff Sgt. He was discharged at Camp Atterbury, Indiana in September 1945.

Russ, son of Frank and Jimmie Nutt Brewer, was born 23 December 1919 in Wayne County, and died 14 October 1989. His brothers are: Carmack, Crevice, Frank, Jr., G. W., Lester and Herbert Gene Brewer. His sisters are: Rubye Anderson and Hester York. His wife is June Vandergriff and children are: Patricia, Bunnee, Rusty and Sandy.

BREWER, WILLIAM WALTER JR., enlisted in the United States Navy on August 8, 1945, and was discharged on January 12, 1948, with the rank of MOMM 3C.

Walter Jr., son of William Walter Sr. and Mabel Stricklin Brewer, was born on July 25, 1927, in Clifton, Tennessee. He died on May 12, 1998, in Maury County Hos-

pital in Columbia and was buried in McGlamery Cemetery in Collinwood.

He was a retired President and CEO of Dixie Chemicals in North Carolina, a member of the Waynesboro United Methodist Church and the Masonic Lodge.

He married Ruby Craig and they had two sons, Robert Brewer of Columbia and Gary Charles (Chuck) Brewer of Forest, Virginia. His siblings are Rita Jane Melton of Hohenwald; Charles Brewer of Sumter, South Carolina; and Gene Brewer of Nashville. He has one sister, Patsy Barnett, who is deceased.

BRIDGES, WILLIAM E., son of Marvin and Nillie Burns Bridges, was born August 10, 1920 at Cardwell, Mo. He moved near Waynesboro, TN and was working as a farmhand when he was inducted into the U.S. Army, October 8, 1942 at Ft. Oglethorpe, Ga. He was a heavy machine gun operator with Co. 1905th Engineer Aviation Batt. and served in the battles of Central-Burma and India-Burma. William E. was awarded the Good Conduct Ribbon and Asiatic-Pacific Theater Ribbon with two Bronze Stars. August 1945 he was discharged at Camp Atterbury, Ind.

William E. was married and has three children, Bessie Mae, Juanita and Billy. He became employed at Indianapolis, Ind. and is now retired from his work there and resides Decatur, Al.

BROCK, HELON N., At the time of his induction into the United States Navy, he was a resident of Clifton. His parents are Charlie and Anna Brock. Helon married Daisy White from Hardin County and they have three children: Donna, Wanda and Freddy. His siblings are: Noah, Kent, John, Hoover, Lee, Woodrow, Vernal, Mincie Brock Walker, Hazel, Mable Brock Turner, and Willie Brock Walker.

BROMLEY, BILLYE R., Serial Number 14 185 186, enlisted 1 November 1942

and entered active service 10 May 1943 at Camp Shelby, Mississippi. He was registered with local Board No 1, Iron City, Lawrence County, Tennessee. He was born 11 July 1921 in Iron City, Tennessee. He finished four years of high school. His civilian occupation was farmer. His military occupation was radar repairman and gun laying equipment. His military qualification was M-1 Carbine Sharpshooter. First Sergeant Bromley was with the 56th Anti-aircraft Brigade, United States Army. The service schools that he attended were AAA School at Camp Davis, North Carolina, and Radar Repairman Gun School. He left the United States for European Theater Operation 11 August 1944 and returned 20 March 1946. The battles and campaigns that he participated in were Northern France, Ardennes, Rhineland and Central Europe. Decorations and citations were: American Theater Ribbon, European-African Middle Eastern Theater Ribbon with four Bronze Stars, Good Conduct Medal and World War II Victory Medal. He was discharged 25 March 1946 at Camp Atterbury, Indiana.

BROMLEY, GUS W., Serial Number 34 189 065, was a Private, First Class with the 31st Fighter Control Squadron, AAF. Gus was born in Lawrence County, Tennessee. He was 32 and 4/12 years old when he enlisted and was a farmer. His description was brown eyes, dark brown hair, ruddy complexion, 5' 9 1/2" height and single. He was honorably discharged at Headquarters Fitzsimmons, General Hospital, Denver, Colorado. He is now deceased.

BROMLEY, JASPER SIMS, Serial Number 965 80 06, enlisted 11 October 1943 in Chattanooga, Tennessee, for two years in the United States Navy. He was born 17 May 1922 in Iron City, Tennessee. His description: blue eyes, brown hair, ruddy complexion, 5'8" height, weight 145 lbs and single. The Service Vessels and Stations that he served on were USNTS Great Lakes, Illinois; UOB Norfolk, Virginia; and Norfolk Naval Hospital, Portsmouth, Virginia. Seaman Second Class Bromley was honorably discharged 10 March 1944 from the Norfolk Naval Hospital, at Portsmouth Virginia.

BROMLEY, JOHN ROBERT, entered service in the United States Navy Cee Bee's 56th Battalion in September 1942 and was discharged in 1945. His overseas duty was in the Hawaiian Islands. After the war, he married Alma Barrett from Paris, Tennessee. They had one daughter, Barbara Jean Boswell, and three grandchildren: Emily, Chad and Brit. Robert attended Murfreesboro Teachers College for two years. He taught in the Wayne County school system and later worked for TVA from which he retired. He is a member of the American Legion. He has made Millington his home for many years. Robert, son of Thomas Carroll and Mollie Chappell Bromley, was born in March 1903 in Flatwoods, Tennessee. His siblings are Mattie Bromley Brewer, Lucille and Thomas Roy Bromley. John died 1 April 1996 in Millington, Tennessee, and was buried in Walker Cemetery in Paris, Tennessee. He was a Methodist.

BROMLEY, THOMAS ROY, son of Thomas Carroll Bromley and Mollie Chappell Bromley, was born October 17,

1910. In 1938, 1 married Mary Louise Shelton. I volunteered for The U. S. Navy on December 22, 1942. While I was in service, Louise worked at Vultee; a factory in Nashville, Tn., that manufactured war related aircraft.

I boarded a troop train at Union Station in Nashville, Tn., along with several other recruits. Our destination was unknown. After several hours on this train we arrived at Camp Perry in the Northern part of Virginia, on the James River. This river is about the size of our own Tennessee River in Clifton, Tn. When we arrived at Camp Perry, there was about 6 to 8 inches of snow on the ground. Our barracks were heated with two potbellied stoves; all we had for fuel was green pine wood that we cut with cross cut saws and axes; chain saws weren't in existence.

We were assigned to the Seventy- Third (73) "CB" Battalion. This is a branch of The U. S. Navy. There was 1500 men in my battalion. We all had phases of experience in construction. I went in as a carpenter with a second class rating; two years later I was promoted to carpenter mate first-class, receiving $95 a month.

We then were divided into companies of about 250, while we were in boot training. We marched, target-practiced, and had

guard duty. Our weapon was a M1 Carbine rifle, a short gun used for jungle warfare. This training lasted for about 2 months.

Soon we all got sick with colds. After this training, we packed up again and pulled out the next day. After 6 days on a troop train, we landed in Port Huenmea, California. We were granted a furlough. Most of us were from the middle and eastern United States. Soon we packed up and pulled out again; destination unknown. We were crammed in a troop ship with our baggage. We had to sleep on the ship's deck at night because of the extreme heat. Everyone got sea sick; no one wanted any food. Our bathing was done in salt water. We spent 19 days and nights on "The President Polk", our ship, sailing in the South Pacific before landing on New Caledonia, a friendly island in the South Pacific, owned by the British. On new Caledonia we built airports, set up radar towers, and built quosent huts, that were used for storage and headquarters for our officers.

Our next move led us to Guadacanal. After the marines had a battle with the Japs, we had to clean up the airport, and bury the dead Japs in trenches dug with bulldozers. The climate was about 100 degrees, and this was a very unpleasant job. We finally set up camp, with 6 men to each tent. We only wore helmets, shoes, and shorts because of the heat.

Soon we all came down with malaria, because of all the flies and mosquitoes. We all had to take atrabine tablets for the malaria. We lived in fox holes at night with coconut logs for a roof. Our church services were held by our Catholic Chaplain. The Catholics had mass at 6 A.M. on Sunday morning, and the Protestants had church at 10 A.M. on Sunday morning. Several of the men got baptized in the South Pacific.

Our next move took us to Pellilew Island. It is a small island about 5 miles long and 2 miles wide. Again we had to clean up and bury the dead Japs- Soon we set up camp again, repaired the airport, and planes were bombing the Japs on New Guinea Island. Here we all got dysentery from all the flies, mosquitoes, and filth.

The Japanese planes that we shot down had pictures of the rising sun under their wings. Everyone was very depressed; several committed suicide. All our mail was censored, in case it got into Japanese hands, to keep them from knowing our location. We would all pray together, especially when the bombs fell around us.

While on Pellilew Island word came that we were going state side. Our battalion was down sized to 500 men. Several died, took their own life, or died from other

causes. We landed on Treasure Island, California, and our 30 day furlough was granted in August of 1945.

After we had reached home, the atomic bomb was dropped on Hiroshima, Japan. This was the end of World War II. I had scored enough points for an honorable discharge while I was home. My discharge took place at Millington, Tn., on Sept., 15, 1945. By faith, hope, prayer, and the Grace of God, I lived through this terrible battle, and remember it well enough to tell the people who read this history about World War II.

BROMLEY, W.D., Serial Number 34 494 867, was inducted in November 1942 at Fort Oglethorpe, Georgia. He was a Private First Class in the 783 M P Battalion of the United States Army. He was born 12 July 1922. His address was Cypress Inn, Tennessee. His civilian occupation before the war was farmhand. He saw 18 months of foreign service. His decorations: Lapel Button, Bronze Star, Good Conduct Ribbon, World War II Victory Medal and a Purple Heart. His education consisted of eight years grammar school and four years in Collinwood High School. He was discharged 25 October 1945 from a Hospital in Daytona Beach, Florida.

His parents are Dallas P. Bromley (1893-1957, buried in Cedar Grove Cemetery, and Lallie Phillips Bromley (1896-). He does not have siblings. His children are: Mary Coral, Shiela, Gregory and Stanley. W. D. retired from Reynolds Company in Alabama after 20 years service.

BROWN, BENTON, Serial Number 44 044 582, was inducted into the United States Army, 19 December 1944 at Fort Oglethorpe, Georgia. His description was hazel eyes, brown hair, 5'6" height, weight 129 lbs and single. His education consisted of four years of grammar school. He was born 11 March 1922 in Lutts, Tennessee. His civilian occupation was farmhand. His military occupational specialty was light truck driver. His military qualification was MM W/Rifle. He attained the rank of Technician, Grade 5 with Company C, 43 Engineers. He was in the battle and/or campaign of Luzon. He received the following decorations and citations: Asiatic Pacific Theater Ribbon, with one Bronze Battle Star, Philippine Liberation Ribbon with one Bronze Battle Star, World War II Victory Medal, Good Conduct Medal, Army of Occupation Medal Japan, Lapel Button and two Overseas Service Bars. He departed the United States 6 July 1945 and returned 30 September 1946. He was discharged 19 November 1946 at Fort Sheridan, Illinois. His permanent mailing address was Route 2, Lutts, Tennessee.

BROWN, CLICE, Serial Number 34 375 249, was a Private, First Class in Company G, 378th Infantry, United States Army. His description was blue eyes, brown hair, 5'8" height, weight 144 lbs, married with 1 dependent. He was born 15 December 1909 in Collinwood, Tennessee. His education consisted of six years in grammar school. His civilian occupation was laborer. His military occupational specialty was Rifleman. Military qualifications given were: Marksmanship Badges and Combat Infantry Badge. He participated in the following battles and campaigns: Rhineland, Central Europe and Northern France. Decorations include: European-African Middle Eastern Theater Operation Medal, Good Conduct Medal and Distinguished Unit Badge. He left the United States on 6 August 1944 for European-African Middle Eastern Theater Operation and returned 29 June 1945. His permanent mailing address was Collinwood, Tennessee. PFC Brown was discharged 6 October 1945 in Camp, Shelby, Mississippi.

BROWN, ERNEST R., was a member of the class 44-J who received their Silver Wings. He graduated as a military pilot from the Army Air Force Training Command Installation at Blackland Army Air Force Field in Waco, Texas. *Wayne County News.*

BROWN, ERVIE RICHARD, "Dick" is the son of Henry and Dora Thompson Brown. He was a United States Army World War II Veteran, a native of Wayne County and a retired mill worker. He died 22 December 1994 at the age of 79 years in the Pulaski Health Care Center. His survivors: two sons, Raleigh and Ricky Brown of Waynesboro, one daughter, Ann Brown of Collinwood, one stepson, Donald Long of Collinwood, one brother, Bill Brown, and two sisters, Gertrude Daniel and Grace Bolin.

Private First Class Brown was the son of Dora T. Brown of Route 1, Cypress Inn, Tennessee. He served in the European Theater area of World War II and was wounded in action.

BROWN, GEORGE R., Serial Number 44 040 794, was a PFC in Company F, 262nd Infantry of the United States Army. He was born 1 June 1920 in Clifton, Tennessee. His description: gray eyes, brown hair, 5'8" height, weight 162 lbs, married with five dependents. His address at time of entry into service was Box 354, Clifton, Tennessee. His education consisted of eight years of grammar school. His civilian occupation was farmer. His military occupation was light truck driver and his military

qualification was Combat Infantryman Badge. He was in battles and campaigns in Northern France and Rhineland, but was not wounded. He received the following decorations and citations: European-African Middle Eastern Theater Ribbon with two Bronze Stars, Good Conduct Medal and World War II Victory Medal. He departed the United States 24 January 1945 for European Theater Operation and returned 7 March 1946. He was discharged 13 March 1946 in Camp Atterbury, Indiana. His permanent mailing address was Route 1, Waynesboro, Wayne County, Tennessee.

BROWN, JAMES E., son of Mrs. Myrtle Brown of R#3, Lutts, TN was wounded in action in the Pacific Theatre Operation.

BROWN, SAMUEL B., was born, September 26, 1925, near Austins Landing, TN. He lived at Paducah, KY and was working as a commercial fisherman, at the time he was inducted into the U. S. Army, December 16, 1943, at Ft. Benjamin Harrison, In. He served as a duty soldier with Co. B. 292nd Engineer Combat Batt. After his training in the states ended he was sent to Europe and landed at Southampton, England, November 2, 1944. Very soon he was in the middle of the action and participated in battles at Thineland and all through Central Europe. He received the following citations; EAME Theater Medal, Good Conduct Medal, Rhineland and Central Europe Campaigns with Silver Stars. After the war, Sam lived at Clifton.

BROWN, TAYLOR, Serial Number 34 193 023, was a Technician Fourth Grade in Company A, 327 Glider Infantry, 101st Airborne Division of the United States Army. His description was: brown eyes, brown hair, height 5' 6", weight 136 lbs, single with no dependents. He had four years of grammar school education. His civilian occupation was farmhand. His military occupational specialty was Cook. His military qualifications were Infantry Marksmanship Badges and Combat Infantry Badge. He was in battles in Normandy, Northern France, Ardennes, Rhineland and Central Europe, but he did not receive any wounds in action. His decorations and citations include: American Theater Ribbon, European African Middle Eastern Theater Ribbon with five Bronze Stars, Good Conduct Medal, Distinguished Unit Badge and World War II Victory Medal. He left the United States 5 September 1943 for European-African Middle Eastern Theater and returned 23 November 1945. He attended Cook and Bakers School in Camp Bogart, Louisiana. He was honorably discharged

29 November 1945 in Fort Knox, Kentucky. His permanent mailing address was Route 2, Lutts, Tennessee.

Taylor was born 8 September 1918 in Lutts, Tennessee, died in September 1991, and is buried in Paulding, Ohio. His wife, June, of Paulding, and four daughters survive.

BROWN, WALTER I., Serial Number 34 494 883, was a PFC in Headquarters Detachment Complement, Fort Logan, Colorado, in the United States Army. He was inducted into active service 29 November 1942 at Fort Oglethorpe, Georgia. His description was brown eyes, brown hair, 5'11" height, weight 150 lbs, married with one dependent. His education consisted of eight years of grammar school. His civilian occupation was farmer. His military occupational specialty was Instrument Observer. His military qualifications: M I Rifle. He was not in any battles but received the following decorations: American Service Medal, World War II Victory Medal, Lapel Button and Good Conduct Medal. Walter was discharged 26 January 1946 at Fort Logan Colorado. His permanent address for mailing was Route 5, Waynesboro, Tennessee.

Walter, son of Frank G. (1884-1969) and Hettie Stockard Brown (1893-), was born 1 March 1921 in Waynesboro, Tennessee. His siblings were Jim Ed, Edith and others.

BRYANT, BARNEY, He entered service 11 April 1944 and was discharged 14 May 1946 as a Tec/4 Sergeant in Bryant Field Artillery. He was a cook with the 624th Headquarters Observation Battalion. He served in the Philippines. Among the decorations he received were the Good Conduct Medal, Sharp Shooters Medal and one Battle Star.

Barney, son of Cypert and Annie Horton Bryant, was born 31 October 1924. His siblings are Joe and Billy Bryant. Barney married Marie Daniel, and they have three children: Barney Keith, Deborah Ann Reaves and Rose Mary Harkey. He worked for Hassell and Hughes and farmed.

BRYANT, JOE WILLIAM, Draft number 64, Serial Number 34 022 576, volunteered for the United States Army. Doris McDonald and Tommy Wilson went the same day Joe did. Joe, son of Cypert Joseph and Annie Horton Bryant, was born 23 April 1919 in the Water Fall community of Wayne County.

Joe tells his story: "I volunteered for the United States Army on 25 February 1941, and went to Fort Oglethorpe, Georgia, From here I was sent to Camp Stewart,

Georgia for 17 weeks basic training in the 70th Antiaircraft Division. In July 1941, I was sent to Brooklyn Army Base. It was here that we were attached to the 1st Division. We boarded an army ship and became part of a convoy of maneuvers off the coast of North Carolina. We had three months of this kind of training (ship to shore maneuvers). After this, we were sent back to the army base in New York harbor and then to Fort Devens, Massachusetts.

In November 1941, we were transferred back to the 70th Antiaircraft Division. At this time, I had been in service for 11 months and was given a holiday leave on 7 December 1941. All leaves were canceled the next day, December 8, when War was declared on Japan. The 70th Antiaircraft received an order to report to New York and be prepared for overseas duty in the Asiatic Pacific Theater. We were loaded aboard the U. S. S. Constong - 6,000 troops. We sailed 23 January 1942 in a convoy with transports and escorts carrying 80,000 men. Landing 12 March 1942 in Melbourne, Australia, we were on and off this ship for about two weeks. After this, we were sent to a small town 80 miles away called Bendigo. We spent two weeks in private homes and, of course, we became close to them. I left here, however, for Melbourne boarded a ship for the French Island, New Caledonia. Almost all of the 80,000 troops landed there. The Maricale Division under General Douglas MacArthur was formed at this time. In April 1942 we went on to Guadalcanal for active service.

The next move was to Bougensville Island, which was under Japanese control. The 3rd Marine Division went into this place and formed a horseshoe perimeter airstrip. We came right in behind the Marines and protected this airstrip they had established. We stayed there for a year, guarding this airstrip for B-24's. At the end of 1943, we gathered on a Guadalcanal point and were sent to New Guinea. Then in December 1944, we were placed on

board a Navy Ship-destination Oakland, California. We bathed and cleaned up and were sent to Fort McPherson, Georgia, to receive a 21-day delay and a leave of 20 days home.

We reported back to Miami Beach, Florida, and stayed at the Rawlings Hotel for two weeks. Then we were sent to El Paso, Texas, on to Fort Bliss. In February 1945, we were assigned to training recruits for overseas duty. From Fort Bliss, I went to Camp Beale, California, in June 1945. I was discharged July 6, 1945 at Camp Stewart, GA.

I received the Good Conduct Medal, American Defense Service Medal and Asiatic Pacific Campaign Medal. I spent over three years overseas. My occupational specialty was machine gun NCO.

I enjoyed and was quite impressed with a humble, polite man with a large frame, called "Rocky," who turned out to be Winfred Rockefeller. I did not know who he was at first. He was in my 1st Army Division as a 1st Lieutenant. He went back to Arkansas and became the state's governor.

I also saw Bryce Morgan, Bert Chambers Jr., Doris McDonald and Tommy Wilson from back home. I went aboard Bert's Navy ship in New Caledonia Bay. (Bert retired from Postal Service in Northern California.)

I came out of service, enrolled in a Barber College in San Diego, California, and worked 31 years at Camp Pendleton as a barber. I also went into real estate before retiring. I was employed in Fall Brook, California.

I married Nadine Thompson from Collinwood and we had one daughter, Jodean Bryant Downing. We have one grandson, Noah Bryant Downing. I have two brothers, Barney and Billy Bryant. Our present home is in Waynesboro.

BRYANT, HERSCHEL, Serial Number 640 30 10, was born 7 April 1913 in Waynesboro, Tennessee. He entered into active service 3 April 1942. He was a Carpenter's Mate, First Class in the United States Navy. The Service Vessels and Stations served on were: NRS Nashville, Tennessee; Const Batt's USNCTC Williamsburg, Virginia; and 54th Naval Construction Battalion. He was discharged 5 January 1946 from the United States Naval Personnel Separation Center in Memphis, Tennessee.

BRYANT, RAYMOND M., Serial Number 34 366 709, was born in Wayne County. He was inducted 26 August 1942 at Fort Oglethorpe, Georgia. His description: blue eyes, brown hair, ruddy complexion, 5'9" tall, single with no dependents and age 32 1/2 years old when he enlisted.

His civilian occupation was elementary teacher. His army specialty was telephone operator. He was a Technician Fifth Grade with the 223rd Army Air Force Base Unit, United States Army. He received a Good Conduct Medal. He was honorably discharged 29 November 1944 at Fort McPherson, Georgia.

BRYSON, J.B., son of Waymon and Noah Bryson, was born May 13,1924, in Wayne County and grew up in the

Shawnettee Community. He was working as a farm hand at the time he received his notice to appear at the selective service office at Waynesboro.

J.B. was inducted into the U.S. Army February 27, 1943, at Ft. Oglethorpe, GA and assigned to Battery D, 483rd AAA AW Bn. He was a light truck driver and classified as a rifle marksman and promoted to a T/5. On June 16, 1944 his unit left for the Asiatic-Pacific Theater. J.B. participated in the campaign of Eastern Mandates and ground combat at Iwo Jima. He received the following citations: World War 11 Victory Ribbon, Good Conduct Medal, American Theater Ribbon, Asiatic-Pacific Theater Ribbon with two Bronze Service Stars. December 19, 1945, they landed back in the states, then J.B. was discharged December 31, 1945, at Camp Chaffee, AR.

He returned home to Shawnettee and married Irma Shepard on May 4,1946. They farmed a short time, then moved to Michigan and J.B. worked with Great Lakes Steel for the next thirty-five years. After retiring they moved back to Wayne County in 1983 and settled on Martin Street in Collinwood, TN.

J.B. became ill in April of 1987, then died of cancer four months later on August 27, 1987. He is buried at McGlamery Cemetery near Collinwood. They have six children; James Barnet (deceased), Brenda (Tittle), Carol Bryson, Karen (Swiney), Ricky Joe (deceased), Jackie (Powell) and

Patrick. J.B.'s siblings are: Walsie (Pulley), Roxie (Moore), Imogene (Daniel), Robbie (Daniel) and Walter Bryson.

J.B. was a member of the Church of Christ, Wyandotte Masonic Lodge and Great Lake Steel Union.

BULLION, EUNICE OVAN "BUSTER", Serial Number 34 882 202, was in 35th Infantry. He entered Army 24

August 1943 and was discharged 9 October 1945. He served 16 months as S/Sergeant in Europe with 1st, 3rd, 7th, 9th and 15th Army. He was in five major battles and received a Bronze Star Medal. The total length of time in service was two years and four months. He served in the Honor Guard for President Truman when he went to Belgium after the war ended.

"Buster," son of Walter Autumn and Martha Merritt (Brown) Bullion, was born 13 August 1920 in Lewis County, Tennessee. His siblings are Eugene Thomas "Elvin," Esmond Cletus "Chip," and Lois Mildred Bullion Fain. He graduated from Peabody and is retired from DuPont in Old Hickory. He was married 15 June 1940 in Linden to Monetta Rasbury, daughter of Van and Florence (Brown) Rasbury. They have made their home in Wayne County, Tennessee, Alabama, North Carolina and Madison, Tennessee. They have two children: Donald Ray and Bonita Bullion. They also have two granddaughters, Denicia and Christie Bullion, and two great-grandsons.

Source: Monetta Rasbury Bullion.

BUMPUS, HENRY C., Private Henry C. Bumpus of Clifton, Tennessee, was born on August 31, 1924. He was the son of Tom and Evana Bumpus. Henry enlisted in Hardin County, Tennessee, for military services and entered on May 25, 1943. He was sent to the European Theater of war in battles in Normanly, France, Ardennes, Rhineland and Central Europe. He was awarded the following medals: Good Con-

duct, World War II Victory, European, African and Middle Eastern Theater Ribbon and one Silver Star. He was discharged on December 18, 1945.

He is at present time residing in Sandusky, Ohio. His siblings are T. J. Bumpus, Raymond Bumpus, Claude Bumpus, Peggy Bumpus and W. H. Bumpus.

BUNCH, CARNIE M., Serial Number 44 071 187, inducted at Fort Oglethorpe, Georgia, into the United States Army where he served three months before he was discharged. His occupation before the war was farmer. Occupation after services was working for the Wayne County Road System and working in the timber business.

Carnie, son of John William "Billy" and Nancy Katherine (Inman) Bunch, was born in 1918 on Cedar Creek in Perry County, Tennessee. He died in 1970 and was buried in Praters Chapel Cemetery. He married Delia Turnbow and their children are Dorothy, Carolyn and Debra Bunch. His brothers are Robert Lee, Barney, Hollie Earl and Roland Bunch. His sisters are Ida Mae McWilliams, Alma Lou Giles and Mildred Berry.

BUNCH, DAN, Serial Number 34 738 923. Private Dan Bunch was born on December 6, 1922, in Clifton, Tennessee. He died on January 22, 1983, and is buried in the Worley Cemetery on Beech Creek in Wayne County, Tennessee. He served in the United States Army during World War II with active duty starting on July 16, 1943. He was attached to Reception Center in Camp Shelby, Mississippi. His description was brown eyes, brown hair, ruddy complexion, 5'7 " tall, single with no dependents, age 20 7/12 years of age and a farmer. Under remarks: "Soldier was transferred to English Reserve Corps on July 2, 1943, and was recalled for active duty on July 16, 1943. " Private Bunch was honorably discharged on October 22, 1943, at Camp Shelby, Mississippi.

He was the son of John William (Billy) Bunch and Nancy Katherine Inman Bunch. Dan married Clara Marie Turnbo on September 25, 1945. Their children are Donald Eugene, Patsy Nell and Robert Daniel. Dan was a Mormon by faith. He was always smiling and a good husband and father. He lived most of his young life in Perry County, Tennessee on Short Creek. Adult life was spent in the Beech Creek area of Wayne County, Tennessee. He was a Tennessee State employee for many years and a state retiree.

His siblings are Carnie Monroe, Robert, Ida Mae, Alma Lou, Barney, Hollie Earl, Mildred and Roland.

BUNCH, LOUIS HUBERT, Serial Number 34 375 241. Hubert was inducted 3 October 1942 and entered active service

17 October 1942 in Waynesboro, Tennessee. His description was blue eyes, brown hair, 6' tall, weight 146 lbs, two dependents. His education was eight years of grammar school. His occupation before service was sales clerk. His military occupation specialty was Ammunition Bearer (motor) and 1607 Carbine Expert. His military qualification was a Combat Infantry Badge. Battles and campaigns listed were Rome-Arno, North Apennines and Po Valley. Decorations and citations were the European-African Middle Eastern Theater Ribbon with three Bronze Stars, Good Conduct Ribbon, plus other medals. He left the United States 1 January 1944 for European Theater Operation, then was transferred to NATO 24 March 1944 and returned to the United States 14 August 1945. PFC Bunch was with Headquarters Company, 2nd Battalion, 337 Infantry, United States Army when he was discharged 8 October 1945 at Camp Atterburg, Indiana. His permanent mailing address was Route 6, Waynesboro, Tennessee.

Hubert, son of Newton David Bunch (1883-1962) and Lou T. (Pulley) Bunch (1889-1962), both buried in Whitehead Cemetery in Topsy, was born 15 September 1915 in Clifton, Tennessee. His siblings are Marvin, Vaughan (deceased 1932), Walter (deceased), Bernecye Venzel "Niecie" Dugger (deceased), Lorene Kelly and Malcolm Dugger. Hubert married Katherine Boyd and they have two children: Ronald Wayne "Ronnie" and Donald DeWayne "Donnie" Bunch. After returning home from the service, he owned and operated a grocery store in the Waynesboro area. He died 21 February 1993 and was buried in Memorial Gardens in Waynesboro with military rites.

BUNCH, WALTER E., Serial Number 34 013 705. Walter was a S/Sergeant

in Company K, 117th Infantry when he was discharged 28 April 1943 in Welch Convalescent Hospital in Daytona Beach, Florida. His permanent mailing address was Route 6, Waynesboro, Tennessee. The description given was blue eyes, light brown hair, height 5'11" weight 155 lbs, married with two dependents. His civilian occupation was sales clerk in a grocery store. He was inducted 22 January 1941 and entered active service 22 January 1941 at Fort Oglethorpe, Georgia. His military occupation was heavy truck driver. He was in the battle of Normandy.

Walter, son of Newton David and Lou T. (Pulley) Bunch, was born 4 June 1918 in Wayne County. He died 27 September 1991 in Waynesboro and was buried in Memorial Gardens in Waynesboro. He was a member of Mt. Hope Methodist Church and the Disabled Veterans. He was married to Corrine Bunch of Waynesboro. They had two daughters, Phyllis Newton of Lawrenceburg and Martha Butler of Waynesboro, and one son, Dwight Gene Bunch, of Hohenwald. He also has five grandchildren and one great-grandchild. His siblings are Marvin, Vaughan (deceased 1932), Hubert (deceased), Bernecye Venzel "Necye" Dugger (deceased), Lorene Kelly and Malcolm Dugger.

BUNDRANT, ROY F., Serial Number 14 148 950. Roy was a T/Sergeant in the 576th Ordnance (MM) Company, Fort Ord, California, of the United States Army.

Roy, son of James Frank and Ora (Steele) Bundrant, was born 26 July 1913 in Clifton, Tennessee. He graduated from Frank Hughes High School in 1932 and then attended Union University in Jackson, Tennessee. He taught in the Wayne County School System, was employed by Jack Yeiser Chevrolet Company as an automobile salesman, and also was part owner of an automobile tire business.

He was married to Ethel Dixon on 24 November 1940. They have one son, James Frank Bundrant, and three grandchildren:

James Marvin, Joy Beth and Jeremy Roy Bundrant. Roy also has one sister, Pearl Bundrant Stanfill.

On December 7, 1941, the Japanese bombed Pearl Harbor and World War II was declared. When it became evident that he was going to be drafted, he enlisted in the United States Army on 3 September 1942 in Nashville, Tennessee, with the rank of Sergeant.

He departed Waynesboro in December 1942 for California, where he received his basic training with Company D 21st Ordnance Training Center, Camp Santa Anita in Arcadia, California. He served as Sergeant from September 3, 1942 to May 4, 1943; S/Sergeant from May 5, 1943 to June 3, 1943; and T/Sergeant from June 3, 1943 to December 3, 1943 when he was given an Honorable Discharge at the Oakland Area Station Hospital in Oakland, California.

He returned to Waynesboro where he became outstanding in the automobile business holding partnership in Bundrant-Whitehead Motor Company.

He was elected Wayne County Commissioner of Highways and Accounts in 1950 and served four two-year terms. In addition, he gained wide recognition as a builder and contractor. His wife and son accompanied him to the state capitol to cast his ballot as one of Tennessee's electors when Dwight D. Eisenhower was elected president of the United States.

He was a member of the Waynesboro Methodist Church, a member of Clifton Masonic Order No. 173, and a member of the Waynesboro Chamber of Commerce.

At the time of his death, February 12, 1964, he was holding partnership in Bundrant- Hassell Motor Company.

BURNS, DURELL, Private, son of Mr. and Mrs. Clyde Burns of Collinwood, received a letter dated December 1945 of commendation from his commanding officer which read:

"To Private Marvin D. Burns, 44 069 665, 21st. RCT Military Police Platoon."

"Your action on 12 December 1945 when you apprehended 10 Japanese carrying bundles containing weapons while you were a passenger enroute to Yonago is highly commended. While it turned out that these weapons were being transported for the purpose of turning them in to the proper authorities, nevertheless you displayed, while off duty, a sense of keen observation and willingness to assume responsibility in a situation which might have been quite dangerous to the Allied Occupation Forces. I am very happy to find that members of my command are so alert and so prompt in assuming responsibility in the face of unusual circumstances. "

Signed *Hugh Cort,* Brigadier General, U. S. Army.

BURNS, JOHN HERSCHEL, son of Erby and Madgie (Martin) Burns, he was born 12 December 1915 in Lutts, Tennessee, died 29 October 1974, and was buried in Lee Memorial Gardens in Lehigh Acres, Florida. He has one sister, Mrs. Eva Smith Luttrell of Florence, Alabama, and one brother, Bobby E. Burns of Waynesboro. His wife is Veda Pebble Hudson of Harrison, Arkansas. His children are John Michael Burns, who married Linda Rolls, and Nancy Catherine Burns, who married Jim Hoarz, His grandchildren are Heather and Danielle Burns and Lona Jean and Madeline Hoarz.

Herschel (Little Erby) enlisted in the United States Navy on 14 October 1939 and served his country and his fellowmen until 9 August 1961. He was at Pearl Harbor, on duty at Hickman Field when Pearl Harbor was bombed. He was injured by flying glass and was hospitalized for three weeks. He recovered and was assigned to the *Lexington* where he was Chief Maintenance Supervisor of the aircraft on board the carrier. Herschel was in the battles of Midway, Iwo Jima and Guam and was in Tokyo Bay when the Japanese surrendered.

After the war, he was sent to Alaska aboard the Randolph as chief of aircraft maintenance. He served there for two years. Next, he was transferred to the Naval Air Station in Anacostia, D. C. where he stayed for 12 years and served as payroll master.

Chief Burns was then sent to Guam aboard the Bon Homme Richard as Line Supervisor of Aircraft. He received the following medals: Asiatic Pacific, American Area, Philippine Liberation, American Defense, World War II Victory and Good Conduct.

BURNS, RALPH, was born on July 6, 1922, in Clifton, Tennessee. He was working as a farmhand at the time he was inducted into the United States Army on October 24, 1942, at Ft. Oglethorpe, Georgia. Ralph served with Company A, 391st Infantry until his discharge on December 21, 1945, at Welch Convalescent Hospital in Daytona Beech, Florida. He participated in battles in the Asiatic-Pacific Theater and received the following citations: Asiatic-Pacific Service Medal, American Service Medal and World War II Victory Ribbon.

BURNS, T.J., was a disabled United States Army Veteran of World War II and a son of Archie and Ollie (Adkisson) Burns. He was born in 1921 in Wayne County. He worked as an assistant foreman for the Brown Shoe Company in Savannah, Tennessee. He was a member of the Savannah Foursquare Church. He died 3 July 1993 at his home in Savannah and was buried in the Memory Gardens of Hardin County.

He married Peggy Burns. His children are Janice Richardson, Peggy Gray and Sandra Butler. His stepchildren are Donnie Rainey and Jeanie Majors. His sisters are Mae Lowe, Myrtle Baker, Gladys Baker and Willodean Burns. His brothers are Robert, Ralph, Billy Gene and John Burns.
Source: Obit in Wayne County News, 14 July 1993.

BUTLER, ARNETT, Private First Class, son of Mr. and Mrs. Joe Butler, Route 1, Collinwood, entered the service 27 July 1944. He received his military training at Fort McClellan, Alabama. He was sent to Fort Meade, Maryland, and was assigned overseas service 20 January 1945. He served with the 3rd Army in Germany. *Wayne County News.*

BUTLER, BILL F., Serial Number 44 121 856. Bill Butler was a Private in Company D 1473 Scu Stu Detachment, Army of the United States, and was given an honorable discharge at 1473 D Scu Regional Hospital at Camp Shelby, Mississippi, on 13 September 1945. His permanent mailing address was Route 2, Iron City, Tennessee. He was born 27 April 1927 in Collinwood, Tennessee. His description: blue eyes, brown hair, 5'9" height, weight 150 lbs,, married with one dependent. His civilian occupation was farmer. He was inducted into service 20 June 1945 at Fort Oglethorpe, Georgia.

BUTLER, BUFORD SCOTT, Private First Class Butler served in Company D, 125th Infantry Division, United States Army. He received his basic training in California. He received a knee injury in San Francisco, resulting in limited service for him. He remembers while being as-

signed to M. P. duty in California, 40 liberated P. O. W. 's from Japan were flown to Fort Baker. These men were placed in command cars to parade from Fort Baker, across the Golden Gate Bridge into San Francisco. Buford drove the number 20 command car that carried three of the P. O. W.'s. He remembers an estimated crowd of 50,000 lining the parade route. Buford received the Good Conduct Medal and Expert Rifleman Medal. He was taught hand to hand Judo training. He was in the CC Camp when war was declared.

Buford, son of Paulie and Mandie Gallaher Butler, married Ella Marie Cummings, and they live in South Wayne County. Their children are Sharon and Hazel Marie. His sisters are Verna, Nola Caperton, Lois McGee and Octavia Brice. His brothers are Edward Earl, Olive and Charles Butler.

BUTLER, CHARLES, Sergeant, son of Mrs. Annie B. Thompson, has been in the service for the past three years. He is a member of a Military Police Unit and has been on duty overseas for 15 months. He was stationed in Calcutta, India. Before entering the service of the United States Armed Forces, he was a member of the CCC.
Source: Wayne County News clippings kept by Clyde Bevis.

BUTLER, EDWARD EARL, served in the United States Navy at Pearl Harbor and Midway Island. His parents are Paulie and Mandie Gallaher Butler. After the war was over, he worked at Genesco Shoe Company in Waynesboro for 26 years and Murray Ohio Company in Lawrenceburg for 11 years. He was born in 1925. He married Lina Daniel and they have three children: Kenneth, Mitchell Ray and Katherine. His siblings are: Buford S., Olive and Charles Butler, Verna, Nola Butler Carpenter, Lois Butler McGee, and Octavia Butler Brice.

BUTLER, ELLIS ARDEAN, son of Elvin and Ella (Franklin) Butler, was born November 14,1925 near Collinwood, TN. He grew up in the Shawantee Community and attended Wayne County High School. September 22, 1943, Ellis entered the U. S. Navy and served at NTS, San Diego, CA.; REC Station PSNY, Bremerton, Washington; USS Makin Island and SLOU #61. He was awarded the Coxswain Victory Medal; American Area and Asiatic Pacific Ribbon; one Bronze Star and three Engagement Stars. He was discharged, April 12. 1946, at the U.S. Naval Separation Center at Memphis, TN.

Ellis and Frances Lee were married in September 1946 and moved to Michigan,

where she was employed. They were employed there until 196 1, when they returned to Waynesboro. Very soon Ellis began working in the automobile parts business, which lasted for more than 35 years. They are very active members at First United Methodist Church. They have two children, Karen of Columbia, TN and Jamie of Waynesboro; they also have four grandchildren.

BUTLER, GERALD E., of Laton, California, 38, entered the service in 1942 and was given an Honorable Discharge August 1943. He is the son of Mrs. Babe Gallien by a former marriage.
Source: Wayne County News 16 February 1942, p. 1.

Gerald had five half-brothers: Charles and James M., who live in Athens, Alabama, Joe R., Archie H. and John R. Gallien. He also has a half-sister, Clara Gallien Stricklin of Iron City.

BUTLER, JESSE W., Serial Number 6 972 371, Jesse W. Butler entered active service 9 October 1939 at Fort McClellan, Alabama. His description was given as brown eyes, dark hair, 5' 5 1/4" height, weight 128 lbs, single without any dependents. His military occupation was driving a heavy truck. His military qualification was Sharpshooter Rifle. His decorations were Central Pacific Medal, American Defense Service Ribbon with one Bronze Star, Asiatic Pacific Theater Ribbon with one Bronze Star and Good Conduct Medal. He was a Corporal in 1079th Army Air Force Base Unit when he was discharged at Fort McPherson, Georgia.

Jesse W. "Mutt" Butler was born 13 July 1916 in Wayne County. He died Thursday, October 8, 1993, at E. C. M. Hospital in Florence, Alabama, and was buried Saturday, October 10, 1993, in the Railroad Cemetery near Iron City. Mr. Butler was a United States Army Veteran of World War II. He was a retired foreman and a mem-

57

ber of the Masonic Lodge. His address was Route 1, Iron City, Tennessee.

His parents were the late Joe and Carrie Keeton Butler. He was married to Carmen Wilson. They had one son, Winston W. His siblings include: Alvin Butler of Iron City; Norman Butler and Jessie Kirkpatrick, both of Warren, Michigan; Nell Horton of Cleveland, Mississippi; Corene Olive of Killen, Alabama; Emmanola Berry and Lillian Whitten of Florence, Alabama; Alene Dickey of Iron City; and Earlene Walker of Waynesboro, Tennessee.

BUTLER, NORMAN M., Serial Number 44 120 492. Norman M. Butler was a Private First Class in the 12th Dep Sup Sq of the United States Army Air Force when he was discharged 18 December 1946 at Fort Sheridan, Illinois. His description: brown eyes, black hair, 5'6" height, weight 156 lbs, single with two dependents, born 22 January 1927 in Florence, Alabama. His education consisted of eight years of grammar school and one year of high school. His civilian occupation was truck loader. His military occupational specialty was guard patrol. His military qualification was MM W/Carbide. His decorations and citations are: Victory Medal, Asiatic Pacific Theater Ribbon, Lapel Button, one Overseas Bar, and Army of Occupation Medal Japan. He departed the United States 26 November 1945 for Pacific Theater Operation and returned 6 November 1946. His permanent mailing address was Route 3, Iron City, Tennessee.

BYLER, EDGAR DONALD, II, was born in Collinwood, Tennessee, on 19 September 1921, in an apartment over the old

Brown and Byler Drug Store building on the corner of 4th and Broadway. He was the son of Edgar and Sarah Dunn Byler.

Following graduation from Collinwood High School in 1938, he went to Houston,

58

Texas, and worked with Western Electric. On 18 December 1939, he enlisted in the United States Army Air Corps. He was first assigned to Brooks Field in San Antonio, Texas, for basic training and light duty with the 32nd Pursuit Squadron. In June 1940, he was stationed at Scott Field in Belleville, Illinois, for schooling, and then Chanute Field in Rantoul, Illinois, in August 1940 for further training.

In June 1941, he was shipped to Losey Field, Ponce, Puerto Rico and joined the 32nd Fighter Squadron (General Aircraft Maintenance). The unit was placed on active alert two weeks prior to Pearl Harbor. They were to serve as the first line of defense for the United States.

On 11 December 1941, the unit was sent to Arecibo for submarine surveillance and the training of fighter pilots. They remained here until March 1943 when the Squadron was transferred to Curacao, Netherland Antilles (West Indies). Here, the Squadron was again involved in submarine surveillance guarding the giant refinery on the island. In June 1943 they moved to Aruba, Netherlands Antilles.

In April 1944, the Squadron was transferred to France Field, Panama Canal Zone to guard the canal against attempts to destroy it. They were again involved with submarine surveillance and training of fighter pilots.

In July 1944, he was sent to Lincoln, Nebraska, for reassignment. Then in August 1944, he was sent to Hays Field, Hays Kansas, for assignment to an Electronics Depot. In March 1945, he was reassigned to Jackson Army Air Base in Jackson, Mississippi, where he was training navigators in a secret navigational school for the Air Corps.

In September 1945, he reported to Fort McPherson, Georgia, where he was honorably discharged with a length of service of five years and nine months. Within three days of his discharge, he returned home to Collinwood.

On 24 August 1951, he married Helen M. Gallien, the daughter of Alvin Clarence and Addie Mae Whitten Gallien. She was born 3 November 1933. They have one child, Edgar D. Byler III, born June 22, 1952.

BYRD, CHARLIE L., Serial Number 34 375 256. Charlie Byrd was inducted 3 October 1942 and entered active service 17 October 1942 at Fort Oglethorpe. His description: blue eyes, blonde hair, 5'11" height, weight 138 lbs, married with four dependents and a farmer. He was born 20 February 1914 in Ruppertown, Tennessee. His military occupational specialty was Rifleman. He was in battles in Northern France and Central Europe. He received

the Good Conduct Medal and European-African Middle Eastern Theater Medal. Private First Class Byrd was honorably discharged from Company K, 378th Infantry, United States Army on 26 September 1945 at Camp Shelby, Mississippi.

BYRD, HARVEL EARL, son of Wylie A. and Ollie (Spann) Byrd, was born October 23, 1922, in Lawrence County, TN

and grew up in the Highland Community in Wayne County near the Lawrence County line. He attended Wayne County Schools, then enrolled in the CCC program, which was formed in, 1933, for young men, to help conserve and developed natural resources, such as planting trees, fighting forest fires and building dams. After World War II started, this program was abolished in 1942.

February 20, 1943, Harvel joined the U. S. Army at Ft. Oglethorpe, Ga. and served as a light truck driver with Hdq. Btry. 483rd AAA AW Btn. After several months training, he was sent to the Pacific Theater, June 24, 1944, where he was involved in Asiatic-Pacific and Western Pacific Battles and participated in ground combat at Iwo Jima. He received the following citations; WWII Victory Ribbon, Good Conduct Ribbon, American and Asiatic-Pacific Theater Ribbons with two Bronze Stars. December 1, 1945, he arrived back in the states, then was discharged, December 31, 1945, at Camp Chaffee, AR.

After his discharge from the army, Harvel married Carolyn Lindsey, daughter of Mrs. Lula Lindsey, who held an office at the Wayne County Courthouse. He opened Wayne Grille Restaurant and formed a country music band, known as Byrd Brothers and the Drifting Tennesseans. This band opened up the Pulaski, TN radio station. They later went to Toledo, OH, where they worked at factories and did radio and night club shows. From there they went to Sedalia, MO, where they worked and played night clubs and did radio and TV shows at Sedalia and Jefferson City. They did a "Smoky the Bear" show for the Forest Conservation Service, played for the first "Porter Wagoner Day" at Springfield, MO and traveled a short time with Jim Reeves and other Opry stars. In 196 1, they came back to Wayne County for a short time, then Harvel was employed with Samsonite, Co. at Laverne, TN. They cut back on their performances as a band and became active in the church and the music department.

Harvel began to have heart problems that required by pass surgery. After several weeks at St. Thomas Hospital, he died, July 26, 1982, and is buried at Highland Cemetery. He and Carolyn have four children, Pat, Pam, Larry and Barry; his siblings are Naomi, Carmie, Ormand, Mack, Ira, Ramona and Dale.

BYRD, JAMES CALVIN, (AMM3/C) was born to George W. and Bertha Mae Spann Byrd on December 18, 1919, in Lawrenceburg, Tennessee. He has one brother, Marshall, and two sisters, Betty Bradley and Emmanola Coxwell. He lived his childhood years in the Ovilla community known by many as the County Line Community.

He met his wife to be while they were both working in Detroit, Michigan. Frances Lay and Calvin Byrd had never met while they were both living in Wayne County. They were married in Detroit on 5 April 1942. They have two sons, James Allen and Jeffery Steven Byrd, and five grandchildren.

Calvin was inducted into the United States Navy on 5 November 1942 and sent to Great Lakes, Illinois, for basic training. After completing his training there, he was stationed in Memphis, Tennessee, where he served until he was honorably discharged on 20 January 1946 at the rank of Aviation Machinist Mate Third Class.

After service Calvin returned to Wayne County where he worked at the Western Auto Store. He then opened a quarry operation until he and his father and brother opened Byrd Pic and Pac Grocery on the east side of the Public Square in Waynesboro. He later entered the small engine business and opened Wayne Chain Saw Company, which he had for several years, in addition to an excavation business. His last job was working for the State of Tennessee until his health forced him to retire.

James Calvin Byrd died 21 March 1988 in the Maury County Hospital and is buried in Memorial Garden in Waynesboro.

BYRD, HENRY L.E. "MARSHALL", Private, was born to George W. and Bertha Mae Spann Byrd on 31 July 1923 in Hudson, Ohio. He has one brother, Calvin (deceased), and two sisters, Betty Bradley and Emmanola Coxwell.

Marshall enlisted in the United States Army on 4 December 1945 and was sent to Fort McClellan, Alabama, to receive his basic training in the Infantry. After completing his training he was sent to New York City, where he boarded his ship for overseas. He arrived in Le Havre, France and then was sent to Germany where he was stationed with the 130th Station Hospital. He was honorably discharged from the service on 17 July 1946 in Fort George G. Meade, Maryland.

Marshall married Tessie Gobbell on 3 July 1943. They have three children: Milton, Shirley Butler and Shelia Glass, and four grandchildren and one great-grandchild. Marshall returned to Ohio after the war and worked there for a couple of years. Then, he returned to Wayne County in 1968 where he has been a businessman for most of his life. At one time, he and his brother Calvin operated a rolling grocery store in Wayne County. He is now retired, and he and Tessie reside in Waynesboro.

CAMFIELD, WALTER RAY, served his country in the United States Army during World War II. He was inducted November 13, 1943, at Fort Oglethorpe, Georgia. He served in Company B, 3rd Battalion Armored Replacement Training Center. He received a medical discharge on April 21, 1944. He was qualified as expert gunner.

He was born in Rockport, Kentucky, on August 25, 1914, the son of William Ora and Audrey Ferguson Camfield. Walter was employed at the button factory in Clifton, Tennessee, before his induction into the service.

He married Ruth Warren, daughter of Arthur and Nannie Powell Warren, on July 11, 1941. They had two sons: Ronnie Warren Camfield and Tommy Ray Camfield.

After returning home form the service,

he was employed at the shoe factory in Waynesboro. He went into his own business selling automotive parts later in life.

Walter loved to fish. He loved the river, boat racing, car racing and hunting. He was a member of the American Legion. His siblings are Connie, Mary Ethel and Hazel. Walter died on January 13, 1978, and is buried in Memory Garden in Waynesboro, Tennessee.

CAMP, JOHN E., Serial Number 34 501 229, was a Private in the 577th AAA AW Battalion in the United States Army. He was born in Sheffield, Alabama. At the time of his enlistment he was 20 years old and a farmer. His description: blue eyes, brown hair, ruddy complexion, 5' 8" in height and single. He was inducted 20 December 1942 at Fort Oglethorpe, Georgia. He was discharged 16 December 1943 at Station Hospital, Fort Bliss, Texas with poor health.

CANNON, JAMES C. "J.C.", Serial Number 34 936 425, served in Company I, 2nd Regiment, 3rd Army, 5th Division of the United States Army. He states, "We joined General George Patton with the 5th Division, immediately after the Battle of the Bulge and fought with General Patton all through Germany. I rode the front tank with him most of the time. He was a great General. His Tank Division was *400 TANKS STRONG*. He was really a great person."

J. C. is the son of Jim and Flora Clayton Cannon, (deceased.) His sisters are Madge Griggs, Anna Belle Baker, Mary Ruth Erdman, and Jessie Morris. His brothers are Carl, Jesse, and Les. His children are Jerry Richard, Debra Ann and Steve Cannon.

Source: J. C. Cannon.

CANNON, LESLIE, Serial Number 34 495 024, was a Technician, 5th Grade at the time of his discharge from Company Y, 335th Infantry, Army of the United

States. His permanent address was Route 2, Waynesboro, Tennessee. He was born 11 May 1923 in Waynesboro, Tennessee. At the time of his enlistment, his description was: grey eyes, black hair, 5'6" in height, weighted 190 lbs and single. His Civilian Occupation was Light Truck Driver. His Military Occupation was Truck Driver too. His Military Qualifications was Combat Infantry Badge. He was in the battles of Ardennes, Rhineland, and Central Europe. He received the following decorations: American Theater Ribbon, European-African Middle Eastern Theater Ribbon with 3 Bronze Stars, Good Conduct Medal, and World War II Victory Medal. He left the US 29 September 1944 for European Theater Operations and returned 22 January 1946. He was discharged 27 January 1946 in Camp Atterbury, Indiana.

CANTRELL, GEORGE R., Serial Number 34 375 245, was a Private. He was inducted 3 October 1942 at Fort Oglethorpe, Georgia. His Civilian Occupation was Carpenter. His Military Occupation was Finance Officer at Camp Swift, Texas. His Army Specialty was General Carpenter. He was discharge 16 October 1943 in Camp Swift Texas.

He married Hazel (Bell) Davis. He was born in 1908 in Pittsburgh Landing, Tennessee and was the son of Rev. and Mrs. B. J. Cantrell. His siblings were Florine, Bernice, Nancy, Oris and a twin sister Grace Cantrell.

CAPERTON, EUGENE, was born in Iron City, Tennessee. I am the oldest son of seventeen children born to John and Tinnie Violet Caperton. In 1937 when I was sixteen, I joined the C. C. C. (Civilian Conservation Corp). I was there for two years. I earned $8. 00 a month, which I sent home to my dad.

In 1941, I joined the Army and received my basic training at Fort Apalene, Texas. I was stationed in New Guinea. My first assignment was dishwasher for the officer's mess hall, then I drove a medical supply truck and an ambulance to pick up wounded personal.

When I returned home in January 1946, I married Gracie Hickerson. We have four children: Robert, Patsy, J. W and Tom Caperton. I went to Detroit in 1951 to find work. We settle there and still live there. - Eugene Caperton.

CARROLL, PETE, was born in 1925 near Clifton, Tennessee. He grew up in this area. He joined the C. C. Camps, and from there he went into the United States Navy. This carried him into active service during World War II.

When he came out of the service, he went to work in the Cotton Mill. He married Alice Walton. They have two daughters, Marylin and Jackie, and one son, Kelley.

They live in Findley, Tennessee.

CARROLL, REX, Serial Number 34 723 059, was a Staff Sergeant in the 93 D Bombardment Squadron of the Army of the United States. His Civilian job before the war was Radio Repairman. He was inducted 20 February 1943 and entered into active service 27 February 1943 at Fort Oglethorpe, Georgia. His Military Occupational Specialty was Radio Mechanic. His Military Qualifications was Marksman Carbine. He was in the battles and campaigns of Western Pacific Air Offensive, Japan. His decorations and citations: Asiatic Pacific Theater Ribbon and two Bronze Service Stars, World War II Victory Ribbon, Good Conduct Medal, American Theater Ribbon, and Lapel Button issued. He left the USA on 18 December 1944 for Asiatic Pacific Theater and returned 28 December 1945. He was discharged 6 January 1946 at Camp Chaffee, Arkansas, Then three years later he reenlisted in the Air Force.

Rex was born 19 January 1923 in Waynesboro, Tennessee, died 8 April 1968 in Murfreesboro, Tennessee and is buried in Stone River National Park in Murfreesboro. He went to Mt. Hope Elementary school and attended Wayne County High school for two and a half years. His parents are Leonard P. Carroll (9 April 1877-25 April 1947) and Inquis M. Carroll (9 October 1884-4 February 1978). Both are buried at Mt. Hope Church of Christ Cemetery in Wayne County. His siblings are Vernon of Mt. Juliet, Tennessee, Ruth Gobble (deceased), Etah DeVasure (deceased), and Jimmie Stanfield of Waynesboro. He married Dola Jean Jeter of Clifton. His children are Pamela and Gary who live in Murfreesboro. There is one grandchild. He worked for the Coco Cola Company in Murfreesboro.

CARTER, LEONARD, Serial Number 832 66 57, was born 28 January 1923 in Wayne County, Tennessee. He served in the United States Navy from 21 March 1943 until November 1945. He held the following ratings: AS, S2/E, S1/C, Cox, and BM 2/C. He was stationed on USNYS Bainbridge, Maryland and USS ARGONNE. His parents were Henry Clay and Susan Nutt Carter. His sisters are Nell Martin, Margie Watson, Melba Clay, Mattie Lue Purdue, and Joyce Flowers. His only brother, Harvell Clay Carter, was killed in action during the war. Leonard

was married 14 June 1947 to Wynelle Haddock. They have one daughter Victoria Ann "Vicky" Carter. His civilian occupation is car salesman and Postal Service Employee in Waynesboro.

CARVER, CORNELIUS ANDREW "NED", was a Tec 5 with Co B, 114 Engineer Combat Battalion. He was inducted

into the United States Army on 23 March 1944 at Ft. Sherdan, Illinois and discharged 20 February 1946 at Camp Grant, Illinois. He served in the Philippines, Luzon and the Occupation Army in Japan. His decorations included two Overseas Bars, Asiatic Pacific Campaign Medal with one Bronze Battle Star, Philippines Liberation Ribbon with one Bronze Star, Good Conduct Medal, and World War II Victory Medal. He was married 18 October 1941 to Grace Wright. They have two children: Carol Sue and Milton Edward "Mel: Carver. They also have eight grandchildren and four great grandchildren. Ned, son of John and Minnie Mae (Vaughan) Carver, was born 11 October 1913 in Dickson, Tennessee, died 28 May 1992 in Wayne County, Tennessee and is buried in McGlamery Cemetery. He attended school in Cypress Inn, Holts and Collinwood.

CARY, WILL FIELDEN, was born in 1917 and died 2 September 1993 in the Henry County Medical Center in Paris,

Tennessee. Burial was in Hardin County Memorial Gardens in Savannah, Tennessee.

He was a native of Hardin County, the son of the late Jack Fielden and Lillie Pool Cary. He was a member of the Puryear United Methodist Church. He came to Puryear Farmers Bank in Puryear in 1962 from Peoples Bank in Clifton. He was an Army World War II Veteran, a Grand Chapter Royal Arch Mason, a member of the Grand Lodge F and AM, a Shriner, a member of the Lion's Club and the Elk's Lodge. He served on the board of directors of the West Kentucky Rural Telephone for 26 years and is a retired president of Farmers Bank and Trust in Puryear.

Survivors include his wife, Gernell Hardin Cary of Puryear, daughters, Nancy Webb of Paris, Billie Jean Henearling of San Antonio, Texas, and Frances Steele of Mt. Juliet, Tennessee; one son, John F. Cary of McKenzie and five grandchildren and several nieces and nephews.

CASNER, WILLIE E., Serial Number 44 040 718, was a Private in the Army of the United States. He was born in Pe-

ters Landing, Tennessee. He was 29 5/12 years old when he was inducted 31 August 1944 at Fort Oglethorpe, Georgia. His description: brown eyes, black hair, ruddy complexion, 5'10" in height and married. He completed three months and 16 days in service. His Military qualification was M M Rifle. He was discharged 16 December 1944 at Fort McPherson, Georgia.

CASTEEL, JAMES T., Serial Number 34 361 752, was a Corporal in the 554 Army Air Force Base Unit of the United

States Army. His permanent mailing address was Waynesboro, Tennessee. He was born 7 March 1924 in Wayne County. His description when inducted into the army: brown eyes, brown hair, 5'7" height, weight 129 lbs, single without any dependents and a farm hand. His home address was General Delivery, Waynesboro, Tennessee. His Military Occupational Specialty was Military Policeman. He was not in any battles. His decorations were American Theater Medal,. European- African-Middle-Eastern Theater Medal, Good Conduct Medal, and World War II Victory Medal. He departed the USA 7 July 1944 for European Theater Operations and returned 18 December 1945. His education consisted of six years in grammar school. He was discharged 26 January 1946 at Maxwell Field, Alabama.

CASTEEL, LAWTON, son of Ken and Minnie Dugger Casteel, was born on December 21, 1916, in Wayne County. He served in the military service until the end of the war. After his discharge, he went to Memphis where he continues to work with the education department as a carpenter. He is married and has two children, Wayne Doyle and Susanne.

CASTEEL, MARION LEON, son of Ed and Mary Belle (Thurman) Casteel, grew up in Wayne County near Collinwood, Tennessee, and attended

Collinwood School. I married Hazel Ayers, and we live on a farm near Collinwood.

On April 11, 1944, I entered the United States Army and received my basic training at Camp Blanding, Florida. After that, I was sent to Europe to join the 28th Infantry Division. I then participated in the battles at Vosneck and Smidth, Germany.

We invaded the Hurtgen Forrest and were there about a month. The Germans surrounded us and I spent three days in a foxhole with my "best buddy" dead beside me. I didn't have water, so I ate snow and had a half of a can of potted meat each day for three days, then the Rangers broke through and relieved us. I spent the next nine months in hospitals convalescing from pneumonia and frozen feet and returned to Wayne County.

Marion Leon Casteel, Serial Number 34 987 504, was a Private in Company B 109th Infantry of the United States Army. His permanent address was Route 1, Collinwood, Tennessee. His description: blue eyes, brown hair, 5'9" height, weight 155 lbs, single and a farmer. His Military Specialty was Rifleman. He was in the battle of Rhineland. He received the European African Middle Eastern Theater Ribbon with one Bronze Battle Star. He departed from the United States on 27 September 1944 for the European Theater and returned 9 March 1945. He was discharged 23 August 1945 at Camp Butler Convalescent Hospital, North Carolina. The reason for the discharge was a Certificate of Disability.

Submitted by Marion Leon Casteel.

CASTEEL, WILLIAM F., Serial Number RA 19 259 595, was a Private in 9956 TSU Medical Section, Letterman General Hospital of the Army of the United States. His permanent mailing address was Waynesboro, Tennessee. His description: blue eyes, blonde hair, 5'3 1/2" height, weight 146 lbs, single with two dependents and a truck driver. He was not in any battles. The decoration that he received was

World War II Victory Medal. He attended the War Attendants school, Letterman General Hospital, San Francisco, California, for two weeks. He attended Grammar school for four years. He was discharged 11 June 1947 at Letterman Hospital in San Francisco, California.

CHAMBERS, CALVIN O., Serial Number 34 882 175, was a Private, First Class in 178th General Hospital, Army of the United States. His Description: blue eyes, brown hair, 5'7" height, weight 140 lbs and has two dependents. He was born 1 April 1925 in Iron City, Tennessee. His Civilian Occupation was Farmer. His home address at time of entry was Iron City, Tennessee. He was inducted 3 August 1943 and entered active service 24 August 1943 at Fort Oglethorpe, Georgia. His Military Qualification was Carbine MKM and Combat Infantryman Badge. He was in the battles of Rhineland and Ardennes. The decorations that he received were: European-African Middle Eastern Theater Ribbon with two Bronze Stars, American Theater Ribbon, Victory Medal, Good Conduct Ribbon, and Purple Heart with one Oak Leaf Cluster. He was wounded in action twice. Once in France on 9 November 1944 and again in Luxembourg on 7 February 1945. He departed the USA 24 August 1944 for European Theater Operations and returned 11 February 1946. His education consisted of eight years of grammar school. He was discharge 18 February 1946 at the Reception Center in Camp Atterbury, Indiana.

He reenlisted the next day, 19 February 1946 at Camp Atterburg and kept his old Serial Number. This time he made Sergeant with the 13th Combat Engineers, United States Army. His Military Specialty was Construction Foreman. His Military Qualification was EMP M-1 Rifle. He received a Lapel Pin and World War II Victory Medal. He left the USA 21 August 1946 for Asiatic Pacific Theater Operation and returned 5 April 1947. Chambers enlisted

as Sergeant in the Reserve. He was discharged 23 May 1947 at Fort Lawton, Washington.

CHAMBERS, FLOYD B., of Cypress Inn, TN served as a Cpl. in the US Army while stationed in Louisiana during World War II. He was presented three medals; Good Conduct, Expert Mechanic and Expert Rifle.

CHAMBERS, JASPER J. "JAP", a native of Iron City in Wayne County, Tennessee, Jasper was the son of Walter and Annie Liles Chambers. He served in the United States Army during World War II.

He was inducted 18 January 1943 and entered active Service 25 January 1943 at Ft. Oglethorpe, Georgia. He was in the battles of China Offensive, and China Defensive. His Military Occupational Specialty was Light Truck Driver. His Military Qualification was Driver. His decorations were: World War II Victory Medal, Good Conduct Medal, American Theater Ribbon, and Asiatic Pacific Theater with two Bronze Service Stars. He departed the USA on 1 November 1944 for Asiatic Pacific Theater and returned 3 January 1946. His education consisted of eight years of grammar school. He was discharged 17 January 1946 at Camp Chaffee, Arkansas.

He was a boiler operator with Tennessee Valley Authority. He served as Collinwood's City Manager and City Commissioner at one time. He was a member of the Collinwood Church of God.

He died on Saturday, June 5, 1999, at the age of 76 years. Burial with military rites were in McGlamery Cemetery near Collinwood.

He had three children: Randy, Rusty and Gail Chambers Horton.

His siblings are Joe, Louise Chambers Butler, Bessie Chambers Balentine and Nora Chambers Stults.

CHANDLER, ALFRED V., Serial Number 34 995 999, was a Private in the 301st Training Company, ATTR of the Army of the United States. His permanent mailing address was Clifton, Tennessee. His description: brown eyes, black hair, 5"8" height, weight 157 lbs, and married with one dependent. His Civilian Occupation was Longshoreman. His Military Occupational Specialty was Basic. His total length of service was 9 months and 29 days. The reason for his discharge was a Certificate of Disability. His race was Black. He had six years of grammar school education. He was discharged 5 October 1935 at Camp Gordon, Georgia. He was born 13 July 1923 in Clifton, died 3 January 1974 and was buried in Lizard Glade Cemetery in Clifton.

Alfred was the son of Etta Witherspoon. He attended school at Rosenwald in Clifton and was a member of the Baptist Church. He married Earmon Harbor in Corinth, Mississippi. He and his wife helped with the care of family children. They had none of their own. He was employed by the State Highway Department as a truck driver in Wayne County, Tennessee.

He had four sisters: Mariatta Davis, Geneva Williams, Mable Green and Edith Mosby. He had four half-sisters: Roberta, Amanda, Lovely and Dorothy. He had three brothers: Jesse, Edward and Alford. He also had two half-brothers: Griff and Leonard.

CHAPPELL, ROBERT A., Serial Number 34 189 100, was a Private in Company F 159th Infantry of the Army of the United States. His permanent mailing address was Waynesboro, Tennessee. His description: brown eyes, brown hair, 5"10" height, weight 118 lbs, and single. He was born 15 March 1922 in Dallas, Texas. His Civilian Occupation was Automobile Mechanic. His Military Occupational Specialty was Special Vehicle Operator. He was in battles in Northern France, Normandy, and Rhineland. His decorations: European-African Middle Eastern Theater Service Medal, and Good Conduct Medal. He Departed the USA on 5 November 1943 for European-African Middle Eastern Theater and returned 21 August 1945. He had eight years of grammar school education. He was discharged 1 October 1945 at Camp Gordon, Georgia.

CHOATE, ERNEST EDWARD, Serial Number 44 040 714, was a Sergeant in the Army of the United States. His permanent mailing address was Route 3, Waynesboro, Tennessee. The date of entry into active training was 31 October 1944 at Fort Oglethorpe, Georgia. He was born 24 November 1922 in Wayne County and was the son of Ab and Lois Choate. He

was married. His Civilian Occupation was Farmer. His Military Occupational Specialty was Rifleman. His citations: American Theater Service Medal, Good Conduct Medal, World War II Victory Medal, and Lapel Button. He was a high school graduate. As Rifleman Instructor, he was assigned to the Infantry Replacement Training Center, Camp Fannin, Texas where he instructed basic trainees in care, maintenance and firing of all small arms, such as M-1 rifle, carbine, automatic rifle, machine guns and 60-MM Mortar. He also instructed the men in bayonet tactics. Each class had fifty men enrolled. He was discharged 30 June 1946 at Fort Bragg, North Carolina. After the war, Ernest worked for the General Shoe Corporation in Waynesboro. He also enlisted for three years in the Army National Guard of the U. S. and Tennessee. He enlisted on 9 June 1955 at Waynesboro and was discharged 8 June 1958. He was a Platoon Sergeant during this time.

CHURCHWELL, JAMES E., was born 17 April 1924. He enlisted February

1942 in the United States Army and was honorably discharged in 1946.

CHURCHWELL, LOUIS C., Serial Number 36 897 794, was a Technician, Fifth Grade in the 3797 Quartermaster Truck Company in the Army of the United States. His permanent mailing address was Clifton, Tennessee. His Description: brown eyes, black hair, 5'5 1/2" height, weight 156 lbs, Negro, married with two dependents. His Civilian Occupation was Casting Cleaner. His Military Occupational Specialty was Light Truck Driver. His Military Qualifications was Carbine Expert. He served as T/5 with the 3797 Quartermaster Truck Company and participated in the battle of Rhineland. His decorations: European-African Middle Eastern Theater Ribbon with one Bronze Star, Good Conduct Medal, World War II Victory Medal.

He left the USA on 17 December 1944 for European Theater Operations and returned 23 March 1946. He had four years of grammar school education. He was discharged 28 March 1946 at Camp Atterbury, Indiana.

Louis C. Churchwell was born on November 8, 1912, in Clifton, Tennessee. He grew up there, married and has two children.

CHURCHWELL, MILTON BURTON, Serial Number 34 325 867, Registrant, was a Private, First Class in Company A, 460th Heavy Construction Battalion of the Army of the United States. His permanent mailing address was General Delivery, Waynesboro, Tennessee. His Description: brown eyes, black hair, 5'7" height, weight 160 lbs, no dependents, and is Black. He was born 1 June 1920 in Clifton, Tennessee, the son of Sam and Celia Churchwell. His Civilian Occupation was Cook's Helper. He was inducted 14 September 1942 at Camp Forrest, Tennessee. His Military Occupational Specialty was Lineman for Telephone and Telegraph. His Military Qualifications was Marksman Rifle. His battles and campaigns included Ryukyu. His decorations: World War II Victory Medal, Good Conduct Medal, American Theater Ribbon, Asiatic Pacific Theater Ribbon and one Bronze Service Star. He had three years of grammar school education at Wayne County Schools. He left the USA on 27 October 1944 for Asiatic Pacific Theater and returned 27 January 1946. He was discharged 24 January 1946 at Camp Chaffee, Arkansas.

He married Lela Wilton Harwell on May 11, 1947. After the war, he worked as a lineman for a telephone company. He left Wayne County to work for the company in Knoxville, Tennessee. He worked for a number of years. He died in Knoxville and is buried there. He was of the Missionary Baptist Faith.

He has a brother, John Frank Churchwell.

CHURCHWELL, RALPH N. JR., was a native of Clifton, Tennessee, a Veteran of World War II, the Korean Conflict, and the Vietnam War. He met his future wife in 1936 in Nashville through a mutual friend. He and Helen were united in marriage in 1938 at the Holy Catholic Church in Nashville. From there, the couple launched forth on a life of adventure as a career Navy family. Now, Ralph and Helen are retired in Portsmouth, Rhode Island where they just celebrated their fifty-fifth wedding anniversary. They are the parents of three children. Their eldest son, Ralph III, is retired from a career as a Naval officer and their son, John, is retired from a career as an Air Force pilot. John is

now back in Clifton, Tennessee where he is manager of the local airport. Daughter Flora Churchwell Prestipino entered the corporate world after graduating from college.

Source: The Wayne County News, 27 April 1994.

CLAY, JAMES W., Serial Number 44 173 955, was a Private First Class in Company L, 35th Infantry Regiment of the Army of the United States. His permanent mailing address was Route 5, Waynesboro, Tennessee. His Description: blue eyes, blonde hair, 5'4" height, weight 153 lbs, Single with one Dependent. He was born 5 September 1925 in Olive Hill, Tennessee. His Civilian Occupation was Farmer. His Military Occupational Specialty was Rifleman. His Military Qualifications was Sharpshooter M-1 Rifle. His decorations: World War II Victory Medal, Army of Occupation Medal- Japan. He departed the USA 13 December 1946 for Pacific Theater Operation and returned 12 May 1947. He had eight years of grammar school education. He was discharged 2 June 1947 at Camp Stoneman, California.

CLAY, MAHON WOOD, Serial Number 9 667 086, was a Seaman First Class in the United States Navy. He was married. He was inducted 24 January 1944 in Waynesboro and entered into active service 31 January 1944. He held the ratings of AS, 2/6, S1/6. Service Vessels and Stations that he served on were: USS ICY (FF) 628, USS FULTON PHIB TRA Base, Maryland, NTS Great Lakes, Illinois. His overseas duty was spent in the South Pacific. His decorations: American Theater Medal, Victory Medal, Asiatic Pacific Medal and others. His last employer was Great Lakes Steel Company, Ecorse, Michigan from 1943 to 1944. His Civilian Occupation was Laborer. He was discharged 11 December 1945 at NAS, Charleston, South Carolina.

His parents were Jacob Thomas and Ida Beckham Clay. He was born 12 October 1907 on the Dick Boyd Farm in the Philadelphia Community on Hardins Creek near Waynesboro, Tennessee. His sisters are Fathie Clay Burns and Lucy Clay Bryant. He married Nellie Nowlin, daughter of Garlin and Opal Balton Nowlin. After the war he was a farmer and employee of TVA and Genesco. He died 8 December 1969 in Veterans Hospital in Memphis, Tennessee and is buried in Mt. Hebron Cemetery on Indian Creek in Wayne County.

CLAY, ROBERT E.L., was born, September 10, 1905, in Wayne County and lived at Rt 6, Waynesboro, Tn. He was working as a sign painter, at the time he was inducted into the US Airforce, May 23, 1942, at Ft. Oglethorpe, GA. Robert served as Supply Sgt. with Sq. Ad 231st Army Air Force Bn. October 15, 1945, he was discharged at Drew Field, FL.

CLAY, WILLIAM LEONARD, JR., went to high school in Clifton at Frank Hughes. He became a star basketball player

and graduated in the 1932 senior class as salutatorian. While here in Clifton he made his home at Lawson and Sally Robert's. After graduation he joined the C. C. Corps. Then he joined the United States Army doing more than 20 years of service before retiring. He died in an Army hospital in San Antonio, Texas, in 1958. He married his wife, Rena Mae, in Lexington, Tennessee. They had one son, William Leonard III. His wife and son live in Memphis, Tennessee. Leonard came to Clifton in 1948 to visit old friends and relatives there.

Submitted by William Leonard Clay Jr.

CLAYTON, J.M., was born in Collinwood, TN, February 29, 1920, the son of Lindsey E. And Minnie B. Clayton.

He grew up on his father's farm in the Shawnettee community during the Great Depression. At the age of 20, he voluntarily enlisted in the United States Army, taking his physical examination for enlistment in Nashville on September 26, 1940, just over a year before America became involved in World War II. Clayton was sent to Ft. McPherson, Georgia to be sworn into the Army. From there, he was sent to Ft. Benning, Georgia for basic training. After basic, he was assigned to the 29th Field Artillery, 4 Division at Ft. Benning for 18 months. He was serving there on December 7, 1941 when Japan bombed Pearl Harbor. In March, 1941, Clayton was reassigned to the 654 T.D. Battalion, an armored cavalry (tank) battalion, stationed at Ft. Gordon, Georgia. He remained in this assignment until Sept. 10, 1943. On that date, he was sent to the Brooklyn Navy Yard's Port of Embarkation in New York for transport to the European theater of action. From there, he boarded the U.S.S. Panama for a ten day sea voyage to Liverpool, England. After disembarking in Liverpool, Clayton and the 654th were sent on a three day voyage across the Irish Sea to a small town in Northern Ireland where they were to be trained for the invasion of Europe. The 654th was attached to the 7th Army under Gen. George Patton. Clayton remembers Gen. Patton as a commander whose very appearance was intimidating, but who also inspired his men with confidence because of his competence.

When this training was completed, Clayton and the men of the 654th were sent back to England. His battalion was chosen to participate in the D-Day invasion on June 6, 1941, but Clayton had broken an arm in training and had to stay behind. On August 6, 1941 he was sent to France as a replacement, joining the 823rd T.D. Battalion as an assistant gunner on an M-10 tank destroyer.

Clayton entered France at Omaha Beach, which was by then fully in America control. The 823rd was attached to the 9th Army's 30th Division under Gen. Simpson and was immediately sent into combat. As a part of the 832rd, Clayton fought his way across France, entering Germany through the Siegfried Line. During this time, he participated in three major campaigns of the war. He was gravely wounded in combat inside Germany during a battle that took place between Achen and Cologne when shrapnel from a shell struck his head. At that point, he began a slow retreat back through France through a series of field and general hospitals, finally arriving in Paris to be prepared for evacuation to England. From Paris, he was flown to England where he remained hospitalized for two and a half months. He was placed aboard the U.S.S. John Erickson in February, 1945 for his second trip across the Atlantic, this time landing in Boston, Massachusetts that same month. From Boston, he was sent to Kennedy General Hospital in Memphis, Tennessee where he remained hospitalized for another month.

On April 19, 1945, three weeks before the final German surrender to Allied Forces, Clayton received an honorable discharge from the U.S. Army with an excellent character rating. He was also rated a disabled veteran due to his combat injuries. As a soldier fighting for his country in this horrible war, he had earned three campaign ribbons, a Purple Heart, a Good Conduct Medal, and Expert medals both with a pistol and a rifle.

After the war, he returned to Wayne County where he still lives.

CLEMENTS, GRADY GLEN, age 69, of Hurricane Meadows Drive, Waynesboro, died 9 March 1997 in St. Thomas Hospital in Nashville, and was buried in Memorial Gardens in Waynesboro. He was a native of Birmingham, Alabama, a son of the late Samuel Grady and Eleanor Inez (Atkins) Clements. He was a veteran of World War II having served in the U. S. Army. He was a parts dispatcher at General Motors in Illinois before moving to Waynesboro and a member of Kelly's Chapel Baptist Church.

Survivors included his wife, Leva N. Bolyn Clements of Waynesboro; one daughter, Janice Marie Webb of Hot Springs, Virginia; three sons, Gerald Clements of Manhatten, Illinois, Thomas and Jeffery Clements both of Joliet, Illinois; seven stepsons; three sisters, Jeannine Watkins of Quinton, Alabama, Eleanor Engleking of Houston, Texas and Mary Russell of Henderson; one brother, David Clements of Joliet, Illinois; twenty-seven grandchildren and two great-grandchildren.

CLENDENIN, LAWTON LEE, There is no discharge filed in the office of Register in Waynesboro. Lawton was born 4 September 1903, died 11 February 1970 and is buried in McGlamery Cemetery on Highway 13 South in Collinwood, Tennessee. He is the son of Frank A. Clendenin (?-16 Oct 1939) and Laura Ella Craig (21 February 1874-31 March 1959). His siblings are, Mary Biffle Clendenin (12 January 1897-16 November 1973), married Dewitt W. Lyles; Frank Carmack Clendenin (1906-23 September 1978), married Lura Conway; and Laura Boyd Clendenin (20 June 1898 ——), married Joe Dunn. Lauton's grandparents are John Rufus Craig (20 October 1844-11 May 1911) and Ursula Annie E. Biffle (1 January 1852- 4 February 1895) Salem Cemetery. Annie is the daughter of Jonathan

Isom and Elizabeth Ann (Hardin) Biffle. John R. Craig is the son of John and Diane Walker Craig. Diane Walker is the daughter of William Burrell and Ann Scott Walker.

COFFMAN, HUBERT HENRY, Serial Number 830-67-91, had the Grade of Shipfitter, Third Class in the United States Navy. He was married. He was born 29 September 1918 in Corinth, Mississippi. He was registered with Selective Service Board in Waynesboro, Tennessee. He was inducted 15 September and entered active service 22 September 1943 in Jacksonville, Florida. His home address at time of entry was Iron City, Tennessee. His Military Qualifications were Shipfitter 3/C-Shipfitting and Welding and Handling Personnel. He held the rating of 3/C (CB). The Vessels and Stations that he served on were: CBD 1028; Quoddy Village, Maine, NCTC Davisville, Rhode Island; 65 NCB; USNFB Tompkinsville, NY; and USNH Shoemaker, California. Decorations awarded to Coffman included: American Area Ribbon, Victory Ribbon and Point System. His last employment was with the St. John Shipbuilding Company, Jacksonville, Florida from 1942 to 1943. His main Civilian Occupations were Shipfitter, Farmer and Foreman on Construction work. He had an eighth grade education. He attended a Vocational or Trade School Course in welding for four weeks. He was honorably discharged on 10 December 1945 at Shoemaker, California.

COGGINS, JOHN EDWARD, was born 4 April 1923 in Collinwood, Tennessee, died 31 October 1960 at the age of 37. He was the son of Henry and Georgia Weaver Coggins. Edd had three sisters: the late Mary Coggins of Collinwood, the late Annie Martin of Waynesboro and Flora Morrison of Waynesboro. He also had one brother, Raymond Coggins of Collinwood.

Edd was a farmer before he was inducted into the United States Army on 18 January 1943 at Ft. Oglethorpe, Georgia. He was then sent to Bowie, Texas. He left Bowie on 25 January 1943 for Normandy, France. His Military Occupational Specialty was Cook. He received two decorations: the Good Conduct Ribbon and the Fame Ribbon. Edd was given an Honorable Discharge on 14 October 1945 in Bowie, Texas.

Soon after Edd was discharge from the Army, he met Jewell Brown of Collinwood. They were married 1 December 1945 in Corinth, Mississippi and shortly thereafter moved to Detroit, Michigan. They both worked there for several years before moving back to Wayne County. Edd and Jewell have four daughters: Shirley Battles and Kay Rippy of Clifton, Tennessee; Thelma Harmon of North Carolina; and Joy Webb of Savannah, Tennessee.

Edd was a loving husband and father. He is greatly missed by his family and friends. Written by daughter Shirley Battles, 24 November 1991.

COLE, CARL LLOYD, age 70, of Leoma died 27 January 1998 at Columbia Crockett Hospital in Lawrenceburg and was buried in Lawrence County Memorial Gardens. He was a native of Wayne County, a son of Henry Luther and Zula May Hodges Cole. He was retired from Murray, Inc., an Army Veteran of World War II and a member of Leoma Church of Christ. Survivors include: six daughters: Wanda M. Cockrell of Columbia, Patricia Moore and Mary Alice Davis both of Lawrenceburg, Gearldean K. Hicks of Waynesboro, Sherry Cotton of Hohenwald and Phyllis Polk of Leoma; three sons: Carl Gene and Randy Cole both of Lawrenceburg and Roger D. of Five Points; one sister Lillian Hazel Pope of Columbia, five brothers: J. C., James Glenn and Grady Lee Cole all of Lewisburg, and Hausard Leo Cole of Mt. Pleasant and Charles Rubin Cole of Lawrenceburg.

COLE, CLAUDE EDWARD, Serial Number 967 13 60 had the Grade of Ship's Cook, Third Class in the United States

Navy. He was born 12 April 1925 in Waynesboro, Tennessee. He entered into active service 10 April 1944. The highest Rank that he held was SC 3/C. The Vessels and Stations that he served on were: Construction Battalion's USNCTC of Williamsburg, Virginia; NAS D NAS Navy 128; NASD Oahu, T. H. ; AV1 Sup Branch NAV Sup Center, Pearl Harbor, T. H. He was discharged 2 March 1946 at US Naval Personnel Center, Memphis, Tennessee.

His parents were the late Fred and Marietta Alley Cole His brothers are James, Robert, Eugene and Billy Cole, all of whom served in the United States Armed Forces. His sisters are Pauline, Nellie and Marietta Cole.

COLE, DON HOWARD, Serial Number 966 28 41, was an Apprentice Seaman in the V 65 Naval Reserve of the Navy. He enlisted 31 December 1943 at Chattanooga, Tennessee for two years. He was born 14 May 1918 in Waynesboro, Tennessee. He was married. He was discharged 21 January 1944 in Farragut, Idaho. The Vessels and Stations that he served on were: NRS, Chattanooga, Tennessee; and NTS, Farragut, Idaho.

COLE, EUGENE, Pvt., was the oldest son of Fred and Marietta "Etta" (Alley) Cole He was born in June 1917 in the

Hardins Creek Community of Wayne County, died 19 December 1981 and is buried at Philadelphia, Hardins Creek on Highway 64 West in Wayne County. His brothers are James, Robert, Claude and Billy Cole, all of whom served in the Armed Forces. His sisters are Nelle Wilson, Pauline and Marietta Cole.

On 4 January 1942, Eugene and Violet Harrison of Killen, Alabama were married. They lived in Wayne County until Eugene was drafted into the United States Army at Fort Oglethorpe, Georgia in March of 1942.

He was sent to Camp Claiborne, Louisiana. Mrs. Cole joined him and lived in Alexandria, Louisiana for several months. She followed her husband from camp to camp. They lived all over the South and Eastern Coast of the United States. She was a cosmetologist and it was very easy to secure jobs in the large cities where they lived. Mr. Cole drew separate rations, so he could live off the post in the nearest town with her.

From Louisiana, Private Cole and wife moved to Fort Bragg, North Carolina. Eugene was placed in the 101st Airborne.

What a relief it was for him to get out of the Infantry. The foot soldier had it hard, thirty miles of hiking with a full field pack, weighing sixty-five pounds, on his back.

After Fort Bragg came Fort Eustis, Virginia. Newport News was a port of embarkation. The huge troop ships slipped in and out at night bound for overseas duty. The huge aircraft carriers would hold four football fields. The "Miss America" docked, stripped of all her luxurious trappings. It was painted a battleship gray and used for a troop carrier. Pvt Cole was in the Anti-aircraft there. His company would assemble the big search lights on the planes flying overhead.

After Fort Eustis came Fort Stewart, Georgia. Fort Jackson in lovely old Southern South Carolina came last. Pvt Cole never had overseas duty but he was a well-trained and proficient soldier. He received an honorable discharge from the United States Army in April 1945 and returned to Wayne County to farm.

His children are Gerald, Pam, Shelia, David and Janela Cole.

Submitted by Violet Cole.

COLE, JAMES F., Serial Number 34 146 878, was a Sergeant in Company 1, 121st Infantry of the Army of the United

States. His permanent mailing address was Route 1, Waynesboro, Tennessee. His Description: brown eyes, brown hair, 5'9" height, weight 134 lbs and single. He was born 31 August 1919 in Waynesboro, Tennessee. His Civilian Occupation was General Farm Hand. He was inducted 3 October 1941 at Fort Oglethorpe, Georgia. His Military Occupational Specialty was Squad Leader. His Military Qualifications were SS Rifle and SS Pistol. His battles and campaigns included Normandy, Northern France, Rhineland, and Central Europe. His decorations: Purple Heart, European-American Middle Eastern Service Medal, with four Bronze Stars, Good Conduct Medal, American Defense Service He was

wounded in action on 25 December 1944 in the Germany European Theater. He had seven years of grammar school education. He left the USA on 5 December 1943 for European Theater and returned 11 July 1945. He was discharged 3 October 1945 at Fort McPherson, Georgia.

His parents were the late Fred and Marietta Alley Cole His brothers are Claude, Robert, Eugene and Billy Cole, all of whom served in the United States Armed Forces. His sisters are Pauline, Nelle and Marietta Cole.

COLE, JAMES TAYLOR, was born 22 September 1920 in Wayne County, Tennessee, and is the son of Guilford and Mary Lou Daniel Cole. Except for a few years in Grand Chain, Illinois, he grew up in Waynesboro and graduated from Wayne County High School in 1938. He worked in Florence, Alabama until 7 February 1942, when he was inducted into the US Navy in Birmingham, Alabama, shortly after the bombing of Pearl Harbor. After boot camp in San Diego, California, duty in Pensacola, Florida, New Orleans and Moffett Field, California, he sailed from San Francisco on the ship, Mormac Port, on 15 April 1943, as part of the Third Amphibious Force. He was a navy medic in a group called Cub 3. From the Fiji Islands, Cub 3 was sent to the Solomon Islands, landing from LST's on Guadalcanal, then Rendova and later Munda where Base Hospital 12 was being established. The most dangerous period was on Rendova where he experienced regular Japanese bombings and sniper fire.

After 21 months, he came back on the Snortin' Morton, landing in San Francisco on New Year's Eve. Since he no longer possessed a full official uniform, he had to wait for a friend to bring one to his ship before he was allowed to disembark to join the festivities.

At his request, he was assigned to the Memphis Naval Station where he stayed for eight months, then was sent to Camp Wallace, Texas, where he helped in processing discharges of naval personnel until he, himself, was discharged on 30 November 1945, as a Pharmacist's Mate First Class.

In June 1949, he received a BS degree from the University of Tennessee in Knoxville, and has spent his entire career as district manager of a wholesale paper company. He was married to Lucy Rowntree of Knoxville December 18, 1948, and has two sons and three daughters, plus eight grandchildren. Their children are Patricia, Barry, Stephen, Mary Lou and Laura. His siblings are Mary Louise, Marie, Doris Jean, Harold, Robert, Jasper, John, Guilford and David Lynn.

Except for 15 months at the Naval Air Station in Corpus Christi, Texas during the Korean Conflict, he has lived in Knoxville since World War II. - James Taylor Cole.

COLE, JENNINGS B., son of John Ellison (Babe) and Sophronia Ann (Jordan) Cole was born August 10, 1899 near Waynesboro. He grew up and received his education in Wayne County. About 1919 he enlisted in the United States Army and served on through World War II. He was serving as a Warrant Officer when he received his discharge, April 30, 1947, at Fort McPherson, Georgia.

He married Cathleen Whitstone during his army years. Bryan was losing his eyesight, so after his discharge, they returned to Wayne County and bought a home on Hardin Creek. They are both deceased and buried at the Ralph Cole Cemetery on Hardin Creek. They have no children. His siblings are Ernest, Meda, Ralph, Rill; Roy, Gertrude, Ruby and Rex.

COLE, JOE PRIMM "JODY", JR., Serial Number 34 194 547, was a Sergeant with Headquarters Detachment SCU of the Army of the United States. His permanent mailing address was Waynesboro, Tennessee. His Description: brown eyes, brown hair, 5'7" height, weight 147 lbs, and single. He was born 19 September 1911 in Wayne County, Tennessee. His Civilian Occupation was Heavy Truck Driver. He was inducted 4 April 1942 at Fort Oglethorpe, Georgia. His Military Occupational Specialty was Motor Transportation NCO. His Military Qualification was M M Rifle. He was not in any battles or campaigns. His decorations: American Service Medal, Asiatic Pacific Service Medal, World War II Victory Medal, and Good Conduct Medal. He left the USA on 25 September 1945 for Pacific Theater and returned 3 December 1945. He finished two years of high school. He was discharged 19 January 1946 at Fort McPherson, Georgia.

Joe was the son of Joe Primm, Sr. and Myrtle Hardin Cole who are buried in the Philadelphia Baptist Church Cemetery. He was a farmer, a member of the Democrat Party, the American Legion and the Waynesboro Church of Christ. He died 27 April 1994 and is buried in the Philadelphia Baptist Church Cemetery on Hardins Creek. He lived with his sister, Lena Cole Youngblood, in Waynesboro.

COLE, JOEL, There was excitement in Jordon Hollow in Wayne County, Tennessee, November 27, 1927. Twin boys, Joel and Noel, were born to James Henry and Elizabeth Griggs Cole.

Joel went to Missouri to work on a farm

and met his wife, Ila Kerr. They were married December 31, 1943.

He entered the U. S. Army July 8, 1946, serving in, the Occupational part of World War II. After basic training was finished at Ft. Leavenworth, Kansas, he was sent to Italy. Joel left Italy February 11, 1947, and arrived at Ft. Dix, New Jersey, February 27, 1947. He was discharged early because of having a small dependent at home.

After he received his Honorable Discharge he returned to Missouri to his wife and daughter and farmed for a few years. Around 1950 they moved to Topeka, Kansas where he worked at ..a Grain Elevator. In 1955 Joel was transferred to a Grain Elevator in . Lincoln, Nebraska. Joel became homesick for the hills of Tennessee in 1957 and moved his family back to Wayne County where he resided until his death.

Joel and Ila have four daughters, Glenda, Jo Nell, Kathy and Janice.

1. Glenda married Milas Davis, Jr. and they have four sons, Joel (Mac), Jeff, Jason and Josh.

a. Joel (Mac) married Renee Blanton and they have two children, Zachary and Macayla.

b. Jeff married Rebecca (Becky) Mathis and they have two children, Ashlee and Cameron.

c. Jason married Carisa Cummings and they have five children, Brittany.

d. Josh is single at this time.

2. Jo Nell married Jerry Baugus and they have two sons, Jeremy and Jerrod.

a. Jeremy married Gwen Rauchle and they have two sons, Braxton and Hayden.

b. Jerrod married Ginger Hasting.

3. Kathy married Vic Barnett and they have two children, Maegan and Joel.

4. Janice married Brian Wood and they have two children, Brianne and Justin.

Joel was a truck driver for Hassell & Hughes Lumber Company, Collinwood, Tennessee, at the time of his death, July 13, 1983. He is buried at the Shawnettee Cemetery behind the Shawnettee Methodist Church.

COLE, MAX, son of Thomas Ben and May Hardin Cole, was born in the Second District of Wayne County near Clifton, Tennessee on, June 28, 1918. 1 attended school in Clifton and graduated from Frank Hughes College in 1937. 1 served in the CC Camp from October 1937 to October 1939. (Times were hard during because of the depression). From 1939 - 41 I worked for Hassell Lumber Co. in Clifton.

During, October 1941, I was drafted into the Army of the United States for one year of service and returned home four years later. I went from Waynesboro to Fort Oglethorpe, Georgia and then on to Ft

Knox, Kentucky for basic training, where I was sent to the 1st Armored Division. I was still at Fort Knox when the Japanese bombed Pearl Harbor. Then in March 1942, my Division was sent to Ft. Dix, New Jersey. In May my Division left the States and landed in Northern Ireland. We stayed there until September and went on to England. In October we were loaded on a boat in Liverpool, England to go to the invasion of North Africa, where we landed November 7, 1942. We went through the Strait of Gibraltar. These were the first ships to pass through since 1939 as the British had it blocked. We landed about six miles from Oran and fought through the African campaign. The war in Africa ended in May 1943. 1 had been in the following cities: Oran, Casa Blanca, Fez, Robat, Tunis, Algiers and Rizirete. After the war was over in Africa, we stayed in a forest of cork trees at Robat and did more training. I fought in three countries Morocco, Algeria and Tunisia.

We made the invasion of Italy on, September 9, 1943, at Salerno and fought up to Cassenio. We were pulled out of there and sent on the invasion of Anzio Beachhead in January 1944, this is where Nero fiddled while Rome burned. We helped capture Rome, June 4, 1944, and fought all the way to the Brenner Pass and up to the mountains that overlooked the Po River Valley. We moved into the valley in, April 1945: then the war for Italy ended, May 1st. We had also been at Naples and Florence. I had come back to Milan, Italy and saw Mussolini's body hanging by his heels in the Square of Milan. They cut him down and laid him on the ground. More than a dozen people were going over spitting on his body. He had been killed at Lake Commo and brought to Milan. Italians were surrendering by the thousands. I left Italy the last of June 1945 and flew to North Africa, then down to Dakar, from there to Brazil, then to Florida. I had a stop at Puerto Rico. I was then sent to Camp Atterbury, Indiana to be discharged in July 1945.

I spent 46 months in the army and was awarded the Bronze Star at Anzio. When I was drafted in 194 1, we were paid $21.00 a month. I can't say that I liked the army, but I am proud that I have served. I spent 550 days in combat and made 3 invasions.

I have lived in Waynesboro since 1949, retired from Genesco in 1982 and worked for the Wayne County Highway Department for 18 years. I married the former Marietta Templeton and we have a son, Thomas Craig Cole. He married Janice Sims and they live in Franklin, Tn. with their two children.

COLE, NOEL, There was excitement in Jordon Hollow, Wayne County, Tennessee, November 27, 1927. Twin boys, Noel and Joel, were born to James Henry Cole and Elizabeth Griggs Cole.

Noel entered the U. S. Army in the early part of 1946. After completing his Basic Training at Fort Bragg, North Carolina he was sent to Germany; serving in the Occupational part of War World II.

One day the Red Cross was serving coffee and doughnuts to the soldiers. As Noel was going in for refreshments a cousin, Ford Griggs, was coming out of the building. They both were surprised because neither one of them knew that the other one was stationed there. Noel said it sure was great to see someone from home. Ford was the only person from home Noel saw while he was stationed overseas.

After Noel's Honorable Discharge in 1948 he came back to Wayne County and farmed.

Later he joined his twin brother, Joel, in Topeka, Kansas, where they both worked at the same Grain Elevator. They both transferred to Lincoln, Nebraska, for the same company and worked there until 1957 when they both became homesick for the hills of Wayne County. They moved their families and have lived here since.

Noel married Reba Skelton and they have three daughters, Kayron Joyce and Rita and one son, Wayne. Because of injuries from a serious car accident they had when they were living in Nebraska, Reba is now in Wayne County Nursing Home and Noel has retired as a Truck Driver for Hassell & Hughes Lumber Company, Collinwood, Tennessee and lives in Waynesboro.

COLE, ROBERT, Serial Number 34 495 120, was a Private First Class with Company F, 141 Infantry Regiment, Thirty-sixth Division of the Army of the United States. His permanent mailing address was Route 1, Waynesboro, Tennessee. His Description: blue eyes, black hair, 5'9" height, weight 145 lbs, and Single. He was born 9 April 1922 in Waynesboro.

His Civilian Occupation was General Farm Hand. He was inducted 22 November 1942 and entered into Active Service 29 November 1942 at Fort Oglethorpe, Georgia. His Military Occupational Specialty was Light Machine Gunner. His Military Qualifications were Rifleman Marksman, Expert Infantry Badge and Combat Infantry Badge. His battles and campaigns included Rome-Arno, Southern France, Rhineland and Central Europe. His decorations: Purple Heart Medal with Oak Leaf Cluster, American Theater Ribbon, Good Conduct Medal, World War II Victory Medal, European-African Middle Eastern Theater Ribbon with four Bronze Service Stars, Distinguished Unit Badge, a Bronze Arrowhead and a Lapel Button. He was wounded in action in France 10 October 1944 and 16 March 1945. He left the USA on 1 July 1944 for European-African Middle Eastern Theater and returned 15 December 1945. He had six years of grammar school education. He was discharged 21 December 1945 at Fort Knox, Kentucky.

He died 11 January 1969 and was buried in Philadelphia Church Cemetery located on Highway 64 West in Wayne County. His parents were the late Fred Cole (1886-1962) and Marietta Alley Cole (1892-1960). His brothers are Claude, James, Eugene and Billy Cole, all of whom served in the United States Armed Forces. His sisters are Pauline, Nelle and Marietta Cole.

COLE, WILLIAM ANDREW, was the only son of Mr. and Mrs. A. E. Cole. He volunteered for the Air Corp in 1942 and received his training in Greenville and Gulfport, Mississippi. Later, he was transferred to Columbus, Ohio, where he was stationed at Lockeborne Army Air Force Base for many months. PFC Cole was assigned to duty overseas and was stationed at Hickman Field in the Hawaiian Islands. He was transferred to special duty with the Navy and served for a time aboard ship. He is now deceased.

COLE, WILLIAM DOUGLAS, was born in Wayne County 22 October 1924 to Ernest and Alma Lay Cole. He lived on the family farm until they moved to Michigan in 1942. In 1943, Douglas came back to Tennessee and enlisted at Tullahoma, Tennessee. He was with the 98th Sea Bee Battalion and was in the South Pacific.

After the war he returned to Michigan and went to work for the Greyhound Corporation. He spent thirty-seven years with them before retirement.

In 1949 he married Mary Gillahan from Cumberland City, Tennessee. They met in Michigan and lived there until both retired. They have no children. They have move back to Wayne County and live on the old home place - Route 1, Waynesboro.

COLLIE, DAVID THOMAS, was the son of George O. and Lena Wilbanks Collie of Wayne County, Tennessee. He graduated from high school in Clifton where he attended with his brothers, Joe and Montie and his sister, Mildred.

He enlisted in the Army Air Force serving from 1941 to 1944 in the 9th Air Force, 44th Bomb Group, 67th Squadron. He was assigned to the photo department and was later transferred to gunnery school. He left Ft. Dix, New Jersey in 1942 for England where he stayed until he was transferred to North Africa to train as a Waistgunner on a B-24 Liberator as part of a special mission. His family received a letter from "Somewhere in the Middle East" dated 28 July 1943, and did not hear from him again until his mother received a telegram on 20 August 1943, informing her that her son was wounded in action 1 August 1943 over Rumania and interned in a neutral country. Never before or since the 1 August 1943, Ploesti mission were so many decorations for heroism and gallantry in action awarded to individuals in a single battle. For this reason a full account is given below.

On Sunday, 1 August 1943, 178 powerful B-24 Liberator bombers took off from bases in North Africa to cross the Mediterranean headed for Rumania. S/Sgt Collie was part of this crew. Their assignment was to cross Yugoslavia's mountains and approach Rumania at treetop level to destroy the oil refineries at Ploesti. This would deal a significant blow to Axis oil production during a critical time period of the war. Hitler's dependence on Ploesti oil, and the German Occupation of Rumania made the mission one of great importance. The strategy was to avoid radar detection and to prevent flak gunners and fighter pilots from getting good shots at them. Five bomb groups were assigned to destroy Ploesti's refineries in one massive raid. Each group was briefed to attack a certain target. During the air raid, a wrong turn was made by one of the lead planes resulting in radio silence being broken. (Participants differ widely in this tragic event and even today survivors are still preparing formation charts, etc.) Axis fighters sporadically attacked all the way to the Mediterranean.

David's plane, "The Horsefly," and other crews fearlessly approached their target through antiaircraft fire, exploding oil fires and smoke. The crews alternated between fighting the enemy and throwing things out of the plane to lighten the load. When David's plane was attacked, the wing and engines were damaged. David and the other waistgunner suffered extreme wounds to both legs and were unable to parachute from the damaged plane. It appeared that both legs were broken. The pilot, 1st/Lieutenant Edward R. Mitchell, made the decision for everyone to stay with the plane. Ordering the co-pilot and bombardier to the rear of the plane in order to keep the nose up, Mitchell gained altitude. He made a crash-landing by hitting the runway short to slow down his speed, and landed his crew in Turkey successfully. A third of the 178 B-24's did not return to base. Many survived as POW's in Rumania or as internees in neutral Turkey. David, along with the other crew members, was hospitalized in Turkey. After a few weeks in the hospital, he and his comrades escaped from Turkey by being smuggled out of a Red Cross hospital in the Middle East. On 30 October 1943, David arrived at Fort Devens, Massachusetts, and stayed in Lovell General Hospital until he was able to be transferred to Lawson General Hospital, Atlanta, Georgia. In February 1944, he underwent surgery on both legs. After he recuperated, he toured on crutches with five decorated World War II veterans along with Lon Chaney, Jr. and Ann Savage, who were movie stars during the forties, promoting war bond sales.

Because of heroic perseverance, technical skill and valiant effort, the Ploesti oil field mission met with great success. This achievement brought high honor to the Army Air Forces. For his contribution, David received nine decorations, including the Distinguished Flying Cross, A Bronze Oak-Leaf Cluster, and the Purple Heart.

Returning home to Clifton, David married Clara Edith Hobbs. They spent their married life in Waynesboro. Their children David T Collie, Jr., Brenda Dianne Rose, James Steven, George Mark and Jonathan Lee attended Wayne County schools. David was a disabled veteran who was an experienced photographer and in later years worked as a contract painter. He was born 22 April 1920, died in Veterans Administration Hospital, Nashville, Tennessee, on 26 December 1982, and was buried in Mt. Carmel Cemetery in Hardin County where a military funeral was held in honor of his contribution to freedom.

"Although the generation that was shaped by WW II fades from memory and sight, there are some who will never let them be forgotten."

Submitted by Brenda Collie Rose, 20 February 1995.

COLLIE, JOSEPH EARL, Serial Number 34 723 017, son of George O. and Lena Wilbanks Collie, was born 19 December 1923 in Clifton. He was educated in the Clifton schools. He enlisted in the United States Army on 27 February 1943 at Fort Oglethorpe, Georgia, and was assigned to the 20th Armored Division in Fort Campbell, Kentucky. This was the only division activated from Fort Campbell during World War II. He serve from 1943 to 1946 and fought in France, Belgium, Holland, Germany and Austria. He received World War II Victory Medal, American Service Medal, European-African-Middle Eastern Service Medal with one Bronze Star. At the end of his military service, Joe held the rank of Sergeant. He was discharged from the 8th Armored Infantry

Battalion on 12 February 1946 at Fort McPherson, Georgia.

After the war he moved to Nashville and worked for Royal Crown Bottling Company until 1985. Although retired, he continues to work in landscaping and is self employed. He and his wife Chris reside in Pleasant View, Tennessee. Each year they attend the 20th Armored Division Reunion at Fort Campbell.

COLLIE, MONTIE BILLY, the youngest son of George O. and Lena Wilbanks Collie, Billy was born 23 May

1926. He was educated in the Clifton schools; however, he left high school to join the United States Navy at the age of 17 in January 1943. He served as a medic on the USS INDEPENDENCE in the South Pacific for 2 1/2 years and was aboard when it was torpedoed. Montie re-enlisted in the Navy in 1948 to serve in the Korean Conflict. He was medically retired in 1951 and lives in Florence, Alabama, where he is a retired contract painter. He has two children Montie, Jr., and Tamara Casares.

Source: Brenda Rose.

COLLINS, FREDDIE LEO, Serial Number 641 89 54, was an Electrician's

Mate Third Class in the United States Navy. His permanent mailing address was P. O. Box 172, Waynesboro, Tennessee. He volunteered 31 August 1943 at Pulaski, Tennessee. His home address when he entered service was Ethridge, Tennessee.

His basic training was at Great Lakes, Illinois, then in November 1943 he was assigned to duty with Company A, 32nd Special Battalion at Naval Construction Center (Seabees) At Camp Peary, Virginia. His overseas service included the South Pacific, Philippine Islands and North China. His qualifications were those of RATE. The ratings that he held were: AS, S2/C, S2/C(CB), S1/C. EM 3/C(CB).

He completed a three and one half-week Diesel School in Camp Endicott, Rhode Island. He was discharged on January 3, 1946, at U. S. N. Separation Center in Memphis, Tennessee. He received an Honorable Discharge Service Button and Service Emblems.

He was born 14 June 1926 in Giles County, Tennessee. He had an eighth grade education. Leo married Rothonell Norton. They have two children: Steven Lindsey and Gilbert Lee Collins. He has one brother, Justin Cleo, and one sister, Zane Bell.

COLLINS, HOLLIS A., was born 20 December 1916. His parents were John Anderson and Nora Coffman Collins, both deceased. His brothers include Sid, Loyd, and Carlton Collins. His sisters were Mildred Moore and Eula. Eula is deceased. Mildred lives in Lobelville, Tennessee.

Hollis was inducted into the Navy while he lived in Ohio. When he returned from war duty, he continued to live in Ohio. He married Eloise McKnight and to this union were born a son, James and two daughters, Shelby Jean and Georgia Ann. Eloise died and later, Hollis married Vada Carpenter. They lived in Texas. Hollis passed away 6 September 1987 and was buried in Whitehouse Cemetery in Tyler, Texas.

COMBS, CHARLES HENRY, Serial

Number 34 713 872, was a Private First Class in the Third Army of the United States with General Patton. Charles Combs left 30 April 1943 with twenty seven other Wayne County boys from Waynesboro to be inducted into active duty at Fort Oglethorpe, Georgia. He entered into active service April 1943 at Camp Stewart, Georgia. He received a Bronze Star for heroic achievement while in actual combat in Luttz.

The 565th AAA A/W Battalion had just been organized on 10 April 1943 at Camp Stewart, Georgia under the command of Lt. Col. Frank Courtenay. Charlie with other soldiers began training in May 1943 for a sixteen week cycle. In November 1943 they moved to the 2nd Army maneuver area (Tennessee), participated until 17 January 1944, then returned to Camp Stewart for further training and restructuring.

On 30 September 1944, Charlie and his group departed Camp Stewart for Camp Kilmer, New Jersey, where they boarded the transport, USAT Cristabal, for overseas duty. They arrived in Plymouth, England 19 October 1944, then went to Midlands for training. They left 7 December 1944 for Camp Hursley then to Rauen, France. On 20 December 1944 they left for combat assignment; they participated in three major campaigns, Ardennes, Rhineland and Central Europe. They departed Germany 8 July 1945 for Rauen, France, then left France 15 August 1945 for Belgium where varied duties were assigned at 13th Port Luchtbal Barracks, Antwerp. They were deactivated 6 October 1945.

Charlie is the son of Jack and Ada Combs. His brother, Edgar J. Combs was in the service, stationed at San Francisco, California at the same time Charles was in service. He received his education in Pinhook School in Lutts, Tennessee. Charlie died in Savannah and is buried in Hardin County.

COMBS, EDGAR JAMES, lived in Lutts, Tennessee, where he received his elementary education. His parents were Jack, a Veteran of World War I, and Ada Combs. His brother Charles Henry was also in World War II in the 3rd Army. E. J. married Juanita Daniels of Lutts. They now live in Adamsville, near Savannah, Tennessee.

CONAWAY, ELMER C., Serial Number 34 366 650, was a Private First Class in Company D, ETMO, ASFTC of the Army of the United States. He was born 20 August 1920 in Clifton, Tennessee. His permanent mailing address was Route 1, Clifton, Tennessee. He was single and a farmer. He was inducted in August 1942 and entered into active service 9 September 1942 at Fort Oglethorpe, Georgia. His Military Occupational Specialty was Duty Soldier. His battles and campaigns included the Central Burma Campaign. Decorations awarded to Conway included the Good Conduct Medal, World War II Victory Medal, and Asiatic Pacific Campaign Ribbon. He left the USA on 20 January 1942 for China-Burma-India and returned in 1945. He was honorably discharged so he could enlist in the regular army 18 December 1945 at Fort Leonard Wood, Missouri.

Elmer reenlisted 19 December 1945 at Fort Leonard Wood, Missouri. This time he received the Army of Occupation Medal and a Lapel Button was issued. He left the USA 17 July 1946 for Mediterranean Theater Operation and returned 14 February 1947. He was discharge the second time 17 March 1947 at Fort Dix, New Jersey.

Elmer's parent are Mr. and Mrs. Turner Conaway of Route 1, Clifton, Tennessee. His siblings are Willie, Richard, Oscar (Buddy), Barney, Harley, Annie Fletcher and Ora Belle. Elmer died 30 April 1969 and is buried in Mt. Carmel Cemetery near Clifton in Hardin County.

CONAWAY, MARVIN D.C., Serial Number 34 185 046 was a Private in TR A 15th CAV RCN Squadron of the Army of the United States. His permanent mailing address was RFD 1, Clifton, Tennessee. His Description: blue eyes, brown hair, 5'11" height, weight 169 lbs, and single. He was a farmer both before and after the war. He was inducted 8 January 1942 at Fort. Oglethorpe, Georgia. He was registered with Selective Service Board in Savannah, Tennessee. His Military Occupational Specialty was Light Truck Driver. His Military Qualifications were Carbine MM and M1 Rifle Marksman. His battles and campaigns included Normandy, Northern France, Rhineland and Central Europe. Decorations awarded to Conaway included the World War II Victory Medal, American Theater Ribbon, and European-African Middle Eastern Theater Service Medal. He left the USA on 1 March 1944 for European-African Middle Eastern Theater and returned 26 November 1945. He was honorably discharged 3 December 1945 at Camp Gordon, Georgia.

Marvin, son of Turner and Martha Julian Conaway, was born 2 March 1918 in Hardin County, Tennessee, died 16 May 1992 and was buried in Mt. Carmel Cemetery in Hardin County. He married Willie Ann Turnbo in January 1946. There were no children. Marvin's siblings are Anna, Willie, Richard, Oscar, Barnie, Harlie, Elmer Cleo and W. H. Conaway, Fleeta Conaway Foster and Ora Belle Conaway Graham.

CONWAY, JEFFERY DELL, native of Clifton, Tennessee, was born on August 19, 1924. He died on October 10, 1992, at Central Baptist Hospital in Memphis, Tennessee, at the age of 68 from surgery.

Parents of Jeff were Henry Eugene Kyle Tince Conway and Adolphus Conway of Clifton, Tennessee.

Jeff enlisted in the United States Navy at the age of 17, serving time on the USS Memphis ship from May 2, 1942, to December 3, 1945, with an honorable discharge. Jeff reenlisted in the United States Navy, serving time on the USS Whitehurst ship from July 15, 1948, to July 7, 1952. Jeff traveled the globe while in the Navy. Total time served was six years, six months and 23 days.

Jeff, as a civilian, attended Los Angeles Barber College and was a barber for over 40 years in Santa Monica, California, at Waynesboro Barber Shop and at Weavers Barber Shop in Adamsville, Tennessee.

Jeff married Francis Stricklin of Clifton and was married 32 years. They had lived in Savannah, Tennessee, for 24 years at the time of his death. He is buried in the Clifton Cemetery.

Jeff's siblings are Bill, Joanne, Anita Sue, Noel, Kenneth Mack, Jewell, Raleigh (Boots) and Rufus.
Submitted by Jeffery Dell Conway.

CONWAY, WAYNE EDWARD, was born on August 21, 1928, the son of Gid and Mattie Locke Conway.

I served my country in three branches of service. I entered the Navy and was sent to San Diego for boot training. I was sent aboard the Franklin D. Roosevelt aircraft carrier to the European Theater of war. I left Frank Hughes School in Clifton at the end of my Junior year in high school. I finished my high school work aboard this ship. I served four years in the navy. I came out with grade BMC 1st.

I went into the Air Force and spent one year and come out with grade S. Sergeant.

I decided to go directly into the United States Army. I spent 16 years here. I served in the Korean Conflict. My grade here was S, F, C. I retired from service in 1968 from Fort Knox, Kentucky.

I enjoyed standing upon hearing the Navy, Air Force and the Army military bands play these special themes for each branch of service.

I married Louise Carroll. We have three children: Ronald, Janice and Beverly, and seven grandchildren. We make our home in Orlando, Florida, where we are active in the Baptist Church. My siblings are Bob, Donald, Dorothy, Jane and Ruth. There are three sets of twins in my family. My twin is Jane.

COOK, JAMES, Serial Number 14 041 079, was a Staff Sergeant in the 2132nd Army Air Force Base Unit of the Army of the United States. His permanent mailing address was Collinwood, Tennessee. His description: grey eyes, brown hair, 5' 9" height, weight 133 lbs, and married. He was born 15 July 1917 in Hamiliton, Alabama. His Civilian Occupation was Farmer. He enlisted 17 December 1940 at Ft. McPherson, Georgia. His Military Occupational Specialty was AP and Engineer-

ing Mechanic. He was not in any battles. He received the American Defense Medal and Good Conduct Medal. He attended the AP Mechanic Service School in Chanute Field, Illinois. He was a high school graduate. He was discharged 18 September 1945 at Maxwell Field, Alabama.

COOK, ODDO, Serial Number 44 120 491, was a Technician Fourth Grade in Company B, 66th Infantry of the Army of the United States. His permanent mailing address was Route 2, Collinwood, Tennessee. His Description: blue eyes, brown hair, 5'9" height, weight 175 lbs, and single. His Civilian Occupation was General Farm Hand. His Military Occupational Specialty was General Clerk. His Military Qualifications was MKM M1 Rifle. He was not in any battles. Decorations awarded to Cook included the World War II Victory Medal, and Army Occupation Medal. He had a high school education. He left the USA on 8 November 1945 for France and returned 30 September 1946. He was discharged 26 October 1946 at Fort George C. Meade, Maryland.

COOK, THOMAS HASSELL "T.H", JR., a native Wayne County World War II veteran, he served in the South Pacific during this time. He also served his country in the Korean Conflict and was awarded the Purple Heart during this Conflict.

He was a member of the American Legion Post 19; V. F. W. Post 4969, a life member of the D. A. V. Chapter 22, and a member of the Riverview Baptist Church. He attended Columbia Central High School and Columbia Business College.

He died on Saturday, April 10, 1999. He was a son of Thomas Hassell Cook Sr. and Corrine Moore Cook.

His children are Barbara Gail Cook Moore and Tommy Cook.

His siblings are Kathleen Cook and Mary Cook Walters.

COOK, WOODROW, of Rt 4f, Waynesboro, TN as reported in The Wayne County News, was discharged at Ft. Knox, KY in December, 1945.

COOKSON, FRED, son of Mark and Mary Jane Cookson, was born September 19, 1919 at Siloam Springs, IL and lived there until his teen years. His family then moved to Camp Point, IL, where he lived until he entered the U. S. Army in 1941. After his training he was assigned to an airborne division at Ft. Benning, GA as a base ambulance driver.

While on maneuvers one day, his unit passed through Clifton, TN. The soldiers threw out their names and addresses as they passed the girls on the streets; this is how

he met Pauline Reeves of the Eagle Creek Community. In, 1943, several months after meeting Pauline, they were married.

Within a short time, Fred was shipped overseas to the Fiji Islands in the South Pacific Theater of War and spent about two years. When he returned they made their home on Eagle Creek and he worked for a short time on a boat for Hassell and Dowdy at Clifton. He was then employed at Genesco, Inc. at Waynesboro, until he suffered a stroke in 1974. About three years later, December 22, 1977, Fred died from a massive heart attack. Ten years later, May 17, 1987, Pauline died from a heart attack; they are buried at McGlarnery Cemetery at Collinwood, TN. They have a son, Fred Cookson, Jr., who lives in the Eagle Creek Community. Fred, Sr. has four brothers and three sisters, who resided in IL

COPELAND, CLARENCE ALBERT, Serial Number 44 042 120, was a Private First Class with the 414th Infantry Regiment of the Army of the United States. His permanent mailing address was P. O Box 142, Waynesboro, Tennessee. His Description: blue eyes, brown hair, 5'10" height, weight 154 lbs, and single. His Civilian Occupation was Prentice Apprentice. He was inducted 19 October 1944 at Fort Oglethorpe, Georgia. His Military Occupational Specialty was Rifleman. His Military Qualification was Combat Infantry Badge. He was in battles in Central Europe. His decorations included the Army of Occupation Medal, European African Middle Eastern Campaign Medal, American Campaign Medal, Good Conduct Medal and World War II Victory Medal. He departed the USA on 7 March 1945 for European-African Middle Eastern Theater and returned 11 July 1945. His education consisted of eight years of grammar school and one year of high school. He was discharged 31 July 1946 at Camp Beale, California.

Clarence, son of Mack (William McNeil) and Ella Lawson Copeland, was born 5 June 1926 in Lutts, Tennessee, died 7 February 1996 in Veterans Affairs Hospital, Mountain Home near Johnson City, Tennessee and was buried Washington County Memory Gardens. His siblings are: James Emery, Joseph, William Howard, Elmer (Elna V.), Leroy, Samuel Ellis, and Lois King. Clarence was survived by five daughters, Gail Copeland of Gray, Donna Church of Johnson City, Pattie and Karen Copeland both of Jonesborough, and Becky Fariss of Allisonia, VA. He was also survived by nine grandchildren and one great-grandson. Although a Wayne County native, Mr. Copeland had lived most of his adult life in Johnson City. He was a retired employee of Johnson City Press. He was a

Baptist and a member of the V. F. W., John Sevier Post No. 2108 where he was a Post Master General and two term past Commander.

Source: Wayne County News, P. 12, 14 Feb 1996.

COPELAND, ELMA V., Serial Number 34 361 751, was a Corporal with the 39th Infantry, Company F of the Army of

the United States. His permanent mailing address was Box 142, Waynesboro, Tennessee. His description: blue eyes, red hair, 5'9" height, weight 130 lbs, and single. He was born 7 June 1921 in Waynesboro, Tennessee. His Military Qualifications were Combat Infantry Man and Gunner. His Military Occupational Specialty was Rifleman He was in battles in Rhineland. His decorations included the Purple Heart, European-African Middle Eastern Theater Service Medal, and Good Conduct Medal. He departed the USA on 10 February 1945 for European-African Middle Eastern Theater and returned 29 May 1945. He was wounded in action 15 March 1945 in the European-African-Middle Eastern Theater. His education consisted of eight years of grammar school and two years of high school. He was discharged 23 October 1945 at Welch Convalescent Hospital in Daytona Beach, Florida with a Certificate of Disability. He is deceased.

His parents are Mack and Ella Lawson Copeland. His siblings are James Emery, Joseph, William Howard, Samuel Ellis, Leroy, Clarence Albert and Lois King.

COPELAND, JOHN D., Serial Number 36 519 484, was a Sergeant with the 23rd Troop Carrier Squadron of the Army of the United States. His Civilian Occupation was Aircraft Riveter. He was registered with Selective Service Station 28 in Wayne County, Michigan. He was inducted 19 August 1942 and entered active service 2 September 1942 in Detroit, Michigan. His Military Occupational Spe-

cialty was Glider Mechanic. He was in battles in Rhineland, Central Europe, Egypt-Libya, Tunisia, Sicily, Naples-Foggia, Rome - Arno, Normandy and Northern France. Decorations awarded to Copeland included the European-African Middle Eastern Theater Ribbon with nine Bronze Stars, Good Conduct Medal and Distinguished Unit Citation. He was discharged 26 September 1945 at Camp Atterbury, Indiana.

John, the son of Judge W. W. and Mamie McClaren Copeland, was born 24 July 1921 in Waynesboro, Tennessee. He married Jaunita Warren. They have three children: Pamela, Johnnie Sue and Keith Copeland.

COPELAND, SAMUEL ELLIS, Serial Number 832 66 78, held the rank of EM2/C V6 in the Navy of the United

States. His permanent mailing address was Box 142, Waynesboro, Tennessee. He was born 2 June 1924 in Lutts, Tennessee. He was single when he was inducted 21 March 1943 and entered in active service 28 March 1943 at Waynesboro, Tennessee. Qualifications held were those of RATE and the Ratings that he held were A/S, S2/C, F2/C, F2/C(EM), EM3/C, and EM2/C1(T). The Service Schools that he com-

pleted were: NT (Electrical) USNTS, Bainbridge, Maryland; NTS Gyro Compass, Navy Yard, Brooklyn, New York (two weeks). The Vessels and Stations that he served on were NTS, Bainbridge, Maryland; NTS, NOB, Norfolk, Virginia; and USS Runnells. He was discharged 8 December 1945 at Memphis, Tennessee. Ellis spent 24 months on the Destroyer Escort Runnells. He participated in the battle of Southern France. He received the European Ribbon with one Battle Star and the Good Conduct Medal.

His parents are Mack and Ella Lawson Copeland. His siblings are James Emery, Joseph, William Howard, Elmer (Elna V.), Leroy, Clarence Albert and Lois King.

COPELAND, WILLIAM H., Serial Number 34 903 997, was a Private in the Detachment Medical Department at Fort Francis E. Warren, Wyoming of the United States Army. His permanent mailing address was Route 2, Waynesboro, Tennessee. His Description: blue eyes, red hair, 5'9" height, weight 139 lbs, and married with four dependents. His Civilian Occupation was Truck Driver. He was inducted 22 January 1944 and entered active service 23 February 1944 at Camp Forrest, Tennessee. His home address was Box 142, Waynesboro, Tennessee. He was born 23 September 1919 in Waynesboro, Tennessee. His Military Occupational Specialty was Medical Aidman. His Military Qualification was Marksman Rifle. He received the Good Conduct Medal. He was discharged 18 October 1945 at Fort Francis E. Warren, Wyoming. He is deceased

His parents are Mack and Ella Lawson Copeland (Deceased). His siblings are James Emery, Joseph, Samuel Ellis, Elmer (Elna V.), Leroy, Clarence Albert and Lois King.

COPOUS, JAMES THOMAS, Serial Number 874 02 00, was a Seaman First Class in the Navy of the United States. He

was born 19 July 1925 in Collinwood, Tennessee. He entered into active service 14 March 1944. The highest rank that he held was S1/C. The Vessel and Stations that he served on were: NTC, Farragut, Idaho; USS Edward C Daley; and USS New Orleans. He received the World War II Victory Medal and Asiatic Pacific Medal. He was discharged 7 May 1948 in Memphis, Tennessee.

CORLEW, LEE BURNS, Serial Number 977 32 80, held the rank of SV6 in the Navy of the United States. He was born 6 September 1926 in Flatwoods, Tennessee. His home address at time of entry was Route 1, Flatwoods, Tennessee. He was inducted into service 27 September 1944 in Nashville, Tennessee. He attended a Signalmen Course Service School in the Naval Training Center in Bainbridge, Maryland. The Vessels and Stations that he served on were: NRS, Nashville, Tennessee; USNTC, Great Lakes, Illinois; USS Warrington; and the USS Marquette. His main Civilian Occupation was Student. He was single and had finished one year of college before he entered service. He held ratings of AS, S2/C, S1/C and SM3/C. Corlew was awarded the Signalman, Third Class and Victory Medal. He was discharged in Memphis, Tennessee. He stated that he wanted additional training in Agriculture Engineering after he was discharge. Lee Burns served on a destroyer for six months in the Atlantic. The war was over by the time he went to sea.

After service he entered the University of Tennessee in Knoxville and graduated in 1949 with a B. S. in Business Administration. His first job was with Universal C. I. T. Credit Corporation. He was with them for five years and was a Branch manager in Montgomery, Alabama when he resigned to become a salesman for Burroughs Corporation in Chattanooga, Tennessee. He resigned from Boroughs in 1963 and became a State Farm Insurance Agent in Rome, Georgia. He resigned in 1988 after 25 years.

He and his wife have three daughters and five grandchildren. One daughter lives in Birmingham, Alabama, one in Chattanooga, and one in Rome. His parents, both deceased, were Nannie Bell and William Claude Corlew who are buried in Bell Cemetery in Wayne County. His brothers, Woodrow and Ross also served in World War II. Woodrow was killed in action.

CORLEW, ROBERT ROSS, Serial Number 640 13 42, had the rank of 1 C in the Navy of the United States. He was inducted 28 January 1942 in Pulaski, Tennessee and discharged 16 December 1945. He was in battles in the Islands in the Pacific. He was stationed at Navy Pier, Chicago, Illinois, San Diego, California and Pensacola, Florida.

Ross was born 17 June 1914 in Flatwoods, Tennessee and died 14 November 1985 in Hohenwald and is buried in Swiss Cemetery. He was the son of William Claude Corlew (1883-1964) and Nannie (Bell) Corlew (1889-1967). Both are buried in Bell Cemetery on Buffalo River in Northern Wayne County. His brothers are Woodrow who was killed in WW II and Lee Burns Corlew who lives in Rome, Georgia. He was married 26 November 1953 to Ann Hinson, daughter of Chess and Lou (Turnbow) Hinson. ANN was born 28 June 1914. They have one son, Robert Ross Corlew, Jr., born 21 January 1955, was married 18 September 1983 at Smyrna, Tennessee to Patricia Wright.

Ross attended elementary school in Wayne County and high school in Flatwoods and in Wayne County High School.

CORNELIOUS, HARVEY ISHMAEL, was one of twenty-eight men registered at Local Board Number I, Waynesboro, Tennessee, who was called to active duty and left from Waynesboro for the Reception Center in Fort Oglethorpe, Georgia. They enlisted 30 April 1943.

Cornelius, with a group of soldiers, was sent to Camp Stewart, Georgia with the 565th AAA A/W Battalion which had been reorganized in April of 1943. This training began in May 1943 for a 16 week cycle. Then they moved to the 2nd army Maneuver area (Tennessee), stayed there until 17 January 1944, and then returned to Camp Stewart for further training and restructuring.

Mr. Cornelius, age 72, of Hohenwald, died 12 September 1995 at Columbia Health Care Center in Maury County. Burial was in Highland Cemetery near Waynesboro. He was a native of Tishamingo, Mississippi, the son of the late Thomas Franklin and Ila Lynn Choate Cornelius. He was a Veteran of War World II, serving in the US Army. He was a surveyor and a musician. He made his home in Dayton, Ohio where he was one of the founders of the Dayton Musicians Club. Survivors included his wife, Hazel Dean Aldridge Cornelius of Hohenwald; two daughters, Lynette Brown of Orlando, Florida and Judith Cornelius of Hohenwald and one grandson.

CRAIG, ALFRED T., Serial Number 34 955 116, was a Corporal in the 149th Port Company of the Army of the United States. His permanent mailing address was Route 3, Waynesboro, Tennessee. His Description: brown eyes, black hair, 5'10" height, weight 185 lbs, and married with two dependents. His race was Black. He was born 21 April 1917 in Waynesboro, Tennessee. He had an eighth grade education. His Civilian Occupation was Laborer. His Military Occupational Specialty was Duty Soldier. His Military Qualification was Rifle Expert. He was inducted 2 April 1944 at Fort Benning, Georgia. His decorations included the Asiatic-Pacific Campaign Medal, American Theater Medal, Victory Medal, and Army of Occupation Medal. He left the USA on 4 June 1945 for Hawaiian Islands, left there 29 June 1945 for Okinawa, and returned to USA 5 March 1946. He was not in any battles. He was discharged 29 May 1946 at Kennedy General Hospital, Memphis, Tennessee.

He served in Okinawa during World War II. He was born in Waynesboro, Tennessee, and attended school in Wayne County. His parents are Myrtle and R. T. Craig. He married first Claudie Craig, and they had two children, Alfred T. Craig Jr. and Barbara. He later married Flora Floyd, and they had no children. He resided in Nashville after the war and was buried in the Nashville Military Cemetery. His siblings are Walter Craig, Laura Mae, Charlotte, Willa Josephine and Waughnell.

CRAIG, JAMES B., Serial Number 34 013 619, was a Private First Class in Troop B, 177th Cavalry Reconnaissance Squad-

ron of the United States Army. His permanent mailing address was Cypress Inn, Tennessee. His Description: brown eyes, black hair, 5'9" height, weight 172 lbs. He was born 2 September 1919 in Tennessee.

His Civilian Occupation was General Farmer. He was inducted 22 January 1941 at Fort Oglethorpe, Georgia. His Military Occupational Specialty was Rifleman. His battles and campaigns included Rome-Arno and Southern France. His decorations included the American Defense Service Ribbon, European Africa Middle Eastern Theater Ribbon, two Bronze Star and a Purple Heart. He was wounded 14 June 1944 in Italy and 15 August 1944 in France. His education include five years in grammar school. He left the USA on 27 October 1942 for the European Theater and returned 4 December 1944. He was discharged 5 June 1945 at Fort McPherson, Georgia.

CRAIG, JOE ARNOLD, He was a son of Thomas Ervin and Mamie Lee Branon Craig, and a Veteran of World War II. He was born 18 September 1924. He married 24 December 1946 Rachel Geneva Wright. They had two sons, Dalton Glennis Craig born 3 October 1947 and Dennis Lynn Craig born 31 October 1952.

CREASY, AUDREY, son of James (Jim) and Amelia Ann (Mathis) Creasy, was born, November 5, 1919, at Peters Landing in Perry County. He grew up in Perry County and attended school there, then moved near Clifton when he was in his late teens. On, November 6, 194 1, Audrey was inducted into the U. S. Army at Camp Forrest, TN. and served as a gun crewman in light artillery with Co. C. 755th Field Artillery Batl. After a few months training, he was sent to Europe, where he participated in battles at Normandy, North-

ern France, Rhineland and Central Europe and was awarded the EAME Theater Ribbon with four bronze stars, Good Conduct Medal and Bronze Arrowhead Medal. October 13, 1945, Audrey was discharged at Camp Atterbury, Indiana.

He worked at the VA Hospital at Nashville several years, but left to help care for his mother when she became ill. After her death, he worked at Dana Corp. at Hohenwald, until his father's health began to fail. After losing his father, Audrey began working at Wayne County Nursing Home, until he became ill from cancer. At this time he became a patient there until he died from a heart attack in 1977. He was buried at Praters Chapel Cemetery near Clifton. Audrey was never married; his siblings are Alton, Ocie, Bonnie and Leland. His brother, Leland served with the U. S. Air Force from January 8, 1950 to November 1, 1964, when he was retired with a disability after a heart attack. Leland served in Viet Nam and Korean Wars.

CREECY, ALFRED, was a Private First Class in the Infantry of the Army of the United States. His permanent mailing address was Route 5, Waynesboro, Tennessee. His Civilian Occupation was Farmer. He was inducted into service 2 November 1944 at Fort Oglethorpe, Georgia. He received his education in the Factory Elementary School in Wayne County. He was discharged in December 1944 at Fort Oglethorpe, Georgia.

His parents were Will Creecy (1876-1940) and Ida (Inman) Creecy (1888-1927). He was born 14 November 1921 on Factory Creek, Wayne County, Tennessee, died 2 February 1989 and is buried in McGlamery Cemetery on Highway 13 South in Collinwood. His brothers are Clyde, Jake (deceased), and Lemuel. He had one sister, Ollie Kilburn (deceased). Alfred married Fayetta Butler and their children are Janice Creecy Jackson of Collinwood and Wade Creecy of Lutts. There are eight grandchildren.

CREECY, ELBERT ORLEAN, Serial Number 34 506 482, Elbert was a Technician Fifth Grade in the 1st Auxiliary Surgical Group of the Army of the United States. His permanent mailing address was Route 1, Collinwood, Tennessee. His description: blue eyes, brown hair, 5'7" height, weight 147 lbs, and married with two dependents. He was born 8 January 1922 in Waynesboro, Tennessee. His Civilian Occupation was General Farm Hand. He was inducted 18 January 1943 and entered into active service 25 January 1943 at Fort Oglethorpe, Georgia. His address at time of entry was Route 5, Waynesboro,

Tennessee. His Military Occupational Specialty was Surgical Technician. He was in battles in Normandy, Northern France, Rhineland, Central Europe and Battle of Bulge. His decorations included the Good Conduct Medal, American Service Medal, World War II Victory Medal, and European-African-Middle Eastern Service Medal with four Bronze Stars. He Departed the USA on 20 September 1943 for European Theater Operations and returned 31 July 1945. He attended a 1st Aux Surgical Op Service School at Fort Sam Houston, San Antonio, Texas. He finished eight years of grammar school at Factory School. He was discharged 20 December 1945 at Fort McPherson, Georgia. His occupation since his discharge has been farmer. His present address is Route 4, Box 968, Waynesboro, Tennessee 38485.

His parents are Hobart and Rose Dugger Creecy. His grandparents were James and Martha Woodward Dugger and Joseph and Hannah Stults Creecy. His brothers are Calvin, Lewis, Gene and Melvin (deceased). His sisters are Lessie Walker and Geneva Prince. He married Lucille Brison 21 July 1943. Their children are Raymond Doyle, Dennis James, Linda Newborn, and Wanda Elaine Creecy Rich. The grandchildren are Christopher and Amy Creecy, Leann and Andrea Creecy, Todd, Timmy, Sheree and Robert Mercier and Micah Todd.

He died at the home of his daughter, Wanda Elaine Rich, on Saturday, May 22, 1999. Burial with military rites was held at Shawnette Memorial Gardens near Collinwood, Tennessee. He was 76 years old. He was a retired factory worker and was a member of the Millrock Freewill Baptist Church. At the time of his death, his survivors included: two sons, Raymond D. Creecy and Dennis J. Creecy; two daughters, Linda Gail Creecy Newborn and Wanda Elaine Creecy Rich; and nine grandchildren and eight great-grandchildren.

CREECY, ELVE, Serial Number 34 234 702, was a Private First Class in the 143rd Anti-Aircraft Gun Battalion of the Army of the United States. He was born 11 March 1917 in Waynesboro, Tennessee His permanent mailing address was Waynesboro, Tennessee. He was married with two dependents. His Civilian Occupation was General Farmer. His Military Occupational Specialty was Field Switchboard Operator. His Military Qualification was Sharpshooter Rifle. He was in battles in Northern France, Ardennes, Rhineland and Central Europe. His decorations: European-African Middle Eastern Theater Ribbon with four Bronze Stars, Good Conduct Medal and World War II Victory Medal. He

Departed the USA on 26 July 1943 for European Theater Operations and returned 15 December 1945. He had an eighth grade education. He was discharged 20 December 1945 at Camp Atterbury, Indiana.

CREECY, JAMES CLYDE, Serial Number 34 495 064, was a Private First Class in Company M, 184th Infantry of the Army of the United States. The date of induction was 22 November 1942 and date of entry into active duty was 27 November 1942 at Fort Oglethorpe, Georgia. His Military Occupational Specialty was Military Machine Gunner. His battles and campaigns: Aleutian Islands, Eastern Mandates, Ryukyus and Philippines. His decorations and Citations: Asiatic-Pacific Theater Ribbon with four Bronze Service Stars and one Bronze Arrowhead, Purple Heart, Two Bronze Oak-leaf Clusters, Philippines Liberation Ribbon and two Bronze Stars, World War II Victory Ribbon, Good Conduct Medal and Combat Infantry Badge. He was wounded in action three times, 11 April 45, 2 May 1945 and 3 May 1945. He Departed the USA on 11 July 1943 for Asiatic Pacific and returned 1945. He was discharged 20 November 1945 at Camp Chaffee, Arkansas.

Pfc Creecy was born 5 August 1920 in Wayne County. His Parents were Will Creecy (29 October 1876-17 May 1940) and Ida Inman Creecy (5 April 1888-26 May 1927). His brothers are Jake (deceased), Lemuel, and Alfred (deceased). He had one sister, Ollie Kilburn (deceased). He married Mayola Poag in 1952. Their children are Randall, Vickie Garrison, Tom and Sherri.

He was engaged in farming on Factory Creek when he went into service. After the war, he was employed by "Chrysler" in Michigan for several years. He now lives in the suburbs of Waynesboro on Highway 99.

CROWE, EDWARD P., Serial Number 34 189 089, was a Staff Sergeant with the 561st Army Air Force Base Unit of the Army of the United States. He was born 12 April 1910 in Lewis County, Tennessee. His permanent mailing address was Route 1, Waynesboro, Tennessee. His description on discharge papers: grey eyes, brown hair, 5'8" height, weight 129 lbs, and single. His Civilian Occupation was Manager Retail Automatic Service. He was inducted 18 February 1942 at Fort Oglethorpe, Georgia. His Military Occupational Specialty was Air Operations Specialist. He was in battles in Air Offensive Europe. His decorations included the European-African Middle Eastern Theater Ribbon with One Silver Star and two bronze Stars, Distinguished Unit Badge, and Good Conduct Medal. He Departed the USA on 30 August 1942 for European-African Middle Eastern Theater and returned 26 September 1944. He had two years of high school education. He was discharged 9 July 1945 at Fort McPherson, Georgia. He is deceased.

CROWE, FARRIS L., Serial Number 34 192 999, was a Sergeant in the 224th Airborne Medical Company of the Army of the United States. His permanent mailing address was 1125 Stainback Avenue, Nashville, Tennessee. His description: brown eyes, black hair, 5'10 1/2" height, weight 162 lbs, and married. He was born 13 March 1920 in Wayne County, Tennessee. His Civilian Occupation was Stock Clerk. He was inducted 14 March 1942 at Fort Oglethorpe, Georgia. His home address at time of entry was Route 1, Waynesboro, Tennessee. His Military Occupational Specialty was Medical. He was in battles in Normandy, Central Europe and Ardennes. His decorations: Purple Heart, European-African Middle Eastern Theater Ribbon with three Bronze Stars and 1 Bronze Arrowhead, Distinguish Unit Citation with one Oak Leaf Cluster, and Good Conduct Ribbon. He was wounded in Action in Holland 19 September 1944. He departed the USA on 3 September 1943 for European Theater Operations and returned 3 February 1945. He left the USA a second time on 24 April 1945 for European Theater Operations and returned 15 September 1945. He had four years of high school education. He was discharged 23 September 1945 at Camp Atterbury, Indiana.

CROWE, RALPH E., Serial Number 34 727 099, was a Private in Headquarters Battery, 89th Division Artillery of the Army of the United States. His Description: blue eyes, black hair, dark complexion, 5'10" height, and married. He was born December 1910 in Hohenwald, Tennessee. His Civilian Occupation was Laborer. He was 33 years old when he was inducted 19 March 1943 at Fort Oglethorpe, Georgia. His Military Occupational Specialty was Machine Gunner. He was not in any battles. He was discharged 18 November 1944 at Camp Butner, North Carolina in fair physical condition. Ralph died in May 1956 and is buried in Prater's Chapel Cemetery, southeast of Clifton. He married Gladys Riley.

CULP, CLAUD DEAN, Chief Petty Officer, was born 5 March 1908 in Wayne County, died 15 December 1964 and is buried in the Golden Gate National Cemetery in San Francisco, California. He joined the Navy at age 17 and made a career out of it. After serving twenty years, he retired but the Navy called him back during the Korean Conflict and he served a few more years.

During the Second World War, he was serving on the Hornet (The largest aircraft ever built at that time.) when the Japanese made a direct hit on it. Claude was in the water 45 minutes, hanging to a piece of the ship, with shrapnel flying everywhere, before being rescued. I have read somewhere that the Hornet was so badly damaged that the U. S. Navy sank it with their own gunfire, rather than let Japanese tow it in and learn about the latest techniques of this great ship.

Claude married Catherine Hudson on 3 July 1938. She was born and reared in Springfield, Missouri. His parents were Bennie S. Culp (12/23/1880-3/7/1917) and Anna L. Waters Culp (3/16/1878-8/16/1928). He was a brother to W. B, Alton and Ethel Culp, all born and reared at Clifton, Tennessee.

By Monnie E. Culp, sister-in-law.

CULP, IKE, Serial Number 34 181 332, was a Private in Company A, 399th Quartermaster Battalion of the Army of the United States. His permanent mailing address was General Delivery, Clifton, Tennessee. His Description: brown eyes, black hair, 5'6" height, weight 131 lbs, race - Black and single. He was born 8 May 1915 in Clifton, the son of Sally Culp and Bud Culp. His Civilian Occupation was Handling Cross Ties. He was inducted 8 January 1942 at Camp Forrest, Tennessee. He was not in any battles. He had four years of grammar school education. He was honorably discharged July 17, 1947, in San Francisco, California.

His siblings are Charley Culp, Jim Culp, J. W. Culp, Nora Culp, Cora Culp, Harry Culp, Lou Vina Culp, and Joe.

CULP, JAMES ROSCOE, "J.R.", a son of Elvis and Otta Steele Culp, was born 19 April 1910 near Clifton, Tennessee, died

24 October 1971 and is buried in the Clifton City Cemetery. His siblings were Gladys Culp Hardin and a younger brother named Palmer who passed away when he was seven years of age, James received his education at Frank Hughes School in Clifton. He was a member of the Masonic Lodge, # 173 in Clifton.

He entered the Army 5 October 1942 at Fort Oglethorpe, Georgia. He received his basic training in Fort Riley, Kansas, from there he was sent to Camp Blanding, and from there he was sent on maneuvers at Camp Forrest near Tullahoma, Tennessee for several weeks. While there, he was able

to come home often for the weekends when his family went after him. From Camp Forrest, he was sent to Normandy in Europe. He went into Northern France, Rhineland and Central Europe. Decoration and Citations awarded to Culp included: American Theater Ribbon, European-African Middle Eastern Theater Ribbon with four Bronze Stars, Good Conduct Medal and Victory Medal. He was discharged 19 December 1945 at Camp Atterbury, Indiana.

Soon after his discharge, he entered the Southern School of Watchmaking in Memphis, Tennessee. After completing the course, he opened a shop in Waynesboro, where he worked for several years. Then he worked for several years for Standard Oil Company in Lima, Ohio as a pipe fitter. For the last fifteen years of his life, he was Postmaster of the U. S. Post Office in Clifton, Tennessee.

CULP, JAMES W., Serial Number 34 181 403, was a Technician, Fourth Grade in the 569th Port Company of the Army of the United States. His permanent mailing address was Clifton, Tennessee. His Description: brown eyes, black hair, 5'4" height, weight 122 lbs, race - Black and single. He was born 6 May 1919 in Clifton. His Civilian Occupation was Barge Loader. He was inducted 8 January 1942 at Camp Forrest, Tennessee. His Military Occupational Specialty was Longshoreman. His battles and campaigns included Algeria, French Morocco, Southern France, Rome, Arno, and Rhineland. His decorations included the European-African Middle Eastern Theater Service Medal, and Good Conduct Medal. He departed the USA 1 July 1942 for European-African Middle Eastern Theater and returned 15 September 1945 He had eight years of grammar school education. He was discharged 28 September 1945 at Camp Gordon, Georgia.

CULP, REX, is the son of Tom and Nora Lineberry Culp. His siblings are: Roy Culp, Sue Culp Trull and Martha Lou Culp Craig. After his discharge, he went to California where he married and raised his family.

CUMMINS, CARL E., Serial Number 34 884 588, was a Private in the 6th Repl Depot of the Army of the United States. His permanent mailing address was Collinwood, Tennessee. His Description: hazel eyes, brown hair, 5'6" height, weight 120 lbs, and single. He was born 14 February 1924 in Cypress Inn, Tennessee. He was inducted 3 September 1943 and entered into active service 24 September 1942 at Fort Oglethorpe, Georgia. His Military Occupational Specialty was Heavy Weapon Crewman. He was not in any battles. His decorations included the

Asiatic-Pacific Campaign Ribbon. He had three years of grammar school education. He left the USA on 18 August 1944 for Hawaii and then went to New Caledonia and returned to the USA 9 February 1945. He was discharged 29 March 1945 at 1318th SCU U. S. Army General Hospital, Camp Pickett, Virginia with a Certificate of Disability.

DANIEL, BASCEL E,. was born on July 21, 1916, in Lutts, Tennessee. He was married and living in Lutts, working as a farmhand, when he received his call to be inducted into the United States Army on December 20, 1942. He was stationed at Headquarters Battalion, Harber Defense of Boston, Ft. Banks, Massachusetts. He was discharged on August 29, 1945, at Waltham Regional Hospital in Waltham, Massachusetts.

DANIEL, CARLIE MADISON "MACK", of Lutts, Tennessee, was inducted into the United States Army in

Waynesboro, Tennessee on November 22,1942. From there he went to Fort Oglethorpe, Georgia, where he was processed and issued the required clothing. He was then sent to Ford Ord , California for basic training as a Heavy Mortar Crewman and Combat Infantryman. It was here that he was assigned to the M Company of the 32nd Regiment 7th Division and shipped to the Aleutian Islands in April, 1943.

During the next year and half, he was involved in combat action in the Aleutians Campaign, the Central Pacific Campaign, and the Southern Philippines Campaign. It was during the fierce fighting on Leyte that he suffered the wound that would eventually cause the left leg to be amputated above the knee. From Leyte he was put a ship to the Admiralty Islands were he was hospitalized for a short time then shipped to a New Caledonia hospital. From here he was flown to California and on to the Percy Jones Hospital Center at Fort

Custer, Michigan, where he was treated and rehabilitated until his discharge on October 4, 1945.

During his active duty, he was awarded the Asiatic Pacific Campaign Ribbon, Three Bronze Campaign Stars, Philippine Liberation Ribbon, Combat Infantryman Badge, Good Conduct Medal, Bronze Arrowhead, and the Purple Heart.

He was born on August 3, 1921, to John Robert (Rob) and Vesta Elizabeth Warrington Daniel. On August 9, 1945, he married Bertha Marie Moris, Daughter of Robert William (Willie) and Ola Dove Hodges Morris. They made their lifetime home on the farm that had belonged to his parents. They had two daughters, Brenda Maxine and Glenda Gayle, four grandchildren and three great - grandchildren.

DANIEL, CARNELL N., son of Sam N. Daniel of Iron City, Tn, enlisted in the US Navy and served as seeaman First Class. He served 34 months on active duty aboard ship in the Pacific Area and wore five Battle Stars. November 20, 1945, he was discharged at the US Naval Center at Memphis, TN.

DANIEL, CLIFFORD E., Serial Number 34 375 255, was a Corporal in Company M, 350th Infantry of the 88th Division of the Army of the United States. His permanent mailing address was RFD 2, Iron City, Tennessee. His Description: blue eyes, brown hair, 5'11" height, weight 153 lbs, and single. He was a farmer both before and after the war. His education consisted of 6 years grammar school. He was inducted 3 October 1942 and entered into active service 17 October 1942 at Fort Oglethorpe, Georgia. His Military Occupational Specialty was Heavy Machine Gunner. His Military Qualification was Combat Infantry Badge. His Battles and Campaigns included North Apennines and Po Valley. Decorations awarded to Daniel included the Good Conduct Ribbon, Purple Heart, European-African Middle Eastern Service Ribbon, Victory Medal and American Theater Ribbon. He was wounded in action in Italy on 25 September 1944. He left the USA on 3 December 1943 for European-African Middle Eastern Theater and returned 7 September 1945. He was discharged 6 November 1945 at Foster General Hospital in Jackson, Mississippi.

Clifford, son of the late Plumer and Fronie Gambrell Daniel, was born 13 January 1916 in Iron City, died 11 September 1993 in the Wayne County Nursing Home in Waynesboro and was buried in Butler Grove Cemetery. His survivors: wife, Emma (Franks) Daniel; sons were Coy E., J. C., and David E., all of Iron City and daughters were Margie Brewer and Dor-othy Kilburn, both of Collinwood. There were seven grandchildren, one step grandchild, and one brother, Clice Daniel of Lawrenceburg, Tennessee.

The following article appeared in the *Wayne County News.*

"Pfc. Clifford E. Daniel, son of Mrs. Fronie Daniel of Butler's Creek near Collinwood entered the service 17 October 1942. He received his training at Camp Gruber, Okla., and was on army maneuvers at Camp Polk, Louisiana. His advanced training was received at Fort Sam Houston, Texas. Pfc. Daniel is with a Heavy Weapon Company of the 305th Infantry of the 88th Division.

He was authorized to serve as squad leader without the formality of advanced rank in order to keep his platoon in readiness for the attack on Mt. Battaglea. After being slightly wounded on September 25, 1944, he was moved to a hospital for treatment but was discharged in a short time and allowed to return to his company. Pfc. Daniel has been awarded the Purple Heart and is still stationed in Italy. " .

DANIEL, ELMER W., Serial Number 34 193 018, was a Private attached to SCU 1959, Army of the United States. Elmer was born in Wayne County, Tennessee. When he was inducted 15 March 1942 at Fort Oglethorpe, Georgia, he was 30 and 9/12 years old and by occupation a laborer. He had brown eyes, red hair, ruddy complexion, was 5' 11" in height and single. He completed one year, four months and five days service for longevity pay. He was honorably discharged 20 July 1943 at Fort MacArthur, California.

DANIEL, EVERETT C., Serial Number 34 936 476 was a Private First Class with Company A, 320th Infantry 85th Division of the Army of the United States. His permanent mailing address was Route 3, Iron City, Tennessee. He was born 3 September 1920 in Waynesboro, Tennessee. When he was inducted 28 July 1944 at Camp Forrest, Tennessee, he had blue eyes, brown hair, was 5' 6" in height, weighted 170 lbs and was married with one dependent. His Civilian Occupation was General Farmer. His Military Specialty was Light Truck Driver. His Military Qualifications were, Combat Infantry Badge. He was in the Battles of Ardennes, Rhineland and Central Europe. He received the following Decorations: European-African Middle Eastern Service Medal with three Bronze Stars, American Theater Service Medal, Good Conduct Medal, World War II Victory Medal and Occupation Ribbon. He had a high school education. He departed the USA for European Theater Operations on 1 January 1945 and returned 10 Sept 1945. He was discharged 2 July 1946 at the Separation Center in Fort Bragg, North Carolina.

DANIEL, GRADY E., served in United States Army from July 1943 until April 11, 1946. His rank was corporal. He was in combat in Italy in 1945, and he served there until end of war. He was born on January 12, 1923, in Wayne County. He died on March 5, 1984, and is buried in Memory Garden at Collinwood, Tennessee. He went to school at Middle Butler and graduated from Collinwood High School in 1943. After his discharge from service, he married Lazelle Kelso. They had five children: Connie Lorraine Warren, Emily Rebecca Gobble, Roger Dwayne, David Kirk and Lewis Bryan. His parents were Henry H. and Elda Nelson Daniels. He had one brother, Everett Daniel, and one sister, Effie Bradley.

DANIEL, GRAYFORD T., S2/C, son of Pinkney Daniel, entered the Navy March 7, 1944. He took his boot training at Bainbridge, Maryland and was transferred to Norfolk, Virginia for specialized schooling. He was assigned to sea duty on September 20, 1945 in the Atlantic Theater of Operations.

His wife is Annie Thompson Daniel. Before entering service, he was employed by Fisher Body Co. in Detroit, Michigan *Source: Wayne County News* .

DANIEL, HARLEY M., son of Mr. and Mrs. J. R. Daniel of Waynesboro, TN, spent twenty-two months in the Pacific Theater of War and was in combat in three major campaigns. -,He remembers his toughest action was on Attu in the Aleutianis, although, he was wounded during the fighting on Leyte. He was hit below the left knee and the left thigh broke, also. Harley was an 8-mm mortar gunner with the seventh infantry division and fought at Attu, Kwajalein, Marshalls and Leyte. He was awarded the Purple Heart, Combat Infantry Badge, Philippine Liberation Ribbon and Asiatic-Pacific Liberation Theater with three Battle Stars.

DANIEL, HOWARD T., Serial Number 34 367 696, was a Private with the Detachment of Patients of the Army of the United States. He was born in Collinwood, Tennessee. When he was inducted 1 September 1942 in Waynesboro, Tennessee, he was 22 1/12 years old and had blue eyes, brown hair, ruddy complexion, 5'6" tall and single. His Civilian Occupation was Farmer. He was discharged 6 April 1843 at Station Hospital, New Orleans Port of Embarkation, New Orleans, Louisiana.

DANIEL, LESLIE, Serial Number 34 983 731, was a Technician, Fifth Grade with Company C, 1268th Engineer Com-

bat Battalion of the Army of the United States. His permanent mailing address was Route 2, Iron City, Tennessee. He was born 8 October 1924 in Iron City. When he was inducted, his description was given as brown eyes, brown hair, 5'6" height, weight 145 lbs, single and a farmer. His education consisted of 5 years grammar school. His Military Specialty was General Carpenter. His Military Qualification was Marksman Carbine. He fought in Battles in Central Europe. The following Decorations were awarded to Daniel: World War II Victory Medal, Good Conduct Medal, European-African Middle Eastern Theater Ribbon with one Bronze Star, Philippine Liberation Ribbon, Asiatic-Pacific Theater Ribbon and Army of Occupation Ribbon (Germany). He left the USA 9 December 1944 for European-African Middle Eastern Theater; left there 10 July 1945 for Asiatic-Pacific and returned to USA 7 May 1946. He was discharged 15 May 1946 at Camp Chaffee, Arkansas.

"Pfc. Leslie Daniel, son of Mr. and Mrs. J. T. Daniel of Route 2, Iron City, Tennessee, entered the service on March 17, 1944. He received his training at Camp Shelby, Mississippi, Camp Bowie, Texas, Ft. Sill, Oklahoma, and Camp Maxey, Texas. He has been in overseas duty in England, France, Belgium and Germany. " Married Carlene Stutts on February 7, 1947. They have 6 children: Janet, Carla, Alan, Margarita, Shea and Bryan.

He makes his home on Middle Butler Creek, Wayne County, TN.

He is a member of the Macadonia Missionary Baptist Church. His siblings are: Laura, Lorene, Lester, Dean, Earline, Lois, J.R. Edward, Barbara and Robert.

Source: Wayne County News .

DANIEL, LESTER - Cpl, son of Mr. and Mrs. J. T. Daniel, was inducted into

service on January 25, 1945. He received his training at Camp Lee, Virginia, Camp Blanding, Florida, Camp John T. Knight, California, Fort Lawton, Washington and Camp Livingston, Louisiana. He married Beulah Simmons from Iron City, Tennessee.

Source: Wayne County News .

DANIELS, JAMES DOIL, was born June 9, 1926 in Wayne County, TN. He was the son of Willie and Bertha Thompson

Daniels. He had two brothers: Johnny (Penny) and Alfred Daniels, and two sisters: Shirley Daniels Stults and Bernice Daniels Simmons, of Iron City, TN.

He was accepted for service in the U.S. Army on June 20, 1945. He had just returned to Camp from a furlough with his parents when he was assigned to overseas duty. He was aboard ship for Okinawa when he became ill from what was thought to be seasickness. He was sent to sick-bay on April 30, 1946. As both Navy and Army doctors gave him their full attention, his condition worsened. The ship course was changed from Okinawa to Yokohama, Japan and a wire was sent for a seaplane to meet the ship. When the plane arrived the sea was so rough that the plane could not land. James died May 7 at 6:45 P.M. before the ship

could reach Yokohama. The cause of death was determined as and abscesses of the brain. It was apparent that the infection had developed sometime before the seasickness.

Memorial Services were held on the ship on May 8, 1946 with several hundred attending the service. Burial was sometime later in Okinawa.

DANIELS, JAMES MARCUS, Staff Sergeant, served his country in the United States Army. He enlisted on June 20, 1945. He served in Europe with the 5th infantry. He was discharged on November 27, 1946. He was awarded the following medals: Army recuperation [Germany] and World War II Victory Ribbon. J. Marcus was the son of Monroe and Meda Brewer Daniel. He was born on January 27, 1929. He married Marie Pigg. They had five children: Linda, Darwin, Roger, Roberta and Debra. His siblings are Lorene, Elsie, Essie, Christine, Paul, Mavolyn, Mary Lou Lois and Carmy.

DANIELS, TED K., Serial Number 34 378 441 was a Private First Class in the Service Battery, 916th Field Artillery Battalion of the Army of the United States. His permanent mailing address was Route 1, Collinwood, Tennessee. His description was given as blue eyes, brown hair, 5'6" in height, weight 135 lbs, and married with 3 dependents. His Civilian Occupation was Farmer. He was born 5 May 1921 in Collinwood. He was inducted 21 October 1942 and entered into active service 4 November 1942 at Fort Oglethorpe, Georgia. His Military Specialty was Truck Driver. His Military Qualifications were Carbine (marksman) and Rifle M-1 (sharpshooter). He was in the Rome-Arno Campaign. He received the European African Middle-Eastern Theater Ribbon with 1 Battle Star. He left the USA 2 April 1944 for the European Theater and returned 30 Sept 1944. His education consisted of 8 years grammar school. He was discharged 28 June 1945 at Wakeman Convalescent Hospital in Camp Atterbury, Indiana with a Certificate of Disability.

"Pfc. Ted K Daniel was inducted into service 4 November 1942. He received his training at Camp White and Camp Adair, Oregon before being sent overseas in April 1944. He saw action in Italy and the Anzio Beach Head. He was wounded in the battle of Rome June 16, 1944. He was granted permission to return to the States in October 1944. He spent time with his parents, Mr. and Mrs. Pinkney Daniel of Butler's Creek and his wife and two children near Collinwood. His wife is the daughter of Rev. and Mrs. J.H. Daniels. Pfc Daniel has been confined for several months in

Nichols General Hospital in Louisville, Kentucky for treatment. "

Source: Wayne County News .

DARBY, LESTER W., Serial Number 34 884 597 was a Private First Class in the Company F, 1308th Engineer's General Service Regiment of the Army of the United States. His permanent mailing address was Route 1, Cloverdale, Alabama. His description was given as blue eyes, brown hair, 5'10" in height, weight 164 lbs, and married with 2 dependents. His Civilian Occupation was Welder Combination. Lester, son of John Thomas and Malinda Boyd Darby, was born 24 February 1908 in Cypress Inn, Tennessee. His home address at time of entry into service was Route 1, Cypress Inn, Tennessee. He was inducted 3 September 1943 and entered into active service 24 September 1943 at Fort Oglethorpe, Georgia. His Military Specialty was Welder Acetylene. His Military Qualification was Sharpshooter Rifle. He was in Battles in Northern France, Ardennes and Rhineland. He received the World War II Victory Medal, Good Conduct Medal, European African Middle-Eastern Theater Ribbon with 3 Bronze Service Stars and Asiatic-Pacific Theater Ribbon. He left the USA 12 May 1944 for the European African Middle-Eastern Theater, then was transferred to the Asian Pacific Theater 14 July 1945 and returned home 8 December 1945. His education consisted of 7 years grammar school. He was discharged 20 September 1945 at Camp Chaffee, Arkansas.

DARBY, MARVIN G., Serial Number 34 936 464 was a Private First Class in the Company C, 137th Infantry Division of the Army of the United States. He was also in Company C, 320th Infantry when he was stationed in France. His permanent mailing address was Route 2, Lutts, Tennessee. His description was given as blue eyes, brown hair, 5'8" in height, weight 146 lbs, and married with 2 dependents. His Civilian Occupation was Farmer. He entered into active service 28 July 1944 at Fort McPherson, Georgia. His Military Occupational Specialty was Rifleman. His Military Qualifications were Rifle and Carbine Combat Infantryman Badge. He was in Battles in Central Europe, Ardennes and Rhineland. He received the European African Middle-Eastern Theater Ribbon with 3 Bronze Service Stars and World War II Victory Medal. He departed the USA 1 January 1945 for the European Theater, and returned home 10 September 1945. His education consisted of 8 years grammar school. He was discharged 4 December 1945 at Camp Breckinridge, Kentucky.

Marvin, son of Mr. and Mrs. W. A.

Darby, was born 12 February 1919 in Lutts, Tennessee. He is a brother of Pauline Lutts and Carl Ernest Darby, who gave his life 9 December 1944 in the European Theater of Operations. Marvin married Eva Newborn and they had one daughter, Jackie Sue Darby Ragland. Jackie has two children Tony and Trace Ragland.

DARNEL, LUTHER W., Serial Number 34 373 139 was a Private First Class in the Company B, 825th Engineer's Aviation Battalion of the Army of the United States. His permanent mailing address was Route 1, Collinwood, Tennessee. His description was given as blue eyes, brown hair, 5'10" in height, weight 147 lbs, and married with 3 dependents. His Civilian Occupation was General Farm Hand. He was born 23 June 1912 in West Point, Tennessee. His home address at time of entry into service was Route 1, West Point, Tennessee. He was inducted 24 September 1942 and entered into active service 8 October 1942 at Fort Oglethorpe, Georgia. His Military Occupational Specialty was General Carpenter. He received the World War II Victory Medal, European African Middle-Eastern Theater Ribbon and Good Conduct Medal. He left the USA 3 May 1943 for the European African Middle-Eastern Theater, and returned home 27 December 1945. His education consisted of 8 years grammar school. He was discharged 4 January 1946 at Fort Knox, Kentucky.

DAVIDSON, FREEMAN COLE, Serial Number 34 189 662, was inducted into the Army of the United States on 21 February 1942. He was a Private. He was discharged 15 April, 1942 from the Detachment Medical Department, Station Complement Citizens Disability, 2nd Inf Headquarters, Camp Davis, North Carolina.

Submitted by Russ Davidson.

Mr. Davidson, 86 of Waynesboro died 25 June 1995 at the Wayne County Nursing Home and was buried in Philadelphia Cemetery. A native of Wayne County, he was the son of Alfred Fagan and Mattie Camille Cole Davidson, a retired farmer and a member of Philadelphia Baptist Church. Survivors include one son, Alfred Davidson; two brothers, Russ and Frank Davidson both of Waynesboro and one sister, Elliott Brown of Clifton; and three grandchildren.

Source: Obit in Wayne County News, 28 June 1995.

DAVIS, BUFORD B., Serial Number RA34 999 789 was a Corporal in the Field Artillery Observation Training Detachment of the Army of the United States. His permanent mailing address was 526 Viola

Street, Florence, Alabama. His description was given as blue eyes, brown hair, 7' 1/2" in height, weight 157 lbs, and married with 1 dependent. He was registered with S. S Board No 2 in Lauderdale County, Alabama. His Civilian Occupation was Radio Repairman. He was born 14 July 1913 in Iron City, Tennessee. He was inducted 28 July 1944 at Fort McClellan, Alabama. His Military Occupation Specialty was Radio Repairman. His Military Qualification was Carbine Expert. He was not in a battle. He received the World War II Victory Medal, and American Campaign Medal. His education consisted of 4 years of college. He attended the FA Sound Ranging Service School in April 1945. He was discharged 26 December 1945 at Fort Sill, Oklahoma so that he could reenlist in the RA.

He reenlisted in the same organization with the same serial number. His permanent mailing address was 112 S. Park Avenue, Little Rock, Arkansas. The address from which employment will be sought was Radio Station KLRA, Little Rock. The highest rating that he held was Technician Fourth Grade. He was discharged again 26 November 1946 at Fort Sill, Oklahoma.

DAVIS, CALDWELL, Serial Number 641 90 30, had the grade of Seaman, Second Class V-6 in the United States Navy. He was born 31 March 1926 in Waynesboro, Tennessee. He enlisted 9 November 1943 in Nashville, Tennessee for two years. He was qualified to do general handiwork aboard ship. The ratings that he held were Apprentice Seaman and Seaman, Second Class. His service (Vessels and Stations served on) are NRS Nashville, Tennessee; NTS, Great Lakes, Illinois, USNH Treasure Island, California and RECSHIP, San Francisco, California. His description was given as blue eyes, brown hair, ruddy complexion, 5' 11" in height, weight 128 lbs, and single. He received an Honorable Service Button. Caldwell was discharged 8 March 1944 from the U. S. Receiving Ship at San Francisco, California.

DAVIS, CLADIS B., served in World War II from Wayne County, Tennessee. Cladis enlisted in the Civilian Conservation Corps at the age of 17 and was enrolled on October 2, 1940, in Lawrenceburg, Tennessee. He was honorably discharged from the War Department on March 26, 1941, at Camp Oakridge, Oregon. He was the son of Ealey Anderson Davis and Mary Ann Pulley Davis. Cladis Brown Davis was born on February 13, 1924, in Wayne County, Tennessee. He enlisted in the Army on February 23, 1945, as a private at Fort Oglethorpe, Georgia. He went to basic training from

April 2, 1945, to July 28, 1945, at Fort Sill, Oklahoma, for field artillery. He was honorably discharged on October 27, 1946, at Fort Sherdian, Illinois. His duties were to operate a crane, wrecker operator and truck driver. Cladis was five feet seven inches with green eyes and brown hair and weighed 177 pounds. He received the Asiatic-Pacific Theater Ribbon, Victory Medal and Good Conduct of Occupation Medal. He married Ardilla Leona Holt on May 10, 1941. He was a farmer in civilian life. The family left Wayne County in 1950 and moved to Missouri. In 1963 he moved to Hollandale, Mississippi. Caldis died on January 25, 1992, in Greenville, Mississippi. His body was brought back to Beech Creek community. A second funeral was held at Old Union Church and his burial was in the Worley Cemetery in Wayne County, Tennessee. He had 12 siblings: Bessie, Hester, Arrie, Roxie, Oma, Taylor, Emma, Hazel, Christine, Ealie Jr. and Earline. Cladis B. Davis.

DAVIS, CLAUDE ERVIN, the son of Lewis and Pearl Warren Davis was born 14 November 1916. He served in the United States Army from 1937 until 1939. In January 1940, he enlisted in the United States Navy. He and Ed Goodman enlisted together in Nashville, Tennessee. They were both sent to Norfolk, Virginia for training. Claude was assigned to an Ammunition ship, the USS Nitro. He also served on the USS Charleston and went to Alaska. When war broke out on 7 December 1941 the docks were bombed in Hawaii. Claude was then assigned to a Retriever YMS mine sweeper from Alaska to Australia. This Retriever was sunk in Sidney. Claude relates, "On October 22, 1944, we participated in two invasions Okinawa and Leyte. From here we went back to the States. We did shore duty in Long Beach, California. After this I was discharged."

Claude reenlisted in the Army Infantry, 5th RTC and went to Korea. He was discharged in 1961.

Claude was reared on Beech Creek and attended the local schools there. He married Jewel Pope, daughter of Wesley and Nora Davis Pope. They had one child, Debby. Later Claude married Mag Anderson and they live in Waynesboro. They do not have children. His siblings are Floyd, Irene and Inez. Claude is a member of the First United Methodist Church in Waynesboro.

"In 1990 Claude Davis and Nashville resident, Bud Farmer met for the first time since June 1945 when they were shipmates aboard the Attack Cargo Ship USS Tyrell, AKA 80 which saw service in the Philippine Islands and the Invasion of Okinawa where she was struck by a Japanese Kamikaze plane on April 2, 1945. For 45 years one didn't know the other was alive or near by. A very pleasant day was enjoyed by the two."

Source: Wayne County News.

DAVIS, EDWARD, Serial Number 44 121 857 was a Private in Company A, 2nd Repl Battalion, 1st Regiment of the Infantry of the Army of the United States. His permanent mailing address was RFD 3, Waynesboro, Tennessee. His Description: brown eyes, brown hair, 5'9" height, weight 133 lbs, and single. His education consisted of 6 years grammar school. He was a farmer before the war. He was born 5 April 1927 in Waynesboro, Tennessee. He was inducted into the service 20 June 1945 at Fort Oglethorpe, Georgia. His Military Occupational Specialty was Rifleman. His Military Qualification was Rifle Marksman. He was not in a battle. He was honorably discharged 13 January 1946 at Camp Pickett, Virginia to enlist in the RA-WD Cir 310, 1945.

He reenlisted with the same Serial Number on 15 January 1946 at Fort McPherson, Georgia. This time he was assigned to Hq and Hq Detachment Harbor Defense of Narragansett Bay and New Bedford. He was discharged again 30 December 1946 at Fort Banks, Massachusetts.

DAVIS, ELMER C., was born December 1, 1919 at Clifton, Tennessee, the son of George W. and Bessie Davis. He was living on Route 2, Clifton, working on a farm when he entered the US Army, 31 January 1945 at Fort Oglethorpe, Ga. He was a field lineman with Co. B. 60th. Signal Battalion, serving in the Pacific Theater from 27 September 1945 until I June 1946. Elmer received the following awards Asian-Pacific Theater Campaign Ribbon, Good Conduct Ribbon, Army of Occupation Ribbon, and Japanese Ribbon with I overseas bar. He received his discharge 14 July 1946. Elmer Clay married Zora Lee Davis, daughter of Monroe and Lucy Davis. Elmer and Zora have one son, David Clay Davis. Omer C. worked as a farmer, and later he was employed at the Genesco Shoe Company, and worked 13 or 14 years there, before moving to Savannah, Tn., where he worked for the city, before retirement. He enjoyed guitar playing and singing gospel and country music. Elmer died on 24 February 1990. He was buried at the Balcolm Cemetery, located on Beech Creek, Wayne County, Tn. Siblings: Sheb, Jessie Virgil, Gladys, Edward, Robert, Buford, Fayand Hazel (Jessie Virgil was killed in action during WWII)

DAVIS, EUNICE EATIE, son of Joseph Allen and Matalda (Ray) Davis, was born in 1897 in the Beech Creek Community of Wayne County and died in 1974. Eatie enlisted in the US Army in June of 1918, the year World War I ended. He did not engage in any fighting in this war. He had a foot injury and came out of the service until he recovered.

He then enlisted in the Navy on 20 February 1920 and served until he retired in 1937. He was recalled in 1940, during World War II and was discharged in 1943.

He married Josephine Pickett and they live in Waynesboro. They had two children Carolyn Davis Seitz and Steven E Davis. Carolyn has two children Thomas Shayne and Gregory Keith Seitz. Steven married Michele Edwards, Daughter of Billy and Martha Anderson Edwards, and they have three children Chelsea Jane, Andrew and Marigrace Davis.

DAVIS, EUNICE MILTON, was born on January 30, 1915, on Beech Creek to William Oscar and Mattie Hill Davis. He

was the youngest of six boys and six girls. Soon after his birth, the family moved to Lawrence County, Tennessee, in the Deerfield community. Eunice married Gladys Wilson on March 4, 1939. They lived with Gladys' parents on the Ira Gillis farm on Green River for about two years until Eunice and Gladys moved to the Evans Chapel community on Eagle Creek in 1941. They moved again in 1944 to the Barlow community near Waynesboro, Tennessee. He was inducted into the Army on March 14, 1945, at Camp Gordon, Georgia, and assigned to the Infantry. After six weeks of basic training, he was reassigned to the medics at Camp Crowder, Missouri. On the very day that he left Camp Crowder the Japanese surrendered! From Memphis,

I traveled by troop train to San Francisco, California. At that point they had orders to go directly to Japan as an occupation Army; however, in the middle of the Pacific Ocean our orders were changed, and we were rerouted to Luzon, Philippines. We landed in Manela, Luzon in October of 1945. Eunice was set up to be at a first aid station as a medic in the 199th Military Police Battalion. His company commander was Captain David Hyman from New York. Our first aid station was located at what was once the University of Manela. He was transferred to Hickam Field on Oahu, Hawaii in late April or early May of 1946. After spending about a month there, he was sent back to the mainland and received an honorable discharge at Fort Sam, Houston, Texas, on June 11, 1946. In the Army he had attained the rank of Private First Class. Upon my discharge, I returned to my home on Barlow for five and one half years before moving to the Red Hill community in Lawrence County, Tennessee, on November 15, 1951. He has resided in that current residence ever since. He and Gladys have one daughter, Sandra Hammond, who resides in Hendersville with husband, Richard, and sons, Jeffery and Wade. Our son, Tommy, lives with me. Tommy's twin brother, Tony, passed away on March 2, 1958, at the age of five. His beloved wife, Gladys, died on July 15, 1997. Eunice is a retired farmer and member of the Macedonia Baptist Church. He enjoys gardening, record collecting and listening to country bluegrass music. Due to poor health he rents his 66 and a half-acre farm. Through good times and bad, he thanks God for all of his many blessings. Eunice Milton Davis, Manila 1945.

DAVIS, FLOYD EUNIS, went into the United States Navy in 1942. He served his country in the South Pacific Theater of War

on the USS Battleship New Jersey. This ship was torpedoed. The ship was afloat about 50 miles out from New Orleans. The

next day, seventeen hours later Floyd was picked up afloat in the water. He was discharged from the Navy in 1946. About a year later, he enlisted in the US Army and served with the 2nd Infantry Division during the Korean Crisis. He retired from the army about 1964. During the Korean Crisis, Claude Davis, Floyd's brother visited him, Billy Cole and B. S. Davis near the front line.

Floyd, son of Lewis and Pearl Warren Davis, was born in 1920, died 1986 and is buried near Hartford, Kentucky. He was reared on Beech Creek in Wayne County and attended the area schools. Floyd married Ruby Massey and they had two children Michael and Delisa Davis. His siblings are, Claude, Irene and Inez Davis.

DAVIS, JOHN BRADLEY, was born in Wayne County, Tennessee, on December 1, 1909. He died at Hardin County

Nursing Home in Savannah on Thursday, September 23, 1998. He was 88. Burial was in the Balcum Cemetery at Beech Creek in Waynesboro, Wayne County, Tennessee. Bradley was the son of William Riley Davis and Ferbie Viola Pulley Davis. Brad was raised on his father's farm with his siblings: Arizona, Charlie and Viola, also with his half-sister, Ella Bawcom, and her four children. In 1936 he married Lona Smotherman. She died in 1938. When World War II was declared, Bradley enlisted in the United States Army. He was assigned to the 31st Field Artillery Battalion, 7th Infantry Division. His division was shipped to the Pacific Theater of war, where they saw action on the Alaskan Aleutian Islands of Attu and Siski, the landing on Leyte and the retaking of the Philippines. Brad said he was one of the men that waded ashore at Leyte with General Douglas MacArthur holding their rifles over their heads. He received many military honors and awards, including the Good Conduct Medal, Asiatic-Pacific Ribbon, Philippine Liberation Ribbon and four

Bronze Stars. He returned home after the war and continued farming. He also drove a school bus for the Wayne County School System. He retired after 19 years. He married Annie Elcia Pope in 1947 and together they raised five children, including Elcia's daughter from a previous marriage: Shirley Ann, James Earl, Joyce Marie, Dennis Lee and Bennie. Bradley married a third time to Hester Orlenia Turnbo. They had no children. John Bradley Davis died September 23, 1998. He was buried at the Balcum Cemetery near Waynesboro, Tennessee.

DAVIS, JOHN HENRY, was born, October 24, 1912, to William Jesse and Minnie (Staggs) Davis and lived near Collinwood, Tn. in Wayne County.

John Henry was inducted into the U S. Army, February 18, 1942 at Ft. Oglethorpe, GA. He served with Btry. A 268th Coast Artillery Br. as a light truck driver keeping food and water supplied to the soldiers. He was sent to Fort Eustus, Virginia, later to New York, then to the South Pacific by way of Guadalcanal and New Guinea. He participated in the battles of New Guinea and Luzon as a T/5 and received the following citations; AP Theater Ribbon with two Bronze Stars, Philippine Liberation Ribbon with one Bronze Star, Good Conduct Medal and WWII Victory Ribbon. He received his discharge at Camp Chaffee, Arkansas, December 4, 1945.

He married Nadine Odle and they have two children, Shirley (Newborn) and James; he has a sister Buleah (Davis) Cook. He was a farmer, then he and Nadine were both employed by the Wayne County Board of Education as janitors at the Waynesboro Elementary School, where they both retired. At the present time they both reside at the Wayne County Nursing Home at Waynesboro. John Henry is of the baptist faith and when he was able enjoyed hunting and fishing.

DAVIS, MILAS M., Serial Number 34 501 371, was a Technician, Fifth Grade with Headquarters Company 24th Corps of the Army of the United States. He was born 21 November 1919 in Waynesboro, Tennessee. His permanent mailing address was Route 5, Waynesboro, Tennessee. His description on discharge papers: blue eyes, brown hair, 6'9" height, weight 190 lbs, and married with 3 dependents. Both his Civilian Occupation and his Military Occupational Specialty was Heavy Truck Driver. He was inducted 20 December 1942 and entered active service 27 December 1942 at Fort Oglethorpe, Georgia. His Military Qualification was Marksman Rifle. He was in Battles in Southern Philippines, and Ryukyus. His Decorations included the World War II Victory Ribbon, Good Conduct Medal, American Theater Ribbon, Asiatic-Pacific Theater Ribbon with 2 Bronze Service Stars and Philippine Liberation Ribbon with One Bronze Star. He departed the USA on 19 December 1942 for Asiatic-Pacific and returned 16 December 1945. He attended an Automotive Mechanic Service School. He had 7 years of grammar school education. He was discharged 29 December 1945 at Camp Chaffee, Arkansas.

"Cpl Milas M. Davis, the only son of Mrs. Annie B. Davis, entered the service December 27, 1942. He took his training at Fort Bliss, Texas, Camp Carson, Colorado, Fort Mead, Maryland, Camp Waters, Texas and Fort Sheridan, Illinois. He was on Maneuvers in Michigan. Davis was transferred overseas in December 1944 and was stationed on Leyte and later on Okinawa.

He was a farmer and truck driver before entering the service. He married Ruby Kilburn. Their children are: Milas, Jr., Glenda, Cathy and Edward. Milas Sr., died December 16, 1987. He is buried at Shields Cemetery in Waynesboro, Tennessee."

Source: Wayne County News .

DAVIS, PERRY PHILLIPS, SR., Serial Number 34 524 976, was a Staff Sergeant in the Air Force of the Army of the United States. He was inducted 21 December 1942 and entered active service 28 December 1942 at Camp Forrest, Tennessee. His Military Occupational Specialty was Sales Clerk and PX Manager. He served in Combat Infantry in the Aleutian Islands, with the AF in Hawaii. He was discharged from the Air Force 31 October 1945, SAD AAF, San Antonio, Texas, 543rd Base Headquarters and ARI Base Squadron.

Perry was born at the Davis Farm home on Kennedy Creek in Wilson County, Tennessee 16 October 1910 and died at his home in Clifton, Tennessee 28 August

1989. He was the son of Mary Henrietta, "Retti" Phillips and William Hatton Davis. His siblings were an older sister, Frances Irene Thomas, a younger sister, Mabel Dorothy Davis and a half-brother Nathan Tarver Davis (deceased).

Perry's education started in a one teacher school on Kennedy Creek. He finished high school in 1927 in Watertown. He received his Bachelor of Science Degree in 1933 from Cumberland University in Lebanon, Tennessee, He later did graduate work at UT Knoxville pursuing a Master's Degree in Education.

He served as an Elementary School Principal in Smithville, Tennessee. Then he began work with Ragland-Potter Wholesale Grocery and later worked for C. B. Ragland Wholesale Grocery in Nashville. He served as purchasing agent for CBR for the Army installations in Camp Forrest, Tullahoma and Paris, Tennessee.

On 23 December 1942 Perry Davis married Flora Mae Keeton and from that time Clifton, Wayne County, Tennessee, was his legal residence. After his discharge from service, the Davises opened Davis Drug Company in Clifton in partnership with Dr. J. T. Keeton, Perry's father-in-law. Perry became the first principal of Cerro Gordo Consolidated Elementary School in Hardin County, Tennessee. In November 1950, Perry was appointed to become Clifton Post Office Rural Route Two carrier and continued at this occupation until his retirement on 27 February 1976.

The Davises have one son, Perry Phillips Davis, Jr., Lt. Col. Retired from USAF, who now works for Reflectone in Tampa, Florida, and lives in Saint Petersburg. He is married to Carol Burnette Davis and has two children.

Perry was a lifelong Southern Baptist, at his death he was a member of Philadelphia Baptist Church. His spare time was spent working with livestock and operating the farm purchased in 1958. His chief interest was working for Veterans and their families. He served as a Volunteer Service Officer for many years and spent untold hours filing claims for those "Buddies" and their families. He never accepted payment. He said that the servicemen's service to our country and their thanks were all he wanted.

He also worked with Boy Scouts of America and Little League Baseball. He was active in Big Brothers and was Ambassador of Al Menah Shrine Temple and in charge of the Paper Sale for the Crippled and Burned Children's Hospital for more than 30 years. He also was active in politics and city government until he became a Civil Service employee.

The American Legion and Disabled American Veterans were two of his favorite organizations and he held many offices locally, District and State. He also was a Mason, Scottish Rite Mason and a Shriner (Al Menah Temple, Nashville).

Submitted by Flora Mae Davis.

DAVIS, RICHARD W., Serial Number 34 886 122, was a Private First Class with the Company A 325th Glider Infantry, 82nd Airborne Division of the Army of the United States. His permanent mailing address was Route 2, Clifton, Tennessee. His description on discharge papers: blue eyes, brown hair, 5'3" height, weight 147 lbs, and married with 3 dependents. His Civilian Occupation was General Foreman. He was inducted 5 October 1943 and entered active service 27 October 1943 at Fort Oglethorpe, Georgia. His Military Occupational Specialty was Rifleman and Glider Pilot. His Military Qualifications included Combat Infantry Badge, Glider Badge and Rifle MI 30 Caliber Rifle Sharpshooter Badge. He was in Battles in Ardennes, Rhineland and Central Europe which included France, Belgium, Luxembourg and Holland. He placed firepower where it would assist advancing troops to break enemy lines. He cleaned and cared for weapons and had knowledge of the use of all hand and shoulder weapons. His decorations included the European-African Middle Eastern Theater Ribbon with 3 Bronze Service Stars, Good Conduct Medal, Croix De Guerre Belgium, World War II Victory Medal, and Netherlands Orange Lanyard. He departed the USA on 2 July 1942 for European-African Middle Eastern Theater and returned 3 June 1946. His education consisted of 5 years in Grammar school. He was discharged 21 January 1946 at Fort Knox, Kentucky.

Richard, son of James Monroe (26 June 1895- 15 May 1928) and Lucy Paralee Hill Davis (22 May 1899 -), was born 12 July 1924 in Clifton, Tennessee, died 12 May 1993 in the Veterans Hospital in Nashville and was buried in the Balcolm Cemetery on Beech Creek. His siblings are Vina Davis Mathis, Zora Davis and Louise Davis Hamilton. He was married 7 February 1943 to Ottie Mae Creasy and they have three children: Richard Glenn, Larry Monroe Davis and Janice Davis Greer. He was reared on Beech Creek in Wayne County. He was a construction worker after he was discharged from the service. He was of the Pentecostal faith.

Additional genealogy notes from the records of Mary Edith Wood - 220 Brookwood Drive, Greer, South Carolina: James Monroe Davis was born 26 June 1895 and died 15 May 1928. He was married 4 February 1917 to Lucy Paralee Hill, born 22 May 1899. James Monroe was the son of Cecil Kansas Davis, born 26 March 1871, and Sarah Francis Pope, born 15 September 1874 and died 2 June 1940. They were married 19 September 1891. Cecil was the son of William Carroll Davis (10 February 1838 - 14 June 1911) and Anna Mahula Davis (20 June 1839 - 12 May 1904). They were married 12 May 1859. William C. was the son of Henry William Davis, Jr., (20 March 1797-4 September 1862) and Sally Winchester who died in 1844. They were married 27 February 1839. H. W., Jr., was the son of Henry William Davis (1754-9 January 1835) and Judith Wolmack (17 August 1762 - 21 October 1843). They were married 17 August 1786.

DAVIS, ROSS H., Serial Number 44 121 847, was a Private with the 805th Engineer Aviation Battalion of the Army of the United States. He was born 14 April 1927 in Waynesboro, Tennessee. His permanent mailing address was Route 6, Lawrenceburg, Tennessee. His description on discharge papers: blue eyes, brown hair, 5'5" height, weight 140 lbs, and married with 1 dependent. His Civilian Occupation was General Farm Hand. He was inducted 3 November 1945 at Camp Blanding, Florida. His Military Occupational Specialty was Truck Driver. His Military Qualifications included SS Rifle M-1. His Decorations included the World War II Victory Medal. He departed the USA on 11 October 1946 for ATO and returned 3 December 1946. He had 4 months and 13 days prior service with AUS. His education consisted of 7 years in Grammar school. He was discharged 10 December 1946 at Fort Bragg, North Carolina.

DAUGHTERY, JESSIE EDWARD, served from January 1943 to February 1946. The war was at fifth scale and the United States and our allies were beginning to make progress against the Axis Powers of Germany, Italy and Japan but the outcome was still in considerable doubt.

The Armed Forces needed warm bodies so I joined the Navy. I was two months in basic training at Great Lakes Naval Training Station in Illinois; home 20 days; then two months Basic Engineering School in Great Lakes; two months ship building yard in Portland, OR; two months in Brenerton, WA, on Puget Sound Commissioning the Aircraft Carrier CVE 10 1 The U. S. S. MATANIKAU. He served all of his sea duty and Navy time aboard the MATANIKAU.

The MATANIKAU, being assigned to the Carrier Task Force of the 90' Fleet, Fleet Commander Admiral Fletcher's area of operation was the Pacific Ocean war zone. He went to sea on the Matanikau qualifying Navy Fliers for carrier duty, landings and takeoffs. They went to the Hawaiian Islands Carrier Base at Pearl Harbor, returned to Alameda Naval Air Station in Oakland, CA, on San Francisco Bay. His oldest brother, "Bud," had been stationed at the Naval Air Station in Corpus Christi, TX When they docked at Alameda and got mail, a letter from Bud was a great surprise. Bud had been transferred to Alameda. Jesse got permission to go looking for Bud. Jesse found Bud sitting on the commode reading a newspaper.

Jesse was involved in qualifying squadrons out of Alameda and San Francisco so he got to see Bud a number of times. Jesse's operation was transferred to Ford Island, Pearl Harbor. Returning to Pearl Harbor for supplies and another squadron, he got mail from Bud saying the he had also been transferred to the same base as Jesse.

Jesse's assignments thereafter included Esperito, Santo, New Hebridges Islands, Guam, Marshall Islands, engaged the Japanese at the battle of Finchaven. Then to New Guinea, Philippine Islands and occupied secondary Naval base on the Northern end of Honshu Island in Japan. They got caught in a typhoon in Yokohama Bay. When the war was over Jesse's unit went up the Yellow and into Tiensen and Peking China where they spent Christmas and New Years. They docked at Long Beach, CA, and left USS. Matanikau, got on a troop train for the Naval Air Station at Millington, TN. He met Bud and family there after three days on February 5, 1946.

The old fear of lack of education was a big problem but relief came in the form of the G.I. Bill of Rights. This let veterans go to Night School five nights a week while working fill time. I qualified for four years and this was my life saver. His marriage failed which caused much heart ache and disappointment.

DEDRICK, JOE B., son of Mrs. Roxie W. Dedrick of Clifton, TN, was wounded in action in the European Theater of War.

DEVERS, BUFORD W., Serial Number 34 373 122, was a Private First Class with the 455th Battalion of the Army of the United States. He was born 21 June 1920 in Ethridge, Tennessee. His permanent mailing address was Route 1, Waynesboro, Tennessee. His description on discharge papers: blue eyes, brown hair, 6'1" height, weight 200 lbs, and married with 4 dependents. His Civilian Occupation was Farmer. He was registered with Selective Service Board No 1, Waynesboro, Tennessee. He was inducted 24 September 1942 and entered active service 8 October 1942 at Fort Oglethorpe, Georgia. His Military Occupational Specialty was Antiaircraft

Artillery. His Military Qualifications included 30 Caliber M1 Rifle Marksman. He was in Battles in Normandy, Northern France, and Rhineland. His Decorations included the World War II Victory Medal, Good Conduct Medal, American Service Medal, European-African Middle Eastern Theater Medal. He departed the USA on 5 September 1943 for European-African Middle Eastern Theater and returned 25 March 1945. He was discharged 12 April 1946 at Welch Convalescent Hospital, Daytona Beech, Florida with a Certificate of Disability.

He was the son of Joseph and Maude Wood Devers. He grew up in the Hardin Creek community and did farm work until he was inducted into the United States Army. On return from the service, he lived in Nashville, Tennessee, and worked as a semi-truck driver until retirement. At that time he returned to Wayne County for several years and now lives in Savannah, Tennessee. He married and has a son, James Buford, who now lives in Waynesboro. Buford's siblings are Hugh, Dena, Jim, Ralph, Anna Lou, Della, Lucille, Lona Bell and Emma Jo. Lonna Bell is the only one living at this time.

DEVERS, JAMES MALCOLM, was born 11 July 1914 in Wayne County, the son of Ward and Ikie Morgan Devers. He

graduated from Wayne County High school in 1932, then worked several years as a clerk for D. N. Morrow Grocery Store. He was employed by the Wayne County Agriculture Department until 15 March 1942, when he was inducted into the 101st Airborne Division as a medical assistant. He received his training at Fort Bragg, North Carolina, then was sent to the European Theater of Operations for the duration of the war.

After his discharge in 1945, he moved to Louisiana for several months to manage a grocery store for his commanding officer. Due to a shortage of housing, he

returned to Tennessee and worked with a government farming program.

In 1944 he married Turney Falls from Savannah. They have two daughters. On 27 January 1978 he died in Melvindale, Michigan from a stroke caused by a malignant tumor on his brain. He was 64 years old and was buried in Michigan.

DEVERS, J.E. "BILLY", was born on the banks of the Red River in a cotton farmers shack in Yarnaby, Oklahoma, on 12

August 1920. I am the son of the late William T. and Meda Cole Devers. About 1923, we migrated to Wayne County, Tennessee where I have spent the remainder of my life, except for 35 Months, 13 days, 18 hours and six minutes, which I spent in service to my country from 29 October 1942 until 15 October 1945, in the United States Army. I was married to the former Verna Mae Castleman at the time of my induction. We were parents of one daughter, Billie Jane. I reported for duty, along with a bus load of friends, to Fort Oglethorpe, Georgia. I conducted services on the bus and had several converts. I was shipped from there to Fort McClellan, Alabama, for basic infantry training. The only piece of clothing I was issued that fit were my shoestrings, and I wrapped them around my legs twice. After six weeks of infantry training, we were shipped to Fort Dix, New Jersey to go overseas as infantry replacements. Due to a training accident I was reclassified and sent to Fort Cluster, Michigan, as a part of a troop to organize and serve as military railway police. I served in North Africa, Italy, France, Southern Germany and Belgium. In North Africa, I met the only person from Waynesboro that I saw while I was in service. This was Floyd "Snooks" Merriman. We both got lost in Algiers for most of two days. In Italy, we were attached to General Mark Clark's Fifth Army at Caserta during the Battle for Cassino. We rode trains as guards and were flown

where we were needed. It seemed as though I would get lost and wind up in Paris, France, for two or three days regardless of where I was sent. In Lyons, France I met a nurse that married a Frenchman during World War I. She would cook special food, especially horse steaks and french fries, and slip it to me. I was discharged at Camp Atterbury, Indiana, on 15 October 1945 with the rank of T/5. God certainly was merciful.

Billy died July 31, 2000. He is entombed in Memory Gardens at Waynesboro.

DEVERS, NATHAN, son of Ed and Lillie (Woods) Devers, was born on February 5, 1916, in Wayne County. He grew up in Clifton and graduated at FHHS. His army record is not available, although he served in Memphis at a supply depot for the duration. He married Virginia Hollis on March 6, 1946, in Memphis and moved to Wayne County where he was employed with Edwards & Hampton John Deere dealership and became a part owner in a laundry. In 1948 he became employed with Metropolitan Life Insurance Company and resided in Blytheville, Arkansas. He transferred to Amory, Mississippi, in 1958. In 1960 he was promoted to staff manager in charge of the Columbus, Mississippi, office and took on Andrew Jackson Life Insurance Agency, also. Nathan served on the official Board of the First United Methodist Church in Amory, Chamber of Commerce, Civitan Club, Masonic Lodge, Alderman-at large from 1966-1970, and County Underwriter for 20 years receiving the National Quality Award. He retired in 1981 suffering from Alzheimer's disease. Six years later on April 30, 1987, he died and was buried in Amory Masonic Cemetery. He and Virginia have three children: James E., Patsy and Dolly.

DIAL, AUGHT BOON, Shipfitter Second Class, was honorably discharged from the United States Naval Personal Separation Center in Memphis, Tennessee on 7 November 1945. Signed by J.M. Libby, Lt. (J.G.) USN By Direction of Commanding Officer.

DIAL, JOHN T., Cpl, son of Mr. and Mrs. Walter Dial of Iron City, was inducted into the service 31 December 1942. He took his basic training at Fort Bliss, Texas, transferred to San Francisco, California before being sent to the South Pacific 6 June 1944 for active duty. He is the brother of Lambert L. Dial who was wounded in Belgium.

DIAL, LAMBERT LEEOLIS, was born on October 25, 1925. He died on

August 10, 1979, and was buried in McGlamery Cemetery located near Collinwood, Tennessee. His parents were Walter Yancy Dial and Mary Lucille Montgomery Dial. He served his country in World War II in the United Stated Army in the European Theater of war. He was wounded in the Battle of The Bulge in Germany. He never mentioned much about the war on his return. He and I, Mary June Reeves married on July 3, 1947. I am the daughter of Willie (Bill) Reeves and Etta Mae Melson Reeves. We had eight children born to us. Freda Janette Lee, Brenda Joyce Reed, Robert Leeois, Carol June Daniel, Jackie, Dwight, Ricky David and Karen Ann Brewer. Leeolis worked for the Tennessee River and Barge Company as Chief Engineer until he became disabled several years before he died. He was born and raised on Middle Cypress Creek in Wayne County, Tennessee. He enjoyed hunting and fishing in his spare time. His paternal grandparents were John and Ada Dial and maternal grandparents were Tom and Annie Montgomery. Siblings: J. T, James Herbert, Lawton, Paul Jerome, Billy Joe, Bobby Eugene, Douglas MacArthur, Annie Faye, Ada Ruth, Shirley and Harlon Ray.

DIAL, RICHARD C., Serial Number 34 189 094, was a Private First Class with the 122nd Cavalry Ren Troops of the Army of the United States. He was born 24 April 1908 in Wayne County, Tennessee. His permanent mailing address was Route 3, Iron City, Tennessee. His description on discharge papers: brown eyes, brown hair, 6'1/3" height, weight 190 lbs, and single. His Civilian Occupation was Farmer. He was inducted 18 February 1942 at Fort Oglethorpe, Georgia. His Military Occupational Specialty was Gun Crewman. His Military Qualifications included 2nd CL Gunner, M 1 Rifle Marksman. He was in Battles in the India-Burma Campaign. His Decorations included the Asiatic Pacific Medal and Good Conduct Medal. He departed the USA on 8 December 1942 for India and returned 25 February 1945. His education consisted of 6 years grammar school. He was discharged 5 October 1945 at Fort Windfield Scott, California.

DIAL, THURMAN DEE, was honorably discharged, as seaman First Class V-6, from the U. S. Naval Personnel Separation Center, Jacksonville, Florida on October 21, 1945. Signed by R. L. Thomas, Jr. For M. M. DeWolf, Captain, USNR Commanding.

DICKEY, CHARLES, was born May 30, 1925, at Collinwood. and enlisted in the U. S. Navy, July 21, 1944, He was a Seaman Second Class serving at NRS St Louis, Mo.; TADC Williamsburg, VA; NCTC Davisville, R. I.; 37th USNCB, 20th USNCB. He received the following citations; American Area Victory Medal; Asiatic-Pacific Medal and was discharged, March 2, 1946, at St. Louis, MO.

DICKEY, GEORGE A., JR., entered the US Army on November 16, 1942, at age 22. He received his training at Ft. Jack-

son, SC and Camp Polk, LA. He received the rank of Staff Sergeant. He saw overseas duty in Hawaii, Philippines and Okinawa. After being wounded in action he was returned to a military hospital in Swannanoa, North Carolina. He was discharged in 1945. G.A. was married to the former Orene Berry and they became the parents to two children; Lowell born in 1943 and Betty Jo born in 1947. G.A. died in September 1949 and is buried in McGlamery Cemetery near Collinwood.

DICKEY, JAMES W., Serial Number 34 494 885, was a Private First Class with the Battery C, 81st Field Artillery Battalion of the Army of the United States. He was born 31 March 1922 in Collinwood Tennessee. His permanent mailing address was Route 1, Collinwood, Tennessee. His description on discharge papers: blue eyes, brown hair, 5'6" height, weight 134 lbs, and single with 1 dependent. His Civilian Occupation was General Farm Hand. He was registered with Selective Service Board No 1, Waynesboro, Tennessee. He was inducted 22 November 1942 and entered active service 29 November 1942 at Fort Oglethorpe, Georgia. His Military Occupational Specialty was Light truck Driver. His Military Qualifications included MKM Carbide and EXP Rifle. He was in Battles in Ardennes, Central Europe and Rhineland. His Decorations included the American Theater Ribbon, Good Conduct Medal, World War II Victory Medal, and European-African Middle Eastern Theater Ribbon with 3 Bronze Stars. He

departed the USA on 9 December 1944 for European Theater Operations and returned 6 February 1946. His education consisted of 7 years grammar school. He was discharged 15 February 1946 at Camp Atterbury, Indiana.

DICKERSON, JAMES KENNETH, was born on March 6, 1923, in Clifton, Tennessee. He enlisted in the United States Marine Corp on September 1, 1942, in St. Louis, Missouri. He participated in battles at Okinawa and Ryukyu Island. On November 10, 1945, he was discharged.

DICUS, LELAND M., son of Oscar and Willie Dicus, was born on October 9, 1910, in Wayne County. He grew up and attended school at Clifton. His responsibility was filling orders for the company he worked for at the time he was inducted into the United States Army on February 18, 1942, at Ft. Oglethorpe, Georgia. He was a telephone switchboard operator at the beginning of his army career. After a few months, he was sent to the European Theater where he participated in the battles at Ardennes, Central Europe and Rhineland. He was awarded the following citations: African Medal, Middle Eastern Ribbon with three Bronze stars, American Theater Ribbon, Good Conduct Medal, World War II Victory Medal and European Theater Ribbon. On November 21, 1945, Leland was discharged at Ft. Knox, Kentucky. He returned to his job, married and lived in Mississippi. His siblings are Guy and Ora.

DIXON, CHARLES W., was a World II Veteran. He went to Florence, Alabama and joined the United States Navy in October 1942. He was discharged January 1946. Charles lives at 574 Malone Circle, Florence, Alabama, at the present time.

DIXON, DELBERT C., P. F. C. #34886120, served in China, Burma India

Theatre of World War II. He was with Base 6th Post Office in Calcutta, India. He is currently residing in Collinwood, Tennessee. He is the son of McKinley and Elgin Todd Dixon. He married Octa Lee Brewer. They have a daughter, Sherrye Lee Dixon Hambree. Delbert has one brother, Glenn Dixon. Delbert C. Dixon.

DIXON, HUGHLET M., Serial Number 34 494 874, was a Private First Class with Company A, 789th Military Police of the Army of the United States. He was born 4 March 1922 in Collinwood Tennessee. His permanent mailing address was Route 2, Collinwood, Tennessee. His description on discharge papers: brown eyes, brown hair, 5'11" height, weight 186 lbs, and single. His Civilian Occupation was General Farm Hand. He was registered with Selective Service Board No 1, Waynesboro, Tennessee. He was inducted 22 November 1942 and entered active service 29 November 1942 at Fort Oglethorpe, Georgia. His Military Occupational Specialty was Military Policeman. He was in Battles in Normandy Northern France, Ardennes, and Rhineland. His Decorations included the European-African Middle Eastern Theater Ribbon with 4 Bronze Stars, Good Conduct Medal, and World War II Victory Medal. He departed the USA on 27 May 1943 for European Theater Operations and returned 13 November 1945. His education consisted of 6 years grammar school. He was discharged 17 November 1945 at Camp Atterbury, Indiana.

Pfc Hughlett M. Dixon is the son of Mr. and Mrs. R. E. Dixon. He was inducted into the service 29 November 1942 and received his training at Fort Custer. He was transferred to a port of embarkation in June 1943 and transported overseas for active service. He served in Belgium.

Source: This was in an album of Wayne County news clippings owned by Clyde Bevis.

DIXON, JOHN W., Serial Number 34 039 056, was a Technician Fourth Grade in the 289th Station Hospital of the Army of the United States. He was born 19 January 1916 in Wayne County, Tennessee. His permanent mailing address was Route 1, West Point, Tennessee. His Civilian Occupation was Buyer. He was registered with Selective Service Board No 1, Waynesboro, Tennessee. He was inducted 15 March 1941 at Fort Oglethorpe, Georgia. His home address at time of entry into service was Route 5, Waynesboro, Tennessee. His Military Occupational Specialty was Medical Technician. His Military Qualifications included Marksman Rifle. He was in Battles in the Western Pacific.

His Decorations included the AF Service Ribbon with 1 Bronze Service Star, Good Conduct Medal, and American Defense Service Ribbon. He was overseas 3 years, 8 months and 20 days. He attended the 147th General Hospital Hawaii Male Nursing Company Service School for 12 weeks. His education consisted of 8 years grammar school. He was discharged 26 October 1945 at Camp Chaffee, Arkansas.

DIXON, JOSEPH F., Serial Number 20 457 382, Volunteered and was a Staff Sergeant with Headquarters Company, 1st

Battalion 417 Infantry of the Army of the United States. He was born 4 April 1922 in Waynesboro, Tennessee. His permanent mailing address was Waynesboro, Tennessee. His Civilian Occupation was Tool Clerk. He enlisted 23 February 1942 at Fort Jackson, South Carolina. His Military Occupational Specialty was Intelligence. His Military Qualifications were Combat Infantryman Badge and Rifle Sharpshooter. He was in Battles in Normandy, Northern France, Rhineland, Central Europe and Ardennes. His Decorations included the European-African Middle Eastern Theater Ribbon with 5 Bronze Stars, American Defense Service Medal, Good Conduct Ribbon, and Purple Heart. He was wounded in France. He departed the USA on 12 February 1944 for European Theater Operations and returned 12 September 1945. His education consisted of 4 years of high school. He was discharged 16 September 1945 at Camp Atterbury, Indiana.

DIXON, PAUL N., Serial Number 34 373 197, and was a Private with the Army of the United States. He was born in West Point, Tennessee. His Civilian Occupation was Farmer. His description on discharge papers: blue eyes, brown hair, ruddy complexion, and 5'10" height. When he was inducted into service 24 September 1942, he was 28 years of age. He was honorably

discharged 30 October 1943 at Fort Blanding, Georgia.

DODD, ARCHIE, son of Berry Wes and Sarah Ada Dodd, was born 26 March 1918, died ca 1974 and was buried in the Susan Moore Cemetery on Weatherford Creek between Lutts and Cypress Inn. His siblings were Hillis, Ellis, Barbara, Guy, Warren and Ethel Dodd. He never married.

Archie was drafted into the United States Army but never served overseas because of a physical impairment to his shoulder. He stayed in the service until the war was ended. He was a farmer.
Source: Warren Dodd.

DODD, ARLIE HUBERT, enlisted in the United States Air Force on 8 August 1942, He received his basic training in Tullahoma, Tennessee and was assigned to the 343rd Air Base Squadron for twenty and a half months. He was sent to Orlando, Florida and was assigned to 916 AAA Squadron Demonstration Group Anti Aircraft Artillery. He spent a total of three years, six months and ten days in service.

Arlie was the son of Johnny and Elvie Franks Dodd. His siblings are Pearl Dodd Burns, Jewel Dodd Snider and Irene Dodd Wain. He married Joyce Bates and they have two sons Keith and Marty Dodd.

DODD, ELLIS R., Serial Number 34 189 073, was a Private First Class with the Enlisted Detachment 1881st Service Command Unit of the Army of the United States. His permanent mailing address was Route 1, Lutts, Tennessee. His Civilian Occupation was Farmer. He was drafted and inducted 18 February 1942 at Fort Oglethorpe, Georgia. He was sent to Fort McClellan, Alabama for training then to Oklahoma He had problems with a crippled leg which prevented him from active service overseas. However, he stayed in service until the war was over. His Military Occupational Specialty was Cook. His Decorations included the World War II Victory Medal and Good Conduct Medal. He was discharged 15 December 1945 at Headquarters, Camp Gruber, Oklahoma.

Ellis, son of Berry Wes and Sarah Ada Dodd, was born 5 April 1911 on Weatherford Creek in Wayne County, died 1972 and was buried in the Susan Moore Cemetery on Weatherford Creek between Lutts and Cypress Inn. His siblings were Elmer, Hillis, Warren, Guy, Archie, Barbara, and Ethel Dodd. He married Willa Mae Cummings and they had four children Ray, Josie, Dean and _____ Dodd.
Source: Warren Dodd
(Parsley Note - Elmer not mentioned as sibling of Archie Dodd).

DODD, LEONARD, Serial Number 34 361 746, was a Private First Class with Company A, 151st Infantry of the Army

of the United States. He was born 9 May 1910 in Wayne County, Tennessee. His permanent mailing address was Route 3, Iron City, Tennessee. His Civilian Occupation was General Farm Hand. He was inducted 24 July 1942 and entered active service 8 August 1942 at Fort Oglethorpe, Georgia. His Military Occupational Specialty was Rifleman. His Military Qualification was Combat Infantryman Badge. He was in Battles in New Guinea, Luzon, and Southern Philippines. His Decorations included the Philippines Liberation Ribbon with one Bronze Star, World War II Victory Ribbon, Good Conduct, and Asiatic-Pacific Theater Ribbon with 3 Bronze Service Stars. Medal. He was discharged 12 November 1945 at Fort Chaffee, Arkansas.

Leonard's parents were Berry Albert and Rose Lee Henson Dodd, He married Ora Heard of Iron City, Tennessee. He has one sister, Edith Brewer of Iron City. Mr. Dodd died Thursday April 1, 1993 in the hospital in Florence, Alabama and burial was in the Cromwell Crossroads Church Cemetery.

DONEGAN, JOE EDWARD, Serial Number 34 713 890, was a Sergeant in Company G, 168th Infantry Regiment of the Army of the United States. His permanent mailing address was Waynesboro, Tennessee. He was single. His Civilian Occupation was Electric Arc Welder. His education consisted of 5 years grammar school. He was inducted 23 April 1943 and entered into active service 30 April 1943 at Camp Forrest, Tennessee. His Military Occupational Specialty was Squad Leader. His Military Qualification was Combat Infantry Badge. His Battles and Campaigns included Naples- Foggia, North Apennines, Po Valley, and Rome-Arno. Decorations awarded to Donegan included the Silver Star, Bronze Star, Good Con-

duct Medal, Distinguished Unit Emblem, European African Middle Eastern Campaign medal with 4 Bronze Stars and World War II Victory Medal. He left the USA on 2 November 1943 for European-African Middle Eastern Theater and returned 3 November 1945. He was honorably discharged 8 November 1945 at Camp Atterbury, Indiana.

Joe, son of Walter and Blanch M. Donegan, was born 19 July 1925 in Centerville, Hickman County, Tennessee. He had two sisters and one brother: Fannie Mae Workman of St. Clair Shores, Michigan, Christine D. Sizemore and Winford S. Donegan, both of Waynesboro. He married Sue Mathis and they have two sons Joel E. Donegan of Nashville and Shawn Donegan of Columbia. There is also one granddaughter.

Silver Star Award- Joe E Donegan-"For gallantry in action on 9 May 1944, in the vicinity of Campomorto, Italy. While their Battalion was occupying a defensive position, Pvt Donegan and two comrades volunteered to help an aid man carry a wounded comrade by litter to a point where he could receive medical treatment. Fully realizing that the route they had to follow was under direct enemy observation and was constantly being harassed by enemy artillery, mortar and machine gun fire, these men in the belief that the man's wounds required immediate attention, obtained permission to carry him back. With utter disregard for their own personal safety they carried the wounded man 700 yards across dangerous terrain to a place of safety. In assuring that immediate medical attention could be given to their fellow comrade, they displayed great courage and initiative and their actions are in keeping with the highest traditions of the Armed Forces of the United States. Entered military service from Waynesboro, Tennessee. " signed by Charles W. Ryder, Major General, U. S. Army

Newspaper article undated (The article is a very bad xerox copy of a newspaper

article with part missing. Some errors may occur.) "With the Fifth Army in Italy- Pvt Archie Adams of Olive Hill and Sgt Joe E Donegan of Waynesboro have been fighting with the 168 Infantry Regiment, veterans of more than 300 days of combat, in its attempt to breach the Gothic Line in Italy.

The 168th arrived in the British Isles in February and April of 1942. In its two and a half years overseas it has fought through 88 days of combat in the Tunisian Campaign and has been on the line in Italy almost constantly since landing at Paestum September 21, 1943, 12 days after Continental Europe was invaded for the first time. Known as the "Rainbow" Regiment, the 168th was part of the 42nd "Rainbow" Division in World War I.

DONEGAN, WINFRED SUTTON, Serial Number 34 713 885 was a Technician Fifth Grade in Company B, 276th In-

fantry of the Army of the United States. His permanent mailing address was Box 221, Waynesboro, Tennessee. His Description: blue eyes, brown hair, 5'4" height, weight 145 lbs, and married with 1 dependent. His Civilian Occupation was Grader. He was inducted 23 April 1943 and entered active service 30 April 1943 in Waynesboro, Tennessee. His Military Occupational Specialty was Field Lineman. His Military Qualifications were Combat Infantryman Badge. His Battles and Campaigns included Naples-Foggia, Rome-Arno, Rhineland, Southern France, and Central Europe. Decorations awarded to Donegan included the European-African Middle Eastern Theater ribbon with 5 Bronze Stars, Bronze Arrowhead, Good Conduct Ribbon, Purple Heart, Distinguished Unit Citation with Oak Leaf Cluster and Bronze Star Medal. He was wounded in France 26 January 1945. He left the USA on 4 October 1943 for NATO, left 14 November 1943 for European Theater Operations and returned 9 October

1945. He was honorably discharged 14 October 1945 at Camp Atterbury, Indiana.

"CITATION—Award of the First Oak Cluster to the Bronze Star - Technician Fifth Grade (then Private First Class) Winfred S Donegan 34 713 885, Infantry, Headquarters Company, Third battalion, 30th Infantry Regiment. For meritorious service in actual combat, from 21 January 1944 until 8 May 1945, throughout fighting on the Anzio Beachhead, in France, Germany, and Austria, Technician Donegan served as a wireman. On the Anzio Beachhead he worked frequently under shelling which continually disrupted communication lines and on occasion wounded wire crew men with him. In Kaysersberg, France, he was wounded in the neck by enemy shell fragments but continued with his mission despite his wound. His sixteen months of service as a wireman has resulted in a major contribution to his organization's combat efficiency. - 25 September 1945"

Winfred, son of Walter and Blanch Donegan, was born 13 August 1923 in Coble, Hickman County, Tennessee. He had two sisters and one brother: Fannie Mae Workman of St. Clair Shores, Michigan, Christine D. Sizemore and Joe Donegan, both of Waynesboro. He married Ruby Pully.

DOWDY, J. JAMES, enlisted in the United States Army Air Corps in Nashville, Tennessee on 6 November 1941. I was sent

to Fort Oglethorpe, Georgia and then on to Keesler Air Force Base, Biloxi, Mississippi. I took my basic training there. From Biloxi, I was sent to Shepherd Field, Texas. Later I was sent back to Barksdale Field, Shreveport, Louisiana and there was assigned to the 348th Air Service Squadron. After formation of the new outfit, we went to Fort Myers, Florida and then up to Lakeland, Florida. We were alerted for overseas assignment and went to Fort Dix, New Jersey, then on to Fort Hamilton, New York.

We boarded the Ship (M/S Zaandam-for me) on 12 July 1942. We were in Convoy and as best I could tell there were approximately twelve vessels in the convoy.

Our first stop was at Recife, Brazil. The next stop for our ship was at Cape Town, South Africa. From Cape Town we went on up to the lower end of the Suez Canal and disembarked from our ship. We arrived 2 September 1942 after 52 days on the ship. We went to a camp near Cairo, Egypt. From Cairo we went to Rayak, Lebanon. This had formerly been a Free French Camp. There were permanent barracks, a landing field and hangars at this location. From here we went back across Palestine and back into Egypt out from Alexandria-to Landing Ground #174. We departed L.G. #174 to move out across North Africa and stopped at Landing Ground #142. From L.G. #142, we went to Salouch, Libya. It was from Berka #2 Air Field that the Mission to Ploesti Oil Fields, Rumania was mounted. They got 164 B-24 Liberators in the air for this mission. The losses were staggering - 53 were shot down, 23 forced down on auxiliary fields and 88 returned to base. Davie Collie was shot down on this mission and was interned in Turkey before being able to return to the States. From Solouch we moved up to Berka #2 near Benghazi, Libya, then to L.G. North (Enfidiaville, Tunisia) and then to L. G South in same town.

From Enfidiaville, we passed on to Tunis, Tunisia and were on our way to Southern Italy. A few were able to fly over in C-47's and some went on ships. I was lucky and got to fly. It took me 3 and 3/4 hours from Tunis to San Pangrazie, Italy. Some who went on ships were bombed by the Germans in the harbor of Bari, Italy. Injuries were received by some but no loss of life occurred. From here we moved up to Grotaglia, Italy. At this time we were a part of the 15th Air Force and were working with the 449th Bomb Group. This was a camp that had paved runways and bombed out hangars.

I had acquired enough points to come back to the States and left for Naples, Italy. I boarded the S/S Argentina (Converted troopship) on 25 December 1944 to come back to Boston, Massachusetts. This for me was a great Christmas present. We docked in Boston 11 January 1945. I had been overseas two and a half years. It was great to be back in the States again.

From Camp Miles Standish, Massachusetts, near Boston, I boarded the troop train headed for Atlanta, Georgia. In Atlanta, I received a furlough and it was good to get back to Clifton after a lapse of more than three years. I reported back to the Camp in Miami, Florida a Happily Married Man. From Miami I was assigned to MacDill Air

Force in Tampa, Florida. Then I was discharged at Camp Blanding, Florida as a Staff Sergeant after almost four years of service in the Air Force. - J. J. Dowdy.

DUCKWORTH, MILBURN L., son of Earnest and Leona (Helton) Duckworth, was born on December 2, 1925, in the

Flatgap community on the Hardin and Wayne County line. He grew up there and attended Flatgap School. At the age of 14, he lived on Hardin Creek. On April 12, 1944, Melburn was drafted into the United States Navy at Camp Perry in Norfolk, Virginia. He was assigned to the U. S. S. Mount McKinley and served on this ship until his time expired. The U. S. S. Mount McKinley had successfully completed her first cruise when she was commissioned as an amphibious force flagship in the United States Navy on May 1, 1944. She became the "Mighty Mac" and set sail for Pearl Harbor on June 8, 1944, with S/1C Duckworth serving as lookout. They participated in battles on Leyte, Kerama, Okinawa, Saipan and Japan. The battle at Palau was described as "a naval bombardment creating an inferno of fiery hell. " On January 2, 1946, S2/C Duckworth boarded the U. S. S. Henry at Pearl Harbor on his way home. He was discharged on January 16, 1946, in Memphis, Tennessee. Melburn worked in timber and farmed several months after the war. Then he became employed in 1951 at Genesco, Inc. making shoes. For the next 44 years he was employed at Murray Ohio Manufacturing Company in Lawrenceburg making bicycles, until he retired on December 15, 1995. Melburn and Ruby Dixon were married in 1955 and made their home in Waynesboro. They are dedicated members at Green River Baptist Church and have two children: Randy, who lives in Florida, and Amy of Nashville, Tennessee. He has two sisters, Louise (deceased) and Margaret in Florida. Melburn L. Duckworth.

DUGGER, ELZA RAYMOND, son of Clay and Mary Etta Casteel Dugger, was born on July 8, 1909, in Wayne County. He married Niecie Bunch and they have a daughter, Mary Lou. Elza worked as a sawmill operator at Dave Anderson Sawmill at the time he received his notice to be inducted into the United States Army at Ft. Oglethorpe, Georgia, on December 30, 1943. He served as a rifleman with the 1564th Engineer Depot Company and was discharged on November 9, 1944, at Ft. Bragg, North Carolina. Elza then worked as a mechanic at Hassell and Hughes Ford Company in Waynesboro several years, but left the company to open his own shop. He did mechanical work until he was forced to retire due to health reasons. Elza was a resident at Wayne County Nursing Home when he died on December 24, 1995, from Alzheimer's disease. He is buried in Wayne County Memory Garden.

DUGGER, J.C., was the son of Clay and Mary Casteel Dugger. He was born on March 11, 1921, in Wayne County, Tennessee, in the Ashland Community. He attended school in the Ashland and Topsy Communities of Wayne County. J. C. had 3 brothers and 3 sisters. J. C. married the former Dena Skelton, and is the father of two sons, Don Dugger of Prattville, Alabama, and Kent Dugger of Waynesboro, Tennessee. He has one grandson, Jeff Dugger of Atlanta, Georgia. In November of 1974, he married the former Barbara Chambers. He is the stepfather of Janice Dixon Crews of McAlester, Oklahoma and step-grandfather of Jennifer and Amanda Crews, also of McAlester.

Before entering service, J. C. was employed by Holthouse and Hartup Handle Factory in Waynesboro, and other odd jobs. After returning from service, he worked for Genesco in Waynesboro for 8 years. He was owner and operator of his own service station located in Waynesboro. In 1962, he sold his service station and started working for the Wayne County Highway Department. He worked for the County Highway Department for approximately 2 years. After leaving the County Highway Department, he went to work for Hassell Kelley Motor Company, in Hohenwald, Tennessee and worked for Mr. Hassell Kelley from 1964 until 1970. In 1970, he started working for the State Highway Department of Tennessee, where he became the Wayne County State Supervisor. In 1974, he left Tennessee and moved to McAlester, Oklahoma, where he worked for the State of Oklahoma until he retired in 1990. Since his retirement, he spends most of his time going fishing, gardening, camping and attending the Northtown Church of Christ.

DUNCAN, HARRY GYRD, was inducted into the United States Army in 1942. He was sent to Colorado Springs for basic training, then to the European Theater of War. He was wounded in action in Germany. He was honorably discharged in 1945.

He came back home and married Maxine Shea. They have five children Harry, Jr., and Larry are Viet Nam Veterans, Janice, Elizabeth Ann and Tommy Joe Duncan. Harry, the son of James Whitten and Sina Wilbanks Duncan, was born in 1920. His siblings are Mary Elizabeth, Ruth, Patsy and Polly Duncan.

DUNN, JOHN F., Serial Number 44 121 849, was a Corporal with the 7105th Surrendered Enemy Personnel Administration Company of the Army of the United States. He was born 25 November 1926 in Collinwood, Tennessee. His permanent mailing address was Collinwood, Tennessee. His Civilian Occupation was Student. He was inducted 21 June 1945 at Fort Oglethorpe, Georgia. His Military Occupational Specialty was Operations NCO. His Decorations included the European-African Middle Eastern Campaign Medal and World War II Victory Medal. He departed the USA on 29 November 1945 for MTO and returned 24 December 1946. He had four years of high school education. He was discharged 6 February 1947 at Fort Dix, New Jersey.

John F Dunn, 1 SGT U S Army Retired, reported to the Wayne County Draft Board on 19 June 1945, went to Fort Oglethorpe for induction then to Fort McPherson, then to Camp Wheeler, Georgia for basic training in Macon, Georgia for seventeen weeks. After graduation a nine day delay enroute through Collinwood to Camp Pickett, Virginia for overseas assignment. I departed from Hampton Roads, Virginia on the MERIPOSA VICTORY Ship for eleven days to Naples, Italy. After two weeks in Replacement Depot, I was assigned to the 15th Field Artillery Observation Battalion in Livorno, Italy. In this unit we transported by rail German Prisoners back to Germany. I got my first promotion to Corporal here and was reassigned to 7105 Sep Adm Company at the Prisoner of War enclosure 339 in Pisa, Italy. I remained here for one year, then on 11 December 1946 I returned to the USA on the NEW BERN VICTORY Ship to Pier 13, Staton Island, New York on Christmas Eve Night. The next day I was transported to Fort Dix, New Jersey for processing and was put on furlough and discharged effective 7 February 1947.

In June of 1953 I enlisted in the Alabama National guard. My first assignment was with 464th AAA BN Co B which had twin 40 MM guns and later 75MM guns. I stayed in this unit for five years. The unit was reorganized in 1958 to 107th Transportation Bn (Helicopter). It was reorganized again in 1959 to 113th Signal BN (Depot), Co E. Reorganized again in 1968 to 151st Engineers Bn Co B. I remained here until 1986 and on 25 November I retired from the US Army as a First Sergeant with 34 years 11 months and 20 days service. I received numerous citations and decorations.

DUREN, FLOYD, was born 17 May 1921 in Waynesboro, Wayne County, Tennessee to Clifford and Flora Scott Duren.

He attended Wayne County schools and worked with his father in the lumber mill business.

Floyd was inducted into the army 26 August 1942, serial number 34 366 697 and went into training 9 September 1942 at Fort McClellan, Alabama as a construction foreman. On 13 April 1943 he sailed to Northern Africa, from there to Sicily and into the campaigns of Naples-Foggia, Rome-arno, Rhineland, Central France and Central Europe. He was hospitalized twice with scraphnel- 17 November 1944 in France and by his truck exploding in Germany. Sgt Duren served 3 years, 2 months and 14 days with Co A, 111th Combat Engineers Battalion. He was discharged 9 November 1945 at Camp Atterbury, Indiana. Decorations awarded to Duren included the European-African Middle Eastern Theater Ribbon with 5 Bronze Stars, Bronze Arrowhead, Good Conduct Ribbon, 2 Purple Hearts, World War II Victory Medal, Distinguish Unit Citation, and Bronze Star.

On November 21, 1947 Floyd married Frankie Duren Lynn. David Michael Duren was born July 26, 1949. This family lived on upper Green River in the 7th District in Wayne County.

David married Christine Moore of Wayne County in November 1967. Their children are Christi Michelle Duren born March 4, 1970, and Michael Wayne Duren born September 4, 1971. Christi is married to Ricky Giles Rice who is a teacher and football coach at Lake County High School. Michael is doing custom work with heavy equipment and farming with his father David. At this time David is married to Cindy Spencer, Extension Agent for Wayne County. She has a son, Christopher Spencer,

Floyd Duren was killed in an automobile accident as he was driving to work February 8, 1981 at the entrance of Lincoln Brass Works in Waynesboro. He was 69 years old. He was buried in Shields Cemetery with full military rites preformed by the Home Guard of Wayne County.

A Memorial Service was held in Louisville, Kentucky June 23, 1991 for 15 of the 36th Division Veterans of which Floyd was one. As Floyd's wife, Frankie was unable to attend the service, Floyd's Captain, James Muller placed a flag for Floyd.

DUREN, SAM, whose wife, Dorothy, resides at Rt 6, Waynesboro, TN, worked as a farmer at the time he was inducted into the US Army. He was promoted to Sergeant and assigned assistant squad leader. He actively engaged in the Western European Theater.

EATON, CHARLIE M., son of FS and Lizzie Eaton, was born 1907 in Wayne County, died 1952 and is buried in Mt. Hebron Cemetery. Southeast of Rayborn and Indian Creeks. His siblings are Don Eaton and Louise Eaton Ellis.

EATON, DON, Serial Number 34 185 054, was a Private in 741st Tank Battalion, Service Company of the United States Army. His permanent mailing address was RFD 2, Waynesboro, Tennessee. He was divorced when he entered service. His Civilian Occupation was Truck Driver. His education consisted of 8 years grammar school. He was inducted 8 January 1942 at Ft. Oglethorpe, Georgia. His Military Occupational Specialty was Ammunition Handler. His Military Qualification was Rifle Marksman. His Battles and Campaigns included the Normandy Campaign. Honors awarded to Eaton included a Presidential Citation and the European- African Middle Eastern Service Ribbon. He was discharged 31 May 1945 at Wakeman Hospital Center in Camp Atterbury, Indiana With a Certificate of Disability. Don, son of F. S. and Lizzie Eaton, was born 10 October 1913 in the Houston Community of Wayne County, Tennessee, died 20 January 1970 at age 52 and is buried in Mt. Hebron Cemetery, Southeast of the

confluence of Rayborn and Indian Creeks. His siblings are Charlie M. Eaton and Louise Eaton Ellis.

EATON, JAMES REX, Serial Number 34 043 128, was a Private First Class with Headquarters Company Detachment

P 6995th Guard Company of the United States Army. Mr. Eaton volunteered for service 25 April 1941 at Fort Oglethorpe, Georgia and received his training at Camp Wheeler and Camp Benning, Georgia. He was sent to Fort Meade, Maryland and was then transferred overseas 22 March 1944 aboard the ship, HENRY GIBBONS. He landed in Northern Ireland, then was sent to England and then on to France and Worms, Germany. He was in the Normandy Campaign and Central Europe. He received the European Theater Operations Ribbon, Good Conduct Ribbon, Pre-Pearl Harbor Ribbon, Expert Infantryman Badge, three Bronze Stars, the American Defense Service Medal and the European African Middle Eastern Theater Ribbon. He was a Military Policeman and spent eighteen months overseas in the Quartermaster Corps. He received an Honorable Discharged 9 August 1945 at Camp Atterbury, Indiana. After returning home, he was a machinist at Bower Roller Bearing in Detroit, Michigan for 21 years. He is now retired and lives at Route 4, Box 750, Waynesboro, Tennessee 38484. James R., son of Joecephus and Tennie (Stowe) Eaton, was born 22 August 1916 in Lutts, Tennessee. He has two brothers, Grady and Luther. He also has two sisters, Esther and Edith. He married Clara Caroline Bratton, 3 February 1943. They had four children, One son, James Rex Eaton, Jr., died at age seven months. (Mr. Eaton never saw his son.) and three daughters Carolyn Sue Eaton Kelley, Judie Fay Eaton Collins and Deborah Ann Eaton Clark.

EDDY, CILDON DAVID, entered the Army July 28, 1944 and he was stationed

at Camp Selby, MS, and Camp Walters, TX, before being shipped over seas. He rose to the rank of PFC during the Goverman and European campaigns. He was involved in the destruction of the Sig Froid Line. He was honorably discharged October 31, 1945.

He earned the following decoration and citations; Bronze Star, Theater Campaign Medal, Purple Heart.

EDWARDS, BLUFORD E., was born in 1905 to Mark Ples and Minnie Devers Edwards on Edwards Branch that flows

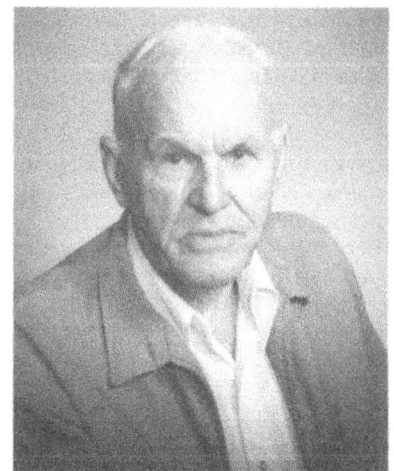

into Buffalo River near Topsy. He had three brothers; Clifford, Hubert and Rankin and one sister, Vesta Stults. Mr. Edwards went into service in 1942. Before he enlisted he was an automobile mechanic, in the service he was an equipment mechanic. He was discharged the 20th of March 1944. After that he helped young people to get started in life because he began his career in Wayne County. Many students from Wayne County have already received B. E. Edwards Scholarships from an endowment that he established in the late seventies. Before Mr. Edwards death in 1990, he gave the University of Tennessee a large farm located off Highway 64 near Natchez Trace. It is currently being used for pasture and research. With additional endowments that are now being established more Wayne and other county students will benefit from his generosity.

EDWARDS, CHARLES WILLIAM,

"I am Charles William Edwards. My wife, Blanche Cole Edwards, and I live at 720

South Main Street in Waynesboro, Tennessee. My parents were Horace and Bessie Edwards who lived in Waynesboro until their death. In 1941, at the age of seventeen, I went to Detroit. Michigan, looking for work. At that time I was registered at the Wayne County, Tennessee Local Board. My work in Detroit was Surface Grinder operator doing work for Defense. In March of 1943 I got my call for the service from the Waynesboro Local Board. I went to the Local Board in Detroit and had my records transferred up there. On 2 April 1943, I was inducted into the service and was assigned to the Army Air Force. I took my basic training in Miami Beach, Florida, and then was stationed at Pope Air Force Base in North Carolina. There I had my schooling and stayed until I went to the European Theater of Operations. I was stationed at Nottingham and Reading, England, then St. Ginivieve, France. My Military record is enclosed. After service I took flying school under the G. I. Bill. I flew around for a while, then I worked for the Natchez Trace Parkway and helped build it. Then I helped wire the Genesco Factory here in Waynesboro. I had a radio and T. V. business for two or three years and then worked at the Airport in Birmingham, Alabama, repairing Military Aircraft radio. While working for the same company, I went into the beginning of the Space Program. A friend and I wired the first panels for the Red Stone Rocket that was the beginning of the Space Program. I worked through the Saturn and Apollo program, and for American Biltrite which later became Dana Corporation in 1960. I retired in 1989.

"Charles W. Edwards An abstract of Charles's Military record - Serial Number 36 592 842, was a Corporal in 76th Troop Carrier Squadron, 451st Troop Carrier Group of the Army Air Force of the United States. His permanent mailing address was RFD 2, Waynesboro, Tennessee. His Description: blue eyes, brown hair, 5'8 1/2" height, weight 121 lbs, and single. His education consisted of 2 years of high school. He was inducted 2 April 1943 and entered into active service 9 April 1943 at Detroit, Michigan. His Military Occupational Specialty was Telephone Switchboard Operator. His battles and campaigns included Rome-Arno, Rhineland, Southern France, Northern France, Central Europe, Ardennes and Normandy. Decorations awarded to Edwards included the Distinguished Unit Badge, Good Conduct Medal, European African Middle Eastern Service Medal with one Silver Star and two Bronze Stars. He was awarded a Bronze Star for each of the above named battles. He left the USA on 21 October 1943 for European Theater Operations and returned 2 August 1945. He was discharged 11 September 1945 at Fort McPherson, Georgia.

EDWARDS, CLARENCE HAROLD,

Serial Number 977 28 80, was a Specialist (I) Third Class in The United States Navy.

His service time was spent at Williamsburg, Virginia; Indianhead, Maryland and Washington, D. C. from 29 July 1944 to 3 July 1946. While serving in the Navy, he received a Victory Medal and American Theater Medal. He entered active service 29 July 1944 and was discharged 2 July 1946 from U. S. Naval Personnel Separation Center in Memphis, Tennessee. Harold, son of Lovic David and Naomi (Gallaher) Edwards, was born 11 October 1923 in Ruppertown, Lewis County, Tennessee. His siblings are Charles Gerald (deceased). Lemuel Eugene and Betty Jo Edwards Cook. He married Nancy Catherine Gillis and they have two daughters, Anna

Catherine Edwards Galbreath and Carole Jean Edwards Crews.

EDWARDS, ENIS O., Serial Number 36 545 633, was a Technician Fourth Grade in Headquarters Detachment, 120th Medical Battalion of the Army of the United States. His permanent mailing address was 407 Perry St, Hicksville, Ohio. His Description: blue eyes, brown hair, 5'10 1/2" height, and weight 160 lbs. His Civilian Occupation was Automobile Mechanic. He was born 6 March 1916 in Waynesboro, Tennessee. His education consisted of 3 years high school. He was inducted 19 November 1942 and entered into active service 1 December 1942 in Detroit, Michigan. His Military Occupational Specialty was Auto Mechanic. His battles and campaigns included Rhineland and Central Europe. Decorations awarded to Edwards included the European African Middle Eastern Service Ribbon, Good Conduct Ribbon, American Theater Ribbon and World War II Victory Medal. He was overseas for 11 months and 7 days. He was discharged 14 November 1945 at Camp Bowie, Texas.

EDWARDS, JAMES DALBERT, Serial Number 965 96 58, was a Seaman First Class in the United States Navy. He was born 24 February 1924 in Waynesboro, Tennessee. He was inducted 15 November 1943 and entered active service 22 November 1943 in Waynesboro. He was single. He held the following ratings: AS S2/C, and S1/C. Stations and Vessels where he served were: NTB Great Lakes, Illinois; Phib Trs Base, Solomons, Maryland; and USS Tuscaloosa. His last employer before entering service was farming with Emory Middleton, Route 1, Waynesboro. Dalbert was discharged 15 December 1945 from U. S. Naval Personnel Separation Center in Memphis, Tennessee.

EDWARDS, RANKIN, son of Pleas and Minnie Dever Edwards, was born on October 14, 1907, in Wayne County. He had three brothers; Clifford, Hubert and Bluford and one sister, Vesta Stults. He married Mary Lowery of Wayne County, and they have two children, James and Eva Jean. He later married Grace Keeton, and they have three children. He was working as a mechanic at the time he was inducted into the United States Army on September 22, 1942, in Nashville. He served as a cook with the 554th Army Air Base and was discharged at Kennedy General Hospital in Memphis, Tennessee. He now resides in Nashville.

ELLISON, J.T., son of James and Elsie (Bums) Ellison, was born, June 9, 1924,

in Jefferson County, AL. He attended school at Warrior, AL. April 15, 1942, he enlisted in the United States Navy and served on the U.S.S. Saratoga. He was discharged, August 24, 1947, at Norfolk, VA with the following decorations; Purple Heart, Asiatic-Pacific Ribbon with eight stars, Victory Medal and Good Conduct Ribbon.

After the war J.T. worked in Michigan, then married Osa Monetta White of Wayne County, February 14, 1954; she is the daughter of Willie and Osa White. J. T. and Osa Monetta lived in Michigan several years, where he worked at construction. They moved to AL, and he worked there until 1983, when he retired and moved to the Eagle Creek Community in Wayne County, TN. J. T. became ill from emphysema, heart problems and a stroke. He died, March 15, 1999, and is buried at Knollwood Cemetery at Canton, MI.

J.T. and Osa Monetta, have three children, Janice Mullins of Waynesboro, TN, Curtis Mitchell Ellison of the Eagle Creek Community and Martha Ann Heimendinger of MI.

ESTES, CARLTON W., was born 2 February 1924, and entered the United States Army Air Corps, 27 March 1943.

His foreign service was with the 20th Air Force in Guam and Mariana Islands. He was discharged as a S/Sgt 6 Oct 1946 and assigned to Air Corps Reserve on 7 October 1946. Carlton enlisted in the Tennessee National Guard on 7 April 1947 and was commissioned 2nd Lt CE 18 November 1948. He completed a basic officer course at Fort Belvoir, Virginia 22 Feb 1951. He served three months A. D. "Operation Longhorn" in Fort Hood, Texas. He was promoted to 1st LT CE, 1 March 1952. Carlton organized and commanded Waynesboro National Guard Company in June 1955. He was promoted to Captain CE 5 Dec 1955. Then he was assigned to Hq 4/117 (M) Inf in Henderson, Tennessee and was promoted to Major Inf 19 March 1965. He was transferred to Retired Reserve 19 March 1965 and placed on U. S. Army retired list 2 February 1984 with a total Federal Service record of 40 years, 8 months and 5 days.

EVANS, LLOYD M., was a Private First Class in 558th Antiaircraft Artillery of the Army of the United States. His permanent mailing address was RFD 6, Lawrenceburg, Tennessee. His Description: green eyes, brown hair, 5'9" height, and weight 163 lbs. His Civilian Occupation was Fire Lookout. He was born 9 May 1924 in Nashville, Tennessee. He was inducted 5 October 1943 and entered into active service 27 October 1943 at Ft. Oglethorpe, Georgia. His home address at time of entry was Route 5, Waynesboro, Tennessee. His Military Occupational Specialty was Light Truck Driver. His Military Qualification was Rifle SS. His battles and campaigns included Rhineland and Central Europe. Decorations awarded to Evans included American Theater Ribbon, European African Middle Eastern Theater Ribbon with 2 Bronze Stars, Good Conduct Medal, and World War II Victory Medal. He left the USA on 30 October 1944 for European Theater Operations and returned 25 April 1946. He was discharged 1 May 1946 at Camp Atterbury, Indiana.

EVANS, THOMAS, was a Private First Class in HQ Company 134th Infantry Regiment with 35th Infantry Division of the Army of the United States. He entered into active service 15 April 1944 from Bedford, Lawrence County, Indiana. His Military Qualification was Combat Infantryman. His battles and campaigns included France, Belgium and Luxembourg. Decorations awarded to Evans not listed but must have included the Purple Heart and other Medals. He was wounded in left leg in action in Luxembourg on 5 January 1945. He returned to active duty as a Hospital Ward Aide in the 21st General Hos-

pital at Nancy, France, where he was when the war ended. He received a medical discharge 11 November 1945. Thomas, son of Wyatt Lemuel "Lam: and Irma Baker Evans, was born 26 August 1906 in Clifton, Tennessee, died 8 August 1980 and was buried in Bennett Cemetery in Avoca, Lawrence County, Indiana. He had one sister, Katherine Evans (1911-1924). His mother, Irma Baker, was the daughter of T.A. Baker. As a young man, Thomas was taught the stonecutter trade by his father and his uncle, Henry A. Evans. They were employed by the Beasley Monument Company in Clifton, and relocated to Paducah, Kentucky when the Beasley Company moved. Thomas went to Lawrence County, Indiana about 1929 to work in the limestone quarries and stone mills as a stonecutter and stone carver. He returned to Wayne County, Tennessee several times and always had warm thoughts of friends and relatives in and around Clifton, Savannah and Waynesboro. After returning from his army service, Thomas was the town marshall Ooletic, Lawrence County, Indiana until 1960. He, then, accepted employment as custodian at Ooletic Elementary and High School until he retired in the early 1970s.

FAIRRIS, EVERETTE EDWARD, was born, January 17, 1917, to Witt and Iva (Ferguson) Fairris at Metropolis, 11 in

Massac County. They moved to Mayfield, KY in Graves County and lived there until Edd graduated from high school. He and his mother moved to Detroit, MI, where Edd enrolled in college and worked at Ford Motor Co. March 24, 1944, he entered the U. S. Army Air Force and served as a Cpl. with Co. 3705 as an air force tech. He trained as an airplane engine mechanic and was discharged, March 27, 1946, at Ft. Logan, CO. He received the following citations; WWII Victory Medal, American Victory and Good Conduct Medals.

After his discharge from the air force,

Edd again enrolled in college at Detroit. His first job was with a radio station at Dallas, TX. The day President Kennedy was killed, Edd was on a bridge covering the parade. Sometime later he was visiting his mother at Lawrenceburg, TN, when Joe Sevier heard that he was an electronic engineer and hired him to manage his TV Shop at Waynesboro.

After several months, William Thomas Helton, hired him to construct and manage a radio station at Waynesboro. He hired Neal Jones as a disc jockey and together they put Radio Station WAAN on the air. The station grew and was very popular several years under their leadership. Edd was the first electronic instructor at Wayne County Vocational School for five years. After his resignation, this position was filled by his step-grandson, Bronson Berry.

Edd had worked with the Wayne County Emergency Unit many years, assisting Bill Askins, Banker at The Bank of Waynesboro, with the organization and building of the unit. When Mr. Askins, health began to decline due to heart problems, Edd devoted full time to the managing of the unit as long as his health permitted.

January 17, 1966, Edd an Lurlean (Lee) Risner were married and made their home on Woodtown Street in Waynesboro. Edd's health began to fail and he died, November 9, 1998, from a bout of pneumonia and heart failure. He is buried at Wayne County Memory Garden.

He has a son by a previous marriage, Marion Thomas Fairris, who lives at Tucker, GA; he has four grandchildren. His five stepchildren are Fred Risner, June Warren, Morris Risner (deceased), Gail Berry, Fonda Corn and Patricia Beckham.

FALLS, FLOYD EDWARD, Serial Number 845 67 05, Rating SIC,SV6, entered into service on 8 July 1943 and into

active service 15 July 1943. He held ratings AS, S2C, and SIC. He served on Vessels and Stations as follows: NRS, Chatta-

nooga, Tennessee; NTS, San Diego, California; Navy Per Distr Center, Pleasanton, California, USS REPUBLIC; USNH Treasure Island, San Francisco, USS HENRY A. WILEY (DM-29), R/S San Francisco, California; and NTS, NOB Norfolk, Virginia. He served in the Ordnance Department. Floyd was awarded the Asiatic Pacific Medal with 3 Stars, World War II Victory Medal, and American Area Medal. He worked as an auto mechanic before entering the service. He was honorably discharged from U. S. Naval Personnel Separation Center in Toledo, Ohio on 30 December 1945. Floyd came home on the USS HENRY A. WILEY DM-29. This ship was presented the Presidential Unit Citation by the President of the United States. It read, "For heroic service fulfilling each assigned mission on schedule, she emerged without damage from every contact with the enemy. By her efficient protection of mine sweeping units, her brilliant performance on radar picket and her accurate gunfire, the HENRY A. WILEY contributed essentially to the success of the forces. Her gallant service throughout the Okinawa Operation attests the valor, skill and devotion to duty of her officers and men and sustains the highest tradition of the United States Naval Service. " Signed by James Forrestal, Secretary of the Navy, for the President. He stated, "You have served in the greatest Navy in the world. It crushed two enemy fleets at once, receiving their surrender only four months apart. It brought our land-based air power within bombing range of the enemy, and set our grand armies on the beach heads of final victory. It performed the multitude of tasks necessary to support these military operations. No other Navy at any time has done so much. For your part in these achievements, you deserve to be proud as long as you live. The nation which you served at a time of crisis will remember you with gratitude. The best wishes of the Navy go with you into civilian life. Good luck. "Floyd also received a Letter from the Chief of Naval Personnel saying that the Citation had been awarded the USS Henry A. Wiley. He received the Facsimile of Citation and Insignia - Ribbon, bar and star- and that by virtue of his service on the Henry A Wiley during the period from 23 March 1945 to 24 June 1945 that he was authorized to wear as part of his uniform the Presidential Unit Citation with a Star. Floyd also received a letter from James Forrestal, Secretary of the Navy, on 29 January 1946 stating that, "Without formality he wanted the Navy's pride in him to reach into his civil life and to remain with him always. "Floyd Edward Falls, son of Fletcher Falls, was born 27 October 1919 in Prairie, Mississippi, died 17 July

1994 and was buried in Georgia. His siblings are: Gaston Falls, Kathleen Davidson and twin brother, Lloyd Falls. Floyd married Ann Holt and they have a son, Larry Edward Falls. Floyd lived in Clifton before entering service. At the time of his death, he lived at 6132 Landover Circle, Morrow, Georgia 30260.

FARMER, LUTHER CLIFFORD, Serial Number 273 30 89, entered into the United States Navy on 23 June 1944. He was born 29 May 1927 in Lawrence County, Tennessee. He held the rating of Seaman Second Class. He served on Vessels and Stations: TADC Camp Perry, Williamsburg, Virginia; NOB Norfolk, Virginia; USNH St. Albans, Long Island, New York; USS YMS 136 USNSH Sea Gate, Brooklyn, New York; Naval Station, Astoria, Oregon; NRS, Nashville, Tennessee; Navy Per Sase, Norfolk, Virginia; NOB Norfolk, Virginia; and USS ARIEL. Luther was awarded the American Theater Medal and World War II Victory Medal. He was honorably discharged 29 March 1946 from U. S. Naval Special Hospital in Brooklyn, New York.

FARMER, RICHARD EARL, volunteered and entered into the United States Navy on 5 March 1940. He was born 23 November 1920 in Collinwood, Tennessee. He held the rating of Aerographer's Mate First Class. He served on Vessels and Stations: NRS, Nashville, Tennessee; USNTS, Bob, Norfolk, Virginia; NAS, Pensacola, Florida; District Headquarters and Naval Radio Station, Balboa, Canal Zone-, Navy Weather Central 15th N.D., US Naval Base, Galapagos Island; Navy Weather Central 15th N.D. USNR ECBKS NTC Lido Beach, Long Island. N.Y.; RS Newport News, Virginia; USS TICONDEROGA (CV14),- US Navy Weather Central, Seattle, Washington; US Naval Hospital, Seattle, Washington,, and US Naval Hospital, Corona, California.

Richard received the American Area Campaign Medal- Asiatic Pacific Medal and Good Conduct Medal He was honorably discharged 25 March 1946 from U.S. Naval Special Hospital in Corona. California.

FARMER, SIE H., son of Dr. Boyd and Rena Kephart Farmer, was born on August 17, 1913, in Wayne County. He was living at Collinwood when he was inducted into the United States Army at Ft. McPearson, Georgia on May 15, 1941. He served with the 9200 Transportation Service Unit, Company C at Myles Standish as Mess Sergeant and was awarded the American Defense Ribbon, American Theater Ribbon and Good Conduct Medal. On October 30, 1945, he was discharged at

Camp Stewart, Georgia. Sie married Dorothy in Great Bend, Kansas, and continued to live there after his Army discharge. They adopted a daughter, Janet Rose. He has two nieces in Waynesboro, Linda Jones and Ann Crews. Several years ago Sie died from cancer and is buried in Grand Bend.

FARRIS, CHARLIE J., JR., Serial Number 34 144 922, was a Staff Sergeant in the 545th Base Headquarters and Air Base Squadron in the Army Air Force of the United States. His permanent mailing address was Route 7, Pulaski, Giles County, Tennessee. He was born 17 June 1917 in Collinwood. He was married when he was inducted. His education consisted of 4 years of high school. He was registered with Selective Service Board in Wayne County, Tennessee. His Civilian Occupation was Tractor Mechanic. He entered into active service 18 August 1941 at Fort Oglethorpe, Georgia. His home address at time of entry was Collinwood, Tennessee. His Military Occupational Specialty was Mess Sergeant. His Military Qualification was SS Carbine. The following decorations were awarded to Farris: Asiatic Pacific Service Medal, American Defense Service Medal, American Service Medal, Good Conduct Medal, and World War II Victory Medal, He left the USA 12 April 1945 for the Pacific Theater; and returned to USA 23 October 1945. He was discharged 3 November 1945 at Fort McPherson, Georgia.

Mr. Farris died Thursday, February 3, at Eliza Coffee Memorial Hospital in Florence, AL.

He was a native of Wayne County, a son of the late Charles Jefferson Farris, Sr. and Effie Byler Farris. He was retired from the US Air Force after serving over 20 years. He was a veteran of WWII and the Korean War. After his retirement from the military service he also served as a chef for Governor Ray Blanton for over 4 years. He was a member of the Collinwood Church of Christ and the Masonic Lodge.

FARRIS, GUY, was born 18 April 1903, died 9 March 1966 and is buried in Mt. Hebron Cemetery on Indian Creek in Wayne County. His parents were Charlie and Minnie Farris. His sibling include Minnie C. Eaton, Frankie Bain and Cecil Farris. His half-siblings include C. J., Allen, Harold Farris and Mary Louise McWilliams. Guy was a United States Army Veteran of World War II. He was in the Aleutian Islands for some length of time. This information was given over the phone by Minnie C. Eaton to Rita Edwards Duncan, August 10, 1992.

FARRIS, JOSEPH FRANKLIN, JR.,

Serial Number 605 09 12, was a Ship's Cook, Second Class (T) V-6 USNR of the United States Navy. He held the following ratings: S2C, S1C, SC3C(CB) and SC2C(T). His permanent mailing address was Collinwood, Tennessee. He was married when he entered service. His main Civilian Occupation was Trucking. He was born 17 June 1919 in Lutts, Tennessee. He was inducted 10 October 1942 and entered into active service 11 November 1942 at Birmingham, Alabama. The Service Vessel and Stations where he served were: NRS Birmingham, Alabama; USNCTC-NOB Norfolk, Virginia; and 56th NCB USNCTC Davisville, Rhode Island. He was discharged 10 October 1945 in Boston, Massachusetts. There are no discharge papers in the Wayne County Court House. J. F. Jr., son of Joseph F. and Ollie Belle (Pigg) Farris, was born 17 July 1919 on Rayborn's Creek in Wayne County. He had seven siblings, Juanita F. Lay (deceased), Evelyn F. Lawson, Beatrice F. Pokorney, Jo Ann F. Little (deceased), Mable F. Murdock, Lawrence Farris, Arthur D. Farris, and Charles Eugene Farris (deceased). J. F. Jr. was reared on a farm where he worked and went to school. Later he moved to Collinwood to live with his Aunt Mattie and her daughter, Ethel Whitt. For several years he was a truck driver for the Natchez Trace and in Courtland, Alabama. He liked everything pertaining to mechanics and trucks. On 29 December 1939, he married Frances McGee, the daughter of John and Ella McGee. Sometime later J. F. and his wife moved to Decatur, Alabama, where he worked as a welder for Ingall's Iron Works. One daughter, Claudella Farris, was born on 17 June 1942 in ECM Hospital in Florence, Alabama. J. F. was drafted soon after her birth. He chose to join the Seabee's 56th Battalion Construction Company. He departed to Virginia to begin his training on 27 November 1942. His wife and daughter moved back to Collinwood to live with her parents. After his training, he was sent to California and

then to Hawaii and Guam. Here he won a Pacific-Asiatic Medal and one Star. J. F. Jr., did not see his daughter from the day he left until he returned in July 1945. He was sent to Providence, Rhode Island to be released from duty. J. F., Frances and Claudella lived there for a few months until his discharge on 10 October 1945. After he was discharged, he came back to Collinwood to live. He bought a truck and hauled whatever was available. One of his dreams was to someday own a fleet of trucks. This dream did come true. His trucks were leased for 20 years to Angelica Uniform Company based in St. Louis, Missouri. He bought the Winford place containing 72 acres where he retired to raise black Angus cattle. Daughter Claudella married Jim Garmon of Burksville, Kentucky. He is now deceased. They lived in Nashville, Tennessee and have one daughter, Tanya Francine Garmon, born 17 May 1970 in ECM Hospital, Florence, Alabama. Jim and Claudella lived and worked in Nashville for fifteen years and then moved to Florence, Alabama. Tanya, at time the article was written, was a senior at Auburn University with a major in Electrical Engineering. Claudella works at ECM Hospital. J. F, Jr., will not get to see his granddaughter graduate from college, because he died 8 August 1988. He was a great believer in education and wanted his family to do better than he. He always insisted that education and religion were the backbone of one's life. "Be honest. " he would say, "Life's to short to fool around. " He had a good life and was loved very much.

FAULKNER, ALBERT L., son of Mrs Jennie R. Faulkner of Clifton, TN was in the US Service.

FERGUSON, AUBREY A., Serial Number 34 377 213, was a Staff Sergeant with Company F, 329th Infantry of the Army of the United States. He was born 23 May 1921 in Priceville, Alabama. His permanent mailing address was Route 1, Lutts, Tennessee. His Civilian Occupation was Farmer. He was registered with Selective Service Board No. 1, Waynesboro, Tennessee. He was married with two dependents when he was inducted 13 October 1942 and entered active service 27 October 1942 at Fort Oglethorpe, Georgia. His Military Occupational Specialty was Rifleman. His Military Qualifications included Combat Infantry Badge. He was in battles in Normandy, Northern France, Ardennes and Rhineland. His decorations included the Purple Heart Medal, American Theater Ribbon, World War II Victory Medal, Good Conduct Medal, and European-African Middle Eastern Theater Ribbon with 4 Bronze Stars. He was wounded in action in France 12 July 1944. He was overseas 1 year, 7 months and 9 days. He was discharged 21 November 1945 at Fort Knox, Kentucky.

FIELDER, JAMES HARRIS, was born 20 September 1909 in Hohenwald, Tennessee. His parents were William Tho-

mas Fielder, a lawyer and former legislator representing his native Hickman County, and Roxanna Merriman Fielder, a school teacher from Wayne County. In 1910 the family moved to Waynesboro in Wayne County, where in November of that year a daughter, Virginia Will, was born. Until his death from typhoid fever in 1911, Will T. Fielder practiced law in Waynesboro, in partnership with Attorney Elisha B. Turman. The widow Fielder (Miss Roxie) and children soon went to live in the home of her father, James H. Merriman, on Upper Green River. After sometime, however, they returned to their house near the Square in Waynesboro. The widow's aging father and bachelor brothers Walter, Dodge and Homer Merriman moved in with them. During those days Grandfather Merriman often told his young grandson and namesake stories about the people, the times and trials of the Civil War. The Grandfather had served as a third lieutenant under the command of General Nathan B. Forrest. These stories, no doubt, helped to kindle in young Harris an abiding love of history and of people. In 1920 Miss Roxie resumed teaching at the nearby country schools. She entered her children in whatever school she taught. Their conveyance was a horse and buggy. Harris graduated from Wayne County High School in 1928. That summer he entered State Teachers College in Murfreesboro to earn a teaching certificate. By the 1934 June graduation he had managed to teach three years on Lower Green River in Wayne County and to obtain a degree from the Murfreesboro college, where he had

been president of the Dramatics Club, active in the men's honorary Sigma Club and served as president of the Senior Class. In September 1934, this Wayne Countian accepted the principalship of a Consolidated School in Trousdale County, remaining there for four years. In 1938 he returned to Waynesboro to help operate the family business of D. E. Merriman & Co. From 1939 he also worked as a clerk in the local post office. He served as president of the Lions Club. In 1941 he married Eva Frances Wilburn, a teacher from Trousdale County. Days of World War II: As one of a bus load of Wayne County recruits, James H. Fielder left the Court House Square at mid morning 15 March 1942, for induction into the U. S. Army at Fort Oglethorpe, Georgia. On May 15, 1942, Pvt Fielder was sent to Fort McClellan, Alabama, for Basic Training. On 22 July 1942, he reported to Key Field, Mississippi, for Ordnance Training in 311th Bomb Squadron 86th Bomb Group. On 7 September 1942, Pfc Fielder applied for attendance at the Army Postal Service Officer Candidate School. On 5 December 1942, Cpl Fielder was enrolled in AG OCS Fort Washington, Maryland. There he served as a Sergeant of Co. D Off. Cand, Bn. (Pov). On 23 February 1943, he was discharged from the U. S. Army to accept a commission. 2nd Lieut. Fielder was assigned on 24 February 1943 to ADG, APS, AGP, CPE, Charleston, South Carolina, as Asst Postal Officer. From June to October of 1943, he activated, trained and prepared for overseas movement of the 585th Army Postal Unit. On October 12, 1943, the 585th APU departed for the European Theater of Operations. Arriving in England October 19, the unit was stationed in London and assisted in operations of APO 887. This was the period of Hitler's buzz-bomb blitz of the London area. On February 11, 1944, 1st Lieut. Fielder as Commanding Officer of 585 APU Special Troops, Twelfth Army Group, activated and supervised the operation of APO 655. The 585 APU through the operation of APO 655 and additional service provided complete postal service to General Omar N. Bradley's Twelfth Army Group Headquarters. The countries into which that service extended were England, France, Belgium, Luxembourg and Germany. In July 1944, the 585 APU was moved to Paris, France. For a time it operated from a portion of the converted stables of the Palace of Versailles. Concurrently, the stables housed theater entertainment for troops of the area, billing popular stars from the U. S. and Allies. In May 1945, the 585 APU was moved to the Weisbaden, Germany Army Base. On June 30, 1945, 1st Lieut Fielder was awarded the Bronze Star Medal by the Army Group Com-

mander with the following citation: First Lieutenant James H. Fielder, 01001781, AGD, US Army, for meritorious service in connection with military operations from 11 February 1944 to 9 May 1945. As Commanding Officer, 585 Army Postal Unit, he secured a high standard of discipline in his command. Under his skillful supervision and planning the unit provided unsurpassed postal service for Headquarters 12th Army Group in spite of the various difficulties that arose. He met all demands for increases in service without fail. Entered military service from Tennessee. Officer Fielder was separated from his Post at the end of October 1945 and departed for the United States on November 1, 1945, debarking in New York, twelve days later. He was directed to Separation Center, Camp Atterbury, Indiana. He was promoted to Captain S. O. 318 at Camp Atterbury 24 December 1945. He was honorably discharged 25 January 1946. On November 17, 1945, 1st Lieut. Fielder had, at Camp Atterbury, accepted appointment as First Lieutenant, AGD, in the Officers Reserve Corps, Army of the United States. He was appointed Captain on 6 August 1946. He remained in the ORC, AGD until April 1, 1953. After The War: On 19 November 1945, James Harris Fielder picked up anew his civilian way of life when, on the trip home from Camp Atterbury to Waynesboro, Tennessee, his folks met him in Nashville. To heighten the joy his "folks" now included his first child, twenty-month-old daughter Mary Cynthia. He always loved to remember the first word he heard her say - the word "airplane" - as she pointed upward to a noisy speck in the sky. The Fielers' second daughter, Virginia Dodge, was born in 1948. He always loved to remember the first step he saw Virginia Dodge take. Mr. Fielder returned to the work he left in 1942, helping with the family business and serving as postal clerk. He went back to the Lions Club for several years and joined the American Legion and the VFW. He became Chairman of the Wayne County Savings Bond Committee in 1948 and remained so for the rest of his life. In 1956 he was appointed rural letter carrier on Route 4, later transferring to Route 1, from which he retired in 1973. He enjoyed his years of retirement, especially his small cattle farm and home garden. A member of the First Christian Church, he was on the official church board for thirty-five years and Chairman for nine years. Mr. Fielder died 7 August 1985 and was laid to rest in Shields Cemetery. In addition to his wife, he was survived by his two daughters, Mary Cynthia Diamond of Shawnee, Kansas, and Virginia Dodge Crye of Miami Beach, Florida; three grandchildren,

Camille Fielder, David Harris and Andrew Frank Diamond, all of Shawnee; and one sister, Virginia Hobbs of Waynesboro.

FISHER, PAULIE MEARINE, 77, of Waynesboro died 1 January 1998 at Maury Regional Hospital in Columbia and was buried in Loretto Cemetery. A native of Lawrenceburg, he was the son of Berry Noble and Florence Hughes Fisher. He was retired from Acme Metal Company, a member of V. F. W. Post 1618, a member of American Legion Post 146 and a World War II veteran.

FLIPPO, FRANK RUSS, was born on January 16, 1922, the son of Cord and Minnie Jobe Flippo, in the Beech Creek

community. He joined the United States Navy in 1941. He was placed with the Submarine Forces and was based most of the time at Pearl Harbor. He received an honorable discharge in 1945. He was married on September 19, 1945, to Kathryn Hardin, daughter of Dick and Viv. Hardin. Frank and Kathryn had one son, Ken, and one grandson, Bryant. Frank moved his family to Jackson, Tennessee, in 1950. He worked at the Milan Arsenal in Milan, Tennessee, for 15 years. He died on May 4, 1980, with lung cancer. He is buried in Highland Memorial Gardens in Jackson, Tennessee. His siblings are Jim, J. C., Carrie and Minnie Lee. Frank Russ Flippo, U. S. Navy 1941-1945, Submarine Forces.

FLIPPO, HENRY FORD, son of Will and Ruth (Harris) Flippo, was born, October 16, 1922, in Wayne County. He grew up in the Ashland and Topsy Communities, then joined the CCC program during the F. D. Roosevelt Administration. With the outbreak of WWII, he enlisted with the U. S. Army and served in Europe during the heaviest battles. He was wounded while in battle in Germany.

After the war, he worked at Nashville and was married there. He is now retired,

living at Hohenwald, Tn. No children. He is a half-brother to W.C. Flippo.

FLIPPO, JOHN C., JR., Serial Number 34 189 104, was a Private in the 1153rd RD Army Air Force Base Unit of the United States Army. His permanent mailing address was Route 1, Peters Landing, Tennessee. He was born 16 January 1920 in Wayne County. He was registered with Selective Service Board in Wayne County, Tennessee. His Civilian Occupation was General Farm Hand. His Military Specialty was Military Policeman. The following decorations were awarded to Flippo: World War II Victory Medal, Good Conduct Medal, American Defense Service Medal, and American Service Medal. He left the USA 20 May 1943 for the American Theater and returned to USA 24 September 1945. He was discharged 17 November 1945 at Fort McPherson, Georgia.

FLIPPO, MALCOLM ARNOLD, entered the United States Navy on 26 May 1942 and was discharged 16 December

1945. He received his Basic Training at Great Lakes Naval Training Center. He participated in the invasion of Northern Africa and Sicily. He served on the USS LEEDSTORUM. This ship was sunk by a German sub while the crew were unloading in Algeria. He also served on the USS WILKES a destroyer and the USS HORADEN, a destroyer. While on the last mentioned ship, they escorted the Aircraft Carrier Bunker Hill through the Panama Canal for the invasion of the Marshall Islands and Guam. Flippo had the rank of Coxswain, 3rd Class Petty Officer. Malcolm, son of the late Jim and Delphia (Riley) Flippo, was born 31 March 1924. His sisters are, Eddie Flippo Williams, Mary Elizabeth Hayes and Ermadine Hurley (deceased.) His half brothers and sisters are, William Isaac Gifford, and Rothie Nell Gifford Lineberry. Malcolm married Bertie Pulley and they have three

children, Malcolm Arnold Flippo, Jr., born 8 September 1961; Patricia Ann Flippo Anderson, born 19 June 1947 and Robert Eugene Flippo, born 12 February 1961.

FLIPPO, WILLIE, Serial Number 34 713 910, was a Private in the Army of the United States. He was born in Waynesboro, Tennessee. He was inducted into active service 23 April 1943 at Camp Forrest, Tennessee. His Military Specialty was Antitank Crewman. His Military Qualification was MM 30 Caliber Carbine and MM 30 Caliber Rifle. He was discharged 9 November 1944 at the Separation Center in Fort Bragg, North Carolina. Remarks stated that he was issued a Discharge Lapel Button at Fort Bragg, North Carolina.

FLOYD, NEWT ALLEN, Serial Number 965 71 35, entered into the United States Navy on 1 February 1944. He held

the rating of Ship Fitter, Third Class (SF3/C). He served on Vessels and Stations: NRS, Nashville, Tennessee; NTS, Bainbridge, Maryland, Repair Unit, Navy 3205; Ship Repair Base Navy 3864 and USS MONADNECK. Mr. Floyd used his skills as a welder to repair ships in the Philippines during his active duty service. The following citations were awarded to Floyd: Asiatic Pacific Medal, Philippines Operation Medal, Victory Medal, and American Theater Medal. He was honorably discharged 24 April 1946 in Memphis, Tennessee. Newt Allen, son of Frank L. and Annie Tucker Floyd, was born 1 October 1922 in Clifton, Tennessee, died 26 March 1984 in William Bowld Hospital in Memphis and is buried in Clifton Cemetery. He married Jeanne Villines and they have two children, Peggy Floyd Richarson and Harry V. Floyd. Newt Allen was a member of the Evans Chapel United Methodist Church, a 32nd degree Mason of Nashville, a member of the Masonic Lodge in Clifton and a member of the board of directors at Peoples Bank.

FOLGER, MORRIS WINFORD, Private First Class, son of Mr. and Mrs. Paul K. Folger of Wayne County received

his basic training at Camp Craft, South Carolina and went overseas on 18 February 1945. PFC Folger is a member of the 99th Division, a part of the 3rd Army. He was stationed in Czechoslovakia. He was awarded the Infantry Badge and two battle stars.

Source: Wayne County News.

Morris, son of Paul and Myrtle (Gower) Folger, was born in Wayne County, died 22 December 1994 in the Veterans Administration Medical Center in Nashville and was buried in the Highland United Methodist Church Cemetery. Survivors were his wife, Iva Thompson Folger, two sons, Douglas and David Folger and three daughters, Barbara Davis, Beverly Price and Belinda Graham, brother, Stanley Folger and sister Connie Jaske. He lived at Route 6, Lawrenceburg, Tennessee. He was a member of the Highland Methodist Church and was retired from the State of Tennessee.

FOLGER, STANLEY RALPH, Serial Number 640 36 41, was born in Wayne County 4 November 1920 near the

Lawrence-Wayne County line. The address was Route 6, Lawrenceburg, Tennessee. His education included three years of high school. His parents were Paul K. and Myrtle (Gower) Folger. He has a sister Connie Jaske and a brother Morris. His great grandparents came to Tennessee from Chicago, Illinois in a covered wagon. His father was only fifteen years old at that time. His father was also a World War I Veteran. Stanley was married on 14 June 1946 to Belle Skelton, daughter of Henry and Goldie Skelton. From May 1941 to May 1942, Stanley was employed as a truck driver for Barker Lumber Co. in Dearborn, Michigan. Stanley registered at the Selective Service Board in Detroit, Wayne County, Michigan. He entered into active service 26 March 1942 in Nashville, Tennessee. His rank was Chief Boatswain's Mate V-6 USNR. The Vessel and Stations he served on included USS LEONARD WOOD, USS THOMAS STONE, USS DORTHA L. DIX, USS LST 308, USS LST 344, USS LST 511 and USS LST 973. On 26 December 1942 he reported to USS Lst 308 in Portsmouth, Virginia. On 2 January 1943 Stanley was a member of the original crew on date of commissioning of the vessel. He aided in the outfitting for operations and participated in the amphibious training maneuvers in the Chesapeake Bay area. He landed with Task Force at Gela, Sicily on "H" hour July 10, 1943. He made six subsequent shuttle trips from North African ports to various parts of the island. Stanley served loyally and faithfully while under fire. On September 9, 1943 he landed with Tank Force on Red Beach at Sale, Italy and participated in the five squint shuttle trips from Sicily, French North Africa and Tripalitania to the Italian mainland, carrying vehicles and men in support of the initial attack. Folger received Special Commendation 12 October 1943 for performance of duty during the time of the Italian Invasion from his Lieutenant Commander S. B. Purdin. Stanley with his company participated in the original assault on the Red Beach of the Italian Invasion. The forces landed through heavy enemy shell fire and retracted under trying conditions. With his rating BM/C, Stanley again reported aboard 19 February 1944 from his previous ship USS LST 344. On 23 July 1944 he transferred to Co USS LST 511 for duty. He participated in the initial assault of the invasion of France. "He took part in the follow up and support, showing great courage and skill. He worked long hours with but one thought in mind, Support the Army" said R. B. Hensley, Lt., USN Commanding officer. On January 27, 1945 Folger, on USS Lst 973 reported aboard from RS, Boston, Massachusetts. He then participated in the initial phase of

the Occupation of Japan in the Tokyo-Yokohama Area from September 12 to September 19, 1945. On 27 September 1945, Folger transferred to Reo Station Navy 3064 FFT to the U. S. for discharge. He was discharged 6 November 1945 in Boston, Massachusetts. Honors Folger received include American Area Ribbon, European African Middle Eastern Theater Ribbon, Asiatic-Pacific Ribbon, Good Conduct Medal, and World War II Victory Medal, On 9 September 1946, Stanley re-enlisted in the Navy at Lawrenceburg, Tennessee. He entered into active service on 14 November 1946 in connection with Station Keeper, as a recall. He was released to inactive duty 1 May 1947. His last employment before recall was with F. M. Ice Company in Oak Ridge, Tennessee as a mechanic from June to September 1946. In Waynesboro, Folger worked at J.O Barnett Funeral Home, Barnett's One Stop Store and recently retired from Folger's Insurance Agency where he spent many years.

FOSTER, GRADY GLENN, was born June 19, 1925 at Lutts, Tn. He enlisted in the U. S. Navy, April 10, 1944, and served at NRS Nashville; Const. Batt's, Williamsburg, VA.; U.S.S. Wyoming and U.S.S. Shadwell. He received the following citations; American Area Campaign Medal, Asiatic-Pacific Ribbon with one star and Victory Medal.

FOWLER, CALVIN W., Serial Number 34 723 006, was a Private First Class in Battery C 483rd Antiaircraft Artillery AW Battalion in the Army of the United States. His permanent mailing address was Route 3 Iron City, Tennessee. He was born 26 August 1923 in Iron City. His education consisted of 2 years of high school. He was registered with Selective Service Board in Wayne County, Tennessee. His Civilian Occupation was Knitting Machine Operator. His Military Specialty was Antiaircraft Artillery Crewman. His Military Qualification was Rifle Sharpshooter. He was in the Battles of Eastern Mandates and was in Ground Combat on Iwo Jima. The following decorations were awarded to Fowler: World War II Victory Ribbon, Good Conduct Medal, American Theater Ribbon, Asiatic-Pacific Theater Ribbon and two Bronze Service Stars. He left the USA 16 June 1944 for the Asiatic-Pacific Theater, and returned to USA 20 December 1945. He was discharged 31 December 1945 at Camp Chaffee, Arkansas.

FOWLER, J.C., JR., was a Seaman Second Class in the United States Navy. He was discharged 29 November 1945 from the U. S. Naval Personnel Separation

Center in Memphis, Tennessee. No other information available.

FOWLER, JAMES R., Serial Number 34 375 234, was inducted into the Army of the United States on October 3, 1942, and was released from active duty and transferred to the Enlisted Reserve Corps, and returned to Waynesboro, Tn. On October 17, 1942 he was called to active duty and reported to Ft. Oglethorpe, GA.

FOWLER, ORBIE LUTHER, was a Baker Second Class in the United States Navy. He was discharged 29 October 1945 from the U. S. Naval Personnel Separation Center in Memphis, Tennessee. Orbie Fowler is the most popular man in the 64th Battalion of Seabees. He is the fellow who makes the ice cream, turning out 75 to 95 gallons daily in 28 delicious flavors. Stationed on "Island X" in the Philippines where the temperatures range around 124 degrees in the sun (There is no shade.) Fowler's product is really popular with the men who are working on a nine hour day, seven days a week schedule. Fowler makes the ice cream with great pride in what the men have termed "Orbie Fowler's Old Fashion Ice Cream Emporium. " Using the most modern equipment, he makes his own mix or uses ready made mix. adding the flavors desired, since the ice cream is served once a day and sometimes twice to the men of the 64th Battalion, Fowler is pretty much of a one man ice cream factory. Prior to joining the Seabees on December 2, 1942, Fowler who is a native of Iron City, Tennessee, was a farmer who raised corn, cotton and hay. Upon entering service, he struck for baker's assistant, and was later promoted to Baker, Third Class and then to his present rating Baker 2/C. He has been with the 64th Battalion since its formation, saw duty with the outfit in Argentina, Newfoundland, Pearl Harbor, Hawaii and is now with the unit in the Philippines. When Fowler is released from the service, he is not certain that he wants to go back to farming. "May set up a little ice cream parlor. " he confides. If he follows the new trade he has learned in the Seabees, Fowler is very likely to do a thriving business. Surely if there is a Seabee within a 100 mile radius he will stop by to sample Fowler's ice cream. Looks as though "Orbie" is due to be as popular in Iron City as he is on "Island X.

FOWLER, ROY NATHANIEL, Serial Number 34 375 254, was a Technician in the United States Army. His permanent mailing address was Route 2, Waynesboro, Tennessee. His Civilian Occupation was General Farmer. He was inducted 3 October 1942 and entered into active service

17 October 1942 at Fort Oglethorpe, Georgia. His Military Occupational Specialty was Utility Repairman. His Military Qualification was Rifle Marksman. He was not in a battle. The following Decorations were awarded to Fowler: World War II Victory Ribbon, Good Conduct Medal, American Theater Ribbon, European-African Middle Eastern Theater Ribbon, Philippines Liberation Ribbon and Asiatic-Pacific Theater Ribbon. He left the USA 2 December 1944 for the European-African Middle Eastern Theater, left there 12 July 1945 for the Asiatic-Pacific Theater; and returned to USA 1 February 1946. He was discharged 8 February 1946 at Camp Chaffee, Arkansas. Mr. Fowler, son of Steve and Ora Casteel Fowler, was born 14 August 1914 in Waynesboro, died 27 October 19?? in Veterans Administration Medical Center in Memphis, and was buried in Jowers Cemetery. He was of the Baptist belief and worked as a brick mason. Survivors included his wife, Pearl Fowler of Savannah; three daughters, Linda Green of Council Bluffs, Iowa, Barbara Wolfe of Fayetteville, and Paula Gammill of Luka, Mississippi, one son, Michael Cox of Fayetteville; one sister, Alvie Brown of Marianna, Arkansas; one brother, Rufus Fowler of Marianna; one half sister Ruby Swift of Bruceton; two step brothers, Walter Ayers of Waynesboro and Lester Ayers of Florida and 11 grandchildren.

FOXX, JAMES PRICE, was born 10 May 1925 in Wayne County, Tennessee. He was the son of James Pearson and Mary Ella Olive Foxx. James attended school at Whitten's School on Little Cypress Creek not far from his home. He attended Collinwood High School. On 10 April 1944, he enlisted in the U. S. Navy at the Naval Receiving Station, Nashville, Tennessee and served until 18 May 1946 when he was honorably discharged in Memphis, Tennessee. During the service he saw duty on the USS Comfort and served in the Philippine Liberation Operation and the Asiatic Theater. His highest rank was Seaman First Class. He received the following medals: Philippine Liberation Medal with one star, Victory Medal, and the Asiatic Pacific Medal with one star. After his discharge, James returned to Florence, Alabama and went to work for the Tennessee Valley Authority as a heavy equipment operator. On 3 September 1949, he married Marcie Faye Gallien in Luka, Mississippi. She was born 25 September 1930 in Wayne County on Little Cypress Creek and was the daughter of Alvin Clarence and Addie Mae Whitten Gallien. They have four children and nine grandchildren: (1) Patricia Ann Foxx, born 4 July 1950, was married 30 August 1969 to Charles Coo-

per Young, born 8 June 1942 and has three children, Charles Foxx Young born 7 January 1971, Chadwick Beau Young born 18 November 1978 and Tristian Tennille Young born 18 September 1978. (2) James Dwight Foxx born 28 July 1952, married on 19 March 1973 Rita Faye Adams, born 20 April 1954 and has three children: April Dawn Foxx born 15 April 1975, Vanessa Lynn Foxx born 27 October 1978 and Karla Leann Foxx born 22 November 1981; (3) Carla Rena Foxx born 11 March 1963, married 15 May 1982 to Ronald Bart Cannon born 4 September 1957 and has two children, Robyn Rena Cannon born 25 April 1985 and Susan Marie Cannon born 23 September 1987; and (4) Karen Leigh Foxx born 20 January 1965, married 4 July 1986, Gregory Dale Michael, born 28 August 1964 and has one daughter, Courtney Leigh Michael born 5 May 1990. James died 3 September 1969 in Florence, Alabama and is buried at Grandview Memorial Cemetery in Florence, Alabama. Marcie lives in the Petersville area of Florence.

FOXX, R.C. MORRIS, Serial Number 34 495 009, was a Private First Class in Company C 184th Infantry of the United States Army. His permanent mailing address was Route 3, Florence, Alabama. He was born 17 August 1922 in Cloverdale, Alabama. His education consisted of 1 year of high school. He was registered with Selective Service Board in Wayne County, Tennessee. His Civilian Occupation was General Farmhand. He was inducted 22 November 1942 and entered into active service 29 November 1942 at Fort Oglethorpe, Georgia. His Military Occupational Specialty was Rifleman. His Military Qualification was Combat Infantryman. He was in the following Battles: Aleutian Islands, Eastern Mandates, Southern Philippines, and Ryukyus. The following Decorations were awarded to Foxx: Good Conduct Medal, Purple Heart, Philippine Liberation Medal with two Bronze Stars, and World War II Victory Medal. He was wounded in the Asiatic-Pacific Theater May 3, 1945. He left the USA 11 July 1943 for the Pacific Theater; and returned to USA 16 November 1945. He was discharged 29 November 1945 at Camp Chaffee, Arkansas.

FRALEY, ALTON, Serial Number 34 506 475, was a Private First Class in Battery A, 602nd Field Artillery Battalion in the Army of the United States. His permanent mailing address was Route 6, Lawrenceburg, Tennessee. He was born 9 May 1920 in Collinwood. His education consisted of 4 years of high school. He was registered with Selective Service Board in Wayne County, Tennessee. His Civilian

Occupation was Burner Regulator Operator. He was inducted 18 January 1943 and entered into active service 25 January 1943 at Fort Oglethorpe, Georgia. His Military Specialty was Gun Crewman and Light Artilleryman. His Military Qualification was Carbine Sharpshooter. He was in battles in Rome-Arno, Southern France, Rhineland and Central Europe. The following decorations were awarded to Fraley: European African Middle Eastern Service Medal with 4 Bronze Service Stars. Good Conduct Medal, American Theater Medal, and World War II Victory Medal. He spent 1 year, 4 months and 22 days overseas. He was discharged 30 October 1945 at Fort Knox, Kentucky.

FRALEY, JULIS FARRIS, Serial Number 44 072 735, was a Technician, Fifth Grade in 174th M P Company in the Army of the United States. His permanent mailing address was Route 2, Clifton Tennessee. He was born 2 December 1926 in Clifton. His education consisted of 8 years of grammar school. He was registered with Selective Service Board in Wayne County, Tennessee. His Civilian Occupation was General Farm Hand. He was inducted 10 April 1945 at Fort Oglethorpe, Georgia. His Military Specialty was Military Policeman. His Military Qualification was Expert Rifleman. The following Decorations were awarded to Fraley: World War II Victory Medal. He left the USA 11 December 1945 for the Pacific Theater Operation; and returned to USA 26 September 1946. He was discharged 3 November 1946 at Fort Sheridan, Illinois. Farris was the son of Willis and Lora Culp Fraley. His siblings are, Pearl, Geneva, Wilton, Stella, Clarice twin to Farris, Nannie, Willie Ann and Kenneth Fraley. Farris married Dean Lineberry and had two children, Glenda and Jill Fraley. Farris grew up in the Beech Creek Community and attended the county schools there. He still lives in the same community.

FRANKS, ALLEN, was son of Mr. and Mrs. H. B. Franks and was wounded in France during World War II, See biography of Wilfred Franks.

FRANKS, HERSCHEL, was the son of Mr. and Mrs. H. B. Franks. See biography of Wilfred Franks.

FRANKS, HERSCHEL WILLIE, "DOC", 72, the son of Hal and Ollie Pearl Pickens Franks, died 9 May 1997 in Florence Hospital. He was buried in Greenview Memorial Park in Florence. He was a native of Wayne County, a retired concrete finisher and a veteran of World War II having served in the US Army

where he received the Purple Heart. He was stationed in Germany during the War. Survivors include his wife, Hassie Faye Davis Franks of Florence; three sons, William of Petersville. Alabama, and Timothy and James both of Florence; one daughter, Linda Gayle Hunt of Petersville, Alabama; four brothers, J. H. and Othear Franks of Arkansas, Grayford Franks of Mexico and Wayland Franks of Hillsboro, Alabama; four sisters, Estelle Cooper of Indiana, Edith Beard of Oregon, Ruby Eskew of Missouri and Reba Franklin of Tennessee and four grandchildren.
Source: Wayne County News, 17 May 1997.

FRANKS, THEODORE LOUIS, was born on February 19, 1925, in Kempsville, Illinois. He entered the United States Navy on February 5, 1943, and served as Seaman First Class with the USNTS in Great Lakes, Illinois; U. S. Naval Section Base in Mobile, Alabama; USS Guide, USN Frontier Base in Burrwood, Louisiana; and USS Helena. On March 1, 1940, he was discharged at the U. S. Naval Personnel Separation Center in Memphis, Tennessee.

FRANKS, WILFRED, Private, son of Mr. and Mrs. H. B. Franks, was inducted into the Army on 26 July 1944. He took his training at Camp Shelby, Mississippi and Fort McClellan, Alabama, and was sent overseas in March 1945. He was attached to the Infantry in Italy. He has two brothers in the service, PFC Allen Franks who was wounded in France and Pvt Herschel Franks who is in Germany. Pvt Franks married Myrtle Holt, daughter of Mr. and Mrs. Joe M. Holt, Lutts, Tennessee.
Source: Wayne County News.

FRAZIER, JOE BROWN, Seaman First Class, went into the Navy 6 December 1943. He went through Boot Camp in

San Diego, California and was stationed at North Island. He was discharged 16

January 1946 . Joe Brown was born 11 October 1917 and died 10 November 1973. He was the son of Clay and Annie (Nutt) Frazier. He had five brothers and two sisters, Arlie Skelton and Margie Hardin. He married Ruth Edwards, daughter of Jack and Mary (Pope) Edwards. They have one son and two grandchildren.

FRAZIER, NORMAN GLYNN, lived near Collinwood, Tennessee. He was inducted into the United States Navy and served as a Third Class Aviation Ordnance Man. In November 1945, he was discharged at the U. S. Naval Separation Center in Memphis, Tennessee.

FRAZIER, ROBBIE L., was a Private First Class in the Infantry in the United States Army. He enlisted 4 December 1943.

He spent his war days in the European Theater and was wounded in Germany. He received the Purple Heart. Robbie was born 8 September 1924 in Wayne County, died 1 September 1968 and is buried in Salem Primitive Baptist Church Cemetery. His parents were H. Clay Frazier (born 30 January 1895) and Annie Nutt Frazier (born 14 June 1897.) Both are buried in the Salem Cemetery. He had five brothers and two sisters. He was married to Ima Jackson of Mt. Hope and to this union was born one daughter. There are three grandsons.

FREE, ALONZO L., was the son of Eugene and Daisy McCuistion Free. He married Lockie Bell Inman, and they had one son. Alonzo volunteered for the United States Army. He was wounded in German during World War II. When he returned to the United States, he spent much time in the hospital. He is buried in Mt. Carmel Cemetery in Decatur County, Tennessee. His siblings are Bertha Free Phillips, George, William and Lewis.

FREE, LEWIS E., was the son of Eugene and Daisy McCuistion Free. He was born on September 5, 1919. He was married to Hazel Fluty, and they had two sons, John and Quincy. Lewis served in the United States Marines during World War II. He was a volunteer. He died on October 17, 1980, and is buried in the Bunch Cemetery in Perry County, Tennessee. His siblings are Bertha Free Phillips, George, William and Alonzo.

GALLAHER, ALFRED E., was the seventh son and last of eight children, born to William James (Billy) Gallaher (August

31, 1869 to April 20, 1940) and Nora Clara (Cole) Gallaher (July 31, 1874 to February 22, 1954). Alfred was born May 6, 1918 on Banjo Branch, also known as Talley Branch, Route #2, Waynesboro, Tennessee. He attended elementary school at Ray School, presently known as Ray's Chapel Baptist Church, on upper Hog Creek and graduated from Wayne County High School in. 1936. Alfred was good at sports, especially baseball and basketball.

Alfred entered college at Austin Peay State, Clarksville, Tennessee in the fall of 1936. He was on first team and played caw on the basketball team, who won the Southeastern. Conference Championship in 1938. Alfred said that "one of the greatest benefits of being on the team was getting to eat free at the athletic training table."

After completion of two years of college, Alfred returned to Wayne County and aught one year (1939) at Holley Creek. His co-teacher at this school was Nanny MaLawson. The next year, in 1940, Alfred was the only teacher at Holt School on Big Cypress Creek. In 1941, the United States role in the war in Europe was becoming a reality and Alfred assist with the sign-up of draftees in the Big Cypress Creek area at the Holt school.

On March 15, 1942, Alfred was inducted into service by the Wayne County, Draft Board. He was among the second group to leave Wayne County, to go to Fort

Oglethorp, Georgia, the induction center. His group left Waynesboro by bus on March 14, 1942. After a few days Alfred was sent to Camp Claiborn, Louisiana for basis training. He soon became a part of the 82nd Infantry Division which was reactivated on the 25th of Match 1942. Alfred said, -they said that I had volunteered for the 82nd, but I don't remember volunteering. The 82nd was under the command of Omar N. Bradley. The division command training was related to doctrines appropriate for an infantry division. Major General Matthew B. Ridgway succeeded to the command on June 26, 1942.

On the 15th day a August, what so many thought was a nasty rumor became a reality. On that day, the 82nd was designated as an Airborne Division. The reorganized division consisted of the 325th and 326th Glider Infantry Regiments and 319th and 320th Glider Field Artillery Battalions, and the 504 and 505 Parachute Infantries were also added. Alfred was assigned to the 325th.

General training of the Division continued at Camp Caiborn until October 1, 1942, when most of the Division was moved to Fort Bragg, North Carolina. At this place, thousands of more recruits were given basic training. Ground and glider training was pushed to the point of exhaustion.

On April 20, 1943 the Division commenced the movement from Fort Bragg to Camp Edwards, Massachusetts to stage for overseas transport by ships. Early on the morning of April 29, 1943, the transport ships were moved out of the harbor. There were two rather distasteful meals a day during passage and much speculation as to the 82nd's destination. Submarine alerts and boat drills, as well as watching the maneuvers of the convoy took up most of Alfred's and the other GI's time during passage. After 12 days the convoy came to a stop in Casablanca Harbor. It was so quiet and peaceful that the war seemed far away. However, it only seemed that way. Casablanca (Casa for house and Blanca for white) translates to mean white house. During the latter part of the war President Roosevelt and Winston Churchill met at Casablanca to discuss the unconditional surrender terms the allies would expect regarding Germany.

What Alfred saw was busy docks in the harbors and the harbors still dotted with hulks of ships sunk in the first fighting in Africa. Streets were crowded with all manner of military vehicles passing among the horse drawn engineless autos, donkey carts and bicycles. The dark Arab men, turbaned and clad in flowering white tunics or patched "coats of many colors% their feet bare or wearing sandals. Veiled Arab women, covered from head to foot in long, flowering robes left much to the imagina-

tion, as to what they looked like. Arab children in dirty, ragged, and jabbering groups were pleading everywhere for something to eat. This is what greeted the men of the 82nd as they went down the gangplank at Casablanca on the afternoon of May 10 1943, just four days past

Alfred Gallaher's 25th birthday. The 82nd marched through the city to Camp Don Barnes the north edge of the city. Death and destruction by war, for the next Low years, was horrible for the 82nd compared to this peaceful first encounter away from American soil.

On July 9, 1943, after two exhausting months of combat training, the 82nd Airborne Division spearheaded the first invasion of Europe with the invasion of Sicily under way. This was the first of five campaigns that T/Sgt. Alfred Gallaher participated in. Three of winch was by glider invasion (Sicily, Normandy, and Hollandia), by sea in Italy, and by land in Belgium. The last major war encounter and one of his most miserable experiences was at the Battle of the Bulge, where the 82nd were napped by the Germans under fierce fighting conditions. Alfred recalled that he and his men survived under outdoor conditions in about two feet of snow that had accumulated continuously from December 22, 1944 to January 21, 1945.

Leaving Africa behind and after flying over the Atlas Mountains Alfred's 325th Glider group of the 82nd was in position for the invasion of Sicily. The battle for Sicily didn't seem to last very long, but at that, there were a large number of casualties. On September 15, 1943 the invasion of Italy began. 'Me 325th was part of the invasion by sm. Alfred Gallaher received his first personal injuries during tins invasion and the account as verified by Pfc. Ollie Hall as follows:

Pfc. Ollie Hall, a cook with Company B was detailed to carry water and rations to his company holding positions on the crest of Mt. Chmunzi. Pvt. Robert Baker from Oak Hill, W. Va., armed with a rifle, was assigned to assist Hall. Baker liked to show Ins toughness and would bluster, "When it is too rough for you boys, it will be just right for me!"

One day as Hall and Baker, each carrying a five-gallon can of water, neared the crest, the roar of an incoming navy shell made them (live for cover. The navy guns were not high-trajectory weapons, so the gunners had to clear the mountain by only a few yards to drop their shells on their target in the valley beyond. Sounding like an express a-an, there was no doubt that this huge shell would not clear the mountain The shell exploded in the center of the heavy machine gun position. As the shell exploded, Hall saw a GI blown off his feet and several feet into the air. When the dust cleared, Hall ran to the GI and saw that he was slowly getting to his feet. "Sergeant, are you all right?" He asked. The GI was T/Sgt. Alfred Gallaher in command of the lst Battalion heavy machine gun platoon.

Gallaher, still dazed and shaken, with dirt in his mouth and blood all over his head, paused, spit several times to clear his mouth, then replied, "I reckon I'm all right!" Realizing that Gallaher was able to walk, Ollie turned in time to see his rifleman Baker drop his rifle and can of water and say, "I'm getting out of here!" He took off down the mountain. Hall continued with his delivery.

Four men of the machine gun platoon - Whitley, Wiggins, Karlen and Tuckerman — were killed by the shell. Gallaher, shell-shocked, ears ringing and head covered with dirt and blood, was assisted to the aid station. As his head cleared, be saw so many men who were seriously injured, much worse off than he, that he turned away without accepting aid and returned to full duty with Ins platoon.

Ollie Hall was from Kentucky and Alfred Gallaher was from Tennessee. Neither knew the other. Fifty-two years after this incident, Gallaher met Hall at the 325th reunion in Cleveland, Ohio on October 7, 1995. Soon the story about the "short round" on Mt. Chimmzi came up; they each related their experience and realized they were the two men involved. In Cleveland the men were asked: "Were you scared?" "Yes, of course, anyone would be scared, but not so scared that I did not do what I had to do!" Replied Gallaher.

Following the above encounter, the 325th went as far as Naples, where they stayed for about three weeks keeping order and seeing that water was being fairly distributed to the city. About the first of December 1943 part of the 82nd boarded the ship O'Hara and on December 9, 1943 arrived at Belfast, Northern Ireland. They bonded a train and moved about 35 miles to Ballymena, den later on to Portgenone. On February 14, 1944 the 325th Glider Infantry boarded a Dutch ship and landed at Liverpool, England, moving on by train to Leciter, England. Training here prepared the 325th for their part in the upcoming invasion of Normandy. On leadership and direction of the company, his courage and coolness under fire and his high sense of responsibility and duty to his in= and the battalion, won the respect and admiration of the entire platoon and enabled it to deliver the maximum fire possible at a critical moment.

Upon returning to Wayne County, Alfred was employed by the Government as an Instructor in the On-the-Farm. Training program. He worked in this capacity from 1945 until 1949. He then was employed once again as a teacher and taught or was principal of Pinhook Elementary School at Lutts, from 1949 to his retirement at age 65, in 1983. He also purchased a firm. On Indian Creek in 1950 and has enjoyed the peace of noncombat up until this date in February 2000. Following the War, Alfred Gallaher has lived a quiet life, has been a model citizen of Wayne County, Tennessee and has dedicated his life to teaching others as well as caring for the wealth of his family, friends and neighbors. He presently resides near the house in which he was born on Banjo Brawk Route #2, Waynesboro, Tennessee. Alfred is a member of the Church of Christ. One thing that is unique about Alfred is his habit of reading the Bible. If you are visiting in his home, you will be treated by Alfred leading the family in a Bible reading, every night before bedtime. Alfred Edward Gallaher is a much loved hero by the Gallaher clan.

Article submitted by R. Noel Gallaher and Glenn W. Gallaher, nephews of Alfred E. Gallaher.

GALLAHER, ARNOLD, son of Noah Gallaher and Mrs. Oscar Martin, lived on Factory Creek in Wayne County with his grandparents Mr. and Mrs. George Gallaher until he was 13 years old. He became a pilot in the US Air Force and served as a First Lt. According to an article released to the Wayne County News, his plane dropped the bombs that helped liberate 15,000 Allied prisoners.

GALLAHER, ALTON, was a native of Wayne County and a World War II Veteran. He was retired from Lincoln Brass

Manufacturing Company in Waynesboro. He was a member of the Green River Baptist Church and of the Masonic Lodge. He died on Monday, 15 February 1993 in the Waynesboro Hospital, age 70. He was buried in Memorial Gardens, Waynesboro. He was married to Louise Garrison. They had one son, Joey Gallaher and one daughter Debbie Gallaher Taylor. There were four grandchildren. His parents were Mr. and Mrs. Walter Gallaher. His sibling were Jane Gallaher Hodges, Mary Jo Gallaher Miller, Margie Gallaher Griggs, Helene Gallaher Hicks and Betty Gallaher Warren.

GALLAHER, CARNELLE RAYMOND, spent two years in the United States Army, serving in Europe. He married Geneva Moore and had one child, Judith (Judy). He was born on November 1, 1924, the son of Charles D. Gallaher and Willie Brewer Gallaher. After the war, C. Raymond and his family went to Toledo, Ohio. He worked and retired from a trucking company there. After retiring, he moved back to his old home place on Factory Creek in Wayne County, Tennessee. He takes care of farming activities there. His siblings are Stella Gallaher Lucker and Thelma Jean Hendrix.

GALLAHER, CHARLES DENSON, was the third son of William Jams (Billy) Gallaher (August 31, 1869 to April 20,

1940) and Nora Clara (Cole) Gallaher (July 31, 1974 to February 22, 1954). He was born October 9, 1902 in Wayne County, Tennessee, Route 2, Waynesboro on Banjo Branch (also known as Talley Branch). He received an elementary education in Wayne County, Tennessee from Ray School on upper Hog Creek (presently Ray's Chapel Baptist Church) and Leadierwood School on Hardin. Creek. His high school education was interrupted for two years with a teaching job in Wayne County. He soon realized the need for more education and returned to complete his high school education. He graduated from Wayne County High School in 1924, Waynesboro, Tennessee.

Charles continued his education by attending Middle Tennessee State Normal College, Murphreesboro, Tennessee from

1924 to 1926; University of Tennessee, Knoxville, Tennessee (B.S.) from 1926 to 1928; Teachers College, Columbia University (Post Graduate); University of Chicago, (Post Graduate) summer sessions, and University of California Berkley (Post Graduate) summer sessions. He was a teaching Fellow at the University of Tennessee from 1929 to 1930, while working on his M.S. Degree. While in college he was a member of CHI DELTA, the Literary and Debating Society, PH[DELTA KAPPA, Educational Fraternity, and ALPHA SIGMA PI, Social Fraternity.

Charles spent all of his career in administration, counseling, and teaching with secondary education He served as teacher or principal at numerous schools in Tennessee. He taught at Cross Roads, RFD Iron City, Tennessee; Pinhook, Lutts, Tennessee; Morrow Valley RFD Waynesboro, Tennessee; and Waynesboro, Elementary and High School.

Charles Denson was principal of Coalfield High School in Morgan County, Tennessee from 1928 to 1929; at Ducktown High School in Polk County, TN; Wayne County High School, Waynesboro, Tennessee m the 1930's; Selmer High School at Selmer", Tennessee in McNairy county from 1942 to 1945; Wayne County High School, Waynesboro, Tennessee in the 1950's; and Frank Hughes High School, Clifton, Tennessee from 1963 to 1966. From 1966 until retirement at age 70 in 1972, Charles served as High School Supervisor of Guidance for all Wayne County High Schools, including Wayne County High, Frank Hughes High, and Collinwood, High Schools. During his employment as principle at Frank Hughes High School, Clifton, Tennessee in the 1960's, he worked for the south integration of the schools there.

Charles was an education role-model for the entire Gallaher clan of Wayne County, Tennessee, as well as for hundreds of other people of Tennessee. He wrote the alma mater that is still sung by the Wayne County High School. Many of the academic program at Wayne County High School were initiated in the early days of Charles' leadership. He even coached basketball.

Charles Denson Gallaher was drafted into the US Army (34366888) (H) (A.A.F.) and served in the Medical Section as a Research Specialist, Nuclear Laboratories, Oak Ridge, Tennessee. He was in the 96th Bombardment Group, 336th Squadron. His service was from August 26, 1942 to April 12, 1943.

Charles was a member of the First Christian Church, the Tennessee Historical Society, Southern Historical Association, American Historical Association,

Masonic Lodge, and served as President of Wayne County library Board, Genealogist, County Historian from 1966 until his death in 1990.

Charles retired from teaching in 1972 at the age of 70, after which he devoted fall time service in the capacity of Wayne County, Tennessee Historian. He was responsible for the society compiling records of cemeteries and the people of Wayne County.

Charles Denson, Gallaher died March 11, 1990. He is remembered as a scholarly man of great honor, love and devotion to his family, friends and Mow Tennesseans. A photograph of Charles in his army uniform accompanies this writing.

Article submitted by R. Noel Gallaher and Glenn W. Gallaher, nephews of Charles D. Gallaher

GALLAHER, CHARLES INO, served in the U. S. Army during World War II from 6 August 1942 until 4 July 1944. He was stationed at O'Rielly General Hospital in Springfield, Missouri during his time in the army. He was born 30 December 1916 in Wayne County in the Ashland-Topsy Community. He was the son of Charlie Edgar and Myrtle Thompson Gallaher. He died 13 January 1986. He was married to Lela Sizemore and had one son, Robert Quentin Gallaher. He also has one grandson, Robert Davis Gallaher. He later married Maudell Gallaher. He had three sisters and one brother, Winfred Bowling, Magnolia Keeton, Irene Clanton and the late Mayhon, "Jack" Gallaher who retired from the U. S. Army.

GALLAHER, DURWARD ELLMONT, Serial Number 966 71 05, had the grade of Ship Fitter, Third Class in the United States

Navy. He enlisted as Apprentice Seaman on 24 January 1944 in Waynesboro, Tennessee. He was born 28 November 1911 in West Point, Tennessee. He held ratings of AS and SF3C. His service included the

following Vessels and/or Stations from 24 January 1944 to 17 January 1945: United States Naval Training Station, Great Lakes, Illinois; Receiving Station, San Diego, California; Receiving Station, Pearl Harbor, T. H. and USS ARD Thirteen. He was discharged 17 January 1945 from the U. S. Naval Hospital, PSNY, Bremerton, Washington. He was issued an Honorable Service Button.

GALLAHER, FLOYD W., Serial Number 34 921 992, was a Private First Class in 390th Medical Collecting Com-

pany in the Army of the United States. His permanent mailing address was Route 1, Waynesboro, Tennessee. He was born 2 July 1913 in Waynesboro. He was registered with Selective Service Board in Wayne County, Tennessee. His Civilian Occupation was Edger Man. He was married when he was inducted 30 December 1943 and entered into active service 20 January 1944 at Fort Oglethorpe, Georgia. His Military Occupational Specialty was Litter Bearer. He was in the battles of Ardennes, Rhineland, and Central Europe. The following decorations were awarded to Gallaher: World War II Victory Ribbon, Meritorious Unit Award, European-African Middle Eastern Theater Ribbon with 3 Bronze Stars and Good Conduct Medal. He left the USA 11 August 1944 for the European Theater Operation, and returned to USA 24 January 1946. He was discharged 28 January 1946 .

GALLAHER, HERSHELL H., son of Joe and Mattie Martin Gallaher, was born on September 4, 1911, in Wayne County and grew up in the West End community of Waynesboro. He was working as a watchman for Holthouse & Hartup at the time he was inducted into the United States Army on February 18, 1942, at Ft. Oglethorpe, Georgia. The next three years he served with Headquarters and Base service Squadron, 552nd Air Service Group and retired on December 17, 1945, at Camp Chaffee, Arkansas. Hershell and Joyce were married and made Elizabethton, Tennessee, their home after his retirement. They adopted a daughter, Shelby Jean. He died and is buried in Elizabethton.

GALLAHER, HUBERT, S/1C, is the son of Mr. and Mrs. W. J. Gallaher of Collinwood. He entered the service in October 1943. He took his basic training in Great Lakes, Illinois. In January 1944 he was assigned to a ship which carried him to the South Pacific and into combat several times. Seaman Gallaher was allowed to return to the States and to attend school for special training.
Source: Wayne County News.

GALLAHER, JOHN B., was the sixth son of William James (Billy) Gallaher (August 31, 1869 to April 20, 1940) and Nora

Clan (Cole) Gallaher (July 31, 1874). He was born April 5, 1910 in Wayne County, Tennessee, Route 2, Waynesboro on Banjo Bunch (also known as Talley Branch). He received an elementary education in Wayne County, Tennessee from Ray School on Upper Hog Creek (presently Ray's Chapel Baptist Church). John is a Mum and a member of the American Legion.

John married Edith (Estes) Gallaher, daughter of Jesse Estes and Anne Huckaba August 24, 1935. That same yen they moved to Detroit, Michigan where John was employed by Bundy Tubing. John worked for Bundy Tubing until he was drafted into die U.S. Army in 1943. At that time his wife Edith moved back to Waynesboro, Tennessee until John was discharged from the army at the end of the Second World War

Following his draft notice in 1943, John reported to the U.S. Army headquarters in Battle Creek, Michigan and was soon on his way south on a train by way of Chicago, Illinois, Cincinnati, Ohio, St. Louis, Missouri, little Rock, Arkansas, Memphis,

Tennessee and to his final destination at Camp Van Dom, Mississippi. Following some training in Mississippi, he was transferred to Fort Lee, Texarkana, Texas where he trained for about 9 months. He recounted an accident among fellow soldiers at Fort Lee, in which a 75 mm shell exploded killing several men and giving him a good scare. From Fort Lee, John received orders to proceed east to prepare for duty in Europe. He traveled to Camp Shanks, New York for a few days, while his Company of 162 men was My deployed. One of the highlights of his short stay in New York was his unit being greeted and encouraged by Joe Louis, a noted prize fighter of the day. He recalled a statement Lewis made in which he said, *Nobody likes war or this kind of fighting." John recalled that at midnight the day before departing for Europe his company was called out of bed and marched to a nearby hilltop where they sang "God Bless America. * The next day his company boarded the ship named "Ex. Checker* and departed for combat in Europe. The crossing took 26 days before landing in England.. He recalled that the water was so choppy that one could hardly sleep and the men were sick most of the trip.

John and his company spent two weeks in England after which they were ordered to board a LSD and embarked across the English Channel. He said they landed on a beach in Frame from which they moved inland. Death and destruction greeted John and his company, "sights that one wishes to forget!" John was designated to be the one to receive special training in recapping motor vehicle tires and traveled across Frame to a small privately owned recapping shop from which he increased his training in this area of war need. John became involved in training others in his company who became responsible for providing recapping services for 40,000 or more military fires.

Near the end of the war in Europe, John recounted an encounter he had with a large group of German soldiers who requested information of him on what they needed to do to surrender. John directed the commanding officer on how they could get through to the rear of the American lines and where to go. The Germans were surrendering for several reason, including hunger. John indicated that his company employed about 300 Germans at the time to assist with cooking and other duties as well as in recapping fires. At another time John provided assistance to three American prisoners of war. He said they were almost skin and bones, because of the lack of food. Even after providing them with food they were not able to consume but a few bites, due to their condition. He indi-

cated that they were routed to health facilities and he thought they likely were sent back to America. John's action in Europe took him to England, Frame, Spain, Luxembourg, and Germany.

John recalled the day of the Germans surrender in Europe. He said he just knew the war was over for him and his company, but it was not to be. John and his company were soon placed on train cars (called 40 and eights for 40 soldiers and eight mules) to be shipped out. It was during this time that John fell getting off the train and received significant injuries, but was moved on out anyway, by ship with his company to Panama. After a delay in the Panama Canal area, he was soon on his way to the Pacific to aid in the war with Japan. The crossing took 47 days and just before arrival in the Philippine Islands, Japan surrendered. John continued his duties supervising the recapping of military fires from a shop set up on board a small ship docked in the Philippines. After slightly over six months in the Philippines John was discharged from, the Army in. 1945. He recalls getting to meet and shake hands with. General Douglas MacArthur the day he received his discharge papers in Luzon, Philippines. John was noted as having the highest ranking in marksmanship Expert Marksman) in every outfit he served with during the war.

Upon his return to Waynesboro, Tennessee, John and his wife Edith purchased a farm on lower Indian Creek, war Olive Hill, Tennessee They lived at this location for only a few years. He also worked for a while for Yieser's Oil company. He eventually returned to the specialty he had learned in the service and took employment with the U.S. Government as Shop Foreman over a recapping facility in the Federal Penitentiary in Petersburg, Virginia. This facility provided two services, one was training of federal prison in a useful trade and the second was providing inexpensive recapped tires for the military and government. Following retirement from this position, John and Edith moved owe more back to Waynesboro, Tennessee in the mid 1960's. Following Ins return to Waynesboro, John served as City Judge for three and one-half years.

During his employment with the Federal Penitentiary in Petersburg, the FBI contacted John to see if he would serve as one of the body guards for the newly elected President John F. Kennedy. He was contacted because of his Expert Marksmanship record during the war and because he was also in a top security position with the Federal Government. John often recounted this story, with some regret that he had turned down the offer.

John and Edith are both members of the

Fim Baptist Church in Waynesboro, TN. They presently reside in the Wayne County Nursing Home, Waynesboro, Tennessee. A photograph of John in his army uniform accompanies this article.

Article submitted by R. Noel Gallaher and Glenn W. Gallaher, nephews of John Bell Gallaher

GALLAHER, SHERLOCK HOLMES, was the first of eight children born to William James Gallaher (August 31, 1869 to

April 20, 1940) and Nora Clara (Cole) Gallaher (July 31, 1874 to February 22, 19:54). Hoiner was born March 13, 1900 on Banjo Branch, also known as Talley Branch, Route #2 Waynesboro, Tennessee. He attended elementary school through the seventh grade at Ray School, presently known as Ray's Chapel Baptist Church, on upper Hog Creek. He also attended Leatherwood School on Hardin Creek and high school at Waynesboro, Tennessee. He served Wayne County as a elementary school teacher for dam years on Little Cypress Creek, in south Wayne County.

Homer served in the US Army in his first enlistment with the 21st Field Artillery (F.A.) at Camp Bragg, North Carolina from February 4, 1921 to February 4, 1922. He and his brother, Spencer Roam Gallaher, also of Wayne County, Tennessee, (born on Homer's birthday, Much 13, 1901. Spencer died February 15, 1992) on an walk to Florence, Alabama met an army recruiter and talked into enlisting in the US Army. See the photograph of Spencer Roam Gallaher in his First World War uniform. After the two brothers completed physical examinations, they traveled by train by way of Adam, Georgia on to Camp Bun, North Carolina. Both of the brothers served the entire yea of military service at Camp Bragg.

Homer was drafted a second time into the US Amy during the Second World War in 1942. During this time of active duty be served with the Military Police (M.P.) Bat-

talion, at Stapelton, Stanten Island, Now York.

Following his military service during the Second World War, Homer returned to Wayne County and married Lillian Neviaiane McClain on July 31, 1943. Homer and Lillian had four children including: 1) Lillian Margaret Tiberio (married to Salvatore Tiberio), 2) Nora Mai Longsworth (married to Ted Longsworth), 3) Loren Vincent Gallaher (married to Claudia Bertenaschi), and 4) Linda Mae Geffrion (married to David Geffrion).

Following a few years of farming in Wayne County, Tennessee, Homer moved his family to Toledo, Ohio where he worked at the American Shipbuilding Co,. retiring in 1965. Following retirement, Homer resided in Oregon, Ohio, a suburb of Toledo, Ohio until his death December 31, 1999. He died less than three months before his 100th birthday. At his death, three of his children and families were still living in Oregon, Ohio and his eldest, Lillian and family were living in Las Vegas, Nevada. He was also survived by eight grandchildren and 9 great-grandchildren.

Homer was a devout patriot of his country. He was a member of East Toledo Baptist Church. Family and friends remember Homer for his great passion for reading and his collection of books on every subject. He was a loving family non and a self educated scholar.

Article submitted by R. Noel Gallaher and Glenn W. Gallaher, nephews of Sherock Holmes (Homer) Gallaher.

GALLIEN, ARCHIE H., son of Richard "Babe" and Nancy Hayes Gallien, graduated from Collinwood High School in 1934. He entered service in December 1943 and received his basic training at Camp Lee, Virginia and Camp Reynolds, Pennsylvania. He was sent to Alaska October 1944. Before he entered the service he was employed by TVA. Archie had four brothers, Charles, James M. lives in Athens, Alabama, Joe R., and John R. Gallien and a half brother Gerald E. Butler, and a sister Clara Gallien Stricklin of Iron City. He married Elizabeth Roberts and they have one son. They make their home in Iron City.

GALLIEN, CHARLES HARDING, SR., Serial Number 34 189 069, was a Sergeant with in the 464th Army Air Force Base Unit. His permanent mailing address was Route 3, Iron City, Tennessee. He entered service 18 February 1942 at Fort Oglethorpe, Georgia. His description was blue eyes, brown hair, 5'7" tall and weighed 158 pounds. He took his training in Florida and Louisiana. He was transferred to England in August 1942. Before

he entered the service he was Farmer. His Military Occupational Specialty was Airplane Armorer. His battles and campaigns included Ardennes, Rhineland, Naples-Foggia, Air Combat in Northern France, Central Europe, Tunisia, Egypt-Libya, Sicily, Air Offensive Europe, and Normandy. Decorations awarded to Gallien include Distinguished Unit Badge, Good Conduct Medal, European-Africa Middle Eastern Service Medal with 2 Silver Stars and 1 Bronze Star. He left the USA on 31 August 1942 for the European Theater and returned 21 June 1945. He was discharged 12 September 1945 at Fort McPherson, Georgia. Charles, son of Richard "Babe" and Nancy Hayes Gallien, was born 1 June 1920 in Collinwood, Tennessee, died on Monday March 8, 1994 in Eliza Coffee Memorial Hospital in Florence, Alabama and was buried in Railroad Cemetery in Iron City. Charles had four brothers, Archie H., Charles, James M. lives in Athens, Alabama, Joe R. lives in Franklin, and John R. Gallien and a half brother Gerald E. Butler, and a sister Clara Gallien Stricklin of Iron City. He was married 26 December 1945 to Lavaughan Roberson of Iron City, Tennessee. They had two sons Charles Gallien, Jr. and Tommy Ray Gallien. Charles graduated from Collinwood High School in 1940. He was a retired carpenter and attended Railroad Methodist Church.

GALLIEN, JAMES M., Serial Number 34 494 858, was a Private First Class with Company B 783rd Military Police Battalion of the United States Army. His permanent mailing address was Route 3, Iron City, Tennessee. He was single. His Civilian Occupation was Truck Driver. He was registered with Selective Service Board No. 1, Waynesboro, Tennessee. He was inducted 22 November 1942 and entered active service 29 November 1942 at Fort Oglethorpe, Georgia. His Military Occupational Specialty was Military Policeman. His Military Qualifications included MM Pistol. He was in battles in Normandy, Rhineland and Northern France. His decorations included the American Theater Service Ribbon, World War II Victory Medal, European African Middle Eastern Theater Service Medal, Meritorious Unit Award and Good Conduct Medal. He left the USA 12 February 1944 for European-African Middle Eastern Theater and returned home 12 September 1945. He was honorably discharged 7 November 1945 at Camp Gordon, Georgia. James, son of Richard "Babe" and Nancy Hayes Gallien, was born 22 February 1922 in Wayne County, He had four brothers Archie H, Charles, Joe R. lives in Franklin, and John R. Gallien and a half brother Gerald E. Butler, and a sister Clara Gallien Stricklin of Iron City. He is a graduate of Collinwood High School and lives in Athens Alabama.

GALLIEN, JOE RAY, Serial Number 604 06 26, Signalman First Class, volunteered and was inducted in the United States Navy on 7 October 1941 at Birmingham, Alabama. He was registered with the Selective Service Board in Inkster, Michigan. His Permanent mailing address was Route 3, Iron City, Tennessee. His Civilian Occupation was Hospital Attendant in Veteran's Hospital in Dearborn, Michigan. Gallien served on the following Vessels and/or Stations: NTS NOB Norfolk, Virginia, AGC Brooklyn, NY; SS Sirocco, SS El Oceana, SS Sandmaster, USS PASTORES, USS HENRY S. GROVE, and USN AGC New Orleans, Louisiana. He was honorably discharged 20 October 1945 in Memphis, Tennessee. Joe was called from inactive duty and reenlisted in the Navy on 7 September 1950 in Nashville, Tennessee, with Service Number 604 06 26. He was discharged 30 November 1951. He had gray eyes, brown hair, 5'7" tall and weighed 210 lbs. After the war he was a postal employee in Franklin until he retired. Joe, son of Richard "Babe" and Nancy Hayes Gallien, was born 6 February 1919 in Iron City, died Sunday September 5, 1993 at his home in Franklin, Tennessee. Burial was in Railroad Cemetery in Iron City. Joe had four brothers Archie H, Charles, James M. lives in Athens, Alabama, and John R. Gallien and a half brother Gerald E. Butler, and a half sister Clara Stricklin of Iron City. He had a foster son, James Cobb of Nashville and a foster daughter Bernice Ward.

GALLIEN, JOHN R., son of Richard "Babe" and Nancy Hayes Gallien, had four brothers Archie H, Charles, James M. lives in Athens, Alabama, Joe R. lives in Franklin, and a half brother Gerald E. But-

ler, and a half sister Clara Stricklin of Iron City. He married Earline Eaton and they had two children at the time of his induction. He was stationed at Camp Shelby, Mississippi. John graduated from Collinwood High School in 1936. He was employed by TVA when he was inducted into service in December 1944.

GALLIEN, LELAND, was born on December 2nd, 1916 and died on March 3rd, 1981. He was the son of the late Med

Warren and Nannie L. Wilson Gallien. He had one brother, Clarence Gallien, and one sister, Lacy Gallien both of whom are deceased. Mr. Gallien attended school in Collinwood, Tennessee and graduated in 1936.

Mr. Gallien left his family to serve his country in World War II from December 1943 to September, 1945. He was a rifleman with Company K, 12th Infantry. Mr. Gallien served in the European Theater, where he fought in two major battles, the Battle of the Rhineland, and the Ardennes. Mr. Gallien was awarded the Purple Heart for wounds he received in Germany on February 9th, 1945. He also received the European African Middle Eastern Theater Ribbon with two Bronze Battle Stars. After being wounded, Mr. Gallien spent several months in military hospitals both in Europe and the United States., He was honorably discharged from the Army on September 14th, 1945 from Camp Butner Convalescent Hospital in North Carolina. Mr. Gallien was always honored and proud to have served his country. He often told his children about the brave and wonderful men he served with. He never forgot them.

After returning home to Wayne County, he married Lila Ruth O'Bryant in 1946. She was the daughter of Little Tom and Lillian Hill O'Bryant. They had five children: Carolyn Mauldon, Janis Cook, Michael Gallien, Gene Gallien and Deborah Jackson.

He was also blessed with seven grandchildren: Dewayne, Chris, and Amy Mauldon, Megan and Matthew Gallien, Corey and Emily Jackson. He also had one great-grandchild, Lexie Mauldon.

Mr. Gallien retired from the Tennessee Valley Authority after 30 years of service. At his untimely death at age 64, he was laid to rest at Whitten's Crossroads Cemetery along side his parents until August 11th, 1999 when he was joined by his wife of 35 years.

GALLOWAY, CHARLES, Funeral services for Charles E. Galloway, 81 of Hwy 64, W Waynesboro, were conducted

Saturday, December 6 at 1 P.M., at the Cumberland Presbyterian Church in Waynesboro with Herbert Carlock Jr. officiating. Burial was in Memorial Gardens in Waynesboro. Mr. Galloway died Thursday, December 4 at Wayne Medical Center in Waynesboro.

GAMBRELL, BUFORD H., Serial Number 34 983 725, was a Private First Class with Company C, 210th Infantry Training Battalion of the Army of the United States. He was born in Waynesboro, Tennessee. His Civilian Occupation was Trailer Truck Driver. He was married and 27 years old when he was inducted. His Military Occupational Specialty was Basic. His Military Qualifications included MM Rifle. He was discharged 28 October 1944 at Fort McPherson, Georgia.

GAMBRELL, LOUIS, Serial Number 34 373 158, was a Private with Second Headquarters, Special Troops, ILL Corps in the Army of the United States. He was born in Iron City, Tennessee. His Civilian Occupation was Truck Driver. He was married and 31 7/12 years old when he was inducted. He had blue eyes, brown hair, ruddy complexion and was 5' 10" in height. His Military Occupational Specialty was

Cannoneer. He was discharged 28 February 1944 at Camp Cook, California.

GARNER, CURTIS BROWN, was inducted into the Army 20 March 1943. He took his basic training in California,

Mississippi and Alabama. He was sent to the European African Middle Eastern Theater. His departure date was 25 November 1944 and he landed in France 8 December 1944. He was wounded in combat 5 January 1945 and returned to the States 11 May 1945. Garner attained the rank of Corporal with Company A, 141st Infantry, 36th Division. He was awarded the Combat Infantry Badge, The M-1 Marksman Badge and the Purple Heart. He spent 2 years, 4 months and 7 days in service before he was honorably discharged with a Medical Certificate on 24 July 1945. Curtis was born 15 June 1923 in Flatwoods, Perry County, Tennessee, died 26 February 1997 in St. Thomas Hospital in Nashville and was buried in Memorial Gardens in Waynesboro. His parents were Ada Agnes Hamm and Samuel Theodore Garner. He had four brothers, Elmer Ernest, Ben Willard, Boyd Atha and John Isaac Garner. He had three sisters, Clora Bell, Mary Tom and Imogene Garner. On 31 May 1945, he married Bonnie Lois Stricklin. They had two daughters and five grandchildren. Pamela Cheryl Garner married David Johnson and they have three children, Samantha Nicole, Ginger Michelle and Adam Tyler Johnson. The other daughter, Shelia Ann Garner married Phillip Ray Harris and they have two children, Matthew Jarrad and Bethany Ann Harris. He was a retired supervisor with Genesco Manufacturing, and a member of Flatwoods Church of Christ.

GEIBEL, REGIS, 76, of Waynesboro died 11 August 1997 in Waynesboro and was buried in Memorial Gardens in Collinwood. He was a native of Herman, Pennsylvania, A World War II and Korean

War Veteran, a Prudential Insurance Agent, a member of St. Mary's Catholic Church in Herman, and a member of the Knights of Columbus and the Elks Lodge. He was the son of Henry and Dorothy Miller Geibel. Survivors included his son Robert Geibel of McAfee, New Jersey, two daughters, Jane Skaggs of Collinwood and Karen Daniel of Iron City; Three brothers, Henry, Jim and Donnie Geibel all of Butler, Pennsylvania; two sisters, Joan Alwiac and Leona Davis both of Butler; nine grandchildren and six great-grandchildren.

Source: Wayne County News, 13 August 1997.

GILCHRIST, JAMES WILLIAM, Serial Number 967 13 53, had the Grade of Storekeeper, Second Class. He was born 30 December 1923 in Cypress Inn, Tennessee. He was inducted in the United States Navy on 10 April 1944. Gilchrist served on the following Vessels and/or Stations: NTS Williamsburg, Virginia, R/S Norfolk, Virginia, NOB Trinidad BWI, Escort Repair Base Trinidad BWI, Independent Unit NOB Trinidad BWI, and US Naval Supply Depot Trinidad BWI. He was awarded the American Area Campaign and Victory Medal. He was honorably discharged 21 March 1946 in Memphis, Tennessee.

GILLHAM, FRED ELLIOTTE, had the Grade of Carpenter's Mate First Class in the US Navy. He was issued an Honorable Discharge Button, Honorable Service Lapel Button and Honorable Service Emblem. He was discharge 2 October 1945 in Memphis, Tennessee. Fred was the son of Archie Harold and Leila Mae Finger Gillham. He married Delia Hime from the Ross Creek Community near Clifton. They resided in Clifton. They had two children, Archie Dee and Fred, Jr. Fred, his wife and Archie Dee are buried in the Clifton City Cemetery. Fred's siblings are Anna Mae Gillham Jeter, Mary, Robbie, and Finley Gillham.

GILLIS, COY HERSCHEL, Serial Number 34 495 080, was a Private First Class with the 167th General Hospital in the Army of the United States. He was also a Combat Medic with the 99th Division, 32th Medical Battalion. His permanent mailing address was Route 2, Lutts, Tennessee. He was registered with Selective Service Board in Wayne County, Tennessee. His Civilian Occupation was General Farm Hand. He was married when he left Waynesboro 22 November 1942 and traveled by bus to Fort Oglethorpe, Georgia where he entered into active service 29 November 1942. His Military Occupational Specialty was Litter Bearer. He was

in the battles of Rhineland. The following decorations were awarded to Gillis: European-African Middle Eastern Theater Ribbon with 1 Bronze Star, American Theater Ribbon, World War II Victory Ribbon, and Good Conduct Medal. He left the USA 29 September 1944 for the European Theater Operation, and returned to USA 13 January 1946. He was discharged 17 January 1946 at Camp Atterbury, Indiana. Coy was born 28 January 1922 in Wayne County. He is the son of James Thomas Gillis (1893-1967) and Susan Artie Rich (1895-1975). His brothers and sisters are: 1. Lora Ocie Gillis, born 29 September 1913, married Wilburn Lee Bevis. 2. Ira Quinton Gillis, born 29 November 1915, married Chrystal Holt. 2. Sarah Irene Gillis, born 19 December 1919, died 30 January 1928. 4. James Carvel Gillis, born 23 February 1925, died 25 December 1944. 5. Zora Iva Nora Gillis, born 5 March 1929, married Walter Lee Bratton. 6. Rhoda Laveda Gillis, born 5 February 1932, married Seab Murphy, Jr. 7. Ima Elvesta Gillis, born 5 January 1935, married George William Murphy. Coy was married 23 June 1943 in Florence, Lauderdale County, Alabama to Edith Berry, daughter of Paulk and Mattie (Vickery) Berry. Edith was born 17 July 1926. Their children: (1) Linda Marie Gillis, born 1 March 1945, married (1) Donald Lee Blalock and (2) Johnny Thompson. (2) J. P. Gillis, born 7 February 1948, married Sandra Chambers. and (3) James Allen Gillis, born 21 March 1951, died 25 September 1957.

GILLIS, DANIEL HARRY, was inducted into the United States Army 12 August 1941 at Fort Oglethorpe, Georgia. He completed basic training at Fort Eustis, Virginia. He was transferred to Fort Knox, Kentucky and then to Warner Robins, Georgia. In 1943 he traveled to Oakland, California where he boarded the Dutch ship Nordam for the South Pacific. First stop was Townsville, Australia and then on to Port Moresby, New Guinea, He flew

through a hurricane on his way to Clark Field in the Philippines. Dan served on various Pacific Islands from New Guinea to Luzon to Le Shima. He was involved in the battles of Bismarck-Archipelago Islands, Papua, New Guinea, Luzon in the Philippines and Ie Shima. Dan was assigned as a military police motorcyclist with the 1131st Military Police Company (aviation) attached to the 5th Air Force. He rode a motorcycle in such duties as traffic control and direction and to guard plane crashes by getting there ahead of other personnel to protect property. His other two years in service included such general duties as a military policeman, a regular town duty, interior and outpost guard duty and prisoner escort. On 20 August 1945, Dan guarded the Mitsubishi G4M-1 (Betty) that landed on Ie Shima. It brought a sixteen man delegation to represent Japan in preliminary peace talks. The Japanese, accompanied by an allied delegation, preceded by C-54 to Manila. Thanksgiving Day 1945, Dan returned to Vancouver, Washington. After serving four year years, three months and twenty-five days, Corporal Gillis received an Honorable Discharge on 6 December 1945 at Camp Chaffee, Arkansas. His decorations and citations included: World War II Victory Ribbon, Asiatic Pacific Theater Ribbon and Four Bronze Stars, Good Conduct Medal, American Theater Ribbon, Philippine Liberation Ribbon, and American Defense Service Ribbon. Dan, the fifth child of Ira Haywood and Maude Catherine Johnson Gillis was born in Wayne County, Tennessee on 18 January 1919. His grandparents were James and Mahulda Sims Johnson and Thomas Jefferson and Fannie Middleton Gillis. Dan had six brothers and two sisters: Frank Hugh, Homer Clyde, Donald Clay, Nancy Catherine, Anna Isophine, George Samuel, James Thomas, and John Dougal Gillis. His brothers Homer C., Donald Clay, James and George Samuel Gillis were also in service for their country during World War II. Dan attended

Lockland and Springdale school in Ohio and Memorial and Three Churches School on Indian Creek in Wayne County. After graduation, he worked with his father on a one hundred acre farm, raising cotton, corn and hay. Livestock included horses, mules, chickens, cattle and hogs. On 2 August 1941, Dan married Lois Evelyn Partain and they had three daughters: Nancy Louise born 10 March 1947, Betty Elaine born 27 August 1948 and Debra Annette born 8 June 1960. Nancy married Lester Paul Heard and they have a son, Derrick Paul born 30 June 1973. Betty married Jerry Travis Risner and they have a son, John Travis Risner born 13 May 1979. Dan and Evelyn purchased a farm in the northern part of Wayne County where Dan enjoyed farming for the next forty-five years, He passed away on 18 December 1990 and is buried in Oak Ridge Cemetery.

GILLIS, DONALD CLAY, Serial Number 34 180 400, the third child of Ira Haywood and Maude Catherine Johnson

Gillis was born in Hardin County, Tennessee on 11 March 1915. His grandparents were James and Mahulda Sims Johnson and Thomas Jefferson and Fannie Middleton Gillis. Don had six brother and two sisters: Frank Hugh, Homer Clyde, Daniel Harry, Nancy Catherine, Anna Isophine, George Samuel, James Thomas, and John Dougal Gillis. His brothers Homer C., Daniel Harry, James and George Samuel Gillis were also in service for their country during World War II. Don attended Lockland and Springdale school in Ohio and Memorial and Three Churches School on Indian Creek in Wayne County. After graduation, he worked with his father on a farm, raising cotton, corn and hay. Livestock included horses, mules, chickens, cattle and hogs. He then moved to Lockland, Ohio and worked one year at Jim Walter Corporation. Don was inducted into the United States Army on 13 November 1941 at Fort Oglethorpe, Georgia. He

volunteered for the United States Air Force. His basic training was completed at Biloxi, Mississippi. Don then went to Key Field, Barksdale in Shreveport, Louisiana. He had motor vehicle training for one month. Then he moved to Greenville, South Carolina where he was a jeep driver for six weeks. Next stop was Ford's giant new Willow Run plant in Ypsilanti, Michigan. Then Don traveled to Fort Stoneman, California near San Francisco. On 3 September 1942, Don was one of thirteen hundred men on the 90th Bomb Squad to board the S. S. REPUBLIC that slipped through the Golden Gate Bridge into the troubled waters of the Pacific. Eight days later they arrived in Honolulu, Hawaii. The 320th lived in rugged isolation in a sugar cane field and trained for night driving and blackouts. On 19 October 1942, Don left for Brisbane, Australia on the Norwegian transport Torrens. Then he went on to Northern Australia, Port Moresby, New Guinea, Markham Valley, Philippines and Ie Shima. His battles and campaigns included Papua, New Guinea, Bismarck-Archipelago and Luzon, Southern Philippines. Sergeant Gillis returned to Seattle, Washington on 16 September 1945. He served three years, two months and twenty eight days. He received an Honorable Discharge 5 October 1945 at Camp Chaffee, Arkansas. Don's decorations and citations included: American Defense Service Ribbon, Good Conduct Medal, Distinguished Badge, Philippine Liberation Ribbon, Asiatic Pacific Service Ribbon and a Silver Service Star. After his discharge from the Army, Don returned to work in Ohio. He married Juanita Catherine Barnes on 19 June 1949. They had two sons: Donald Eugene born 6 June 1950 and Charles David born 23 December 1952. Juanita passed away on 4 April 1954. Don married Grace Lucille Lawson on 1 March 1959. He worked at the Jim Walter Corporation for twenty-seven years doing various jobs. His son Donald married Sharon Metzer and they have two children, Donald Keith and Kimberly Ann. Don retired in 1977 and he and Grace returned to Wayne County where they still reside.

GILLIS, GEORGE SAMUEL, Serial Number 34 501 405, was a Private First Class in Squadron F 137th Army Air Force Base Unit in the Army of the United States. His permanent mailing address was Route 2, Waynesboro, Tennessee. He was registered with Selective Service Board in Wayne County, Tennessee. His Civilian Occupation was General Farm Hand. He was inducted 20 December 1942 and entered into active service 27 December 1942 at Fort Oglethorpe, Georgia. His Military Occupational Specialty was Salvage Tech-

nician. His Military Qualifications were MM Rifle and SS Carbine. The following Decorations were awarded to Gillis: American Service Medal, World War II Victory Ribbon, and Good Conduct Medal. He was discharged 19 February 1946 Fort McPherson, Georgia. George received his basic training at Fort Ruckman, Massachusetts. After being stationed in that area for several months, he was transferred to Camp Hood, Texas, and from there to the Air Force at Shepherd Field, Texas, then on to Charlotte, North Carolina. George, son of Ira Haywood and Maude Catherine Johnson Gillis was born in Waynesboro, Tennessee on 16 September 1922. His grandparents were James and Mahulda Sims Johnson and Thomas Jefferson and Fannie Middleton Gillis. George had six brother and two sisters: Frank Hugh, Homer Clyde, Donald Clay, Daniel Harry, Nancy Catherine, Anna Josephine, James Thomas, and John Dougal Gillis. His brothers Homer C., Daniel Harry, James and Donald Clay Gillis were also in service for their country during World War II. George finished one year of high school. After that, he worked with his father on a farm, raising cotton, corn and hay. Livestock included horses, mules, chickens, cattle and hogs.

GILLIS, HOMER CLYDE, Serial Number 34 713 894, was a Private First Class in 163rd Engineers Combat Battalion of the United States Army. His permanent mailing address was Route 2, Waynesboro. His Civilian Occupation was Wire Puller. He was inducted 23 April 1943 and entered active service 30 April 1943 at Camp Forest, Tennessee. His Military Occupational Specialty was Rigger General. His Military Qualification was Marksman Rifle. He fought in battles in Normandy, Northern France, Rhineland, and Central Europe. Gillis received the following decorations: Croix Guerre with Palm Fourragere Free of Provincial Government of France, World War II Victory

Medal, Good Conduct Medal, and European African Middle Eastern Theater Ribbon with 4 Bronze Service Stars. He left the USA on 27 February 1944 for European-African Middle Eastern, and returned to the USA 28 December 1945. He was discharged 4 January 1946 at Fort Knox, Kentucky. PFC Gillis received his basic training at Camp Van-Dorn, Mississippi. After completing basic training, he went on maneuvers in Louisiana and was soon assigned to overseas duty with an engineering unit. Prior to entering service he was employed by Briggs Manufacturing in Detroit. He married Lucille Nowlin, daughter of Mr. and Mrs. Walter Nowlin Four brothers, Donald Clay, James, George Samuel and Daniel are also in the service.

Source: Wayne County News.

Homer, the son of Ira Haywood and Maude Catherine Johnson Gillis, was born 22 September 1913 in Olive Hill, Tennessee. His grandparents were James and Mahulda Sims Johnson and Thomas Jefferson and Fannie Middleton Gillis. Homer had six brother and two sisters: Frank Hugh, Donald Clay, Daniel Harry, Nancy Catherine, Anna Josephine, George Samuel, James Thomas, and John Dougal Gillis.

GILLIS, IRA, Serial Number 966 28 38, enlisted in the Navy 31 December 1943 and entered into active service 7 January 1944. He was a Seaman First Class. He was discharged 11 January 1946 in Memphis, Tennessee. He took six weeks of boot training at Farragut, Idaho, and four weeks of gunnery training at San Diego, California before being assigned to a ship. He was an armed guard serving as a gunner on four ships. He was on active duty in the Pacific, Australia, New Guinea and the Philippines. On the 6th of April 1945, his ship, Hobbs Victory, was sunk off Okinawa by a Japanese suicide plane. The ship, although heavy loaded with ammunition, lost only thirteen men. The other Vessels and Stations that he served on are: SS Fort George,

USN TADCEN Shoemaker, California and USS Casa Grande. Ira was born 29 November 1915 in Cypress Inn, Tennessee. His parents were James Thomas Gillis (1893-1967) and Susan Artie Rich (1895-1975). His brothers and sisters are:1. Lora Ocie Gillis, born 29 September 1913, married Wilburn Lee Bevis. 2. Sarah Irene Gillis born 19 December 1919, died 30 January 1928. 3. Coy Herschel Gillis, born 28 January 1922, married Edith Berry. 4. James Carvel Gillis, born 23 February 1925, killed 25 December 1944 in World War II. 5. Zora Iva Nora Gillis, born 5 March 1929, married Walter Lee Bratton. 6. Rhoda Laveda Gillis, born 5 February 1932, married Seab Murphy, Jr. 7. Ima Elvesta Gillis, born 5 January 1935, married George William Murphy. Ira was married 21 December 1935 to Chrystal Holt. They make their home in Collinwood. Their children are:1. Glen Edwin Gillis, born 26 November 1941, married Judy Nipper October 1962. They have one daughter, Michelle Rae born 21 September 1963. Michelle married Randy Robinson and has one daughter Amanda Lauren Robinson born 5 January 1990 and a son Tyler Lynn born 14 October 1992. Glenn's second marriage was to Maude Bentley in March 1970. Glen also has a stepson, Johnny Helton. Glenn and Maude make their home in Greenhill, Alabama. 2. Kathy Renae Gillis, born 9 June 1951, married Larry Toungette August 15 1970. They have three children: Brandon Scott born 9 October 1974, Beth Renae born 23 December 1978 and Adam Matthew born 29 June 1981. Kathy and her family live in Collinwood. 3. Ira and Chrystal also had three babies to die shortly after birth and they are buried in Piney Grove Cemetery in Cypress Inn.

GILLIS, JAMES T., Serial Number 44 044 573, was a Technician Fifth Grade with 762nd Engineer L E Company in the Army of the United States. He was born 6 September 1925 in Cincinnati, Ohio. His per-

manent mailing address was Box 143, Waynesboro, Tennessee. He entered the service on 19 December 1944 at Fort Oglethorpe, Georgia. His civilian occupation was student in high school. His Military Occupational Specialty was Crane Operator. His Military Qualification was MM W/Rifle. His decorations included Asiatic Pacific Theater Ribbon, Victory Medal, Good Conduct Medal, and Army of Occupation-Japan Medal. He was also issued a Lapel Button and two Overseas Bars. He left the USA on 6 August 1945 for Pacific Theater Operations and returned 26 September 1946. He was discharged 23 November 1946 at Fort Sheridan, Illinois. Pvt James F. Gillis, son of Mr. and Mrs. Ira H. Gillis, received his basic training at Camp Blanding, Florida. Before induction into service Pvt Gillis was employed by Holthouse and Hardup Hickory Mill in Waynesboro. He married Iva Mae Jackson from Ohio and they had one son, Stephen.

Source: Wayne County News. Album of Clyde Bevis.

GILLIS, TOM E., Serial Number 34 373 127, was a Staff Sergeant in Squadron A 813 AAFBU of the United States Army.

His permanent mailing address was Route 1, Waynesboro. His Civilian Occupation was Riveter Aircraft. He was married when inducted 24 September 1942 and entered active service 8 October 1942 at Fort Oglethorpe, Georgia. His Military Qualification was Carbine SS. He fought in battles in Rome-Arno, Southern France, Northern France, Ardennes, Rhineland and Central Europe. Gillis received Seven Bronze Stars for the above campaigns per Ltr's MTOUSA, NTOUSA, European Theater Operations USA; a Distinguished Unit Badge Medal, European-African Middle Eastern Theater Ribbon, Lapel Button, Good Conduct Ribbon and Two Overseas Bars. He left the USA on 27 February 1944 for England, and returned to the USA 18 July 1945. His education consisted of 4 years of high school. He was discharged 19 October 1945 at Scott Field, Illinois. Tom graduated from high school in 1939 in Clifton. He lived in the Flat Gap area while growing up. Tom, son of Van and Willie Ricketts Gillis, was born 3 December 1919 in Olive Hill, Tennessee, died August 1985 and is buried in Philadelphia Church Cemetery on Highway 64 West. He had one sister, Frances Gillis who married Lee Roy Patterson. Tom married Jessie Atwell and they had one daughter, Beverly Gillis who married Gary Adams.

GIPSON, VELMA YAPMAN, Serial Number 966 28 43, was an Apprentice Seaman V6s in the United States Naval Reserve. He was discharged from US Naval Training Station, Farragut, Idaho on the 4 February 1944. He was born 10 October 1906. He spent his time in service at Naval Reserve Station, Chattanooga, Tennessee and Naval Training Station in Farragut, Idaho. Gipson's description was brown eyes, black hair, ruddy complexion, 5'6" height, weight 147 and married. His monthly rate of pay when discharged was $50. 00. He was furnished five cents per mile from Athel, Idaho to Waynesboro, Tennessee and was paid $136. 62 in full to date of his discharge.

GIVENS, LOUIS R., Serial Number 34 903 949, was a Private First Class with Company A, 23rd Armored Infantry Battalion of the Army of the United States. His permanent mailing address was Route 3, Iron City, Tennessee. He was born 14 October 1913 in Florence, Alabama. His Civilian Occupation was General Farmer. He was inducted 22 January 1944 and entered into active service 11 February 1944 at Camp Forrest, Tennessee. His Military Occupational Specialty was Rifleman. His Military Qualifications included Rifle Combat Infantry Badge. Givens participated in battles in Ardennes, Rhineland and Central Europe. He was awarded the European African Middle Eastern Service Medal, American Service Medal, Victory Medal, Three Bronze Stars in the European Area and Good Conduct Medal. He left the USA 30 August 1944 for European Theater Operations and returned 9 August 1945. He was discharged 6 February 1946 at Fort McPherson, Georgia.

GOBBELL, FRED M., Serial Number 34 373 133, was a Private First Class with 510th Quartermaster Railhead Company of the Army of the United States. His permanent mailing address was Route 6, Lawrenceburg, Tennessee. He was born 17 November 1913 in Lawrenceburg, Tennessee. His Civilian Occupation was Light Truck Driver. He was registered with Selective Service Board in Wayne County, Tennessee. He was inducted 24 September 1942 and entered into active service 8 October 1942 at Fort Oglethorpe, Georgia. His Military Occupational Specialty was Warehouseman. His Military Qualifications included Rifle SS. He was awarded the World War II Victory Medal, Pacific Service Medal, and Good Conduct Medal, He left the USA 31 July 1943 for the Pacific Theater and returned 13 November 1945. He was discharged 19 November 1945 at Fort McPherson, Georgia. The highest grade held was Corporal.

GOBBELL, ODELL, Serial Number 34 936 457, was a Private First Class with Company H, 164th Infantry of the Army of the United States. His permanent mailing address was Route 6, Lawrenceburg, Tennessee. He was born 1 February 1919 in Wayne County, Tennessee. His Civilian Occupation was General Farm Hand. He was registered with Selective Service Board in Wayne County, Tennessee. He was married when he was inducted 28 July 1944 at Camp Forrest, Tennessee. His Military Occupational Specialty was Heavy Mortar Crewman. His Military Qualifications included SS Rifle Combat Infantry Badge. He fought in battles in the Southern Philippines. He was awarded the World War II Victory Medal, Asiatic-Pacific Theater Ribbon with One Bronze Battle Star, Philippines Liberation Ribbon with One Bronze Battle Star, Three Overseas Service Bars, Army of Occupation Medal and Good Conduct Medal. He left the USA 9 February 1945 for the Pacific Theater and returned 9 August 1946. He was discharged 15 August 1946 at Fort Meridan, Illinois.

GOBBELL, WILEY CLAYTON, was the son of Charlie and Elzadia Gobbell, was born 11 February 1922 on Forty Eight Creek in Wayne County. The youngest of seven children, I attended school in Savannah and Waynesboro, Tennessee. I went into the United States Army

on 20 December 1942. I took my basic training at Fort Sheridan, Illinois in the 476th AAA, then went to Camp Stoneman, California. From there I was sent to Sydney, Australia, then to Brisbane, Australia and next to Townsville, Australia. Here we received training for nine months for warfare in the Pacific. Next I was sent to Orlaundia, New Guinea, then to Netherland Indies. This is the first action that we saw. I was a jeep driver for the officers of the 476th AAA. We set up around the air strip to fire on enemy planes coming in. We left here and went to Palawan, Philippines. From there on to Luzon, Philippines. We were taking training to go to Japan. The war ended before we went and I was shipped back to the United States and discharged in January 1946 at Fort Smith, Arkansas after thirty-seven months in the United States Army. On 22 December 1946, I married Ellen Harris of Centerville, Tennessee. We have four children, Ricky, Sherry, Gary and Jackie Gobbell. We have five grandchildren and two step grandchildren. We live in the Mink Branch subdivision in Waynesboro, Tennessee dated 1 December 1991.

GOBBELL, WILLIAM W., JR., son of William Wylie, Sr. (Billy) and Minnie (Hooks) Gobbell, was born, September 2, 1919, at West Point, Tn. He and Helen Clayton were married, September 10, 1939 living at Shawnatee and he was working in timber when he was inducted into the U.S. Army, September 2, 1945, at Ft. Oglethorpe, GA. From there he was assigned to Ft. Hood, TX. for thirteen weeks training, then to the Pacific Theater.

GOODMAN, ALBERT LOUIS, Service Number 295 14 67, enlisted in the United States Navy 18 July 1942 in Nashville, Tennessee, as AMM2C, V-6, USNR, Mate Second Class. He served satisfactorily on active duty from U S Naval Recruiting Station, Nashville, Tennessee; US Naval Air Station, Memphis, Tennessee; and US Naval Hospital, Memphis. He was discharged 31 July 1945 at the U S Naval Hospital in Memphis, Tennessee. Albert, son of Ewing and Bessie L. Davis Goodman, was born 21 December 1910 in Clifton, Tennessee, died in 1977 and was buried in Anderson Davis/Holt Cemetery, one half mile West of Old Union Church on Beech Creek. He married Opal Ray, daughter of William and Lily Conaway Ray. They had two children Conrad and Sandra Goodman. Albert had one brother, Edgar Daniel Goodman who was also a World War II Veteran. Albert and Opal made their home near Clifton and later in Waynesboro.

GOODMAN, EDGAR DANIEL, "Edd" is the son of James Ewing and Bessie L. Davis Goodman and was born 1911, died 14 January 1997 and was buried Memorial Gardens in Waynesboro. Edd was inducted into the United States Navy January 1940 in Norfolk, Virginia. He was sent to the Atlantic Theater of War and was in active service in the Normandy Invasion. He stayed in the Navy for six years. He worked with Civil Service in Florida after he was discharged from the Navy. He is now retired. Edd married Ada Mozelle Gobbell from Waynesboro. They have one son, Timothy Shane Goodman. They live near Scott Hill, Tennessee. Edd had one brother, Albert Louis Goodman who was also in the Navy during World War II.

GOODWIN, OTIS L., Serial Number 34 735 447, was a Private First Class in the 708th Ordnance Company of the Army of the United States. He was born 30 April 1918 in Calhoun City, Mississippi. His permanent mailing address was Box 113, Waynesboro, Tennessee. He was married with two dependents. His Civilian Occupation was Fireman Stationary Boiler. He was registered with Selective Service Board No. 1, Waynesboro, Tennessee. He was inducted 2 June 1943 and entered active service 16 June 1943 at Fort Oglethorpe, Georgia. His Military Occupational Specialty was Cook.

His Military Qualifications included Marksman Rifle. He was in battles in Normandy, Northern France, Rhineland and Central Europe. His decorations included: European African Middle Eastern Theater Service Medal with four Bronze Service Stars and Good Conduct Medal. He left the USA 5 December 1943 for the European Theater and returned 9 July 1945. He was discharged 16 October 1945 at Fort Francis E. Warren, Wyoming.

GOWER, CARMEL E., Serial Number 14 022 616, was a Staff Sergeant with 247th Army Air Force Base Unit of the Army of the United States. He was born 21 August 1918 in Wayne County, Tennessee. His permanent mailing address was Route 6, Lawrenceburg, Tennessee. His Civilian Occupation was Farmer. He was registered with Selective Service Board No. 1, Waynesboro, Tennessee. He volunteered and entered active service 25 September 1940 in Montgomery, Alabama. His Military Occupational Specialty was Airplane and Engine Mechanic. His Military Qualifications included AAF Tech Badge. He was in battles in Northern France, Southern France, Air Combat Control-Europe, Naples- Foggia Tunisia, Sicily Air Offensive Europe, Normandy, Rome-Arno Po Valley, Rhineland and Northern Apennines. His decorations included the American Defense Service Medal, and European African Middle Eastern Theater Ribbon with Two Silver Stars. He finished four year of High school. He left the USA 13 January 1943 for the European Theater and returned 24 May 1945. He was discharged 9 September 1945 at Fort McPherson, Georgia.

GRAHAM, J.C., Serial Number 34 494 853, was a technician fifth Grade with the Company B. 47th Engineer Construction Battalion of the Army of the United States. He was inducted into the Army November 22, 1942 and entered into active service on November 29 at Fort Oglethorpe, GA. His Military Occupational Specialty was Con-

struction Foreman. His Military Qualifications included Rifle Marksman. He was in battles in the Western Pacific Ryukus. His decorations included WWII Victory Ribbon, Good Conduct Medal, American Theater Ribbon, Asiatic Pacific Ribbon with two Bronze Service Stars and Meritorious Unit Award. He left the USA April 4, 1944 for the Asia Pacific Theater and returned June 6, 1946. He was discharged January 14, 1946 at Camp Chaffee, AK.

J.C. son of Columbus and Mary Hill Graham, was born March 11, 1921 on Beech Creek, Wayne County, TN. His siblings are Alice Graham married Wesley Prater, Nola Graham married Lenzie Ray, Mae Graham married Ellis Johnson, James Graham married Ora Belle Conaway and Bonnie Graham married W.E. Culp. He completed the 8th grade at the community elementary school. He attended church on a regular basis. He played the guitar and was a vocalist in the church choir. He did general farm work before entering the service.

GRAHAM, JAMES EDWARD, Serial Number 977 28 96, was a Carpenter's Mate Third Class in the Navy of the United

States. He entered into active service 19 June 1944. He served on USNTADC Williamsburg, Virginia; CBRD Camp Parks, California and CBMU509 - CBMU618. He was discharged 13 February 1946 at US Naval Personnel Separation Center in Memphis, Tennessee. James, son of Columbus and Mary Hill Graham, was born 11 March 1916 on Beech Creek in Wayne County. His siblings are Alice Graham married Wesley Prater, Nola Graham married Lenzie Ray, Mae Graham married Ellis Johnson, J. C. Graham married (1) Willie Mae Walker and (2) Margie Duren, and Bonnie Graham married W. E. Culp. James was reared in this community and attended the community school and church. He met and married Ora Belle Conaway, daughter of Turner and Martha Elizabeth "Dolly" Julian Conaway from

near Clifton. He helped with farming and was later hired by Genesco Shoe Company in Waynesboro. He and Ora Belle bought a home on Green River near Waynesboro. They have four children, (1) Eugene married Edith Ayers. (2) Joyce married Larry Pully and they have two children, Bryan and Jennifer. (3) Jerry married Susan Fraley and they have one child, Tana. and (4) Jimmy married Belinda Folger.

GRAMBELL, LOUIS, Serial Number 34 373 158, was a Private with Second Headquarters, Special Troops, 111 Corps of the Army of the United States. He was born in Iron City, Tennessee. His Civilian Occupation was Truck Driver. He was married and 31 years old when he was inducted 24 September 1942 at Fort Oglethorpe Georgia. He had blue eyes, brown hair, ruddy complexion and was 5'10" tall. His Military Occupational Specialty was Cannoneer. He was discharged 28 February 1944 at Camp Cooke, California.

GRAVES, ROBERT T., Serial Number 34 022 534, was a Private First Class with Headquarters and Headquarters Detachment, Section 1, Station Complement SOU of the United States Army. His permanent mailing address was Route 6. Trenton, Tennessee. He was divorced. His Civilian Occupation was General Farm Hand. He was registered with Selective Service Board No. 1. Waynesboro, Tennessee. His address at time of entry into service was Route 1. Flatwoods, Tennessee. He was inducted 25 February 1941 at Fort Oglethorpe. Georgia. His Military Occupational Specialty was Searchlight Crewman. He was in battles in Northern Salnions. His decorations included the American Defense Service Ribbon and Asiatic Pacific Theater Ribbon with one Bronze Star. He left the USA 23 January 1942 for Pacific Theater and returned home 25 July 1944. His education consisted of eight years of grammar school. He was honorably discharged 24 August 1945 at Fort McPherson, Georgia.

Robert, son of Jesse and Mattie Graves, was born 14 May 1910 in Waynesboro, Tennessee, and is buried in Graves Cemetery in Perry County. Siblings: Moncy L, Willie married Jim Bartley and Bess Graves, Bonnie E., and Roy Graves.

GREESON, BILLY CARROLL, is the son of Matthew Herman and Cora E. Kilburn Greeson, was born 20 November 1926 in Waynesboro, Tennessee. He is the grandson of William David and Mary Victoria Emmaline Parker Greeson and Carol L. and Janie Copeland Kilburn. He graduated from Wayne County High School in 1945. On 1 April 1945, he mar-

ried Peggy Jean Stricklin. He was inducted into the Army on 20 June 1945, and was a Private with the 129th Military Police Company. He spent most of his enlistment in Egypt, and received his Honorable Discharge on 7 July 1946. Billy was a printer for most of his working years. He also owned a service station. He retired in 1990. He and Peggy now live in Hermitage, Tennessee. They have two sons, Larry Carrol Greeson of Kennesaw, Georgia and Jerry Randall Greeson of Hermitage. Larry, married Deborah Kelly, served in the Army during the Vietnam War. Jerry is married to Debra Oaks and they have three children, Benjamin Kyle, Andrew Ellis and Etta Lee, all of Hermitage.

GREESON, HERMAN CHARLES, son of Matthew Herman and Cora E. Kilburn, and the grandson of William David and Mary Victoria Emmaline Parker Greeson and Carol L. and Janie Copeland Kilburn. He was born 4 December 1916 in Wayne County, and attended several different schools in the county, including Waynesboro, as both his parents were teachers and taught in many of the rural schools at that time. In 1934, he graduated from Wayne County High School. Charles entered the Army in May of 1941 and, after serving as senior drill instructor at Fort Benning, Georgia for more than three years, volunteered for overseas duty. He was wounded in Germany during the Battle of the Bulge while on duty with the Third Army near Hitler's hideout. S/SGT Greeson was evacuated by plane to a hospital in England, then returned to the United States and spent time in hospitals in Florida and Texas, recovering from painful but not critical injuries. He received his discharge in 1945. In October 1945, he left Tennessee and went to Flint, Michigan, where he went to work for General Motors Corporation, Buick Division. On 24 December 1948, he married Ethel Spivey. They were the parents of three children, one daughter and two sons. In 1977 he retired from GM. Charles passed away on 4 September 1989 and was buried in Sunset Hills Cemetery in Flushing, Michigan. An active member of the Lutheran Church, he was survived by his wife, Ethel of Flushing; two sons, Charles Edward of Bancroft, Michigan and David of Flushing; one daughter Susan Plummer of Lambertville, Michigan; three grandchildren, Christopher and Jeniffer Plummer and Megan Greeson; one brother Billie Carrol Greeson of Hermitage, Tennessee and one sister, Marie Stricklin of Waynesboro.

GREESON, LEMUEL, son of Parker and Montie Shipman Greeson. He grew up in Clifton and Waynesboro. He attended both schools but graduated from Memphis Tech. It was here that he met his wife Mildred Dalton. They had five children, Bennie Parker, France Leigh, Davis Lemuel, Alfred

Yancy and Mona Lisa Greeson. Lemuel had one sister Lorraine. He was inducted into the US Army on 26 February 1944 and was discharged in 1946. He received his training at Camp Butner, NC. Then he was sent to Camp Kilmer, NJ to be shipped to the European Theater of War. His unit was in England. He was sent in a detached service to France and on toward the Battle of the Bulge. He was near the place where some of our local men were taken P. O. W.

GREESON, WILLIAM EDGAR, JR., SI/C, is the son of William Edgar and Era Lawson Greeson of the Hardin's Creek Community in Wayne County. Edgar, Jr. 's siblings were Bobby, and Ronnie Joe Greeson and Betty Greeson Turnbo. He volunteered for the Navy in November 1943 in Los Angeles and took his boot training in San Diego, California. He was stationed later at the Naval Hospital in Cronona, California for a brief time before being transferred to Shoemaker Training Center for advanced overseas training. Before entering the service he was employed several months with the American Airlines in Los Angeles where he completed a course in blueprint and electrical welding. He served in the South Pacific.

Source: Album of Wayne County News clippings owned by Clyde Bevis.

GRIGGS, ARVIE, Serial Number 44 069 664, was a Private in Company D, 6th Replacement Battalion Regiment in the Army of the United States. His permanent mailing address was General Delivery, Waynesboro, Tennessee. He was born 8 January 1919 in Waynesboro, Tennessee. He was registered with Selective Service Board in Wayne County, Tennessee. His Civilian Occupation was Automotive Mechanic. He was inducted 31 January 1945 at Fort Oglethorpe, Georgia. His Military Occupational Specialty was Rifleman. His Military Qualification was M1 Rifle Marksman. He was honorably discharged 27 November 1945 in Camp Pickett, Virginia so he could

enlist in the R. A. He reenlisted 28 November 1945 in Camp Pickett, Virginia. His Military Occupational Specialty was Automotive Mechanic. His Military Qualifications were MKM M1 Rifle and Gunner. He was not in any battles. The following decorations were awarded to Griggs, American Theater Ribbon, World War II Victory Ribbon, and Good Conduct Medal. He departed the USA 16 February 1946 for Europe and returned 4 July 1946. He was discharged 27 December 1946 at Strategic Service Unit in Washington, DC.

GRIGGS, CLAUDE E., Serial Number 34 366 663, was a Technician, Fifth Grade with Company A, 554th Signal Air Warning Battalion of the Army of the United States. He was born 27 February 1921 in Waynesboro, Tennessee. His permanent mailing address was Waynesboro, Tennessee. His Civilian Occupation was Shipping Checker. He was registered with Selective Service Board No. 1, Waynesboro, Tennessee. His Military Occupational Specialty was Light Truck Driver. His Military Qualifications included Driver and Mechanic Badge. His decorations included the American Service Medal, World War II Victory Medal, Good Conduct Medal and a lapel Button. He left USA 20 April 1943 for American Theater and returned home 3 December 1945. He was discharged 7 December 1945 at Fort McPherson, Georgia.

GRIGGS, CLIFFORD FRANKLIN, Serial Number 36 879 046, was a Private First Class with the 968th Quartermaster Service Company of the Army of the United States. He was born 9 September 1917 in Waynesboro, Tennessee. His permanent mailing address was Waynesboro, Tennessee. He was married with two dependents. His Civilian Occupation was Multiple Spindle Drill Press Operator. He was registered with Selective Service Board in Wayne County, Michigan. His Military Occupational Specialty was Duty Soldier. His decorations included the European-African- Middle Eastern Theater Ribbon and Good Conduct Medal. He was in the European Theater Operation 1 year, 0 months and 12 days. He was discharged 28 August 1949 at Percy Jones Hospital Center in Fort Custer, Michigan with a Certificate of Disability. Griggs, son of Mr. and Mrs. Elmer Griggs of Waynesboro entered the service on 23 September 1943. He took his basic training at Fort Custer, Michigan and Fort Sheridan, Illinois and was then sent overseas in May 1944. He served thirteen months in England and France. He came back to the States and later entered the Percy Jones Convalescent Hospital at Fort Custer. Wayne County News from Clyde Bevis Album.

GRIGGS, FORD, Serial Number 44 126 817, was a Private with Headquarter Army Security Agency with the World War

II Army of Occupation. I was inducted into the Army 1 November 1945 at Fort Oglethorpe, Georgia at the age of eighteen. I took my basic training at Fort Knox, Kentucky in an armored unit and became a medium tank driver. Shortly after basic training, I was selected for the army security agency. I took my training at Vint Hill Farm Station, Warrenton, Virginia. I was given several courses in intelligence, surveillance and trained as a "799" high speed radio interrupt operator. Vint Hill Farm Station was a high security post. It was the number one communication center for all federal agencies. Every phase of the operation was classified including the schools, etc. While there I was given the opportunity to take courses that prepared me to take and pass the army security agency high school equivalence test. I finished my training the 1st of September and shipped out for the European Theater Operations "Germany" on 10 September 1946. I landed at Bremerhaven, Germany on 21 September. I was sent to Marburg first and then to the army security agency Headquarters in Frankfurt. Most of my duties were performed in and around the Frankfurt area. I also pulled duty at Herzo Air Base and the Nuremberg area. I was at Nuremberg when General Goering killed himself. Although the fighting had stopped over a year earlier, the cold war was heating up. Most of our surveillance was directed toward the Russians at that point. We received instructions in January 1947 that all those drafted before a certain date in 1945 would be going home and be discharged in March 1947 at the convenience of the Government. We sailed from Bremerhaven on 4 February 1947 for the USA and we landed in New York on 13 February 1947. I was discharged 9 March 1947 at Fort Dix, New Jersey. I enlisted in the Army Security Agency Reserve for three years and was discharged 9 March 1950. I was born 1 June 1927 on Factory Creek and attended Factory elementary school and Wayne County High School. I am the youngest of five children born to James G. and Virginia Cole Griggs. My brothers and sisters are, Marie Griggs Borden, Forest Cole, and James Quinton Griggs and Edith Evelyn Griggs Lynch. I left the farm where I was raised and Wayne County in 1944 for Toledo, Ohio. Shortly after arriving there, I went to work for the Willis Overland Motor Co. and worked there as a dispatcher until I was drafted into the Army. This company made jeeps, trucks, shells, airplane parts, buzz bombs and many other items used in the war. After my discharge, I returned to my old job in Toledo. I worked there as an assembler and line leader in master assembly. I was married 29 April 1950 to Lillie Frances Matthews and we moved to Nashville. After a short time, we moved to Amarillo, Texas and I went to work for a large wholesale company as a department manager. I attended the Amarillo secretarial school at night under the G. I. Bill of Rights. I studied accounting and business administration. Frances and I have three children, Ford Durand "Randy", James Matthew "Jimmy and Pamela Gail "Pam" Griggs, all of whom were born in Amarillo. We moved back home to Wayne County in 1957 and went into the cafe business. We operated the cafe until 1965. At that time I went to work for the W. J. Schoenberger Company as a supervisor. I worked there until 1972 when I entered private business again. I built and operated the Shady Grove Trailer Park and the 7-Springs Park. I sold these businesses in 1986 and retired. Signed: Ford Griggs 1 December 1991.

GRIGGS, HOMER LEO, Private, enlisted in the United States Army on August 17, 1945. He served in Company C, 343rd Engineers General Service Regiment. He was discharged on January 21, 1947, and was awarded the Army of Occupation and World War II Victory Medals. He was born in 1927, the son of Elmer and Thelma Lands Griggs. He married Ethelens C. Butler. They have four children: Homer Jr., Roger Neal, Sheri Diane and Cyndi Jo. His siblings are Willie Ruth, Clifford Franklin, Mamie Louise, Claule Elward, Wilton Estella and James Henry.

GRIGGS, JOHN WASHINGTON, Serial Number 34 373 132, was a Private First Class in Company C 473rd Infantry Regiment in the Army of the United States. His permanent mailing address was Route 4, Waynesboro, Tennessee. He was registered with Selective Service Board in Wayne County, Tennessee. His Civilian Occupation was Farmer. He was inducted 24 September 1942 and entered active service 8 October 1942 at Fort Oglethorpe.

Georgia. His Military Occupational Specialty was Rifleman. He was in the battles of Tunisia, Sicily, Rome-Arno, North Apennines and Po Valley. The following decorations were awarded to Griggs: European-African Middle Eastern Theater Medal and Good Conduct Medal. He left the USA 5 March 1943 for the European-African Middle Eastern Theater Operation, and returned to USA 29 August 1945. He was discharged 30 October 1945 at Camp Shelby, Mississippi. John was born 12 April 1913 in Waynesboro, died 2 August 1991 in the Wayne County Hospital and was buried Memorial Gardens in Waynesboro. He was the son of Alfred Franklin Griggs (born 15 April 1884) and Mary Jane Dixon Griggs (born 3 November 1887). He was survived by two sisters, Lizzie Poag of Waynesboro and Lorine Dunmire of Florence, Alabama. He also had two brothers, L. C and Alfred Griggs both deceased.

GRIGGS, WADE, was born, June 11, 1921, at Waynesboro and was living at Collinwood at the time of his induction into the U. S. Army. No battles listed, but he received the following citations; Good Conduct Medal, Army of Occupation (Japan) Medal, WWII Victory, Asiatic-Pacific Theater medal. He was discharged, July 21, 1947.

GRIMES, ARVIE, Serial number RA 44 069 664, was a Technician Fifth Grade in the Army of the United States. His per-

manent mailing address was General Delivery, Waynesboro, Tennessee. He was married and his description was given as blue eyes, brown hair, 5'6" tall and 170 lbs weight. His Civilian Occupation was Truck Driver. He enlisted 28 November 1945 at Camp Pickett, Virginia. His Military Occupational Specialty was Rifleman and M1 Rifle Marksman. He was an automotive mechanic and performed all types of general mechanic repairs. He was in

charge of seven German civilian employees. He can drive all type of vehicles in the United States and Germany. He was responsible for maintenance of vehicles driven and drove between the principal cities of Germany. His related Civilian occupation was auto mechanic, auto repair serviceman, and motor analyst. His decorations included the American Theater Ribbon, World War II Victory Medal, and Good Conduct Medal. He received an Honorable discharge 27 December 1946 from Headquarters Det SSU in Washington, DC. He was born 8 January 1919, died 21 March 1977 and was buried in Mt. Herman Cemetery in Hardin County. He was married 11 September 1937 to Edith Bridges.

GRIMES, BONNIE JACKSON, 77, of 2311 Clearview Place, S. W., Decatur, Al, died 19 July 1997 at Decatur Hospital and was buried in Grandview Memorial Park. A native of Iron City, Mr. Grimes was a former resident of Florence before moving to Decatur. He retired from TVA with 35 years of service as an electrician, was a U. S. Army veteran of World War II and a member of the Elks Lodge of Decatur. Survivors included his wife, Jean Hassell Grimes; a daughter, Linda Grimes of Decatur; a brother, James Grimes of Tampa, FL; a sister, Hazel Grimes of Florence; and one granddaughter.
Source: Wayne County News, 30 July 1997.

GRIMES, CLARENCE H., Serial Number 34 194 558, was a Sergeant with Company A, 44th Armored Infantry Battalion of the Army of the United States. He was born 3 November 1917 in Wayne County, Tennessee. His permanent mailing address was Route 2, Collinwood Tennessee. His Civilian Occupation was Routeman. He was registered with Selective Service Board No. 1, Waynesboro, Tennessee. He was inducted 4 April 1942 at Fort Oglethorpe, Georgia. His Military Occupational Specialty was Chief Radar Operator. His Military Qualifications included Infantryman Badge. He was in battles in Ardennes, Central Europe and Rhineland. His decorations included Silver Star Medal, World War II Victory Medal, American Service Medal, European African Middle Eastern Service Medal with Three Bronze Stars and Good Conduct Medal. He left the USA 23 May 1943 for American Theater, left there 8 January 1945 for European Theater and returned 14 August 1945. He had an eighth grade education. He was discharged 6 November 1945 at Fort McPherson, Georgia. "Sgt Clarence H. Grimes, son of Mr. and Mrs. V. C. Grimes of the McCall Community entered the service 3 April 1942 and took his basic training at Fort Benning, Georgia. From there he was transferred to Fort Eustis, Virginia where he stayed until he went overseas in January 1945. He served in Germany with the Third Army. He was awarded the Silver Star for gallantry in action as follows: Sergeant Grimes, Army Serial number 34 194 558, Infantry United States Army for gallantry in action in the vicinity of Germany on 7 February 1945 was forced to swim from an overturned assault boat while trying to land on the opposite bank of the river. Sergeant Grimes in bitter cold weather volunteered to swim to the enemy side of the river to secure cables necessary for the pontoon over which a bridge was installed. The area was then subjected to heavy enemy artillery, mortar and sniper fire. His rare courage, devotion to duty, and perseverance, are in keeping with the finest traditions of the service, and reflect the highest credit upon himself and the United States Infantryman. He entered the service from Tennessee. By command of the Division."

Source: Wayne County News from Clyde Bevis album.

GRIMES, EATHEL IRIS, Serial Number 34 377 050, was a Private First Class in Company A, 270th Engineer

Combat Battalion of the Army of the United States. His permanent mailing address was Route 4, Waynesboro, Tennessee. He was married. His Civilian Occupation was Automobile Serviceman. He was registered with Selective Service Board No. 1, Waynesboro, Tennessee. He was inducted 13 October 1942 and entered active service 27 October 1942 at Fort Oglethorpe, Georgia. His Military Occupational Specialty was Light Truck Driver. His Military Qualifications included Light Truck Driver and Rifle Marksman. He was in battles in Normandy, Northern France, Rhineland, Central Europe and Ardennes. He participated in the Normandy Invasion

as a truck driver. His decorations included: European African Middle Eastern Theater Ribbon with five Bronze Stars, Purple Heart and Bronze Star Medal. He was wounded 15 January 1945 in Luxenburg. He left the USA 18 January 1944 for the European Theater and returned 15 October 1945. He attended grammar school for seven and a half years. He was discharged 22 October 1945 at Camp Atterbury, Indiana. He was born 28 December 1920 in Waynesboro, Tennessee, died 15 March 1985 and is buried in Memory Gardens in Waynesboro. He was married 1 March 1941 to Alora Brewer and they had two children, David and Wanda Grimes.

GRIMES, JAMES C., Serial Number 34 189 099, was a Staff Sergeant with Battery C, 247th Antiaircraft Searchlight Battalion of the Army of the United States. He was born 2 July 1916 in Iron City, Tennessee. His permanent mailing address was 2509 Woodard Avenue, Florence, Alabama. His description was given as blue eyes, brown hair, height 6', weight 165 lbs and married with one dependent. His Civilian Occupation was Soldier. He was registered with Selective Service Board No. 1, Waynesboro, Tennessee. He entered active service 18 February 1942 in Fort Oglethorpe, Georgia. His address at time of entry was General Delivery, Iron City, Tennessee. His Military Occupational Specialty was Searchlight NCO. He finished eight years of grammar school. He was discharged 13 January 1945 at Fort McPherson, Georgia. He had prior service from 5 May 1938 to 4 May 1941 and 9 January 1935 to 10 April 1937.

GRIMES, JOHNNIE FRANK, Serial Number 845 48 76, had the grade of AM 2/O in the United States Navy. His mailing address was Route 3, Iron City, Tennessee. He was born 4 July 1924 in Iron City. He was registered with Selective Service Board No. 1, Waynesboro, Tennessee. He was single when he was inducted 3 June 1943 and entered into active service 10 June 1943 at NRS in Chattanooga, Tennessee. He did not see any foreign service. He completed the following service schools, NATTC Norman, Oklahoma; NT School Line Maintenance PBHY and NAS Minneapolis, Minnesota. Service Vessels and Stations that he served on are, USNTS San Diego, California; NAS Key West, Florida; and Hedron 14-2 Fleet Air Wing 14 Headquarters, Squadron 5. Grimes was awarded the Aviation Metal , Victory Medal and American Theater Medal. He was a student in Collinwood before he enlisted. He finished four years of high school. He was discharged 4 May 1946

Memphis, Tennessee. Johnnie's parents were the late Floyd and Annie McCain Grimes. His residence address is 2044 Alpine Drive, Florence, Alabama 35630.

GRIMES, MONTIE JOHNSON, Serial Number 34 141 806, was a Technician Fourth Grade with 13th Station Hospital

in the Army of the United States. His permanent mailing address was Box 333, Clifton, Tennessee. He entered active service on 25 June 1941 at Fort Oglethorpe, Georgia. His civilian occupation was Maintenance Mechanic. His military occupational specialty was Utility repairman. His decorations included Good Conduct Ribbon, American Defense Service Ribbon, Philippine Liberation with one Bronze Star and Asiatic-Pacific Theater Ribbon with three Bronze Stars, He was also issued a Lapel Button. He left the USA on 17 February 1942 for Southwest Pacific Theater Operations and returned 21 April 1945. He was discharged 8 June 1945 at Fort McPherson, Georgia. Montie was born 7 January 1915 in Clifton, Wayne County, the son of Hundley and Martha Collie Grimes. He was a retired mail carrier with the United States Postal Service and a member and former elder of the Olivet Cumberland Presbyterian Church, a former Boy Scout Leader in Clifton for many years, and a United States Army Veteran of World War II. He married Anita Neil Grimes. They had one son, Dr. Gary L. Grimes of Paris, Tennessee. Montie died 29 November 1993 in Jackson-Madison County General Hospital and was buried in Neil Cemetery near Savannah, Tennessee. He was 78 years old.

GRIMES, OPHNIE CHARLES, was born on September 26, 1914, near Waynesboro, Tennessee. He lived near Collinwood, Tennessee, and was working as a farmer when he entered the United States Navy on January 5, 1944, in New Madrid, Missouri. He served as Seaman First Class and served on the USS Rocky

Mount, at Puget Sound Navy Yard and at Bremerton, Washington. Ophnie Charles was awarded the American Campaign Medal, Asiatic-Pacific Medal and World War II Victory Medal. He was discharged on December 13, 1945, in Bremerton, Washington.

GRIMES, RAYMOND FOY, Serial Number 273 51 31, was born 27 October 1927 in Wayne County, Tennessee. He entered into active service in the United States Navy on 3 November 1944. Service Stations and Vessels that he served on were, Naval Training Center, Great Lakes, Illinois; Amphibious Training Base, Fort Pierce, Florida; Let. Personnel Replacement Pool; Amphibious Training Base, St. Andrew Bay, Panama City, Florida, USS LST 111C; and USS WILLIAMSBURG. His decorations included: American Campaign Ribbon, Asiatic-Pacific Campaign Ribbon; World War II Victory Medal and Honorable Service Button. Grimes was discharged 29 July 1946 at US Naval Hospital, Bethesda, Maryland.

GRIMES, WALTER W. "BUD", son of the late Claude W. and Gladys Crews Grimes, was born in Wayne County 20 October 1922. He received his education in Wayne County, having graduated from Wayne County High School in May of 1943. Walter entered the United States Navy 3 June 1943 and received Recruit Training at the Naval Center, San Diego, California. Upon completion of recruit training, three months of additional duty with the Base Security Force (Seaman Guard), he began training to be an Aircraft Metal Smith at Manual Training Center, Navy Pier, Chicago, Illinois. On completion of T R G in June 1944, he was ordered to the Naval Air Station in Norfolk, Virginia, where he was assigned to the Overhead and Repair Department, working on carrier based-combat aircraft which were heavily damaged. This assignment lasted until March 1946. Therefore, he did not see "combat" in World War II, nor was he in "combat" during the other wars between 1946 and his retirement on 1 July 1973. During his years of service, he advanced from Seaman Recruit to Master Chief Aircraft Maintenanceman, and served in many various squadrons, stations and organizations. He served on Fleet Aircraft Service Squadrons 13, 14, and 119. Thirteen was located at Naval Air Station (NAS) Orote, Guam; 14 at Kobler Field, Saipan and 119 at NAS, Tanapeg, Saipan, USS PHILIPPINE SEA CVS 38. Squadron 44 was located at NAS, Moffett Field, Sunnyvale, California, and later at Corpus Christi, Texas. The Squadron performed heavy maintenance modification and re-

pair of Aircraft Boeing used in the Berlin Airlift. The Air Anti-Submarine Squadron 20 and 21, on which he served, was located at Naval Auxiliary Air Station, North Island, San Diego, California. Between the two squadrons, assignment lasted approximately forty-seven months. In the addition to maintenance of aircraft, he served as an air crewman operation surface search radar electronic counter, measuring equipment and airborne magnetic detective equipment. Duty required frequent flights from aircraft carriers including one six month deployment to the West Pacific operating from the carrier USS Princeton CUS 237 and a seven month deployment aboard the carrier USS Philippine SEA CUS 38. Another duty station at which Walter served was Attack Squadron, 76 which was home based at NAS, Lemore, California (near Fresno.) The squadron flew all Skyhawk Jet Attack planes. Walter served as the main control officer. When he reported to the squadron, they were deployed aboard the carrier USS INDEPENDENCE in the Mediterranean Sea. He served aboard the carrier approximately six months. During his 30 years and 28 days of service, approximately 11 years was spent in Technical Training Billets, both as an instructor and supervisory, including Naval Tech Training Center, Memphis, Tennessee and Naval Air Maintenance Training Detachments NAS, North Island, San Diego and NAS Imperial Beach, California where Grimes retired 1 July 1973. Grimes was awarded the following medals: Good Conduct with seven Stars, American Defense, World War II Victory and Navy achievement Medal. Walter and wife, Barbara Walohager Grimes now live 612 Green River Road, Waynesboro, Tennessee 38484. They have four children, Stanley, David, Patricia and Richard, eleven grandchildren and three great-grandchildren.

GROSSMAN, SIGUARD SANDOR, Serial Number 302 414, was a Sergeant in the United States Marine Corps. He was born 30 March 1920 in Hohenwald, Lewis County, Tennessee. He enlisted 29 November 1940 at Nashville, Tennessee for four years. His description was 67 3/4" high, brown eyes, dark brown hair, and ruddy complexion. His Weapons Qualifications were Sharpshooter-rifle, 21 January 1942 and Marksman-Pistol, 9 January 1941. His Special Military Qualifications were Radio Operator and Message Center Clerk. His Service (Sea and Foreign) Reykjavik, Iceland from 7 January 1941 to 13 March 1942, South, Central and Western Pacific areas from 3 December 1942 to 29 September 1944. His battles, engagements and expeditions were: participated in action

against enemy at Russell Islands on 17 March 1943, and at New Guinea Islands from 13 September 1943 to 13 February 1944. He was recommended for a Good Conduct Medal. Grossman was discharged 17 September 1945 at First Separation Company, San Diego, California.

HADDOCK, ARDELL JOHN, JR., Serial Number 273 30 85, had the grade of Seaman, First Class in the United States Navy. He entered into service 23 June 1944. The highest rating held was that of S1/C. His service included the following Vessels and/or Stations NRS, Birmingham, Alabama; REC. TRG. Com. and USNTADC, Williamsburg, Virginia; USS HALSEY POWELL; and USS YMS 219. He was discharged 23 May 1946 from the U. S. Naval Personnel Separation Center in Memphis, Tennessee. His decorations included the Asiatic Pacific Ribbon with Four Bronze Stars, Philippine Liberation Ribbon with One Bronze Star, American Area Ribbon and World War II Victory Medal. Ardell, son of the late Ardell and Mollie (Bryson) Haddock, was born 17 April 1927 in Collinwood, Tennessee, died Sunday, August 30, 1992 in Wayne County Hospital and was buried in Copeland Cemetery near Collinwood. His sisters are Vivian Copous of Waynesboro and Marie Thomas of Fort Worth, Texas. He married Teresa Odle and their children are Ricky Ardell of the U. S. Marines in California and Jeffery Shawn of Collinwood. His occupation after the war was disabled laborer. He was a member of the VFW in Lawrenceburg.

HADDOCK, CLARENCE S., Serial Number 34 189 087, was a Private First Class with 843rd Engineer Aviation Battalion of the United States Army. His permanent mailing address was Route 1, Collinwood, Tennessee. He was born 6 October 1917 in Wayne County. His Civilian Occupation was General Farm Hand. He was registered with Selective Service

Board No. 1, Waynesboro, Tennessee. He was inducted 18 February 1942 at Fort Oglethorpe, Georgia. His Military Occupational Specialty was General Carpenter. He was in battles in Central Europe. His decorations included the European African Middle-Eastern Theater Ribbon with one Bronze Star, World War II Victory Medal, and Good Conduct Ribbon. He left the USA 6 August 1942 for European Theater Operations and returned home 7 November 1945. He was discharged 12 November 1945 at Fort Knox, Kentucky.

HADDOCK, CLYDE D., Serial Number 34 713 911, was a Technician Fifth Grade in Battery A 365th Antiaircraft Artillery Automatic Weapons Battalion in the Army of the United States. His permanent mailing address was Route 2, Waynesboro, Tennessee. He was born 17 May 1924 in Wayne County. He was registered with Selective Service Board in Wayne County, Tennessee. His Civilian Occupation was General Farmer. He was inducted 23 April 1943 and entered into active service 30 April 1943 at Fort Oglethorpe, Georgia. His Military Occupational Specialty was Power Generator Operator. His Military Qualifications included Rifle MM Carbine, Sharpshooter Driver and Mechanic Badge. He was in the battles of Ardennes, Rhineland, and Central Europe. The following decorations were awarded to Haddock: American Theater Ribbon, Europe-African Middle Eastern Theater Ribbon with 3 Bronze Stars, Good Conduct Ribbon and World War II Victory Medal. He left the USA 6 October 1944 for the European Theater Operation, and returned to USA 8 March 1946. He was discharged 13 March 1946 at Camp Atterbury, Indiana.

Upon discharge from the United States Army he returned to Wayne County and resided with his parents, Arlie (Adkisson) Haddock and James K. Polk Haddock on Indian Creek. On, July 22, 1947, he wed Jean Brewer daughter of Ora (Moore) Brewer and Leonard Brewer of Waynesboro.

He was a driver for Shull Truck Line. He was also a local businessman and farmer. Over the years the family resided in different places in Tennessee due to his line of work and had three children: Brenda Gaye Haddock born on August 25, 1950, Jonathan Douglas Haddock born June 27, 1957 and Holli Jan Haddock on January 5, 1970.

Later, they built a house on their farm on Indian Creek (close to the place where he was raised as a child), where he lived until his death on October 21,1973.

HADDOCK, JAMES H., Serial Number 34 373 145, was a Private First Class in Battery A 455th Antiaircraft Artillery Air Warning Battalion in the Army of the United States. His permanent mailing address was Route 1, Collinwood, Tennessee. He was born 9 June 1915 in Waynesboro. He was registered with Selective Service Board in Wayne County, Tennessee. His Civilian Occupation was Farmhand. He was inducted 24 September 1942 and entered into active service 8 October 1942 at Fort Oglethorpe, Georgia. His Military Occupational Specialty was AAA Automatic Weapons Crewman. His Military Qualifications included Rifle Marksman. He was in the battles of Normandy, Northern France, Rhineland, and Central Europe. The following decorations were awarded to Haddock: Europe-African Middle Eastern Theater Ribbon with four Bronze Stars. He left the USA 5 September 1943 for the European Theater Operation, and returned to USA 16 October 1945. He was discharged 22 October 1945 at Camp Atterbury, Indiana.

HAGGARD, ROBERT ROY, JR., Serial Number 574 20 92. Roy Jr. had the grade of Apprentice Seaman in the United

States Navy. He entered into service on December 2, 1942, in Nashville, Tennessee for four years. His description was 5'5 1/4" tall, weight 114 lbs, blue eye, brown hair, fair complexion, and he was single. He was discharged on December 10, 1943, from the United States Naval Personnel Separation Center in Charleston, South Carolina. He was born on June 9, 1924, in Clifton, Tennessee. He grew up in Waynesboro, where his father was an attorney. He was the son of R. R Haggard Sr. and Anna Lou (Montague) Haggard. Roy Jr. and Betty Jean Skelton were married and lived in Waynesboro, where he was an attorney. They have two children, Ann and Robert Roy III (Bob).

He died on May 27, 1968, and was buried in Greenwood Cemetery in Waynesboro.

HAITHCOCK, ROY W., a native of Warrenton, North Carolina, he was the son of Early D. and Cynthia Rose Overby

Haithcock. He served in the 283rd Combat Engineers in the United States Army. He owned and operated a Ben Franklin Variety Store in Waynesboro for twenty years.

After his return from the US Service, he continued work with Roses, sometime later he accepted a position with Butler Brothers of St. Louis, who owned the franchise for Ben Franklin variety store chain, as a store manager.

He soon was advanced to Middle Tennessee zone manager, and then to District manager of the southeast.

After sometime in the chain management, Roy became interested in a location for a store of his own, an opportunity for this occurred in Waynesboro, TN in the year 1965.

Roy, being a civic minded person, was soon caught up in the civic web. He served as city commissioner two terms, vice mayor the last term, president of the Chamber of Commerce eight years. He became a member of the Lion's Club, the American Legion and the VFW.

After retiring in 1985, he and Doris have continued making their home in the peaceful small town, enjoying their friends and surroundings.

Roy died February 22, 1998 and was buried at the Shields Cemetery in Waynesboro. He was instrumental in establishing the Green River Country Club. He was a very active member of the First United Methodist Church serving the church in many positions during his lifetime. Survivors include his wife, Doris Harris Haithcock of Waynesboro, one son Roy W. Haithcock, Jr., of Memphis; two daughters, Cynthia Sawyer of Houston, Texas and Jean Rolen of Atlanta, Georgia; one half-brother, Earl Haithcock of Raleigh, North Carolina; one half-sister, Betty Lou Peoples of Raleigh and five grandchildren.

HALL, WARREN W., Serial Number 34 377 038, was a Private First Class in Company K, 390th Infantry of the United States Army. His permanent mailing address was Route 1, Lutts, Tennessee. He was born 19 November 1921 in Lutts, Tennessee. His Civilian Occupation was General Farmer. He was registered with Selective Service Board No. 1, Waynesboro, Tennessee. He was inducted 13 October 1942 and entered active service 27 October 1942 at Fort Oglethorpe, Georgia. His Military Occupational Specialty was Light Machine Gunner. His Military Qualifications included Expert Infantryman. His decorations included: World War II Victory Medal, Good Conduct Ribbon, American Theater Ribbon and Asiatic-Pacific Theater Ribbon. He left the USA 29 April 1944 for Asiatic-Pacific and returned home 25 January 1946. He was discharged 1 February 1946 at Camp Chaffee, Arkansas. Pfc Warren Hall, son of Mr. and Mrs. P. J. Hall of Route 1, Lutts was in basic training at Fort McClellan, Alabama, Fort Benning, Georgia and Mobile, Alabama. He also spent a short time in Seattle, Washington. He was then sent overseas for active duty.

Source: Wayne County News.

HAMACK, WILLIAM D., Serial Number 34 013 665, was a Private First Class in Company M 409th Infantry in the Army of the United States. His permanent mailing address was Route 1, Lutts, Tennessee. He was born 24 September 1915 in Morgan County, Alabama. He was registered with Selective Service Board in Wayne County, Tennessee. His Civilian Occupation was Saw Mill worker. He was inducted 22 January 1941 at Fort Oglethorpe, Georgia. His Military Occupational Specialty was Rifleman. His Military Qualifications included Infantryman Badge. He was in the battles of Northern France, and Central Europe. The following decorations were awarded to Hamack: Europe-African Midde Eastern Theater Ribbon with two Bronze Stars, and American Defense Service Medal. He left the USA 6 August 1942 for the European Theater Operation, and returned to USA 18 September 1945. He was discharged 25 September 1945 at Camp Atterbury, Indiana.

HAMM, JOHNNY B., was a Sergeant in the United States Army Air Force. He was discharged after World War II but re-enlisted to serve in the Korean Conflict. He was born 1 December 1921, died 17 November 1972 in Washington, D. C. and was buried there. He lived on Beech Creek until he was inducted into service. He was married and lived in Washington several years before his death. He had no children. He was the son of Johnny and Essie Mae Hickerson Hamm. His known siblings are Irene and Myrtle Lois Hamm.

HAMPTON, TALMAGE WADE, son of Lola Copeland and Charlie Hampton, was born 20 September 1912 in Wayne County. He was educated in the Waynesboro's schools. He married Ruth Ella McWilliams December 25, 1935. He entered service 23 July 1943, and was honorably discharged 28 January 1946. He served in Company B 880th Airborne English Aviation Battalion, in New Guinea and the South Philippines. While in the service he earned the World War II Victory Medal, Good Conduct Medal, Asiatic Pacific Theater Ribbon, two Bronze Service Stars and the Philippines Liberation Ribbon. He was the father of one son, Talmage Allen Hampton and the grandfather of five grandsons, Allen Wade Hampton, John Robert Hampton, Christopher Thomas Hampton, Chadwick Hampton and Anthony Hampton. He also is the great-grandfather of Christopher and Christi Hampton.

HANBACK, ALVIN LEE, Serial Number 34 361 785, was a Technical Sergeant in the 319th Ordnance Maintenance Depot Company in the Army of the United States. His permanent mailing address was Route 3, Lutts, Tennessee. He was born 4 February 1917 in Cypress Inn, Tennessee. He was registered with Selective Service Board in Wayne County, Tennessee. His Civilian Occupation was General Farm Hand. He was married when he was inducted 25 July 1942 at Fort Oglethorpe, Georgia. His Military Occupational Specialty was Motor Transportation. He was not in any battles. The following decorations were awarded to Hanback: Europe-African Midde Eastern Theater Ribbon, Good Conduct Ribbon and World War II Victory Medal. He left the USA 21 August 1943 for the European Theater Operation, and returned to USA 14 December 1945. He had an eighth grade education. He was discharged 18 December 1945 at Camp Atterbury, Indiana. Alvin Lee was the son of James Bailey and Vina Drucilla Montgomery Hanback. He had a brother, Arlie Craiton Hanback.

HANBACK, ARLIE C., Serial Number 34 936 470, was a Private First Class in Company F 320th Infantry in the Army of the United States. His permanent mailing address was Route 2, Iron City, Tennessee. He was born 26 December 1918 in Cypress Inn, Tennessee. He was regis-tered with Selective Service Board in Wayne County, Tennessee. His Civilian Occupation was Farmer. He was married with two dependents when he was inducted 28 July 1944 at Camp Forrest, Tennessee. His home address at time of entry into service was Route 1, Cypress Inn. His Military Occupational Specialty was Rifleman. His Military Qualifications included Rifle, Carbine, Bar, and Combat Infantry Badge. He was in the battles of Rhineland, Central Europe and Ardennes. The following decorations were awarded to Hanback: Europe-African Midde Eastern Theater Ribbon with three Bronze Stars, and World War II Victory Medal. He left the USA 1 January 1945 for Glasgow and returned to USA 10 September 1945. He was discharged 16 November 1945 at Camp Breckinridge, Kentucky. Arlie Craiton Hanback was the son of James Bailey and Vina Drucilla Montgomery Hanback. He had a brother, Alvin Lee Hanback.

HANBACK, DUMONT, Serial Number 34 042 220, was a Technician Fifth Grade in Battery A 286th Field Artillery Observation Battalion in the Army of the United States. His permanent mailing address was Collinwood, Tennessee. He was born 17 March 1919 in Cypress Inn, Tennessee. He was registered with Selective Service Board in Wayne County, Tennessee. His Civilian Occupation was Tractor Driver. He was inducted 16 April 1941 at Fort Oglethorpe, Georgia. His Military Occupational Specialty was Light Truck Driver. He was in the battles of Northern France, Ardennes, Rhineland, and Central Europe. The following decorations were awarded to Hanback: Good Conduct Medal, World War Victory Medal, American Defense Ribbon, American Theater Ribbon, and Europe-African Midde Eastern Theater Ribbon with four Bronze Service Stars. He left the USA 2 July 1944 for the Europe-African Midde Eastern and returned to USA 29 October 1945. He was discharged 20 January 1946 at Fort Knox, Kentucky. Dumont Hanback had a brother, James Bomount Hanback. They were sons of Arthur and Cora Stowe Hanback.

HANBACK, EVERETTE DALTON, Serial Number 34 378 430, was a Private First Class in Private Headquarter Company 1604th Service Unit in the Army of the United States. His Civilian Occupation was Farmer. He was single when he was inducted 21 October 1942 at Fort Oglethorpe, Georgia. His description was blue eyes, brown hair, ruddy complexion, 5' 8 1/2" in height, and 21 5/12 years of age. He was honorably discharged 26 February 1943 at District, Sault Ste. Marie, Fort Brady, Michigan. Everett Dalton

Hanback was born 9 May 1921 in Iron City, Tennessee, son of Jasper Lee and Thuna Etta (Holt) Hanback. He died 7 July 1990 at the age of 69. At the time of his death, he was married to Loraine Anders. He is the father of three children, Lee Allen, Ricky and Shelia Hanback.

HANBACK, JAMES B., Serial Number 34 506 479, was a Private in Casual Detachment, Station Complement in the Army of the United States. He was born Cypress Inn, Tennessee. His Civilian Occupation was Farmer. He was 19 10/12 years of age when he was inducted 18 January 1943 at Fort Oglethorpe, Georgia. He was discharged 31 January 1943 at Camp Blanding, Florida in poor physical condition.

HANBACK, MARVIN, Serial Number not given, was a Private in Company B 719th Railway Operating Battalion in the Army of the United States. He was born 14 April 1901 in Waynesboro, Tennessee. He was inducted 21 October 1942 at Fort Oglethorpe, Georgia to serve for the period of emergency and entered into active service 4 November 1942. He was discharged 23 March 1943.

HARBIN, PRICE, Serial Number 34 936 420, was a Private in Company D, 28th Infantry Training Battalion in the Army of the United States. His permanent mailing address was Route 1, Collinwood, Tennessee. He was born 11 January 1922 in Cloverdale, Alabama. He was registered with Selective Service Board in Wayne County, Tennessee. His Civilian Occupation was General Farm Hand. He was married when he was inducted 28 July 1944 at Camp Forrest, Tennessee. He spent six months and eleven days in foreign service. He was discharged 8 February 1945 at Fort McPherson, Georgia. He was issued a Lapel Button.

HARDIN, CHARLES, son of Ruby and Katie Hardin, was born in the Dog Creek Community of Wayne County, TN. and attended the Forty-Eight Creek School. He was inducted into the United States Army and served through the duration of the war.

After his discharge, he settled at Rocksboro, N. C. and worked as a truck driver. His brother, Walter Woodrow, soon moved to Rocksboro to be near him. Both of them died from cancer in the 1990's, about a year apart and are buried at Rocksboro.

Charlie was married and has children. He is the uncle of Tom Frank, David and Charles Brewer.

HARDIN, FRANK GIPSON, age 81

of Clifton died 7 May 1991 in the Wayne County Nursing home in Waynesboro and was buried in the Clifton Cemetery. He was a native of Hardin County, the son of Will and Mamie Warrington Hardin, a retired towboat engineer with the Counce Corporation, an Army veteran of World War II, and a member of the Clifton United Methodist Church. Survivors include a daughter, Mrs. Patricia Downey of Houston, Texas; a son, David Hardin of Waynesboro and one brother, Burnice Hardin of Clifton and three grandchildren. (Wayne County News, 15 May 1991).

HARDIN, JAMES, was the son of James (Jim) Hardin and Lula Stutts Hardin. He graduated from Frank Hughes School in Clifton in 1938 and was the only graduate that year at Clifton. He left from there on July 24, 1941, with Vernon Jeter and J. E. Pickett to join the United States Navy in Norfork. Virginia. From there, James was sent to the Great Lakes for training. He served in the Navy during the World War II. After returning home, he married and operated a dairy business in the Detroit, Michigan, area. He has no children. His siblings are Florine, Monetta, Louise, Gerldine and Kenneth.

HARDIN, JAMES L., served in WWII, TN Tech 4, USA. He was born on November 24, 1911, and he died on April 1, 1959. He is buried in Greenwood Cemetery in Waynesboro, TN.

He became on of Waynesboro's business men and operated a Dry Goods and Shoe Store on the city's square.

He married Virginia Boyd, a local girl, daughter of Lawyer Claude and Vera Cypert Boyd.

HARDIN, JOHN EDWARD, Serial Number 34 995 555, was a Private First Class in Infantry Replacement Training Center in the Army of the United States. His permanent mailing address was Clifton, Tennessee. He was born 27 August 1919 in Clifton. He was married with three dependents. He was registered with Selective Service Board in Wayne County, Tennessee. His Civilian Occupation was Truck Driver. He was inducted 30 October 1944 at Fort Benning, Georgia. His Military Occupational Specialty was Truck Driver. His Military Qualifications included MM 30 Cal Rifle M1. He was not in any battles. The following decorations were awarded to Hardin: American Theater Service Medal, Good Conduct Medal and World War II Victory Medal. He had an eighth grade education. He was discharged 3 August 1946 at Fort Bragg, North Carolina. He was issued a Lapel Button.

He was the son of Lane Hardin and Estelle Witherspoon. He married Lily Mae Clemmons first. Later he married Dorothy?. He has one stepdaughter, Juanita Whitmore. John Edward was born in Clifton and attended school there. He is a truck driver and owns his own cleaning business. He lives in Detroit, Michigan.
Source: Earmon Chandler.

HARDIN, WALTER WOODROW, son of Ruby R. and Katie Hardin, was born in Wayne County in 1919. He grew up in

the Dog Creek Community and attended the local schools. As the threat of war became closer, he enlisted in the United States Navy and served during the duration of the war.

After his discharge, he settled at Chattanooga, TN as a truck driver for a few years, then moved to Rocksboro, N. C., where he died in the 1990's from cancer. He is buried at Rocksboro.

Walter was married and has children.

HARKEY, ALLEN B., Sergeant, was born on December 16, 1926, and was farming when he enlisted in the United States

military service on November 13, 1941. He served with the 1020th Army Air Force

Base Unit and participated in the following battles: East Indies, Paupa, New Guinea, Bismark and Archipelago. He was awarded the following medals: Asiatic Pacific Theater Campaign Medal with 4 Bronze Service Stars, Distinguished Unit Badge, Good Conduct and American Defense Service Medal. Allen married Mary Lynn Moore, daughter of Arch Creed and Bess Rinehart Moore. His children are Barbara, Linda, Jimmy and David.

HARPER, CHESLEY CLYDE, Serial Number 34 739 368, was a Technician Fourth Grade in Headquarters Detachment SCU 2407 in the Army of the United States. His permanent mailing address was Cypress Inn, Tennessee. He was born 31 July 1913 in Cypress Inn. He was married. He was registered with Selective Service Board in Wayne County, Tennessee. His Civilian Occupation was Sticker. His address at time of entry into service was Route 3, Iron City, Tennessee. His Military Occupational Specialty was Truck Driver. The following decorations were awarded to Harper:: American Service Medal, Good Conduct Medal and World War II Victory Medal. He left the USA 15 November 1943 for the American Theater and returned to USA 3 February 1945. He was discharged 7 April 1946 at Fort McPherson, Georgia. He was issued a Lapel Button.

HARPER, EVERETT G., Serial Number 44 121 846, was a Private First Class in 13th Traffic Regulating Group in the Army of the United States. His permanent mailing address was Route 1, Cypress Inn, Tennessee. He was born 15 October 1926 in Cypress Inn. He was registered with Selective Service Board in Wayne County, Tennessee. His Civilian Occupation was Farm Hand. He was inducted 21 June 1945 at Fort Oglethorpe, Georgia. His Military Occupational Specialty was General Clerk. His Military Qualifications included MKM M1 Rifle. The following decoration was awarded to Harper: World War II Victory Ribbon. He left the USA 23 March 1946 for France and returned to USA 2 October 1946. He had a high school education. He was discharged 17 October 1946 at Fort George G. Meade, Maryland. He was issued a Lapel Button.

HARPER, EVERETT SANFORD, Serial Number 34 701 733, was a Private First Class in Company 1 424th Infantry Regiment, 106th Infantry Division in the Army of the United States. His permanent mailing address was Route 2, Iron City, Tennessee. He was born 1 March 1922 in Hamilton, Alabama. He was registered with Selective Service Board in Lauder-

dale County, Alabama. His Civilian Occupation was Sales Clerk. He was inducted 18 January 1943 and entered active service 25 January 1943 at Fort McClellan, Alabama. His Military Occupational Specialty was Rifleman. His Military Qualifications included Sharpshooter 45 Cal Revolver. He fought in battles in Northern France and Rhineland. The following decoration was awarded to Harper: American Theater Ribbon, Europe-African Midde Eastern Ribbon with two Bronze Service Stars, Good Conduct Medal and World War II Victory Medal. He left the USA 10 February 1945 for European Theater Operations and returned to USA 2 December 1945. He was discharged 13 December 1945 at Fort Knox, Kentucky. He was issued a Lapel Button. Everett Sanford Harper, was the son of the late George and Julia (Stidham) Harper, a retired truck driver with TVA, a member of Teamster Union, an Army Veteran and a Baptist. Mr. Harper died 1 September 19?? at Elize Coffee Memorial Hospital in Florence and he was buried in Memorial Gardens in Collinwood. Survivors include his wife Nola Brewer Harper of Florence, Alabama, two sons Gregory and Stanley Harper both of Florence; and one daughter, Edith Brewer of Iron City.

HARPER, WARREN G., was born 13 September 1920 in Wayne County. He was the son of Luther Franklin Harper (1 Sept 1875, AL - 4 Feb 1949, TN) and Jennie Louise Berry (8 Jan 1880, TN - 22 Mar 1953, TN) His parents were married 24 December 1896. Warren's siblings are Lillie Mae (1897-1975), Ada Bell (1900-1973), Wiley Lonzo (1903-1981), Jesse Granville (1906-1988), Roy Lee (1909-1974), J. B. (1911-), Chesley Clyde (1913-1991) and Ida Lorene (1917-). Warren was married (1) 4 June 1942 to Evelyn Ayers (1911-1942) and (2) 23 December 1946 in Corinth, Mississippi to Ona Lorraine Dixon, born 10 May 1920. Warren's children are Warren G., Jr., born 1947, Ronnie Lee born 1951, Stanley Franklin born 1952, Mischa Anne born 1959, and Barney Keith born 1961. Warren is a Methodist and lives in Greenville, Mississippi.

HARRIS, DANIEL R., Serial Number 34 044 877, was a Staff Sergeant in Company H, 326th Glider Infantry in the Army of the United States. His permanent mailing address was Route 6, Waynesboro, Tennessee. He was born 9 December 1916 in Lewis County, Tennessee. He was registered with Selective Service Board in Wayne County, Tennessee. His Civilian Occupation was General Farmer. He was married with two dependents when he was inducted 27 May 1941 at Fort Oglethorpe,

Georgia. His Military Occupational Specialty was Section Leader. His Military Qualifications included Pistol MM 8 MM 1st C1, Gunner, and M1 Rifle MM. He was in the battles in Central Europe. The following decorations were awarded to Harris: American Defense Service Medal, Good Conduct Medal, American Theater Service Ribbon, Europe-African Midde Eastern Theater Service Medal, and World War II Victory Medal. He left the USA 26 January 1945 for the European-African Middle Eastern Theater Operation, and returned to USA 25 August 1945. His education consisted of one year of high school. He was discharged 9 November 1945 at Camp Gordon, Georgia.

HARRIS, EDD A., of Waynesboro enlisted in the US Navy. After his training was completed, he served in the European Theater of Operations and was discharged at the Anaval Separation Center in Memphis, Tn.

HARRIS, HERMAN, Serial Number 34 193 020, was a Corporal in 571st Airborne Signal Company in the Army of the United States. His permanent mailing address was Route 1, Flatwoods, Tennessee. He was born 7 April 1907 in Wayne County, Tennessee. He was registered with Selective Service Board in Wayne County, Tennessee. His Civilian Occupation was Light Truck Driver. His Military Qualifications included MM Rifle and MM Carbine. He was inducted 15 March 1942 at Fort Oglethorpe, Georgia. His home address at time of entry into service was Route 6, Waynesboro, Tennessee. His Military Occupational Specialty was Antitank Gun Crewman. He was in the battles in Normandy, Northern France, Rhineland and Ardennes. The following decorations were awarded to Harris: Europe-African Midde Eastern Theater Ribbon with Four Bronze Stars, and a Bronze Arrowhead, Good Conduct Ribbon, Distinguished Unit Citation with One Oak Leaf Cluster and a

Bronze Star Medal. He left the USA 5 September 1943 for the European Theater Operation, and returned to USA 15 September 1945. He was discharged 23 September 1945 at Camp Atterbury, Indiana. He was issued a Lapel Button.

HARTUP, JAMES HUGO, JR., Serial Number 640 84 56, had the Grade Chief Carpenter's Mate in The United States Navy. He was born 14 February 1912 in Munice, Indiana. His permanent mailing address was Waynesboro, Tennessee. He enlisted 24 March 1943 in Pulaski, Tennessee. He completed a Carpenter's School in Williamsburg, Virginia. He served on the following Vessels/Stations: NCTC, Williamsburg, Virginia, 94th NCB. He was awarded the American Theater Ribbon, Asiatic Pacific Ribbon and Victory Medal. He had three years of college when he entered service. His last employer was Holthouse and Hardup in Waynesboro from 1934 to 1943. His main civilian occupation was Superintendent of Operations. He was discharged 25 December 1945 at US Naval Personnel Separation Center in Nashville, Tennessee.

HASSELL, BOB ADKINS, Serial Number 605 29 29, volunteered and enlisted in 1942 in the United States Navy.

He was born 28 November 1917 in Wayne County, Tennessee, in the home of his maternal grandparents in the Eagle Creek Community. Bob was the only child of Joel Adkins Hassell, born 30 September 1894, died 19 October 1962 and Ora Maude (Brown) Hassell, born 19 November 1894, and died 28 August 1977. Bob's paternal grandparents were William Amos Hassell, born 17 December 1868, died 20 October 1938 and Lily Irene (Hartley) Hassell, born 21 July 1873, died 15 January 1948. His maternal grandparents were Robert Andrew Brown of Wayne County, Tennessee and Clara (Medley) Brown from Ohio. (The Browns lived most of their life in Medford,

Oklahoma.) Bob lived his first years at Furnace Landing near Clifton, Tennessee. The family moved to Clifton and Bob attended school at Frank Hughes College until he was twelve years old. The family then moved to Waynesboro and he completed his public school years there, graduating from Wayne County High in 1936. Some of Bob's happiest memories were made as a team player on the WCHS basketball team and on the "historic football team - the first squad formed at WCHS. After graduation, and before joining the Navy, he worked as an employee of the Wayne County Highway Department. Bob married Martha Adeline Old of Waynesboro on 22 May 1938. Their first of two children was born 2 September 1941, a son named Thomas Jerrold Hassell. World War II was raging around the globe so in 1942, Bob volunteered for service in the United States Navy. The three member family lived in Ohio and Louisiana during his naval training months. When Bob was assigned to duty on the USS PATOKA, a tanker, his wife and son returned to live in Waynesboro. Bob saw active sea duty both in the Atlantic Ocean and the Pacific war zone. He was on duty on ship in the Japanese waters when World War II ended. In 1945, Bob was honorably discharged from the Navy. He returned to his family in Waynesboro and began working with his uncle at the Tom Hassell Sinclair Oil business where he continued to work until his death 17 March 1974. The Hassell's had a second son, Robert Edward Hassell, born in Waynesboro on 31 December 1948. Both of the Hassell sons, "Jerry" and Robert volunteered, as their father had, for service in the U. S. Navy and saw active duty during the Vietnam Conflict. "Jerry" served twenty years as a sailor, retiring with the rank of Lieutenant Commander (submarine). He now lives in Delaware with his wife, Margie (Berlin) Hassell and works at his second career as a consultant for Dupont. Robert, after a four-year tour of duty in the Navy, was honorably discharged in 1974, and he choose the field of law for a career. He was serving in Wayne County as General Sessions Judge and County Attorney at the time of his death in January of 1989. Adeline resides in Waynesboro at the present time. She and Bob have three grandchildren, Tommy, Sharon and Karen Hassell, the children of Jerry and Margie Hassell. They all live in Delaware.
Source: Adeline Old Hassell, Waynesboro, Tennessee.

HASSELL, HOWARD, Serial Number 34 325 962, was a Private in 827th Tank Destroyer Battalion in the Army of the United States. His permanent mailing address was 5726 Williams Street, Detroit, Michigan. He was born 24 September 1924

in Waynesboro. His race was Negro. He was registered with Selective Service Board in Wayne County, Tennessee. His Civilian Occupation was Heavy Truck Driver. He was inducted 13 September 1942 at Fort Benning, Georgia. His Military Occupational Specialty was Light Truck Driver. His Military Qualifications included Carbine - Marksman. He was in the battles of Naples-Foggia, Northern France, and Central Europe. The following decorations were awarded to Hassell: Europe-African Midde Eastern Theater Ribbon with two Bronze Stars, and World War II Victory Medal. He left the USA 21 August 1943 for the European Theater Operation, and returned to USA 2 December 1945. He was discharged 9 December 1945 at Camp Atterbury, Indiana.

He was the son of Cicera and Alice Hicks Hassell. He attended school in Wayne County and was of the Baptist Christian Faith. His birth and death dates are unknown, but he is buried in Waynesboro. He had three sisters: Dorothy, Mozella and Opal, and three brothers: Columbus, Edward and Waiden McCulley.
Source: Opal Bumphas.

HASSELL, RICHARD FRANK, Service Number 63 91 39, was a Seaman, First Class in the United States Coast Guard. He enlisted as A. S. on the 11 December 1942 at Nashville, Tennessee for three years. He was born 31 December 1923 near Clifton, Tennessee. He held the ratings of A. S, S2C and S1C. The Vessels and Stations that he served on are; Man Beach Trasta, CG BKS, Providence, Rhode Island; St. Louis, 9th Naval District; MBNAD Hastings, Nebraska and Trasta Curtis Bay, Maryland. His active duty was from 19 January 1943 until 9 April 1946 when he was discharged from regular reserve. Hassell was awarded a Good Conduct Medal, Honorable Discharge Button and Honorable Service Lapel Button and Emblem.

HAYES, CECIL ARTHUR, Serial Number 273 50 91, was a Seaman, Second Class in the United States Navy. He entered service on 23 November 1944. He was born 26 November 1926 in Wayne County, Tennessee. The Vessels and Stations that he served on are, NRS, Birmingham, Alabama; USNTC Great Lakes, Illinois and USNH, Memphis, Tennessee. He was discharged 19 February 1946 in Memphis, Tennessee.

HAYES, ERNEST L., Serial Number 34 044 873, was a Private in 4th Service Command (ASGD) Special Army in the Army of the United States. He was born in Wayne County. His Civilian Occupation was Farmer. He was 30 9/12 years old when he was inducted 21 February 1942 at Fort Oglethorpe, Georgia. His stations were: Headquarters Company, 725th, MP Battalion, Fort Jackson, South Carolina February 27, 1942 to June 30, 1942; Company D, 725th M. P. Battalion, Fort Jackson from June 30, 1942 to December 7, 1942; and Special Unit Rec. Center Fort Jackson from December 7, 1942 to July 3, 1943. He was discharged 3 July 1942 at Fort Jackson, South Carolina.

HAYES, JAMES HIRAM, Serial Number 34 494 866, was a Private First Class with Company F 350th Infantry of the United States Army. His permanent mailing address was Route 1, Cypress Inn, Tennessee. He was born 22 May 1921 in Cypress Inn. His Civilian Occupation was Student. He was registered with Selective Service Board No. 1, Waynesboro, Tennessee. He was inducted 22 November 1942 and entered active service 29 November 1942 at Fort Oglethorpe, Georgia. His Military Occupational Specialty was Light Machine Gunner. His Military Qualifications included Rifle Marksman. He was in battles in the Italian Campaign. His decorations included the European African Middle Eastern Campaign Medal, Two Bronze Battle Stars, Purple Heart with One Bronze Oak Leaf Cluster, Combat Infantryman Badge, and Good Conduct Medal. He was wounded 11 July 1944 and 1 October 1944 in the European Theater. He left the USA 7 December 1943 for North Africa, then left there 17 February 1944 for Italy and returned home 19 November 1944. He was honorably discharged 29 June 1945 at Kennedy General Hospital, Memphis, Tennessee He was the son of Jacob McCoy and Lillie (Moser) Hayes and he had a high school education.

HAYES, JOHN LOUIS, Serial Number 965 96 55, had the grade of Shipfitter, Third Class in the United States Navy. He was born 4 August 1925 in Wayne County, Tennessee. He entered service 22 November 1943 and was honorably discharged 5 January 1946 at US Naval Personnel Separation Center in Memphis, Tennessee. He served on the following vessel and stations: NTS Great Lakes, Illinois, NATTC Navy Flier, Chicago, Illinois and USS SARATOGA. John L. Hayes was the son of Mr. and Mrs. J. D. Hayes of Route 1, Lutts, Tennessee. He spent 25 months in the Navy - 18 of which was aboard ship in the South Pacific. He participated in two invasions and received two Battle Stars.
Source: Wayne County News, 18 January 1946.

HAYES, ROBERT FIELDER, Serial Number 44 171 594, was a Private First Class in C Battery 339th Field Artillery Bat-

talion, 88th Division in the Army of the United States. His permanent mailing address was Route 1, Lutts, Tennessee. He was born 3 April 1927 in Iron City, Tennessee. He was registered with Selective Service Board in Wayne County, Tennessee. His Civilian Occupation was Farmer. He was inducted 3 March 1946 at Fort Oglethorpe, Georgia. His Military Occupational Specialty was Light Truck Driver. His Military Qualifications included Rifle Expert. The following decorations were awarded to Hayes: Army of Occupation Medal, and World War II Victory Medal. He left the USA 9 June 1946 for the Mediterranean Theater Operation and returned to USA 4 May 1947. He finished a year and a half of high school. He was discharged 7 June 1947 at Camp Kilmer, New Jersey. He was issued a Lapel Button. Mr. Hayes died 29 March 1996 in Florence, Alabama and was buried in Mt. Hope Cemetery in Cypress Inn. He was the son of Jacob Dumont and Beulah Elizabeth Fowler Hayes; he was retired from the Ford Motor Company. Survivors included his wife, Charla Mae Holt Hayes of Florence; One son Danny Michael Hayes of Florence; two brothers, Thomas Hayes of Florence and Ray Hayes of Joliet, Illinois and two grandchildren.
Source: Wayne County News, 3 April 1996.

HEARD, CLARENCE EDWARD, Serial Number 34 040 790, was a Private First Class with Company K 390th Infantry of the United States Army. His permanent mailing address was General Delivery, Collinwood, Tennessee. He was born 8 September 1915 in Wayne County, Tennessee. His Civilian Occupation was Circular Head Saw. He was registered with Selective Service Board No. 1, Waynesboro, Tennessee. He was inducted 3 April 1941 at Fort Oglethorpe, Georgia. His Military Occupational Specialty was Light Mortar Crewman. His Military Qualifications included Marksman Rifle. His decorations included the Good Conduct Medal, American Defense Service Ribbon, and Asiatic-Pacific Service Ribbon. He left the USA 27 January 1942 for Asiatic-Pacfic Theater and returned home 10 December 1944. He left the USA the second time 31 January 1945 for Asiatic-Pacfic Theater and returned home 19 August 1945. He was honorably discharged 26 August 1945 at Camp Chaffee, Arkansas. "Pvt Clarence E. Heard, son of Henry Heard of Collinwood, entered the service in 1941. He took his basic training at Camp Wheeler, Georgia. He served overseas four years. He was stationed in Hawaii for a long period of time."
Source: Wayne County News.

HEARD, JAMES ROSS, Serial Number 970 01 77, enlisted in the United States Navy for two years on the 18 March 1944

in Memphis, Tennessee. He was born 23 November 1922 on Indian Creek in Wayne County, Tennessee. The Vessels and Stations that he served on were: USNTS, San Diego, California and NRS, Memphis, Tennessee. He was discharged 28 April 1944 at the US Naval Training Center in San Diego, California with a grade of Seaman Second Class. He was married.

HEARD, REUBEN, Serial Number 970 01 76, was inducted into the United States Navy 18 March 1944 at Waynesboro, Tennessee. His permanent mailing address was Route 2, Collinwood, Tennessee. His Civilian Occupation was Farmer. The Vessels and Stations that he served on were: NTC, San Diego, California; USNAS, Kahului, Maui, T. H. ; Personnel and Training Command NRS, New Orleans, Louisiana, and USS BONHOMME RICHARD. He was discharged 8 December 1945 at the US Naval Training Personnel Separation Center in Memphis, Tennessee with a grade of Seaman Second Class. He was awarded the American Theater Ribbon, World War II Victory Medal and Asiatic-Pacific Ribbon. Reuben, son of George W. and Ella Heard, was born 5 February 1914 in Collinwood, Tennessee. He married Vivian Dodd who lived in the Indian Creek Community. He took boat training in San Diego, and was sent overseas where he spent seven months in the Hawaiian Islands.

HELTON, HAROLD, was a Veteran of the United States Navy. He was born in 1927 in Wayne County, Tennessee and died

17 December 1992 in Longview, Texas. He was buried in Hillcrest Memorial Gardens in Bridge City, Texas where he had lived for a long time. His parents were John and Katie Duren Helton. His wife was Bettie Helton of Longview. He also had two nephews and three nieces. He was a retired operator for DuPont Salune River Works.

HELTON, JAMES CATON, In 1942

and 1943 there were not too many Draft Dodgerslat least not from Wayne County. I heard after the war that fourteen hundred men from the county had served in the war.

I wanted to join the Navy right out of High School but my dad talked me out of it saying I would be signing up for the draft soon enough. I signed up for the draft on June 24, 1943 my eighteenth birthday, and was sworn into the Navy in Chattanooga on Sept. 4, 1943. After a six day train ride I arrived at the Navy Training Station in San Diego, Cal. I went on active duty Sept. 11, 1943.

We went through seven weeks of Boot Camp with Taps at 4:30 A.M. and Reviley at 9:30 P.M. It must to have been good for me because I gained twenty five pounds in those seven weeks.

After basic training we were either sent to Sea or to other schools for training. I was sent to Hospital Corps School located in Balboa Park, also in San Diego. After completing six weeks of corp school I was sent to the Navy Hospital at Corona, Cal. where I served three months. I was then sent to Shoemaker, Cal. to embark for overseas.

I love the ocean and wanted to join the Navy but this was the most terrifying part of my whole military career. We embarked WOW #1 troop ship named the S.S. General George 0. Squire, with seven thousand five hundred men. There were six hundred and forty men in our sleeping compartment which was deep down the bottom of the ship. If we had been torpedoed there would have been no way to get out. Consequently I spent more time on the top deck than I did in my bunk. Breakfast was served between 4:30 A.M. and noon which consisted of two pieces of fruit. Dinner was served between noon and 8:30 P.M. I don't see how the cooks did as well as they did.

After thirty one days at sea I was at Base Hospital . 817 on the southern tip of New Guinea. I had ward duty for about three months and then transferred to the operating room where I worked for about seven months. We had no set schedule here, every one worked until they were exhausted.

After ten months I was glad to be transferred to the 22nd Spec. C.B. Battalion on the Admiralty Islands. Manous Island was the largest of the group and Los Negros was slightly smaller but most of this island was perfectly flat and was a natural air field. This was the major supply depot for the Pacific during that part of the war. C.B. Spec. Battalions are made up with Stevedore Gangs whose primary duties are loading and unloading ships and planes 0 1 worked in a dispensary near the airport. Our duties besides taking care of the sick and injured in our Battalion was to keep an ambulance at the airport. All types of planes were coming in to pick up supplies or to refuel.

I arrived back in the states at Seattle, Wash. on Jan. 2, 1946. I was transferred to the Navy Air Station where I served, three months and was discharged there on April 6, 1946. 1 served thirty one months and - three days with about twenty one months in the Pacific. I consider myself as one of the very lucky ones. I saw a lot of war without being deeply involved in it, had some bad and good experiences but interesting, was very few times in great danger, and came out without a scratch.

HELTON, TOLBERT MAXEY, was the son of William B. and Lucy Flippo Helton. He had two brothers, John and Leon,

and a sister who died as a child. Talbert was a medic in the United States Army. He served in active battles, picking up wounded in the field. In fact, he received a Purple Heart for a shoulder wound in Germany. He received a military disability pension.
Source: Pat Taylor.

HELTON, TOM, Serial Number 34 377 042, was a Private First Class in Battery D 397th Antiaircraft Artillery in the Army of the United States. His permanent mailing address was Route 2, Lutts, Tennessee. He was born 10 December 1921 in Lutts. He was registered with Selective Service Board in Wayne County, Tennes-

see. His Civilian Occupation was General Farmhand. He was inducted 14 October 1942 at Fort Oglethorpe, Georgia. His Military Occupational Specialty was Antitank Gun Crewman. He was in the battles of Normandy, Northern France, Ardennes, Rhineland, and Central Europe. The following decorations were awarded to Helton: Purple Heart, World War II Victory Medal, American Theater Ribbon, and European-African-Middle-Eastern Theater Ribbon with four Bronze Stars. He left the USA 7 April 1944 for the Europe-African Midde Eastern Theater Operation, and returned to USA 3 December 1945. He was discharged 13 December 1945 at Fort Knox, Kentucky. Newspaper clipping not dated (very poor xerox copy-parts not readable)- Pfc Helton... and took his training at Camp Atterbury, Indiana and Camp Breckinridge, Kentucky, and was transferred to active duty overseas in April 1944. He was with the 83rd Division, 330 Infantry. He saw action in France and took part in the battle for Brest, Germany and was awarded the combat Infantry Badge. He was wounded 14 December 1944 in Germany. He writes he is now able to go to the mess hall and hopes to be back with his outfit soon. Helton's mother, Mrs. Frank Harbour, lives in the Martin Mill's community.

HENDRIX, J.T., age 68, died 1 March 1984 at his home in Florence, Alabama, and was buried in Memorial Gardens in Collinwood. He was the son of James T. and Mattie Keeton Hendrix. He was a retired store operator and a member of Bethel Berry Church of Christ. Survivors include his wife, Roxie Butler Hendrix; three sons, Douglas of Florence, Michael and Floyd both of Portland, Oregon; a daughter, Sheila Harris of Florence; three brothers, Bernon, R. V. and Oval Hendrix all of Florence; four sisters, Lela Holt, Earline Hines, Vernice Thomason and Ethel Purser all of Florence; and eleven grandchildren.

HENDRIX, JACK WILLIAM "BILLY", son of Jim and Nona Hendrix was born, April 14, 1922, in Wayne County. He lived in the Buffalo Valley Community at Rt. #6, Waynesboro, TN and was farming, when he was inducted into the U. S. Army. Billy was sent overseas and promoted to Sgt. and Assistant Rifle Squad Leader with the 6th Armored Infantry Battalion, 1st Armored Division and served in Italy with the Fifth Army under Gen. Mark W. Clark. He was awarded the Combat Infantry Badge.

Billy married Sarah Lou Mathis and had a good life living near the Buffalo River. They have seven children, William Dwight (deceased), Melissa, Connie, Rhonda, Deborah, Tracy and Travis. October 14, 1978, he died suddenly from a cerebral hem-

orrhage and is buried at the Whitehead Cemetery in the Topsy Community. His six siblings are Maurice (deceased), Margie, (twins) Helen and Ellen, Geraldine and Betty.

HENDRIX, LESTER, Serial Number 34 040 083, was a Sergeant with Medical Detachment Service Command Unit, Moore General Hospital of the United States Army. His permanent mailing address was Route 3, Florence, Alabama. He was born 18 November 1919 in Lauderdale, Alabama. His Civilian Occupation was Farmer. He was registered with Selective Service Board No. 1, Waynesboro, Tennessee. He was inducted 26 March 1941 at Fort Oglethorpe, Georgia. His Military Occupational Specialty was Medical Aidman and Lab Technician. He was in battles in the East Indies Campaign, and New Guinea Campaign. His decorations included: the Asiatic-Pacific Service Ribbon with two Bronze Battle Stars, and Good Conduct Ribbon. He left the USA 17 February 1942 for Australia, departed from there 27 July 1944 for Holland and returned home 30 December 1944. He was honorably discharged 20 September 1945 at Moore General Hospital, Swannanos, North Carolina. His parents were James T. and Della (Keeton) Hendrix. His brothers are, Roland V., Orval twin to Roland, Clyde killed in action, J. T., and Vernon. His sisters are, Lela Holt, Earlene, Bernice Pollock Thomason and Ethel Handback Purser. Lester is buried in the City of Florence Cemetery.

HENDRIX, ORVAL, was inducted 19 January 1942 into the Infantry of the United States Army. He was wounded in action in Italy and was sent back to a Maryland Hospital. He was discharged in 1944. He died 3 May 1985 and was buried in McGlamery Cemetery in Collinwood. He was survived by his wife, Lydia O'Mally Hendrix and children, Earline, Betty, Shirley and Lisa Hendrix. His parents were James T. and Della (Keeton) Hendrix. His

brothers are, Lester, Orval twin to Roland, Clyde killed in action, J. T., and Vernon. His sisters are Lela Holt, Earlene, Bernice Pollock Thomason and Ethel Handback Purser.

HENDRIX, ROLLAND V., Serial Number 975 90 81, was a Seaman, First Class in the United States Navy. He entered into service 17 October 1944 and received his basic training at Great Lakes, Illinois. The Vessel he served on was USS TYPHOON. The area of his battles and campaigns were in the South Pacific Theater of War and the islands in this area. His Civilian Occupation was Farmer in Cypress Inn in the southern part of Wayne County. He was discharged 27 June 1946. His parents were James T. and Della (Keeton) Hendrix. His brothers are, Lester, Orval twin to Roland, Clyde killed in action, J. T., and Vernon. His sisters are, Lela Holt, Earlene, Bernice Pollock Thomason and Ethel Handback Purser. He married Doris Givens and his children are James, and twins, Jerry and Shirley Hendrix.

HENRY, JAMES "JIM" MELVIN, age 79, died 27 October 1996 at his home in Clifton and was buried in Praters Chapel Cemetery. A native of Waterloo, Ohio, he was the son of Will and Effie Mitchum Henry. He was an Army veteran of World War II, a retired steel mill worker and a member of the Beech Creek Church of Christ. Survivors include his wife, Rheba A. Henry of Clifton. (Wayne County News 30 October 1996) .

HENSLEY, BILLY L., Serial Number 44 173 403, was a Technician, Fifth Grade with Headquarters Company 2nd Major Port of the United States Army. His permanent mailing address was General Delivery, Collinwood, Tennessee. He was born 11 July 1927 in Iron City, Tennessee. His Civilian Occupation was Student. He was registered with Selective Service Board No. 1, Waynesboro, Tennessee. His Military Occupational Specialty was Clerk Typist. His Military Qualifications included Expert Rifle Caliber 30 M-1. He left the USA 21 August 1946 for Pacific Theater Operation and returned home 2 April 1947. He was honorably discharged 7 May 1947 at Camp Stoneman, California. He had a high school education.

HENSON, VIRGIL L., entered the U.S. Army from his home, Route 1, Lutts,- Tennessee, on March 15,1942, at age 25 years, with service entry at Fort Oglethorpe, Georgia. After training, and stateside service, he departed for the European Theater Operation on September 5,1943, as a member of the 10 1st. Airborne Division

(Screaming Eagles). He did not return home until November 20,1945. During his over two years overseas war service, the Screaming Eagles distinguished themselves 'in battle. Although Mr. Henson would -not cite his individual exploits, he always spoke highly of his unit and the members with which he served. His medal awards were- Distinguished Unit Badge, American Theater Ribbon, European African Middle Eastern Ribbon with 4 bronze service stars,, Good Conduct Medal, Bronze Star,, Bronze Arrowhead, and the World War 11 victory Medal. He was a Marksman with the Garand rifle, and was awarded the Aviation Glider Badge. His battles and campaigns were Normandy, Ardennes, Rhineland, and Central Europe. His total military time was 3 years, 8 months, and II days. He was separated from the service at Fort Knox, Kentucky, with an Honorable Discharge.

To his family, Mr. Henson was the strong silent type, generous, supportive and a man of his word. He was somewhat shy with strangers, until he got to know them, then he could display a great sense of humor. Mr. Henson always said he served his country when needed and it was a price for the privilege of freedom. His feet bothered him after the war from frostbite, or actually having been frozen to some degree. He always commented on how cold it was, and that the soldiers had to endure the harshest winter that part of the world had seen in 50 years! One personal story he told, was of driving the famous actress, singer and entertainer, Marlene Dietrich as an assignment, after she entertained the, troops in his service area. His discharge papers show his military specialty as a light truck driver. Allowing for his quiet, shy demeanor, his commanding officer made an excellent choice for Ms. Dietrich's driver.

Virgil Henson never married,, and after the war,- he moved to Georgia along with members of his family,. He remained in Georgia until his death on January 12, 1999, at age 91. His family is extremely proud to have had him represent Wayne County, Tennessee, in defense of our country. To his family, Virgil Henson is a much loved hero and family member, who has left a great void with his death. Thanks to the production of books like these, our heroes, treasures and loved ones, of the greatest generation, will live on in our hearts and memories!

HICKERSON, KENNETH REECE, age 66, of Route 4, Waynesboro died 24 July 1997 in Maury Regional Hospital in Columbia and was buried in Memorial Gardens. He was a native of Perry County, a son of Fount and Elsie Thelma Culp Hickerson. He was a truck driver, mechanic and a member of the Methodist Church. Survivors include his wife, Robbie June Joines Hickerson of Waynesboro; two sons, Larry of St. Louis, Missouri and Barry Hickerson of Augusta, Georgia; two brothers, W. C. of Waynesboro and Earl Gene Hickerson of Collinwood; four grandchildren and one great-grandchild.

Source: Wayne County News 30 July 1997.

HICKERSON, WALTON F., Serial Number 13 104 327, I enlisted in the Army Air Force 6 October 1942. I left Baltimore, Maryland, went to Camp Lee, Virginia, and was sent from there to Bowman Field in Louisville, Kentucky for six weeks basic training. From there I was sent to Chanute Field, Illinois for thirteen weeks. While there I enrolled in a sheet metal school. After this I was transferred to Detroit, Michigan to a self sealing gasoline tank school. Leaving Detroit, I went to Savannah, Georgia to Hunter Field and stayed there from March until October 1943. Then I went to Plant Park in Tampa, Florida for eight days. We were issued winter clothing. We couldn't understand why, but what we didn't know was that we were being prepared to be sent overseas. We were sent to Camp Kilmer, New Jersey. Here we boarded a ferry boat that carried us to New York where we were put aboard the luxury ship, LONDON ORION. We were in a convoy of ships, about 45, I guess. It took us eleven days to go to Glasgow, Scotland. A ferry boat carried us from the ship to the bank. Then we boarded a train that was blacked out in Scotland and went to England. After staying there a few days, we were shipped to Belfast, Northern Ireland. While there I enrolled in a driver education school to learn how to drive vehicles in Europe. Then, I was sent to London to a welding school for six weeks. Back to Northern Ireland for a short time until the entire troop that I was with was sent back to London. This is where I was when the invasion took place. My job was to help carry supplies to troops as they needed them, repair planes, and refuel them. Later, we got leave and went to Brighton, England and was on the coast near the White Cliffs of Dover when news came that the war in Europe had ended. I was then sent to Paris, France where I stayed about nine months before I received orders to be shipped to Hickman Field, Hawaii. The war in Japan ended before I left France and they started sending the boys home. I received 4 Battle Stars while I was there. I left Marseille, France 7 December 1945, went down the Mediterranean to Gibraltar, took ten hours to refuel the ship. Gibraltar was a beautiful town. We were on the ship 14 days coming home before we landed in Hamptom Road, Virginia. After staying there a few days, we took a train to Fort Knox, Kentucky where we were discharged. After spending three years, two months and twenty-two days in service, I got home 1 January 1946.

(For more family information see William Thirl Hickerson biography.)

HICKERSON, WILLIAM THIRL, was born in the Beech Creek Community of Wayne County on 9 March 1915. His parents were William Jackson and Florence (Denton) Hickerson. Ten of their twelve children survived infancy. They were Grady, Jewell Mae, Lotus, Herschel, Arnez, Paul, Stanley, W. Thirl, Lorrene and Walton. In 1936, Thirl transferred from Frank Hughes High School in Clifton to Perry County High School in Linden to play football, and during this time he boarded with the Denton family. Vivian was a fourth grader. Thirl, a senior, immediately became her hero. After graduation Thirl returned home and worked at odd jobs. On 5 October 1939, he traveled from Wayne County to Nashville and enlisted in the United States Navy. At the time he had $7. 50 in his pocket and a few clothes in a suitcase. When the Japanese hit Pearl Harbor on 7 December 1941, Thirl was aboard the USS WEST VIRGINIA and had to swim to safety after the ship was bombed. He lost all of his belongings and had to wear a pair of officer's pants and mismatched shoes that he had found until he was reassigned and new clothes were issued. He was later assigned to the USS FANNING and participated in the Doolittle Raid on Tokyo, April 18-22, 1942. Vivian and Thirl met again while he was on leave in 1943, and he proposed to her on their first date. They were married in Rossville, Georgia, 25 June 1945. Mattie Vivian Hickerson was born in the Cedar Creek Community of Perry County on January 18, 1925. Prior to her marriage Vivian worked for the Fulton Syphon Company in Knoxville. After her marriage she lived with Thirl near several Naval installations. Their first child, Janis Denton Hickerson, was born in Nashville on 3 August 1946. After eight years in the Navy, Thirl decided to return to Tennessee. Jobs were scarce and he turned to farming to make a living for his family. On 28 October 1947, the Hickersons purchased a 430 acre farm near Bakersville, Tennessee, for the enormous sum of $37,500. But after a year they sold this property and returned to Perry County. When it was announced that TVA was planning to build a power plant in New Johnsonville, Vivian and Thirl again decided to look for a permanent place to live in Humphreys County. Thirl was positive that his work with steam boilers on ship would qualify him for a position at the new power plant. Walter Murphy of Waverly contacted the couple and showed them the old R. L. Parnell place on Trace Creek Road, and they purchased the property and moved in immediately. Five months later William Bruce Hickerson was born 10 December 1949. To make a living Thirl raised hogs and cattle and used his G.I. benefits to learn more about agriculture. A second daughter, Rita Gail Hickerson, was born 29 June 1951. When TVA started cutting powerline right-of-ways Thirl and his neighbor B. H. Atkins snaked logs by mule for $16.00 a day. On 25 February 1952, Thirl went to work permanently for the TVA steam plant and retired from the job 31 May 1976. A fourth child Trudy Diame Hickerson was born 27 May 1959. The Hickersons have now lived in Humphreys County for 43 years, and all their children are grown. Janis married Joe Patterson, Jr., and they had one son Christopher. Janis and her son live near Hustburg. William Bruce is married to Kathleen Bradford and they live on the Trace Creek farm. Rita Gail married James D. Pratt, III, they had one daughter, Angelia. Rita Gail is now married to Robert Moreland and they live in Memphis. Trudy attended Middle Tennessee University and major in business. She is married to Joe David Satterfield and they live in Gallatin with their son David William Satterfield. Thirl and Vivian look forward to many more happy years in Humphreys County.

Source: Vivian Denton Hickerson 1992.

HICKERSON, WILLIE FLOYD, Serial Number 34 713 895, was a Private First Class with 275th Armored Field Artillery Battalion and was attached to the 1st and 9th Army of the United States Army. His permanent mailing address was Route 1, Flatwoods, Tennessee. His Civilian Occupation was Farmer. He was registered with Selective Service Board No. 1, Waynesboro, Tennessee. He was inducted 22 April 1943 and entered active service

30 April 1943 at Fort Oglethorpe, Georgia. His Military Occupational Specialty was Cannoneer. His Military Qualifications included Expert Carbine, 30 Caliber and Expert Submachine Gun. He was in battles in Northern France, Central Europe, Rhineland and Ardennes. His decorations included: the Good Conduct Medal, and European-African Middle Eastern Campaign Medal. He left the USA 2 July 1944 for Europe-African Midde-Eastern Theater and returned home 3 July 1945. His education consisted of seven years of grammar school. He was discharged 15 October 1945 at Camp Beale, California. Willie received his basic training at Selina, Kansas, then was sent to England. Two months later he went into combat at Breast, Germany. He was on the front line in Seigred, Germany, then crossed the Rhine River for the Battle of the Bulge. Willie, son of Johnny and Mandy (Jones) Hickerson, was born 4 January 1924 in Flatwoods, Tennessee. His brothers are Leonard, Tom, Albert, William, Rex and Ray and his sisters are, Grace Caperton, Reba Baxter, and Virgie Money. He married Wilma Griggs and their children are Margaret Riley of Ypsilanti, Michigan, Boyd of Coldwater, Michigan, Katherine of Clifton, Linda of Detroit, Michigan, Richard of Waynesboro, and Kenneth Hickerson of Greensboro, North Carolina. Willie, age 72, died 30 March 1996 in Columbia and was buried in the Forty-Eight Creek Frewill Baptist Church Cemetery in Waynesboro.

HICKS, BROYLES T., 3104QN Service, served in World War II (1943-1946) in the European Theatre, England, Germany and Holland. Broyles T. was born in Clifton, Tennessee. He attended the Rosenwald School in Clifton.

HILL, ANDREW, was born on January 26, 1921, the son of Miles Brison and Roxie Staggs Hill. He was born on Beech Creek in Wayne County, Tennessee. Andrew lost his parents at an early age and was reared in the home of Jack and Ollie Culp on Beech Creek. He received two years of high school before being inducted into the Army Infantry in the academic field at Fort Benning, Georgia, on January 5, 1943. He received the Good Conduct Medal with 4th Clasp, National Defence Service Medal and Sharpshooter Medal (rifle). He retired with an honorable permanent disability on March 7, 1958, at the Sch. Brig. at Fort Benning, Georgia. His occupation duty was as Specialist-Office Manager. Andrew died while at Fort Benning with leukemia at the age of 37. He was buried one mile from Fort Benning. He married his sweetheart, Ethel. They had one son, Miles Eugene, and has three grandchildren: Billy, Scotty and Dawn. He had five brothers: Barney, Hubert, Claiborn, Clayton and Chesley. He has one sister, Ruby Hill Staggs, and two half-sisters, Lucy Hill Davis and Mary Jane Hill Graham. Andrew Hill.

HILL, CHESLEY BROWN, son of Miles Brison and Roxie Staggs Hill, was born on March 23, 1923, in Beech Creek

in Wayne County, Tennessee. Near the age of 2 due to a tragedy, he lost his parents and was orphaned. He was adopted. His name was changed to Chester Leon Parman. His family did not know where he was for several years. Fours of these boys served in the United States Service during World War II. Claiborn, one of Chesley's brothers who was residing in California, decided to launch out on a lifetime dream or purpose to find his adopted brother, Chesley. He came to Tennessee in the search. He found him in Memphis, Tennessee. The family had a great reunion with their baby brother, Chesley. Claiborn went back to San Francisco, California, and was killed in a car wreck not long after the reunion with the family. Chesley's sister, Ruby, began receiving mail from his sta-

tion at Camp Polk, Louisiana. Chesley also served in Hawaii during his service. He married and had three children: Robert, Raymond and Sharon. Chesley died on October 15, 1984. His Army rank was Sergeant. He had five brothers: Clayton, Barney, Claiborn, Hubert and Andrew. He had one sister, Ruby Hill Staggs, and two half-sisters, Lucy Hill Davis and Mary Jane Hill Graham. Chesley Brown Hill (Chester Leon Parman-adopted name).

HILL, CLAYBORN B., was born on March 9, 1909, in Beech Creek in Wayne County, Tennessee, the son of Miles Brison

Hill and Roxie Staggs Hill. Clayborn was inducted into the United States Service for World War II on February 18, 1942, at Fort Oglethorpe, Georgia, as a Marine Engineman. He received a marksman rifle. He was awarded the Good Conduct Medal. He was honorably discharged with a certificate of disability on June 14, 1945, as a Technician 5th grade Mine TNG. Det. Ca. Sch. Fort Monroe, Virginia, after three years, three months and 27 days. Clayborn never married. He was killed in a car wreck in San Francisco, California, in 1945. He was brought home to Beech Creek in Wayne County, Tennessee, to be buried in the Balcom Cemetery. He fulfilled a dream of locating his adopted baby brother, Chesley B. Hill, before he died. He also found that Chesley also served his country in World War II under another name. He had five brothers: Barney, Hubert, Clayton, Andrew and Chesley. (Hubert was killed in World War II). He had one sister, Ruby Hill Staggs, and two half-sisters, Lucy Hill Davis and Mary Jane Hill Graham. Clayborn B. Hill.

HILL, CLAYTON H., son of Miles Brison and Roxie Staggs Hill, was born on September 17, 1906, in Beech Creek in Wayne County, Tennessee. He served his country in the United States Army during World War II in the 831st Engineer Battal-

ion from February 18, 1942, to September 6, 1945, in England and France. His rank was Sergeant, Tech 4. He was awarded the EAME Ribbon and Good Conduct Ribbon. He married an English girl, Sylvia Mary Newell, in England on January 4, 1944. Their first child, Marion Roxy, was born in England in December 1945. Their other children (Margaret Ann, Kenneth and William) were born in America. Clayton worked as a carpenter after returning home with his family. He made his home in Pine Bluff, Arkansas. He was a Methodist by faith. He died on September 7, 1997, and is buried in Monticello, Arkansas. He had five brothers: Barney, Hubert, Claiborn, Andrew and Chesley. He had one sister, Ruby Hill Staggs, and two half-sisters, Lucy Hill Davis and Mary Jane Hill Graham. Clayton H. Hill.

HILL, EVERETT LEE, was born on February 19, 1926. His parents are James Hill and Virgie Jones Hill of Collinwood, Tennessee. Everett joined the Navy directly after high school and was sent to Fort Oglethorpe, Georgia, on April 21, 1944. Everett never served overseas or saw any active duty. He was discharged on July 4, 1946, from the United States Naval Personnel Separation Center in Shelton, Virginia. Everett Lee Hill married Imogene Brewer on January 27, 1951. They have two sons, Jimmy Lee Hill and Charles Douglas Hill, both live in Florence, Alabama. They also have five grandchildren. Everett worked as a builder of homes and a contractor of buildings until his death by a massive heart attack on July 11, 1983. He died at the age of 57 in St. Thomas Hospital in Nashville, Tennessee. He was buried July 13, 1983, in Memorial Gardens in Collinwood. His wife Imogene still lives in Collinwood, and his mother, Ms. Virgie Hill, lives in Wayne County Nursing Home at the age of 96. He has two brothers, G. W. of Iron City and Clarence Hill of Collinwood, and one sister, Anna Harris of Nashville.

HILL, GARLAND, son of George and Virgie Jones Hill, was born on March 11, 1924, near Collinwood, Tennessee, and grew up there. After graduating at Collinwood High School, he worked a short time on the Natchez Trace Parkway, then traveled to another state and worked at a shipyard. About 1942 he volunteered for the United States Navy and served as Chief Petty Officer in Europe during World War II. At the end of the war, he returned home and began working as a bricklayer; he worked in several different states. Garland and Willodean Burleson were married on March 2, 1957, and lived in Collinwood where she was employed at City Hall until she retired. They have four children: Brenda, Kenneth David, Robert Jeffery and Amy Dean. Garland died from a stroke on January 4, 1971, and is buried in McGlamery Cemetery near Collinwood.

HILL, MARVIN, joined the armed forces for World War II in 1942. He became a part of the Signal Corps assigned to the 8th Air Force. This led to intensive schooling in Washington, D. C. in electricity and radio maintenance, followed by additional technical training in a school in Florida. The next move was to England where he served until the end of the war. Marvin, a native of Clifton, was the son of Allen and Oda Bell Hill. He graduated from Frank Hughes School in 1937. Marvin made his first visit to Humboldt to visit his sister in the summer of 1935. Three days after his arrival, he had a job with the West Tennessee Power and Light Company helping to clear brush for the construction of its new power line to Fruitland. After a busy summer he returned to Clifton to finish school, then returned to Humboldt to resume a career that lasted until retirement age. After service in World War II, he returned and found his job awaiting him in the electrical department. He served as department head until retirement. Marvin married in 1942 to Jane Lurine Arnold of Humboldt. They have one son, Dr. Kenneth W. Hill, of Humboldt and two grandchildren. His siblings are Eva Hill Rose, Vera Hill Tilghman, Clara Hill Dodson, Bonnie Hill, Harris and Burnes Hill.

HILL, WAYNE D., Serial Number 34 936 467, was a Private First Class in 406th Infantry Regiment, 102nd Infantry Division in the Army of the United States. His permanent mailing address was Lutts, Tennessee. He was born 10 February 1916 in Lutts and was the son of James and Jennie (Reeves) Hill. He was registered with Selective Service Board in Wayne County, Tennessee. His Civilian Occupation was General Farmer. His home address at time of entry into service was Route 2, Florence,

Alabama. His Military Occupational Specialty was Rifleman. His Military Qualifications included Combat Infantryman Badge and MKM Rifle. He was in the battles of Rhineland, and Central Europe. The following decorations were awarded to Hill: Europe-African Midde Eastern Theater Ribbon with two Bronze Stars, Good Conduct Medal, WWII Victory Medal, and Army of Occupation Medal (Germany). He left the USA 1 January 1945 for the European Theater Operation, and returned to USA 17 June 1946. He was discharged 22 June 1945 at Camp Atterbury, Indiana.

HILL, WILLIAM ARTHER, enlisted in the United States Army in August 1943. While he was in the service, he received the Purple Heart, two Bronze Stars and a Good Conduct Medal for active service in the Rhineland Central Europe. Other medals were three Overseas Bars, Victory Ribbon and Lapel Button, no time loss. After the armed services, he moved to Michigan where he worked in a factory. He lived in the Detroit area. Later, he went to Flint. It was here that he found his wife. He was married to Vivian Herndershot in 1963. They had four children: Raymond Bruce, Lynda Marie, Homer and Wayne Arther. He retired in Flint in December 1985. He returned to the Beech Creek area of Wayne County, Tennessee, on Route 2. Here he died on May 17, 1989. Burial was in Flint Memorial Park in Clio, Michigan. William Arther was the son of Thomas Martin and Virgie Griffin Hill. He was happy to return and purchase a home in Beech Creek to live out his life where his roots went back to the settlement in Beech Creek in Wayne County, Tennessee, in 1820. His siblings were Monetta, Jackolyn, Myron Dee, Shirly Jean, Max B., John and Thomas.

HINTON, FLOYD GLEN, age 82, died 20 January 1996 at St. Thomas Hospital in Nashville and was buried in Cloverdale Church of Christ Cemetery in Cloverdale, Alabama. A native of Wayne County, he was the son of Lonnie and Sallie Fraley Hinton. He was an Army veteran of World War II, a retired employee of Uniroyal in Indiana and a member of the Freewill Baptist Church.

HODGES, JASPER "JIMMY" E., was born, April 27, 192 1, to Clarence Farris and Nannie E. Hodges in Montgomery County, TN. He joined the United States Air Force in 1942 and served as an airplane mechanic during WWII, working on B-17 Bombers. His service time overseas was in India and Okinawa. In 1946 he received his discharge and returned to Montgomery County.

126

After a short time Jimmy opened a jewelry store at Dickson, TN, then sold it about a year later. He came to Waynesboro in 1947 and opened Waynesboro's first jewelry store, "Hodges Jeweler". Waynesboro then became home. He met Dortho Jane Gallaher and they were married, February 1, 1948. They operated the jewelry store until, January 1, 1980, when he retired and devoted his time to his checker games.

Jimmy and Jane have two daughters. Dianne married Frederick Gaines Ramsey, III, September 30, 1972. They have three children; Kim, Craig and Keri. Pam married James Allen Scott, March 20, 1987. They have a son, Allen Scott.

HOGAN, CHARLES L., Serial Number 34 501 353, was a Private First Class in Battery A 476th Antiaircraft Artillery Air Warning Battalion in the Army of the United States. His permanent mailing address was Route 3, Iron City, Tennessee. He was born 15 January 1922 in Florence, Alabama. He was registered with Selective Service Board in Wayne County, Tennessee. His Civilian Occupation was Farmhand. He was inducted 20 December 1942 and entered into active service 27 December 1942 at Fort Oglethorpe, Georgia. His Military Occupational Specialty was Cannoneer. His Military Qualifications included Sharpshooter Rifle. He was in the battles in New Guinea, and Southern Philippines. The following decorations were awarded to Hogan: WW II Victory Ribbon, Good Conduct Medal, Asiatic-Pacific Ribbon with two Bronze Service Stars and one Bronze Arrowhead, Philippines Liberation Ribbon with one Bronze Star and Distinguished Unit Badge. He left the USA 27 October 1943 for the Asiatic-Pacific Operation, and returned to USA 20 January 1946. He was discharged 28 January 1945 at Camp Chaffee, Arkansas.

HOGAN, JOHN RALPH, Serial Number 967 13 58, had the grade of Fireman, First Class in the United States Navy. He entered into active service 10 April 1944. His service included the following Vessels and/or Stations: Concept Battalion, NCTC Williamsburg, Virginia, USS DAHLGREN and R/S NYD Philadelphia, Pennsylvania. He was discharged 19 January 1946 from the U. S. Naval Personnel Separation Center in Memphis, Tennessee. He was born 6 January 1926 in Florence, Alabama.

HOGAN, LEAMON G., Serial Number 34 194 537, was a Staff Sergeant with Headquarters and Service Troop, 16th Cavalry Reconnaissance in the Army of the United States. His permanent mailing address was Iron City, Tennessee. He was born 9 April 1916 in Jackson County, Alabama. His description was given as hazel eyes, black hair, 5'8", height, weight 160 lbs. and single. He had an eighth grade education. He attended a Cavalry Service School in 1942. He was registered with Selective Service Board in Wayne County, Tennessee. His Civilian Occupation was Farmhand. He was inducted 4 April 1942 at Fort Oglethorpe, Georgia. His Military Occupational Specialty was Automotive Mechanic. His Military Qualifications included Pistol mm Carbine, ss M1 Rifle. He was in the battles in Rhineland, and Central Europe. The following decorations were awarded to Hogan: American Theater Service Ribbon, Good Conduct Medal, Europe-African Midde Eastern Theater Service Medal, and WW II Victory Medal. He left the USA 21 November 1944 for European-African Middle-Eastern Theater Operation, and returned to USA 24 August 1945. He was discharged 9 November 1945 at Camp Gordon, Georgia.

HOLDER, CLINT, Serial Number 34 501 350, was a Private First Class in Company C 386 Military Police Battalion in the Army of the United States. His permanent mailing address was Route 2, Clifton, Tennessee. He was born 25 January 1918 in Clifton, Tennessee. He was registered with Selective Service Board in Wayne County, Tennessee. His Civilian Occupation was Truck Driver. He was inducted 20 December 1942 and entered into active service 27 December 1942 at Fort Oglethorpe, Georgia. His Military Occupational Specialty was Cook. His Military Qualifications included Combat Infantryman Badge. He was in the battles in Sicily, and Normandy. The following decorations were awarded to Holder: Purple Heart, Good Conduct Medal, European African Middle Eastern Service Medal with two Bronze Stars. Holder was wounded in action in Normandy 12 July 1944. He left the USA 14 July 1943 for the European Theater Operation and returned to USA 12 October 1945. He was discharged 18 October 1945 at Fort McPherson, Georgia.

HOLDER, HOLLIS HERMAN, was born 4 February 1908 in Clifton, Wayne County, Tennessee. His parents were John Jefferson and Hugh Betty Turnbo Holder. He had five brothers, John Jefferson, Jr., Willie Edward, Fred, Wallace Preston and Hugh Oscar. He also had five sisters, Hester Lee, Nora Ann, Lilly May, Nannie and Lena Bell. He married Katherine Bevins and they had two daughters Rita and Nelda.

HOLDER, JESSE BROWN, was born on September 12, 1914, in Wayne County, Tennessee, the son of Lee and Laura C. Pulley Holder. He grew up in the Beech Creek community and married Nannie Fraley Rippy. They have a son, Eddie. Jessie was inducted into the United States Army on December 9, 1942, at Ft. Douglas, Utah, and served with the 374th M. P. EG Company. He was discharged on October 3, 1942, at Ft. Oglethorpe, Georgia. After his discharge, he worked with Lewis Products in Hohenwald, Tennessee. On February 13, 1981, Jessie died from a heart attack and is buried in Wayne County Memory Garden.

HOLDER, WINFRED BROMLEY, son of John Jefferson Jr. and Mary Jose Lineberry Holder, was born on August 25,

1921. He was a World War II veteran. Winfred's father was a World War I veteran. He retired from the United States Air Force in 1963. He worked for Challenger Mobile Homes in Columbia, Tennessee, at the time of his death on February 22, 1981. He was buried in Polk Memorial Gardens in Columbia. He was married to Geneva McCarty on March 20, 1948. Hey had one son, David Richard, and one daughter, Dorothy Lynn. He was a member of the American Legion and V. F. W. His siblings were Rothie Holder Moore, Wallace Earl

Holder, Hollie Holder, Nellie and Billy Holder.

Submitted by Winfred Bromley Holder.

HOLLANDER, DONALD J., son of Mr. and Mrs. Joe Hollander of Rt 3, Iron City, TN, entered the US Service, July 1944 and was sent to Europe in December 1944. March 30 1945, he was wounded in Germany.

HOLLIS, A.N., JR., was the son of Dr. and Mrs. A. N. Hollis Sr., both deceased. Dr. and Mrs. Hollis had four sons to serve in the armed services and one son to serve in the Merchant Marines during World War II. Dr. Hollis was pastor of First Baptist Church in Waynesboro, Tennessee, for many years. A. N. entered the Navy on April 6, 1943, and was discharged on December 2, 1945. He served as an Electrician's Mate 2nd Class on a Destroyer Escort 767 Oswald. On the Destroyer he made six missions from the United States to Europe protecting 100 Merchant ships. Education Background: Coyne Electrical School in Chicago (12 Months); University of Tennessee (3 years); Florence State Teacher's College (BS); Southern Baptist Theological Seminary (BD and MA-4 years); and Bowman Gray School of Medicine (MA in Pastoral Counselling Years). Positions held after World War II: Pastor of Ridgeway Baptist Enka, North Carolina (9 years); V. A. Hospital Chaplain in August, Georgia, and Johnson City, Tennessee; and retired as Interim Pastor at several Baptist churches in Johnson City, Tennessee.

HOLLIS, ALLAN RAY, SR., was born in Lawrence County, Tennessee, on 17 September 1915, to A. N. Hollis, Sr.,

and Maude Shutt Hollis. Dr. and Mrs. Hollis had four sons to serve in the armed services and one son to serve in the Merchant Marines during World War II. Dr. Hollis was pastor of First Baptist Church

in Waynesboro, Tennessee, for many years. He had three sisters: Naoma Hollis Innanen, Ruth Hollis Miller, and Mary Nell Hollis Findley. He had four brothers: Tom Hollis, A. N. Hollis, Jr., Paul J. Hollis and Herbert Hollis. He married Lillian Turman in Sioux Falls, South Dakota, on 27 November 1942. They are the parents of two children, Allan Ray Hollis, Jr. and Ethel McKennon Hollis. They have one granddaughter, Ruthanna Hollis. Mr. Hollis was drafted into the Army in August 1942. Shortly thereafter he went to Atlantic City, New Jersey, and from there was transferred to Sioux Falls, South Dakota Air Base. He was soon sent to Boca Raton Air Force Base in Florida where he taught radar and radar jamming techniques. He entered Officer's candidate School at Fort Monmouth, New Jersey, in the fall of 1943 and there received a commission as a Second Lieutenant in the Signal Corps. After studying fixed station radio in Hicksville, Long Island, New York, he was flown directly to the Philippines where he became a Staff Officer in General MacArthur's Headquarters. When the Japanese surrendered, he was sent to Tokyo, Japan, where he continued as a member of General MacArthur's staff. At the outbreak of the Korean War, Lt. Hollis was recalled as a Reserve Officer and was sent to Tennessee Tech in Cookeville, Tennessee. He taught Military Science IV to ROTC cadets. He was promoted to the rank of Captain in the Signal Corps near the end of his service there.

Ray died 13 December 1996 in Waynesboro and was buried in Greenwood Cemetery in Waynesboro.

HOLLIS, COLEMAN FRAZIER, SR., a native of Wayne County, was born ca. 1919 and died 15 January 1994 in Florence, Alabama. Burial was in Blair Cemetery in West Point, Tennessee. He is the son of David Harrison and Annie Nelson Hollis. He was a World War II Veteran a member of Mills Hunting Club, Whorton Coffee Club, a 21-year member of AA American Legion Post No. 11, and a retired automobile dealer. He had lived in Florence since 1950. Survivors include his wife, Rachel Johnson Hollis of Florence Alabama; two sons, Coleman Frazier, Jr. and Joseph Johnson Hollis.

Source: Obit.

HOLLIS, EDWIN CARNELL, volunteered for service in 1942 on his 17th birthday and joined the United States Navy. He had the Grade of Signalman First Class and Petty Officer Third Class. He took his basic training in San Diego, California and was stationed in Norfolk, Virginia too. He was one of the members of the crew of the

first ship to cross the Channel for the historic invasion of the French Coast. (They transported the US Army for the Normandy-France Invasion.) He was discharged 21 November 1945 in Memphis, Tennessee. After he was discharge from service, he worked for an elevator company in Memphis until he bought his own service station and garage there. Edwin, the son of James Boyd and Nona Ann (Lee) Hollis, was born 29 January 1925. His siblings are, Buford, Leroy, Frances Ricketts, Josephine and Anna Lou Gobbell. He married Estella Moore and they have two children, Edwin, Jr., and Cynthia Hollis. He attended Wayne County High School until he was inducted into service.

HOLLIS, FRED T. "TOM", was the son of Dr. and Mrs. A. N. Hollis Sr., both deceased. Dr. and Mrs. Hollis had four sons to serve in the armed services and one son to serve in the Merchant Marines during World War II. Dr. Hollis was pastor of First Baptist Church in Waynesboro, Tennessee, for many years. Tom was drafted in February 1942 into the Army Air Force and served with the 8th and 9th Air Forces in the ETO for 26 months. He achieved the rank of T/Sergeant in the 22nd Air Deport Group as an aircraft electrical specialist on P47 planes. He was discharged in October 1945 after serving 49 months. Public school experience teaching prior to military service was at Darnell Elementary and Lutts Junior High in Wayne County. Public school experience after World War II was 10 years in North Carolina high schools and four years as a principal. College teaching: Pfeiffer College, Misenheimer, North Carolina (32 years); Appalachian State University (2 years); and North Carolina State University (2 summer schools). Education Background: Guilford College 1936-37; Middle Tennessee State University 1938-41 (B. S.); Vanderbilt-Peabody 1948-49 (MA); and Penn State University 1959-63 (D. Ed). He was married to Louise Shaver Hollis for over 50 years. They have three children, five grandchildren and one great-grandchild.

HOLLIS, JAMES OLIVER PERRY, was the only son of James Perry (called Perry) Hollis and his wife, Bertha Franklin. James was born 26 April 1922 in Wayne County, Tennessee in the area known as Double Branches. James had one sister, Rosa Lee, and another little sister who died in childhood. Her name was Rachel. On 24 December 1940, James married Myrl Lucille Blankenship. Myrl was the daughter of Robert Joshua and Carrie Blankenship, natives of North Alabama. James was a farmer before he entered the military. James was called for the draft at the same time his cousin, Hollis Story, was called. James's induction was deferred because he had "crops in the field', a wife and baby with no immediate family to care for them, his father having died in 1926. When James was inducted on 23 February 1945 at Fort Oglethorpe, Georgia, he was shipped to Fort Providence, Louisiana for Basic Training. He served with Company M of the 14th Infantry Division. He was trained as a rifleman and qualified on a 39 caliber M-1 Rifle. Because of his deferment, James was en route to Europe when the war ended. He was a part of the occupation forces that went into war-torn Germany to maintain peace and begin the reconstruction. He was always eternally thankful that he did not see battle. His cousin, Hollis Story, had written him frequently and told of the horrors of war. In spite of serving in no battles, James was decorated with a World War II Victory Medal and an Occupation Ribbon (European Theater of Occupation). He was discharged, a Private First Class, July 18, 1946 at Fort Bragg, North Carolina. James Oliver Perry Hollis died 25 January 1985 from heart failure associated with cerebral stroke. He was buried in the Lawrenceburg Memorial Gardens. He was survived by his wife, one son, James Perry Hollis, Jr., and two daughters, Mary Nell Franks of the Dunn Community in Lawrence County, Tennessee and Shirley Hollis Rice of Lawrenceburg.
Submitted by Shirley Hollis Rice.

HOLLIS, JOHN HERMAN, was born 30 August 1899 in Wayne County, died 10 March 1965 in Dearborn, Wayne County, Michigan and was buried in Cadillac Memorial Cemetery in Detroit, Michigan. He was married 19 December 1920 to Mamie Lee Ella Robertson who died in 1923. He married secondly in 1945 Alvina Adela Nelson who was born in Wiffyn, Sweden and now lives in Columbia, Tennessee. John was the son of David

Franklin Hollis and Martha Ada Caperton. His children were Lydle J. Hollis and Mary Ruth Redlin. John Herman was about 42 years old when he was drafted. His wife had been dead since 1923. In the fall of 1942 he was at Fort McClellan, Alabama and left there for an Army Base near Parsons, Kansas. Then he was transferred to Alaska. He was in an engineering outfit and they built the Alcon Highway. Because of his age he was assigned to this part of the Army. He was released from the Army in late winter of 1943 or early spring 1944 for the purpose of going to work in an essential industry. So he went to Detroit to work for the automotive industry, and after the war was over he was to receive his discharge. After the war, he married again and lived in Lawrenceburg for about a year. He later moved to Michigan and worked for the Auto Association. Related by his son, Lytle J. Hollis.

HOLLIS, LAWRENCE, Serial Number 641 76 84, was born 9 March 1926 in Wayne County, Tennessee. He entered into active service of the United States Navy 27 July 1943. He had the grade of Machinist's Mate Third Class. The Vessel and Stations that he served on were: USNTC San Diego, California; R/S San Diego, and USS GEMINI. He was discharged 11 May 1946 at US Naval Personnel Separation Center, Memphis, Tennessee. He was awarded the World War II Victory Medal, Asiatic-Pacific Ribbon and American Area Ribbon.

HOLLIS, LEE ROY, son of James Boyd and Nona Ann (Lee) Hollis, was born 22 July 1927 in Waynesboro, Tennessee.

His siblings are, Buford of Waynesboro, Anna Lou Gobbell of Waynesboro, Edwin of Memphis, Frances Ricketts of Norfolk, Virginia, and twins, Josephine Dodd of Dallas, Texas and Nadine Sims of Florida. Lee Roy enlisted on 28 July 1945 as Aviation Radioman and trained at the Naval

Aviation Technical Training Center in Memphis, Tennessee. Most of his service was in the Naval Aviation Station in Anacostia, D. C. He was honorably discharged 17 December 1946 in Washington, D. C. During his high school career, Lee Roy worked as a linotype operator for the Wayne County News. After his discharge from the Navy he worked at the same type of business in Nashville, Chattanooga, and Washington, D. C. He eventually became part owner of York Graphic Service, Inc. in York, Pennsylvania from 1953 to 1975. Lee graduated from Wayne County High School in Waynesboro. He graduated from York College with a Bachelor of Science Degree, majoring in Business, on 27 May 1972. This degree was earned while working and rearing three daughters. In fact, his middle daughter, Debbie, graduated at the same time from high school as his college life ended. All three daughters are married and Debbie has made him a grandfather with a beautiful little girl who is now four years old. Lee Roy married (1) Martha Ann Bailey (she is the mother of all three children) and (2) Patricia "Terri."

HOLLIS, LYTLE J., Serial Number 18 167 934, was a Corporal with 3702 Army Air Force Base Unit of the United States Army. His permanent mailing address was Route 5, Box 10, Dekalb, Texas. His Civilian Occupation was Truck Driver. He was registered with Selective Service Board No. 1, Waynesboro, Tennessee. He volunteered and enlisted 27 October 1942 at Camp Robinson, Arkansas. His Military Occupational Specialty was Construction Equipment Serviceman. His decorations included the World War II Victory Medal, and a Lapel Button was issued. He had a high school education. He was honorably discharged 15 October 1945 at Lowery Field, Colorado. Lytle stated' "I was on limited service during the war as I was blind in one eye and did not do any foreign service. After entering Camp Robinson, I stayed about fifteen days, then transferred to Ft. Worth Army Air Field, Ft. Worth, Texas where I stayed one day. Next, I was transferred to Strother Field, Winfield, Kansas for eighteen months. I spent twelve months at Selman Field, Monroe, Louisiana, then I went back to Ft. Worth Airfield for two months. The next two months were spent at Buckley Field, Denver, Colorado. After six days at Lowery Field, Denver, I was discharged in 1945. "Lytle, the son of John Herman and Mamie Lee Ella (Robertson) Hollis was born 17 September 1921 in Iron City, Tennessee. His sister is Mary Ruth Redlin, and his half sister is Ada Christine Harrison. He married Audie Venita Champion and they have a son, James Herman Hollis.

HOLLIS, PAUL JUDSON "P. J.", was the son of Dr. and Mrs. A. N. Hollis Sr., both deceased. Dr. and Mrs. Hollis had four sons to serve in the armed services and one son to serve in the Merchant Marines during World War II. Dr. Hollis was pastor of First Baptist Church in Waynesboro, Tennessee, for many years. P. J. served in Seabee construction, Battalion as Electrician's Mate and Rank-1st Class. He served in the Alentian Islands for 3 years with a total service of 42 months. Education (before Service): Middle Tennessee State University (BS) and Coyne Electrical School. Occupation before and after service was a professional magician. He spent several years in the V. A. Hospital in Murfreesboro, Tennessee, with service connected problem. He is now deceased.

HOLLIS, WILLIAM PRATER "BILL", born November 1905, died 29 August 1989 and is entombed in Greenwood Cemetery in Waynesboro. He married Nelle Turman. Their children were Martha Nell, Billie Jean and Lige Turman. Bill was a Private in the United States Marine Corps during World War II.

HOLT, ALBERT FRANKLIN, son of William G. "Bud" and Perlee Parthanie (Davis) Holt, was born 15 January 1903, died 9 July 1994 and is buried in Copeland Family Cemetery near his home. He married Mattie Copeland, a local Wayne County school teacher. They had no children. His siblings are Colbert Anderson, John Thomas, Bentley, Charles Johnson, Ida Belle Riley, Bertha Warren, Callie and Edna Anna. Mr. Holt enlist in 1942 in the United States Army in the Medical Corps during World War II. Most of his service time was spent in Alaska. He had a high school education. He retired from Chrysler Corporation in Michigan. Then the family returned to Wayne County to buy a home on Highway 13 North, about four miles from Waynesboro. Albert died 9 July 1994. He and his wife are buried in the Copeland Cemetery near their home.

HOLT, ALTON CHARLIE, Serial Number 34 494 878, was a Technician Fifth Grade in the Twentieth Field Hospital in the Army of the United States. His permanent mailing address was Route 1, Clifton, Tennessee. He was registered with Selective Service Board in Wayne County, Tennessee. His Civilian Occupation was Student. He was inducted 22 November 1942 and entered into active service 29 November 1942 at Fort Oglethorpe, Georgia. His Military Occupational Specialty was Surgical Technician. He served with the 20th Field Hospital. He administered medicines and blood plasma; changed bandages and dressings; and made patients as comfortable as possible. He served 28 months in the ETO. His Military Qualifications included Rifle Marksman. He was in the battles of Rhineland, Central Europe and Luzon. The following decorations were awarded to Holt: Asiatic-Pacific Theater Ribbon with one Bronze Star, World War II Victory Medal, European-African Middle Eastern Theater Ribbon with two Bronze Stars and Good Conduct Medal. He left the USA 24 April 1943 for the Asiatic-Pacific Theater Operation, and returned to USA 17 March 1944. He left the USA again 2 September 1944 for the European-African Middle Eastern Theater Operation, and returned to USA 16 December 1945. He had a high school education. He was discharged 21 December 1945 at Fort Knox, Kentucky. After his discharge from the Army, he worked as a mechanic for Barnett Motor Company, Hassell & Dowdy and T. V. A. He was born 15 June 1922 in Clifton, Tennessee to John Thomas Holt and Jenney Mayo Holt. He lived his entire life in the Clifton, Tennessee, area. He married Jewell Tinin Holt on April 1, 1945. Their son is Kenneth Ray Holt, who married Sussie Halford Holt. They have two grandchildren, Keith Ray and Timothy Wayne Holt. Alton died on February 7, 1991, preceding his wife, Jewell, in death after 45 years of marriage. He was laid to rest in the Riverside Cemetery. He was a member of the Clifton Masonic Lodge #173 and of the Riverside United Methodist Church. He sang base in the church quartet. His favorite song was "Let Us Have a Little Talk with Jesus. "Alton C. Holt.

HOLT, CHARLES WILLIAM, was born 29 May 1911. He was the son of Virgil Garfield Holt (24 December 1881-29 May 1959) and Laura Lydia La Croix (5 February 1884-1967) who were married 22 December 1907. His siblings were Virgilia born 24 May 1909, Harold B. (1913-1981), Joy Elizabeth (1916-1966), and Margaret Floy (1916-1916). Holt was married 20 July 1939 in Lawrence County to Robert Nell Gibbs, born 4 November 1916. Their children were Rebecca Charlene (1943-1943), Nelda Kay, born 1946, Laura Lee born 1947, Charles William, Jr., born 1951 and Sara Jane born 1962. Mr. Holt was a school teacher, principal and superintendent of Education. He lived in Wayne and Lawrence County, Tennessee.
Source: C. Harper.

HOLT, HOLLIS ANDREW, was born in November 1919 in Wayne County, Tennessee. He was the son of John Henry Holt

(November 7, 1887-February 20, 1964) and Ruthie H. Holder (March 7, 1891-December 6, 1974). Both of them were born and died in Wayne County, Tennessee, and are buried in the Worley Cemetery in Wayne County, Tennessee. Hollis joined the Army and served in the South Pacific in the Infantry division during World War II. He married Jean Massey and had five children: Three boys (Donald, Tim and Johnny) and two girls (Andrea and Deborah). Hollis died on November 22, 1977, and is buried in the Memorial Gardens in Red Bay, Alabama.
Submitted by Edith Wood. Hollis Andrew Holt.

HOLT, HOMER L., Serial Number 34 713 919, was a Private with Medical Detachment Service Command, ASF of the United States Army. He was born in Waynesboro, Tennessee. He was married. He was 27 years old when he was inducted 23 April 1943 at Camp Forrest, Tennessee. His Military Occupational Specialty was Cook. He was honorably discharged

24 September 1943 at Camp Stewart, Georgia.

HOLT, JAMES F., Serial Number 34 987 507, was a Private with 3702nd Army Air Force Base Unit of the United States Army. He was born 12 August 1923 in Lutts, Tennessee. His permanent mailing address was Route 1, Waynesboro, Tennessee. He was married. His Civilian Occupation was Farmer. He was registered with Selective Service Board No. 1, Waynesboro, Tennessee. He was inducted 11 April 1944 at Camp Shelby, Mississippi. His Military Occupational Specialty was Duty Soldier. His Military Qualifications included Combat Infantryman Badge. He was in battles in Central Europe. His decorations included the World War II Victory Medal, European African Middle Eastern Theater Ribbon, and Good Conduct Medal. He left the USA 5 October 1944 for England and returned home 14 August 1945. He was honorably discharged 20 November 1945 at Barksdale Field, Louisiana.

HOLT, JOE SILAS, Serial Number 977 28 97, had the Grade of Shopfitter Third Class in the United States Navy. He was born 8 February 1924 in Iron City, Tennessee, His address at time of entry was Route 2, Iron City, Tennessee. He entered into active service 29 July 1944 at Nashville, Tennessee. He held the following ratings, AS, S2/C, S1/C, and SF3/C. He was registered with Selective Service Board No. 1, Waynesboro, Tennessee. Vessels or Stations that Holt served on were: Rec. Trg. Com and USN TADC, Williamsburg, Virginia; 20th USN Const Battalion, and 36th Usn Construction Battalion. Last employer before service was his brother, Bud H. Holt of St. Joseph, Tennessee. His civilian occupation was farmer. Holt was discharged 13 February 1946 at Memphis, Tennessee.

HOLT, JOHN CALVIN, was born on July 20, 1923, in Wayne County, Tennes-

Willis, Elvis and Andy Holt with Taylor and J.C. Hollis.

see. He was the son of John Henry Holt and Ruthie Holder. J.C. joined the Army and served in the 634 Q Master Battalion during World War II. He married Etheline Coats and had a son, Norris L. Holt. He married second to Inez Yielding and had a daughter, Fay. He married third to Chlorice Webb. There are no children of this marriage. J. C. is presently living in Russellville, Alabama, with his wife, Chlorice.

HOLT, LOUIS W., Serial Number 34 495 063, was a Private First Class with Company H 184th Infantry of the United States Army. He was born 24 February

1922 in Clifton, Tennessee, son of Harvey Dixon Holt and Bessie Sally Holder. His permanent mailing address was Route 2, Clifton, Tennessee. His Civilian Occupation was general farmhand. He was registered with Selective Service Board No. 1, Waynesboro, Tennessee. He was inducted 22 November 1942 and entered active service 29 November 1942 at Fort Oglethorpe, Georgia. His Military Occupational Specialty was Machine Gunner. His Military Qualifications included Combat Infantryman Badge. He was in battles in Aleutian, Eastern Mandates, Ryukyus and Southern Philippines. His decorations included the Purple Heart 17 February 1944, Good Conduct Medal, World War II Victory Medal, Philippine Liberation Medal with two Bronze Battle Stars, American Theater Service Ribbon, and Asiatic-Pacific Theater Ribbon. He was wounded in battle on Kwajalein Island on 4 February 1944. He left the USA 11 July 1943 for Asiatic-Pacific and returned home 18 June 1945. He was discharged 3 December 1945 at Camp Butler Convalescent Hospital, North Carolina with a Certificate of Disability. Louis marred Hazel B. Davis (born December 3, 1931), daughter of Ealy Anderson Davis (September 8, 1888-June 1964) and Ruby Carter Fisher Davis. Their children are Melvin, Wanda, Wendell and Debra Holt. Louis died in Missouri and is buried in the Memorial Gardens in Caruthersville, Missouri. His siblings are Mae, Melton, Nelle, Willie, Lockie and Margie. Louis Winfred Holt.

HOLT, MELTON JOHNNY, was born on March 21, 1924, in Booneville, Mississippi. He is the son of Harvey Dixon and Bessie Sally Holder Holt. He served in the United States Navy for eight years, including World War II. Mae Tatum, who has his discharge papers, said he was all over the waters during this time. He was married to Ocie Walker for a short time and had no children. He died in Wayne County in 1950 and is buried in the Calvin Holt Cemetery. His siblings are Mae, Louis, Nelle, Willie, Lockie and Margie.

HOLT, MERRELL ODOUS, JR., was born 22 April 1924 in Wayne County. He is the son of Merrell Odous Holt, Sr., (1894-1965) and Garner Esther Chandler (1896-1983). His siblings are Edsel A Holt (1922-1923), Paul Holt (1935-1935), Price Holt (1926-), Margaret Holt, Kathryn Holt (1929-), Coral Holt, Barbara Holt, and John Emerald Holt (1931-). He was married 18 May 1946 in Lauderdale County, Alabama, to Hazel Virginia Moomaw, born 12 April 1928. Their children are Larry Rayborn Holt, born 21 February 1947, Sarah Emmajean Holt born 14 August

1949, and Teresa Darlene Holt born 29 May 1957. He now lives in the Underwood-Petersville Community in Florence, Alabama 35633.

Source: Carolyn Harper.

HOLT, MOUNTIE ARK., Serial Number 845 38 13, was a Seaman Second Class with the United States Naval Reserve. He enlisted as, ASS USN-1 on 24 April 1943 at Nashville, Tennessee for two years. His description was given as married, height 5'9", weight 160 lbs, blue eyes, brown hair, and fair complexion. He was born 9 March 1910 in Collinwood, Tennessee. He was honorably discharged 4 September 1943 from Naval Hospital, Norfolk, Virginia. The reason given was Medical Survey. His monthly pay was $54.00 and he was furnished 5 cents per mile from Norfolk, Virginia to Waynesboro, Tennessee.

HOLT, PRESTON M., Serial Number 34 723 066, was a Private with Headquarters, 488th Antiaircraft (AW) Battalion of the United States Army. He was born in Waynesboro, Tennessee. His Civilian Occupation was Farmer. He was 19 years old when he was inducted 20 February 1943 at Fort Oglethorpe, Georgia. His Military Occupational Specialty was Telephone Operator. He was honorably discharged 3 September 1944 at Hoff General Hospital, Santa Barbara, California with fair physical condition.

HOLT, PRICE C., Serial Number RA 44 120 527, was a RA Sergeant with Headquarters Company First Battalion, 350th Infantry of the United States Army. He was born 29 November 1926 in Wayne County, Tennessee. His permanent mailing address was Route 3, Iron City, Tennessee. His Civilian Occupation was Farmer. He was registered with Selective Service Board No. 1, Waynesboro, Tennessee. His Military Occupational Specialty was Squad Leader. His Military Qualifications included Rifle M-1. His decorations included the Army of Occupation Medal and World War II Victory Medal. He left the USA 3 January 1946 for Mediterranean Theater Operation and returned home 20 March 1947. He was honorably discharged 22 April 1947 at Fort Dix, New Jersey. Mr. Holt was enroute from his home in Birmingham, Alabama to Florence, Alabama, to attend the funeral of his brother, John, when he was involved in an automobile accident which claimed his life. Both Price and John passed away 27 May 1997. Price was buried in Forest Grove Cemetery. He was retired from US Steel with 35 years of service, and was a member of the First Baptist Church of Pleasant Grove. Survi-

vors included his wife, Dean Holt of Birmingham; a daughter Karen Cobb of Memphis; a son, Robert Holt of Birmingham; four sisters, Margaret Bretherick of Greenhill, Alabama, Kathryn Grinnell of Lawrenceburg, Coral Bromley of Iron City, and Barbara Holt of Muscle Shoals and two grandchildren.

Source: Wayne County News, 4 June 1997.

HOLT, RALPH E., Serial Number 34 367 273, was a Private First Class with Section 40, Base Air Depot, No. 1 of the

United States Army. He was born 30 September 1920 in Wayne County, Tennessee. His permanent mailing address was Route 3, Waynesboro, Tennessee. His Civilian Occupation was Light Truck Driver. He was registered with Selective Service Board No. 1, Waynesboro, Tennessee. He was inducted 29 August 1942 and entered active service 12 September 1942 at Fort Oglethorpe, Georgia. His Military Occupational Specialty was Supply Clerk. His Military Qualifications included Marksman Carbine. His decorations included the American Theater Service Ribbon, World War II Victory Medal, European-African Middle Eastern Theater Service Medal, and Good Conduct Medal. He left the USA 14 November 1942 for European-African Middle Eastern Theater and returned home 11 May 1943. He left the USA the second time 27 February 1944 for European-African Middle Eastern Theater and returned home 26 December 1945. He was discharged 31 December 1945 at Fort Knox, Kentucky.

HOLT, ROBERT HIGHTOWER, JR., was born 27 November 1927. He is the son of Robert Hightower Holt, Sr (16 January 1889-6 May 1957) and Ethel Myrtle Spain (20 June 1894-22 May 1973). His siblings are: Roy Burl born 8 February 1915, Ruth Camile born 6 November 1916, Infant brother born 1919, Frances

Mabel born 28 April 1921, Rachel Sue 9 March 1923, infant brother 1930, Betty Jane 2 April 1931, Ruby Nell 24 March 1933, and Mary Ann 6 January 1938. Holt was married to Marion Okerlene Prentice, 17 September 1949 in Corinth, Mississippi. She was born 1 December 1929. They have two daughters, Janet Lynn born 25 January 1954 and Jennifer Eve Holt born 4 June 1956.

Submitted by Carolyn Harper.

HOLT, ROY BURL, was born 8 February 1915 in Wayne County; died 26 April 1967. He is the son of Robert Hightower Holt, Sr. (16 January 1889-6 May 1957) and Ethel Myrtle Spain (20 June 1894-22 May 1973). Roy's parents were married 22 January 1914. His siblings are: Ruth Camile born 6 November 1916, Infant brother born 1919, Frances Mabel born 28 April 1921, Rachel Sue born 9 March 1923, Robert Hightower, Jr., born 27 November 1927, infant brother born 1930, Betty Jane born 2 April 1931, Ruby Nell born 24 March 1933, and Mary Ann born 6 January 1938. Holt was married to Bonnie Ruth Davis, 21 October 1939 in Waynesboro. She was born 29 June 1919. They have one son William Robert Holt born 4 May 1949.

Submitted by Carolyn Harper.

HOLT, TAYLOR, was born on December 1, 1911, in Wayne County, Tennessee. He was the son of John Henry Holt (November 7, 1887 February 20, 1964) and Ruthie H. Holder (March 7, 1891-December 6, 1974). Both of them were born and died in Wayne County and both are buried in the Worley Cemetery in Wayne County, Tennessee. Taylor joined the Army and served in the 500th field Artillery in Europe during World War II. Taylor died on September 4, 1994, in Russellville, Alabama. He was buried in Memorial Gardens in Russellville, Alabama. Taylor was never married.

HOLT, THURMAN C., from Lutts, TN enlisted in the US Army Air Force and received his basic training at Greenville Army Flying School, then six weeks training at Miami Beach, FL. He was promoted to S/SGT and stationed in England.

HOLT, VERNIE L., Serial Number 44 042 782, was a Private First Class with Company B 19th Infantry of the United States Army. He was born 25 May 1917 in Lutts, Tennessee. His permanent mailing address was Lutts, Tennessee. His Civilian Occupation was Farmer. He was registered with Selective Service Board No. 1, Waynesboro, Tennessee. He was inducted 10 November 1944 at Fort Oglethorpe,

Georgia. His Military Occupational Specialty was Rifleman. His Military Qualifications included Combat Infantry Badge, MM with Rifle M-1. He was in battles in Luzon. His decorations included the Asiatic-Pacific Theater Ribbon with one Bronze Battle Star, Philippine Liberation Ribbon with one Bronze Battle Star, World War II Victory Medal, Good Conduct Medal and Army of Occupation Medal in Japan. He left the USA 28 April 1945 for Pacific Theater Operation and returned home 25 September 1946. He was honorably discharged 22 November 1946 at Fort Sheridan, Illinois.

HOLT, WILLIAM D., Serial Number 44 072 741, was a Private with Special Training Unit SCU 3402nd of the United States Army. He was born 26 July 1925 in Iron City, Tennessee. His permanent mailing address was Route 3, Florence, Alabama. He was married with one dependent. His Civilian Occupation was General Farm Hand. He was registered with Selective Service Board No. 1, Waynesboro, Tennessee. He was inducted 10 April 1945 at Fort Oglethorpe, Georgia. His Military Occupational Specialty was STU Trainee. He was honorably discharged 18 July 1945 at Fort McPherson, Georgia.

HOLT, WILLIS, was born on November 24, 1921, in Wayne County, Tennessee. He was the son of John Henry Holt (November 7, 1887-February 20, 1964) and Ruthie H. Holder (March 7, 1891-December 6, 1974). Both of them were born and died in Wayne County and both are buried in the Worley Cemetery in Wayne County, Tennessee. Willis joined the Army and served in the South Pacific during World War II. He was in the first Calvary Division. He married Emma Hastings and had two sons, Terry and Berry. He died in August 1991 and is buried in Muscle Shoals, Alabama.

HORTON, CLARENCE W., Serial Number 34 040 099, was a Private First Class with Headquarters Company, 3 Battalion, 271st Infantry of the United States Army. He was born 22 December 1912 in Wayne County. His permanent mailing address was Route 1, Collinwood, Tennessee. His Civilian Occupation was Farmer. He was inducted 16 March 1942 at Fort Oglethorpe, Georgia. His Military Occupational Specialty was Truck Driver. His Military Qualifications included Rifle Marksman. He was in battles in Normandy, Rhineland, Northern France and Central Europe. His decorations included European African Middle Eastern Theater Ribbon with 4 Bronze Stars, and Good Conduct Medal. He left the USA 16 April 1944

for European Theater Operation and returned home 20 September 1945. He was honorably discharged 27 September 1945 at Camp Atterbury, Indiana.

HORTON, EDWARD, Serial Number 34 373 146, was a Private First Class with Battery A, 455th Coast Artillery Battalion of the United States Army. He was born 30 April 1915 in Lutts, Tennessee. His permanent mailing address was Route 2, Lutts, Tennessee. His Civilian Occupation was General Farm Hand. He was registered with Selective Service Board No. 1, Waynesboro, Tennessee. He was inducted 24 September 1942 and entered active service 8 October 1942 at Fort Oglethorpe, Georgia. His Military Occupational Specialty was AAA Auto Weapons Crewman. His Military Qualifications included Rifle Sharpshooter. He was in battles in Normandy, Rhineland, Northern France and Central Europe. He was a member of General Patton's Third Army. His decorations included the European African Middle Eastern Theater Service Medal with 4 Bronze Stars. He left the USA 5 September 1943 for European Theater Operation and returned home 16 October 1945. He was honorably discharged 22 October 1945 at Camp Atterbury, Indiana. His mother was Mrs. Sallie Horton of the Bear Creek Community near Lutts, Tennessee. His brother, John E. Horton was honorably discharged from the service too.

HORTON, HOMER F., Serial Number 34 375 236, was inducted into the Army of the United States 3 October 1942, and was released from active duty, and transferred to the Enlisted Reserve Corps, and returned to Waynesboro, Tennessee. On 17 October 1942, he was called to active duty and reported to Fort Oglethorpe, Georgia.

HORTON, JAMES PAULK, Serial Number 34 043 793, was a Corporal with 90th Airdrome Squadron of the United States Army. He was born 12 December 1916 in Wayne County, Tennessee. His permanent mailing address was Route 2, Lutts, Tennessee. His Civilian Occupation was Farmer. He was registered with Selective Service Board No. 1, Waynesboro, Tennessee. He was inducted 15 May 1941 at Fort Oglethorpe, Georgia. His Military Occupational Specialty was General Carpenter. His Military Qualifications included Expert TSMG. He was in battles in China. His decorations included the Asiatic-Pacific Theater Ribbon with 1 Bronze Star, American Theater Ribbon, American Defense Service Medal and World War II Victory Medal. He left the USA 26 December 1941 for American Theater Operation and returned home 24 November 1942. He

left again 1 November 1944 for the China Burma India Theater and returned 1 November 1945. He was honorably discharged 6 November 1945 at Camp Atterbury, Indiana. His parents are Lonzo and Melissa (Southerland) Horton. His brother, Wayne E. Horton was also in World War II.

HORTON, JOHN E., Serial Number 34 375 252, was a Private First Class with Headquarters Camp, Livingston, Louisiana, of the United States Army. He was born in Lutts, Tennessee. His Civilian Occupation was Laborer. His age was 33 years and 7 months when he was inducted 3 October 1942 at Waynesboro, Tennessee. Under remarks, "Soldier transferred from 349th Infantry, Shreveport, Louisiana 17 July 1943. " He was discharged 10 August 1943 at Camp Livingston, Louisiana. He was the son of James William and Sarah Jane King Horton of the Bear Creek Community near Lutts. His brother, Edward Horton served with the Third Army under Patton. Mr. Horton, 86, of Route 2, Collinwood, died 17 February 1996 in Waynesboro and was buried in Cromwell Crossroads Cemetery. He was survived by his wife, Josie Evelyn Reeves Horton, five sons, Edward Doyle, James Arlie, George William, Johnny Lee and Kenneth Howard Horton all of Collinwood; five daughters, Linda Sue Cypert of Bristol, Indiana, Judy Ann Thompson of Collinwood, Barbara Arlene White of Elkhart, Indiana, Teresa Kay Bramlett of Jackson and Janice Gail Hunt of Waynesboro; one brother, Edward Horton of Collinwood; one sister, Myrtle Melton of Stuart, Florida, nineteen grandchildren, nine great-grandchildren and several nieces and nephews.
Source: Wayne County News, 21 Feb 1996.

HORTON, RAYMOND E., Pvt, husband of Mrs. Catherine Horton and the son of Mrs. Leona Horton of Cypress Inn, entered the service in January 1944 and was stationed for a time at Camp Wheeler, Georgia. He was then transferred to France where he was wounded in September 1944. He came back to the States on a thirty day furlough and then returned to Oklahoma. He has a brother, PFC William H. Horton serving in Germany.
Source: Wayne County News.

HORTON, WAYNE E., Serial Number 34 194 570, was a Private First Class with Headquarters Company 15th Army Group of the United States Army. His permanent mailing address was Route 2, Lutts, Tennessee. He was born 7 September 1906 in Wayne County. He was married. His Civilian Occupation was Truck Driver. He was registered with Selective Service Board No. 1, Waynesboro, Tennessee. He was inducted 4 April 1942 at Waynesboro, Tennessee. His Military Occupational Specialty was Truck Driver. He was in battles in Tunisian, Rome-Arno, and North Apennines. His decorations included the European African Middle Eastern Theater Service Ribbon with 3 Bronze Stars, Lapel Button and Good Conduct Medal. He left the USA 22 April 1943 for NATO and returned home 12 October 1945. He was discharged 18 October 1945 at Camp Atterbury, Indiana. His parents are Lonzo and Melissa (Southerland) Horton. His brother, James Paulk Horton was also in World War II.

HORTON, WILLIAM H., "PFC William H. Horton, son of Mrs. Leona Horton of Cypress Inn, entered service in August 1944. He took his boot training at Camp Hood, Texas. He was sent overseas in January 1945. He married Marie Morris, daughter of George Morris of Lutts."
Source: Wayne County News.

HOSKINS, TOM FRANK, was born the son of Joseph J. and Cassie Elizabeth Turnbo Hoskins on July 14, 1925. He

served in the United States Army as Staff Sergeant during WWII in the European Theater of War.

When he was discharged in 1945, he returned to the Clifton area to make his home. He married a local girl, Wanda Anderson, daughter of Richard (Rich) and Eddith Stricklin Anderson. He and Wanda had three children, Frankie, Jo, and Tommy.

Tom Frank was employeed with the towboat company. He started on the ground floor and soon was promoted to Boat Captain. He worked 40 years without having an accident. He and his family moved to Savannah, TN to live.

He became active in his church and was a member of the V.F.W. He loved life and enjoyed traveling, especially to the mountains and camping.

Tom Frank died with a heart attack on May 16, 1997. He was burried at the Memorial Garden in Savannah.

His siblings are Gerldine Hoskins Cook, Jo Ethel Hoskins Franklin, Caroline Hoskins Manoogian, and Robert Holland (Bobby) Hoskins.

HOUSTON, LEAROY, Serial Number 44 120 943, was a Private with Headquarters Field Artillery Replacement of the United States Army. He was born 24 January 1919 in Hazard, Mississippi. His permanent mailing address was Route 1, Cypress Inn, Tennessee. He was married. His Civilian Occupation was Warehouse Man. He was registered with Selective Service Board No. 1, Waynesboro, Tennessee. He was inducted 29 May 1945 at Fort Oglethorpe, Georgia. His Military Occupational Specialty was Basic. He was discharged 3 November 1945 at Fort Bragg, North Carolina.

HOWE, EDDIE, was born 1 March 1920 to his parents, Edward and Roxie (Rose) Howe. His grandparents were James E. and Elsie Howe and Calvin and Roxie Rose. His siblings include Cora Green, Mary Bartley, Vada Hughes, Esther Seals, Jim and Norman Howe. Eddie was married to Margaret Slaughter of Hicksville, Ohio. Her parents were former Wayne Countians, Okie and Isabel (Skelton) Edwards Slaughter. Eddie and Margaret had two daughters, Linda Piersma and Lynette Bechtal. Before entering the service Eddie worked for Holthouse and Hartup Hickory Mill in Waynesboro. After the war he was employed in Hicksville, Ohio with Federal Civil Service and New Haven, Indiana with storage and depot work. Eddie was inducted into service 21 November 1942. He spent twenty-one months overseas which included Africa, Italy, France, and Germany. He saw combat in Anzio, Southern France all the way into Germany. He was wounded in his right leg.

HOWE, NORMAN, Serial Number 34 713 925, was inducted into the Army of the United States prior to 30 April 1943, and was released from active duty, and transferred to the Enlisted Reserve Corps, and returned to Waynesboro, Tennessee. On 30 April 1943, he was called to active duty and reported to Fort Oglethorpe, Georgia.

He was born on February 18, 1919, in Waynesboro, Tennessee, and was inducted into the United States Army on April 23, 1943, at Camp Forrest, Tennessee. He served as a heavy truck driver and participated in battles in Northern France, Ardennes, Rhineland and Central Europe. He was presented the following citations:

World War II Victory Ribbon, American Theater Ribbon, EAME Theater Ribbon and Good Conduct Medal. Norman was discharged on November 14, 1945, at Camp Gordon, Georgia.

HOWELL, ALBERT B., Serial Number 34 987 505. He was a Private First Class with Company F 335th Infantry, 84th

Division of the United States Army. He was born 11 February 1923 in Clifton, Tennessee. His permanent mailing address was Clifton, Tennessee. He was married. His Civilian Occupation was General Farmer. He was registered with Selective Service Board No. 1, Waynesboro, Tennessee. He was inducted 11 April 1944 at Camp Shelby, Mississippi. His Military Occupational Specialty was Rifleman. He was wounded 4 March 1945 in the European Theater. He was in battles in the Germany Campaign. His decorations included the European African Middle Eastern Theater Campaign Medal with one Bronze Battle Star, American Theater Medal, World War II Victory Medal, Purple Heart and Combat Infantryman Badge. He left the USA 12 October 1944 for England, left there 21 October for France, left 20 December 1944 for Belgium, left 2 February 1945 for Holland, left 23 February 1945 for Germany and returned to the USA 11 May 1945. He was discharged 4 March 1946 at Kennedy General Hospital in Memphis, Tennessee.

HOWELL, JESSIE ELLIS "BABE", Serial Number 966 28 53, had the Grade of Seaman 1/C in the U. S. Navy. He was

born 5 October 1911 in Clifton, Tennessee. His home address at time of entry into service was Route 2, Clifton. He was married. He was registered with Selective Service Board No. 1, Waynesboro, Tennessee. He was inducted 31 December 1943 and entered the Navy 18 January 1944. He held Ratings of AS, S2C and S1C. His Service was at USNTS Great Lakes, Illinois; USS WHITMAN (De-24) used in the invasion of Guam and Saipan. Howell was awarded the American Theater Ribbon, World War II Victory Medal and Asiatic-Pacific Campaign Ribbon. His last employer before entering service was Edd Howell of Clifton. His Civilian Occupation was General Farmer. He was discharged 11 November 1945 in Nashville, Tennessee. His parents were Wade W. and Tennie (Riley) Howell. His sisters were Eva Howell Thompson, Pearl Howell Simmons, and Alma Howell Prater. His brothers are Tom, Edd, Elvis and James Howell. He married Myrtle Warren. Their children are Shirley Howell Bulter and Loyd Howell. "Babe" made the following statement about his war experience: "We carried ship convoys from Pearl Harbor, deep down into the South Pacific; maybe twenty-five or thirty different types of ships would compose a convoy. We would go along the side of them, then pass to search the waters for depth charges and to detect submarines. Our duty was to keep the waters safe for the convoys. We also picked up pilots when the aircraft carriers made a bad landing.

HUGHES, BOYD, Pfc. son of Mr. and Mrs. Sidney T Hughes of Iron City, TN, was wounded in action, July 27, 1945.

HUNT, CRAIG VAUGHN, was born on January 23, 1922, in Wayne County, Tennessee, the son of Cicero and Zada Nutt

Hunt. He was inducted into the United States Navy on October 16, 1942, and served as Aviation Radioman Third Class during World War II. On January 20, 1946, he received his discharge at the Naval Separation Center in Memphis, Tennessee. Craig and Virginia Nutt were married on March 1, 1948. They lived in Wayne County a short time, then moved to Detroit, Michigan, where they remained until 1961. At that time, they returned to Waynesboro and built a home. Craig retired as an inspector with the Tennessee Department of Transportation. On November 16, 1995, he died with Alzheimer's and is buried in Wayne County Memory Garden near Waynesboro, Tennessee. He was a retired inspector with the Tennessee Department of Transportation. He was a member of the American Legion. Surviving him are his wife, Virginia Nutt Hunt of Waynesboro; two daughters, Faye Beauchamp of Kingston and Cindy Hunt of Waynesboro; four brothers, Ira and Arnold Hunt, both of Waynesboro, and Freeman and David Hunt, both of Memphis; a sister, Leva Nell McCroy of Waynesboro; six grandchildren, Lee, Craig, Brooks, April Erin and Hayden; and several nieces and nephews.
Source: Wayne County News, 22 November 1995. Submitted by Craig V. Hunt.

HUNT, FREEMAN S., age 73, died 19 March 1998 in Methodist Central in Memphis and was buried in Memorial Gardens in Waynesboro. He was employed as Finance/Office Manager for National Mortgage, a member of the Wells Station Baptist Church, and a World War II Veteran serving as Staff Sergeant in the Air Force. He was also a Corporal in the U. S. Army. He was born in 1929. Survivors include his wife, Mary Louise Hunt of Memphis, three daughters: Mary Alice Greeson of Knoxville, Kathy Elizabeth Hunt of New Orleans and Karen Louise Troutman

of Memphis; one sister, Leva Nell McCroy of Waynesboro; two brothers, Arnold Ray Hunt of Waynesboro and David Leon Hunt of Memphis, and three grandchildren.

HUNT, JACK ROCKY, of Route 1, Cypress Inn, died Saturday 6 June 19?? in Eliza Coffee Memorial Hospital in Florence, Alabama and was buried in Florence Cemetery. A native of Florence, Alabama, he was the son of the late Albert and Josie (Pounders) Hunt, a military and postal service retiree, a World War II and Korean War Veteran, a member of the Florence American Legion Post No. 11 and a National Air Force Sergeant's Association. Survivors included his wife, Helen Harveston Hunt of Cypress Inn; one son, Jack R. Hunt, Jr., of Chattanooga; four brothers, A. L., Warren G., and Edsel Hunt all of Florence and Stinson Hunt of Muscle Shoals; one sister Miss Irene Hunt of Lawrenceburg and two grandchildren.
Source: Obit in Wayne County News.

HURST, JAMES STERLING, Serial Number 14 219 406, was a Private First Class with First Food, S V Squadron, FTR

Jet First ABGP of the United States Air Force. His permanent mailing address was P PO Box 244, Waynesboro, Tennessee. He was born 20 December 1928 in Waynesboro, Tennessee. His Civilian Occupation was Truck Driver. He was not registered with any Selective Service Board. He enlisted 5 January 1946 for three years. His Military Occupational Specialty was Cook. His Military Qualifications included Carbine MM. His decorations included the World War II Victory Medal of Occupation of Germany, AFLSA with one Silver Oak Leaf Cluster and AFOCM with two Bronze Oak Leaf Clusters and AFM. He left the USA 26 July 1946 for Germany and returned home 5 February 1947. He was discharged 4 January 1949 at March Field, California. Hurst reenlisted and spent a total of 24 years in the United States Air Force. He was stationed in Germany, Alaska, Africa, Turkey and Greenland. He rose to the rank of Technical Sergeant. His specialty title was Steward Superintendent. His last duty was with the USAF Academy Hospital. He was honorably discharged 20 April 1970 and permanently retired by reason of disability. On 21 April 1965 Major Harry S. Schwab extended his personal appreciation for James's excellent supervision of military personnel, as well as management of the various activities in his position as NCOIC. His mission of the Officers Open Mess was well carried out. January 13, 1966 a letter of appreciation from Commander William W. Dick, Jr., Lieutenant General, USA, Detachment 118-1, TUSLOG, was sent to T/Sgt Hurst. After his retirement from the Air Force he was employed as a private club consultant. His experiences at various clubs include: Manager of Yanche Country Club in Crown Point, Indiana; later took over a fifty year old club that had lost its chef through death and was very successful in doing so. At one time he was manager of the Broadview Country Club in Carthage, Missouri and another time he was manager of the Stones River Golf and Country Club in Murfreesboro, Tennessee. He retired in 1982 in order to take care of his property in Tennessee. James was the son of Vera (Moore) and James N. Hurst of Waynesboro. His mother died and his father married secondly, Evie Edwards. They live in Collinwood. James is married to Hazel Dudley and has one stepdaughter, Verna Owens Caruthers. Verna has one son, William Wesley.

HURST, WADE B., was born on December 23, 1909, in Waynesboro, Tennessee, the son of Fielding and Rachel Hurst. He grew up in Waynesboro and graduated at Wayne County High School. He and Elizabeth Gray were married and have two children, Gene and Jerri Lou. Wade and Elizabeth were divorced. A few years later, Wade and Hazel Smith were married and lived in Savannah, Tennessee. They have a daughter. On April 23, 1941, Wade entered the United States Army at Ft. Benning, Georgia, and served with the 1350th Engineer Base Depot Group. He participated in the following battles: Tunician, Sicilian, Naples-Foggia and Philippines. He received the following citations: Good Conduct, Tunician with four Bronze Stars, Sicilian Medal, Naples-Foggia Ribbon, Asiatic-Pacific Theater Campaign Ribbon, American Defense Service Ribbon, European-African Middle Eastern Theater Campaign Ribbon and Philippine Liberation Ribbon with one Bronze Star. Wade was discharged on July 22, 1945, at Jefferson Barracks, Missouri. He is deceased and buried in Greenwood Cemetery in Waynesboro, Tennessee.

INMAN, JOHN WILLIAM, was born on January 25, 1925, the son of Duke and Stella (Holder) Inman. He married Frances

Ray on January 16, 1945. They had four children: Dale, Freddie, Kathy and Joy Inman. Will and Frances lived and reared their family on Morrison Creek and Beech Creek in Wayne County, Tennessee. He entered the United States Navy on August 12, 1943, and was discharged on December 24, 1945, at the United States Naval Center in Nashville, Tennessee. He served as Seaman First Class with V-6 SV USNR during World War II. He served in Bainbridge, Maryland; Norfolk, Virginia; Cuba; Guantanima Bay; Phib. Tra. Base, Solomons, Maryland; USS LCI (L) 658, YNT-7 (LDTDC); NOB, St. Thomas, V. I. ; NSTA Roosevelt RDS, P. R. He was awarded the American Theater Medal and the Victory Medal. He worked for Genesco for 15 years and in 1976 developed terminal kidney failure. He was on a home dialysis machine for four years before he died on March 11, 1981. He is buried in the Worley Cemetery in Wayne County. He was an avid coon hunter. When he became ill, he would drive the dogs in his truck to the woods just to hear the dogs barking. He enjoyed other kinds of hunting and fishing. John Will was of the Mormon Faith.

INMAN, SAMUEL CURTIS, was the son of Duke Norrie and Stella Holder Inman. He was born on March 21, 1923. He was inducted into the United States Army Air force in January 1943. He was sent to Okinawa, and at the end of World War II, he was sent on to Gwam for seven months before returning to the states. He was discharged in 1946. He was married first to Hazel Roberta Warren, daughter of Luke Warren and Lily Turnbo Warren. They had five children: Kenneth, Donald, Ronald, Dennis and Dianne. His siblings are Carrie, Betty Jo and Will. He married second to Edna Earl Bryson, and they had no children. Curtis is a member of the American Legion and the V. F. W.

IRWIN, CHARLIE BURT, Serial Number 34 903 955, was born 7 May 1906 in Wayne County, Tennessee, died 16 August 1961 at age 55 and is buried in McGlamery Cemetery in Collinwood. His parents were the Reverend William N. and Hannah (Martin) Irwin. He had one brother, Sherman Irwin, and two sisters, Waymon Irwin Baker and Martha Irwin Long. At the time this article was written, all were deceased except Waymon who lived on Melson Drive in Waynesboro and was 92 years old. Charlie was married to Ruby Smith on 26 May 1929. They had five children: Norma Sue Creasy, Robert Smith "Bobby" Irwin, Emma Frances Jones, Willie Ann Scott and Melba Jean Staggs. They had fifteen grandchildren (two deceased - Charles Creasy and Robert Irwin) and twelve great-grandchildren. Charlie attended the Wayne County schools and was employed since the age of 16. He worked for the State, Cadillac Motors in Detroit, Hayes Aircraft in Birmingham, was self employed as a taxicab driver, and was working for the County Highway Department at the time of his death. He was drafted into the U. S. Army on 22 January 1944, at age 38 and was stationed during the war at Fort Leonardwood, Missouri as a member of the D Company, 28th Engineering Training Battalion and was honorably discharged on 19 May 1944, as a Private.

IRWIN, LEIGHTON BUNDRANT, was born 11 July 1908, died 12 September 1983 and was buried in Greenwood Cemetery in Waynesboro. Sergeant Irwin served with the 281st Combat Engineers, during the Third Army's advance through France, Germany, and Austria. He received an Honorable Discharge at Fort Knox, Kentucky on the 6th of December 1945. He married Lucille Eaton. They had five children at the time of his discharge. He was the son of John N. and Cora Irwin. He had a sister Gladys.
Source: Wayne County News, 14 December 1945.

IRWIN, WALTER G., Lutts, TN as reported in the Wayne County News was discharged in December 1945 at Ft. Knox, KY.

JACKSON, CHESTER, son of Mr. and Mrs. Lester Jackson of Rt. 6 Waynesboro, TN entered the US Navy in May 1945, and received his training at the Naval Training Center at Great Lakes, IL.

JACKSON, CLARENCE BAKER, "C.B.", Serial Number 34 727 058, was a Technician Fourth Grade in Headquarters Company 1101st Army Corps of Engineers Group in the Army of the United States. His permanent mailing address was Box

337, Clifton, Tennessee. He was registered with Selective Service Board in Wayne County, Tennessee. His Civilian Occupation was Automobile Mechanic. He was inducted in March 1941. He was attached to the Cee Bee's. He was stationed in England during the Normandy Invasion, then he was sent on into France. He was captured in Belgium and stayed in captivity for about a week. His mother had a Service Caller to tell her he was missing in action. Luck would have it, she received a letter the same day to say he was out of captivity. His Military Occupational Specialty was Automotive Mechanic. He was in the battles of Normandy, Northern France, Rhineland, and Central Europe. The following decorations were awarded to Jackson: Europe-African Middle Eastern Theater Ribbon with 4 Bronze Stars, Good Conduct Ribbon, Purple Heart, and World War II Victory Medal. He was wounded in action in France on 24 August 1944. He left the USA 23 December 1943 for the European Theater Operation, and returned to USA 10 December 1945. His education consisted of 8 years grammar school and one year of high school. He was discharged 15 December 1945 at Camp Atterbury, Indiana. "C. B. " was the son of Jack and Goldie (Baker) Jackson. He was born 24 July 1924 in Dewitt, Arkansas, died 16 August 1992 in Telzer, South Carolina, and was buried in the White Plains Baptist Church Cemetery in Pelzer. He had two sisters, June and Mary Ann Jackson of Clifton. He married his hometown sweetheart, Mary Lou Williams, of Telzer. She is the daughter of E. C. Williams Jr. (Bub) Williams and Maude Williams. They had two sons: Thomas V. (Tommy) of Telzer and C. Michael (Mike) of Pickens. He also had three grandchildren and three great-grandchildren. Clarence worked on a riverboat for awhile, then went into construction as a welder. He was a welder in South Carolina when he died.

JACKSON IRA L., Serial Number 34 738 879, was a Corporal in Headquarters 53rd Troop Carrier Wing in the Army of the United States. His permanent mailing address was General Delivery, Collinwood, Tennessee. He was born 8 April 1921 in Cypress Inn, Tennessee. He was registered with Selective Service Board in Wayne County, Tennessee. His Civilian Occupation was Assembly Line Worker. He was inducted 2 July 1943 and entered into active service 16 July 1943 at Fort Oglethorpe, Georgia. His Military Occupational Specialty was Heavy Truck Driver. He was in the battles of Rome-Arno, Southern France, Normandy, Northern France, Ardennes, Rhineland, and Central Europe. The following decorations were awarded to Jackson: Europe-African Middle Eastern Theater Ribbon with 7 Bronze Stars, Good Conduct Medal, Distinguished Unit Badge, and Lapel Button. He left the USA 14 March 1944 for the European Theater Operation, and returned to USA 10 October 1945. His education consisted of four years in high school. He was discharged 16 October 1945 at Camp Atterbury, Indiana.

JACKSON, REX, Pfc, son of Mr. and Mrs. Charlie Jackson, Waynesboro, went into service 20 March 1943. He took his basic training at Camp Robinson, Arkansas, and was then sent to Camp Livingston, Louisiana. He left for overseas duty in December 1943 and spent four and a half years in service. He served ten months in England and three in France. Jackson was in the Medical Corps 23 months, then transferred to the Infantry to serve in Germany. Prior to entering the service, Jackson was employed with the A. C. Spark Plug Co. at Flint, Michigan.

JACKSON, SAMUEL, of Rt. #6, Waynesboro, TN, served with the 398th Antiaircraft Artillery Battalion in the 7th Army. This unit left the states, June 22, 1944 for Scotland. They crossed the channel into Northern France at Utah Beach, July 28th and supported the 3rd Army in Normandy. Samuel was wounded and sent back to Oliver General Hospital, Augusta, GA.

JACKSON, ULIS MOORE, was a Technician Fifth Grade in the Army of the United States. He was inducted 4 April 1942. He was in the battles in the European Theater and African Theater. His war services began at Fort Sam Houston, Texas in the Medical Department. He was a supply clerk. He received and issued medical materials according to size and kind. He was Discharged 11 November 1945 at Fort Belvior, Virginia. Ulis was born 14 July 1913 in Wayne County, died 5 January 1983 and was buried January 6 in Swiss Cemetery in Hohenwald, Tenn. His parents were Daniel A. and Lola J. Jackson. His brothers were Ezra (Edd), and Lawrence Jackson. His sisters were, Grace J. Bridges, Edna J. Matney, Earlene J. Whitehead, Bertha J. Runions, and Jerry Lou J. Whitehead. He was married to Myrtle Lou Skelton on 23 May 1944. He has one daughter, Janet Elaine Jackson Williams.

JASKE, DONALD LEE, who has listed Waynesboro, Tennessee as his home for the last 34 years of his life, was born 2 January 1917 in Beverly, Kansas to Frank and Emma Bennet Jaske. He was educated in different rural schools in Kansas, graduating from high school in 1934. He worked on the farm for the next five years. On 7 April 1939 he joined the Civilian Conservation Corps. On 7 November 1939 he was honorably discharged to volunteer in the Regular Army. He was stationed at Fort Lewis, Washington and Fort Ord, California. When World War II broke out, he was shipped to Europe. Landing at Normandy, serving in Central Europe, his battles took him to Southern France, French Morocco, Sicily, Naples Foggia, Rome-Arno, Anzio, Tunisia, Algeria and the Rhineland. While there he served as an auto mechanic and as a supervisor in charge of motor transportation. Jaske was awarded thirteen battle Stars, several Good Conduct Awards for his demonstration of honor, fidelity and efficiency, the American Defense Service Ribbon, Five Silver Clasp with 1-2-3-4-& 5 Bronze Loops, Medal with Germany Clasp and French Fourrageres with Colors of Croix De Guerre with Palm Dest. Unit Badge. There were many other awards. When the war ended he received an Honorable Discharge. He came to Tennessee to live where he met and married Connie Folger. To this union a son, Gale Lynn Jaske, was born on 30 October 1946. In about three years he returned to the military, this time the Air Force. He served one year in Korea, three in England, one year in Thailand and Vietnam. He also was stationed in the Philippines, New Jersey, New York, Michigan, Kentucky, North Carolina, Mississippi, Tennessee, and Ohio. On 2 June 1972 he was temporally discharged with service connected disability.

He had just had cancer surgery. On 4 January 1974, he was honorably discharged with over 31 years to his credit. He returned to Waynesboro to live until he died with cancer 5 July 1979. He was entombed in the Shiloh National Cemetery with full military honors. He had two grandchildren, Michele Lee and Donald Lynn Jaske. They were his pride and joy in the last years of his life.

JETER, PAUL, volunteered for the United States Army in 1937. He served in the Calvary, spending two years at Fort Oglethorpe, Georgia, before going to the Philippines. He returned to the United States in 1941. He was sent to Europe during World War II and stayed until the war was over. He came back to the states settling in California. He worked for the Shell Oil Company. He retired from there and came back to home grounds around Clifton, Tennessee. He was born on January 30, 1917, the son of John Thomas Jeter and Mary Jane (Molly) Pevahouse Jeter. He married Virginia Biggert. They have three children: Billy, John Paul and Barbara. His siblings are Robert, Jack, Edd, Ada, Ida and Polly.

JETER, ROBERT WOODROW, was born 31 January 1914 in the Ross Creek Community near Clifton, Tennessee. His

parents were John Thomas and Mollie Jane (Pevahouse) Jeter. His brothers include Paul, Jack and Edd Jeter. His sisters are Ada, Polly, and Ida Prater Jeter. Half brothers include Neal and Carl Jeter. Half sisters are Ola Jeter Williams, and Minnie Jeter Lineberry. He married Thelma Bowling on 17 May 1946. They have three children, Larry Robert, William Thomas of the U. S. Navy and Cynthia Carol Jeter Culp. They also have three grandsons, John Lawrence Jeter, Robert Harris Jeter and William Buck Culp, III. Robert W. Jeter, TEC, 4th U. S. Army served in the CCC camps before his induction into the U. S. Army on 24 September 1942. He served in the European Campaigns under General G. S. Patton, Jr., being active in the

battles and campaigns of Normandy, Northern France, Rhineland, and Central Europe. He was in communications as a radio operator. Robert was discharged 9 October 1945. Returning to his home in Clifton, he was one of the first radio, television and electrical repairman in Wayne County. He continued in this line of work most of his life. Robert also farmed and raised cattle. Robert died 7 May 1979 after a long battle with Lou Gehrig's disease. He was laid to rest in his beloved town of Clifton, in the Clifton Cemetery.

JETER, VERNON J., was born 29 January 1917. My parent were James Ira and Ermin (Benham) Jeter. I have four brothers,

two older and two younger. They are Russell, Ralph, William and David. I attended Frank Hughes High School in Clifton, graduating in 1935. I attended West Tennessee State Teachers College in Memphis for one year, then attended Austin Peay Normal School in Clarksville for a year. After this I worked in the Civilian Conservation Corp (CCC Camp) for two years. Next, I taught in the Hardin County Elementary School system for two years. In 1942 I married Velma Land of Savannah. We have three children, Daniel, Joseph, and Brenda and three grandchildren, Bryan Scott, Danielle and Gabriel. In 1941 I joined the U. S. Navy and continued on active duty until 1964. My career in the Navy took me to many interesting places in the line of duty as listed below: July 1941 - Recruit Training in Norfolk, Virginia. October 1941 - AMM School in Norfolk, Virginia. March 1942 - ADV Carrier Training in Norfolk, Virginia. July 1942 - Link Training School in Pensacola, Florida. October 1942 - NAS, Cecil Field, Florida. February 1943 - VSB-3, Daytona Beach, Florida. September 1944 - HEDRON-3, Coco Solo, Canal Zone. January 1945 - VPB-74, Coco Solo, Canal Zone. January 1947 - NAS, Lakehurst, New Jersey. June 1949 - NATTC, Memphis, Tennessee. January 1950 - LTA School, NAS, Lakehurst, New Jersey. August 1950

- HU-2, NAS, Lakehurst, New Jersey. March 1951 - USS Block Island "CVE-106". January 1953 - Naval Airship Training Unit, Glynco, Georgia. April 1955 - FASEON-2, Quonset Point, Rhode Island. June 1956 - NAS Port Lyautey, Morocco. June 1959 - NATTU, Philadelphia, Pennsylvania. August 1959 - USS Antietam "CVS-36. "August 1960 - NAS, Agana, Guam. September 1962 - NATTC, Memphis, Tennessee October 1964 - retired. After retirement from the Navy, I worked with the mentally handicapped people in Memphis, Savannah and Waynesboro for fifteen years. In 1979 I retired to my hometown of Clifton, Tennessee, on the banks of the Tennessee River where Velma and I still live.
Submitted by Vernon Jeter.

JETER, W.J., the eldest child of Neal T. Jeter and Verna Eliza Churchwell- and lived in the Eagle Creek area of Wayne Co., TN. His mother died in 1928 and he dropped out of school to help his dad and younger brother, Arnold. They farmed and logged to furnish wood to the local sawmills.

He received his draft notice in the fall of 1941 and chose to report a month early. Along with another local, Gavin Pulley, he reported to the induction station at Camp Forrest, Tullahoma, TN, on May 8, 194 1. They were then sent to Fort Oglethorpe, GA for about a week. It was here that he decided that this might be better than looking at the backside of a mule all of the time, so he and Gavin Pulley decided to join the Regular Army for a three year hitch. They were sent to Camp Lee, VA for basic. On December 7, 194 1, their three-year hitch was extended indefinitely. On January 31, 1942, they left for Brooklyn, NY for embarkation. They left by boat on February 18, 1942, and arrived 12 -13 days later in Belfast, Northern Ireland. It was here that W. J. and Gavin were separated. W. J. stayed in Belfast, pulling various garrison duties, until Christmas, 1942. He was sent to Crane and Winch Operator School at the docks at Groomsby England. He, along with a higher ranking Sgt, were the only two out of the group to make excellent, although the instructor pointed out that "poor old Jeter could barely read or write". Then it was back to Belfast until late in January 1943. The unit moved first to Scotland, then England, and finally to Oran Africa, in the spring of 1943. In July 1943, they began the invasion of Sicily. They stayed here about a year before moving on to Naples, Italy. They stayed on the ship's deck for 14 days before sailing. They began the invasion of Southern France on August 15, 1944. They first landed at the small vacation towns of St. Raphael, St. Maxine, and St. Tropaz. W.J. was a crane operator assigned to a small loading barge ferrying supplies up the coast toward Marseille, where he stayed until the end of the war. In January 1945, the Army began taking 2-3 people from different units to use as prisoner guards to be sent back to the US. W. J. had been selected as a guard when they got word of V-E Day, May 8, 1945. He was sent to New York, spending from May 8 to May 29, 1945 on the deck of a ship. They were not allowed to go below decks. He spent 2 days in New York before leaving by train for Fort McPherson, GA. The Army started a discharge system of points based on your time in service, time overseas, etc. You needed 85 points to be discharged, and at this time, W. J. had 130, so he was discharged on June 9, 1945. He went by train to Chattanooga. The train arrived too late for him to catch the bus towards Memphis, so he spent the night sleeping in an old rocking chair at the YMCA. The next morning the caught the bus, and arrived at Olive Hill about 1:00 PM on June 10, 1945.

W. J. Jeter courted and married Mary Edith Ray, the daughter of Arthur Ray and Dora Culp Ray, on December 1, 1945. They have raised four children. Mary Edith died August 4, 1993. W. J. Jeter is retired and lives in Benton, KY.

JETER, WILLIAM H., "BILL", son of James Ira and Ermin (Benham) Jeter, was born 15 June 1921 near Clifton, Tennessee.

He graduated from Frank Hughes High School in 1940. He went to Detroit, Michigan, soon after graduation to live with his older brother, Ralph Jeter. He was employed by the Aircraft Division of Briggs Manufacturing Company, a maker of auto bodies for Chrysler Corporation. On 7 October 1942, Bill was inducted into the Air Corps as a sheet metal specialist. After Basic Training in St. Louis, Missouri, he was assigned to Curtis Wright Technical School in Glendale, California. After completing five months of schooling, he was assigned to Kelly Air Force Base in San Antonio, Texas. Over the next year he spent some time at Dale Mabry in Tallahassee, Florida; Tinker

Air Force Base, Oklahoma City, Oklahoma; Walker Air Base in Pratt, Kansas and then back to Oklahoma City. In July 1944, he left Long Beach, California to make Saipan in the Marianna Islands his home for the next year and a half. He was discharged on 31 December 1945. Bill was married on 6 April 1946 to Reginia Harris of Detriot, Michigan. They are the parent of two sons and two daughters. They also have two grandsons and two granddaughters. After forty years with Chrysler Corporation, Bill retired in 1980. He and Reginia live in Clifton, Tennessee on the Beautiful Tennessee River.

JOHNSON, DALTON D., Serial Number 44 042 760, was a Technician Fifth Grade in the 30th Infantry Regiment, 3rd Division in the Army of the United States. His permanent mailing address was Route 1, Lutts, Tennessee. He was born 1 June 1926 in Lutts, Wayne County to Mr. and Mrs. C. B. Johnson. He was registered with Selective Service Board in Wayne County, Tennessee. His Civilian Occupation was General Farmer. He was inducted 11 November 1944 at Fort Oglethorpe, Georgia. His Military Occupational Specialty was Supply Clerk. His Military Qualifications included MM 30 Caliber Riffle M1. He was in the battles of Central Europe - France, Germany and Austria. The following decorations were awarded to Johnson: Europe-African Middle Eastern Theater Service Medal with one Bronze Service Star, Good Conduct Medal, World War II Victory Medal and European Theater Operation Occupation Ribbon. He left the USA 7 April 1945 for the European Theater Operation, and returned to USA 15 May 1946. He finished two years of high school. He was discharged 31 July 1946 at Fort Bragg, North Carolina. Johnson's was sent from Fort Oglethorpe to Fort McPherson, Georgia and later transferred to Camp Wheeler, Georgia where he received his Basic Training. After going home on furlough, he reported to Fort Meade, Maryland and from there he was transferred overseas. Dalton served with General Patton's Armored Division.

JOHNSON, JAMES EDWIN, was born in Clifton in Wayne County, Tennessee. He was the son of Jim and Cindy Sinclair. He had one brother, John, and one sister, Ada. He went to Michigan after the war and was buried there.
Source: Earmon Chandler.

JOHNSON, KERRY PAULK, Serial Number 34 141 812, was a Technician Fourth Grade in Company D 254th Infantry in the Army of the United States. His permanent mailing address was General Delivery, Collinwood, Tennessee. He was registered with Selective Service Board in Wayne

County, Tennessee. His Civilian Occupation was Blocker. He was inducted 25 January 1941 at Fort Oglethorpe, Georgia. His Military Occupational Specialty was Surgical Technician. His Military Qualifications included Combat Medical Badge. He was in the battles of Rhineland, Central Europe, and Asiatic-Pacific. The following decorations were awarded to Johnson: Europe-African Middle Eastern Theater Ribbon with 2 Bronze Stars, American Defense Service Medal, Good Conduct Ribbon and Lapel Button. He left the USA 19 March 1942 for the China Burma India Theater, and returned to USA 12 August 1944. He left the USA again 19 February 1945 for the European Theater Operation, and returned to USA 28 September 1945. He finished two years of high school. He was discharged 2 October 1945 at Camp Atterbury, Indiana. Kerry, son of Alvin Paulk and Lena (Reeves) Johnson, was born 30 July 1917 in Lutts, Tennessee, and died 19 March 1977. He had one sister Geneva Johnson Fore.

JOHNSON, THOMAS I., Serial Number 34 529 216, was a Private First Class in Headquarters 66th Armored Infantry Battalion in the Army of the United States. His permanent mailing address was P. O. Box 347, Clifton, Tennessee. He was born 19 November 1923. He was registered with Selective Service Board in Wayne County, Tennessee. His Civilian Occupation was Timber Packer. He was inducted 10 February 1943 at Camp Forrest, Tennessee. His Military Occupational Specialty was Rifleman. His Military Qualifications included Combat Infantryman Badge. He was in the battles of Normandy, Rhineland, Northern France and Central Europe. The following decorations were awarded to Johnson: Good Conduct Medal, Europe-African Middle Eastern Theater Ribbon with 4 Bronze Stars, World War II Victory Medal and Lapel Button. He left the USA 20 September 1943 for the European Theater Operation, and returned to USA 19 September 1945. He finished one year of high school. He was discharged 22 November 1945 at Fort McClellan, Alabama.

JONES, GEORGE D., Serial Number 34 039 990, was born 24 January 1919 in Wayne County, Tennessee. He was the son of Herbert C. and Hughie (Flippo) Jones. His sisters were Gladys, Grace, and Mary Elsie Jones. His brothers were Grady, Delano and Bobby Jones. He joined the Army in March 1941 and was inducted at Fort Oglethorpe, Georgia. He was discharged in August 1945 at Camp Atterbury, Indiana. He was a Technician Fifth Grade in Company C, 20th Engineer Regiment, an Old World War I outfit in the Army of the United States. He served as a Bugler.

He was with the first troops to land in North Africa, going to Casablanca. From North Africa, he went to Sicily and from there to England, across the Channel to Normandy the second day of the invasion. He was in Czechoslovakia when the war ended. It took nineteen days to go over.

JONES, J.P., Serial Number 34 983 726, was a Private in Company D, 210th Infantry Training Battalion in the Army of the United States. His permanent mailing address was Iron City, Tennessee. His Civilian Occupation was Section Hand on the Railroad. He was 24 10/12 years of age and married when inducted 18 March 1944 at Camp Shelby, Mississippi His Military Qualifications included MM Rifle Ml. The following decorations were awarded to Jones Discharge Lapel Button. He was discharged 8 October 1944 at Fort McPherson, Georgia.

Married Loretta DeLouth Tinsley. Children: Michael Roy Jones born Oct 24, 1955. Mike served 2 years in the Navy Reserves. Darrin Blake Jones born Nov 28, 1965, died May 10, 1991.

Roy served in the Army from 1941 to 1945, six months after the war was over he was discharged, rank was T. Sgt. He was stationed in Ohio, Guam and New Guinea.

After the war in 1946, Roy drove the Shreveport Trolly and worked part time for the Carpenter saw shop for eight years and in 1955 Roy purchased the Saw Shop and worked there until he retired in 1991.

Roy was a hero in the eyes of his brothers and sisters. His father passed away when he was seventeen and he became the head of the household. He took care of his mother and raised five brothers and sisters. He unselfishly gave up his life for his family. He did not begin living his own life, until all his brother and sisters were married.

JONES, JOSEPH WARREN, was the son of Marshal and Flora (Copeland) Jones and grandson of Joe A. and Betty Jo (Helton) Jones and James Dougal, Jr., and Denice Leora (Lona) Copeland. He was

bo.. 1 November 1920 on Indian Creek in Wayne County, Tennessee., died 5 January 1975 and was buried in Lutts Cemetery. He enlisted in the Navy before the beginning of World War II. He was Chief B. M. on a P. T. Boat in the South Pacific, then returned to Washington, D. C. where he had the honor of serving on the color guard at the White House. After he was discharged from service, he joined the police force in Washington, D. C. until ill health forced an early retirement. He returned to his parents home in Lutts, and later purchased his own home. He died at the early age of 55.

JONES, RALPH B., Serial Number 14 210 687, was a Private First Class in 342nd B M Squadron, 197th Bomb Group in the Army of the United States. His permanent mailing address was General Delivery, Collinwood, Tennessee. He was born 31 March 1928 in Camden, Alabama. His Civilian Occupation was Farmer. He volunteered and was inducted 22 January 1946 at Fort Oglethorpe, Georgia. His Military Occupational Specialty was Airplane and Engine Mechanic. His Military Qualifications included Carbine MKM. He was not in any battles. He attended the following service schools: Airplane Turbo Supercharger at Chanute Field, Illinois. The following decorations were awarded to Jones: World War II Victory Medal and Lapel Button. He was discharged 18 January 1947 in Shaaf, Kansas.

JONES, ROY LEE, was born July 29, 1921 to Earl and Pearl Jones, of Wayne County, TN.

He married Loretta DeLouth Tinsley and had two children: Michael Roy Jones, born October 24, 1955, who served two years in the Navy Reserves; Darrin Blake Jones, born November 28, 1965, who died May 10, 1991.

Roy served in the Army from 1941 to 1945, six months after the war was over when he was discharged with rank of T/Sgt. He was stationed in Ohio, Guam and New Guinea.

After the war in 1946, Roy dorve the Shreveport Trolly and worked part time for the arpenter saw shop for 80 years. In 1955 he purchased the Saw shop and worked there until he retired in 1991.

Roy was a hero in the eyes of his brothers and sisters. His father passed away when he was 17 and he became the head of hte household. He took care of his mother and raised five brothers and sisters. He unselfishly gave up his life for his family. He did not begin living his own life, until all his brothers and sisters were married.

He died March 26, 1999. He is buried near Shreveport, LA.

JONES, WILLIAM A., son of Mr. and Mrs. Willie Lee Jones of Collinwood, TN, worked as an electric welder before entering the U. S. Navy, October 3, 1944 and received his training at the U. S. Naval Training Center, Great Lakes, IL He served as seaman first class at the Naval Supply Department.

JORDAN, JAMES H., Serial Number 34 495 008, was a Private First Class in Company H, 395th Infantry Regiment, 99th Infantry Division in the Army of the United States. His permanent mailing address was Box 4, Lutts, Tennessee. He was born 28 July 1922 in Cypress Inn, Wayne County. He was registered with Selective Service Board in Wayne County, Tennessee. His Civilian Occupation was Light Truck Driver. He was married when he was inducted 22 November 1942 at Fort Oglethorpe, Georgia. His Military Occupational Specialty was Light Truck Driver. His Military Qualifications included Combat Infantryman Badge. He was in the battles of Ardennes, and Rhineland. He was wounded 18 December 1944 in Belgium. The following decorations were awarded to Jordan: American Theater Ribbon, European African Middle Eastern Theater Ribbon with 2 Bronze Stars, Good Conduct Ribbon, World War II Victory Medal, and Purple Heart. He left the USA 29 September 1944 for the European African Middle Eastern Theater Operation, and returned to USA 27 November 1945. He finished four years of high school. He was discharged 4 December 1945 at Fort Knox, Kentucky. Jordan received his military training at Camp Van Doren, Mississippi; Camp Maxey, Texas and maneuvered in Louisiana, near Shreveport. In 1944 he was assigned to duty and transferred overseas.

KEA, WILLIAM RAYMON, son of John and Antha (Jordon) Kea, was born in 1909 in Wayne County and attended Waynesboro schools. He married Ruby Nell Stockard of Wayne County. They have four children: Hilda, Raymon Harold, Larry and Robert. Raymon was inducted into the United States Navy during World War II and was discharged on October 16, 1945, at the Naval Separation Center at Memphis, Tennessee. Raymond had the Grade of Seaman First Class in the United States Navy. After his discharge he accepted the position of manager of Wayne Farmers Co-op. He resigned this position a few years later to become postmaster of the Waynesboro Post Office. He retired from this position on March 9, 1973. Seven months later, October 19, 1973, he died in an automobile accident in Florida and is buried in Wayne County Memory Gardens. His siblings are Wilma Kea Echols and Ruth Kea.

KEETON, CLIFFORD, Serial Number 34 713 917, was a Technician Fifth Grade in Battery A 565th Coast Artillery Antiaircraft in the Army of the United States. His permanent mailing address was Box 53, Collinwood, Tennessee. He was born 29 April 1924 in Wayne County. He was registered with Selective Service Board in Wayne County, Tennessee. His Civilian Occupation was Peddler. He was married when he was inducted 23 April 1943 and entered into active service 30 April 1943 at Fort Oglethorpe, Georgia. His Military Occupational Specialty was Light Truck Driver. His Military Qualifications included Driver and Mechanic Badge with Bar, Rifle M-1, MM and T H Submachine Gun MM. He was in the battles of Ardennes, Rhineland, and Central Europe. The following decorations were awarded to Keeton: American Theater Ribbon, Europe-African Middle Eastern Theater Ribbon with 3 Bronze Stars, Good Conduct Ribbon and World War II Victory Medal. He left the USA 6 October 1944 for the European Theater Operation, and returned to USA 8 March 1946. The Service Schools that he attended were: Cooking CRSE, Bakers and Cook's School at Camp Blanding, Florida. He was discharged 13 March 1946 at Camp Atterbury, Indiana.

On 30 April 1943, he and twenty-seven other inductees left Waynesboro by bus for Fort Oglethorpe, Georgia. From there fourteen of the Wayne Countians went on to Camp Stewart for Military training. While at Camp Stewart, they participated in the Tennessee maneuvers. Then they went back to Camp Stewart and left for Europe. This group included Talmage Kelley, Lincoln Brewer, James West, Ishmael Cornelius, Lonzo Sherrills, Clyde Haddock, Lemuel Rainey, Olen E. Southerland, H. B. Rose, Charles Combs, Homer Holt and Lee R. "Goat" White.

KEETON, GEORGE Z., JR., volunteered 7 January 1942 for the Army of the United States. He received his Training in Fort Knox, Kentucky, Camp Bowie, Texas and Camp Pickett, Virginia. He left the USA January 1943 to go overseas. †He was in the Battles in the North Africa Invasion in Salerno, Italy, where his Tank Unit was destroyed. He was next with a Paratroopers Division. He was wounded in right hand, losing his index finger February 1943. His parents are Mr. and Mrs. George Keeton, who lived in Collinwood. He had one brother, John Isaac Keeton.

KEETON, HENRY CLAYBORN, Serial Number 34 361 748, was a Technician Fourth Grade in 3533rd Ordinance Me-

dium Automotive Maintenance Company in the Army of the United States. His permanent mailing address was Collinwood, Tennessee. He was registered with Selective Service Board in Wayne County, Tennessee. His Civilian Occupation was Automobile Mechanic. He was inducted 25 July 1942 and entered into active service 8 August 1942 at Camp Wheeler, Georgia. His Military Occupational Specialty was Auto Mechanic. He was not in any battles but was in France and England Campaigns. The following decorations were awarded to Keeton: American Theater Ribbon, Europe-African Middle Eastern Theater Ribbon, Good Conduct Medal, World War II Victory Medal and Lapel Button. He left the USA 12 February 1944 for the European Theater Operation,

and returned to USA 17 January 1946. He was discharged 22 January 1946 at Camp Atterbury, Indiana. Clayborn, son of William Alfred Keeton (11-4-1884 to 8-16-1968) and Ella Ann (Brewer) Keeton (2-18-1887 to 2-29-1968), was born 19 March 1915 in Collinwood, Tennessee. His siblings were Carter Keeton, Maggie Berry, Grace Edwards, Arland Jones, and Joetta Lester. Clayborn finished eight grade at McCall Elementary School, and graduated from high school at Collinwood in 1935. After high school, he joined the Civilian Conservation Corp and served from 10 April 1939 until 12 July 1939. After his discharge, he worked for Barnett's in Waynesboro as a mechanic. Later he moved to Michigan and worked for Detroit Molding Engineering for thirty years before he retired. He married Margie Cole 13 June 1948 and was the father of six children: Jeff, John, Joel, Jamie, Jerrell and Jennifer Keeton. He also had one adopted daughter, Janet Keeton. He married secondly, 30 August 1974 Magnolia Gallaher Bundrant. Clayborn died 5 June 1985 and is buried in McGlamery Cemetery in Collinwood, Tennessee.

KEETON, HERBERT, was a Private First Class in Battery 170 CA in the Army of the United States. He is buried in Shields Cemetery, East of Green River Baptist Church.

KEETON, JAMES A., Serial Number 34 501 223, was a Private First Class in the 787th Military Police Battalion in the Army of the United States. His permanent mailing address was Route 6, Lawrenceburg, Tennessee. He was born 12 August 1922 in Waynesboro, Wayne County. He was registered with Selective Service Board in Wayne County, Tennessee. His Civilian Occupation was Light Truck Driver. He was married when he was inducted 20 December 1942 and entered into active service 27 December 1942 at Fort Oglethorpe, Georgia. His Military Occupational Specialty was Light Truck Driver. His Military Qualifications included Marksman Rifle M1. He was in battles in Northern France. The following decorations were awarded to Keeton: American Theater Ribbon, Europe-African Middle Eastern Theater Ribbon with 1 Bronze Star, Good Conduct Ribbon and World War II Victory Medal. He left the USA 27 December 1943 for the Europe-African Middle Eastern Theater Operation, and returned to USA 4 December 1945. He was discharged 13 December 1945 at Fort Knox, Kentucky.

KEETON, JOHN I., son of Mr. and Mrs. George Keeton of the McGlamery Community near Collinwood, worked with a gasoline supply company before entering the U. S. Army, April 30, 1943. He was inducted at Camp Campbell, KY and received further training at Camp Phillips, KS. In 1944, he was sent to the European Theater and participated in battles in Europe, France, Holland and Germany. He was married to Ethel Simmons.

KEETON, NELSON, Serial Number 966 28 47, had the Grade of Apprentice Seaman V6 in the Navy of the United States. He was married when he volunteered. He was born 6 July 1911 in Hines, Alabama. His description was brown eyes, black hair, ruddy complexion, 6' 0", and weight 192 lbs. He was discharged 26 August 1944 from the United States Naval Training Center (location not given) and returned to Waynesboro.

KEETON, WILLIAM CARTER, "I was the oldest child of William Alfred and Ella Ann (Brewer) Keeton, and was born

31 October 1911 on Middle Butler Creek into a family of what was to be seven children. I finished eight grade at McCall Elementary School, and high school at Collinwood (1926-1930). I taught school at various places in Wayne County (1931-1939). On 10 July 1939, I married Katie Mae Hatchett. I worked in various places in Detroit, Michigan from 1940 to 1943. Then I was inducted into the Army in Wayne County, Michigan 1 November 1943. My basic training was at Camp Blanding, Florida (1943-1944). I left Fort Meade, Maryland for the European Theater on 20 April 1944 and was in Naples, Italy. That summer I was in Infantry Replacement Depot close to the front lines. I was assigned to Company G 350th Infantry, 88th Infantry Division in late September 1944 as a light machine gunner. In January 1945, I was promoted to Sergeant and was wounded in action 19 April 1945 during the push through the Po Valley. I was hit by shrapnel which affected my right arm. I return to the States in August 1945 and was honorably discharged at Camp Gordon, Georgia, 14 December 1945. " Dr. Keeton died 29 June 1996 in Decatur General Hos-

pital, Decatur, Alabama and was buried in Roselawn Cemetery in Decatur. He was founder of Parkway Medical Center and was a member of Westminster Presbyterian Church. At one time he was a doctor at the Lewis County Hospital. He was survived by his wife, Katie Keeton of Hartselle, Alabama; one daughter, Stacie Keeton Herbert of Decatur, Alabama; two sisters, Arland Jones of Collinwood and Joetta Lester of Florence, Alabama, and one granddaughter.

KELLEY, ALBERT FRANKLIN, was born 3 April 1921 to John Marion "Bay" and Lessie (Copeland) Kelley.

Albert grew up in North Wayne County, on Forty-eight Creek in the Kelly's Chapel Community near Topsy. Mr. and Mrs. Kelley had thirteen children, Albert being one of the middle children. The children in order of birth are, Marion Anna Lou, Robert Howard, Homer Johnson, Bessie Hazel, James Hassel, Albert Franklin, Clyde Talmage, Alfred Stanley, Clara Katherine, Joel Wade, Edna Sue, Hester Rosetta and Martha Quincy Kelley. Howard, Bessie, Talmage, Stanley and Martha are deceased. On 11 October 1941, Albert married Goldie Irene Edwards, daughter of Jack and Mary (Pope) Edwards, also of the Topsy Community. Albert worked as a farm hand and logger on the family farm until 1942 when he was called to active duty in the United States Army. Albert was inducted 4 November 1942 in Fort Oglethorpe, Georgia, then went on to Camp White and Camp Adair in Oregon. In April 1944, Albert shipped out for overseas duty with Battery A, 346th Field Artillery Battalion of the 91st Division in Italy and Northern Africa. His job was setting up, operating and repairing field switchboards for Army communications. While in the Army, Albert earned the rank of Corporal and received the Good Conduct Medal, American Service Medal, European African Middle Eastern Service Medal and World War II Victory Medal. Mr Kelly was honorably discharged in November 1945. Two of

his brothers, Talmage and Stanley, also served in the Armed Forces. After his discharge in 1945, Albert returned to work on the family farm and worked for Genesco in Hohenwald. In 1953, he opened a grocery store on the Square in Waynesboro. Business prospered, and in 1964, he established Kelley's Food Town in the Barlow Shopping Center. Later, in 1971 he opened Kelley's Food Town #2 in Clifton. Albert sold his stores to his sons, Eddie and Gene and retired. Albert died 16 March 1998 and was buried in Memorial Gardens in Waynesboro. Over the years, Albert has been a dedicated hunter and musician. With his band, the Merry Makers, they have cut three albums, and had their own radio and television show. Albert and Irene celebrated their 50th wedding anniversary 11 October 1991. They have four children: Eddie Gerald Kelley, Gary Gene Kelley, Teresa Jane Pope and Nancy Lucinda Mathis. They also have eight granddaughters, three step-granddaughters, two great granddaughters and one step-great granddaughter.

KELLEY, ALFRED STANLEY, was born on July 27, 1925, in Wayne County to Bay and Lessie (Copeland) Kelley. He

was inducted into the United States Navy on January 4, 1944, and went to sea serving as Seaman First Class on a transport ship out of California. He received his discharge on April 23, 1946, in Memphis, Tennessee. Two of his brothers served in the United States Army: Albert in Italy and Talmadge in German. Stanley returned to Wayne County and married Virginia Turnbo on April 6, 1947. They bought a farm in the Topsy community and Stanley became a cattle farmer. They raised their three children (Danny, Wanda and Shelia) there and attended Kelley's Chapel, where they were members. Later he drove a school bus and worked in timber, in addition to farming. At the age of 66 on October 1, 1991, he died in a timber accident and was buried in Wayne County Memory Garden.

KELLY, BILL, Private, of Waynesboro was born on March 10, 1924, and worked as a farmer until he was inducted into the United States Service on January 28, 1943, at Camp Forrest, Tennessee. He served with the 898th Quartermasters Company and participated in the battles at Normandy and Northern France. He was awarded the European, African Middle Eastern Theater Ribbon with two Bronze Stars, Good Conduct and World War II Victory Medals. After three years, he was discharged on January 10, 1946, at Fort Knox, Kentucky.

KELLEY, CLYDE TALMAGE, was born and reared in the Northern part of Wayne County, on Forty-Eight Creek in Kelley's Chapel. He was one of thirteen children born to Bay and Lessie (Copeland) Kelley. Talmage was inducted in the United states Army 30 April 1943. His brother, Albert, was called to the Army six months before and his brother, Stanley, followed in his footsteps six months later. Talmage was married 29 April 1944 in Corinth, Mississippi to Freda Turnbow, daughter of Johnst and Mary (Floyd) Turnbow. They had three children: Ronald, Janice Lynn and Karen Houser. On the 30 April 1943, Talmage and twenty-seven other inductees left Waynesboro by bus for Fort Oglethorpe, Georgia. From there fourteen of the Wayne Countians went on to Camp Stewart for Military training. While at Camp Stewart, they participated in the Tennessee maneuvers. Then they went back to Camp Stewart and left for Europe. This group included Talmage, Clifford Keeton, Lincoln Brewer, James West, Ishmael Cornelius, Lonzo Sherrills, Clyde Haddock, Lemuel Rainey, Olen E. Southerland, H. B. Rose, Charles Combs, Homer Holt and Lee R. "Goat" White. They sailed from Pier 17, Staten Island, New York at noon on 16 October 1944 on the ATSS CHRISTABAL debarking in Plymouth, England, where they had their first glimpse of a bombed-out area. They next boarded the SS JOSEPH STORY across the English Channel and up the Seine River to Rauen, about ten miles from France. Going to Luxembourg, they could see artillery fire in the Battle of the Bulge. Next was the battle in the Ardennes where this group joined General Hodges First Army. Next, they transferred to General Patton's Third Army with headquarters at Luxembourg. The mission was antitank protection. At night the soldiers slept in a hole in the ground where it was 15 degrees below zero. The Third Army started its offensive across the Saner River, where they found themselves in Germany. They visited Orthdrof concentration camp and got a look at the kind of people these Nazis were. This group was the first American troops to enter Larch. They spent some time patrolling the Danube River and guarding P.O.W.s.

They spent 140 days in combat with the First and Third Army. Talmage was discharged in February 1946. He and Freda lived on a farm in the Ashland Community. He is a former sheriff of Wayne County and later served as Wayne County Road Commissioner for seventeen years until he died 25 April 1996 and is buried in Memorial Gardens in Waynesboro.

KELLEY, EMERL H., Serial Number 34 284 328, was a Technician Fourth Grade in 477th Engineer Maintenance Company of the Army of the United States. His permanent mailing address was Route 3, Iron City, Tennessee. He was born 6 October 1917 in Wayne County to Samuel and Inez Isabell (Montgomery) Kelley. He was registered with Selective Service Board in Wayne County, Tennessee. His Civilian Occupation was Steam Fitter Helper. He was inducted 23 May 1942 at Fort Oglethorpe, Georgia. His Military Occupational Specialty was Welder Combination. His Military Qualifications included Marksman Rifle. He was in the battles of New Guinea and Southern Philippines. The following decorations were awarded to Kelley: American Pacific Theater Ribbon with 2 Bronze Service Stars, Philippines Liberation Ribbon with 1 Bronze Star, Good Conduct Ribbon, World War II Victory Medal and Lapel Button. He left the USA 26 February 1943 for the Asiatic-Pacific Theater Operation, and returned to USA 20 November 1945. He attended Ord Welding School. He was discharged 1 December 1945 at Camp Chaffee, Arkansas.

KELLEY, GUY HUGHES, was born 23 November 1922 in the Kelly's Chapel community of Wayne County, Tennessee.

His parents were S. S. and Nona Belle (Kelley) Kelley. He had three sisters, Christine, Louise and Monella, and two brothers, John Richard "J. R." and Roy Kelley. Guy was married 20 December 1941 to Theo Shann, daughter of Walter and Bessie (Galloway) Shann. They had one daughter, Nona

Faye Kelley Byrd and two grandchildren. Kelley Renee Byrd Dixon and James Michael Byrd. Guy was inducted into the United States Navy on 18 October 1943. He received his Basic Training in Great Lakes, Illinois. From there he was transferred to Minneapolis, Minnesota and finally to Oxnard and San Diego, California. His training in California was to ferry men and supplies from ship to shore by way of amphibious landing craft. Guy served aboard the U. S. S. JENKINS and was discharged from the service on 25 January 1946 at the rank of Seaman First Class. After returning to Wayne County, Guy continued to farm. Later he worked for Genesco for several years and continued to farm. He then trained as an auctioneer and started his own company of Kelley's Realty and Auction which he worked at until his retirement. Guy Hughes Kelley died 12 June 1988 and is buried in Memorial Gardens in Waynesboro, Tennessee.

KELLEY, J.D., S2/C, son of Mr. and Mrs. DeWitt Kelley of Route 3, Iron City Tennessee, was inducted into the Navy 30 August 1944. He took his boot training at Camp Peary, Virginia.
Source: Wayne County News.

KELLY, MACK, son of Andrew Jackson and Mamie (Gallaher) Kelly, was a World War II veteran of the United States Navy. His siblings were, Eugene and Woodrow Kelly and Clarice Ferguson. He married Nell Auburn. They had one daughter, Auburn Diane Kelly Johnson and one granddaughter, Kelly Johnson.

KELLEY, NOLAN, Serial Number 34 375 235, was a Private First Class with General Patton's 9th Army of the United States Army. He was inducted 17 October 1942. He received his training at Camp Swift, Texas; Fort Sam Houston, Texas; Camp Polk, Louisiana; Los Angeles, California; and Indian Town Gap, Pennsylvania. He was sent overseas in August 1944. He participated in battles in France, Germany and Belgium. His occupation before he entered service was farmer. He married Nell Brewer from near Collinwood.

KELLY, PAUL H., Serial Number 44 121 848, was a Private First Class in the Army of the United States. His permanent mailing address was Box 7, Waynesboro, Tennessee. He was born 29 December 1926 in Lawrence County. He was registered with Selective Service Board in Wayne County, Tennessee. His Civilian Occupation was High School Student. He was inducted 20 June 1945 at Fort McPherson, Georgia. His Military Occupational Specialty was General Clerk. His Military Qualifications included Rifle

MKM LMG, 2nd Class. He was not in a battle. The following decorations were awarded to Kelly: Europe-African Middle Eastern Theater Ribbon, World War II Victory Medal and Lapel Button. He left the USA 29 November 1945 for the European Theater Operation, and returned to USA 8 March 1946. He had a high school education. He was discharged 24 March 1946 at Camp Atterbury, Indiana.

KELLEY, RALPH J., Serial Number 34 327 540, was a Private First Class in Company C, 354th Engineer Regiment in the Army of the United States. His permanent mailing address was Route 2, Box 2, Waynesboro, Tennessee. He was born 30 May 1921 in Waynesboro, Wayne County. He was registered with Selective Service Board in Wayne County, Tennessee. His Civilian Occupation was Farmer. He was inducted 10 August 1942 Camp Forrest, Tennessee. His Military Occupational Specialty was General Carpenter. His Military Qualifications included Marksman 30 Caliber Rifle. He was in the battles of Northern France, Rhineland, and Central Europe. The following decorations were awarded to Kelley Europe-African Middle Eastern Theater Service Ribbon, Good Conduct Ribbon and Lapel Button. He left the USA 1 July 1943 for England, and returned to USA 11 August 1945. He was discharged 28 October 1945 at Fort George Meade, Maryland.

KELLEY, RAY F, Honorable Discharge from the Army of the United States for Ray F. Kelley: Pvt. first and then PFC. Company "1", 346th. Infantry Regiment.

Separated with: EAME Service medal with 2 Bronze Stars, Good Conduct Medal, WW II Victory Medal, Lapel Button issued 2 Sep. 45, ASR Score 26. Combat Inf. Badge: MM 30 cal Rifle M-1 Military occupational Specialty and no. Rifleman (745) Battles and campaigns: Rhineland; Central Europe. Date of induction: 29 Sep. 44 Date of entry in active service: 29 Sep. 44 Place of entry: CP Forrest, Tennessee. Total length of service: Continental ser. 1 yr. 4 mo. 4 days Foreign ser. 0 yr. 5 mo. 0 days. Date of departure outside Continental US and return: 19 Feb. 45 Destination: ETO Date of arrival: 25 Feb. 45 No record USA 28 July 45

I was about 20 years of age, single, and 3 dependences. My mother, sister and brother.

When I left Waynesboro, Tn. I went to Camp Forrest for my induction then on to Camp Landen, FL for basic training. Came home on furlough then over seas. When I went into the Army we got 0 D's to wear, an M-1 rifle and 30 dollars a month.

When we left to go over seas I was put on the Queen Mary. Not as we know it to-day but it was a troop transport accommodations. Some of us got sick going over because we ran into at storm and the ship was tossed about. It took about a week. We landed at Scotland, crossed Scotland to England. We crossed England in boxcars. 40 men or 8 horses in a boxcar. I had a cold on the ship then on the boxcars my feet got frost bitten. We crossed the English Channel to France. While in France we stayed the night. That's when a plane flew over but didn't do anything. We wondered if there was another reason it flew over, like for instance drop a bomb. We then entered Germany near the Rhine River. Crossed the Rhine and up through Germany.

I had 13 weeks of basic training but when I got to the front lines in the war there was no comparison between the two. We were called a replacement group so we moved around a lot. There were many who got hurt or killed. There were bombs and shells hitting all around and homes and buildings knocked down. Whole towns and cities destroyed. I am glad we were over there fighting if it had to be, if it was over here the people would go crazy. The U.S. helped rebuild the country but we didn't cause the war so I don't know why we had to help rebuild it. If we

Leaders to lead our country and others, maybe things like that wouldn't happen. But people cause wars. Like Germany trying to take over other countries.

The German people were pretty nice acting people. Soldiers were strictly soldiers. I didn't even think about wanting to marry a girl from over there. We were too busy fighting for our lives most of the time. We were moving so much, it was hard for anyone to keep up with us to deliver mail or packages. We were on guard duty every 2 hrs. So we didn't have time to do much reading or anything. When we got food on the front lines, it was gotten from the German people. We got whatever they had. We didn't have K-rations very often, not that we wanted them. Some of the K-rations were fit to eat, especially if you were hungry. The chocolate was traded for cigarettes among other things, it was good. We wore our 0 D's all the time. Didn't have much use for better clothing. Not when we were sleeping of the ground and wading creeks and sometimes riding tanks. We dug fox holes if we had a chance. Other times we didn't take the time to, we kept moving or fighting. We had what we called a short range war, now they would have a long range war. The type of equipment would make the difference. No war is a pleasant place to be so the soldiers were under a lot of stress. When they were under so much stress they would make promises to God how they would change and when the battle or war was over they went back to being the same person they were before.

There were Russian Soldiers, French, German and of course American Soldiers.

The day the war was over I got sick. They took me to a field hospital. Stayed there for a week, then on to Paris, France. Funny thing happened on the way. The airplane we were on, we were told, was running out of fuel. We had to make a landing in Luxembourg. We stayed over night there, then on to Paris and the US. I ended up staying in the hospital for 26 months. I was very glad to get back home. I didn't want to go, in the first place. It was my duty to fight for my country if we wanted to be free people. The American people, at least some were glad to see us come back home. Others were not so glad because they had good jobs and run up debts and didn't know how they would pay the debts if they lost their jobs to the service men who left them. I come back to the farm to make a living. All I ever knew before the war. Guess I was a stronger man because of that.

There are about 6 million WW II Vets. living now and 1 thousand dying each day. I was surprised when our Minister at church recently ask how many WW II Vets. were present and I was the only one there. I still have two good friends living outside this state and some in the county that were in the war.

KELLEY, VIRGIL, Private First Class Kelley, son of Mr. and Mrs. Dick Kelley of Iron City, Route 2, entered the service in June 1944. He received his basic training at Camp Shelby, Mississippi, and Camp Wheeler, Georgia, then on to Fort Meade, Maryland to be transferred to overseas duty. Kelley was wounded in action in Germany and was confined to a English hospital for many months.
Source: Wayne County News.

KELLEY, WILLIE V., Serial Number 34 040 793, was a Private in Company K, 102nd Infantry in the Army of the United States. He was born in Collinwood, Tennessee. His Civilian Occupation was Truck Driver. He was 18 years old and single when he enlisted 2 April 1941 at Waynesboro, Tennessee. He was discharged 22 June 1946 at Camp Atterbury, Indiana in poor physical condition.

KELLY, THOMAS S., 75, Noblesville, Indiana died 27 June 1997 at his home and was buried in Cedar Grove Cemetery in Iron City. A native of Iron City, he was retired from Don Hinds Ford in Noblesville, a US Army Veteran of World War II, lifetime member of the American Legion, lifetime member of Veterans of Foreign Wars, a member of the Moose Lodge and the Eagles Club. He was the son of Sim P. and Hattie Mae Hollis Kelly. Survivors include a son Jerry Kelly; three daughters, Mary Sue, Sheila, and Lesa; four sisters, Marie Crowell,

Alma Williams, Hazel Hall and Mabeline Marlow; one brother Frank Kelly and several grandchildren.

Source: Wayne County News, 2 July 1997.

KELLY, ORBIE OKLEY, was an apprentice Seaman with the US Navy and was discharged, July 20, 1946 from San Diego, CA.

KELSO, JOE BETHEL, Serial Number 272 32 12, was a Carpenter's Mate First Class in the Navy of the United States. He was inducted 5 June 1940. Some of the Vessels and Stations he served on: USS HENDERSON; USS McCAULEY; Des Rep Unit No 2, San Diego, California; Ship Repair Unit, Pearl Harbor; and IND COM REP Base, San Diego, California. Medals awarded Kelso: Asiatic Pacific, American Area, American Defense, World War II Victory and Good Conduct Medals. Kelso was discharged 7 June 1946 in San Pedro, California. When Pearl Harbor was attacked, J. B. was sent to that area. He spent six years in the Navy. J. B., the only son of Joe and Mabel (Brewer) Kelso, was born 17 July 1920 in Lawrence County, Tennessee. He lived with his parents at the foot of Blair Hill on the Lutts-Collinwood Road until he joined the Navy. After his discharge, he worked for many years in the Nashville U. S. Post office. He and his wife lived in Brentwood. He died in November 1991 and was buried in Harpeth Hills Cemetery on Highway 100 about ten miles West of Nashville.

KEPHART, JAMES RICHARD, Serial Number 34 160 381, was a Private in Company M, 271st Infantry in the Army of the United States. His permanent mailing address was Collinwood, Tennessee. He was born 21 October 1921 in White Bluff, Tennessee. He was registered with Selective Service Board in Wayne County, Tennessee. His Civilian Occupation was General Farm Hand. He was inducted 13 September 1941 at Fort McCellan, Alabama. His home address was Cloverdale, Alabama. His Military Occupational Specialty was Light Truck Driver. He was in the battles of Normandy, Northern France, Rhineland, and Central Europe. The following decorations were awarded to Kephart: Europe-African Middle Eastern Theater Ribbon with 4 Bronze Stars, American Defense Service Medal, Good Conduct Ribbon and Lapel Button. He left the USA 16 April 1944 for the European Theater Operation, and returned to USA 20 September 1945. He was discharged 27 September 1945 at Camp Atterbury, Indiana. James died 23 January 1998 at Columbia-Crockett Hospital in Lawrenceburg and was buried in McGlamery Cemetery with Military rites at the Cemetery. He was the son of

William James "Jim" and Alice Izora Spann Kephart. He was a retired truck driver. Survivors include one daughter, Carolyn Austin and three sons, Richard, William "Butch" and Jimmy Kephart all of Collinwood. One sister Lenora Cummins of Collinwood, ten grandchildren and three great-grandchildren.

Source: Obit in Wayne County News 28 January 1998.

KEYMON, CLAUDE A., was born on May 20, 1920, in Clifton, Tennessee. He entered the United States Army on November 29, 1942, at Ft. Oglethorpe, Georgia. He went into the 333rd Infantry as a combat infantryman. He was in battles in Central Europe and the Rhineland. He was awarded the American Theater, EAME Theater with three Bronze Stars, World War II Victory Medal and the Good Conduct Medal. He was discharged on January 29, 1946, at Camp Atterbury, Indiana.

KIDDY, J.C., son of Henry Clay and Martha Vina Conway Kiddy, was born on October 9, 1917. He grew up in Clifton and joined the C. C. Camp during the 1930's, then served his country in the United States Navy during World War II. After his discharge, he returned to Clifton and worked as a cook on a boat for Crounce Boat Company of Calhoun, Kentucky. J. C. and Jewell Goodman were married and divorced; they have three children: Dwayne, Ronnie and Elaine. He later married Lucille and they have a son, Clay. J. C. was an avid fisherman, who enjoyed catching and cooking them for his family and friends. On August 20, 1991, he died in Kentucky and was buried there. His siblings are Altie Reed, Alvin and Frank Kiddy, Broady, Vetree, Clara Keanam, Willie Creed and Myrtle Leeper.

KILBURN, EDGAR BERRY, He was a Lieutenant Colonel in the United States Air Force. He was born 1924 in Wayne County and was the son of Chester and Emma (Berry) Kilburn. His wife was Leota Kilburn. They had two sons and a daughter. After he retired from General Motors, he and his family moved back to Wayne County. Kilburn died 21 May 1993 in ECM Hospital in Florence, Alabama.

KILBURN, MARVIN, Serial Number 44 069 657, was a Private in Special Training, Unit Detachment 1473 SCU in the Army of the United States. His permanent mailing address was Route 5, Box 26, Waynesboro, Tennessee. He was born 10 August 1911 in Waynesboro, Tennessee. He was registered with Selective Service Board in Wayne County, Tennessee. His Civilian Occupation was General Farmer. He was married when he was inducted 31 January 1945 at Fort Oglethorpe, Georgia.

He was discharged 23 March 1945 at Regional Hospital in Camp Shelby, Mississippi with a Certificate of Disability.

KILBURN, NIEL, Serial Number 34 375 251, was a Private in 347th Military Police Escort Guard Company in the Army of the United States. He was inducted 3 October 1942 and discharged 15 February 1943 at Florence Internment Camp, Florence, Arizona.

KILBURN, WAFORD H., Serial Number 34 373 142, was a Private First Class in Battery B 455th Coast Artillery Battalion in the Army of the United States. His permanent mailing address was Waynesboro, Tennessee. He was born 8 May 1917 in Waynesboro. He was registered with Selective Service Board in Wayne County, Tennessee. His Civilian Occupation was Blacksmith Helper. He was married when he was inducted 24 September 1942 and entered into active service 8 October 1942. His Military Occupational Specialty was Field Control Instrument. He was in the battles of Normandy, Northern France, Rhineland, and Central Europe. The following decorations were awarded to Kilburn: Europe-African Middle Eastern Theater Ribbon with 4 Bronze Stars, and Lapel Button. He left the USA 5 September 1943 for the European Theater Operation, and returned to USA 16 October 1945. He was discharged 22 October 1945 at Camp Atterbury, Indiana.

KILBURN, WALTER N., Serial Number 34 377 039, was a Private First Class in Company L, 390th Infantry in the Army

of the United States. His permanent mailing address was Route 5, Waynesboro, Tennessee. He was born 13 August 1921 in Waynesboro. He was registered with Selective Service Board in Wayne County, Tennessee. His Civilian Occupation was High School Student. He was inducted 13 October 1942 and entered into active service 27 October 1942 at Fort Oglethorpe,

Georgia. His Military Occupational Specialty was Light Morter Crewman. His Military Qualifications included Expert Infantryman. He was not in any battles. The following decorations were awarded to Kilburn: World War II Victory Ribbon, Good Conduct Medal, American Theater Ribbon, Asiatic-Pacific Theater Ribbon, and Lapel Button. He left the USA 29 April 1944 for the Asiatic-Pacific Theater Operation, and returned to USA 25 January 1946. He had a high school education. He was discharged 1 February 1946 at Camp Chaffee, Arkansas.

KILPATRICK, OLLIE K., Serial Number 34 373 140, was a Technician Fifth Grade in Battery B, 267th Field Artillery Battalion in the Army of the United States. His permanent mailing address was Box 181, Waynesboro, Tennessee. He was born 13 February 1919 in Flatwoods, Tennessee. He was registered with Selective Service Board in Wayne County, Tennessee. His Civilian Occupation was Farmer. He was inducted 24 September 1942 and entered into active service 8 October 1942 at Fort Oglethorpe, Georgia. His Military Occupational Specialty was Low Speed Radio Operator. His Military Qualifications included Sharpshooter Carbine. He was in the battles of Northern France, Ardennes, Rhineland, and Central Europe. The following decorations were awarded to Kilpatrick: American Theater Ribbon, World War II Victory Medal, Europe-African Middle Eastern Theater Ribbon with 4 Bronze Service Stars, Good Conduct Medal and Lapel Button. He left the USA 23 July 1944 for the Europe-African Middle Eastern Theater Operation, and returned to USA 30 December 1945. He was discharged 25 January 1946 at Fort Knox, KY.

KING, MALCOLM R., Serial Number 34 717 141, was a Technician Fifth Grade in Company A 163rd Engineers Combat Battalion in the Army of the United States. His permanent mailing address was Waynesboro, Tennessee. He was born 13 November 1915 in Waynesboro, Tennessee. He was registered with Selective Service Board in Wayne County, Tennessee. His Civilian Occupation was Light Truck Driver. He was inducted 28 April 1943 and entered into active service 5 May 1943 at Camp Forrest, Tennessee. His Military Occupational Specialty was Cook. He was in the battles of Northern France, Rhineland, Central Europe and Air Offensive Europe. The following decorations were awarded to King: Europe-African Middle Eastern Theater Ribbon with 4 Bronze Service Stars, Good Conduct Ribbon, World War II Victory Medal and Lapel Button. He left the USA 27 February 1944 for the Europe-African Middle Eastern Theater Operation, and returned to USA 28 December 1945. His

education consisted of eight years in grammar school. He was discharged 4 January 1946 at Fort Knox, Kentucky.

LACHER, ALLEN, JR., After being notified by the Selective Service System, Allen Lacher, Jr. left Waynesboro, TN via

bus on October 8, 1941 for Fort Oglethorp, GA to serve in the U.S. Army for the next 36 months. He was sent to Fort Bragg, NC for Army camp and then to Camp Clayborn, LA for AIT (Advanced Individual Training). After all this training he was then off to Fort Lewis, WA to set up guard on the coast "Dexter by the Sea".

Next he went to Camp Stoneman, CA and after a short stay there, left in August and sailed under the Golden Gate Bridge whose slogan was "Golden Gate in 48 if you're alive in '45", to the Island of Kawaii and the town of Kapau (which was approximately 60% Japanese) to set up guard.

Later they went back to Oahu (Fort Hassey) and from there to Gaul Canal - New Britain - into combat. There they had Australian troops whom they fought along side. Then into Luzon Lingaon Gulf and fought a bloody battle where they "mopped up - ass kicked" and lost bad at Clark Field, then into Manila when General MacArthur arrived and said "I have returned".

On to the Isle of Mendora, Philippines - Isle of Mendanou where he helped load up for Japan but having earned over 100 points which was required for rotation back home, he and 3 or 4 others boarded a boat and headed for the United States landing at Peugeot Sound, WA (Fort Lawton, WA). They were greeted by the German prisoners who served them donuts and coffee. They were served good food while there.

While serving in the Army, Allen fought in the following battles and campaigns: Bismarck Archipelago GO 33 or D 45 Eastern Mandates GO 48 WD 45 Luzon Southern Philippines GO 67 WD 45. His decorations and citations received: American Defense Service Ribbon; American Service Ribbon

Good Conduct Medal; Philippines Liberation Ribbon and One Bronze Star GO 23 USAFFE 45 AP Service Ribbon and Four Bronze Service Stars.

For all this service he was earning approximately $100/month and paying $6.59/month for insurance premium.

LACHER, BRANFORD RILEY, After graduating from Wayne County High School, Waynesboro, TN in 1943,

Branford R. Lacher went to Buckeye Lake, OH to live with his brother, Bluford T. Lacher & wife Evelyn. He worked in Newark, Ohio until the Selective Service System found him. His orders referred him from Waynesboro, TN to the local board in Newark, OH for preliminary physical examination, then return to Waynesboro, TN for reporting. Before receiving these orders he had written his brothers Joe Lacher, Robert A. (Bob) Lacher and Allen Lacher for advice about which branch of the service he should select. They definitely told him anything but the ARMY!!!

From there he left on a bus for Fort Oglethorpe, GA, then to San Diego, CA. After boot camp he received a two weeks leave and came home to Waynesboro, TN. Enroute he arrived rode a train into Amarillo, TX and they told him there wasn't anything out of there, but he conned them into selling him a ticket and he rode on the trains observation post (it was very cold) to Memphis, TN. He arrived there very early in the morning and there wasn't a bus out of there til late that afternoon, so he hired a taxi to take him to the eastern outskirts of Memphis and caught a ride on a flat bed truck to Waynesboro. It was very cold and 2 or 3 other guys were also on the flat bed with him. After returning from leave he reported to Mare Island, CA, he boarded a merchant vessel to a Pearl Harbor submarine relief crew. For approximately two months he was aboard the Proteose submarine to and from the Midway Islands. Then when he returned to Pearl Harbor he boarded the USS REDFISH (SS395) patrolling the Pacific off coast of Japan, Formosa, China Sea.

The USS REDFISH (SS395) arrived from the Panama Canal on June 12, 1944 and reported to the Pacific Fleet for duty. She arrived at Pearl Harbor, June 27, 1944 and there continued her training until July 23, 1944 when she got underway from the Submarine Base in company with the U.S.S. PICUDA and the U.S.S. SPADEFISH, fretting a coordinated attack group under the command of the commanding officer of the U.S.S. PICUDA enroute to her assigned area between Formosa and Luzon.

The REDFISH first attack in her wartime career resulted in damaging one 4,000 ton freighter out of a heavily escorted convoy on August 18, 1944, in an early morning surface attack. The first enemy vessel to be sunk by the REDFISH was a large tanker which was sent to the bottom by two torpedoes fired in a similar attack on August 19 off Takao, Formosa. Five days later, while submerged off Cape Bojeador on Northern Luzon, a large convoy which had been previously attacked by the U.S. S. PICUDA, was sighted, and two ships, one a medium transport and the other a medium-sized unidentified ship, were sunk by torpedo fire. On 27 August, the REDFISH left patrol area for Saipan for a reload of torpedoes from the U.S. S. HOLLAND and returned to same patrol area on 10 September. Action against the enemy was resumed on 16 September when two torpedoes severely damaged a large Jap tanker. This attack was made thirty seconds after the submarine was straddled by bombs from one of the escorting planes. Again back on the scene at Cape Bojeador, on September 2 1, REDFISH sent two enemy ships to the bottom, a small transport and a large freighter and damaged a large tanker in a single salvo of six torpedoes. Her first trek into enemy waters done, the REDFISH proceeded to Midway where the submarine tender PROTEUS refitted the ship and put her back in fighting shape. Results of this first "successful" patrol was 5 ships sunk totaling 35,500 tons and 3 ships damaged for 24,500 tons. The coordinated attack group of PICUDA, SPADEFISH and REDFISH known as "Donk's Devils" accounted for the sinking of 15 ships and the damaging of 6 ships for a total of 142,500 tons.

October 25, 1944 was the date upon which the REDFISH set forth upon her second and, little suspecting, her last patrol against the Japanese. The Japanese were not likely to forget this patrol for a long while.

On November 20, 1944 after several fruitless days on her area near the north-east tip of Formosa, the REDFISH, while at periscope depth, sighted an antisubmarine patrol vessel which looked like an excellent target for the as yet untried 5 inch gun. The REDFISH battle surfaced and commenced firing. Return fire, while generally ineffective, injured one man of the 40 millimeter gun crew. VAN DE CAR, Rodney W., 622 34 91, E.M.3c V-6, U.S.N.R. was struck on the top of the head by a ricochet from the machine gun of the enemy vessel. He remained at his battle station in spite of his wound. Eighteen minutes later the target was finished off in a similar manner.

The following evening, a seven ship convoy was attacked by the U.S.S. BANG, and the U.S.S. REDFISH. Together, they finished off six of the seven ships in a series of devastating torpedo attacks. Two of these ships, one of them an unidentified freighter and the other a heavily loaded freighter, were accounted for by the REDFISH. After this attack, the REDFISH returned to Saipan for a reload of torpedoes and a few days rest before returning to hunting grounds. This time her area assigned was the East China Sea.

About 2000 (10 PM), December 8, 1944, contact was made on the submariner's dream come true - a task force consisting of a large aircraft carrier and a battleship, escorted by three destroyers. Six hours later the REDFISH delivered a torpedo into the side of the aircraft carrier which had previously been hit by another submarine. The battleship moved off at high speed to safer waters. The carrier meanwhile, had made emergency repairs and was still afloat. The REDFISH moved in and hit her once again with one torpedo. But that carrier could take plenty and the REDFISH was forced to break off the attack. Credit for the damaging of this 29,800 ton aircraft carrier of the Shokaku or Hayataka, Class was assigned the REDFISH by the Force Commander.

Ten days later, the REDFISH, while patrolling at periscope depth in the East Chine Sea about 50 miles north of the northern tip of Formosa, sighted another large aircraft escorted by three destroyers. Later information disclosed that this was the UNRYU on her maiden voyage, laden with planes and obviously headed southward to help stave off the Mindoro invasion which was progressing favorably for us at the time. She never completed her mission - whatever it was. At 1630 (4:30 PM) on that fateful December 19th, the REDFISH fired her four remaining torpedoes from the bow tubes. One terrific hit stopped this pride of the Jap Navy dead in the water, burning furiously and listing about 20 degrees to starboard. But one damaged carrier was more than the skipper of the REDFISH could stomach. This one had to down. A diversion was provided by firing four torpedoes from the stem tubes at the closest escorting destroyer. A reload was completed aft and careful aim taken at the stricken carrier. The torpedo ploughed into the carrier exactly as aimed - a tremendous explosion accompanied the hit and ten minutes later the aircraft carrier disappeared from view with, as later information proved, all hands lost. A great blow for freedom had been struck. But the fury of the escorts knew no bounds and they lashed out at the REDFISH with everything they had. The submarine was forced to the bottom in 230 feet of water and stayed there while the destroyers vented their wrath upon the instrument that had caused them to lose their most valuable charge. At nightfall, the REDFISH badly damaged and taking water into the forward torpedo room at an alarming rate, shuddered to the surface and left the scene of the attack at maximum speed. Visualize the sigh of relief that went through the men of that ship when they surfaced and opened the range between them and the attacking destroyers who had been so successfully vengeful.

He spent two weeks of R&R (Rest & Recreation) at Royal Hawaiian Hotel.

On January 2, 1945, Commander L. D. McGREGOR, U.S. Navy, was relieved by Commander R.S. Andrews, U.S. Navy, and on the same date the REDFISH sailed eastward to San Francisco for repair of her battle damage which was extensive, for rehabilitation of her crew and for general overhaul. Arrived San Francisco on January 12th and here again the command of the REDFISH changed hands. On January 26th, Lieutenant Commander R.L. GURNEE, U.S. Navy, REDFISH Executive Officer since commissioning, relieved Commander R.S. ANDREWS, U.S. Navy of command and on January 27, 1945 the REDFISH was once again underway, this time enroute to Portsmouth, N.H., her birthplace, to return for repairs and overhaul. She arrived there on February 17, 1945, and the overhaul was begun on the same date. Upon completion thereof the ship was run through trials to check the overhaul work and then once again, on July 2, 1945, the REDFISH left for the Pacific on the same route that had carried to her such success before. On July 13, 1945, she once again reported for duty to the Commander-in-Chief of the Pacific Fleet. She arrived at Pearl Harbor July 23, 1945 and was completing her training period for war patrols when on August 15, 1945, the end of hostilities was announced, and with it the end of opportunity for the REDFISH to damage the enemy any further. On August 17, 1945, the Chief of Staff, Submarines, Pacific Fleet, Commodore G.C.

CRAWFORD, U.S. Navy, in the name of the President of the United States, presented the Presidential Unit Citation to the U.S.S. REDFISH in recognition of her accomplishments against the enemy.

On September 6, 1945, the REDFISH was ordered to proceed to Guam in the Marianas Group where she arrived on September 18, 1945.

During the time the REDFISH was being repaired, Branford was sent home for approximately one month's leave. Then back to the Pacific to Pearl Harbor and as they crossed the equator they were initiated (had picture, but could not get a clear copy)

LACHER, JOE A., I joined the Army October 23, 1940 and was assigned to the 6th Cavalry at Fort Oglethorpe, GA. Our

training equipment consisted of horses, motor cycles, and scout cars. We put sticks on the cycles and called them tanks as we trained. We moved to Camp Blanding, FL in 1942 and received tanks for our horses and motorcycles. We trained in the sand pits and destroyed pine trees. Our name was changed to the 28th Calvary Reconnaissance Squadron. We moved to Fort Jackson, SC in 1943 training there and on maneuvers into Tennessee in preparation for overseas.

We landed in Belfast, Ireland, October 1943, worked and played in Ireland, Scotland and England. It was not much fun, we were all blacked out majority of the time.

Crossed the English Channel in 1944 on landing craft. The landing craft was quite scary, I saw what I took to be bodies and equipment all over. Overheard a lot of planes and all sorts of noise. We unloaded our tanks fast and headed for an apple orchard which would service as a place to hide.

While we were in Ireland, the 3rd Army was formed with George S. Patton in command. We were part of that Army for the duration of the war.

We were in France, Czechoslovakia, Luxembourg, Germany, performing recon-

naissance for armor divisions. We were looking for trouble, which was not hard to find. A major source were Tiger Tanks. One day we believed there was a battle taking place up north. We were asked to come take part and after 12 hours on the road we were in the "Battle of the Bulge" and I missed my Christmas dinner.

There were lots of operations after December 1944, 1 can't really remember much of what happened. I was awarded the Silver Star Medal for gallantry in action in connection with military operations against an enemy of the United States on 29 March 1945 in Germany. "When the forward elements of his task force were ambushed and cut off in the town of Schmitten, Germany, Staff Sergeant Lacher, as platoon sergeant of a light tank platoon, took his tank into the town under heavy small arms and antitank fire on two occasions, dismounted, helped wounded men into his tank and delivered them into the town a third time and returned slowly so that fifteen men who had been pinned down by machine gun fire could be afforded protection by walking beside his tank. Observing that a tank abandoned by our forces was being used by the enemy to harass our forces, Staff Sergeant Lacher maneuvered his tank into a favorable position and destroyed the captured vehicle without damaging his own vehicle. Staff Sergeant Lacher's gallant actions contributed materially to the successful outcome of his platoons mission and were an inspiration to his fellow soldiers." Harvel Carter of Waynesboro, Tennessee lost his life in this operation.

I do remember returning to the states in June 1945. 1 arrived in the hole of a liberty ship that landed in Newport News, VA. From there I went to Camp Attermury, IN. I was discharged June 25, 1945 and lived and worked in Nashville and Columbia, TN for two years. In 1947,

I was back in the Army and after 17 years and 15 countries, I retired as a Staff Sergeant in June 1964 from Fort Mead, MD.

LACHER, ROBERT A., Serial Number 34 727 018, was a Staff Sergeant in 371st Bomb Squadron in the Army of the United States. His permanent mailing address was Route 3, Waynesboro, Tennessee. He was born 11 August 1923 in Wayne County. He was registered with Selective Service Board in Wayne County, Tennessee. His Civilian Occupation was Structure Steel Worker. He volunteered, was inducted 20 March 1943 and entered into active service 27 March 1943 at Fort Oglethorpe, Georgia. His Military Occupational Specialty was Aerial Photographer. His Military Qualifications included AAF Tech Badge with Photographer's Air

Crew Member Badge (Wings). He was in the battles of Bismarck, Archipelago, China, New Guinea, Northern Salmons, South Philippines (Liberation), Luzon, and Western Pacific. The following decorations were awarded to Lacher: Asiatic Pacific Theater Ribbon with 1 Silver Star and 2 Bronze Stars, Good Conduct Ribbon, Philippine Liberation Ribbon with 1 Bronze Star, Air Medal Ribbon with 2 Bronze Clusters, and Lapel Button. He left the USA 19 March 1944 for the South West Pacific Area and returned to USA 23 July 1945. The service schools that he attended were, ACTS Keesler Field, Mississippi, 315th AAFTTD, and AAFWTTC, Camp Consair, San Diego, California. He had a high school education. He was discharged 9 October 1945 at San Antonio, Texas. The following letter was sent to Robert's sister, Mrs. Lucille Mathis: Dear Mrs. Mathis: Recently your brother, Sergeant Robert A. Lacher, was decorated with the Air Medal. It was an award made in recognition of courageous service to his combat organization, his fellow American Airmen, his Country, his home and you. He was cited for meritorious achievement while participating in aerial flight in the South West Pacific area from 29 November 1944 to 4 January 1945. Your brother took part in a sustained operational flight mission during which hostile contact was probable and expected. These flights included bombing missions against enemy installations, shipping and supply bases and aided considerably in the recent successes in this theater. I would like to tell you how genuinely proud I am to have men such as your brother in my command. Signed Lieutenant General George C. Kenney.

Source: Wayne County News.

LAKEY, JOE E., Serial Number 965 96 23, had the grade of Cook Third Class in the Navy of the United States. He was born 6 February 1922 in Collinwood, Tennessee. He entered into Active Service 22 November 1943 and was discharged 17

January 1946 from the US Naval Personnel Separation Center in Memphis, Tennessee. He served on the following Vessels/Stations: USNTS Great Lakes, Illinois; Construction Battalion's USNCTC Williamsburg, Virginia; USNCTC Davisville, Rhode Island (Repair Group) and 103 Naval Construction Battalion. Joe E, Lakey SC3C, husband of Mrs. Marjorie Lakey of Collinwood, Tennessee, is one of 1357 high point Navy Veterans whom the Navy is returning to the States for discharge aboard the USS DUPAGE, an attack transport of the Navy's famed "Magic Carpet" fleet. This ship left from Guam.

Final rites for Joe Ed Lakey 77, of Collinwood were conducted Sunday, February 6 at the Shackford Funeral Home Chapel in Collinwood with Earnest Rich and Glen Richardson officiating. Burial was in Memorial Gardens.

He was a native of Wayne County, a son of the Late Ed and Mattie White Lakey. He was retired from General Motors in Detroit after over 30 years of service as a craftsman die engineer. He was a veteran of WWII serving in the US Navy. He was a member of the Collinwood Masonic Lodge #702, the Al Menah Temple of Nashville and a lifetime member of the Veterans of Foreign Wars and the American Legion. He was also a member off McGlamery Community Church.

Source: Wayne County News.

LANCASTER, JAMES, Serial Number 34 723 048, was a Private First Class in the Coast Artillery in the Army of the United States. His permanent mailing address was Box 68, Collinwood, Tennessee. He was born 11 February 1923 in Collinwood. He was registered with Selective Service Board in Wayne County, Tennessee. His Civilian Occupation was Light Truck Driver. He was inducted 20 February 1943 and entered into active service 27 February 1943 at Fort Oglethorpe, Georgia. His Military Occupational Specialty was AAA Auto Weapons Crewman. His Military Qualifications included Marksman. He was in the battles in the Western Pacific. The following decorations were awarded to Lancaster: Asiatic Pacific Service Medal and Lapel Button. He left the USA 16 June 1944 for the Asiatic Pacific Theater Operation, and returned to USA 30 April 1945. He was discharged 20 July 1945 at Foster General Hospital in Jackson, Mississippi.

LANCASTER, REEDER, Serial Number 34 506 510, was a Private in Company D, 25th Training Battalion in the Army of the United States. He was born in Iron City in Wayne County, Tennessee. His Civilian Occupation was Farmer. He was 27 10/12 years old and single when he was inducted 18 January 1943 at Fort Oglethorpe, Georgia. He did not participate in any battles. He was discharged 29 April 1943 at the 4th Ind. Headquarters QMRTC in Camp Lee, Virginia.

LAWSON, ULYS H., Serial Number 34 375 233, was an Army veteran of World War II. He was born 23 October 1908 and died 25 December 1954. His parents were Johnny and Mary (Holt) Lawson. He had a twin brother, Qulis V. Lawson (1908-1914). Ulys married Verdie Bratcher. They had one daughter Annie Ruth Lawson.

LAY, ANANIAS, was born on December 30, 1916, to David Paris and Mary Ann McGee Lay. Ananias married Ruby Lee Winters. Ananias entered military service on March 15, 1942, and was assigned to the 81st Airborne Division. He took part in six major invasions as a member of the Paratrooper Glider attack group. He was awarded a decoration star for each invasion. He was honorably discharged on September 21, 1945, as a Staff Sergeant; however, he was acting First Sergeant prior to his discharge.

Submitted by Mary Eva Kimbel.

LAY, JAMES JORDAN "JAMIE", Serial Number 34 884 586, was a Technician Fifth Grade in Company H, 175th In-

fantry Regiment 29th Division in the Army of the United States. His permanent mailing address was Box 135, Clifton, Tennessee. He was registered with Selective Service Board in Wayne County, Tennessee. His Civilian Occupation was Light Truck Driver. He was married when he was inducted 3 September 1943 and entered active duty 24 September 1943 at Fort Oglethorpe, Georgia. His Military Occupational Specialty was Light Truck Driver. His Military Qualifications included Ex-

pert and Combat Infantryman Badge and Driver Badge. He was in the battles of Northern France, Rhineland, and Central Europe. He was wounded in action in France September 1944. The following decorations were awarded to Lay: Purple Heart, World War II Victory Medal, Europe-African Middle Eastern Theater Ribbon with 3 Bronze Stars, and Good Conduct Ribbon. He left the USA 6 April 1944 for the European African Middle Eastern Theater Operation, and returned to USA 1 December 1945. He was discharged 10 December 1945 at Fort Knox, Kentucky. Jamie, son of Will and Alice Jordan Lay, was born 16 December 1908 in Waynesboro, Tennessee, died 15 March 1982 and is buried in Clifton, Tennessee. His siblings were: Kennie, Joe, Raymond, Norman, Almon Lay, Mary Lay Ledbetter, Lillian Lay Griggs, Nellie Lay and Frances Byrd. Jamie married Rachel Montague. After her death, he married Irene Dicus.

LAY, LEONARD H., Serial Number 34 377 041, was a Private First Class in Company E, 390th Infantry in the Army

of the United States. His permanent mailing address was Route 2, Waynesboro, Tennessee. He was born 31 August 1920 in Waynesboro, Tennessee. He was registered with Selective Service Board in Wayne County, Tennessee. His Civilian Occupation was General Farm Hand. He was inducted 13 October 1942 and entered into active service 27 October 1942 at Fort Oglethorpe, Georgia. His Military Occupational Specialty was Rifleman. His Military Qualifications included Expert Infantryman. He was not in a battle. The following decorations were awarded to Lay: Asiatic Pacific Theater Ribbon, Good Conduct Ribbon, World War II Victory Medal and Lapel Button. He left the USA 29 April 1944 for the Asiatic Pacific Theater Operation, and returned to USA 25 January 1946. He was discharged 1 February 1946 at Camp Chaffee, Arkansas.

LEE, CURBY L., Serial Number 44 020 844, was a Private in Company B, 1473 SCU, STU Det in the Army of the United States. His permanent mailing address was Route 4, Waynesboro, Tennessee. He was born 22 February 1911 in Lawrenceburg, Tennessee. He was registered with Selective Service Board in Wayne County, Tennessee. His Civilian Occupation was Farmer. He was married when he was inducted 29 September 1944 at Camp Forrest, Tennessee. The following decorations were awarded to Lee: Lapel Button. He was discharged with a Certificate of Disability 29 March 1945 at Regional Hospital, Camp Shelby, Mississippi.

LEE, HOWARD TAFF, Serial Number 966 79 27, had the grade of Apprentice Seaman in the Navy of the United States. He enlisted for two years on 8 March 1944 in Nashville, Tennessee. He was born 3 May 1914 in Hickman, Kentucky. His service (Vessels and Stations served on) included: US Navy Recruiting Station in Nashville, Tennessee; US Naval Training Station in Great Lakes, Illinois; US Naval Hospital in Great Lakes, Illinois. He was discharged 20 April 1944 at the US Naval Training Station in Great Lakes, Illinois.

LEE, JAMES LAWRENCE, Serial Number 641 74 64, had the grade of Yeoman Third Class in the Navy of the United

States. He enlisted 15 June 1943. He was born 19 July 1925 in West Point, Tennessee. His service (Vessels and Stations served on) included: USNTS San Diego, California; Landing Craft School LCS PAC; USNH PRE Flight SCH, Delmonte, California; SLCU No. 34 , Morro Bay, California; Morro Bay DET PRIS TRA Base in Morro Bay; USS Harris Asiatic-Pacific Area 2 Com Trans RON 13, California; US Naval COMM India Burma Malay States Area. The following decorations were awarded to Lee: World War II

Victory Ribbon, American Area Campaign Ribbon, and Asiatic Pacific Area Campaign Ribbon. He was discharged 17 May 1946 at the US Naval Personnel Separation Center in New Orleans, Louisiana. His parents are Mr. and Mrs. Henry Lee. He has one sister, Mrs. Hobart Risner of Collinwood. He attended Collinwood High School.

LEWIS, LAWRENCE DELBERT, Serial Number 272 72 89, had the Grade of Watertender First Class in the Navy of the United States. His permanent mailing address was Route 2, Iron City, Tennessee. He was born 22 October 1919 in Anderson, Alabama. He was registered with Selective Service Board in Wayne County, Tennessee. His last employer was L. M. Bromley, Iron City, Tennessee. His Civilian Occupation was Farming. He finished two years of high school. He enlisted 3 September 1941 in Birmingham, Alabama. He held the following ratings: AS, S2, F3, F2, F1, WT2, and WT1. His service (Vessels and Stations served on) included: USS TEXAS, USS IOWA, and USS HELENA. Lewis completed the NTS MM Norfolk, Virginia service school. The following Medals were awarded to Lewis: Asiatic Pacific with 2 Stars, American Area; African European with 2 Stars, Philippine Liberation, American Defense, World War II Victory Ribbon, and Good Conduct Medal. He was discharged 31 August 1947 in San Pedro, California.

LEWIS, THURSTON, Serial Number 34 32 05, enlisted for four years in the United States Marine Corps on 24 December 1941 at D. H. S., Nashville, Tennessee. He was a Corporal. He was born 23 September 1920 in Mercer, Tennessee. His Special Military Qualification was Field Artillery Crewman. His service took him to the Southwest and Central Pacific Area from 16 June 1942 to 13 December 1944. He participated in defense occupation of Guadalcanal from 12 November 1942 to 19 February 1943 and participated in action against the enemy at Guam, Marinas Islands from 22 July 1944 to 10 August 1944. Lewis was awarded the Good Conduct Medal and issued a Honorable Discharge Button and Service Lapel Button when he was discharged 27 December 1945 at Paris Island, South Carolina.

LINDSEY, HUGH F., Sgt, son of Mrs. Joe C. Lindsey of Lutts, entered the service on 15 December 1943 and received training at Keesler Field, Mississippi; Denver, Colorado; Fort Myers, Florida; and Columbia and Greenville, South Carolina. He was based at Muroc and San Francisco, California before transferring overseas in

May. Sgt Lindsey is a graduate of the Department of Armament of Lowery Field, Colorado and a graduate of AAF Commands Flexible Gunnery School at Buckingham Field near Fort Myers, Florida. He has served as a tail gunner on a B-25 bomber and was in the Hawaiian Islands, then in the Netherlands, East India. Lindsey received his education in the Pinhook and Collinwood High School, and took a course of training with the Anderson Airplane School in Nashville. After this he was employed with the air utilities at Sky Harbor near Murfreesboro, Tennessee.

Source: Wayne County News from Clyde Bevis.

LINEBERRY, COY WILLIAM "MUTT", JR., was born on April 7, 1926. He died on June 2, 1961. He was the son

of Coy W. Lineberry and Minnie Jeter Lineberry. He is buried in the Prater Cemetery near Clifton, Tennessee. Mutt served his country during World War II in the United States Army TEC4 873 Ord. Ham Company. After the war he continued in the service in Japan for some time. After he was discharged from the Army, he and I met and married. I am Nannie Mae, the daughter of Charlie Garrard and Nancy Prater Garrard. Mutt and I lived around Clifton; he worked at General Shoe Company in Waynesboro for some time. He worked at the Limestone Rock Crusher near Clifton and later went to work on the riverboat, Staton Kay Smith, traveling on the Tennessee River. It was at this work that he lost his life in an accident at the Wilson Dam in Alabama on June 2, 1961. We have no children. His siblings are John D., Perry, Mary Elizabeth and Mattie Lou.

LINEBERRY, JEFF DAVID, Serial Number RA 44 121 855, was a Private First Class in the Armed Forces of the United States. His permanent mailing address was Route 2, Clifton, Tennessee. He was registered with Selective Service Board in

Wayne County, Tennessee. He was inducted 19 January 1945. He was in the Campaign of Dermstad, Germany. The following decorations were awarded to Lineberry: Army Occupation Medal (Germany) and World War II Victory Medal. He was discharged 17 December 1948 at St. Louis, Missouri. Lineberry reenlisted 18 December 1948 and retired 1 August 1979 Lineberry's occupation after his discharge was tug boat hand. He was born 27 June 1927 in Clifton, Tennessee, died at his home 20 May 1993 and was buried in Praters Chapel Cemetery in Clifton, Tennessee. His parents were Pleas and Bertha (Pigg) Lineberry. His brothers were: John Ralph of Savannah, Ray and Rex both of Clifton, and J. R. Lineberry of Baxter, Tennessee.

LINEBERRY, RICHARD, was born 11 March 1927 to the late Robert Eli and Lona Bell (Inman) Lineberry in Wayne

County, Tennessee, near the Perry County line. Also born to this union were my sister, unnamed, who died shortly after birth 19 January 1924 and my brother, Curtis Glen born 10 November 1936. I attended Richardson Elementary School in our community and Frank Hughes High School in Clifton. My wife, Rothie Nell Gifford, and I were married 2 April 1946. We have one daughter, Gloria Jean, born 12 November 1947. I was inducted into the Army 27 July 1945 and after arriving that same day at Fort Oglethorpe, Georgia was assigned Serial Number 44 123 730. Three days later I was sent to Fort McPherson, Georgia for one week, then on to Camp Blanding, Florida. There the entire company had two weeks of leisure time due to lack of food. Almost four weeks passed from the time of my induction until I actually started Basic Training. I received twelve weeks of a sixteen week program before being pulled out and sent to Fort Knox, Kentucky, as a Military Policeman. I served there until my discharge 23 March 1946. On this date

I reenlisted and remained at Fort Knox for one more year until my second discharge 22 April 1947. Before the war ended, I had risen to the rank of Corporal at which time all ranks were frozen. My reenlistment time was spent as acting Sergeant of the guard in charge of American prisoners in the stockade.

LINEBERRY, WINFRED, was born on November 15, 1926, son of Fred Sam Lineberry and Marie Inman Lineberry. Winfred entered the United States Army after leaving school. He was inducted on March 30, 1945, at Ft. Oglethorpe, Georgia, serving in the Infantry T-5 Motor Pool. He served one year in Japan, and eight months and nine days in the states. He was discharged at Camp Beale, California, with a Asiatic Pacific Campaign Medal, Army Occupied Medal and World War II Victory Medal. Before Winfred entered the army, he had worked with his father in well drilling. After returning home, he continued this work, the second generation making well drilling their lifetime work. He married Faye Westbrooks on June 18, 1950. They have four children: Dianne, Janet, Patricia (Patty) and Steve. His siblings are Frank, Betty Jo, Dorothy Sue and Wayne.

LINVILLE, CLYDE H., husband of Lois Linville, Rt 2, Iron City, TN served in the US Navy and received his training at the Naval Training Center at Great Lakes, IL.

LINVILLE, JAMES H., JR., Serial Number 34 723 014, was a Corporal in the 278th Military Police Company in the Army of the United States. His permanent mailing address was Iron City, Tennessee. He was born 14 May 19?? in Iron City, Tennessee. He was registered with Selective Service Board in Wayne County, Tennessee. His Civilian Occupation was General Farm Hand. He was inducted 27 February 1943 and entered into active service 27 February 1943 at Fort Oglethorpe, Georgia. His Military Occupational Specialty was Military Police. His Military Qualifications included Rifle MKE. He was not in any battles. The following decorations were awarded to Linville: American Service Medal, Lapel Button and World War II Victory Medal. He left the USA 30 July 1943 for the American Theater Operation, and returned to USA 7 January 1946. He had a high school education. He was discharged 13 January 1946 at Fort McPherson, Georgia.

LINVILLE, LEWIS P., Serial Number 34 495 071, was a Private First Class with the 1135th School Squadron in the Army Air Force of the United States. His permanent mailing address was Route 2,

Iron City, Tennessee. He was born 29 July 1909 in Wayne County. He was registered with Selective Service Board in Wayne County, Tennessee. His Civilian Occupation was Farmer. He was single when he was inducted 22 November 1942 at Waynesboro, Tennessee. He was not in any battles. He was discharged 29 May 1943 at Camp Luna, Las Vergas, Mexico. He continued farming after his discharge. He married Marie Pigg. Their children were Guinda Horton and Curtis Linville. The Linvilles live on Highway 13 South. Obit in the Wayne County News, 10 Sept 1997 stated that Louis P. Linville of Route 1, Iron City, died 4 Sept 1997 in the Wayne County Medical Center and was buried in Memorial Gardens in Collinwood. He was the son of Pink and Lula Bromley Linville, a retired Reynolds Alloy employee, and a Baptist. Survivors included his wife, Mary Pigg Linville, a son, Curtis Linville and a daughter, Guinda Horton, both of Collinwood; two brothers, P.W. Linville of Florence and Hardison Linville of Indiana; one sister, Gladys Prince of Indiana, and three grandchildren.

LINVILLE, PAUL M., Serial Number 44 069 588, was a Technician Fourth Grade in 1789th Engineer Service Flat. in the Army of the United States. His permanent mailing address was Route 3, Iron City, Tennessee. He was born 26 October 1926 in Iron City. He was registered with Selective Service Board in Wayne County, Tennessee. His Civilian Occupation was Light Truck Driver. He was inducted 31 January 1945 at Fort Oglethorpe, Georgia. His Military Occupational Specialty was Cook. His Military Qualifications included MM W/M-1 Rifle. He was not in any battles. The following decorations were awarded to Linville: Asiatic Pacific Theater Ribbon, Good Conduct Medal and World War II Victory Medal. He left the USA 22 August 1945 for the Pacific Theater Operation, and returned to USA 19 August 1946. He finished one year in high school. He was discharged 27 August 1946 at Fort Sheridan, Illinois.

LINVILLE, ROSS M., Serial Number 36 118 256, was a Private First Class with the 7th Armored Division in the Army of the United States. He was born 18 December 1917 in Iron City, Wayne County. He was registered with Selective Service Board in Wayne County, Tennessee. His Civilian Occupation was Former Supervisor. He was inducted 14 June 1941 in Detroit, Michigan. His Military Occupational Specialty was Cook. His Military Qualifications included Carbine MM, and Combat Infantry Badge. He was in the battles in Northern France, Ardennes, Rhineland,

and Central Europe. The following decorations were awarded to Linville: American Defense Ribbon, Europe-African Middle Eastern Theater Ribbon with 4 Bronze Stars, and Good Conduct Ribbon. He left the USA 7 June 1944 for the European Theater Operation, and returned to USA 10 October 1945. He was discharged 16 October 1945 at Camp Atterbury, Indiana.

LOMAX, THOMAS ALLEN "TRUMAN", was born on June 27, 1908, in Wayne County. He is the son of Thomas Andrew and Mary Ann (Davis) Lomax. He was inducted into the United States Navy in March 1944. Truman received his boot training at San Diego, California, then he was stationed at several different bases until he was assigned to Patrol Craft #1378 as fireman first class. After 17 months he was discharged in 1945. Truman and Inis Davis were married on December 19, 1935, and settled in Waynesboro where she taught at the Waynesboro Elementary School until she retired, and he worked at Holthouse and Hartup Company until the business closed in 1965. He then worked construction until he retired in 1980 at the age of 72. Inis died on July 19, 1999, from cancer, and Truman continues to live at their home in Waynesboro. Thomas Allen Lomax and the late Inis Lomax have a son, Thomas Allen (Tommy) Lomax, born on September 29, 1940. He married Floziada Gobbel, daughter of Rex and Rotha Nell (Stricklin) Gobbell. They reside in Moore, South Carolina. Tommy is retired from MEMC Chemical Company, and Floziada works as a RN at the local hospital. They have two children and three grandchildren. His siblings are Anna, Jane, Magaline and Alfred.

LONG, CLYDE SYLVESTER, Serial Number 34 373 186, was a Private in Battery A 103rd Coast Artillery Training Battalion in the Army of the United States. He was born in Waynesboro, Tennessee. His Civilian Occupation was Farmer. He was 36 3/12 years old when he was inducted 24 September 1942 at Fort Oglethorpe, Georgia. He was discharged 6 February 1943 at Camp McQuaide, California. He was the son of Sylvester Lewis and Emily (Keeton) Long. He was a farmer and a member of the Mt. Hope United Methodist Church. He died 9 July 1994 at the age of 88 years. Burial was in Shields Cemetery in Wayne County. He married Bernice Cook. They had two children, Wanda Jeanette who married Paul Skelton and Gloria Jo who married Franklin Pope. His siblings were Newt, Dave, Pearl (Mrs. Joe Kotthoff) and Ada Leek Flippo and a half brother, Taylor Long.

LONG, GROVER C., second son of Robert Newt and Martha (Irwin) Long, was born on March 3, 1924, in Wayne County. I was inducted into the United States Navy on September 4, 1943. After six weeks of boot camp, I was sent to the Asiatic-Pacific and assigned to the Navy amphibious force LCI(L) Boat #5, LCI(L) 436. I spent the remainder of World War II invading islands held by the Japs, from the Solomons, New Guinea and Philippines to Okinawa. We were at Okinawa getting ready to invade Japan when the war ended. Our ship was then ordered to China for occupation duty. I returned to the United States in December 1945 and was discharged. I lived in Wayne County from December 16, 1945, until I reenlisted in the Navy on September 8, 1947. I served 22 years in naval aviation and made two six-month deployments to Korea during the Korean War and one eight-month deployment to Vietnam in the early part of that war. When I retired from the Navy, I worked for the Navy in a civil service position. In 1985 I retired with 40 years United States Government service, including the 22 years of Navy service. Dorothy Morrow and I were married on September 6, 1945, (56 years in 1999) and now live in Florida. We have three daughters: Margaret Ann Mulford in Florida, Peggy Sue Mills in Oregon and Emily Kaye Smith in Florida. We also have two grandsons, three granddaughters, one great-grandson and two great-granddaughters. I have an older brother, Robert G., and a younger sister, Nadine Long. Nadine has lived in Florence, Alabama, most of her adult life. Robert lived at Florence, Alabama, when he went into the United States Navy the early part of 1942. He spent most of the war in the Pacific with the Navy's CB's. When he was discharged, he returned to Florence and worked for TVA until he died in 1977.

LONG, ROY H., Serial Number 14 054 385, was a Staff Sergeant in the Army Air Corp RA. I was inducted 16 September 1941 at Fort Oglethorpe, Georgia and was discharged 14 September 1945 at Fort McPherson, Georgia. I had previously enlisted 18 July 1941 into the Aviation Cadet Air Corps Training Detachment in Jackson, Mississippi but was Honorably discharge by reason of Flying Deficiency. I attended Keesler Field Aviation School, Keesler Field, Mississippi, I completed and was assigned as Airplane and Engine Mechanic to Spence Field Air Base, Moultrie, Georgia with the 89th Material Squadron. In August 1942, the 89th Service Squadron was transferred to Walterboro Air Force Base, Walterboro, South Carolina. It was joined with the 323rd Service Squadron and Headquarters Squadron to form the

305th Service Group. Here the group made preparation for overseas shipment. Preparation complete, we traveled to Charleston, South Carolina staging area for final preparations. On 6 October 1942 the group was transported by troop train to New Port News, Virginia and boarded the RMS MAURETANIA, a luxury ship of Cunard Line. The nurses and 7,000 service men on board left 7 October 1942 for parts unknown, on what was to be the longest unescorted voyage of the war. The course was South to Rio de Janeiro, then across the Atlantic to Durban, South Africa, where troops were allowed two days shore leave. The MAURETANIA then left port but returned hurriedly while military planes flew out and sank a waiting submarine. The MAURETANIA then preceded up the coast of Africa, past the island of Madagascar while a battle was being fought. On up the coast and through the Red Sea to Suez where 5,000 troops were off loaded and German prisoners, guarded by Australian and New Zealand troops were brought aboard bound for Australia. The ship crossed the Red Sea and the Indian Ocean to Colombo, Ceylon, where 305 Service squadrons were transferred to two small vessels, The CITY of PARIS and the KOSCIUSK bound for Bombay, India. Three days later, on 29 November 1942, after 56 days on the water, the 89th disembarked in Bombay, India. Later we were shipped by train to Agra, India. After a one month stay and chance to visit the Taj Mahal and the Red Fort, the 89th Service Squadron left Agra in January 1943 for Ondal, India, to open a new air base serving all types of air craft needed in the war against Japan. The 89th Service Group personnel serviced all types of aircraft in India and all points of Burma and China. By the spring of 1945 the original members of the 89th, after spending over two and a half years overseas, were returned to the United States and assigned to other units. I was assigned to the Air Base at Marianna, Florida. Then I was discharged

14 September 1945 at 137th Army Air Force Unit Separation Center, Fort McPherson, Georgia. The following decorations were awarded to me: Europe-African Middle Eastern Service Medal, American Defense Service Medal, American Theater Service Medal, Asiatic-Pacific Service Medal with 3 Bronze Stars, and Good Conduct Medal. I was born 14 June 1919 in Wayne County to Taylor and Nellie Long. My sisters are Myrtice McNair, Naomi Pevahouse, Edith Elrich, and Neva Duckworth. My brothers are Lewis and Everette Long. I was married 10 June 1942 to Kittie Bell Parker, daughter of Rev. Charles Parker. We had two daughters, Janice, born 17 September 1946 and Elaine, born 9 June 1951. After service, I graduated from the University of Tennessee. Then I had the position of Plant Supervisor for Pet Milk in Mayfield, Kentucky, Greenville, Illinois, and Greeneville, Tennessee. The family moved to Lawrenceburg in 1953, where I was local agent for State Farm Insurance for 30 years. I retired in 1984 and am enjoying good health and traveling extensively.

LONG. WILLIAM B., Serial Number 34 377 194, was a Private in Company D, 12th Infantry in the Army of the United States. His permanent mailing address was Route 4, Waynesboro, Tennessee. He was born 30 May 1917 in Waynesboro. He was registered with Selective Service Board in Wayne County, Tennessee. His Civilian Occupation was General Farm Hand. He was inducted 13 October 1942 and entered into active service 27 October 1942 at Fort Oglethorpe, Georgia. His Military Occupational Specialty was Ammunition Handler. His Military Qualifications included Rifle M1 Sharpshooter and Combat Infantry Badge. He was in the battles of Rhineland Campaign, Normandy and Northern France Campaign. The following decorations were awarded to Long: Europe-African Middle Eastern Theater Service Medal. He left the USA 6 April 1944 for the European-African-Middle Eastern Theater Operation, and returned to USA 2 February 1945. He was discharged 23 July 1945 at Welch Convalescent Hospital, Daytona Beach, Florida with a Certificate of Disability.

LOVE, B. RAYMOND, was born 23 February 1915. He was the son of Carroll T. and Officer W. Love.

He saved in the Calvary of the United States Army, 1941-1945, during WWII.

He was at Camp Forrest when war with Japan started. He remembered sitting in a 1941 Ford car, listening to a radio when they announced the declaration. He went

to camps in Louisiana, Texas, California, and Tennessee for service. He never received orders for overseas duty. He married Joanie Kelley. Their children an Raymond Carroll, Sonya, Melody and April. Raymond is the owner and operator of a restaurant.

LOVE, LEONARD L., was born 16 August 1913. He was the son of Carroll T. and Ollie W. Love. He served his Country

during WW II in the infantry of the United States Army, 1942-1945. He told the story of so many getting seasick on the ship on the way overseas, and also the same on the way back. He remembered the hardships endured during tins tune, sleeping in snow, eating frozen beam. They tried to warm the beans on truck exhausts, however this method was not too successful. He sure got tired of beans. He served in France, Belgium, and Germany. He fought in the Battle of the Bulge. He helped in the liberation of a concentration camp in Germany- He did not talk too much about the war. He said that no one would believe it anyway. He died 20 September 1979, and was buried in the Mt. View Cemetery in Hardin County, Tennessee. Siblings: brothers; Raymond, Tim, Bill, and Pink sisters; Louvenia.

LUKER, OTTO, Serial Number 14 020 523, was a Staff Sergeant in the Company B, 531st Engineers in the Army of the United States. His permanent mailing address was Route 1, West Point, Tennessee. He was born 17 December 1912 in Wayne County, the son of Lee Andrew and Hulda Hollis Luker. His Civilian Occupation was General Farm Hand. He entered into active service 18 September 1940 at Fort McPherson, Georgia. His Military Occupational Specialty was Mess Sergeant. He was in the Algerian, Sicilian and Italian Campaigns. The following decorations were awarded to Luker: European African Middle Eastern Theater Medal, American Defense Medal, Good Conduct Medal, and 3 Bronze Stars. He left the USA August 1942 for the European Theater Operation, and returned to USA 8 November 1942. He was discharged 10 January 1945 at Fort McPherson, Georgia. Otto married Willie McCaig. They had two boys, Danny and Dennis. Otto worked and retired from Chrysler Corporation in Detroit. He died in November 1985. He was buried in the Bethlehem Cemetery in Wayne County, Tennessee. His siblings are Ozro and Dottie Mae Luker Nelson.

LUKER, OZRO, Serial Number 36 523 695, was a Private First Class in the 32nd Infantry Regiment in the Army of the United States. His permanent mailing address was Route 1, West Point, Tennessee. He was born 18 November 1915 in West Point, the son of Lee Andrew and Hulda Hollis Luker. He was single when he entered into active service 15 September 1942 at Fort Cluster, Michigan. His Military Occupational Specialty was Light Mortar Crewman. His Military Qualifications included Combat Infantry Badge. He was in battles in the Aleutian Islands, Eastern Mandates, Luzon, Southern Philippines and Ryukyu. The following decorations were awarded to Luker: Asiatic Pacific Campaign Medal, Good Conduct Medal Philippines Liberation Medal and a Purple Heart while he was with the 7th Infantry Division. He received his wounds in Okinawa 10 April 1945. He left the USA 15 April 1943 for the Asiatic Pacific Theater Operation, and returned to USA 15 September 1945. He was discharged 19 September 1945 at Camp Beale, California. Detroit, Michigan was the address given from which he will seek employment. Ozro married Stella Gallaher. They had five children: Joy Sue, Herbert, Lillie, Teddy and Peggy. He is a member of the V. F. W. His hobbies are hunting and fishing. His siblings are Otto, Dottie Mae Luker Nelson.

LUNA, GOLA A., Serial Number 965 77 38, was an Aviation Ordnance Man, Second Class in the Navy of the United States. He was discharged 8 December 1945 in Jacksonville, Florida. His permanent mailing address was Route 2, Waynesboro, Tennessee. He was born 4 January 1915 in Ethridge, Lawrence County, Tennessee. He was registered with Selective Service Board in Wayne County, Tennessee. He was married when he was inducted 6 October 1943 at Waynesboro and entered into active service 13 October 1943. He held the following ratings: AS, S2C, S1C, AOM3C, and AOM2C. He completed the following Service Schools: AOM Turret School NSTTC, Jacksonville, Florida for eight weeks, and AOM NATTC Memphis, Tennessee for fourteen weeks. The Vessels and Stations that he served on were: NRS, Chattanooga, Tennessee; NTS, Great Lakes, Illinois; NATTC, Memphis, Tennessee; NATTC and NAGS in Jacksonville, Florida. He was issued the USNR Honorable Service Button, Service Lapel Button and Discharge Emblem. He had a high school education. His Civilian Occupation was Repairman for Hudson Motor Car Company, East Jefferson, Detroit, Michigan from March 1942 to October 1943. He and his wife Mary Lou live in Waynesboro, Tennessee.

LUNA, JOHN THOMAS "J.T.", Serial Number 34 366 646, was a Staff Sergeant in 713th Signal Aircraft Warning

Company in the Army of the United States. He entered into active service 9 September 1942 at Fort Oglethorpe, Georgia. On 16 August 1943 he was transferred to foreign service in the Aleutian Islands in the Pacific Theater where he served two years, two months and 22 days as an Information Center Operator of radar equipment to detect enemy aircraft. He was awarded the American Service Medal, Asiatic Pacific Service Medal, World War II Victory Medal and the Good Conduct Medal. He

returned back to the States 9 November 1945 and was honorably discharged 23 November 1945 at Fort McPherson, Georgia. J. T. was born in Hollabaugh Bend on Buffalo River, Allens Creek, Wayne County, Tennessee on 19 December 1920, died 20 February 1972 and is buried in Memorial Gardens in Waynesboro. His parents were Nick Cox and Tessie (Wisdom) Luna. His siblings are Nesbie Luna, Shirley Dixon and Queenie Turman. J. T. was married in 1949 to Rita Jane Brewer, daughter of Walter and Mabel (Stricklin) Brewer. They had four children Joe Darryl, Jancy Belle, Johnita and Talitha Luna.

LUNA, NESBIE CLINTON, Serial Number 34 003 833, was a Private First Class in the 373rd Ordinance MVA in the Army of the United States. His Civilian Occupation was Truck Driver. He was 24 years old and single when he was inducted 12 December 1940. His Military Occupational Specialty was Welder. His Military Qualifications included Rifle Marksman. The following decorations were awarded to Luna: American Theater Ribbon, and American Defense Ribbon. He was discharged 12 September 1944 from Atlanta Ordinance Depot, Atlanta, Georgia with his physical condition being poor. His occupation after service was with Murray Ohio Manufacturing Company in Lawrenceburg, Tennessee Nesbie was born 15 November 1916 in Wayne County, died 24 December 1978 and is buried in Memorial Gardens in Waynesboro. His parents were Nick Cox and Tessie (Wisdom) Luna. His siblings are J. T. Luna, Shirley Dixon and Queenie Turman. Nesbie was married 11 April 1945 to Helen Camillo, originally of Italy and later of Detroit. They had two children, John Clinton and Mary Emily "Dolly" Luna. Nesbie and Helen divorced and he later married Irene Brown Devers and had a stepson James Buford Devers.

LYNCH, CLYDE ALTON, Serial Number 30 64 29, was a Technical Sergeant in the Marine Corps of the United States. His permanent mailing address was Route 5, Waynesboro, Tennessee. His Civilian Occupation was farmer for five years. He was last employed March 1939 on his father's farm. He planted, cultivated and harvested grain, operated all types of machinery and cared for livestock. He had an eighth grade education. Clyde volunteered while he was at CC Camp in East Tennessee. He enlisted in Nashville, Tennessee 17 March 1941 for four years. He was a Gunnery Sergeant at the time of his discharge. His Weapons Qualifications included Rifle Marksman and Pistol Marksman. His duties took him to the South Pa-

cific Area from January 1944 until 2 August 1945. He received a gunshot wound in the neck at Pelelin Island, Palan Islands. He participated in landing, assault, occupation and defense of Pelelin Island, Palan Islands from 15 September until 25 October 1944. He also participated in landing, assault, occupation and defense of Okinawa, Shima, Rynkyer Islands from 1 April 1945 until 2 August 1945. He was discharged at Second Battalion, Seventh Marines, United States Marine Corps Reserve 2 August 1945. He reenlisted 3 August 1945 to serve four more years at Headquarters 7th, 1st Marine Division, FMF, PAC. His Special Military Qualification was Infantry Chief. He served in the Asiatic-Pacific Area from 3 August 1945 until 27 April 1946. He participated in landing, occupation and relief of Japanese Garrison in the Tung Ku-Taku Area, Hopei Province, North China from 30 September 1945 to 12 April 1946. He was discharged 3 April 1947 at Marine Barracks, Norfolk Naval Shipyard, Portsmouth, Virginia. He was issued HS and Honorable Discharge Lapel Button. Marine Corps Combat Correspondent Dispatch: (From Okinawa) -"The Jap sniper who came racing out of his cave had fire as well as smoke in his eyes. "He was plenty mad and sort of bewildered. " said Marine Platoon Sergeant Clyde A. Lynch of Waynesboro, Tennessee. Lynch had flushed the sniper from the cave with a smoke grenade. The Jap, weaponless, rushed out while Lynch was reaching for a second grenade, according to Sergeant Joseph F. Donahue, a Marine Corps Combat Correspondent. "He seemed to want to fight it out, hand to hand," said Lynch, "and we grappled for a few seconds. But all of a sudden, he jerked away and ran back into the cave. " A heavy demolition charge sealed the Jap in the cave. Lynch is the son of Mrs. Mazie Lynch, RFD 5, Waynesboro, Tennessee. " -USMC. After the war, Lynch received congratulations for service and contributions he made toward ultimate victory from General Omar N. Bradley. President Harry Truman sent his heartfelt thanks for Lynch's help in bringing about total defeat of the enemy and said that the Government looks to Lynch and other service men for leadership and example in the future for our county in time of peace. He was born 4 April 1919 in Waynesboro, Tennessee. His parents were Hardie B. Lynch (1885-1972) and Mazie (Clay) Lynch (1892-1954). Both are buried in Mt. Hebron Cemetery, South East Confluence of Rayburn and Indian Creeks. Clyde married Ruby Lynn. They have two children, Brenda Lynch Skimmehorn and Charles Lynch and two grandchildren. They all live in Waynesboro. His siblings are: Carrie

Moore, Katherine Brewer, Virginia Whitten, and Geneva Ray, Lester, Rex, and Edward W. Lynch.

LYNCH, EDWARD W., Serial Number 34 146 880, was a Technician Fourth Grade in Headquarters and Service Troop 117th Cavalry in the Army of the United States. His permanent mailing address was Route 5, Box 71, Waynesboro, Tennessee. He was registered with Selective Service Board in Wayne County, Tennessee. His Civilian Occupation was Truck Driver. He enlisted 4 October 1941 at Fort Oglethorpe, Georgia. His Military Occupational Specialty was Low Speed Radio Operator. His Military Qualifications included Rifle Ex and Pistol Ex. He was in the battles of Rhineland, Rome-Arno, Southern France and Central Europe. The following decorations were awarded to Lynch: Europe-African Middle Eastern Theater Ribbon with 4 Bronze Stars, American Defense Service Medal, Good Conduct Ribbon and Lapel Button. He left the USA 26 September 1942 for the European Theater Operation, Left 26 December 1942 for NATO, Left 13 May 1944 for ETO and returned to USA 12 October 1945. He had a grammar school education. He was discharged 18 October 1945 at Camp Atterbury, Indiana. He was born 22 February 1918 in Clifton, Tennessee died 10 October 1993 at Allenbrooks Nursing Home in Memphis after a long illness and was buried in Memorial Park Southwoods Cemetery in Memphis. His parents were the late Hardy and Mazy Clay Lynch of Waynesboro. His survivors were his wife, Hazel M. Lynch, and son Kenneth Wayne Lynch of Memphis. His siblings who survived him were Carrie Moore, Katherine Brewer, Virginia Whitten, Geneva Ray, and Clyde Lynch all of Waynesboro. Lester Lynch of Memphis and Rex Lynch of Tucson, Arizona.

LYNCH, REX, Serial Number 34 043 124, was a Staff Sergeant with the 235th Army Air Forces Base Unit in the Army of the United States. His permanent mailing address was Route 5, Waynesboro, Tennessee. He was born 9 April 1914 in Wayne County. He was registered with Selective Service Board in Wayne County, Tennessee. His Civilian Occupation was Farmer. He was inducted 25 April 1941 at Fort Oglethorpe, Georgia. His Military Occupational Specialty was Cryptographic Technician. He was in the battles of Normandy, Northern France and Germany. The following decorations were awarded to Lynch: European African Middle Eastern Theater Ribbon with 3 Bronze Stars, American Defense Service Ribbon, and Good Conduct Medal. He left the USA 31 May 1942 for the European Theater Op-

eration, and returned to USA 4 December 1944. He attended the AAF Teletype Maintenance Service School for three weeks in 1942. A lapel button was issued to Lynch. He was discharged 4 June 1945 at Fort McPherson, Georgia. Rex was one of the first four men to volunteered from Waynesboro, Tennessee to serve for his country. Rex went overseas with Head Squadron, 8th Air Force and was stationed at Kingston, England. He spent 18 months there, became ill with asthma and was sent to Oxford Army Hospital. He, then, transferred to 235th Air Force, went to France where he spent the rest of his duty before being sent back to the United States before the war was over. Rex was stationed at El Paso, Texas with big bombers, heading for Japan. The point system was set up and he had enough points to be discharged on 4 June 1945. After his discharge, Rex spent the next thirty years in the grocery business and has been retired for sixteen years. Rex married Helen Edro Peacock of Waynesboro and lives in Tucson, Arizona. To them were born three sons, Rex, Jr., Marcus Kent, of Tucson and Billy Dan of Camp Hill, Pennsylvania. They have four grandchildren, Geoffery, Kristen and Jeanne of Tucson and Billy Dee of Pennsylvania. His parents were Hardy and Mazy Clay Lynch. He had six brothers, four of whom were in the Army at the same time he was. They were Clyde, Lester, Roy, and Edward. He also had four sisters: Carrie Moore, Katherine Brewer, Virginia Whitten and Geneva Ray, .

LYNN, GEORGE H., son of Sam Lynn, grew up in Wayne County and attended school at Waynesboro. He was inducted into the U. S. Navy and spent the next thirty seven months in the service, twenty eight months aboard ship. He served as coxswain in all major theaters of operation and was discharged in 1945 at the Naval Training Center at Memphis, IN.

LYNN, JOHN ANDREW, Serial Number 14 036 020, was a Technician Fifth Grade in Headquarters and Service Troops, 28th Cavalry Reconnaissance Squadron in the Army of the United States. His permanent mailing address was Route 5, Waynesboro, Tennessee. He was registered with Selective Service Board in Wayne County, Tennessee. His Civilian Occupation was Farmer. He was married when he enlisted 26 October 1940 at Fort Oglethorpe, Georgia. His Military Occupational Specialty was Light Truck Driver. His Military Qualifications included Pistol Sharpshooter. John took his basic training in Fort Oglethorpe, Georgia. He served overseas as part of the 28th Cavalry Reconnaissance Squadron. His overseas tour

included Normandy, Northern France, Rhineland, Central Europe and Ardennes. His decorations and citations include Europe-African Middle Eastern Theater Ribbon with 5 Bronze Stars, American Defense Service Medal, and Good Conduct Medal. He left the USA 13 October 1943 for the European Theater Operation, and returned to USA 10 October 1945. He received an Honorable Discharge 15 October 1945 at Camp Atterbury, Indiana. John was born 17 January 1915 in Wayne County. His parents were George and Emily (Cole) Lynn. He had one brother, Hershel Dotson Lynn and three sisters, Mary Cole Lynn Meador Cross, Martha Lynn Owens and Katherine Lynn Davis. John married Mildred Jewel Warren from Perry County, Tennessee, June 25, 1943. To this marriage were born six children, John William, Sally Joyce, Herschel Dee, Geraldine Warren Blalock, George Edward and Michael Brown Lynn. They made their home in Waynesboro, Tennessee. John died 27 March 1991 and was buried in Memorial Gardens in Waynesboro.

MAPLES, NEWTON HUGHES, Serial Number 44 720 490, was with 34th Station Hospital in the Army of the United States. He enlisted 29 May 1945. His Military Occupational Specialty was Automotive Mechanic. His Military Qualifications included MKM M-1 Rifle. He was stationed in Italy and Germany. The following decorations were awarded to Maples: World War II Victory Ribbon, Army Occupational Medal, and Lapel Button. He left the USA 29 November 1945 for Italy, and returned to USA 13 August 1946. He was discharged 24 August 1946 at Fort George G. Meade, Maryland. He was born 26 December 1916, died 16 February 1980 and was buried in Mt. Olive Cemetery in Union Grove, Alabama. His parents were Hathro Bascum and Frances T. Cora (Clark) Maples. His brothers were: Lawrence Conrad, John Howard, and Guy Maples. His sisters were: Parthenia

Clementine Maples Hendrix, Roxie Dimple Maples King, Dixie Margie Maples McClure, Corene Maples Bean and Nellie Louise Maples Kennedy. Newton was married 31 August 1938 to Carlene Price. Their children were: Mary Sue, born 14 August 1939; Jessie Ruth, born 9 June 1941; Martha Ann, born 31 September 1948; Verna Mae, born 14 January 1950; Charles Elbert, born 13 May 1951; and Brenda Lee, born 6 October 1954.

MARTIN, BUFORD WATT, was born 11 June 1912 in Wayne County. He was the son of James William and Eula

(Griggs) Martin. His grandparents were Mr. and Mrs. Cicero Griggs. He was married 26 December 1935 to Louise Kelley, daughter of S. S. and Nona Bell Kelley. Their children were Alwilda and James Harrison, "Jay" Martin, both deceased. He attended the Waynesboro Elementary School and the Wayne County High School. His occupation before the war was owner and operator of a service station in Waynesboro and worked in a Defense Factory in Detroit, Michigan. He had a pilot license for pleasure flying. After the war, he was secretary to Barnett Motor Company in Waynesboro, Owner of Silo Service Station, Supervisory job for the Nashville-Banner and Tennessean, and Insurance agent. He had to quit work because of cancer, passing away 27 May 1960 in the V. A. Hospital in Nashville and was buried in Greenwood Cemetery, West Side, Waynesboro, Tennessee. Buford enlisted 20 January 1944 and entered into active service in the United States Navy 27 January 1944 at Detroit, Michigan. He held the ratings of AS, S 2/C, S 1/C, and SC 3/C. He served on the following Vessels: USNTS Farragut, Idaho; USS LS 468 in the areas of Philippine Liberation, Asiatic Pacific, and American Area. He was awarded the World War II Victory Medal. He was discharged 4 December 1945 at Great Lakes, Illinois as Ships Cook Third Class.

MARTIN, ELZO, was a Private First Class who served with the 333rd Infantry of the United States Army in World War II. He was the son of the late Harrison and Allie (Reeves) Martin. He was a native of Wayne County and a retired mechanic and of the Baptist faith. . He died 27 December 1993 in the Maury Regional Hospital in Columbia, Tennessee and was buried 29 December in the Jackson Cemetery at Cypress Inn, which is located about six miles South of Collinwood and about one mile East of the Natchez Trace. He was 67 years old. His children were Michael Martin of Linden, Kathy White of Memphis and Pamela Souza of Tauton, Massachusetts. His stepdaughters were Judy Cummings and Wanda Savage. His siblings included W. B. Martin of Florence, Alabama; Orville of Lobeville, Ada Greeson and Iveta Cummins, both of Linden; Iva "Billie" Wilson of Nashville, Jesse W. and J. T. Both Jessie and J. T. served in World War II. The following poem was sent to the Wayne County News and was published on Friday, 14 December 1945. My Fallen Comrades by Elzo Martin. Come, living friends, gather round me, Closely listen while I tell the story of my fallen Comrades. These, the boys, we loved so well!" Where are they?" You ask so quickly. Some of them I do not know. Some are safe; some are dead. The thought that hurts me so. In the past, at morning's dawning, "Here", they answered at morning's call. Now, I stop and look around me. So easily count, the number small. Some fell HERE, some fell THERE. Of the others, I wish I knew. I know where some are sleeping, Neath the old red, white and blue. In colors my flag, you speak for them, For here beneath you, my comrade sleep. Yea, in the words that have no sound for silent tongues the crimson speaks. One by one, they fell beside me, For everyone I shed a tear. They are gone but not forgotten; In my memories, they are here. Now we look into the future and the past, we can't forget a price was paid, our prize was won, And Old Glory's waving yet. And now, my friends, let my comrades forever in your memories be. They fought for you and died like heroes, They preserved for us our Liberty.

MARTIN, JAMES DOLPH, "J.D.", 68, of Waynesboro died 11 April 1995 in Wayne County Hospital in Waynesboro, and was buried in Waynesboro Memorial Gardens. He was a native of Wayne County, a U. S. Army Veteran of World War II, a retired factory worker and of the Baptist faith. He was the son of the late Wiley Filmore and Edna (McGee) Martin. Survivors include one sister, Jean Alley of Waynesboro, a half-brother, Jerry Martin

of Florence, a half sister, Connie Smith of Florence., two nephews and four nieces.
Source: Obit in Wayne County News, 19 April 1995.

MARTIN, JAMES ROSS, SR., Serial Number 36 555 350, was a Sergeant in Company A 702nd Tank Destroyer Battalion in the Army of the United States. His permanent mailing address was 19962 Russell Street, Detroit, Michigan. He was born 29 April 1921 in Collinwood, Tennessee. He was registered with Selective Service Board in Wayne County, Michigan. His Civilian Occupation was Aircraft Riveter. He was inducted 6 January 1943 in Detroit, Michigan. His Military Occupational Specialty was Tank Destroyer Crewman. He was in the battles of Normandy, Northern France, Ardennes, Rhineland, and Central Europe. The following decorations were awarded to Martin: American Theater Ribbon, Europe-African Middle Eastern Theater Ribbon with 5 Bronze Stars, Good Conduct Ribbon, World War II Victory Medal, Purple Heart, and Belgium Government Fourragere Citation. He was wounded in Action in Germany 7 October 1944. He left the USA 15 February 1944 for the European Theater Operation, and returned

to USA 20 November 1945. He had a high school education. He was discharged 25 November 1945 at Camp Atterbury, Indiana. James married Frances Carline Smith on 25 December 1946. Their three children are: James Ross Martin, Jr., born 8 February 1948; Charles Richard Martin, born 12 June 1950; and Stephanie Carol Martin, born 27 September 1964.

MARTIN, J.T., was a Private First Class in the United States Army. J. T, was the son of the late Harrison and Allie (Reeves) Martin of Cypress Inn, Tennessee. A native of Wayne County, he died 16 March 1987 in Collinwood, Tennessee. His siblings included W. B. Martin of Florence, Alabama; Orville of Lobeville, Ada Greeson and Iveta Cummins, both of Linden; Iva "Billie" Wilson of Nashville, Jesse W. and Elzo. Both Jesse W. and Elzo served in World War II. J. T. worked in Michigan before the war and was employed in Collinwood after his discharge.

MARTIN, JESSE W., Serial Number 34 013 717, was a Sergeant with the Supply Detachment Division, Section No. 1, Station Complement in the Army of the United States. He was born in Wayne County. His Civilian Occupation was Truck Driver. He was 24 10/12 years old and married when he was inducted 22 January 1941 at Fort Oglethorpe, Georgia. His Military Occupational Specialty was Auto Mechanic. He attended an Ordinance Automotive School to study General Automotive Mechanics in Atlanta, Georgia in 1942. He was not in any battles. A Lapel Button was issued to Martin. He was discharged 28 October 1943 at Camp Mackall, North Carolina in fair physical condition. Jesse was the son of the late Harrison and Allie (Reeves) Martin of Cypress Inn, Tennessee. His siblings included W. B. Martin of Florence, Alabama; Orville of Lobeville, Ada Greeson and Iveta Cummins, both of Linden; Iva "Billie" Wilson of Nashville, and J. T. and Elzo Martin. W. B., J. T. and Elzo served in World War II.

MARTIN, JOEL O., son of Thomas Henry and Martha Alice Jane Smith Martin, was born on October 10, 1919, in Hopewell, Alabama, in Cleburne County. His parents moved to Leoma in Lawrence County, Tennessee, and he attended Lawrence County Schools. He registered in Lawrence County and was inducted into the United States Army in Chattanooga, Tennessee. He served with the 81st Infantry "Wildcat" Division in the South Pacific. The name Wildcat was given to this Division during World War I when a wildcat was captured while this division was in

battle. World War I soldiers named him "Tuffy," and he became their mascot. Joel, a two-year veteran, had been in the Anguar and Peleliu battles. This article was taken from the Division Newspaper, "Out near Bloody Nose Ridge on Peleliu, Sergeant Joel Martin and a patrol ran into about 100 Japs dressed in U. S. Marine uniforms. The Japs opened up and Sergeant Martin was hit in the shoulder. Before being brought in, Sergeant Martin had the satisfaction of seeing the bazooka man in his squad get the Jap who shot him. " The Japs were often noticed wandering through the lines completely equipped with marine uniforms. Everyone had thought they were just another Marine Company. Joel was taken to a General Hospital in New Caledonia and arrived there for his 25th birthday. A week later, a hospital ship took him back to the states. He reached Thayer on November 12, 1944. He was awarded the Purple Heart. The next seven to eight months were spent in the hospital. He was discharged on January 31, 1946 at Camp Blanding, Florida. He left immediately for New Jersey where his fiancee, Sarah, had worked during the war. Joel and Sarah Elizabeth Guttery of Lawrenceburg, Tennessee were married in Natley, New Jersey, on February 3, 1946. She had worked in the Civil Service with the Army Service Forces Finance Division office of Dependency Benefits at Newark from 1942 until 1946. In August 1972, she became an LPN and worked at Wayne County General Hospital and Nelson's Nursing Home until May 31, 1981, when she retired. They settled down in Waynesboro, and Joel worked his first job at J. O. Barnett's "One Stop Store. " On May 30, 1950, he was employed at the Waynesboro Postal Department as a rural mail deliverer and worked afternoons and nights at Helton Drug Company. Joel has been involved in several organizations and received numerous honors. He was second of the local Masonic Lodge about 40 years, Right Worshipful Master Mason of Tennessee,

32nd Degree Scottish Rite Mason, York Rite Mason, Excellent High Priest of Royal Arch Masons, Illustrious Master of Cryptic Mason, Shriners and Eastern Star. Joel and Sarah built their home on Highway 64 east of Waynesboro and raised their five children there: Joel O. Jr., Patricia Ann, Roger Lee, Shelia Gail and Alicia Kay. They are members of the 48 Freewill Baptist Church, where Joel has served as deacon since 1952.

MARTIN, JOHN M., of Collinwood, who served in the US Service as a Cpl. stationed at San Francisco, CA, was awarded the Good Conduct Medal.

MARTIN, LUTHER CARLTON, Serial Number RA 14 216 016, was a Private First Class in the 89th Station Complement Squadron of Army Air Force in the Army of the United States. His permanent mailing address was Collinwood, Tennessee. He was born 15 February 1928 in Florence, Alabama. His Civilian Occupation was Light Truck Driver. He enlisted 20 February 1946 at Fort Oglethorpe, Georgia. His Military Occupational Specialty was Cook. His Military Qualifications included Pistol Expert, April 1946. He was not in any battles. The World War II Victory Medal was awarded to Martin: He left the USA 29 August 1946 for the European Theater Operation, and returned to USA 26 January 1947. He finished eight years in grammar school. He was discharged 19 February 1947 at Fort Dix, New Jersey. Carlton died 16 April 1993 in H. C. A. Hospital in Palatka, Florida. The funeral was held in Collinwood with burial in Memorial Gardens in Collinwood. At the time of his death, the family lived at Route 2, Box 782, Satauma, Florida. His wife is Delores Martin and his children are: Carlton Martin, Jr. of Killen, Alabama, Bobby and Billy, both of Huntsville, Alabama, Michael Wendell Martin of Fayetteville, South Carolina; and Martha Brown of Tuscumbia, Alabama. He had one step daughter, Kim Rouse of Savannah, Georgia. His siblings are: Taylor Martin, Jr., of Collinwood; Betty Smith, Dean Walters, and Marie Brown, all of Collinwood. His parents are the late Joe Taylor and Mamie (Thompson) Martin. Carlton was a member of the Collinwood Masonic Lodge and the Palatka Shriners. He retired from the Air Force in 1967.

MARTIN, MAHON, Serial Number 34 189 076, was a Private with the Military Police in the Army of the United States. He was born in Wayne County. His Civilian Occupation was Farmer. He was 31 10/12 years old when he was inducted 18 February 1942 at Fort Oglethorpe,

Georgia. His Military Occupational Specialty was Basic Assignment. He was discharged 13 October 1943 at Brooks General Hospital, Fort Sam Houston, Texas.

MARTIN, THOMAS J., served as a Cpl. with the 57th Airway Detachment and was discharged, January 11, 1947.

MARTIN, VERNON, Serial Number 34 936 414, was a Corporal with the 1st Quartermaster Company in the Army of the United States. His permanent mailing address was 609 Delmar, Sikeston, Missouri. He was registered with Selective Service Board in Wayne County, Tennessee. His Civilian Occupation was General Farmer. He enlisted 28 July 1944 at Camp Forrest, Tennessee. His Military Occupational Specialty was Light Truck Driver. His Military Qualifications included MKM Rifle. He was in battles in Rhineland, and Central Europe. The following decorations were awarded to Martin: Europe-African Middle Eastern Theater Ribbon with 2 Bronze Stars, Good Conduct Medal, World War II Victory Medal, Army of Occupation Medal in Germany and a Lapel Button. He left the USA 3 January 1945 for the European Theater Operation, and returned to USA 19 June 1946. He had a one-year high school education. He was discharged 25 June 1946 at Camp Atterbury, Indiana. Vernon was born 28 March 1926 in Collinwood, died 12 January 1981, and was buried in Railroad Cemetery. The cemetery is located in the Northeast corner of the intersection of Tennessee Highway 227 and 13 South in the Fairview Community. He was the son of Willie and Madgie (Woods) Martin. He had a sister, Burnsie Martin Griggs. His children were: Judy Barclay of Cookeville, Tennessee; Joan Berry of Iron City; and Janice Martin of Nashville. His occupation after his discharge was farming, carpenter and working for TVA.

MARTIN, VIRGIL L., had the grade of Seaman First Class in the Navy of the United States. He was inducted September 1914 and received his training at Norfolk, Virginia. The USS SAVANNAH was the ship that he served on. He sailed to Cuba, Puerto Rico, Trinidad and Brazil. Then he returned to the USA 6 May 1944 to await his next assignment.

MARTIN, W.B., was a Private First Class in the United States Army. He was inducted 21 November 1942 and received his training in California, Camp Maxey, Texas and Fort George Meade, Maryland. When he went overseas, he landed in North Africa in March 1943 and fought through Sicily. He was in three major engagements

and was also in France with a Military Police Battalion. He was wounded in action on Anzio Beachhead 29 June 1944 and was awarded the Purple Heart. He was the son of the late Harrison and Allie (Reeves) Martin. His siblings included Jesse W., J. T., Elzo, Orville of Lobeville, Ada Greeson and Iveta Cummins, both of Linden; and Iva "Billie" Wilson of Nashville. Brothers Jesse W., Elzo and J. T. served in World War II.

MARTIN, WILLIAM FRANK, Serial Number 34 043 840, was a Staff Sergeant with the 423rd Replacement Company in the Army of the United States. His permanent mailing address was Route 2, Collinwood, Tennessee. He was born 9 May 1915 in Cypress Inn, Tennessee. He was registered with Selective Service Board in Wayne County, Tennessee. His Civilian Occupation was General Farmer. He was inducted 15 May 1941 at Fort Oglethorpe, Georgia. His Military Occupational Specialty was Quartermaster Supply Technician. His Military Qualifications included Sharpshooter Carbine. He was in the battle of Luzon. The following decorations were awarded to Martin: American Defense Service Ribbon, Good Conduct Medal, American Theater Ribbon, Philippine Liberation Ribbon, Asiatic Pacific Theater Ribbon with one Bronze Service Star and a Lapel Button. He left the USA 10 May 1943 for the Asiatic-Pacific Theater Operation, and returned to USA 22 November 1945. He had a seventh grade education. He was discharged 4 December 1945 at Camp Chaffee, Arkansas.

MARTIN, WILLIAM J., Serial Number 34 375 353, was inducted into the Army of the United States 3 October 1942, and was released from active duty, and transferred to the Enlisted Reserve Corps, and returned to Waynesboro, Tennessee. On 17 October 1942, he was called to active duty and reported to Fort Oglethorpe, Georgia.

MATHENY, WALTER JUNIOR, volunteered and enlisted in the United States Army. He was born near Collinwood, Tennessee. His father was Walter Matheny (18 December 1866- 30 November 1931). His mother was Cordie Pennington Matheny (8 April 1881 - 19??). They are buried in McGlamery Cemetery in Wayne County. His siblings are Dicie Kephart, Bertha (died young), Elvin Matheny (a World War II Veteran killed in Action), and Vera Jean Sandy of Florence, Alabama.

MATHIS, EDD LEWIS, Serial Number 34 922 024, was a Private with the Service Command Unit 3402, Special

Training Unit in the Army of the United States. His Civilian Occupation was Farmer. He was 36 1/12 years old and married when he was inducted 22 January 1944 . He was discharged 11 July 1944 at Fort Jackson, South Carolina. Edd, son of Lewis and Susie (Hickerson) Mathis, was born 6 December 1907 in Hohenwald, Tennessee, and died July 1967. He was buried at Phillips Chapel Cemetery, on the Lawson Bundrant farm, five miles South of Green River. He married Lucille Lacher. His children are Helen and Tubby Mathis.

MATHIS, FRED A., SR., Serial Number 34 494 868, was a Private First Class with Company A, 240th Military Police

Battalion in the Army of the United States. His permanent mailing address was Flatwoods, Tennessee. He was born 7 January 1920 in Wayne County. He was registered with Selective Service Board in Wayne County, Tennessee. His Civilian Occupation was Carpenter's Helper. He was married when he was inducted at Fort McPherson, Georgia. He received his basic training at Fort Custer, Battle Creek, Michigan. His Military Occupational Specialty was Military Police and Infantry Basic Training. His Military Qualifications included Sharpshooter Pistol and Sharpshooter Rifle. The following decorations were awarded to Mathis: American Service Medal, Good Conduct Ribbon and World War II Victory Medal. He was discharged 4 February 1946 at Fort McPherson, Georgia. As a Military Policeman, Fred served in Hyde Park, New York. He assisted in the enforcement of military laws, regulations, maintenance of order and control of traffic, in and around the home of Franklin Delano Roosevelt. He assisted in furnishing information regarding the locations of various installations within the estate to the proper authorities. His job include guarding and patrolling the personal property of the President and his family, as well as controlling the circulation of authorized visitors in the estate. He worked in conjunction with the United States Secret Service. He preformed these duties both on foot and in vehicles, and had the knowledge in the use and care of such weapons as the pistol, riot gun and sub-machine gun. Prior to entering the service, Fred was with the CC Camp from 5 July 1939 to 19 April 1941 at Bristol, Tennessee with Company 420. He was also with Company 448 in Lawrenceburg, Tenn. This company helped lay the rocks atop Lookout Mountain. Fred was the son of David Leroy and Duffie (Hickerson) Mathis. His brothers were Oscar, Perry, J. B., Floyd and Bernice Mathis. His sisters were Pauline, Emma, Lillian, Lillie and Berdie Mathis. He was married May 1941 to Ruby Lomax. His children are Janice Stooksberry and Allen Mathis. There are four grandchildren and four great grandchildren. Fred died May 1982 from a stroke on his way to the VA Hospital and was buried in Whitehead Cemetery in the Topsy Community. His grandparents were Bryant and Sally (Hickerson) Mathis and John and Addie (Treadwell) Hickerson.

MATHIS, HUBERT M., Serial Number 34 936 481, was a Private in Company C 16th Infantry Regiment, 1st Infantry Division in the Army of the United States. His permanent mailing address was Box 281, Clifton, Tennessee. He was born 27 June 1919 in Peters Landing, Tennessee. He was registered with Selective Service Board in Wayne County, Tennessee. His Civilian Occupation was Heavy Truck Driver. He was married with four dependents when he was inducted 28 July 1944 at Camp Forrest, Tennessee. His Military Occupational Specialty was Rifleman. His Military Qualifications included Expert M1 Rifle and Combat Infantryman Badge. He was in the battles of Ardennes Campaign and Rhineland Campaign. The following decorations were awarded to Mathis: Europe-African Middle Eastern Theater Ribbon with 2 Bronze Stars, Purple Heart, Good Conduct Medal and a Lapel Button. He was wounded in action 24 February 1945 it the European Theater. He left the USA 3 January 1945 for the European Theater Operation, and returned to USA 12 April 1945. He had an eighth grade education. He was discharged 1 August 1945 at Nichols General Hospital, Louisville, Kentucky. Hubert was the son of James H. and Pearlie Mae (Butler) Mathis. He was born 27 June 1919 in Peters Landing, Tennessee, and died 27 January 1993 at home in Savannah. He was buried in Hardin County Memory Gardens. His siblings are: Grace Hardin of Florence, Alabama, and Laura Brown of Stuart, Florida, His children are: Wilda Mabry of

Savannah, Betty Reno of Tishmingo, Mississippi; Dale Powers of Dennis, Mississippi; Jerry Mathis of Lake Stevens, Washington; Hubert M., Jr., Jimmy, and Joe Mathis of Savannah. His stepchildren are, Georgie Jarrett, Teresa Pickens and Bobby Brewer of Savannah, There were 12 grandchildren and 15 great grandchildren.

MATHIS, OSCAR LEROY, was born 3 August 1916 and died 30 November 1948. He enlisted in the United States Navy

21 September 1942 and was discharged 10 October 1945. He was a Carpenter's Mate second Class. His duty stations were: NTS Great Lakes, Illinois; NTS, Memphis, Tennessee; NATTC- Chicago, Illinois; NATTC- Memphis; and NAS, Coco Solo, Panama Canal Zone. He was the son of David Leroy and Duffie (Hickerson) Mathis. His grandparents were Bryant and Sally (Hickerson) Mathis and John and Addie (Treadwell) Hickerson. His brothers were Perry, Fred, J. B., Floyd and Bernice Mathis. His sisters were Pauline, Emma, Lillian, Lillie and Berdie Mathis. He married Maureen Haley 7 January 1944 in Millington, Tennessee. Their children are: Patricia Marlene Mathis, born 13 July 1946 and Daniel Leroy Mathis, born 2 March 1948. The grandchildren are: Jason Polley, born 23 September 1970; Gena Polley, born 6 July 1974; Mindy Mathis, born 19 July 1973; Emily Mathis, born 5 April 1977; and Daniel Mathis, born 22 May 1980.

MATHIS, PERRY DAVID, Serial Number 34 506 472, was a Private in the Administrative Section Headquarters Company, 1620th Service Unit in the Army of the United States. His permanent mailing address was Route 6, Waynesboro, Tennessee. His Civilian Occupation was Farmer. He was 19 9/12 years old and single when he was inducted 18 January 1943 at Fort Oglethorpe, Georgia. His Military Occupational Specialty was Mes-

senger. His Military Qualifications included MM M1 Rifle. He was not in any battles. He was discharged 27 August 1943 at Camp McCoy, Wisconsin with his physical condition being poor. Perry, son of Dave Leroy and Duffie (Hickerson) Mathis, was born 2 May 1923 in Flatwoods. His brothers were Oscar, Fred, J. B., Floyd and Bernice Mathis. His sisters were Pauline, Emma, Lillian, Lillie and Berdie Mathis. He was married 16 August 1947 to Norah Whitehead. Their children are Elsie and Martha Ann Mathis. His grandparents were Bryant and Sally (Hickerson) Mathis and John and Addie (Treadwell) Hickerson.

MATLOCK, J.W., Serial Number 34 713 924, was inducted into the Army of the United States about 1942 at Ft. Oglethorpe, Georgia, and spent his Army days in Georgia. On 30 April 1943, he was called to active duty and reported to Fort Oglethorpe, Georgia. He was released from active duty, and transferred to the Enlisted Reserve Corps, and returned to Waynesboro, Tennessee. After his discharge, he married and settled at Lepanto, Arkansas. J. W. Matlock was born in 1923 near Waynesboro, Tennessee, to William J. and Estella Walker Matlock. On November 23, 1996, J. W. died at his home and is buried in Garden Point Cemetery in Osceola. He has a son, Robert Glen, who lives in Osceola, and a sister, Esther Mae Reeves of Waynesboro, Tennessee.

MATNEY, JOHN A., Serial Number 34 378 436, was a Private First Class with Battery A 883rd Field Artillery Battalion in the Army of the United States. His permanent mailing address was Route 4, Waynesboro, Tennessee. He was born 21 September 1921 in Wayne County. He was registered with Selective Service Board in Wayne County, Tennessee. His Civilian Occupation was General Farmer. He was inducted 21 October 1942 and entered into active service 4 November 1942 at Fort

Oglethorpe, Georgia. His Military Occupational Specialty was Light Truck Driver. His Military Qualifications included Carbine Sharpshooter. He was in the battles of Rhineland, and Central Europe. The following decorations were awarded to Matney: American Theater Ribbon, Europe-African Middle Eastern Theater Ribbon with 2 Bronze Stars, Good Conduct Ribbon and World War II Victory Medal. He left the USA 8 January 1945 for the European Theater Operation, and returned to USA 1 March 1946. He finished one year of high school. He was discharged 6 March 1946 at Camp Atterbury, Indiana.

MATNEY MARCUS E., Serial Number 44 071 210, was a Technician Fifth Grade in the Infantry in the Military Occupation Army of the United States. He was born 13 December 1914 on Factory Creek in Wayne County. He was inducted 14 March 1945 at Fort Oglethorpe, Georgia. His Military Occupational Specialty was General Carpenter. The following decorations were awarded to Matney: Asiatic-Pacific Theater Ribbon, World War II Victory Medal, Meritorious Unit Medal, and Army of Occupation Medal. He spent eleven months in Japan. He was discharged 18 October 1946 at Fort Sheridan, Illinois. Marcus was the son of Mosie and Elvie Matney. His siblings were: Lucille Ray, Fronie Clayton, Edward, Equilla Springer, Eugene, Emma Nola Andrews, Reba Fisher, Marshall, Sue Gatlin and Tommy Matney. He married Emma Nola Crews. Their children are Marcus Dale, Nona Faye (deceased) and Melba Joyce Self.

MATNEY, WILLIAM T., Serial Number 34 042 227, was a Private First Class in Company B, 97th Chemical Mortar Battalion in the Army of the United States. His permanent mailing address was Route 4, Waynesboro, Tennessee. He was born 12 April 1919 in Wayne County. He was registered with Selective Service Board in

Wayne County, Tennessee. His Civilian Occupation was Farmer. He was married with one dependent when he was inducted 16 April 1941 at Fort Oglethorpe, Georgia. His Military Occupational Specialty was Supply Technician. He was in the battles of Central Europe. The following decorations were awarded to Matney: Europe-African Middle Eastern Theater Ribbon, Good Conduct Medal and Lapel Button. He left the USA 3 February 1945 for the European Theater Operation, and returned to USA 6 July 1945. He was discharged 5 November 1945 at Camp Polk, Louisiana.

MAY, ROBERT UNDERWOOD, was born in 1910 to David Montoe and Catherine Broadfoot May. He spent six

years in the Navy. Much of his service time was spent aboard a submarine destroyer assigned to the coast of Alaska and Japan.

After his military service Robert married Evie Borden. For many years they lived on their farm just north of the Alabama state line in Wayne County. He died in 1995.

McCLAIN, ALTON A., was born 22 January 1922 in Pemiscott County, Steel, Missouri. He was the son of Hugh L. and Lester Morton McClain of Route 2, Waynesboro, Tennessee. He completed the eight grade at Ray School on Hog Creek. He was drafted into service in November 1942 and did his basic training at Camp Van Dorn, Mississippi. Then he was transferred to Camp Maxey, Texas, then sent to Fort Dix, New Jersey where he was sent to Europe. He served with the 395th Infantry in the 99th Division and was a Private First Class. He was in the battle of the Bulge, (the break through in Belgium.) PFC McClain was discharged 20 January 1946. Alton had three sisters, Lottie, Monnie, and Josephine McClain and two brothers, Vernon and Arnold McClain. He married Jackie Doctorman of Toledo,

Ohio. They had six children: Garry, David, Jeffery, Richard, Sharon and Cathey McClain. Alton died 5 July 1987 from a heart attack and is buried in Ottawa Hills Cemetery in Toledo, Ohio.

McCLAIN, CALVIN, was a World War II veteran stationed in Tacoma, Washington. He was born in Waynesboro, Ten-

nessee, on December 18, 1917. He was the son of Russ McClain and Mary Elizabeth Brusth McClain. He married Christine Donegan, daughter of Walter and Blanche Hart Donegan. She was from Waynesboro, Tennessee. They had four children: Mary Elizabeth McClain Skelton, Hubert McClain, James McClain and Butch McClain. His brothers are Hubert, James, Edd and Arlie. His sisters are Lillian and Betty. Calvin died on August 4, 1986. He was buried in Mountain View Memorial Park in Tacoma, Washington. Calvin McClain.

McCLAIN, REX JEWELL, Serial Number 44 020 039, was a Private First Class in Company 1, 271st Infantry in the Army of the United States. His permanent mailing address was Waynesboro, Tennessee. He was born 24 February 1921 in Waynesboro, Tennessee. He was registered with Selective Service Board in Wayne County, Tennessee. His Civilian Occupation was Inspector. He was married with three dependents when he was inducted 17 August 1944 at Camp Forrest, Tennessee. His Military Occupational Specialty was Machine Gunner. His Military Qualifications included Combat Infantryman Badge. He was in the battles of Ardennes, and Rhineland. The following decorations were awarded to McClain: Purple Heart, Europe-African Middle Eastern Theater Ribbon with 2 Bronze Battle Stars, Lapel Button and Emblem. He was Wounded in Action in Germany 28 February 1945. He left the USA 8 January 1945 for the European Theater Operation, and returned to USA 15 May 1945. He finished one year high school. He was discharged 24 September 1945 at Camp Butler Convalescent Hospital, North Carolina with a Certificate of Disability. His parents are Virgil Slaton and Sarah "Sally" (Patterson) McClain. He married Osa Prater. Their children are Linda Kay, George Slaton and Nancy Ann McClain.

McCROY, MALCOLM KENNETH, was a Seaman First Class in the United States Navy. He was born 16 April 1925 in West Point, Tennessee. He was inducted 5 December 1941 and received his basic training at Great Lakes, Illinois. He was in battles in the Coral Sea, Guadalcanal, Talangi, and Savo Islands. The following decorations were awarded to McCroy: European Theater Ribbon, Atlantic Theater Ribbon and Pacific Theater Ribbon with 7 Stars. He was also in Nova Scotia, Iceland, Ireland and Scotland. He was stationed on the USS NEVILLE in the North Atlantic and Europe. In April 1942 he saw active service in the Pacific Ocean in New Zealand, Australia, New Heberdies, New Caladonia, and Frendley Islands. He was discharged 18 June 1945. Malcolm's parents were David Emmett and Bess (Williams) McCroy. His siblings are: Lorene Brewer, Dolly Dixon, Marguerite Stafford, Hallie Smith, Glenn, Freddie Jane and Emmett Jr. He was married 27 December 1944 to Nadine Dixon. Their Children are Kennie Frances Parker, Ronnie and Eddie McCroy. He was a Methodist minister. Malcolm died 26 June 1986 and was buried in Shawnetee Cemetery in Collinwood.

McCURRY, FRANK, Serial Number 34 494 871, was a Private First Class in Company E 184th Infantry in the Army of the United States. He was registered with Selective Service Board in Wayne County, Tennessee. His Civilian Occupation was General Farmer. He was inducted 22 November 1942 and entered into active service 29 November 1942 at Fort Oglethorpe, Georgia. His Military Occupational Specialty was Automatic Rifleman. His Military Qualifications included Combat Infantryman. He was in the battles in the Aleutian Islands, Eastern Mandates, Southern Philippines, and Ryukus. The following decorations were awarded to McCurry: Purple Heart, Good Conduct Ribbon, Philippine Liberation Ribbon and two Bronze Stars, Asiatic Pacific Ribbon with four Bronze Service Stars and one Bronze Arrowhead, and World War II Victory Medal. He was wounded in the Asiatic Pacific Theater 8 April 1945. He left the USA 11 June 1943 for the Asiatic Pacific Theater Operation, and returned to USA 16 November 1945. McCurry as an automatic rifleman, loaded, aimed and fired the rifle to provide fire power support to tactical units. He fired either semi-automatically or in short burst, as the situation demanded and then disassembled, cleaned, oiled, and reassembled the piece. McCurry served 28 months in the Asiatic Pacific Theater of Operations. He was discharged 29 November 1945 at Camp Chaffee, Arkansas. He had a seventh grade education. Frank was born 23 May 1921 in Wayne County and died 17 October 1983 in Waynesboro. His parents were Elmer and Mary (Creecy) McCurry. Frank worked at General Motors for twenty-five years before retiring in 1976 and returning to Waynesboro. He never married.

McCUTCHEON, CARLIE D., was born September 26, 1921, in the Culps Chapel Community in Perry County, TN. My parents are Wade and Ottie (Creasy) McCutcheon. My brothers are Henry, J. D. and Edward McCutcheon and my sisters are Kathleen Howell and Edna Cole. My brother, Edward, served in the Korean War and my brother, Henry, served in World War II during the same period of time I served.

I joined the C. C. Camp. I had a girl friend during this time. She was Miss Bonnie Powell, daughter of "Mr. Jack and Miss Nancy Powell". Bonnie and I were married, February 9, 1942, while I was still in the C. C. Camp.

In, 1944, 1 was drafted into the military and served in the U. S. Navy. My tour of duty was mostly aboard the ship, LST 574, in the South Pacific Ocean. I was honorably discharged in 1946. My brother-in-law, Coy Powell, served in the army and was killed during the war in Holland. After receiving my discharge, I returned to Perry County to the farm, my wife, parents and siblings.

My sister, Kathleen, was married to A. B. Howell. She and their young daughter, Diane, were killed in a tragic automobile accident, one Sunday night on their way to church. My other sister, Edna married Harold Cole and they have lived in Waynesboro all their married lives. They have a son, Thomas, who grew up at Waynesboro.

My wife and I moved to Waynesboro in 1950. 1 did carpenter work and refinished furniture for awhile, then was employed at Genesco, where I worked for eighteen years, until I retired due to health problems. In 1982 my wife died. We were not blessed with children, but had a truly wonderful life together. Life has been good.

I am a member of the Waynesboro Church of Christ and the American Legion. I try to be faithful to my God and my country and treat my friends and comrades with respect. I live alone and take care of my responsibilities very well. I am proud to have been able to donate such a small part to this book.

McDONALD, DON MACK, Serial Number 34 936 469, was a Sergeant in Company A, 242nd Infantry in the Army of the United States. His permanent mailing address was Route 2, Clifton, Tennessee. He was born 14 January 1925 in Clifton, Tennessee, the son of William (Willie) McDonald and Cora Conway McDonald. He was registered with Selective Service Board in Wayne County, Ten-

nessee. His Civilian Occupation was General Farm Hand. He was inducted 28 July 1944 at Camp Forrest, Tennessee. His Military Occupational Specialty was Rifle NCO. His Military Qualifications included MKM M1 Rifle and Combat Infantryman Badge. He was in the battles of Rhineland, and Central Europe. The following decorations were awarded to McDonald: European African Middle European Theater Ribbon, Army Occupation Medal (Germany), Good Conduct Ribbon, World War II Victory Medal and Lapel Button. He left the USA 6 January 1945 for France, and returned to USA 4 July 1946. He finished two years of high school. He was discharged 8 July 1946 at Fort George G. Meade, Maryland. Don married Louise and they had a son, William. He is buried near Detroit. His siblings are Vernal McDonald Morrow and Eva McDonald Warren.

McDONALD, DORIS C., Serial Number 34 022 575, was a Technician Fifth Grade in 725th Antiaircraft Artillery

Searchlight Battery in the Army of the United States. His permanent mailing address was Route 3, Waynesboro, Tennessee. He was born 27 July 1915 in Wayne County. He was registered with Selective Service Board in Wayne County, Tennes-

see. His Civilian Occupation was General Farm Hand. He was inducted 25 February 1941 at Fort Oglethorpe, Georgia. His Military Occupational Specialty was Searchlight Crewman. He was in the battles of Bismarck-Archipelago and Luzon. The following decorations were awarded to McDonald: American Defense Service Ribbon, Good Conduct Medal, Philippine Liberation Ribbon, Asiatic-Pacific Ribbon and two Bronze Service Stars, and Lapel Button. He left the USA 23 January 1942 for the Asiatic-Pacific Theater Operation, and returned to USA 17 December 1944. He left the USA again 28 February 1945 for the Asiatic-Pacific Theater Operation, and returned to USA 13 August 1945. He finished two years of high school. He was discharged 21 August 1945 at Camp Chaffee, Arkansas.

MCDONALD, HOMER, Serial Number 34 378 432, was a Private First Class in Battery B, 348th Field Artillery Battal-

ion in the Army of the United States. His permanent mailing address was Route 3, Waynesboro, Tennessee. He was born 4 October 1917 in Waynesboro, Tennessee. He was registered with Selective Service Board in Wayne County, Tennessee. His Civilian Occupation was General Farm Hand. He was inducted 21 October 1942 and entered into active service 4 November 1942 at Fort Oglethorpe, Georgia. His Military Occupational Specialty was Light Truck Driver. His Military Qualifications included MM Rifle and MM Carbine. He was in the battles of Rome, Arno, Northern Apennines and Po Valley. The following decorations were awarded to McDonald: Europe-African Middle Eastern Theater Ribbon with 3 Bronze Stars. He left the USA 12 April 1944 for the European Theater Operation, and returned to USA 5 August 1945. He had a eighth grade education. He was discharged 11 August 1945 at Fort McPherson, Georgia. Homer's parent were Alvin and Clara (Ray)

McDonald. He had one brother, Doris and he was in WWII too. He married Mavis Warren. Their children are: Barbara Holt of Bloomington, Indiana, Wanda Durham of Christiana, Darlene Ables of Louisville, Kentucky and John McDonald of Waynesboro. Homer and Mavis live on Lower Green River in Wayne County. Mr. McDonald died 10 May 1997 at his home and was buried in Memorial Gardens in Waynesboro with Masonic and Military Rites. He was a retired factory worker and farmer, a fifty year member of the Masonic Lodge and of the Baptist faith. Besides the above mentioned family, he was survived by eight grandchildren and four great-grandchildren.

Source: Wayne County News, 17 May 1997.

McDONALD, LEONARD, was a Private First Class in the United States Army. He was inducted 11 November 1943 and was discharged 18 April 1945. Leonard was the son of Jim and Rachel McDonald. He was married 22 October 1949 to Thelma Harville. They had one son Freeman Eugene McDonald. Leonard died 20 July 1985 and was buried in Neil Cemetery in Hardin County, Tennessee.

McFALL, DOUGAL, Serial Number 34 506 505, was a Private First Class in 96th Fighter Control Squadron in the Army of the United States. His permanent mailing address was Route 1, Lutts Tennessee. He was born 2 February 1923 in Lutts, Tennessee to George and Ola (White) McFall. He was registered with Selective Service Board in Wayne County, Tennessee. His Civilian Occupation was General Farmhand. He was married when he was inducted 18 January 1943 and entered into active service 25 January 1943 at Fort Oglethorpe, Georgia. His Military Occupational Specialty was Guard Patrolman. He was not in any battles. The following decorations were awarded to McFall: American Theater Ribbon, Asiatic-Pacific Theater Ribbon with 2 Bronze Stars, Good Conduct Ribbon and World War II Victory Medal. He left the USA 23 May 1944 for the China Burma India Theater Operation, and returned to USA 1 November 1945. He was discharged 8 January 1946 at SAD AAF Personnel Distribution Center in San Antonio, Texas.

McFALL, JESSIE, of Clifton enlisted in the U. S. Army, October 21, 1941. He served with the AAF Redistribution Station #2 at Miami Beach and became a member of the permanent party personnel. After receiving his training, he spent 31 months in the Asiatic-Pacific Theater. January 12, 1945, an article in the Wayne

County News, stated that he had been presented the Good Conduct Medal. His wife, Eva L. lived at Clifton, Tn.

McFALL, LAWRENCE S., Serial Number 34 040 786, was a Technician Fifth Grade in 2nd Platoon 312nd Quartermaster Sales Company in the Army of the United States. His permanent mailing address was Route 4, Florence, Alabama. He was born 16 March 1906 in Lutts, Tennessee. He was registered with Selective Service Board in Wayne County, Tennessee. His Civilian Occupation was Teacher. He was inducted 3 April 1941 at Fort Oglethorpe, Georgia. His address at time of enlistment was Route 1, Cypress Inn, Tennessee. His Military Occupational Specialty was Military Policeman. His Military Qualifications included MM Rifle. He was not in any battles. The following decorations were awarded to McFall: Good Conduct Ribbon, Europe-African Middle Eastern Theater Ribbon, Defense Service Medal and Lapel Button. He left the USA 20 December 1942 for the European Theater Operation, and returned to USA 12 September 1945. He finished two years of college. He was discharged 15 September 1945 at Fort McPherson, Georgia. Lawrence's parents were Elias and Hettie Margaret McFall. He is retired after many years teaching in the Wayne County School System.

McGEE, C. G., Serial Number 44 040 706, was a Private in Company F, 210th Infantry Training Branch of the Army of the United States. His permanent mailing address was Route 3, Lutts, TN. He was born 6 February 1926 in Lutts. He was registered with Selective Service Board in Wayne County, Tennessee. His Civilian Occupation was General Farm Hand. He was inducted 31 August 1944 at Fort Oglethorpe, Georgia. His Military Occupational Specialty was Basic MOS (521). He was discharged 4 January 1945 at Fort McPherson, Georgia. He received a Lapel Button.

McGEE, C.G., was a Private in Company F, 210th Infantry Training Branch of the Army of the United States. His permanent mailing address was Route -3. Lutts. Tennessee. He was born 6 February 1926 in Lutts. He was registered with Selective Service Board in Wayne County, Tennessee. His Civilian Occupation was General Farm Hand. He was inducted August 1944 at Fort Oglethorpe, Georgia. His Military Occupational Specialty was basic MOS (521). He was discharged 4 January 1945 at Fort McPherson, Georgia. He received a lapel Button.

McGEE, EARL W., served his country for a total of five years. He first entered when he was sixteen years of age. After this was discovered he was given an honorable discharge and sent home for being under age. He later joined the Air Force during WWII. After service he began attending schools to prepare him for a his Bachelor's Degree at Randolph Macon College in Virginia and graduated with the highest average on record. He completed requirement for his Doctorate Degree at the University of Kentucky. He taught at Alabama for about 33 years before he retired. He passed away in 1995.

McGEE, FOSTER, Serial Number 6 928 716 Regular Army Reserve, was a Private First Class in the Regular Army Reserve; Air Corps. of the United States. He enlisted 13 September 1940 at Fort McDowell, California. His prior service as a Private in the Air Corps Unasgd (Unassigned?), was from 10 November 1937 to 13 September 1940. His Civilian Occupational was Mechanic. He was discharged 12 December 1940 at Headquarters, Fourth Corps Area, Atlanta, Georgia, so that he could reenlist in the Regular Army. He was a Staff Sergeant with Base Headquarters, 17th Air Base Squadron, Hickman Field, T. H. Foster was born 7 March 1918 in Collinwood, Tennessee to John G. and Ella (Collaway) McGee. He was a member of a family of eight children: John Ella McGee Patterson, Calla Mae McGee, Gypsy McGee Branson, Edna Earl McGee Thompson, Frances McGee Farris, N. C. McGee, and Ted W. McGee. Foster lived in Collinwood until his second year of high school. At this time he decided to leave school and tour the USA. He and three boys left and were gone almost a year. After this tour, he joined the Army. He was sent to Hawaii. His tour of duty was over just before Pearl Harbor was bombed. The Army was not his choice so he came home to work for awhile. He later joined the Air Force. He spent most of his time in Germany and Tripoli. He married Dorothea, a German girl, with two sons, named Rainer and Helga, which he adopted. They had one son, Foster McGee, Jr. Leaving Germany when he retired, he brought his family to the USA to settle in Colorado Springs, Colorado. While there his wife died and was buried in Colorado. Foster was a Mess Sergeant in the service. Since he always enjoyed cooking, he leases a restaurant in Jackson Hole, Wyoming in the summer time and goes to Scottsdale, Arizona in the Winter. He married Sylvia, a lady from Scottsdale, built a home there and continues this same pattern each year.

McGEE, H.D., had the grade of V-C USNR Gunners Mate, First Class in the Navy of the United States. His permanent mailing address was Route 5, Waynesboro, Tennessee. He was born 12 August 1925 in Wayne County. His last employer before he entered service was Theodore McGee, Route 5, Waynesboro and his job was farming. He was married when he volunteered and enlisted 7 August 1943 at Pulaski, Tennessee. He held the following ratings: AS, S2/C, S 1/C, GM 3/C, GM 2/C AND GM 1/C. The Vessels and Stations that he served on were: Naval Training Center, Great Lakes, Illinois; USS ELIZABETH C. STANTON, USS LST no. 386; and USS Eldridge (DC-173). The following decorations were awarded to McGee: World War II Victory Medal, Asiatic Pacific Ribbon, American Theater Ribbon, and Europe-African Middle Eastern Theater Ribbon with 2 Bronze Stars. He was discharged 9 December 1945 at US Naval Personnel Separation Center, Nashville, Tennessee. H. D. took his boot training at Great Lakes, Illinois. He was assigned to active duty in the Mediterranean Theater of Operations in November 1943. He saw action at Angio, then was later transferred to duty in England where he was at the time of D-Day Invasion of Normandy. H. D. married Eastaline Buttrey of Nashville. His parents were Mr. and Mrs. T. R. McGee of Route 5, Waynesboro, Tennessee.

McGEE, JAMES GRADY, I was born October 2, 1926 between California Branch and Holly Creek. My parents were William Edd McGee and Ollie Nelson McGee. I was raised in the California Branch and Bethlehem area and lived near West Point for awhile. There were eight children, two girls and six boys, but one boy died at birth. My four brothers served in the service, two of them retired with 20 years in the Air Force. My great-grand father was Francis Marion McGee, who served in the Civil War Company G Regiment 10 Tennessee volunteers. He went into service April 13, 1862 and was discharged 1865. His widow was Emily Wade Morrow McGee.

I served in the army in 1945 and 1946. I went through training at Camp Blanding, Florida and Ft. Belvoir, Virginia near Washington D.C. On my 19th birthday, I landed on Leyte. I served in the South Pacific and in Guam with the 20th Air Force.

After I was discharged from the service, I went to college for two years. On December 24, 1948, I married Wilma L. Duren McGee and went to work in Indiana for Sears Roebuck & Company. Later, they wanted to send me to work in Chicago so I moved back to Wayne County and have been here ever since. I worked for Nowlin Hardware Company for awhile, and then later went to work for Shull Truckline working in the office. Later, I started driving one of the trucks, because I could make more money. Also, I went into the Grocery business. When I sold the Grocery store, I built a feed mill and elevator, which was known as Waynesboro Grain & Elevator. At this time, I raised and fed chickens, turkeys, hogs and cattle. Also, I contracted and built houses. In 1966, some of my customers that traded with me asked me to run for County Trustee. After talking with some people and getting some encouragement, I decided to try for it. At that time I was pretty green on politics. I only had about six or seven weeks to campaign door to door before the election. At that time the old paper ballots were used and it took all night for them to be counted at the City Hall. They were getting through about the time the shoe factory people were going to work. I was lucky enough to win by a narrow margin. The people of Wayne County were good to me, they let me serve 20 years (1966-1986) as County Trustee and I thank the people very much.

I have served on different types of boards. I was Service Officer for ten years and I am now the American Legion Service Officer. Also, I have served as Treasure of the American Legion Post 130. I have served as Commander several times. One of the most satisfying committees I serve on is the Big Brothers. We helped needy children and the elder people at Christmas with food, shoes or whatever they needed. I have seen some sad situations. I served on the Tennessee Opportunity Program, which is a federal training program. I was Chairman of this board for about 22 or 24 years. I have been to Washington D.C. to help this program get a several million dollar budget approved. Also I have been to other cities to get budgets approved for this Program.

My wife and I still live on Chalk Creek, where we moved to in the early 60's. We purchased my father in-law, Bill Duren's farm. Also, we purchased Monroe Daniel, Orbie Fowler and Eunice Brewer's farms, all on Chalk Creek. It is a great place to live. My wife and I have two children: Jerry Wayne born September 29, 1950 and LaDonna born August 10, 1966. Jerry married Shirley Malone and they have two children: Jason Wayne born December 4,1973 and Jennifer Ann born March 3, 1975. Jerry served a term in the Vietnam War. LaDonna married Timothy Lee Weaver and they have six boys: Thomas James (T.J.) born December 26, 1982, Colby Jake born July 24, 1990, Taylor Channing and Tanner Chance born May 27, 1992, Christian Isaiah born April 27, 1997, Carson Lee born August 14, 1999. In 1986, I retired and now I raise cattle, enjoy camping and spending time with my grandchildren. I am currently active with the American Legions Post 130.

McGEE, JOHN W., JR., Sergeant, age 23, son of Mrs. Mary McGee, Route 1, Lawrenceburg, Tennessee, a ball turret gunner on a B-24 Liberator based in Italy returned from a mission to Vienna in a battered and scarred bomber of the Fifteenth Army Air Force.
Source: Wayne County News.

McGEE, LOYD GEORGE, Serial Number 34 723 378, was a Private First Class in 6702 Second Leadership and

Battle Training School Replacement Command of the Army of the United States. His permanent mailing address was % of Mrs. T. A. Harvey, Route 2, Smyrna, Tennessee. He was born 16 October 1923 in Collinwood. He was registered with Selective Service Board in Wayne County, Tennessee. His Civilian Occupation was Engineering Operator. He was inducted 24 February 1943 and entered into active service 3 March 1943 at Fort Oglethorpe, Georgia. His Military Occupational Specialty was Light Truck Driver. His Military Qualifications included Driver and Mechanic Badge. He was in the battles of Rome-Arno. The following decorations were awarded to McGee: World War II Victory Medal, Europe-African Middle Eastern Theater Ribbon with 1 Bronze Service Star, Good Conduct Ribbon, Drivers Medal with 2 Battle Stars and a Lapel Button. He left the USA 25 August 1943 for the Europe-African Middle Eastern Theater Operation, and returned to USA 4 December 1945. He was discharged 14 December 1945 at Fort Knox, Kentucky. Loyd served in Africa for fifteen months and in Italy for twelve months. He was a mail truck and jeep driver, hauling mail and officers. His parents were John and Pearl (Dixon) McGee of the Double Branches Community in Wayne County. His siblings were William Frank, Pebble Harvey, Thelma Jewell Thompson, and Dixie Mabel Canby. Loyd married Norma Jean Mann. They have one son, Dennis McGee.

McKIBBON, HERBERT T., Serial Number 34 735 472, was a Staff Sergeant with the 420th Army Air Force Base Unit

in the Army of the United States. His permanent mailing address was Waynesboro, Tennessee. He was born 16 December 1924 in Winter Haven, Florida. He was registered with Selective Service Board in Wayne County, Tennessee. His Civilian Occupation was High School Student. He was inducted 16 June 1943 at Fort

Oglethorpe, Georgia. His Military Occupational Specialty was Airplane and Engine Mechanic. His Military Qualifications included AAF Air Crew Member Badge (Wings) Aerial Gunner. He was not in any battles. The following decorations were awarded to McKibbon: American Service Ribbon, Good Conduct Ribbon and World War II Victory Medal. He had a high school education. He was discharged 24 March 1946 at Fort McPherson, Georgia. Corporal McKibbon was sent to Keesler Field, Mississippi for his basic drill and specialized training in aviation mechanics after brief graduation exercises, he was transferred to Harlenger Army Air Field, Texas, for courses in gunnery, completing this successfully, he was ordered to Fresno, California, for advanced instructions in the same courses. He also received additional courses of instruction in Aviation Engineering at Tonopak, Nevada before he was sent to Hamilton Field, California to await orders for additional duty. He was stricken with a severe ear infection and was confined to Hamilton Field Hospital which delayed his actions in service. Herbert was the son of Mr. and Mrs. McKibbon, mother was former Addie Taylor. He married Maxine Nichols of Selmer. She was employed in Memphis during Herbert's service in World War II.

McNUTT, EDWARD, was born on October 20, 1924, near Waynesboro, Tennessee. He was working as a trackman when he received his notice to be inducted in the United States Army on September 24, 1943, at Ft. Oglethorpe, Georgia. He served as a light truck driver with Btry. A 190th Field Artillery Battalion. On December 26, 1945, he was discharged at Ft. Knox, Kentucky.

McQUIRE, PETE, married Helen Moore, daughter of Mr. and Mrs. Sam Moore of Wayne County, and was engaged in fanning when he was inducted into the U. S. Service, November 25, 1943. He served with the 11 7th Airborne Division in Germany.

McWILLIAMS, HORACE, Serial Number 34 146 953, was in Signal Headquarters Company, Aircraft Warning Squadron, 5th Fighter Command in the Army of the United States. His permanent mailing address was Route 2, Collinwood, Tennessee. He was registered with Selective Service Board in Wayne County, Tennessee. His Civilian Occupation was Rodman. He was married when he was inducted 3 October 1941 at Fort Oglethorpe, Georgia. His Military Occupational Specialty was Water Supply Technician. His Military Qualifications included Marks-

man Rifle. He was in the battles of Bismarck-Archipelago, Papus, New Guinea, Southern Philippines, and Luzon. The following decorations were awarded to McWilliams: Good Conduct Ribbon, Distinguished Unit Badge, American Defense Service Ribbon, Philippine Liberation Ribbon with one Bronze Star, and Asiatic Pacific Service Ribbon and one Silver Service Star. He left the USA 27 October 1942 for the Asiatic-Pacific Theater Operation, and returned to USA 4 October 1945. He finished three years of high school. He was discharged 14 October 1945 at Camp Chaffee, Arkansas. Horace was born 4 January 1916 in Collinwood. Final rites were held 10 May 1993 in Collinwood and burial was in McGlamery Cemetery in Collinwood. His parents were Isaac and Lou Ella (Rinks) McWilliams. His wife was Mary Neal and his children were: Linda Lou Rigsby of Lawrenceburg, and Jay Alton McWilliams of Waynesboro. Horace was retired from TVA and a member of the American Legion.

McWILLIAMS, JASPER M., Serial Number 34 366 645, was a Technician Fourth Grade in Headquarters Company 3rd Battalion, 127th Infantry in the Army of the United States. His permanent mailing address was General Delivery, Waynesboro, Tennessee. He was born 13 August 1920 in Waynesboro, Tennessee. He was registered with Selective Service Board in Wayne County, Tennessee. His Civilian Occupation was Marker. He was inducted 26 August 1942 and entered into active service 9 September 1942 at Fort Oglethorpe, Georgia. His Military Occupational Specialty was Low Speed Radio Operator. His Military Qualifications included Combat Infantryman. He was in the battles of New Guinea, Southern Philippines and Luzon. The following decorations were awarded to McWilliams: Philippine Liberation Ribbon with one Bronze Service Star, Asiatic Pacific Theater Ribbon and three Bronze Service Stars, World War II Victory Medal and a Lapel Button. He left the USA 12 February 1943 for the Asiatic Pacific Theater Operation, and returned to USA 30 October 1945. He attended a Signal Corps International Morse Code Service School for six weeks. He had four years of high school at battle Ground Academy. He was discharged 8 November 1945 at Camp Chaffee, Arkansas. Jasper's parents were John Melton and Dora Josephine (Bryant) McWilliams. He was married 27 July 1946 to Pebble Johnson. The children are Nita Nailey, Joby Lillard and Cindy Basham. The grandchildren are: Christopher Nailey, Joshua, Josiah, Jesse and Amanda Lillard, and Jason and Chase Basham. He has a

brother, John Quentin McWilliams. Mr. McWilliams died 3 December 1997 in Garden City, Michigan, and was buried in Memorial Gardens in Waynesboro. He was retired from General Motors and a member of Waynesboro United Methodist Church.

McWILLIAMS, JOHN QUENTIN, was born. April 6, 1918 to John Melton, McWilliams and Josie Dora Bryant

McWilliams. He was born in Waynesboro, Tennessee which is in Wayne County. He was one of ten children. His siblings include Lora Davis, Pearle Coleman, Blanche Styles, Bas McWilliams, Dona Adkisson, James Grey McWilliams, Theodore McWilliams, Ruth Ella Hampton, and Jasper Hogan McWilliams. On September 25, 194 1, John Quentin was married to Mary Louise Farris. They had three sons-James Quentin, Jeffrey Keith, and Ted Byler. Today, they have 7 grandchildren and 3 great-grandchildren

During World War II, my grandfather, John Q. McWilliams served in the 28th Infantry Division for 25 months. He spent those months in Franck Belgium, Luxembourg and Germany as a Heavy Weapons Squad Leader. There, he was responsible for a 7 man, 30 Caliber Machine Gun Crew who used all types of hand weapons. They were dressed in camouflage and were engaged in hand-to-hand fighting tactics. He was awarded several decorations and citations. They include the following: American Theater Ribbon, Good Conduct Medal-World. War IL Victory Medal European-African-Middle Eastern Theater Ribbon and 3 Bronze Service Stars for Normandy, Rhinelands, and Northern France.

After talking to my grandmother about this time, she had this story to tell.

"Experiences that happened overseas we do not talk about, but we do have memories and experiences that we can talk about."

"After John was drafted into the army, it was some time before our government decided to give us an allotment. So, it was a while before I could even think about going to visit him. However, I was fortunate enough to make three different visits while he was in the states. I saw him at Camp Livingston, LA; Camp Gordon Johnston, FL; and Camp Pickett, VA."

"At Camp Livingston, we had a room in a big house. It had a one burner oil stove and at night we had to use John's Army Coat for warm&. We found out quickly that Louisiana had very cold winters as I recall that the last time I saw John there he had ice on his face from where the vapor from his mouth and nose had frozen to him."

"The second visit was quite a change. At Camp Gordon Johnston, FL, the weather was nice and warm. We had a room in Sopchoppy, FL. I remember that there was plenty of music coming from the tavern across the street. The record "No Letter Today" played continually while we were there."

"Me third and final visit before his departure overseas was Camp Pickett, VA. Time will not allow me to tell about all the things that happened to us there. We found out that not all Americans were as patriotic as they should have been and we also found ourselves in all kinds of situations. We wives knew this was our last visit, but finally the orders for the 110th infantry to ship out became reality. No one, except those of us who experienced it, can express the emotions that overcame us as we watched our soldiers disappear into the street lights. All that was left was our trip home and our long wait with all its uncertainty. "

"John was one of the lucky ones and after 3 1/2 years in service to his country, he was home again to try to rehabilitate. We made it though, as did many others, and are growing old together in Collinwood, Tennessee, surrounded by our children and grandchildren."

"Our grandson gave his granddaddy a book by Tom Brokaw, "The Greatest Generation" and signed it: 'To A Wonderful part of the Greatest Generation, Andy and Brandy and he sure is."

Submitted by his granddaughter, Amanda McWilliams

MELSON, CLYDE M., Serial Number 34 377 047, was a Private in Casual Detachment of Patients in the Army of the United States. He was born in Lutts, Tennessee. His Civilian Occupation was Truck Driver. He was 27 years old when he was inducted 13 October 1942 at Waynesboro, Tennessee. His Military Occupational Specialty was Basic. He was discharged 16 February 1943 at Camp Atterbury, Indiana with poor physical health.

He is the son of John Jack and Mary

Jessie (Farris) Melson, married Linnie Poole in 1935. They have a daughter, Wanda Bevis. Linnie died in 1941 In, 1946, Clyde married Hazel Repp. November 25, 1965, he died and is buried at McGlamery Cemetery.

MELSON, FRANK, Serial Number 34 146 922, was a Private in the Army of the United States. He was born in Lutts, Tennessee. His Civilian Occupation was Farmer. He was 27 9/12 years old when he was inducted 4 October 1941 at Fort Oglethorpe, Georgia. He was accepted for induction at Waynesboro, Tennessee. He was discharge 7 October 1941 by reason of the Convenience of the Government so that he could reenlist in the Regular Army. Melson reenlisted 9 October 1941 at Fort Oglethorpe, Georgia for a period of three years for service in the Regular Army.

He married Nona Eaton and they have three sons, Danny, Lancie and Ronnie. Frank died and is buried at Cromwell Crossroads Cemetery.

MELSON, HAYES COOLIDGE, Serial Number 44 020 823, was a Private with Company A, 206th Infantry Training Bat-

talion in the Army of the United States. He was born in Lutts, Tennessee. His Civilian

Occupation was Student. He was 20 5/12 years old when he was inducted 29 September 1944 in Camp Forrest, Tennessee. He had a high school education. He was discharged 3 January 1945 at Camp Blanding, Florida with a Certificate of Disability because of poor health. His occupation after his discharge: Factory work for a short time, then Insurance Agent. He returned to school and earned both a B. S. and M. A. Degree from the University of Tennessee. He married 25 May 1963, Martha Williams of Knoxville. There are no children. His parents are Joe Henry and Laura Ethel (Hayes) Melson. His siblings are: Ruby Opal Franks, Rudolph Melson, Theo Dodd, J. P. Melson, all deceased and Maureen Rich, Etheleen, Wylo Mae and Charles Ray Melson.

MELSON, J.P., Serial Number 34 043 122, was a Sergeant in 1250 AAF, Base Unit NAD in the Army Air Force of the

United States. His permanent mailing address was Route 1, Cypress Inn, Tennessee. He was inducted 25 April 1941 and received his military training in Hunter Field, Alabama; Seymour Johnson Field, North Carolina; Berry Field, Nashville; a Memphis Base, then was assigned to Air Transport and overseas he went. He was on active duty in Africa for one year, two months and twenty-four days and spent over three years in the States. The following decorations were awarded to Melson: American Defense Theater Ribbon, Europe-African Middle Eastern Theater Ribbon, Good Conduct Ribbon and World War II Victory Medal. He was discharged 19 November 1945. J. P., son of Joe and Ethel (Hayes) Melson, was born 2 September 1919 in Lutts, Tennessee, died at his residence, 2 September 1993, and was buried in Collinwood Memorial Gardens. He was a retired crew leader with Champion Company and a member of International Brotherhood of Pulp and Sulphite. He married Walcie Montgomery. His children are:

Freddie Gene, deceased; Cledith of Florence, Donald of St. Joseph, Joe of Iron City, and Charlie D. Melson of Cypress Inn. His siblings are: Charles Melson of Phoenix, Arizona;, Theo Dodd of Lawrenceburg, Maureen Rich of Florence, Etheleen Berry of Collinwood, Wylo Mae Melson of Cypress Inn. Deceased siblings are; Rudolph, Hayes C., and Ruby Opal.

MELSON, JESSIE, was born 15 October 1925, the son of Jay and Pead Bums Melson on Rayborn Creek, Wayne County,

Tennessee. He attended the Rayborn and Houston schools.

In November 1943 he was inducted into the United States Army-He took his training at Camp Blanding, Florida, then was sea to Camp Rucker, Alabama, where he was assigned to the 264th. Infantry, 66th. Division. From Camp Rucker he was sent to England.

Jessie J. was wounded on December 24, 1944 when the ship transporting them to France through the English Channel was torpedoed. The ship sank. The survivors were sent on to France to relieve another division. This division went on to the Battle of the Bulge. He spent most of his time in France, until he was sent to Vienna, Austria. He was in the service until his discharge in June, 1946. He received various medals. When he returned home from the Army, he married Mary Belle Robbins on December 24, 1946. They made their home on Rayborn Creek. Jessie continued farming and trucking. In 1958 he began driving a bus for the Wayne County School System which lasted until 1973. He and Mary Belle have two children, Wanda Melson Robertson and Michael Melson. They also have two grandchildren, and two great-grandchildren. Jesse and Mary Belle live at the present tone in Collinwood. He continues to work in the woods, and on his form. He teaches the Adult Sunday School Class at Rayborn Chapel Church.

MELSON, JOHN EDGAR, SR., was born. September 25, 1921 on Rayburn Creek, to Jay Melson and Pearl (Bums)

Melson. I have two brothers Jessie J. Melson and Joda Melson, and one sister Jewell (Melson) Stricklin.

At the age of twenty, I was drafted to the Army Air Force. On July 25, 1942 I went to Fort Oglethorpe, Georgia for my physical. Then I went to Atlantic City, New Jersey for basic training. September 1, 1942 I was sent to Pecos Airfield in Pecos, Texas. I was trained to be a special vehicle operator #932. October 31, 1944 I was sent to Fresno, California. In December 1944 I joined the 558 Air Service Group and went to Tinkerfield, Oklahoma. On February 5, 1945 I went to Grand Island, Nebraska where I ranked corporal. On June 21, 1945 I went to Seattle, Washington to board a ship going to Okinawa, Japan.

While I was serving in the states I was in the 20th Air Force division, when I got to Okinawa I was changed to the 8th Air Force division. The base was Pine Tree B29 airbomber. Jimmy Doolittle was my commander while overseas. I served with 993rd air material squadron on Okinawa for seven months. I operated large semitrailers, trailer trucks, wrecking equipment. I refueled units and other special purpose vehicles used in connection with which vehicles were outfitted. I checked operation of brakes, lights, steering mechanism and other working parts. I made minor roadside repairs to vehicles when the occasion arose. I operated hoist, fuel pump and other special equipment mounted on vehicles.

On September 2, 1945 the war was over. I left Okinawa in January 1946 on a ship coming back to the states. The first stop back in the states was Riverside, California and then on to Camp Chaffee, Arkansas, where I was discharged on January 27, 1946. Lt. N.B. Snodgrass signed my dis-

charge. I received the World War II victory ribbon, good conduct medal, American theater ribbon, AP theater ribbon, and sharpshooter carbine.

After the war I returned home to my wife, Eunice Irene (Whitten) Melson, born May 6, 1926 to Sherman Whitten and Isa (Bailey) Whitten. We bought a farm on Rayburn Creek, from my grandfather, and built a house. I made a living raising cattle, farming, and driving a lumber truck. We raised seven children, John Jr., Kenneth, Linda, Carylon, Brenda, Judy, and Norma. We have thirteen grandchildren and eleven great-grandchildren. We have been married fifty-five years and still live on the farm.

MELSON, JOHN W., was inducted 9 September 1942 into the Army of the United States. He was in the battles of Normandy, Northern France, Ardennes, Rhineland, and Central Europe. The following decorations were awarded to Melson: one Service Stripe, Three Overseas Bars, American Campaign Medal, Europe-African Middle Eastern Theater Ribbon with a Silver Battle Star, Good Conduct Ribbon and World War II Victory Medal. John spent eighteen months overseas. He was discharged 24 November 1945 at Camp Grant, Illinois. His parents were Mr. and Mrs. William H. Melson, Route 2, Lutts, Tennessee. At the time of his discharge, he was married and had a son, John W. Melson, Jr.

MELSON, JOHNNIE D., Cpl., son of Mr. and Mrs. J. J. Melson of Lutts, is with the 95th Division and the 3rd Army stationed in Belgium. He has been awarded the Combat Infantryman Badge. Cpl. Melson was employed as a truck-driver by A. M. Gobbel before entering service. He was inducted into service 17 October 1942. He received his training at Fort Sam Houston, Texas, Shreveport, Louisiana, Los Angles, California, and Indiantown Gap, Pennsylvania. He was transferred overseas in August 1944. He has served in England, France, Germany, Holland and Belgium. He has a wife and son, Jerry Lee. He also has a brother, S/Sgt. Peter F. Melson, who has been with the United States Army for 22 months, spent 19 months overseas with the U. S. 5th Army in North Africa and Italy.

MELSON, PETER F., was born on February 22, 1903, in Collinwood, Tennessee. He was living in Lutts and working as a farmer when he was inducted into the United States Army on November 27, 1941, at Ft. Benning, Georgia. He served as Platoon Sergeant with Btry. A 213th AAA AW Battalion. Peter participated in the following battles: Tunis Campaign, North Italy, South Italy and Kasserine Pass. He was decorated with the following citations: EAME Theater Ribbon with four Bronze Stars, Good Conduct and American Defense Ribbon. On October 31, 1945, he was discharged at Ft. Benning, Georgia.

MELSON, RUDOLPH ASTOR, entered the service 25 April 1941. He was a Corporal in the United States Air Force,

Third Air Force Staging Wing, 488 AAF Base Unit, Hunter Field, Georgia. He had base patrol and post office duties. He received the Good Conduct Medal. After serving four years, six months and twenty-nine days, he received and Honorable Discharge on 24 November 1945. At the end of the war, A. A. Arnold, Commanding General of the Army Air Force extended his gratitude to Rudolph, who contributed to successful prosecution of World War II against those who sought to subjugate the Civilized World. Rudolph, son of Joe Henry and Laura Ethel (Hayes) Melson, was born 8 June 1913 in Lutts, Tennessee, died 6 June 1988, and was buried in Collinwood Memorial Gardens. He married Alma Lou Gallaher, 10 March 1951. She was born 22 June 1913. They have one son, Jerry Thomas Melson who married Rhonda Smithson of Franklin, Tennessee. His siblings are: Charles Melson of Phoenix, Arizona;, Maureen Rich of Florence, Etheleen Berry of Collinwood, Wylo Mae Melson of Cypress Inn. Deceased siblings Hayes C., and J. P. Melson, Theo Dodd, and Ruby Opal Franks. Rudolph grew up on a farm. After his discharge, he worked in Detroit, Michigan. Upon returning to Wayne County, he owned and operated service stations; he was a partner in a Chrysler-Plymouth Dealership, and in the Jackson-Melson Grocery in Collinwood. Later he purchased a lot across the street from the Grocery store and built a commercial building. While returning from a business trip to Nashville in 1971, his car

was struck by a tractor-trailer rig which seriously injured Rudolph. He was unable to work again.

MELTON, AUSTON PEAY, enlisted in the United States Navy in 1940 and served during most of the war on supply

ships between Seattle and Alaska. The ships were constantly attacked by the Japanese trying to gain control of Alaska. Auston retired as a Chief Petty Officer in November 1960. He was aboard a ship in Tokyo Bay on V-J Day. Auston, son of William Harvey and Velma (Cool) Melton, was born 12 January 1923 in the Factory Community in Wayne County. He passed away 15 August 1989 and was buried in the National Cemetery in Nashville, Tennessee. His grandparents were James Richard and Dora Anna (Brewer) Melton and George and Sarah Jane (Lay) Cool. His brothers are Buford, William, Jr., and Graford Melton. His sisters are Georgie, Clara, Dora Jane and Lunell. Auston was married 6 November 1948 to Lola Jean Dixon. Their children are Steven, Rose and Janice Melton.

MELTON, ELI JAMES, He was born 26 November 1920 in Wayne County, Tennessee. He was the son of Terry C. and Laura (Merriman) Melton. He had one sister, Edith Nell Bromley and one brother, Charles Ray Melton. At about age 17, he joined the U. S. Navy. He was young enough that his parents had to sign for him to join. He stayed in the Navy seven years. He received a medical discharge about 1946. He served on the mighty battleship, the USS WASHINGTON and the USS MARYLAND. On the USS Maryland, he served with Pat Warren from Waynesboro. He traveled all over the world and was in active service in World War II. He had just left Pearl Harbor when it was bombed by the Japanese. He crossed the equator twice and was in various battles. His father served in the Army during World War I and

his younger brother, Charles Ray, served in the Marines during the Korean War. About 1942, he married Alicia Flores of Brooklyn, N. Y. They had three children: Michael James Melton of Memphis, Tennessee. Charles Ray Melton and Patricia Rivers of Orlando, Florida. After his discharge from the Navy, the family returned to Waynesboro, where he worked at various jobs for a few years. Then, they moved to Memphis, where he worked at the Mallory Depot until it closed. Next, he worked for the Post Office Department in Memphis until he and his wife were divorced. At this time, he returned to Waynesboro to live with his mother who was in ill health. He was a member of the Christian Church and a 32nd degree Mason. After his mother died in 1974, he was in ill health and was soon confined to Hillview Haven Nursing home in Columbia, Tennessee, where he was very active in helping the staff and patients. While there, he was the recipient of two Eli Melton days. He also received many trophies and awards for his participation in events and activities at the nursing home. He died 9 May 1991 and was laid to rest at Walnut Grove Cemetery in Wayne County, beside his mother and father. President Bush sent a certificate in memory of Eli, deceased Veteran, in recognition of devoted and selfless consecration to the service of our country in the Armed Forces of the United States.

MELTON, JAMES WILLIAM, was born 27 October 1923 in Wayne County. His parents were Loyal Denoble Melton, born 15 August 1896 in Wayne County and Maudie Lucille (Brewer) Melton, born 8 February 1900 in Wayne County. Loyal was killed in a car wreck in Waynesboro on 7 September 1936 and was buried in Cedar Grove Cemetery in Southern Wayne County. They had six other children: Mary Edith Tharp, Chapel Melton, Reba Mae Clay, Glenn Houston Melton, Edward Gene Melton, and Jimmy Ray Melton.

James left Waynesboro 19 February 1943 for Fort Oglethorpe, Georgia and was sworn in the Army 20 February 1943. He took a train to Fort Bliss, Texas and his outfit was the 483rd AAA Automatic Weapon Battalion. After thirteen weeks of basic training in the Mexico and Texas deserts, his outfit went to Marysville, California for field training, to San Diego for amphibious training. Later they trained at Camp Cook, San Louis Obispo and from Seattle, Washington to Honolulu, Hawaii to the rain forest to go through jungle training. Later James was put with the 81st Army Wildcat Division and invaded the Palau Islands to take them from the Japanese. After the successful battle he was assigned to help protect the 3rd Fleet Navy from Japanese planes and went to the Ulithi Islands. After three months, he was assigned to the 3rd, 4th and 5th Marine Division and invaded Iwo Jima Island in the Volcano Islands in the Pacific on 19 February 1945. They guarded the airports while US B29's flew from Saipan and Guam coming over Iwo Jima and would be escorted by P51 Mustangs to bomb Japan. After nine months and the war was over, he had enough points to be eligible to return home. He was discharged from the service 31 December 1945 at Camp Chaffee, Arkansas, He gladly packed and returned home 1 January 1946. Charles Kennedy from Lawrence County was James's bosom Pal and foxhole companion all during his military career. James was married 13 February 1948 in Corinth, Mississippi to Louise Griggs. She was born 10 September 1932, died 30 December 1993 and was buried in Waynesboro Memory Gardens.

MELTON, LEWIS GRAFORD, was a student before enlisting in the United States Navy on 2 July 1945. During his service he made Fireman First Class. He was discharged in Seattle, Washington on 9 October 1947. He is now a retired U. S. Postal Service employee and lives in

Cherokee, Alabama. Graford, son of William Harvey and Velma (Cool) Melton, was born 7 July 1927 in the Leatherwood Community in Wayne County. His grandparents were James Richard and Dora Anna (Brewer) Melton and George and Sarah Jane (Lay) Cool. His brothers are Buford, William and Auston P. Melton. His sisters are Georgie Gobbell, Clara Morrow, Dora Jane Carr and Lunell Smith. Graford was married 17 March 1951 to Catherine Cosby. Their children are Marilyn, Donna and Michael Melton.

MELTON, WILLIAM HARVEY, JR., enlisted in the United States Navy in 1939. He was an Aviation Machinist Mate First Class when the war started. He served during World War II and the Korean War. He retired from the Navy in 1960, and later retired from the Tennessee Valley Authority. Bill, son of William Harvey and Velma (Cool) Melton, was born 14 November 1920 in the Factory Community in Wayne County, died 22 September 1989 and was buried in Walnut Grove Cemetery in Wayne County. His grandparents were James Richard and Dora Anna (Brewer) Melton and George and Sarah Jane (Lay) Cool. His brothers are James Buford, Graford and Auston P. Melton. His sisters are Georgie Gobbell, Clara Morrow, Dora Jane Carr and Lunell Smith. Bill was married February 1951 to Patrica Bonifay. Their children are Betty, Donna, David, William H., III, John and Michael Melton.

MEREDITH, JOEL DONALD, was born March 20, 1914 in the Moccasin community on Moccasin Creek, Wayne County, Tennessee. He is the son of Samp Russ Meredith (1889-1972) and Myra Jane Edwards Meredith (1892-1914). Myra Meredith died when J.D. was about six months old. Sophie and Nanne Higgins cared for J.D. and his sister Malvena for several months. J.D. lived in Waynesboro and Collinwood up to about 1922 when the family moved to Memphis, Tennessee.

Russ Meredith worked there for the electric power company. They lived on Adams Street and J.D. attended public school at Christine School. In 1925, he was recognized by the local Memphis newspaper for saving the life of a school mate while swimming in the Hatchie River. The Christine School principal, Florence Dreyfus, nominated J.D. for a Carnegie Medal.

J.D.'s father was injured in an electrical accident in 1927. The family moved first to Frayser and then east of Memphis to Hollywood. J.D. attended Hollywood School where he played football and baseball. He also began boxing about this time. In 1929, J.D. moved to the area of Crawfordsville, Arkansas where, with some assistance from his father, he cleared land and set up farming. He often walked from the farm in Arkansas to Memphis to fight in boxing tournaments and then after boxing walked back to Arkansas. He made several crops, but early in 1933 he set out on an adventure and began riding trains across the country. He traveled and spent time in Missouri, Minnesota, Montana, Washington, California, Kansas, and Texas. He finally settled in Chicago, Illinois in late 1933. While in Chicago he worked for Lightner Publishing Company, Kino Theatre, Liberty Highway, and Bell & Thornton Manufacturing Company.

J.D. enlisted in the United States Coast Guard in Chicago, Illinois after the attack on Pearl Harbor. He attended recruit training at the Coast Guard Training Station at Manhattan Beach, New York. His first assignment was guard duty at New Orleans, Louisiana where he patrolled the area around Lake Pontchartrain for saboteurs. He was transferred to the USS Calcaterra, a newly commissioned ship which had been recently built in a Houston, Texas shipyard. The Calcaterra (DE-390), an Edsall class Destroyer Escort, was designed for antisubmarine warfare and convoy escort duties. J.D. served in the American, European, African, and Middle Eastern Theaters of war. He manned the number two main battery of the ship and served as the gun crew director. He was on the Calcaterra from late 1943 until the middle portion of 1945. The normal tour for a destroyer escort was two or three months convoy duty or antisubmarine duty and then six days in port for resupply. As the European war wound down in mid-1945, J.D. was transferred to a coast guard cutter on the east coast. He reported aboard the patrol cutter CGC Kimball (WPC-143) in August of 1945. Patrol cutters spent six days patrolling the coastline and six days in port for repair, replenishment, and training. He served on the Kimball until a week before he was honorably discharged at the end of his enlistment. J.D. was discharged February 26, 1946 in Detroit, Michigan.

His professional duty during the war was that of ship's cook. He was rated as SC2c at the close of the war and declined promotion to SC1c so he could return to civilian life. All during the war J.D. participated in boxing tournaments and sparing sessions.

After the war, J.D. lived in Waynesboro from 1946 to 1948. He worked for the local power company as a lineman. J.D. moved to Memphis and began working for Memphis Light, Gas and Water in 1948. He worked for MLG&W for nearly 30 years. He was a lineman and later a troubleshooter. As a troubleshooter, he was widely recognized for his knowledge of obscure Memphis area streets. He helped construct many of the large transmission line towers that still stand in Memphis and vicinity. In 1949, he married Sallie Crews of Waynesboro, in Corinth, Mississippi. Sallie is the daughter of Van Vernon (Jack) Crews (1901- 1975) and Marion Temperance Cole Crews (1901-1982). Sallie and J.D. moved to Memphis where they resided in the north Memphis area and later in Frayser.

While in Memphis, Sallie and J.D., raised three children, Don, Myra, and Sandi.

J.D. retired in 1977 and moved back to Wayne County. While living in Wayne County, J.D. has farmed and raised livestock for personal satisfaction rather than monetary gain. He and Sallie are members of the Church of Christ at Waynesboro.

MEREDITH, PAUL B., had the Grade of Seaman First Class in the United States Navy. He was born 7 May 1925 in Waynesboro, Tennessee. His permanent mailing address was Route 3, Waynesboro, Tennessee. He was registered with Selective Service Board in Wayne County, Tennessee. His Civilian Occupation was General Farmer. He was employed from January 1933 to August 1943 on his father's farm. He was inducted 4 August 1943 and received his boot training in Norfolk, Virginia. He served on the following Vessels and Stations: NTS Bainbridge, Maryland; NTS, NOB, Norfolk, Virginia; USS CUSHING, and USS HALSEY POWELL. The following decorations were awarded to Meredith: American Theater Medal, Asiatic-Pacific Theater Ribbon with 6 Stars, Philippine Liberation Medal with two Stars and World War II Victory Medal. He had an eighth grade education. He was discharged 23 December 1945 at U. S. Personnel Separation Center, Nashville, Tennessee. His parents were Clifford B. and Ada (Higgins) Meredith. He married Flora Carroll and they had three daughters, Zada Theresa, Ramona Kay and Carol Denise Meredith.

MEREDITH, STANLEY D., served his country in the United State Army in World War II. He studied to be a doctor in Lubbock, Texas. Stanley was born 12 August 1919 and died in the summer of 1987. He was the son of Russ and Ellen (Thompson) Meredith. He had a sister, Mary Elizabeth Meredith. Stanley also had half- brothers and sisters: Malvena Verda Beasley, Joel Donald "J. D. ", Margaret Ann Jones, and Shirley Jean Maples. He was married 6 November 1943 in Lompoc, California to Virginia Dee Stewart, daughter of Melvin Elmer and Eula Mae (Palmer) Stewart. She was born 30 October 1923 in Gibson County, Tennessee. They made Murfreesboro, Tennessee their home. They had three daughters: Patrica Dee, born 17 May 1943 in Lompoc, California, Walter McCoy ; Diane Dee, born 8 August 1953 in Humbolt, Tennessee, married Dennis James; and Teresa Dee, born 8 June 1957 in Columbia, Tennessee. The grandchildren are: David and Michael McCoy, and Amanda Meredith James.

MERRIMAN, FLOYD SHIELD "SNOOKS", was born 20 October 1913 in Wayne County, died 10 June 1988 and

is buried in the Shields Cemetery. His parents were David Harris and Flora (Whitby) Merriman. "Snooks" was educated in the Wayne County Public School System. He entered the U. S. Navy on 23 May 1942 and served until 16 December 1945. He was a disabled Veteran. After the war he was associated with the U. S. Postal Service for forty-one years. He was active in the community, was elected to the Waynesboro City Commission in 1976, attaining the position of Mayor in 1979, a position he held until February 1988. He married Bonnie Johnson and to them were born Jerry Floyd Merriman and Bridget Johnson Merriman Berman. Their grandchildren are Robert Whitby and Jonathan Harris Merriman. Luella Carter, deceased and Florine Manning of Fall Church, Virginia were his sisters. His brother, Tom Harris Merriman is deceased.

MERRIMAN, GID, Serial Number 34 361 749, was a Private First Class in 84th General Hospital in the Army of the United

States. He was born in Waynesboro, Tennessee. His Civilian Occupation was Farmer. He was 41 9/12 years of age when he was inducted 25 July 1942 at Fort Oglethorpe, Georgia. He was discharged 24 February 1943 at Camp McCoy, Mississippi. Gid's parents were Eli G. and Mary Merriman. His sisters are Rachel Lay, Mary Lee Alexander, Elizabeth Merriman and Lula Martin. He married Delphia Broadway. Gid is now deceased.

MIDDLETON, J.C., Serial Number 34 506 485, was a Private First Class in 141st Infantry Regiment First Battalion Medical Section in the Army of the United States. His permanent mailing address was Route 1, Peters Landing, Tennessee. He was born 30 November 1922 in Peters Landing, Tennessee. He was registered with Selective Service Board in Wayne County, Tennessee. His Civilian Occupation was General Farm Hand. His Military

Occupational Specialty was Medical Aidman. His Military Qualifications included Medical Badge. He was in the battles of Northern France, Rhineland, and Central Europe. The following decorations were awarded to Middleton: Europe-African Middle Eastern Theater Ribbon with 3 Bronze Stars, Good Conduct Ribbon and World War II Victory Medal. He left the USA 9 October 1943 for the European-African-Middle Easter Theater Operation, and returned to USA 15 December 1945. He was discharged 21 December 1945 at Fort Knox, Kentucky.

MILLER, CHARLES, was inducted 25 August 1942 into the Army of the United States and received his basic training at Camp Forrest, Tennessee. His parents were Mr. and Mrs. A. M. Miller, of Route 1, Cypress Inn, Tennessee. He was a farmer before he was inducted.
Source: Wayne County News.

MILLER, COY MARCELL, Serial Number 966 28 54, had the Grade of Fireman First Class in the Navy of the United States. His permanent mailing address was Route 2, Lutts, Tennessee. He was born 12 March 1910 in Barton, Alabama. He was registered with Selective Service Board in Wayne County, Tennessee. His Civilian Occupation was General Farmer. He was married when he was inducted 31 December 1943 and entered into active service 7 January 1944 at Waynesboro, Tennessee. He held the following ratings: AS, S2C, and F1C. The Vessels and Stations that he served on were: NRS Chattanooga, Tennessee; NTS, Great Lakes, Illinois; Nav Rec BKS, Shoemaner, California; and USS HAGGARD. He was discharged 4 November 1945 at US Naval Personnel Separation Center, Shelter, Virginia.

MILLER, PERLIS, was born, September 11, 1923, at Waynesboro, TN. He enlisted in the U. S. Navy, February 21, 1943, and served as seaman second class on the following stations and vessels; NRS Chattanooga, TN., NTS Bainbridge, MD., AGC Brooklyn, N. Y., NOB Iceland SS, SS Matinicock, SS Culpepper, SS Salvator., February 24, 1946, he was discharged at Memphis, TN.

MILLER, RICHARD, DR., was a Major in the United States Army. His parents were Warren and Minnie (Patrick) Miller of Clifton, Tennessee. His brother was W. B. Miller, Jr. He was married and was discharged in late 1945. After his discharge, he returned home to Memphis to resume his medical practice.
Source: Wayne County News, 18 January 1946.

MILLER, SAM, JR., was born on June 10, 1919, the son of Sam and Octa (Adkins) Miller. Sam was inducted into the United States Army on March 15, 1942. He was sent to the European Theater of war. He served with the 82nd Airborne Division Artillery in France, Belgium and German. He was a Staff Sergeant and cooked for 125 men each day and was in charge of six other men during K. P. and cooking. He served 16 months overseas. He was given an honorable discharge on January 4, 1946. He was awarded the American theater Ribbon, European African Medal, Eastern Theater Ribbon, three Bronze Stars, Good Conduct Medal, Bronze Arrowhead, World War II Victory Medal and the Glider Badge-M. M. Rifle. He was married to Walsie Morgan Miller. Their children are Larry E., Dale Miller and Marie Berry. Sam died on April 10, 1994, at the age of 76 in Maury County Regional Hospital in Columbia, Tennessee, and was buried in Collinwood Memorial Gardens. He was a retired saw operator for Hassel and Hughes Lumber Company. His siblings are At age 76, he died 10 April 1994 in Maury County Regional Hospital in Columbia, Tennessee, and was buried in Collinwood Memorial Gardens. He was a retired saw operator for Hassel and Hughes Lumber Company. His siblings were Lawrence, and Euin Miller and Maxine Morgan.

MILLER, WARREN BLAIR, JR., was the son of Warren B. Miller Sr. and Minnie Patrick Miller. He was born on January 31, 1911. He served his country in World War II in Technician 4 HQ Company 14 Armored Division. He was married to Mary Elizabeth Helton, daughter of Edgar and Delia Culp Helton. W. B. and Mary Elizabeth had one son, Warren B. Miller III. W. B. went into the merchandise business with his father-in-law. Later, he operated a Western Auto franchise store in Clifton. W. B. died on May 24, 1964, at his home in Clifton and was entombed in the Clifton City Cemetery. He was a member of the Clifton Civitan Club. He served on the Board of the city as a commissioner. He had one brother, Dr. Richard W. Miller.

MILLIGAN, VIRGIL LEE, was born on September 25, 1915, in Warrior, Alabama. He married Mary Alice Prater, daughter of William B. and Lou Griffin Prater, and lived near Clifton, Tennessee where they raised their nine children: Marlin, Norris, Dean, Lee Elden, Barry, Gary, Dale, Alton and Keith. Virgil was working as a miner at the time he was inducted into the United States Army Air Force on September 11, 1942, at Ft. McClellan, Ala-

bama. He served as Corporal in the supply room. He spent several months in the Pacific Theater and was awarded the Asiatic-Pacific Service Medal, American Service Medal and Good Conduct Medal. He was discharged on October 29, 1945, at Ft. McPherson, Georgia. On July 24, 1993, Virgil died and is buried in Praters Chapel Cemetery near Clifton. Virgil Lee Milligan.

MITCHELL, CHARLES E., son of Charlie and Pearl Matlock Mitchell was born February 17, 1922 at Waynesboro,

TN, where he grew up and attended school. He was working at a sawmill when he was inducted into the U.S. Army on December 27, 1942 at Ft. Oglethorpe, GA. He served as a Tech 5 with Co. B, 71st Chemical Mortar Bn. and received the following citations: Good Conduct Ribbon, WWII Victory Ribbon, American Theater Ribbon and AP Theater Ribbon. He was discharged November 13, 1946 at Camp Chaffee, AR.

Charles and Irma Lee Walker were married and live near Waynesboro. They had three children: Ricky, Tommy and Imogene.

MITCHELL, HILMAN, was born on July 13, 1914, in Bon Air, Tennessee, near Collinwood, Tennessee. He is the son of

Mr. and Mrs. Charlie Mitchell. They moved near Waynesboro when Hilman was a small child and within a short time his mother died. He was listed as a laborer when he was inducted into the United States Army on January 22, 1941, at Ft. Oglethorpe, Georgia. While serving in Europe he was wounded during the battle of Normandy Beach in France and was awarded the following citations: Good Conduct Medal, American Defense Service Ribbon, EAME Service Ribbon and the Purple Heart. On August 2, 1945, he was discharged at Camp Stewart, Georgia. Hilman never married; he is deceased and buried in Walnut Grove Cemetery in Wayne County.

MITCHELL, S.J., Serial Number 34 361 765, was a Private First Class in Company F, 8th Infantry in the Army of the

United States. His permanent mailing address was Route 2, Lutts, Tennessee. He was born 17 January 1919 in Cherokee, Alabama. He was registered with Selective Service Board in Wayne County, Tennessee. His Civilian Occupation was General Farmer. He was inducted 25 February 1942 and entered into active service 8 August 1942 at Fort Oglethorpe, Georgia. His Military Occupational Specialty was Light Machine Gunner. His Military Qualifications included Combat Infantryman Badge. He was in the battles of Normandy, Northern France, Rhineland, and Central Europe. The following decorations were awarded to Mitchell: Distinguished Unit Badge, Europe-African Middle Eastern Theater Ribbon with 3 Bronze Service Stars and Bronze Arrowhead, and Good Conduct Ribbon. He left the USA 18 January 1944 for the European Theater Operation, and returned to USA 10 July 1945. He was discharged 18 October 1945 at Camp Butner, North Carolina. S. J.'s parents were Wheeler and Emma Mitchell. S. J. was married 13 February 1943 in Cloverdale, Alabama to Cleo Berry. He was in service

and she was in high school, so they had one week together, and off he had to go back to the service and Cleo back to school. Their present address: 604 South Street in Mishawaka, Indiana but they were formerly from Lutts. They celebrated their 52nd anniversary in 1995 and stated, "Through the years and through the tears, we have made it this far, and hope to have many more. " Their children are Beverly Howard, S. J. Mitchell, Jr., and Shelia Bolhnlein and they have six grandchildren.

MIXON, ANDREW H., JR., "TOMMY" son of Andrew H. Mixon Sr. and Martha Elizabeth Russ Mixon. His

grandfather was Tom Russ, and his grandmother was Cordie Ricketts, daughter of Charlie Ricketts. Tommy's roots were of the old settlers of Clifton, Tennessee. He had lots of friends there. Tommy was reared by his Aunt Marietta Russ Hartwell in Clifton. He was a junior in high school when he joined the United States Navy at 17 years old. He was wounded while in the service (shell-shocked). He was sent to the Great Lakes Naval Training Center out of Chicago for his basic training. He found his wife, Marion, in California. They had three children. Tommy was buried in California. His siblings are Mary Carolyn and Virginia Joy. They lived in Arkansas.
Source: Carolyn Waters and Dorothy Norman.

MOISON, GORDON B., Serial Number 35 78 71, rating was Messman in the United States Navy. Below is a list of the ships Moison served on with the story of each voyage: 1. ANDREW HAMILTON (Liberty Ship) left New York City 16 April 1943 in a convoy to Algiers, North Africa to haul food, medicine... returned 12 June 1942 - Official Number 242059. 2. SHILOH (C-2 Tanker) Sailed three times in 1943 -(30 July 1943 - 14 Aug 1943), (16 August 1943 - 1 Sept 1943), and (2 Sept 1943-2 Nov 1943). It was a convoy

to Algiers, Oran, North Africa, and Liverpool, England and return. His rating was Wiper, FM WT. 3. ROBERT SWEN -(18 Jan 1944- 17 Apr 1944) Foreign trip, Liberty Ship. 4. JOSEPH M. MEDILL (Liberty Ship) (15 May 1944-4 Aug 1944) Convoy to Liverpool-Channel to Manchester, on load-deck cargo (Trucks). They went to Omaha Beech Head to unload medicine and food supplies for Duku's and Loup's Red Ball trucks. 5. JOSEPH HOLT (Liberty Ship) (24 Aug 1944-17 Jan 1945) Convoy to Portsmouth, England anchored off Isle of Wight and went to Antwerp. It was the only ship with a Christmas tree. This was during Belgium Battle of the Bulge. The Red Ball outfit unloaded there. His rating was FM-WT. (Fireman.) 6. GULF WAX (24 Feb 1945-14 Mar 1945) was a foreign trip from Philadelphia, Pennsylvania to discharge at Charleston, South Carolina. 7. S. S. HAMLIN GARLAND (21 Mar 1945 - 24 May 1945) Foreign from Philadelphia, Pennsylvania and back to New York. His rating was Deck Engineer. 8. GEORGE E. BADGER (26 June 1945-2 Sept 1945) Liberty- from Philadelphia convoy to Algiers, Naples, Savanna, Marseilles, loaded with 6x6 half-tracks, jeeps and armor going to Manilla but while we were enroute JAPAN SURRENDERED. The crew stayed in Panama and were discharged in Cristobal, Canal Zone. They were sent back to Philadelphia where Gordon Moison signed off because it was the end of his service duty.

MOORE, WILLIS, son of Edgar and Blanche Bundrant Moore, was born in 1916 in Wayne County. He was inducted into the United States Army and stationed in Alaska. He married Lena Mae Palmer of Hardin County. Willis was employed by Tennessee Valley Electric Cooperative in Savannah, Tennessee. They made their home there, and he worked with the company 35 years until he retired. He and Lena Mae have five children: Ancil, Johnny, Freddy, Jimmy and Nelda.

MONTAGUE, JAMES JACK, Serial Number 641 29 69, was a Ship's Cook First Class in the United States Navy. He was

born 27 December 1921 in Clifton, Tennessee. He was single when he reenlisted 20 February 1946 at Norfolk, Virginia. His mailing address was P. O. Box 135, Clifton. The Vessels and Stations that he served on were: USS TANAGER (AM 385), and USS MINAH (AMC 204). The following decorations were awarded to Montague: American Area Medal and World War II Victory Medal. He had previously served in the United States Navy Reserve from 8 October 1942 to 19 February 1946. His Occupation before the war was Student. He was discharged 23 December 1947 in Norfolk, Virginia. Jack's parents were Isaac Newton and Martha Virginia "Virgie" (Hudiburg) Montague. His siblings were Virginia, Bill Jack, Nettie Jane and Joe Hughes Montague, Rachel Lay, and Alva Lena Moak.

MONTGOMERY, GRAYFORD EUGENE, was born 8 July 1924 in Wayne County, Tennessee to Lemuel Gid and Ber-

tha (Creasey) Montgomery. He had two brothers, Lee Onis and Ermen L. B. Montgomery. He had five sisters, Eula

Markham, May Hayes, Ruby Berry, Ida Pearl Berry, and Opal Geans. Lee, Ermen, Eula, and Mae are deceased. He married Delphia Williams on 9 April 1944. They had ten children: five boys, Barry, Jarry, Gary, David and Daniel Montgomery; five girls, Patricia Berzett, Gail Partain, Nancy Tilley, Sherry Crosslin, and Melissa Moore. They have twenty-two grandchildren and four great grandchildren. Mr. Montgomery was drafted into World War II on 20 March 1943, and served in the 359th Air Service Group. He served eighteen months in the South Pacific on the Tenian Island. He was discharged as a Sergeant in February 1946.

MONTGOMERY, LEE O., son of L. C. and Bertha Montgomery of Cypress Inn, Tennessee, entered the United States Army 8 October 1942 at Fort Oglethorpe, Georgia. After completion of his basic training, Tec. 5 Montgomery left for his European tour 5 May 1943. He was a heavy truck driver, served with 819th Engineer Aviation Battalion in the European Theater of Operations. He drove trucks, trailers, semi tractors from three to ten ton capacity, transporting heavy equipment over rough terrain under combat conditions. Technician 5 Montgomery returned to the United States 8 December 1945. He received the Europe-African Middle Eastern Theater Ribbon, Good Conduct Ribbon and World War II Victory Medal. He received an Honorable Discharge 25 December 1945 at Camp Atterbury, Indiana. Montgomery returned to his home in Cypress Inn and to his wife, Lillian Horton Montgomery and their first son, George Lee. He made Cypress Inn his home where he was a farmer and a carpenter. Mr. Montgomery passed away 13 March 1987. He was survived by his wife, Lillian, children, G. L., Bobby, Donnie, and Melba and eight grandchildren. We are proud of our Daddy for serving his country. We love him and miss him very much. -The Montgomery children.

MOORE, ALVIN, was a Private First Class in the Armed Forces of the United States. His mailing address was Collinwood. He was inducted in May 1943. He received his basic training at Fort Leavenworth, Kansas. His occupation before service was farming with his father.
Source: Wayne County News.

MOORE, ARCH CREED, JR., Serial Number 845 49 11, had the rate of Fire Control Man Second Class in the Navy of the United States. He entered the Navy 10 June 1943 at Chattanooga, Tennessee and was discharged 19 March 1946 at Millington Air Station, Memphis, Tennessee. He received his boot training at

Bainbridge, Maryland and attended Fire Control School there. He served on the following Vessels and Stations: Naval Training Station, Naval Operating Base in Norfolk, Virginia; Orange, Texas to board and commission the USS ROBERT BRAZIER Destroyer Escort 345; served on USS ROBERT BRAZIER until eligible for discharge. He served in the American Theater, Atlantic Theater and Asiatic Pacific Theater. He participated in the Macajalar Bay Landing and the Philippine Invasion. Moore earned the American Theater Ribbon, Asiatic Pacific Ribbon, Philippine Liberation Ribbon and World War II Victory Medal. A. C.'s parents were Arch Creed, Sr., and Bessie G. Moore. His siblings were Roy H. Moore, deceased, a Paratrooper during World War II; Lon E. also a WWII Veteran; Jack R., and Mary Len Moore Harkey. A. C. married Ann Jones, 24 June 1950. Their children; Theresa Ann Strong, Marcia Gayle Nelson, and Anita Kaye Gilland. Their grandchildren are: Shauna Lei Strong, Allison Marie and Clifton Avery Nelson, and Jonathan Ryan and Daniel Shawn Gilland. A. C. is now retired from TVA and lives in Gallatin, Tennessee.

MOORE, EARLY W., Serial Number 34 495 077, was a Private First Class in 54th Military Police Company in the Army of the United States. His permanent mailing address was Route 1, Collinwood, Tennessee. He was born 9 August 1922 in Collinwood, Tennessee. He was registered with Selective Service Board in Wayne County, Tennessee. He was married with two dependents when he was inducted 22 November 1942 and entered into active service 29 November 1942 at Fort Oglethorpe, Georgia. His Military Occupational Specialty was Military Policeman. His Military Qualifications included Marksman Rifle. He was in the battles of Naples, Foggia, and Rome-Arno. The following decorations were awarded to Moore: Asiatic Pacific Theater Ribbon,

Europe-African Middle Eastern Theater Ribbon with 2 Bronze Stars, Good Conduct Ribbon and World War II Victory Medal. He left the USA 25 June 1943 for the Europe-African Middle Eastern Theater Operation, left there 29 June 1945 for the Asiatic Pacific Theater, and returned to USA 31 October 1945. He was discharged 14 November 1945 at Camp Chaffee, Arkansas. Mr. Moore of Route 2, Waynesboro, died 8 April 1995 in the Wayne County Hospital and was buried in Macedonia Cemetery near Collinwood. He was a son of Rosie Brewer Moore and the late Odie Moore. Survivors included his mother, his wife, Mary Jane Moore, four sons, Larry of Collinwood, Ronnie and Donnie both of Forsyth, Georgia, and Terry of Waynesboro. Three daughters, Frankie Peskopos of Griffin, Georgia., Dian Peters of Forsyth, Georgia, and Sandy Jackson of Juliette, Georgia. ; two stepsons, Jeffery and Glen Reeves, Jr., of Waynesboro. ; one stepdaughter, Sherry Ann Melton of Waynesboro; one brother James Moore of Collinwood; one sister, Lois Rich of Collinwood; nineteen grandchildren, and seventeen great grandchildren.

MOORE, ELIX DOSS, a Veteran of the United States Air Force, died 9 July 1983 in VA Hospital in Nashville, Tennessee and was buried in Piney Grove Cemetery in Wayne County. He was the son of William S. and Willie Ann (Hill) Moore. His daughters are, Linda Dice of Nashville, and Ann Capitano of New Orleans, Louisiana. His sisters were Nipsy Tally of Nashville, Rhoda Clanton and Anna Marie Morgan of Florence, Alabama, two half-sisters, Dorothy Klatt of Santa Anna, California and Lillian P. O'Bryant of Florence. He was a factory worker.

MOORE, FLOYD F., Serial Number 34 903 958, was a Private First Class in the 185th 2nd Service Command Unit, Prisoner of War Camp in the Army of the United States. His permanent mailing address was Route 6, Lawrenceburg, Tennessee. He was born 15 December 1909 in Waynesboro, Tennessee. He was registered with Selective Service Board in Wayne County, Tennessee. His Civilian Occupation was Tractor Driver. He was married with five dependents when he was inducted 22 January 1944 and entered into active service 13 February 1944 at Camp Forrest, Tennessee. His Military Occupational Specialty was Military Police. His Military Qualifications included Marksman Rifle M1. He was not in any battles. The following decorations were awarded to Moore: American Theater Ribbon, and World War II Victory Medal. He was discharged 7 December 1945 at Fort Bliss, Texas.

MOORE, JAMES E., Serial Number 34 193 028, was a Private in Battery B 680th Glider Field Artillery Battalion in the Army of the United States. His permanent mailing address was 214 Hughes Street, Lawrenceburg, Tennessee. He was born 18 August 1919 in Waynesboro, Tennessee. He was registered with Selective Service Board in Wayne County, Tennessee. His Civilian Occupation was Painter. He was inducted 15 March 1942 at Fort Oglethorpe, Georgia. His Military Occupational Specialty was Gun Crewman L Artillery. He was in the battles of Sicily, Naples-Foggia, Rome-Arno, Ardennes, Rhineland, and Central Europe. The following decorations were awarded to Moore: Europe-African Middle Eastern Theater Ribbon with 6 Bronze Stars, and 4 Bronze Arrowheads. He left the USA 29 April 1943 for NATO, departed 10 July 1943 for the European Theater Operation, and returned to USA 14 September 1945. He was discharged 19 September 1945 at Camp Atterbury, Indiana.

MOORE, LON E., Serial Number 34 506 477, was a Private First Class in 3654th Quartermasters Truck Company in the

Army of the United States. His permanent mailing address was Route 1, Waynesboro, Tennessee. He was born 11 May 1923 in Clifton, Tennessee. He was registered with Selective Service Board in Wayne County, Tennessee. His Civilian Occupation was General Farm Hand. He was inducted 18 January 1943 and entered into active service 25 January 1943 at Fort Oglethorpe, Georgia. His Military Occupational Specialty was Light Truck Driver. He was in the battles of Sicilian, Rome-Arno, Southern France, Rhineland, and Central Europe. The following decorations were awarded to Moore: Meritorious Unit Award, Bronze Arrowhead, Europe-African Middle Eastern Theater Ribbon with 5 Bronze Stars, Good Conduct Ribbon and Lapel Button. He left the USA 6 June 1943 for the North

Africa Theater Operation, departed 13 August 1943 for European Theater Operations and returned to USA 1 June 1945. He was discharged 5 November 1945 at Camp Atterbury, Indiana. Lon's parents were Arch Creed, Sr., and Bessie (Gideon) (Rinehart) Moore. His siblings were Roy Hardin Moore, deceased, a Paratrooper during World War II; Arch Creed, Jr., also a WWII Veteran; Jack Rinehart, and Mary Len Moore Harkey. Lon married Virginia Evelyn Lineberry. Their child; Dennis Harold, married Sandra Lynn Williams. Lon received his education in Frank Hughes High School in Clifton. Lon Edward still corresponds with seven members of the 46th.

MOORE, PAUL J., Serial Number 34 193 026, was a Private First Class in 9207 TSU Oper Det. in the Army of the United

States. His permanent mailing address was Route 1, Waynesboro, Tennessee. He was born 24 March 1914 in Wayne County, Tennessee. He was registered with Selective Service Board in Wayne County, Tennessee. His Civilian Occupation was Light Truck Driver. He was married with four dependents when he was inducted 15 March 1942 at Fort Oglethorpe, Georgia. His Military Occupational Specialty was Light Truck Driver. His Military Qualifications included Marksman M1 Rifle. He was in the Battles of the Sicilian Campaign (Italy, Africa and Sicily.) The following decorations were awarded to Moore: Europe-African Middle Eastern Service Medal and Good Conduct Medal. He left the USA 29 April 1943 for the African-European Theater Operation, and returned to USA 22 April 1944. He was discharged 17 October 1945 at Fort Lewis, Washington. Paul's parents were William Edgar and Blanche (Bundrant) Moore. His siblings are, William C., deceased, Willis E. of Savannah, James E. of Lawrenceburg, and Louise Stovall of Lawrenceburg. Paul married Mildred Morris. Their children,

Paula, deceased, Guy, Richard, and Tony all of Waynesboro, Margaret Coln of Savannah, Marilyn Gipson of Waynesboro, and Patricia Plunk of Michie, Tennessee.

MOORE, ROY HARDIN, Serial Number 34 146 951, was a Staff Sergeant in Company C, 38th Infantry Battalion in

the Army of the United States. He was inducted 4 October 1941. He was in the Battles of the European Theater Operation with the 502nd Parachute Infantry, making the JUMP D-Day at Normandy Beach. He graduated from Wayne County High school in 1938. Roy's parents were Arch Creed, Sr., and Bessie (Gideon) (Rinehart) Moore. His siblings were Arch C., Jr., and Lon E. both WWII Veterans; Jack R., and Mary Len Moore Harkey. Roy married Frances Jane Gallaher, 31 March 1945. Their children; Gloria Carole and Robert Creed Moore. Roy died 24 November 1978 and was entombed at Philadelphia Cemetery on Hardin's Creek, Highway 64 West in Wayne County.

MOORE, WILL J., Serial Number 44 125 304, was a Private in 467th AAF Base Unit in the Army of the United States. His permanent mailing address was Route 2, Iron City, Tennessee. He was born 22 August 1927 in Iron City, Wayne County, Tennessee. He was registered with Selective Service Board in Wayne County, Tennessee. His Civilian Occupation was Farmer. He was inducted 5 September 1945 and entered into active service 6 September 1945 at Fort McPherson, Georgia. His Military Occupational Specialty was Basic. His Military Qualifications included Carbine Cal. 30 MKM, and Pistol Cal. 45 SS. He was not in any battles. He had an eighth grade education. He was honorably discharged to enlist Regular Army AR at AAF Overseas Replacement Depot, Kearne, Utah.

MORGAN, BRICE BUNDRANT, was born and raised in the Martin's Mill

area and was the son of John Wesley and Lucy (Bundrant) Morgan. He joined the Navy in Nashville, Tennessee, on 6 February 1940 and was sent to Naval Training School in Norfolk, Virginia, for basic training. Then he was sent to the Pacific Fleet, San Diego, California, and served aboard the destroyers USS PYRO, USS BROWN and USS WATERS, during World War II. He was honorably discharged 18 August 1945 at Terminal Island, San Pedro, California. Brice married Edna Saxen of Astoria, Oregon in Seattle, Washington on 15 February 1942 and their daughter, Cheryl Jean, was born in the U. S. Navy Hospital in Long Beach, California on 3 September 1943. Upon discharge from the Navy, the family moved to Portland, and St. Helens, Oregon where Brice learned meat cutting on the G. I. Bill. He worked for Safeway stores until the family moved back to California where he went to work for Lucky Lager Brewery in Azusa, California and then Budweiser Brewery in Van Nuys, California. A death in his wife's family caused a move back to Oregon and he finished his working days as a meat cutter, retiring in 1972. He enjoyed razor clam digging, fishing, gardening and latch-hooking. He passed away 1 November 1993 in the Veteran's Administration Hospital in Portland, Oregon and is buried in Williamette National Cemetery, Portland, Oregon. His survivors are his wife, Edna, daughter Cheryl Malinen, both of Astoria, Oregon; granddaughters, Juli Ann Malinen, Lari M'Liss Gascoigne and great-grandson, Alan James Gascoigne of Mehama, Oregon, and a sister, Marie Melson of Savannah, Tennessee.

Submitted by: Edna Morgan and Cheryl Malinen, 1654 SE 2nd Street, Astoria, Oregon 97103.

MORGAN, EDWIN ISSAC, was a hard-working farmer and family man who. He was a gentle man, changed by World War IL Decades after the war, he would sob at photographs of fellow soldiers —

young men who perished after their 13- 17 was shot down over the German countryside. Her father,, she said, was one of only two men who survived that mission in 1944. He died Feb. 3 at Doctors Medical Center. He was 78.

Mr. Morgan was born May 6, 192 1, in Wayne County, Tenn., but spent most of his teenage years farming his uncle's land in Madera.

In 1943, Mr. Morgan joined the Army Air Corps and was stationed in Scotland. Then 22, he flew missions over Germany as a waist gunner in a 13- 17.

Mr. Morgan wasn't even supposed to be on the plane the day it was shot down, but someone was ill, so he took over. Shrapnel wedged into Mr. Morgan's abdomen and legs, but he managed to parachute from the plane and land in enemy territory.

"And as he came down in the countryside, he saw the people come out of their farmhouses," his daughter, Sharon Morgan Chandler, 5 1, said, recalling her father's story. "It was one of the strangest feelings he ever had."

German farmers held Morgan at bay with their pitchforks until soldiers arrived. Mr. Morgan was taken to Stalag 17.

At the camp, Mr. Morgan learned how to gamble, an obsession that would last the rest of his life, his daughter said.

Mr. Morgan returned to California a decorated war veteran, earning the Distinguished Flying Cross and a Purple Heart.

Weeks after his return home, Mr. Morgan married his high school sweetheart, Shirley Lee Goode of Madera.

Chandler, the middle child, said she and her brothers grew up among alfalfa fields, cattle and rows of fresh vegetables.

"Wherever we lived, we always had a vegetable garden," she said. Mr. Morgan went to work as a foreman for Marathon Paper, a division of American Can Co. in 1958. While still working for American Can, he began a card room business in Delhi with his wife, who made and served Thanksgiving, Christmas and Easter dinners for the gamblers.

Later, the Morgan home became a "marked house" — a place where people could go to get a free meal, Chandler said.

"The strangest people would come to our door, and my dad would never turn anyone away," she said. "He would offer them a bed in the garage, three meals and work to do... My mom and my dad could never stand to see a hungry person."

Mr. Morgan became owner of Scotty's card room in Turlock during the 1970s and later managed several card rooms in the Modesto area and Manteca.

"The men at the poker games know my dad better than any of us," Chandler joked. "Today, at one of the clubs, they were talking about my daddy and said he never did an unkind, selfish or dishonest thing to any person, ever."

Mr. Morgan was a member of the Sportsmen's Club in Modesto.

In addition to his daughter, he is survived by his son, Bradley Wade Morgan of Modesto; and three grandchildren and one great-grandchild.

A memorial service will be at 2 P.M.. Saturday at Living Faith Community Church in Modesto. Allen Mortuary, Turlock, in charge of arrangements.

MORGAN, ELZIE WILLIAM, was a Private First Class in the United States Army. He served in the European Theater. Elzie, son of Jim and Chessie (Robinett) Morgan, was born 18 August 1911 on Forty-Eight Creek in Wayne County, Tennessee, died 3 July 1978 in Wayne County Hospital and was buried in Walnut Grove Cemetery in Wayne County. He married Mary Frances and they had twin daughters, Lois, deceased and Joyce. He had one granddaughter, Mary Jo (Munn) Creecy.

MORGAN, EZRA A., was born April 23, 1918 in Wayne County. He was working as a farm hand when he entered the U. S. Army, October 20, 194 1. at Jefferson Barracks. MO. He served with the 15th Calvary Reconnaissance Sqd. as a light mortar crewman and participated in battles at Normandy, Northern France, Rhineland and Central Europe. He received the following citations: WWII Victory Medal. American Defense Ribbon. American Theater Ribbon, Good conduct Medal. European -African Theater -Medal and Middle Eastern Theater Ribbon with four bronze service stars. He was discharged November 21. 1945 at Ft. Knox. Ky.

MORGAN, GENE BOSWELL, Serial Number 783 79 74, was a Radarman Third Class in the Navy of the United States. He was born 30 September 1926 in Collinwood, Wayne County, Tennessee. He entered into service 27 October 1944. He served at the following Station and/or Ships: NTC Great Lakes, Illinois; RS Tadger, San Diego, California; and USS TOPEKA. The following decorations were awarded to Morgan: American Theater Ribbon, Asiatic Pacific Theater Ribbon with 2 Stars, and World War II Victory Medal. He was discharged 10 June 1946 at US Naval Personnel Separation Center, Memphis, Tennessee.

MORGAN, JASPER W., Serial Number 34 921 955, was a Private First Class in Company E, 351st Infantry in the Army of the United States. His permanent mailing address was 1011 Maxwell Avenue, Nashville, Tennessee. He was born 5 September 1916 in Lutts, Tennessee. He was registered with Selective Service Board in Wayne County, Tennessee. His Civilian Occupation was Postal Clerk. He was married with two dependents when he was inducted 30 December 1943 and entered into active service 22 January 1944 at Fort Oglethorpe, Georgia. His Military Occupational Specialty was Light Mortar Crewman. His Military Qualifications was CIB SR. He was in the battles in Rome-Arno, North Apennines and Po Valley. The following decorations were awarded to Morgan: Europe-African Middle Eastern Theater Medal, Good Conduct Medal and World War II Victory Medal. He left the USA 28 July 1944 for the Europe-African Middle Eastern Theater Operation, and returned to USA 1 September 1945. He had a high school education. He was discharged 14 November 1945 at Camp Shelby, Mississippi.

MORGAN, JOHN F.H., Serial Number 34 494 890, was a Private First Class in Company B, 184th Infantry in the Army of the United States. His permanent mailing address was Route 2, Olive Hill, Tennessee. He was born 6 February 1921 in Waynesboro, Tennessee. He was registered with Selective Service Board in Wayne County, Tennessee. His Civilian Occupation was General Farm Hand. He was married with one dependent when he was inducted 22 November 1942 and entered into active service 29 November 1942 at Fort Oglethorpe, Georgia. His home address at time of entry was Route 1, Waynesboro. His Military Occupational Specialty was Messenger. His Military Qualifications included Combat Infantry Man. He was in battles of the Aleutian Islands, Eastern Mandates, Southern Philippines and Ryukyu. The following decorations were awarded to Morgan: Asiatic Pacific Theater Ribbon with 4 Bronze Service Stars and one Bronze Arrowhead, Good Conduct Ribbon, World War II Victory Medal and Philippines Liberation Ribbon with two Bronze Stars. He left the USA 11 July 1943 for the Asiatic Pacific Theater Operation, and returned to USA 16 November 1945. He had nine years of grammar school education. He was discharged 29 November 1945 at Camp Chaffee, Arkansas.

MORGAN, SAMUEL PAUL, had the Grade of Carpenter's Mate Third Class in the United States Navy. He was discharged 19 October 1945 from the Receiving Station, Navy Yards, Washington, D. C.
Source: Discharge Papers. No additional information.

MORGAN, TAYLOR T., was born on August 29, 1921, in Collinwood, Tennessee, and worked as a progress clerk. Taylor (Serial Number 34 375 242) entered the United States Army on October 3, 1942, in Ft. Oglethorpe, Georgia. On October 17, 1942, he was called to active duty and reported to Fort Oglethorpe, Georgia. He served with Company L, 311th Infantry as Platoon Sergeant. Taylor participated in battles at Ardennes and Central Europe and was awarded the following citations: Good Conduct, EAME Theater Ribbon with three Bronze Stars, Victory Medal and American Theater Ribbon. He was released from active duty and transferred to the Enlisted Reserve Corps, and returned to Waynesboro, Tennessee. He was discharged on January 15, 1946, at Camp Atterbury, Indiana.

MORGAN, WILLIAM DAVID, Serial Number 273 52 88, was a Seaman First Class in the United States Navy. He was born 17 November 1926 in Lauderdale County, Indiana. He volunteered and entered active service 30 November 1944. Vessels and Stations that he served on were: NTC Great Lakes, Illinois; and NTSCH (Radio) 190 N. State Street, Chicago, Illinois. He was discharged 17 July 1946 at the U. S. Naval Personnel Separation Center, Great Lakes, Illinois. He was awarded the American Theater Ribbon, and World War II Victory Medal.

MORRIS, EDD A., was a Seaman First Class in the United States Navy. He was discharged 13 October 1945 from the U. S. Naval Personnel Separation Center in Memphis, Tennessee.
Source: Discharge Papers. No additional information.

MORRIS, EVERETTE, volunteered for the draft and was inducted into the Army 12 August 1941 at Fort Oglethorpe,

Georgia. From there I went to Fort Eustus, Virginia for basic training. I was trained

on 155mm guns. From there I went to Fort Hancock, New Jersey where there were permanent gun emplacements for harbor defense. I was stationed here when Pearl Harbor was attacked. I was on a pass in New York City that night. I came out of a movie and the news boys were crying, "Pearl Harbor Attacked!" When we got back to our barracks, we had to help man our guns which were already on alert. After being at Fort Hancock for about a year, I was sent across the harbor to a section of Coney Island beach where we had 105mm gun emplacements. Then, later we got some of the 90mm Anti-Aircraft, which could be used for water targets as well. Then, I was sent to the Panama Canal Zone from Fort Meade, Maryland, where I had overseas training. We went down the Florida coast and by Cuba with a destroyer escort. From Panama I was sent to Galopagas Island of the coast of Ecuador, which was part of the Canal Zone Defense. On Galopagas, we had 155 mm guns for harbor defense. I stayed there for 18 months; while there I flew back to Panama twice for schooling and received a Hyperterrestrial Hopper certificate. I was sent back to Panama on the Pacific side in a permanent placement for harbor defense. I was here when the war ended. I came back to the States on a former cruise ship which came up the Gulf of Mexico to New Orleans. From here I was sent to Fort McPherson, Georgia and was demobilized on the 11 November 1945. I was a Technician Fourth Grade Plotter. As a Plotter, I acted as a member of a plotting team of fifteen men while serving with a coast artillery battery in the American Theater. We performed various duties in connection with determination of firing data for seacoast artillery of 155 mm Howitzer; calculated and plotted uncorrected range and azimuth on a mechanical plotting board; measured distance between points and calculated and set forward point; using a special slide rule to determine point at which target should be when projectile landed; calculated corrected range and deflection for nonstandard ballistic conditions and relayed correct data to guns for firing. I was also a telephone operator on a field switchboard. My Serial Number was 34 144 825, was a Technician Fourth Grade of Battery C, 4th Coast Artillery Battalion. My crew left for the American Theater 23 February 1944 and arrived back in the States November 1945. I was awarded the American Service Ribbon, Good Conduct Medal and World War II Victory Medal.

Everett Morris 11 October 1991.

MORRIS, FRED J., Serial Number 34 377193, was a Staff Sergeant in Company D, 12th Infantry in the Army of the United States. His permanent mailing address was Flatwoods, Tennessee. He was born 13 November 1920 in Linden, Tennessee. He was registered with Selective Service Board in Wayne County, Tennessee. His Civilian Occupation was Well Driller. He was married with two dependents when he was inducted 13 October 1942 and entered into active service 27 October 1942 at Fort Oglethorpe, Georgia. His Military Occupational Specialty was Squad Leader. His Military Qualifications included Command Infantry Badge, 35 Pistol, 1st CI Gunner 81 MM Mortar. He was in the battles of Normandy, North France, Ardennes, Rhineland, and Central Europe. The following decorations were awarded to Morris: Europe-African Middle Eastern Theater Service Medal and Purple Heart. He was wounded in Action in the Europe-African Middle Eastern Theater 17 June 1944. He left the USA 18 January 1944 for the Europe-African Middle Eastern Theater Operation, and returned to USA 12 July 1945. He was discharged 17 September 1945 at Camp Gordon, Georgia.

MORRIS, GUILFORD RAY, enlisted in the United States Navy 3 July 1943 for two years. His ratings in the Navy were, Seaman 2C, and Seaman First Class. The Vessels and Stations that Morris was assigned to were: NTS, San Diego, California; Landing Craft School LCS, PAC; USS PRINCE GEORGE, USN Base Hospital No. 8; Navy Air Base, Disp Navy Number 3237; USNH Navy Number 10; US Navy Base Navy Number 3245, USNH CAHU, T. H USNH, Navy 10, USNH, Portsmouth, Virginia. His rating at discharge was Seaman First Class V6 3V, USNR. Ray saw action in the South Pacific, was wounded, spent time in the hospital in Hawaii and was discharged 7 September 1945 at US Naval Hospital in Portsmouth, Virginia. Morris was awarded a Discharge Button and Honorable Service Emblem. Ray, son of George and Mary Ellen "Molly" (Berry) Morris, was born 9 October 1914 in Lutts, Tennessee. He lived the early part of his life with the family at their home on Weatherford Creek in South Wayne County. His siblings are: Inez born 8 October 1910; Ruth born 18 July 1912; Lawton born 3 November 1916, died 18 November 1934; Juanita born 15 September 1918, died 7 July 1920; Marie born 10 December 1920; Raymond born 14 January 1922; Maydon born 1925; Beatrice born 1927; Billy born 1930; Rex died an infant 1932; and an Infant born and died 14 July 1934. Ray married 24 March 1940 Mary Patterson. Mr. Morris, 82 of Lutts, died 14 June 1997 at Glenwood Convalescent Center in Florence and was buried in Memorial Gardens. He was a retired General Motors employee, a member of Liberty Baptist Church, and a member of the Disabled American Veterans. Survivors included his wife, Mary Patterson Morris of Lutts; three daughters, Janet Roldan of Crofton, MD, Judy Vickers of Waterford, MI. and Joann Kannegieter of PeePaw, MI; one brother, Billie L. Morris of Chula Vista, CA; three sisters, Ruth Wright of Waynesboro, Marie Horton and Maedon Haddock both of Florence and six grandchildren.

Source: Wayne County News, 18 June 1997.

MORRIS, HAROLD, Serial Number 976 65 98, was a Seaman First Class in the Navy of the United States. His perma-

nent mailing address was Route 1, Waynesboro, Tennessee. He was born 30 July 1926 in Waynesboro, Wayne County, Tennessee. He was registered with Selective Service Board in Wayne County, Tennessee. His Civilian Occupation was General Farmer. He was inducted 19 October 1944 at Chattanooga, Tennessee. Below is a list of the ships and stations that Morris served on: NTC Great Lakes, Illinois; USN TAD CEN Shoemaker, California; R/S Navy 128; Naval Supply Depot Navy 926 (Guam and Saipan). The following decorations were awarded to Morris Asiatic-Pacific Theater Medal, World War II Victory Medal, Honorable Discharge Button, Honorable Service Lapel Button and Honorable Service Emblem. He had an eighth grade education. He was discharged 27 March 1946 at US Naval Separation Center in Memphis, Tennessee. Harold's parents were John Herman and Mary Ann (Walker) Morris. He had a brother, John Dee Morris. His children are, Brenda married Kenneth Thompson has three children and lives in Collinwood; James Herman "BO" Junior, has three children and lives in Collinwood; and Brenda Kathryn married Daryl West, two children and lives in Collinwood. Ray's occupations after his discharge were, putting siding on homes, and working for the Wayne County Road System. He is now retired and lives at PO Box 115, Collinwood, Tennessee.

MORRIS, HOWARD, Serial Number 34 194 584, was a Private in Medical Detachment, 44th Ordinance Battalion in the Army of the United States. His permanent mailing address was Route 1, Waynesboro, Tennessee. He was born 28 November 1910 in Wayne County, Tennessee. He was registered with Selective Service Board in Wayne County, Tennessee. His Civilian Occupation was General Farm Hand. He was single when he was inducted 4 April 1942 at Fort Oglethorpe, Georgia. His Military Occupational Specialty was Surgical Technician. He was in the battles of Southern France, Rome-Arno, Rhineland, and Central Europe. The following decorations were awarded to Morris: American Theater Ribbon, Europe-African Middle Eastern Theater Ribbon with 4 Bronze Stars, Good Conduct Ribbon, World War II Victory Medal and Lapel Button. He left the USA 31 March 1944 for the European Theater Operation, and returned to USA 16 December 1945. He had an eighth grade education. He was discharged 21 December 1945 at Camp Atterbury, Indiana. Harold's parents were Mr. and Mrs. Frank Morris. His siblings were, Herman, Georgia Ray, Lillian Barnett and Earl Brock. Harold married Katherine Galloway.

MORRIS, JAY W., was born 30 August 1915 in the Hardin's Creek area of Wayne County, Tennessee. His parents were Jake and Minnie Ola (Shipman) Morris. He was the youngest of seven children and the only one to serve in the armed services of the United States. He was inducted into the Army on the 14 March 1942 at Fort Oglethorpe, Georgia. He had his basic training in Camp Claiborne, Louisiana and was placed in the 82nd All American Division. While at Camp Claiborne, the Army created from the 82nd, another Division- the 101st. There were over 15,000 men in this group. This was the birth of the paratroopers and glider troopers. These men were from all over the United States. Jay was in the Glider Company. The day these two divisions were formed, a World War I hero from East Tennessee came to speak to these men. He was Alvin C. York. He made a very patriotic speech and he also elaborated on the changing tactics of fighting in WWI and WWII. The men from Tennessee felt a sense of pride in his being there. In early summer of 1942, the two divisions were transferred to Fort Bragg, North Carolina. Some glider training was done at Camp McCall in Pine Hurst, North Carolina. Jay made the rank

of Corporal at this time and in less than two years attained the rank of 1st Sergeant. In February 1944, Jay was sent with a cadre of noncommissioned officers to Camp Pickett, Virginia to form the 1004th Engineers Service Battalion and was sent to the European Theater Operation 3 January 1945. He was stationed in Holland. Their job was to lay and service a gasoline pipe line from Antwerp, Belgium to the front lines, to supply General George Patton and his 3rd Army. As Jay can attest, Patton was a difficult man to keep up with. This line was so well camouflaged it was never bombed. Jay's Serial Number was 34 193 030. His Military Occupational Specialty was Construction Foreman. His Military Qualifications included Rifle M1 Expert. The following decorations were awarded to Morris: American Theater Service Ribbon, Europe-African Middle Eastern Theater Service Ribbon, Good Conduct Ribbon and World War II Victory Medal. Jay was honorably discharged 20 November 1945 at Fort Belvoir, Virginia. He attended the University of Tennessee in Martin and majored in Agriculture. His civilian job included farming, teaching 6th, 7th and 8th grades in rural schools and coached boys and girls basket ball teams. Also in Sandusky, Ohio in December 1941, he worked as a carpenter on construction of igloos for the storage of high explosives. He also did rough carpentry on railroad bridges. Jay married Norma Jean Boyd, daughter of Ralph W. and Pauline (Merriman) Boyd, on 31 December 1942. They have two daughters, Jaynette W. Meidinger and Bettie Rae Gobble, seven grandchildren and three great-grandchildren. Jay has two sisters, Nellie and Atrell Nowlin. His brothers are Charlie, Marvin, Roy and Raleigh.

MORRIS, JOHN DEE, Serial Number 967 13 71, was a Seaman Second Class, V-6, in the Navy of the United States. He was born 14 May 1924 in Waynesboro, Wayne County, Tennessee. He was single when he volunteered and enlisted 11 April 1944 at Nashville, Tennessee for two years. Below is a list of the ships and stations that Morris served on: USNRS, Nashville, Tennessee; and USNTADC, Williamsburg, Virginia; The Honorable Service Lapel Button was awarded to Morris: . He had a high school education. He was discharged 2 June 1944 from the US Naval Training and Distribution Center at Camp Peary, Williamsburg, Virginia because he was not physically qualified for reenlistment. His parents were John Herman and Mary Ann (Walker) Morris. He had brother, Harold. J. D has one son, David Morris of Toledo, Ohio and two granddaughters. After his

discharge, J. D worked for seventeen years for Auto-Lite. Then he worked for Toledo Scales until he retired. His residence is now Route 4, Waynesboro, Tennessee 38485.

MORRIS, RAYMOND, enlisted in the United States Navy in 1941 and served on the USS COLUMBIA. He was a Quarter-

master Second Class. Raymond, son of George and Mary "Molly" (Berry) Morris, was born 14 January 1922. He lived the early part of his life with the family at their home on Weatherford Creek in South Wayne County. His siblings are: Inez born 8 October 1910; Ruth born 18 July 1912; Guilford Ray born 9 October 1914; Lawton born 3 November 1916, died 18 November 1934; Juanita born 15 September 1918, died 7 July 1920; Marie born 10 December 1920; Maydon born 1925; Beatrice born 1927; Billy born 1930; Rex died an infant 1932; and an Infant born and died 14 July 1934.

MORRIS, RAYMOND G., Serial Number 34 144 899, was a Technician Fifth Grade in Headquarters Battery, 633rd Artillery Battalion in the Army of the United States. His permanent mailing address was Route 2, Lutts, Tennessee. He was born 14 January 1919 in Wayne County, Tennessee. He was registered with Selective Service Board in Wayne County, Tennessee. His Civilian Occupation was General Farm Hand. He was married with two dependents when he inducted 12 August 1941 at Fort Oglethorpe, Georgia. His Military Occupational Specialty was Light Truck Driver. He was in the battles of Tunisian Sicily, Naples, Foggia, and Rome-Arno. The following decorations were awarded to Morris: American Defense Service Medal, Europe-African Middle Eastern Theater Ribbon with 4 Bronze Stars, and Good Conduct Medal. He left the USA 6 August 1942 for the European Theater Operation, and returned to USA 12 June 1945. He had one year of high school education. He was discharged 23 June 1945 at Fort McPherson, Georgia.

MORRIS, REEDER THOMAS, son of Willie and Ola (Hodges) Morris, received his letter from Uncle Sam in September 1942. He was to report for duty with the U.S. Army at Fort Oglethorpe, Georgia on October 21, 1942. Reeder left his new bride, Waymon (Stricklin) Morris, whom he had married only one month earlier, and with his brother-in-law J.R. Combs headed for Fort Oglethorpe. From Georgia he was sent to Medford, Oregon to begin his basic training at Camp White. He was placed in the 346th Field Artillery Battalion, 91st Division Battery "A". He operated a 105 Howltizer gun and drove a kitchen truck part time.

In May 1943 he finished his training, received a furlough and left for Tennessee to see his family and to get his wife and take her back with him to Camp White in Oregon. Waymon stayed with him in Oregon for six months before he was sent to Yakima, Washington for more training. From Washington he was sent to Camp Adair in Corvallis, Oregon. While at Camp Adair he became ill and received a Medical Discharge on February 1, 1944.

After his discharge, Reeder returned to Tennessee to continue his life with his wife Waymon. They have three children, a daughter, Betty (Morris) Martin, two sons, Larry Thomas Morris and Teddy Matthew Morris, (deceased). They have four grandchildren, Deb (Martin) Staggs, Shane Martin, Kim (Morris) Chandler, and Jennifer (Morris) Krieger. They also have seven great grandchildren, Derek and Hunter Martin, Blake and Morgan Chandler, Colby and Bailey Staggs, and Charlee Ann, Cody, and Nathan Krieger.

Reeder said that he Thanks God everyday for his Country, his family and his life.

MORRISON, JOEL REECE, was born 31 March 1925, the oldest child and only son of William Greyford and Clarice Alberta (Duren) Morrison. He was the oldest grandchild of William Semour and Ora (Cypert) Morrison and Samuel Wayne and Viola Belle (Morgan) Duren. Joel has two sisters, Mary and Margaret. Joel entered the United States Navy in June 1943. He was sent to San Diego, California. SM2C (Petty Officer, Signal Man 2nd Class) Morrison was assigned to Min. Division 34-7th Fleet Operation and served on the USS SCRIMMAGE Am 297 (Auxiliary Mine Sweeper) in the Pacific. Petty Officer Morrison received an Honorable Discharge in March 1946 at Memphis.

MORROW, EDWARD EUGENE, son of Mr. and Mrs. Guy Morrow of Waynesboro, attended Wayne County Schools and graduated from the University of Chattanooga. August 1943, he volunteered for the Army Air Corp. and received his basic training at Keesler Field, MS, then received his preflight training at Maxwell Field, AL.

MORROW, MACK GENTRY, was born 17 May 1908 in Waynesboro, Tennessee. Mack, the son of Cicero L. and Mattie Lee Morrow, died 18 April 1970 and was buried in Greenwood Cemetery in Waynesboro. He was the sixth of ten children, three brothers, Clay, Esco and Harry, who died in infancy. One sister, Susie was struck and killed by lighting at the age of five. These are buried in the old Morrow Cemetery on Upper Green River. Another sister, Ione, died of whooping cough and pneumonia when she was eight years old and is buried in Greenwood Cemetery. Four brothers lived to manhood: Forrest, Austin, Roy and Edward. Austin is buried in Greenwood and Roy in Waynesboro Memorial Gardens. Forrest, the oldest is 89 years old and lives in Savannah. Edward, the youngest, entered the US Air Force after graduation from University of Tennessee. He was sent to the Pacific and flew one of the early missions over Japan. His plane was reported missing in action. Later he was declared dead. After WWII was over, his ashes were found in Japan where his body had been recovered and cremated. Mack was married 18 August 1949 to Bessie Pigg. They had two daughters, Linda and Cindy. Linda is married to Steve Nowlin and they have one daughter. They live in Dothan, Alabama. Cindy is married to Wayne Holly of Cornersville, Tennessee. They live in Boston, Massachusetts. Mack enlisted in the Air Force 15 February 1942. After an extensive training period at Keesler Field, Mississippi and Wendover Field, Utah, he was given the rating of Sergeant and assigned to a base "some where in England.

" He was attached to the 306th Bomb Group, 423rd Squadron. His Serial Number is 34 189 083. A summation of the year's accomplishments (1942) included proof, that despite the fact that only 50 to 72 aircraft participated in the missions, the 306th had succeeded where the RAF had failed. They were the first over Germany. Mack, with his first Bombardment Division was awarded a Presidential Citation for "extraordinary heroism, determination and esprit de corps in action against the enemy on 11 January 1942. " This is the highest citation that can be given to a unit, equivalent to the Distinguished Service Cross. Mack came back from England on the famous Queen Mary, and docked in New York.

MORROW, MILLARD HOWARD, son of the late Millard Franklin and Edna Florence (Rippy) Morrow, was born 3 Feb-

ruary 1922 in Cookeville, Tennessee while his father was a student at Tennessee Tech. Howard's siblings include Grayford Frank, Mary Margaret Morman, and Dorotha Elizabeth Stinnett of Jonesboro, Arkansas. Grayford and Mary are deceased. His maternal grandparents were Dr. Willie Wilson and Mary Melinda (Martin) Rippy of Collinwood His paternal grandparents were Robert Luther and Margaret Henderson (Brewer) Morrow. Howard married Bessie Corinne Van Buskirk 11 July 1948 at Aberdeen, Mississippi. They have two children, William Howard Morrow and Judy Corinne Perris and several grandchildren. Howard attended Waynesboro Elementary School, Mound Elementary School in Caruthersville, Missouri, Frank Hughes High School in Clifton, Collinwood High School, and Chapman College in Los Angles, California. He also attended several service schools, including, Naval Technical Training Center in Chicago, Illinois, Naval Air Technical Training Center in Memphis, Tennessee, Faetulant Electronic School in

Jacksonville, Florida, Trades Training Institute of Mississippi State College, Starkville, Mississippi, and several Lockheed Aircraft Company sponsored schools in Marietta, Georgia. Howard was inducted into the United States Navy 14 October 1942 and was discharged 9 December 1945 in New Orleans, Louisiana. He served on the following Vessels and Stations: NTS, San Diego, California; NTSCH, Los Angeles, California; NATTCEN, Chicago, Illinois; NATTC, Memphis, Tennessee; NAS, Jacksonville, Florida; NATS, FLT Unit, NASS, Cecil Field, Jacksonville, Florida; and Carrier Aircraft Service Unit 36, Pacific Area. He held the following ratings: AS, S3C, EM3C, AEM3C, AEM2C, and AEM1C. He also served in the US Navy during the Korean Conflict from 13 October 1951 to 16 February 1953. After graduating from high school, Howard joined the Plumbers and Steamfitters Union at Sheffield, Alabama. He also worked at Reynolds Metal Company in Sheffield and Red Stone Arsenal in Huntsville. Copper Tubing Plant, Decatur, Alabama; McDonald Aircraft Company, St. Louis, Missouri; Lockheed Aircraft Corporation, Marietta, Georgia; Douglas Aircraft Company and Northrop Aircraft Company, both of Cape Canaveral, Florida; Lockheed-Georgia Company, and Lockheed Aeronautical System Company both of Marietta, Georgia. Howard was associated with the research, development, production, delivery and product support of the following projects: F4F, C-130 and Jet Star Aircraft, Thor and Snark Missile, Humming Bird, C-141, C-5 and C-117 Aircraft. The C-130, C-141 and C-5 Aircraft have a long history of service for the US Military. The C-117 is a Radar Avoidance Aircraft and was used successfully during the Gulf War. He was also associated with the project to rescue the hostages in Iran during President Carter's Administration. He helped launch several missiles at Cape Canaveral. Once, he was assigned to Andrews Air Force Base in Camp Springs, Maryland and was associated with the SAM Squadron. These were Jet Star Aircraft used by the president, vice-president and other high ranking Government officials. Howard is now retired from Lockheed and lives with his wife at 1100 Wingate Drive, Southwest, Marietta, Georgia, where they enjoy visits from their children and grandchildren.

MORROW, ROBERT ALLEN, Serial Number 34 361 767, was a Private First Class in Company E, 1306th Engineer General Service Regiment in the Army of the United States. His permanent mailing address was % Allen Rose, Route 2, Harriman, Tennessee. His home address was Route 1, Collinwood. He was born 29 July 1921 in Collinwood, Tennessee. His Civilian Occupation was General Farmer. He was inducted 25 July 1942 at Fort Oglethorpe, Georgia. His Military Occupational Specialty was Carpenter, Heavy Construction. His Military Qualifications included Sharpshooter Rifle. He was in the battles of Ardennes, Rhineland, Northern France and Central Europe. The following decorations were awarded to Morrow: American Theater Ribbon, Europe-African Middle Eastern Theater Ribbon with 4 Bronze Service Stars, Asiatic Pacific Theater Ribbon, Philippines Liberation Ribbon and World War II Victory Medal. He left the USA 20 March 1944 for Europe-African Middle Eastern, left 23 June 1944 for Asiatic Pacific Theater Operation, and returned to USA 25 November 1945. He spent twenty months in England, Belgium, Luxembourg, Germany, Austria, Philippine Islands and Japan. He had an eighth grade education. His work during his service included constructing bridges, hospitals, warehouses... reading blue prints and sketches. Also, he was in salt mines when they found much gold that Germans had stored. He was discharged 10 December 1945 at Camp Chaffee, Arkansas. Robert's parents were Ernest L. and Christine (Murdock) Morrow. Robert enrolled in the Civilian Conservation Corps 16 July 1940 at Lawrenceburg, Tennessee at age 17 and was discharge 30 June 1942 at Fort Oglethorpe, Georgia. His company was 4436 CCC.

MORTON, EUNICE D., Serial Number RA-44 124 526, was a Private First Class in 7025th Area Service Unit Enlisted Detachment in the Army of the United States. His permanent mailing address was Route 6, Waynesboro, Tennessee. He volunteered and was inducted 13 March 1946 at South Post, Fort Myer, Virginia. His Military Occupational Specialty was General Clerk. His Military Qualifications included Rifle Marksman. The following decorations were awarded to Morton: American Theater Ribbon, Lapel button and World War II Victory Medal. His prior service was from 16 August 1945 to 12 March 1946. He had a fourth grade education. He was discharged 8 May 1947 at Fort Myer, Virginia. Eunice, was born 22 May 1927, died 19 May 1983 and was buried in Whitehead Cemetery in Topsy, Wayne County. He was a son of Charlie Denton (20 June 1897-13 March 1976) and Lidia Ann Morton (9 February 1904-14 February 1978).

MOSER, CHARLES L., was born August 14, 1925 in Wayne County, Tennessee. The son of Charles Sherman Moser and John Ella Melson Moser of Wayne County, Tennessee. Charles was drafted into the United States Army on November 18, 1943 at Fort Oglethorpe, Georgia. His Army Serial Number was 34 88 9156. After completion of basic infantry and military police specialized training he spent a short time stateside. Then in March 1945 he was sent to France where he participated in the central European campaign until the end of the war. His military occupational specialty was Military Policeman and he was assigned to 1st Battalion, 253rd Infantry Regiment, 63rd Infantry Division in General Patton's 3rd Army. After Germany surrender in 1945, he was assigned as part of the occupation forces in Germany until May 1946. In May 1946 he was shipped back to the United States and released from service at Camp Atterbury, Indiana on May 31, 1946.

He was discharged as a Private First Class and had served two years, six months and fourteen days in the Army. His decorations include; Combat Infantryman Badge, Army of Occupation Medal Germany, American Theater Ribbon, EAME Theater Ribbon w/I Bronze Star, Army Good Conduct Medal and World War II Victory Medal.

MURPHY, RICHARD, Serial Number 34 378 559, was a Private in Troop B, 161st Engineer Squadron in the Army of the United States. He was born in Lutts, Wayne County, Tennessee. His Civilian Occupation was Farmer. He was 38 years old when he was inducted 21 October 1942 at Fort Oglethorpe, Georgia. He was discharged 17 February 1943 at Fort Bliss, Texas.

NANCE, EDWARD, Serial Number 34 362 618, was a Private in Headquarters and Headquarters Squadron, 9th Service Group, Army Air Force in the Army of the United States. His permanent mailing address was Route 1, Clifton, Tennessee. He was registered with Selective Service

Board in Wayne County, Tennessee. His Civilian Occupation was General Farm Hand. He was married when he was inducted 1 August 1942 and entered into active service 15 August 1942 at Fort Oglethorpe, Georgia. His Military Occupational Specialty was Light Truck Driver. His Military Qualifications included MM Carbine. He received his training in Texas. He was in the battles of Normandy, Ardennes, Rhineland, and Northern France. The following decorations were awarded to Nance: World War II Victory Medal, American Service Medal, Good Conduct Ribbon, and Europe-African Middle Eastern Theater Ribbon with 4 Bronze Stars. He left the USA 6 April 1944 for the European Theater Operation, and returned to USA 12 September 1945. He was discharged 5 November 1945 at Fort McPherson, Georgia.

He was born 13 August 1915, died August 1976 and was buried in Prater's Chapel Cemetery. He was the son of Robert and Leamer (Evans) Nance. His brothers were, Forrest, Kenny and Oliver "Penny" Nance. His sisters were Allie, Mae, Bessie and Tellie Nance. Tellie married Albert Pulley. He married Carlene Frazier, daughter of Jim Frazier. Their children were, Jeannie, Gayle and Austin Nance.

NANCE, JOHN CORNELIUS, Serial Number 14 039 248, was a Private in Military Police Company, Service Command Unit 1100 in the Army of the United States. His permanent mailing address was Route 1, Waynesboro, Tennessee. He was born 5 January 1920 in Wayne County. His Civilian Occupation was General Farmer. He was inducted 7 February 1941 in Fort Bragg, North Carolina. His Military Occupational Specialty was Heavy Machine Gunner. He was in the battles of Guadalcanal and Central Pacific. The following decorations were awarded to Nance: Asiatic Pacific Theater Campaign Ribbon with 2 Service

Stars, Good Conduct Medal and American Defense Service Medal with Clasp. He left the USA 28 May 1941 for the Asiatic Pacific Theater Operation, and returned to USA 18 May 1944. He had an eighth grade education. He was discharged 31 May 1945 at Convalescent Hospital, Camp Edwards, Massachusetts.

NANCE, OLIVER "PENNY", Serial Number 34 377 187, was a Private First Class in the 329th Infantry, Eighty-Third

Division in the Army of the United States. His permanent mailing address was Route 1, Clifton, Tennessee. He was born 2 April 1921 in Clifton, Tennessee. He was registered with Selective Service Board in Wayne County, Tennessee. His Civilian Occupation was General Farm Hand. He was inducted 13 October 1942 and entered into active service 27 October 1942 at Fort Oglethorpe, Georgia. His Military Occupational Specialty was Heavy Mortar Crewman. His Military Qualifications included Combat Infantryman Badge. He was in the battles of Normandy, France, Ardennes, Rhineland, and Central Europe. The following decorations were awarded to Nance: Middle Eastern Theater Ribbon with 5 Bronze Stars, Good Conduct Ribbon, World War II Victory Medal, European African Distinguished Unit Badge and American Theater Ribbon. He left the USA 6 April 1944 for the Europe-African Middle Eastern Theater Operation, and returned to USA 14 December 1945. He was discharged 18 December 1945 at Fort Knox, Kentucky. Nance had brown eyes, brown hair, was 5'9" tall, weight 158 lbs, and had zero dependents.

"Penny" is the son of Robert "Doc" and Leamer (Evans) Nance. His brothers were, Forrest, Kenny and Edward Nance. His sisters were Allie, Mae, Bessie and Tellie Nance. Tellie married Albert Pulley. He married Wanda Sue Wilson, daughter of Connie and Maude Wilson of Clifton. They have one son, Dennis Wayne Nance and

three grandchildren, Donna, Josh Evan and Gabriel Nance. "Penny" has worked as a general timber worker, State bridge painter and Genesco Shoe Company in Waynesboro for twenty-five years before he retired.

Penny's comments: "I was sent to the European Theater of War. We went over on a British ship. The Colonel called us together and spoke to us about the war and our part in it. He mentioned that not all of us would come back. Some were seasick and it was terrible, but I was lucky not to be sick. I remember seeing two submarines. They sunk one of them. Lawrence Woods and I left here together and we stayed together during the entire time over there, however, he got home a week or two before I did. We landed in Liverpool, England. It took us fourteen days to get there. From Liverpool we boarded a train, which carried us almost to the camp of our unit. They let us out to walk quite a distance to our destination. We arrived on April 18th. This was somewhere in England. We left here on 6 June 1944 going toward France. We went in there, two or three days after the Normandy Invasion. We stayed behind the front lines about two weeks. Then we were heading for the battle of the Bulge area. On the 12th day of December, as we were having our supper, orders came to be ready to leave in five minutes. We were transported about forty miles away. During this move three volunteers in a jeep turned back for our food and they did not return until late in the night. We were attacked at dawn. A rifle shot went right by the side of my head. I slumped down in a hedge row. There were hedge rows everywhere. They were used to fence fields and plots of ground. I didn't know what was going on. I could not tell or find my unit. It was about a week before we all got together again. Some went back toward the beach. Some had received cuts and wounds.

After returning home I found that J. W. Boyd, Curtis Northcutt, a Ricketts boy from Clifton, Clayton Staggs and Edd Thompson were not too far from all the rest of us. We were all in the same unit, left Fort Oglethorpe together. Lawrence Woods was the only one who stayed right with me and that meant a lot. We had a picture made at the Wayne County Court House before we left that day. All did not return home."

A copy of his Unit Citation from APO 83rd Headquarters, 83rd Infantry Division dated 4 September 1945 was enclosed. It read in part: "Third U. S. Army, the Second Battalion, 329th Infantry Regiment is cited for outstanding performance of duty in armed conflict with the enemy from 12 December 1944 to 16 December 1944. On the morning of the 12th December 1944 the unit from positions in the Hurtgen Forest in Germany initiated an attack toward Duren, with Gurzenich as its objective. In two days of bitter fighting it advanced three thousand yards, It traveled thru dense, heavily mined coniferous woods, constantly menaced by deadly artillery and mortar tree bursts and heavy machine gun and small arms fire. For twenty-five hundred yards it traversed an open plain against an enemy firmly entrenched astride the only flanks, and in the face of direct observation by the enemy. It suffered severe causalities, but its men never faltered carrying on with a determination that forced a fanatical foe to give ground although possessing every advantage of terrain, disposition and observation.

NANCE, TOMMIE, Serial Number 34 495 082, was a Private attached to 28th Tng Group in the AAFTTC, Jefferson Barracks, Missouri in the Army of the United States. Pvt. Nance honorably served in active Federal Service in the Army of the United States from 22 November 1942 to 8 April 1943. He was discharged 8 April 1943 with excellent character.

NELSON, ELLIS, Serial Number 19 020 522, was a Technician Fifth Grade in Battery A 365th Antiaircraft Artillery Automatic Weapons Battalion in the Army of the United States. His permanent mailing address was Route 2, Waynesboro, Tennessee. He was born 17 May 1924 in Wayne County. He was registered with Selective Service Board in Wayne County, Tennessee. His Civilian Occupation was General Farmer. He was inducted 23 April 1943 and entered into active service 30 April 1943 at Fort Oglethorpe, Georgia. His Military Occupational Specialty was Power Generator Operator. His Military Qualifications included Rifle MM Carbine, Selective Service Driver and Mechanic Badge. He was in the battles of Ardennes, Rhineland, and Central Europe. The following decorations were awarded to Nelson: American Theater Ribbon, Europe-African Middle Eastern Theater Ribbon with 3 Bronze Stars, Good Conduct Ribbon and World War II Victory Medal. He left the USA 6 October 1944 for the European Theater Operation, and returned to USA 8 March 1946. He was discharged 13 March 1946 at Camp Atterbury, Indiana.

NORMAN, CHARLES LAFAYETTE, was drafted 1 October 1942, and entered Service 11 November 1942. He was scheduled to report 4 November 1942 but his son Charles Cleveland was born that day and his departure was delayed until 11 November 1942. He went to Fort Oglethorpe, Georgia, transferred to Richmond,

Virginia, H&S CO. 851 ENGR. A. V. N. B. N. where he went to Engineering school, then he went to Jefferson Barrack, Missouri, and from there to Salt Lake City, Utah, U. S. Air Base Squadron 14, then to Spokane, Washington 851 A. V. N. Gieger Field Air Base. Next, he went to New York and was shipped to England in April 1943. He stayed in England until November 1944, when he returned to North Carolina to guard German prisoners, then to South Carolina. He was discharged at Fort Oglethorpe, Georgia after spending 2 years, 11 months and 28 days in service.

Charles was born 9 December 1905 in Waynesboro, Tennessee. He died 21 February 1971 and was buried in Greenwood Cemetery in Waynesboro. He was the son of Dr. Frank Harvey and Kate (Morrison) Norman. He had two brothers, Paul Eve and Frank Harvey, Jr. His four sisters were, Sallie Helton, Mildred Davis, Mary Butler and Katherine Brooks. He married Sherman Evelyn Skelton and they had two sons, Charles Cleveland and James Allen Norman. He had one stepdaughter, Nina Racine Piller.

NORMAN, FRANK HARVEY, JR., was born 15 August 1915 in Waynesboro, Tennessee. My parents were Dr. Frank Harvey and Kate (Morrison) Norman. My maternal grandparents were William David "Dee" and Ruth Elizabeth "Lizzie" (Burns) Morrison. My paternal grandparents were William M. and Sarah Jane (McLean) Norman. My two brothers are, Paul Eve and Frank Harvey, Jr. My four sisters are, Sallie Helton, Mildred Davis, Mary Butler and Katherine Brooks. I was married 8 October 1941 to Dorothy Russ of Clifton, Tennessee. Our two children are Frank Harvey Norman, III and Mary Alice Norman. Mary Alice is married to Gary David Smith, and they reside in Tullahoma, Tennessee. They have two sons, Steven Norman and David Lewis Norman.

My first paying occupation was that of assistant postmaster in Waynesboro. In 1939 my brother Paul and I purchased the Waynesboro Funeral Parlor, and I managed that until I volunteered for service during World War II. I was a Seaman First Class in the Naval Reserve, stationed at the U. S. Naval Training Station, Great Lakes, Illinois. My first assigned duty was that of delivering mail. After that, I was assigned to Clothing Supply. I received an Honorable Medical Discharge 12 October 1942.

After coming back to Waynesboro, I applied for work with the U. S. Postal Service and was assigned to the Arcade Post Office in Nashville. In 1943, I purchased a grocery store in Waynesboro and managed it for ten years. During this time, I became interested in the automobile busi-

ness having my store between two dealerships, the Ford and the Dodge dealerships. In October 1953, I heard that a Buick Dealership in Tullahoma was for sale. A partner, Donald J. Ellis and I purchased the business and I remained in the Buick sales and service for twenty-one years. I sold the business in 1984 for health reasons. Since that time, I have worked with and partially owned an interest in both Ford and Chrysler-Plymouth Dealerships in Tullahoma. I have lived in Tullahoma for thirty-eight years. Our address is 800 Stone Blvd. I presently work with Russell Barnett Ford in Tullahoma.

NORMAN, JAMES, Serial Number 14 153 649, was a Private First Class in 3111th Signal Service Battalion in the Army of the United States. His permanent mailing address was Route 5, Waynesboro, Tennessee. He was born 1 January 1922 in Waynesboro, Tennessee. He was registered with Selective Service Board in Wayne County, Tennessee. His Civilian Occupation was Student. He enlisted 5 October 1942 at Nashville Tennessee. His home address at time of entry was 1042 W. Eastland Avenue, Nashville. His Military Occupational Specialty was Light Truck Driver. His Military Qualifications included Marksman 30 Caliber Rifle. He was in the battles of Normandy, Northern France, Ardennes, Rhineland, and Central Europe. The following decorations were awarded to Norman: American Theater Ribbon, Europe-African Middle Eastern Theater Ribbon with 5 Bronze Stars, Good Conduct Ribbon and World War II Victory Medal. He left the USA 31 March 1944 for the Europe an African Middle Eastern Theater Operation, and returned to USA 7 December 1945. He had one year of college before he entered service. He was discharged 15 December 1945 at Fort Knox, Kentucky.

NORMAN, PAUL EVE, was born 9 September 1907 in Waynesboro, Tennes-

see. I was sworn into the United States Army on 22 January 1944 at Camp Forrest, near Tullahoma, Tennessee and arrived at Camp Shelby, Mississippi on 13 February 1944. I was in several camps during the war, graduating from the Counter Intelligence School of the Army at Camp Ritchie, Maryland. I was discharged 19 October 1945 at A. P. Hill Military Reservation in Virginia, My Military Occupational Specialty was Military Policeman. My Military Qualifications included Marksman Rifle M1903. The Good Conduct Medal was awarded to me.

He was the son of Dr. Frank Harvey and Kate (Morrison) Norman. He had two brothers, Charles LaFayette and Frank Harvey, Jr. His four sisters were, Sallie Helton, Mildred Davis, Mary Butler and Katherine Brooks. He married Mabel and they had two children, Paul, Jr. and Lucy.

NORRIS, ELMER F., of Clifton, TN served with Co. A 61st Signal Battalion, during World War 11. He received a letter of commendation, endorsed by his commanding general for dangerous work with hot electrical wires where one error might have meant death, while on an emergency assignment after a storm at Pueblo Air Base.

NORTHCUTT, CURTIS HUGH, served his country during WWII in the US Army. He was the son of Will and Lee Northcutt of Wayne County. He was born September 17, 1921.

He married his wife Billie Faye in West TN. They had two children; David and Mary Ruth.

NOWLIN, WALTER, JR., When asked why he chose to join the Marines rather than another branch of the service, Walter Nowlin, Jr., (W. J or "Dub") told his family he liked the Marine uniforms better than any of the others. He said he thought he would look best in the dress blues of the United States Marine Corps. This become a family joke and the source of a great deal of teasing for W. J. for years to come.

Walter Nowlin, Jr., son of Walter, Sr., and Parilee (Shelton) Nowlin of Collinwood, was sworn into the U. S. Marine Corps on 23 April 1943 in Nashville, Tennessee. He took his basic training at Camp Pendleton, California, and was assigned to the 4th Battalion of the 14th Regiment, 4th Marine Division. The 14th was a gunnery regiment assigned to the larger artillery. Though he trained on many weapons, his gunnery crew was assigned to the 105mm guns.

On 6 January 1944, the Fourth Marine Division boarded ships and headed to their new home base on Maui, Hawaiian Islands. While there he wrote home and mentioned that he had seen fellow Wayne Countians, J. B. Kelso and Leslie Bryson. His letters home always seemed to refer to friends he had seen or spoken with briefly.

As the Fourth Division moved out to their first combat in the Pacific, the first objective was the Marshall Islands. It was the largest of these, the twin islands of Roi-Nemur, that many of the troops, including Private Nowlin, saw their first fighting. Though the U. S. troops secured the Marshalls in less than two weeks, the casualties were very high. The Fourth arrived back at Maui 25 February 1944. While at home base, they trained for future missions and built on the camp there.

The next step toward Japan for the Fourth Division was the Marianna Islands. Saipan was the first of these islands to be targeted. On 15 June 1944, the landings began. On his first day in Saipan, a sniper narrowly missed Pfc. Nowlin's head with a bullet, grazing his right ear. Also during this campaign, Nowlin lost about a half inch of the long finger on his right hand while loading ammo into his gun during battle. The Marines encountered a whole different terrain in the Marianna's than they had in the Marshall's. Saipan was dotted with scores of coral-limestone caves, tunnels and caverns which the Japanese soldiers used to their full advantage by striking and escaping through this network of tunnels. On 9 July 1944, after 25 days of continuous fighting, "Old Glory" was hoisted to mark the securing of the island.

Two weeks later, the men of the Fourth made the beachhead of nearby Tinian. The landing date was 24 July 1944 and nine days later the island was secured. On 14 August 1944, the last units of the Fourth boarded ships for home base, Maui. The Marines had made one more big step toward Japan. The brave and costly accomplishments of the Fourth Division were recognized with the awarding of the Presidential Unit Citation. It was during this campaign, 14 July 1944, that Private Nowlin became Corporal Nowlin.

The landings began on the most strategic and costly island in the Pacific on 19 February 1945. The invasion of Iwo Jima signaled one of the fiercest and most intense battles to date. The gunnery crew Sergeant was hit by shrapnel before leaving the ship and he instructed Nowlin to take care of his men for him. During the landing, Corporal Nowlin's landing craft was overturned in the surf as it was being bombarded by enemy fire. He made certain all his men were clear first and as he jumped, the craft went over, taking all his gear with it. All that he reached shore was his ammo belt and canteen. He found his buddy, Johnson, a fellow member of the gun crew who had a carbine and a forty-five handgun, so he gave Nowlin one of them. It was about ten o'clock at night when he and three others dug in and managed to survive till light.

In letters sent home later he told his mother about losing his pack with everything in it. One item specifically mentioned was a can of sausage she had sent to him along with all his extra clothes, etc. In a letter dated 10 March 1945, he told his family he had on the same trousers for more than 15 days. He also later told them he didn't have his boots off for 42 days during this campaign.

On 12 March 1945, the 14th regiment fired their last round -the 156,000 on Iwo Jima. The greatest battle in Marine Corps history was over. Corporal Nowlin witnessed the raising of the American flag on Mt. Surabachi on Iwo Jima. The picture taken of this flag raising became the inspiration for a monument to honor those who fought so courageously. Twenty-six days and nine hours after the troops first landed, Iwo Jima was declared secured for the United States.

The Fourth Marine Division had started out with more than 20,000 men before the first battle in the Marshalls and now there were less than 2,000 left. They became known as the "Famous Fighting Fourth. "

Corporal Nowlin came home just in time for Christmas in 1945. He and his brother-in-law Homer Gillis, who had been in the Army, tried to see who could eat the most of the fine welcome dinner prepared by Mama Nowlin. Walter, Jr., married Lena Stults in 1946 and they lived in Collinwood until his death in 1986. Mrs. Nowlin still resides there. Their children are Steve, Jerry, Stella and Judy Nowlin.

Source: Prepared by Stella Nowlin Matney from old letters, memories of family members, and The Fourth Marine Division in World War II, published by Infantry Journal Press, and distributed gratuitously to former members of the Division and next of kin to those who died.

NUSZBAUM, JOHN WILLIAM, Serial Number 967 13 70, was a Seaman Second Class in the Navy of the United States. He was born 30 January 1926 in Belmont, Mississippi. He entered into active service 11 April 1944. The Vessels and Stations that he served on were: NTS Camp Perry, Williamsburg, Virginia, USS R WIND DD 404 and USS CARIBOU. The following decorations were awarded to Nuszbaum: Asiatic Pacific Ribbon, American Area Ribbon, Europe-African Middle Eastern Theater Medal, and World War II Victory Medal. He was discharged 16 February 1946 at the US Naval Personnel Separation Center in Shoemaker, California. His parents were Harrison and Bonnie (Skillern) Nuszbaum.

NUTT, DOYLE F., son of Mr. and Mrs. Charlie Nutt of Waynesboro, TN, served as S/Sgt. and engineer gunner with Hdq. 13th Army Air Force in the Southwest Pacific. He went overseas in, March 1943, and participated in over 29 bombing strikes against the Japanese in South, Southwest and Central Pacific. Before the service he worked in Delano, CA. (Taken from an article in a December 1944 issue of the Wayne County News).

NUTT, HOMER SHIELDS, Serial Number 966 28 51, was a Seaman First Class with SV6 US Naval Reserve in the Navy of the United States. He enlisted 31 December 1943 at NRS, Chattanooga, Tennessee for two years. He served on the following Vessels/Stations: NRS Chattanooga, Tennessee; NTS Great Lakes, Illinois; Const Battalion's US NC TC in Williamsburg, Virginia; Station Crew, USN ADC, Peary, Williamsburg, Virginia; USN TADC, Williamsburg, Virginia; TADCEN, Shoemaker, California; Con Ser For 7th Fleet R/B (EDUR); USS La VALETTE: US Naval Rec Hospital in San Francisco, California and USNSH in Santa Cruz, California. He was married when he was discharged 17 October 1945 at US Naval Special Hospital in Santa Cruz, California. Before entering the Navy, he worked for Fabricated Metals Company in Detroit, Michigan.

NUTT, MARVIN JAMES, was born February 3, 1918, in Wayne County, Tennessee. He departed this earthly life October 6, 1998, at his home in Crosby, Texas, surrounded by his family.

He is a child of God, beloved husband of Edith Alene Staggs Nutt whom he married December 27, 1944, and beloved father of daughters Karen Michaelson, Carol, Taylor (both of Houston), Sherry Wheeler, Lynnette Tyler and son Terry Nutt (all of Crosby).

Mr. Nutt was affectionately known as "Pa-Daddy" to his 11 grandchildren: Michelle (Michaelson) Cason, Monica Michaelson, Leslie (Taylor) Nelson, Jon Wheeler, Jay Wheeler, Jason Wheeler, Lindsay Tyler, Lauren Tyler, Susan Tyler, Ryan Nutt and Courtney Nutt; his five foster grandchildren: James, Alex, Jeffrey, Brock and Bridget; and his four great-grandchildren: Kayla Cason, Justin Cason, Tyler Cason and Kelly Cason.

A veteran of World War II, Mr. Nutt served his country in the Civilian Conservation Corps in 1936. He served in the United States Army from 1937 to 1940 and the United States Navy from 1940 to 1946,

stationed on the USS Cincinnati as Chief Gunner's Mate in the South Pacific. Upon moving to Houston in September 1952, he worked for Shur-Start Battery Company and later acquired M&S Battery Company in partnership with his brother-in-law cousin Harlan Dugger, who was also his closest friend.

Mr. Nutt was baptized into Christ in 1953 and served as deacon of the Church of Christ for many years.

One brother, Herman Nutt, and one sister, Lois Brewer, preceded him in death. He is survived by one sister, Lillie Kelley, of Waynesboro and a host of nieces and nephews and many friends who will miss him dearly.

Funeral services were held Friday, October 19, 1998.

Source: Wayne County News, October 21, 1998.

NUTT, PAUL, son of Fred & Monetta Dee Kelley Nutt. Born in Wayne Co. Tennessee, June 10, 1925. 1 Graduated from

Wayne Co High School, May 1944. Drafted into US Military Service July 1944. Did basic training in Macon, Georgia.

Served under General George S. Patton, 3d Army, 80 division, 3 1 9th infantry regiment. Company A awarded 3 bronze stars for major battles, Ardennes, Rhineland and Central Europe. Was wounded in action on the Zig-Freed line in Luxenburg Feb. 7, 1945. Awarded Purple Heart and returned to states May 1946. Discharged at Camp Atterbury Indiana May 1946.

Oct. 1948 married Ima Jean Dickey, daughter of Clint & Ada Daniel Dickey of Collinwood. We have 4 children Lynn, Susan, Steve, and Lisa. We still live in Wayne Co. about 2 miles from where I was born.

NUTT, RAY B., was in the Army of the United States. His permanent mailing address was Waynesboro, Tennessee. He entered into active service 13 October 1942 at Fort Oglethorpe, Georgia. His Military

Occupational Specialty was excellent Rifleman. His Military Qualifications included Qualified Bayonet. He was stationed at Fort Oglethorpe for his basic training. Then, he was transferred to Fort Benning, Georgia for further training but was honorably discharged 16 March 1944 at Lawson General Hospital Atlanta, Georgia because of a back injury.

Ray was born 10 August 1920 in Waynesboro, Tennessee. His parents were Grady and Inez (Churchwell) Nutt. His siblings are, Willard, Wilton, Rex, Rachel, Bedford, Craig, and Brooxie Nutt. Ray married Dena Mae Quillen and they had one son and three daughters.

NUTT, T.J., son of Mr. and Mrs. Fred Nutt of Waynesboro, entered the Service 20 August 1942 and received his training

at Fort McCellen, Alabama and Lakeland, Florida before being assigned to overseas duty. He was with the Quartermaster Corps in North Africa and Italy. After thirty-three months overseas, he was honorably discharged from Fort McPherson, Georgia.

T/5 Nutt attended the schools of Wayne County and was enrolled at Austin Peay Normal for two years prior to entering the service. He was associated with the teaching staff of Wayne County. His wife is the former Margaret Ferguson of Lewisburg. They have two daughters: Margaret O'Neal and Amelia Churchwell Nutt.

Source: Wayne County News .

NUTT, TRESTER STEELMAN, Serial Number 34 903 944, was a Private in Company F, 206th Infantry Training Battalion in the United States Army. On 22 January 1942, Trester was inducted at Camp Forrest, Tennessee and was stationed at Camp Blanding, Florida for the entire period of his enlistment. He was honorably discharged on 23 June 1944 at Fort Blanding, Florida.

Trester was born 17 May 1916 in Waynesboro, Tennessee to Pleas Green and Nettie (Dabbs) Nutt. Trester had two sisters, Vesta Nutt married Willie Rasbury and is now deceased and Opal Nutt married Emery Copeland. Opal now resides in Nashville. He also had two older half brothers, Lytle Nutt married Ada Brewer and Fred Nutt married Dee Kelley. He had two older half sisters, Jimmie Nutt married Frank Brewer and Theo Nutt married Dolph Brewer. All of these are deceased.

Trester spent his early life on Forty-Eight Creek in Northern Wayne County, living with his parents on the family farm where his grandfather, James A. Nutt, had lived. He attended school in his home community through eighth grade and two years high school. He started to school at the age of five and was a very quick learner. He graduated when he was just seventeen. Many of the teachers "boarded" in his home and he was exposed to a lot of education and training that many did not receive. The last two years of high school, Trester drove to and from school and had as passengers, his sister Vesta and others who needed to go to school but had no other way. His family was interested in and promoted education and they were always willing to help those who wanted to further their education, whether it was providing transportation, a place "to stay" or

in may cases, money for their school expenses.

After graduating from high school in May 1933, Trester attended Freed Hardeman College in Henderson, Tennessee. He later attended Austin Peay College in Clarksville, Tennessee. He taught in the schools of Wayne County for three years, first at Blowing Springs, second at McGleamery near Collinwood and the third at Morrow Valley where he had attended school. During this school year he was appointed to serve as a rural mail carrier and on 8 February 1937, he started carring mail on Route 4 out of the Waynesboro office. He carried the mail for almost 41 years, retiring in 1977. He served five of the six routes out of the Waynesboro office during this time.

On 30 October 1937, Trester married Evelyn Brewer, daughter of Snow M. and Wilton (Morrow) Brewer. Evelyn was also a teacher and was teaching on Beech Creek, her fourth school, when they married. At the end of the school year, they moved into their new home in Waynesboro and lived there sixteen years. At this time they bought the old home place on Forty-Eight Creek and in March of 1954 they moved into a new house that they had built on the farm and have lived there ever since.

Trester and Evelyn had seven children: James Harville, Sarah Margaret, Frank McMillan, Jewell Carolyn, David Morrow and a little girl, stillborn. They have fifteen grandchildren and thirteen great-grandchildren.

Trester and Evelyn still live on their farm on Forty-Eight Creek. Trester continues to raise beef cattle. They are both active in church and community affairs. Trester has been an elder in the Waynesboro Church of Christ for many years.

NUTT, WILTON LELAND, was the second of ten children born to Grady and Inez (Churchwell) Nutt. He attended the Forty-Eight Creek School in Wayne

County, through the eighth grade, and graduated from Wayne County High School in 1938.

Wilton enlisted in the Army in 1940 and was stationed at Fort Jackson, South Carolina for a period of one year with Company G. 177th. On 25 July 1942, Wilton was inducted into the military at Fort Oglethorpe, Georgia and went into active service 2 August 1942. He fought in the European Theater and was engaged in battles in Central Europe including the Rhineland and Ardennes. He received the Bronze Star Medal for Meritious Service in Connection with Military Operations against the enemy during the period from 13 December 1944 thru 16 April 1945 in Germany. During this period T/Sgt Nutt performed consistently outstanding service as Platoon Sergeant of the Anti-Tank Platoon, Second Battalion, 309th Infantry Regiment. On numerous occasions he served as Platoon leader, displaying outstanding leadership and tactical ability in the selection and establishment of gun positions to provide support for the Rifle companies. His ability, untiring efforts and devotion to duty are in accordance with the highest Military traditions.

For exemplary conduct in ground combat during the Rhineland campaign, he received the First Oak Cluster to the Bronze Star Medal, American Defense Medal and Good Conduct Medal. He was honorably discharged 17 October 1945.

In 1947, Wilton went to work for the State of Tennessee as State Trooper and was promoted to Lieutenant before his death 1 December 1965. He was buried in the Walnut Grove Cemetery in Wayne County. He was survived by his wife, Mary Lois Long Nutt, whom he married 19 July 1947, and two sons, Gary Wilton and Stephen Douglas Nutt. Wilton was a member of the First Street Church of Christ.

OAKLEY, WILLIAM OTIS, was a Seaman 1/C (Cee Bee's) in the United States Navy. He volunteered for service in 1941 and took his basic training at Camp Peary and Camp Allen, Virginia. He was in active service in the Philippines and other locations in the South Pacific. He was discharged in 1945 in California. He worked as a labor foreman for DuPont in Pryor, Oklahoma and in Akin, South Carolina as an assistant superintendent after the war.

He was born 5 Oct 1914 and was the son of Ten and Mary (Gray) Oakley. He married Mildred Terry. They have one daughter, Martha Oakley Newman and two sons, Frank and Robert Oakley. He had a brother, Frank Oakley. He now resides at 2323 Clara Avenue S. W., Decatur, Alabama 35601.

ODLE, HENRY, Private, of Wayne County was the son of Neil and Emma Gower Odle. He was born on September 17, 1919. He worked as a farmer until he was inducted into the United States Army on March 12, 1944, at Camp Shelby, Mississippi. He served in Company K, 97th Infantry Regiment 3rd Division. He was in battles in Central Europe, Naples-Foggia and Rhineland. He was awarded the European African Middle Eastern Services Medal, World War II Victory, Good Conduct and Army of Occupation Medals. After more than two years, he was discharged on July 3, 1946, at Brooke General Hospital at Ft. Sam in Houston, Texas. He worked for the TVA. He belonged to the American Legion.

He was married to Willodean Franklin. Their children are Doyle, Wanda Odle Thompson, Elbert and Jerry. His siblings are Edgar Odle, Andy Odle, Della Odle Murphy, Alberta McDonald, Nellie Gambrell and Norma Jean Odle.

Henry Odle died on April 13, 1987, and is buried in the Copeland Cemetery.

ODLE, RUBEN, Serial Number 34 193 014, was a Corporal in Battery B, 80th Airborne Antiaircraft Battalion, in the

Army of the United States. His permanent mailing address was Route 1, Collinwood, Tennessee. He was registered with Selective Service Board in Wayne County, Tennessee. His Civilian Occupation was General Farm Hand. He was inducted March 1941. His Military Occupational Specialty was Gunner Antiaircraft. His Military Qualifications included 2nd CI Gunner and SS Pistol. He was in the battles of Normandy, Rhineland, Sicily, Rome, Arno, and Northern France. He was wounded in action in France 23 December 1944. The following decorations were awarded to Odle: Good Conduct Ribbon, and European-African-Middle Eastern Theater Ribbon with 5 Bronze Stars. He left the USA 29 April 1943 for the European Theater

Operation, and returned to USA 5 May 1945. He was discharged 28 June 1945 at Fort McPherson, Georgia.

He was born 15 March 1919 in Wayne County, Tennessee. He was the son of Mr. and Mrs. Jesse Odle of Route 1, Collinwood, Tennessee.

ODLE, VAN ALBERT, Dr., was the son of A. A. (Dick) and Mattie Odle. He was a native of Clifton, Tennessee. He served in the United States Army Medical Corps during World War II.

He was a graduate of the University of Tennessee in Knoxville and received his medical degree from U. T. Memphis. He did graduate work in radiology at Georgetown University in Washington, D. C. He had practiced medicine 35 years before he died at his home in Bullhead City, Arizona. Funeral services were conducted in Needles, California where he also lived. Burial was in River View Cemetery in Needles. Survivors included his widow, Opal Martin Odle, his mother, Mrs. A. A. Odle of Cornersville, Tennessee, a brother C. B. Odle of Peoria, Illinois, and a sister, Mrs. Alfred (Martha) Overholser of Nashville.

Source: Undated Obit.

OLD, TALMAGE J. "BUDDY", was born 6 Feb 1920 in Nashville, Tennessee. Buddy was the third of four children and

only son of Talmage J. Old, Sr. ,(24 June 1891-24 May 1942) and Grace Leo (Ricketts) Old (5 Feb 1890 - 24 Oct 1972). Buddy's paternal grandparents were Hugh Shields Old and Martha Adeline (Morrison) Old, both of Wayne County. His maternal grandparents were Charles Samuel Ricketts of Clifton and Willie Shannon (Hawkins) Ricketts, a native of Louisiana.

Buddy's three sisters were (1) Mary Ruth (Old) Baird, born 20 April 1915 in Watertown, Wilson County, Tennessee, and died 1 Sept 1981 from Cardiac Arrest in Walnut Creek, California. (2) Martha

Adeline (Old) Hassell, born 20 Sept 1917 in Watertown and is currently living in Waynesboro. and (3) Margaret Ellen (Old) Rains, born 5 Aug 1928 in Nashville, Tennessee and is currently living in Waynesboro.

Buddy's family moved from Nashville to Waynesboro when he was ten years old, here he completed his elementary and high school education, graduating from Wayne County High School in 1936. Opportunities for the young graduate were scarce; the Depression and the war in Europe clouded the future. A family cousin, Mrs. Ebin Morrison, helped by offering Buddy an apprenticeship at the Morrison Electrical Works in Bloomington, Indiana. Buddy could board with the Morrison family while learning a trade. This offer Buddy accepted and stayed in Indiana for a year.

At seventeen, Buddy returned to Waynesboro, and went to work (another on-the-job-training situation) at the *Wayne County News* office with Editor H. D. Bailey as his mentor. Work at the newspaper plant challenged Buddy's mechanical abilities (press work, Linotype keyboard, etc) and his mental capabilities (writing articles, reporting, etc.). Buddy liked it all. A fast learner and a creative thinker, Buddy enrolled in the Southern School of Printing in Nashville. After his graduation, Buddy accepted a position with a newspaper in Rocky Mount, North Carolina. There he gained more experience in his profession as he worked as a writer, proofreader, printer - and even as a weather forecaster - until 1940.

By then, all the printed news was centered on the efforts to stop Adolph Hitler, and on America's involvement in those efforts. In September 1940, the National Guard was mobilized. Buddy returned to Waynesboro, and along with several hometown friends volunteered for service in Company G, 117th Infantry, Unit of the 30th (Old Hickory) Division. The young Privates were sent to Fort Jackson, South Carolina, for training.

In June 1942, Buddy's latest talents came to the forefront, and he was selected to attend Infantry Officer Candidate School at Fort Benning, Georgia Graduating from OCS and receiving a commission as second lieutenant, Buddy was assigned to the 13th Armored Division, Camp Beale, California. He remained with this division through the war, serving in the European Theater where he won the Bronze Star and Combat Infantryman Badge as S-3 (Operation Officer) of the 67th Armored Infantry. Buddy participated in the Rhineland and Central Germany Campaigns and was promoted to Major by the U. S. Third Army

Major Old returned to the States with his division in July 1945, and the war ended while the division was assembling at Camp Cooke, California, in preparation for the scheduled November Trans-Pacific amphibious assault on Japan. Buddy was released from active duty in December 1945. He remained in Active Reserve for several years after his discharge.

Buddy married Margaret Held of Lawrenceburg in 1942. From 1945 until his death in 1985, Buddy and Margaret made their home in Memphis, except for one year spent in Tarboro, NC and one year at the U. S. Government Printing Office in Washington, DC.

During his career in Memphis, Buddy worked in the composing room of *The Commercial Appeal* and the *Memphis Press-Scimitar*, at Kelly & Jamison Typesetters, and at Murdock Printing Company where he was Plant Superintendent and Intertype Operator. He attended Memphis State University as a part time student, completing three years toward a B. S. degree in history.

Buddy and Margaret had two sons, Michael Talmage and Thomas Quentin Old. Mike and wife Helen live in Memphis and have three children, Jeff, Leo and Laura Old. Tom and wife Becky live in Mississippi and have two children, Mickey and Sarah Old. Margaret continues to live in Memphis where she is active in church work and helping with the grandchildren.

Buddy's main interest and efforts were centered around his family, his church (St. Paul in Whitehaven) and his work. As a man of keen intellect, he enjoyed lively discussions on a wide variety of subjects: reading biographies and Civil War works, a challenging game of Chess, spectator sports, and involved himself in the organized activities within his church and within his field of work. He was elected to numerous offices of responsibility in these organizations.

Buddy (even his grandchildren called him Grandbuddy) died unexpectedly in his home in Memphis (Whitehaven) On 5 July 1985, the victim of a massive heart attack at the age of 65. His burial was in Calvary Cemetery in Memphis. He was a devoted son to his widowed mother, a dedicated and competent soldier, a capable and productive printer/newspaperman, a faithful and loving husband, father and grandfather, a loyal and helpful friend to many, a devout Christian and the ideal brother.

Source: Margaret Ellen (Old) Rains, 105 E. Songer Street, Waynesboro, TN 38485, 5 July 1991.

OLIVE, CAROL CLAYTON, 70, of 143 Danley Road, Iron City died 1 April 1997 at his home and was buried in Wolf Creek Cemetery with Military Services at grave side. A native of Lawrence County, he was the son of Wince and Mary Susan

Butler Olive. He was retired from TVA, a member of Iron City Church of Christ, a Army Veteran, a member of American Legion Post 146 and Labor Local 366 in Sheffield, Alabama. Survivors include his wife, Mattie Olive, three daughters, Tina Kelley of Florence, Teresa Johnson of Iron City, and Sabrina Musgrove of Summertown; a son Dwight Olive of Iron City; three brothers, Clinton Olive of Wayne, Michigan, R. C. Olive of Nashville, and Lincoln Olive of Iron City; two sisters, Artue Jackson and Gladys Aldridge of ST. Joseph; and three grandchildren.
Source: Wayne County News.

OLIVE, WILLIAM DAVID, JR., Serial Number 34 506 476, was a Staff Sergeant in 323rd Troop Carrier Squadron in the Army of the United States. His permanent mailing address was Route 3, Iron City, Tennessee. He was registered with Selective Service Board in Wayne County, Tennessee. His Civilian Occupation was Welder Acetylene. He was single when he was inducted 18 January 1943 and entered into active service 25 January 1943 at Fort Oglethorpe, Georgia. His Military Occupational Specialty was Aerial Engineer. His Military Qualifications included AAF Air Crew Member Badge. He was in the battles of Normandy, Northern France, Rhineland, and Central Europe. The following decorations were awarded to Olive: Europe-African Middle Eastern Theater Ribbon with 4 Bronze Service Stars, American Theater Ribbon, Air Medal, Distinguish Unit Badge, and World War II Victory Medal. He left the USA 25 Feb 1944 for the Europe-African Middle Eastern Theater Operation, and returned to USA 20 December 1945. He was discharged 28 December 1945 at Fort Knox, Kentucky.

He was born 1 January 1923 in Wayne County, Tennessee. His parents were William David and Annie (Bailey) Olive. He graduated from Collinwood High School and attended college for eleven weeks.

OVERTON, THOMAS W., Serial Number 34 373 143, was a Technician Fifth Grade in Company B 825th Engineer Aviation Battalion in the Army of the United States. His permanent mailing address was Clifton, Tennessee. He was born 15 June 1920 in Collinwood, Tennessee. He was registered with Selective Service Board in Wayne County, Tennessee. His Civilian Occupation was Deck Hand. He was inducted 24 September 1942 and entered into active service 8 October 1942 at Fort Oglethorpe, Georgia. His Military Occupational Specialty was Heavy Truck Driver. His Military Qualifications included Marksman Rifle. The battles that he was in are not available but the follow-

ing decorations were awarded to Overton: Europe-African Middle Eastern Theater Ribbon, Good Conduct Medal, and World War II Victory Medal. He left the USA 5 May 1943 for the Europe-African Middle Eastern Theater Operation, and returned to USA 27 December 1945. He was discharged 4 January 1946 at Fort Knox, Kentucky.

OVERTON, VIRGIL GRANVILLE, Serial Number 34 373 148, was a Technician Fourth Grade in Battery C 455th An-

tiaircraft Artillery Automatic Weapons Battalion in the Army of the United States. His permanent mailing address was Russelville, Alabama. He was registered with Selective Service Board in Wayne County, Tennessee. His Civilian Occupation was Mechanic. He was married when he was inducted 24 Sept 1942 and entered into active service 8 October 1942 at Fort Oglethorpe, Georgia. His Military Occupational Specialty was Cook. He was in the battles of Normandy, Northern France, Rhineland, and Central Europe. The following decorations were awarded to Overton: Europe-African Middle Eastern Theater Ribbon with 4 Bronze Stars and Good Conduct Ribbon. He left the USA 5 Sept 1943 for the European Theater Operation, and returned to USA 16 Oct 1945. He was discharged 22 October 1945 at Camp Atterbury, Indiana. He had an eight grade education.

Virgil Granville was born 26 November 1919 in Collinwood, Tennessee. He was the son of John William Overton (born 4 June 1895) and Mary Luesenda Hathcoat Overton, both born in Wayne County. Virgil was married 12 April 1941 to Mary Nell Rumbaugh. They have one daughter, Virgie Nell Overton Gifford, born 17 January 1943 in Wayne County, Tennessee. He also has two grandchildren and three great grandchildren. Virgil Granville's brothers and sisters are: (1) Harvey B. Overton born 24 August 1913 in Wayne County; (2) Virginia Overton Staggs born 26 Dec 1921 in Wayne County; (3) Don Robert Overton born 4 Nov 1924 in Wayne County; (4) James Willard Overton born 30 Nov 1927 in Wayne County; (5) Willie Ray Overton born 14 August 1929 in Lauderdale County, Alabama; (6) Billy Overton born 10 Nov 1933 in Wayne County and (7) Mary Helen Walles born 11 Feb 1936. Virgil married 12 April 1941, Mary Nell Rumbaugh and they have one daughter, Virgie Nell Overton, born 17 January 1943 in Wayne County. He has 2 grandchildren and 3 great-grandchildren.

OWENS, J.T. LAWRENCE, Serial Number 34 189 091 was a Sergeant in Headquarters and Headquarters Squadron,

12th Air Depot Group, in the Army of the United States. His permanent mailing address was Route 2, Collinwood, Tennessee. He was registered with Selective Service Board in Wayne County, Tennessee. His Civilian Occupation was General Farmer. He was single when he entered into active service 19 Feb 1942 at Fort Oglethorpe, Georgia. His Military Occupational Specialty was Light Truck Driver. The battles that he was in are not available but the following decorations were awarded to Owens: American Theater Ribbon and World War II Victory Medal. He left the USA 24 March 1943 for the South West Pacific Theater Operation, and returned to USA 26 Nov 1945. He was discharged 8 December 1945 at Fort Bliss, Texas.

He was born 1 June 1920 in Lawrenceburg, Tennessee, the son of Roy Jack and Mittie Owens of Route 2, Collinwood. Jack was born on March 14, 1875, in Illinois, and Mittie was born on June 17, 1899, in Lawrence County, Tennessee. Lawrence had a brother, William Thomas (Bill), born on October 19. 1917, in Lawrence County. Bill died in September 1952. He is buried in Sunnyside Memorial Park on Cherry Avenue, Long Beach, California. He also has a sister, Ellen Pearl, born on May 15, 1924, in Wayne County. She lives in Diamond City, Arkansas.

After the war ended Lawrence married Martha Naomi Keeton on December 15, 1945, in Arkansas. They came to Wayne County, Tennessee to live. Their daughter, Sonja Elaine, was born on June 13, 1947, in Wayne County. Lawrence grew up in Wayne County on Indian Creek near the Three Churches area and was a farmer.

Lawrence, Naomi, and their baby daughter moved to California where they lived until he retired. Lawrence and Naomi then moved to Arkansas where he had a cattle farm.

Lawrence's mother, sister and brother all moved to California in the late 1940s. Mittie died December 23, 1986, and is also buried in the Sunnyside Memorial Park in Long Beach, California. Her husband Jack is buried in McGlamery Cemetery in Wayne County, Tennessee. He died on March 14, 1945.

"Sgt J. T. Lawrence Owens is a member of a Far East Air Service Command Depot. He recently received a letter of Commendation from the Headquarters of Lieut. General George C. Kenney, Commander of the Allied Air Forces, S.W.P.A.

Owens, who has been overseas for 18 months, was among those commended for the part played in making the "Townsville Depot" one of the best Air Depots in the world. The commendation referred to "amount of work turned out, general over all efficiency, and the ability to expeditiously accomplish any task imposed upon it at any time, have made it the main stay of the 5th Air Force effort throughout the campaign. " Owens was a farmer prior to his enlistment. "

Source: Album of Wayne County News Clippings owned by Clyde Bevis.

PALMER, JAMES T., Serial Number 34 735 452, was a Sergeant in 112th Army Air Force Base Unit in the Army of the United States. His permanent mailing address was Waynesboro, Tennessee. He was born 6 March 1924 in Lawrenceburg, Tennessee. He was registered with Selective Service Board in Wayne County, Tennessee. His Civilian Occupation was Student. His Military Occupational Specialty was Airplane Armorer Gunner. His Military Qualifications included Sharpshooter Carbine Marksman Pistol and Aviation Badge for Aerial Gunner. He was not in any battles. The following decorations were awarded to Palmer: World War II Victory Medal, Good Conduct Ribbon, and American Theater Campaign Ribbon. The Service Schools that he attended were: Air Cadet for 14 months, Airplane Mechanic School at Napier Field in Alabama, and Aircraft Armor School at Lowery Field Colorado. He was discharged 24 February 1946 at Fort Devens, Massachusetts. He had one year of college education.

PARKER, AUTIE, Serial Number 34 494 873, was a Technician Fifth Grade in Company D, 568th Signal Aircraft Warn-

ing Battalion in the Army of the United States. His permanent mailing address was General Delivery, Waynesboro, Tennessee. He was born 25 May 1919 in McEwing, Tennessee. He was registered with Selective Service Board in Wayne County, Tennessee. His Civilian Occupation was Heavy Truck Driver. He was inducted 22 November 1942 and entered into active service 29 November 1942 at Fort Oglethorpe, Georgia. His Military Occupational Specialty was Light Truck Driver. His Military Qualifications included Marksman Carbine. He fought in ground combat in Iwo Jima. The following decorations were awarded to Parker: World War II Victory Ribbon, Good Conduct Ribbon, American Theater Ribbon, and Asiatic Pacific Theater Ribbon with 1 Bronze Service Star. He left the USA 2 May 1944 for the Asiatic-Pacific Theater and returned to USA 18 December 1945. He was discharged 1 January 1946 at Camp Chaffee, Arkansas.

PARKER, CARROL J., Serial Number 34 494 861, was a Private First Class in Company H, 306th Infantry in the Army of the United States. His permanent address was General Delivery, Collinwood, Tennessee. He was born 28 July 1921 in Collinwood, Tennessee. He was registered with Selective Service Board in Wayne County, Tennessee. His Civilian Occupation was Trailer Truck Driver. He was married when he was inducted 22 November 1942 and entered into active service 29 November 1942 at Fort Oglethorpe, Georgia. His Military Occupational Specialty was Light Truck Driver. His Military Qualifications included Combat Infantryman. He was in the battles in Eastern Mandates, Southern Philippines and Ryukyu. The following decorations were awarded to Parker: Asiatic Pacific Theater Ribbon with 3 Bronze Service Stars and one Bronze Arrowhead,

Good Conduct Ribbon, World War II Victory Ribbon, American Theater Ribbon, and Philippine Liberation Ribbon with one Bronze Star. He left the USA 25 March 1944 for the Asiatic Pacific Theater Operation, and returned to USA 29 November 1945. He was discharged 12 December 1945 at Camp Chaffee, Arkansas.

PARKER, CHARLIE, According to an item in The Wayne County News, November 10, 1944, Mst/Sgt. Charlie Parker had served in the U. S. Army twenty-seven and one half years. He was with the 7th Command and had been a farm worker on the old home place of the late Dr. E. R. Yeiser. His sister was Ennie Kelley of R#2, Waynesboro.

PARKER, JOHN, was inducted into the United States Army in 1941. He served in French Morocco and the European Theater of War. When he was discharged, he reenlisted in the Air Force. His air Force training was received in Biloxi, Mississippi, Ohio, Georgia, and Rantouf, Illinois. He retired from the Air Force in 1962. Later he retired from Wayne Metal in Waynesboro where he worked for five years.

John attended school at Frank Hughes in Clifton and completed his high school work while in service. He worked in the Enlistment Service office in Texas.

John, son of Robert Bradley and Eliza (Crossnoe) Parker, was born 30 November 1915 and died 2 May 1986. His siblings were, Richard, Pete, Louise Parker Poole, Dovie Parker Pevahouse, Ora Parker Goodman, Kennie Parker Boyd and Nancy Parker Prater. John married Mattie Sword. John's two sons, Robert Daniel and John, Jr., were born while he was stationed in Rantouf, Illinois.

PARKER, JOHN D., He was inducted into the United States Navy June 1943 and had the rank of Seaman First Class. He spent several months overseas. He was employed by Fallbrook Citrus Association in Fallbrook, California before he entered service. He was a former resident of Waynesboro.
Source: Wayne County News .

PARKER, ZAN M., Serial Number 34 377 051, was a Private First Class in the Army of the United States. He was born in Wayne County, Tennessee. He was 38 years old and single when he was inducted 13 October 1942 at Fort Oglethorpe, Georgia. He was discharged 18 June 1943.
Source: Wayne County News .

PARTAIN, CECIL W., Serial Number 14 100 168, was a Sergeant in 982nd Ordinance Depot Company of the Army of the United States. His permanent mailing address was Route 5, Waynesboro, Tennes-

see. He was born 8 July 1918 in Lawrenceburg, Tennessee. His Civilian Occupation was Clerk Typist. He was married with four dependents when he was inducted 11 September 1942 and entered into active service 14 November 1942 at Chattanooga, Tennessee. He was in battles in Normandy and Northern France. His decorations: American Theater Ribbon, European-African Middle Eastern Theater Ribbon with 2 Bronze Stars, Good Conduct Medal and World War II Victory Medal. He departed the USA on 5 Sept 1943 for European Theater Operation and returned 6 November 1945. He had four years of high school education. He was discharged 11 November 1945 at Camp Atterbury, Indiana.

PARTAIN, HAROLD B., son of Ben and Ethel Partain, grew up on Hurricane Creek and attended school at Waynesboro. He entered the U. S. Army during WWII and served for the duration. After his discharge from the service, he married and moved to Copper Hill, TN. They have a son.

PARTAIN, HERMAN P., son of John and Beatrice (Henson) Partain, was born, February 10, 1920 in Lawrence County, Tn. In, 1934, his parents bought a farm on Indian Creek in Wayne County, so Herman spent the rest of his growing up days in that community and attended Wayne County Schools. He worked on the farm until he received his call for induction into the U. S. Army in 1942, where he served with the 803rd Tank Destroyer Division. After several months training in the states, he was sent to the European Theater as a M/Sgt. and participated in various battles, where he was wounded and received the Purple Heart. At the end of the war he reenlisted and made a career of the service, retiring after twenty years; he then served ten years in the U. S. Army Reserve.

Herman married and had two daughters, Shirley (deceased) and Georgette of Texas. He made his home at Ft. Walton Beach, Florida and worked as an automobile parts salesman until, 1990, when he retired. He died from cancer, December 28, 1999, and is buried in Florida. His siblings are Lou Ella Phillips, Evelyn Gillis and Carol Partain.

PASCHALL, ROBERT H., Serial Number 34 495 025, was a Technician Fifth Grade in the Medical Department, 361st Infantry of the Army of the United States. His permanent mailing address was Waynesboro, Tennessee. He was born 7 November 1922 in Waynesboro, Tennessee. His Civilian Occupation was College Student. He was registered with Selective Service Board in Wayne County, Tennessee. He was inducted 22 November 1942 at Fort Oglethorpe, Georgia. His Military Occupational Spe-

cialty was Clerk Typist. His Military Qualifications included Medical Badge. He was in the battles of North Apennines, Rome-Arno, and Po Valley. The following decorations were awarded to Paschall: Bronze Star, European-African Middle Eastern Theater Service Ribbon, American Theater Ribbon, World War II Victory Medal, and Good Conduct Ribbon. He left the USA 3 July 1944 for the European-African Middle Eastern Theater and returned to USA 30 Aug 1945. He had three and a half years of College. He was discharged 12 November 1945 at Camp Gordon, Georgia.

PATTERSON, JAMES HERSCHEL, Serial Number 94 32 20, was a Private First Class of the United States Marines. He was born 11 December 1914 in Lutts, Tennessee. He was married when he enlisted 6 January 1944 at Nashville, Tennessee to serve for the duration of the emergency.
Source: Wayne County News .

PATTERSON, LEROY, son of Frank and Lizzie (Kelley) Patterson, grew up in Waynesboro and attended Waynesboro schools. He married Frances Gillis of near Clifton. Within a short time he was inducted into the U. S. Service and served in the Air Force.

After he was discharged from the service, they lived in the northern states, where he was a truck driver. He became a baptist minister and sometime later moved with his wife and children to Hardin County, TN, where he pastored a church. He is deceased.

PEACOCK, CHARLES, A graduate of Wayne County High School, he volunteered in the United States Air Force. He graduated and received his Gunner Wings from the Aerial Gunner School in Harlingen, Texas. He was stationed in Greenville, Mississippi. He attained the rank of Sergeant.

Charles is the son of Charlie and Bertha (Jeter) Peacock of Delano, California and former residents of Wayne County. His wife is Geraldine Throgmorton, daughter of Mr. and Mrs. J. F. Throgmorton of Eagle Creek in Wayne County.
Source: Wayne County News .

PEACOCK, JAMES, son of Grover and Lela (Helton) Peacock, was born in Wayne County and graduated at Wayne County High School. During World War II, he served in the United States Navy.

After his discharge, James married Loretta and settled in Nashville where they raised their two sons. He worked as a cameraman at WSM-TV station. Several years later he retired from that due to failing health. They remain in their home in Nashville.

PEACOCK, QUENTIN, Serial Number 34 193 031, was a Private First Class with 101 Quartermaster Detachment "A", 187 8th Unit Camp, Claiborne, Louisiana, in the Army of the United States. He was born in Wayne County. His Civilian Occupation was Saw Mill Worker. He was 27 years and 11/12 months of age and was married when he was inducted 15 March 1942 at Fort Oglethorpe, Georgia. His Military Occupational Specialty was Basic. He was discharged 17 march 1943 at Camp Claiborne, Louisiana in poor physical condition.

PERRY, GRADY FRANKLIN, Serial Number 273 09 28, was a Quartermaster Third Class in the Navy of the United States. He was born 18 Feb 1926 in Lutts, Tennessee. He was inducted 13 April 1944. The Vessels and Stations served on were: NTC Williamsburg, Virginia, NTS NOB Norfork, Virginia, and USS HANK. The following decorations were awarded to Perry: World War II Victory Medal, American Area Service Medal, Asiatic Pacific Theater ribbon and Philippine Liberation Ribbon. He was discharged 21 May 1946 from the U S Naval Personnel Separation Center in Memphis, Tennessee.

PERRY, JASPER T., Serial Number RA 14 219 182, Non Registrant (volunteered), was a Private First Class in Company A 808th Engineer Aviation Battalion in the Air Corps of the United States Army. His permanent mailing address was General Delivery, Collinwood, Tennessee. He was born 17 June 1929 in Collinwood. His description when inducted into the army: brown eyes, brown hair, 5'9" height, weight 180 lbs, married with three dependents and was a Mechanic Helper. He was inducted 15 August 1946 at Fort Oglethorpe, Georgia. His Military Occupational Specialty was Auto Equipment Mechanic. His Military Qualifications were Rifle and Pistol Sharpshooter. He was not in any battles. His decorations were World War II Victory Medal, and Army of Occupation Medal-Japan. He departed the USA 19 Nov 1946 for Pacific Theater Operation and returned 3 June 1947. His education consisted of eight years in grammar school. He was discharged 22 June 1947 at Camp Stoneman, California.

PERRY, JESSIE NEWTON, JR., Serial Number 295 59 15, was a Seaman First Class in the United States Navy. He was born 28 June 1921 in Lutts, Tennessee. He enlisted 10 February 1940 in Nashville, Tennessee. His Civilian Occupation was Farmer. He was discharged 22 May 1942 at the United States Naval Hospital in Pensacola, Florida because of physical disability.

PEVAHOUSE, ANDY, was born on July 16, 1905, the son of George Wesly and Maudie Mae Queen Pevahouse. He died on March 7, 1982, and is buried in the Culp Cemetery on Little Beech Creek in Wayne County, Tennessee.

He served in World War II in the Army.

Andy married Bonnie Riley, born on October 11, 1923, daughter of Charlie Riley and Bessie Smith Riley. Andy and Bonnie were the parents of Emma Lee, David Andrew and Sharen Kay. Andy and his family are members of Methodist Church.

His siblings are Fred, Ada, Clyde, Ernest Brown and twins, William Clay and Annie Mae.

PEVAHOUSE, CLYDE ODLE, was born on December 20, 1907, the son of George Wesley and Maudie Mae Queen Pevahouse. He married Lassie Thompson, and they are the parents of three children: Austin, Wallace and Wanda. They have four grandchildren and one great-grandchild.

Clyde served during World War II in the United States Army and was inducted at Ft. Oglethorpe, Georgia.

He was a member of Mt. Auburn Church in Perry County, Tennessee, and served as church treasurer for many years. He saw the church grow during his time there. On February 14, 1998, Clyde died and is buried in Mt. Auburn Cemetery.

His siblings are Fred, Ada, Andy, Ernest Brown and twins, William Clay and Annie Mae.

PEVAHOUSE, ERNEST BROWN "DICK", was born on July 16, 1911, to George Wesley and Maudie Mae Queen Pevahouse. He grew up in the Beech Creek community and joined the Civilian Conservation Corp. (C. C. C. Camp), which

was the first agency of the New Deal in the early 1930's.

Dick served as T/4 in the United States Army during World War II.

After the war, he returned home, but never married. On December 13, 1981, he died and is buried in Culp Cemetery on Little Beech Creek in Wayne County.

His siblings are Fred, Ada, Clyde, Andy and twins, William Clay and Annie Mae.

PEVAHOUSE, HOLLIS BROWN, served his country in the United States Army during World War II.

He was born on June 13, 1912, and died on October 14, 1987. He is buried near Clifton in the Riverside United Methodist Church Cemetery. He was the son of Chesley Pevahouse and Ada Warren Pevahouse.

He was married (1) to Estelle Ricketts. They had one daughter, Yuvonne. He married (2) to Wilma (Kitty) Graves. They had three children: Ronnie, Carolyn and Jerry Wayne. His siblings are Hester Orlenia, Forrest Lee, Milbourne J., Lockie Mae and W. C.

PEVAHOUSE, MALCOLM OBE, worked at public works and farmed until he volunteered for military service and was inducted into the United States Army in 1937. He spent two years in the Panama

Canal Zone in Panama, then was honorably discharged. At this time he became a part of the Regular Army Reserve and spent two years in the engineering department of the Civilian Conservation Corps in Oregon. In 1941, Pevahouse was recalled to active duty and served until 1943 in the Complaint Division of the 1318th Infantry at Camp Claiborne, Alexander, Louisiana where he attained the rank of Sergeant. He and his brother, Sergeant Joseph Pevahouse were stationed here at the same time. In 1943, Sergeant Pevahouse was transferred to North Camp Hood, Texas, where he served in Field Engineering. He was also stationed at Camp Pope, Louisiana and Camp Bowie, Texas. He was honorably discharged from the Army in November 1945.

After the war was over, Pevahouse worked for General Shoe Company in Hohenwald, Tennessee for two years before moving to Folkville, Alabama to work in construction with Brooks and Mixon. After working there for twenty-nine years, he retired and still lives there.

Sergeant Pevahouse, son of Mr. and Mrs. Oscar Lee Pevahouse of Clifton, Tennessee, was born 22 March 1917 in Clifton. He attended Little Beech Elementary School near Clifton. He married Iris Delaney while he was stationed at Camp Claiborne. They have four children, three boys and one girl.

PEVAHOUSE, ROBY, was born in Wayne County, Tennessee, near Clifton and lived in this area. He attended the

schools and was a member of the Methodist Church in Clifton.

He was the son of John J. and Hattie M. Waters Pevahouse. He went into the United States Navy in 1934 and came out in 1954. His rating was Chief Petty Officer. He was a veteran of World War II and also the Korean War.

He was a member of the Fleet Reserve Association, the Masonic Lodge and the American Legion. He joined the staff of ARO at Arnold Center in 1962 as an in-

strument technician in the Karman Facility where he remained until he retired in January 1977.

Roby died on January 14, 1979, at age 63 in the hospital at Huntsville, Alabama, after a long illness. He was entombed in the Shiloh National Park Cemetery on January 16, 1979.

He was married to Marie Freeman. His siblings are Delta Pevahouse Pugh, Lorene Hardin, Freddy Lee Hardin, Christine Franks, Maudie Lee Sandiege and Marie Parrish.

Submitted by Roby Pevahouse.

PHILLIPS, CHARLIE GRADY, Serial Number 966 79 26, entered the United States Navy 8 March 1944 and was a Seaman First Class. He was born 5 May 1918 in Waynesboro, Tennessee. The vessels and Stations served on: NTS Great Lakes, Illinois; Construction Battalion USNCTC Williamsburg, Virginia; Asiatic Pacific A REC BKS Naval Station, Seattle, Washington; USS LYCOMING (APA155); and USS BISCAYNE. Service medals include: Victory Ribbon, Asiatic Pacific Ribbon with one Star and Philippine Liberation Ribbon. Charlie was discharge 5 April 1946 in New Orleans, Louisiana.

PHILLIPS, HENRY CLAY, JR., was honorably discharged from U.S. Naval Service after serving three years, 5 months.

He was born in Autanga County, AL, August 2, 1920. He entered active service September 2, 1942, assigned to the Naval Aviation Candidate Selection Board, Atlanta, GA, Sqd. VPB2#1 as a yeoman, P class. This office closed September 15, 1944. He spent the next 2 1/2 months in Jacksonville, FL, and San Francisco, CA. He was transported to the battleships, USS Mississippi on duty in the Pacific, assigned to the Executive Officer. Like most veterans he talked very little about his experiences aboard the "Old Miss." They were hit by a suicide plane, and engaged in several encounters with the enemy. His ship was in Tokyo Bay for the signing of the surrender and peace treaty. Most of the ships returning to the states after the signing were battered by a dangerous storm.

The Mississippi, along with the aircraft carrier, Ranger, came into port in New Orleans in October of 1945. Most long serving officers and men were discharged here. The ship proceeded to the naval base in Virginia where more crew were discharged. On February 8, 1946, Phillips received his discharge in Jacksonville, FL, as a yeoman, First Class.

Mr. Phillips grew up in Dothan, AL, moving to Luverne, AL, for his junior and senior years in high school. His parents having moved to Georgia before his graduation, he attended Business School in Atlanta. At 19 he was working for the Atlanta, Birmingham and Coast Railroad in Atlanta, then in Savannah, GA, as Secretary to the manager of the Freight-Sales Dept. In November, 1940, he was transferred to the same department in Nashville. He left AB&C in August of 1942 to visit with his family before enlisting.

While in Nashville he met Clara Nell Yeiser, a student at Vanderbilt University. They were married February 1, 1943, in Waynesboro. They lived in Atlanta until he was transferred in September of 1944. Their first son was born in Atlanta in October of 1944. Mrs. Phillips and son returned to Waynesboro for the duration of the war.

After his discharge, Mr. Phillips worked in Georgia for three years before moving the family to Waynesboro to take a job with the Bank of Waynesboro. For the next 20 years he was active in the Lions Club, Little League baseball and was the voice of the Wildcats. He was a City Commissioner and Mayor, President of the Chamber of Commerce, Elder in the Christian Church.

Upon leaving the Bank of Waynesboro with the officers in 1969, he joined the new Mallory Corp. as Personnel Officer. In 1971, he was recruited to help found a new bank in Dunlap, TN, which is now called Tri-County Bank. After his retirement he was asked to return to the Bank of Waynesboro as President and CEO. In 1989 he retired due to approaching blindness. He had a stroke in August of 1991, and died from an aortic aneurysm on October 4, 1991. He is survived by his wife and sons Henry II, Jay Yeiser Phillips, Warren W. Phillips - four grandchildren and one great-grand child.

PHILLIPS, HUBERT L., Serial Number 34 190 396, was a Technician Fifth Grade in the Army of the United States. He was born 15 Aug 1916 in Iron City, Lawrence County, Tennessee. He was inducted 26 February 1942. He was in the battles of Africa, Sicily, Naples, Foggia,

Rome-Arno, Rhineland, Southern France and Central Europe. The following decorations were awarded to Phillips: European-African Middle Eastern Theater Ribbon with 6 Bronze Stars and Bronze Arrowhead and Good Conduct Ribbon. He was discharged 27 September 1945 at Camp Atterbury, Indiana

He left Fort Dixon, New Jersey, for Casablanca, North Africa and arrived there in February 1943. He joined General Patton's 5th Army and fought across North Africa from West to East. He then boarded a ship at Bizirte, Tunisia, with the 5th Army and sailed to Sicily, and then to Salerno, Italy. There they joined the British 8th Army. From there, they went to Naples, boarded another ship and made the invasion of Anzio Beachhead. After spending four and a half months here, they went North and took Rome and then North to Piza. Next, they turned around and went back to Naples to board a ship for the invasion of Southern France with the American 7th Army commanded by General Patch. They fought North to Sauerbruken, Germany. There they were under the command of the 70th Infantry-"Bloody Hatchets" Division. From here they fought to Frankfurt, Germany, where they were when the war ended. After that he spent six months in the Army Occupation. Then he went to LaHavre, France, and on to South Hampton, England where they spent three weeks before boarding the Queen Elizabeth to sail for home. They arrived in New York 27 September 1945.

PHILLIPS, JAMES THELBERT, was born on May 14, 1922. He was the son of Coy Francis Phillips and Ada Walker Phillips. Thelbert married Joan Conway, daughter of Adolphus and Tince Kyle Conway of the Clifton area.

He served with the 236th Army Engineers during World War II. He was in combat in Burma.

He worked at Genesco for several years. He went on to work with Reynolds Aluminum Company in Lister Hill, Alabama,

as an ironworker. He was a member of the Waynesboro Church of Christ. Thelbert and Joan had one son, Darryl Jeffrey. Thelbert died on February 3, 1992. He was buried in Memorial Gardens in Waynesboro, Tennessee. His siblings were Willie Kate, Audry, Doland and Rex.

PHILLIPS, REX, was born on June 14, 1927, son of Coy Francis Phillips and Ada Walker Phillips. He married Mary Janette Odle. They had three children: Ondra, Cynthia and Charise.

Rex served in the United States Navy during World War II. He worked as a towboat pilot on the Mississippi River after returning to civilian life.

His wife Janette died in 1977. He married his second wife, Ella Chloe Alexander Davis. His siblings are Willie Kate, Audrey, Doland and James Thelbert.

PHILLIPS, JESSIE TAYLOR, Serial Number AF 34 189 082, was with the Army Air Force of the United States. His Civilian

Occupation was Mail Clerk. He was married when he entered into active service 29 September 1945. The following decorations were awarded to Phillips: Good Conduct Ribbon. He had no foreign service. He was honorably discharged 27 September 1948 at Camp Livingston, Louisiana.

Taylor, son of Peter Riley and Dora (Hill) Phillips, was born 9 July 1910 in Wayne County, and died 26 May 1980 in Hohenwald, Tennessee. He had two brothers, Woodfin Walter and Conred Phillips and two sisters, Sallie Lee Phillips McNutt and Edith Phillips Daniels. He had one half sister, Elizabeth "Betsy" Horton Galloway. Taylor was married 17 April 1943 to Lena Tharp. They had one son, Kenneth Phillips.

PHILLIPS, NORMAN, Serial Number 14 003 255, was a Private First Class in Company K, 34th Infantry in the Army of the United States. His permanent mailing address was Route 1, Waynesboro, Tennessee. He was born 10 March 1916 in Wayne County, Tennessee. His Civilian Occupation was General Farmer. He was married with one dependent when he entered into active service 18 July 1940 at Fort McClellan, Alabama. His Military Occupational Specialty was Rifleman. His Military Qualifications included Combat Infantry Badge. He was in the battles in the Asiatic-Pacific Theater of Operations. The following decorations were awarded to Phillips: Asiatic Pacific Theater Operation Campaign Ribbon, Good Conduct Ribbon, Purple Heart, and American Defense Service Medal. He was wounded in action 1 July 1944 Asiatic-Pacific Theater of Operations. The wounds were to his ears. He left the USA 16 December 1941 for the Asiatic-Pacific Theater of Operations, and returned to USA 13 December 1944. He was discharged 19 April 1945 at Deshan General Hospital, Butler, Pennsylvania because of disability.

PHILLIPS, WOODFIN WALTER, Serial Number 34 013 682, was with the 1468th Engineer Main Company in the

Army of the United States. He entered into active service 22 January 1941. He spent seven months and one day in the Rhineland in Central Europe participating in the battles and campaigns of that area in 1945. Woodfin was honorably discharged 18 October 1945.

Woodfin, son of Peter Riley and Dora (Hill) Phillips, was born 26 April 1913 in Wayne County, and died 24 July 1974. He had two brothers, Jesse Taylor and Conred Phillips and two sisters, Sallie Lee Phillips McNutt and Edith Phillips Daniels. He had one half sister, Elizabeth "Betsy" Horton Galloway. Woodfin was married 21 September 1945 to Marie Dixon. Her death occurred 14 March 1961. He then married Ruby Gallaher Young 5 November 1961. He had one stepdaughter, Martha Jo (Young) Foster.

PICKETT, JESSE ELIZA, J. E.

Pickett, Vernon Jeter and James Hardin left the Clifton area in Wayne County, Tennessee, on July 24, 1941, for the United States Navy to be trained in Norfolk, Virginia. They were still together in the Pacific. J. E. went to radio school and was radar and radio operator and gunner on a dive bomber.

J. E. was born in 1917 an only child of Jess and Grace Hill Pickett. He graduated from Frank Hughes School in Clifton in the Class of 1936. After the war he was on the West Coast when he met his wife, Grace English, a native of Waukegan, Illinois.

He retired from the Johnson Outboard Motor Company in Waukegan. In semi-retirement, he had a second career as a land developer in Hamilton, Alabama.

J. E. died on Thursday, July 15, 1982, with a heart ailment in Tupelo, Mississippi. At this time he was living in north Mississippi. His wife preceded him in death.

They had two daughters, Roxie Pickett and Carol Pickett Arrelola; two sons, Mark and Lance; and two grandchildren. He was carried back to Waukegan to be buried by his wife, Grace.

PICKETT, W.C., JR., Serial Number 44 123 378 was a Corporal in Company A, 383rd Military Police Battalion in the Army of the United States. His permanent mailing address was %Postmaster, Clifton, Tennessee. He was registered with Selective Service Board in Wayne County, Tennessee. His Civilian Occupation was Machinist. He was married when he was inducted 20 July 1945 at Fort Oglethorpe, Georgia. His Military Occupational Specialty was Military Policeman His Military Qualifications included M1 Rifle. He was not in any battle. The following decorations were awarded to Pickett: World War II Victory Medal. He left the USA 3 January 1946 for France, and returned to USA 25 June 1946. He was discharged 8 July 1946 at Fort George Mead, Maryland.

Pickett, the son of Walter Clarence, Sr., and Oasie (Jeter) Pickett, was born 14 November 1915 in Clifton, Tennessee, died 11 February 1993 at Centennial Pavilion in Nashville, and was buried in Clifton Cemetery. He married Mary Jack Pickett. Their children were Vickie Powell of Savannah, Bob of Memphis, Walter of Clifton and Danny of Cullman, Alabama. There were eleven grandchildren.

PIGG, ASHEL J., Serial Number 34 144 822, was a Private in 175th Quartermaster Gas Supply Company in the Army of the United States. His permanent mailing address was General Delivery, Waynesboro, Tennessee. He was registered with Selective Service Board in Wayne County,

Tennessee. He was born 21 May 1923 in Collinwood, Tennessee. His Civilian Occupation was Laborer. He was inducted 12 August 1942 at Fort Oglethorpe, Georgia. His Military Occupational Specialty was Duty Soldier. His Military Qualifications included Rifle Sharpshooter. He was not in any battles. The following decorations were awarded to Pigg: American Defense Service Medal, American Theater Campaign Medal, Asiatic-Pacific Campaign Medal, World War II Victory Medal, One Service Stripe and 2 Overseas Service Bars. He left the USA 16 February 1944 for the AF Operation, and returned to USA 25 February 1945. He had a seventh grade education. He was discharged 18 November 1945 at Fort Sam Houston, Texas.

PIGG, DEWEY, son of Archie and Mary Melinda Jane (Rich) Pigg, he, was born 7 September 1920 in Wayne County,

Tennessee. He had two brothers living, Noah and Richard Pigg, and two brothers deceased, J. H. and Allen Pigg. He has two nieces, Patti Stults and Sheila Smith and one nephew, Jamie Pigg. He also has two great nieces, Janila Pigg and Michelle Smith and two great nephews, Brian Smith and Matthew Stults. Dewey married Mary Elizabeth McClendon on 26 December 1958.

Dewey was inducted into the Army of the United States 22 November 1942 at Fort Oglethorpe, Georgia. Dewey and his brothers, J. H. and Noah served in the Army at the same time. His Military Occupational Specialty was Military Policeman. His Military Qualifications included Marksman Rifle. He was in the battles of Normandy, Northern France, and Rhineland, The following decorations were awarded to Pigg: World War II Victory Medal, Good Conduct Medal, American Theater Ribbon, European-African Middle Eastern Theater Ribbon, with three Bronze Service Stars, Philippine Liberation Ribbon, American Theater Ribbon, and Belgium Fourragere. He was overseas one year, ten months and four days. He was discharged 27 December 1945 at Camp Chaffee, Arkansas.

PIGG, HERSCHEL, Pfc Herschel Pigg son of Mrs. Emma Pigg of Iron City Route 2, entered the service on 17 October 1942 and took his basic training at Camp Gruber, Oklahoma. He was on maneuvers in Louisiana and was then transferred to Fort Sam Houston, Texas. From there he was sent to overseas duty in November 1943. He landed in North Africa and then went to Italy. Before entering service, he was engaged in farming.
Source: Wayne County News .

PIGG, JALMER, SR., son of Walter and Leslie (Keeton) Pigg, was born in 1917 on Indian Creek in Wayne County, TN. He entered the U. S. Army Air Force at the beginning of World War 11 and participated in the African Campaign. After he returned to the states, he settled his family at Memphis, TN and studied radiology at U. T. Memphis.

Mr. Pigg was a radiology technician at LeBonhr and John Gadston Hospitals. During the course of his daily work he became aware of the need of some way to hold infants and children totally immobile for x-rays. He invented such a device during the early 1960's. The Pigg-O-Stat infant immobilizer has been in use world wide since it's invention. The government has endorsed and requires its availability at all government subsidized hospitals.

He died in, 1995, at the age of 78.

PIGG, JAMES N., was born on October 9, 1923, in Iron City, Tennessee, and was living in Cypress Inn, Tennessee, working as a farmhand when he was inducted into the United States Army on July 28, 1944, at Camp Forrest, Tennessee. He served as a T/5 with Company D, 4th Tank Battalion as an ambulance driver. He was in the battle in Central Europe and was awarded the Good Conduct Medal, Euro-

pean African Middle Eastern Theater Ribbon, Army Occupation Medal (Germany) and World War II Victory Medal. James was discharged on January 1, 1946, at Ft. George G. Meade, Maryland.

PIGG, JAMES R., Pfc, son of Mr. and Mrs. E. C. Pigg, of Waynesboro, Tennessee, was wounded in action in the Marshall

Islands on the night of Feb 3. PFC Pigg was not removed from the battlefield until the following day when he was immediately placed aboard a hospital ship and taken to a base hospital in Pearl Harbor. His injuries were the loss of his left eye and the hearing in his left ear. He was permitted to return to the United States and was placed in a hospital in Springfield, Missouri.

PFC Pigg entered the service 21 November 1942 and took his training at Fort Ord, California, He remained there until he was assigned to overseas duty Aug 1943. He was awarded the Purple Heart, Infantry Badge, Good Conduct Medal and a Service Ribbon with 2 Stars. Before service he was employed at the Reynolds Aluminum Plant in Sheffield, Alabama. He left the USA 11 July 1943 for the Asiatic Pacific Theater and returned to USA 14 April 1944. He was discharged 19 October 1945. He married Marie Stafford from Lawrenceburg.

PIGG, JOHN H., was in the Army of the United States. His Civilian Occupation was Farm Hand. He entered into active service 23 February 1943 at Fort Oglethorpe, Georgia. His Military Occupational Specialty was Amphibian Tank Crewman. He was in the battles of Eastern Mandates, Southern Philippines, Western Pacific and Ryukyu. The following decorations were awarded to Pigg: World War II Victory Medal, Good Conduct Medal, Asiatic Pacific Theater Ribbon with 4 Bronze Service Stars, Philippine Liberation Ribbon, Purple Heart and Distinguish Unit Badge.

He was discharged 18 December 1945 at Camp Chaffee, Arkansas

John, son of Archie and Mary Melinda Jane (Rich) Pigg, was born 3 Sept 1922 in Cypress Inn, Tennessee, died 12 Sept 1973 and is buried in Memorial Gardens in Collinwood. He had four brothers Noah, Richard, Dewey and Allen Pigg. He married Reba Rich and they had one daughter Shelia (Pigg) Smith and two grandchildren, Brian and Michelle Smith. He attended school at Scotts Chapel. He worked for the Natchez Trace Parkway for more than twenty-two years before he retired.

PIGG, JOHN I., Serial Number 34 361 755, was a Private First Class in Company 1, 8th Infantry Regiment in the Army of the United States. His permanent mailing address was Route 3, Florence, Alabama. He was born 9 February 1918 in Cypress Inn, Tennessee. He was registered with Selective Service Board in Wayne County, Tennessee. His Civilian Occupation was General Farmer. He was single when he was inducted into active service. His Military Occupational Specialty was Machine Gunner. His Military Qualifications included MKM Rifle. He was in the battles of Rhineland, Normandy, Northern France and Central Europe. The following decorations were awarded to Pigg: European-African Middle Eastern Theater Ribbon with 4 Battle Stars and Arrowhead, Purple Heart, Distinguished Unit Citation Badge, and Good Conduct Ribbon. Pigg was wounded in action 29 November 1944 in Germany. He left the USA 18 January 1944 for the European Theater Operation, and returned to USA 12 July 1945. He was discharged 12 October 1945 at Hospital Center Separation Point, Camp Butner, North Carolina.

PIGG, JOHNNY B., Serial Number 34 501 225, was a Private First Class in Battery D, 476th Antiaircraft Artillery A W Battalion in the Army of the United States. His permanent mailing address was Route 1, Cypress Inn, Tennessee. He was registered with Selective Service Board in Wayne County, Tennessee. His Civilian Occupation was General Farmer. He was inducted 20 December 1942 and entered into active service 27 December 1942 at Fort Oglethorpe, Georgia. His Military Occupational Specialty was Cannoneer. His Military Qualifications included Marksman Rifle. He was in the battle of New Guinea. The following decorations were awarded to Pigg: World War II Victory Medal, Good Conduct Ribbon, Asiatic Pacific Theater Ribbon with one Bronze Service Star and one Bronze Arrowhead, Philippine Liberation Ribbon and Distinguished Unit Badge. He left the USA 27 October 1943 for the Asiatic Pacific Theater Operation, and returned to USA 20 January 1946. He was discharged 28 January 1946 at Camp Chaffee, Arkansas.

Johnny, son of Andrew Thomas and June Elizabeth (Trousdale) Pigg, was born 29 June 1921 in Florence, Alabama, died 20 April 1993 in Humana Hospital in Florence and was buried in Cromwell Crossroads Cemetery near Collinwood. He married Etta Hanback of Cypress Inn. His children are, Johnny, Jr., Larry of Iron City, Ronnie, "Pete" of Smyrna, Gary, Jerry, Sherry Stults and Janie Pigg of Cypress Inn. He has one sister, Annie Blanche Holt of Florence, Alabama. He was a retired carpenter.

PIGG, MARSHALL, Private First Class, was born 29 August 1922 to Lige and Sally (Daniel) Pigg. He was their third child.

He was born and reared on Little Indian Creek and attended the Masonic Hall School. On 9 June 1945 he and Clara Nell Berry were united in marriage. To them were born two children, Margaret Ann and Travis Hugh Pigg. Marshall died of service related illness 7 August 1981 in the VA Hospital in Nashville and was buried in the Memorial Garden in McGlamery, Tennessee.

He was inducted into the United States Army 20 December 1942 at Fort Oglethorpe, Georgia. After basic training, he was

sent with the 476th AAA Battalion to Sydney, Australia. Due to illness he was returned to Camp Lee, Virginia. He worked in the medical department until he was honorably discharged 19 September 1945.

PIGG, NOAH, son of Archie and Mary Melinda Jane (Rich) Pigg, he was born 9 December 1924 in Wayne County, Tennes-

see, died 12 Sept 1973 and is buried in Memorial Gardens in Collinwood. He had four brothers J. H., Richard, Dewey and Allen Pigg. He married Hazel Arlean Arnett in 1952 and they had two children, Patti Kim Pigg Stults and Jamie Kirk Pigg and two wonderful grandchildren, Jamila Nicole Pigg and Matthew Ray Stults. Noah and his brothers Dewey and J. H were all in the service at the same time.

Noah was inducted 5 October 1943 and entered into active service 26 October 1943 at Camp Shelby, Mississippi. His Military Occupational Specialty was Rifleman. His Military Qualifications included Combat Infantryman Badge. He was in the battles of Northern France, Ardennes, and Rhineland. The following decorations were awarded to Pigg: World War II Victory Medal, Middle Eastern Theater Ribbon with 3 Bronze Battle Stars, Good Conduct Ribbon, and Purple Heart. He was wounded 15 January 1945 in the Ardennes Forest. He was shot in the right leg in Belgium. He was overseas one year, one month and twenty-seven days. He was discharged 4 December 1945 at Fort Jackson, South Carolina.

PIGG, SAMUEL H., Serial Number 34 375 246, was inducted into the Army of the United States 3 October 1942, and was released from active duty, and transferred to the Enlisted Reserve Corps, and returned to Waynesboro, Tennessee. On 17 October 1942, he was called to active duty and reported to Fort Oglethorpe, Georgia.

PIGG, WALTER W., JR., W. W., Jr.,

son of Mr. and Mrs. Walter W. Pigg of Cypress Inn, joined the Merchant Marines December 1943. He took his Maritime schooling in St. Petersburg, Florida and was sent overseas in October 1944. He returned in May 1945 to Savannah, Georgia.
Source: Wayne County News.

PITTS, ANDREW JOE, was a Seaman First Class in the Navy of the United States. He was born 17 December 1916 in Waynesboro, Tennessee. His home address was Waynesboro, Tennessee. His permanent mailing address was Flatwoods, Tennessee. He was registered with Selective Service Board in Wayne County, Tennessee. His Civilian Occupation was Mechanic and Truck Driver. He was married when entered into active service 4 September 1942 at NRS, Memphis, Tennessee. The Vessels and Stations that he served on were: NRS Memphis, Tennessee, USNTS, Great Lakes, Illinois, USNAS, Memphis, USNATS, Fort Pierce, Florida. The following decorations were awarded to Pitts: One Bronze Star for Okinawa Campaign and Good Conduct Ribbon. His last employer before entering service was the Tennessee State Highway Department in Nashville, Tennessee from July 1941 to August 1942. He was honorably discharged 26 October 1945 in Nashville, Tennessee.

On July 19, 1942, Joe married Marguerite Bastin. They had four children. Sandra Nell Pitts Martin, born May 23, 1943, married Chester Darrol Martin, one child, Chester Darrol Martin, Jr., married Angie Spurlock, one child, William Chester Martin.

Brenda Jane Pitts Davis Whitehead, born October 29, 1947, married Tafford Davis, two children, Seelley Marguerite Davis Bunch married James Bunch, two children, Andrew Brian Bunch and Alora Katherine Kittrell Bunch married Ted Whitehead. Brenda passed away November 9, 1998.

Joe Anthony Pitts, born June 23, 1949, married Lydia Joy Moore, two children, Jane Anna Pitts Cummings, married Jeff Cummings and Jason Pitts. Children Johna Kay Pitts, Martha Evelyn Pitts, and John Ross Pitts.

Joe and Marguerite lived most of their married lives in Wayne County. They were members of the North Highland Church of Christ. Joe passed away on July 4, 1970 and Marguerite passed away on November 30, 1998.

PITTS, JACK, Serial Number 34 366 647, was a Corporal in Company A, 113th Engineer (Combat) Battalion in the Army of the United States. His permanent mailing address was 438 N. Walnut St., Florence, Alabama. He was registered with

Selective Service Board in Wayne County, Tennessee. His Civilian Occupation was Catcher Steel Mill. He was married with one dependent when he was inducted 26 August 1942 and entered into active service 9 September 1942 at Fort Oglethorpe, Georgia. His Military Occupational Specialty was Rigger. His Military Qualifications included MKM. He was in the battles of New Guinea, South Philippines and Luzon. The following decorations were awarded to Pitts: ARO Medal, Asiatic Pacific Theater Operation Medal, Philippine Liberation Ribbon with one Bronze Star, Good Conduct Medal, Bronze Indian Arrowhead, and World War II Victory Medal. He left the USA 31 December 1943 for the Asiatic Pacific Theater Operation, and returned to USA 2 November 1945. He had a high school education. He was discharged 12 November 1945 at Camp Shelby, Mississippi.

Jack, son of Joe Pitts, Sr. and Lulu Belew Pitts ,was born 8 July 1921 in Waynesboro, Tennessee. His siblings were Joe Pitts, Jr., Sallie Pitts Hendrix and Mary Nelle Pitts.

PITTS, LEONARD WOODROW, Serial Number 970 01 75, was a Carpenter's Mate Second Class in the

Navy of the United States. He was born 17 May 1919 in Waynesboro, Tennessee. He entered into active service 18 March 1944. The Vessels and Stations that he served on were: NTS San Diego, California, Hedron 14-1 FAW 14, and FLT A RECL Center, Coronado Heights Annex. He was honorably discharged 18 January 1946 in Memphis, Tennessee.

PITTS, MARION LIOYD, Serial Number 966 19 96, was a Seaman First Class in the Navy of the United States. He was born 30 April 1925 in Waynesboro, Tennessee. He entered into active

service 23 December 1943. The Vessels and Stations that he served on were: NTS, San Diego, California; Hedron Fleet Air Wing - 14; and USS Ka Dashan Bay. He was honorably discharged 7 January 1946 in Memphis, Tennessee.

He was born to Ross Montgomery (Sam) Pitts and Mary jane Hickerson Pitts. He was the seventh of eight children, five girls and three boys. He attended school in Lewis County and in Wayne County.

He married Dorothy Frances Kelley in 1947. While living and working in Waynesboro, he and Frances had two sons, Ron in 1948 and Terry in 1950. Shortly after the birth of their third son, Roger in 1960 they moved to Savannah, Tn., where four years later the had their fourth son, Keith.

Lloyd worked for 17 years in Savannah where he owned and operated a dry cleaning business. In 1977, they moved to Lawrenceburg where he operated another dry cleaning business.

At present, Lloyd is retired and living in Savannah, Tn. Lloyd served his country proudly during WWII. He now enjoys relaxing and enjoying his grandchildren.

POAG, CHARLES H., was born to Bruce and Lillie Poag, November 17, 1916. He grew up on Forty-Eight Creek, the youngest of seven children. About the age of nineteen he went to Keiser, Arkansas to help on his brother's cotton farm. Sometime later he moved in with his sister and took over forty acres of rich land on Milligan. About this time he met Jewell Rowlett. After an extended courtship they were married. She became an elementary school teacher and Hughes continued farming until he was drafted into the U. S. Army during October 1942.

Hughes was assigned to Co. A, 96th Infantry Division as a cook and sent to

the west coast for his basic training. Within a short time, Jewell followed and was living there when their oldest child, Melba, was born in, April 1944. Shortly after her birth, Hughes got a furlough and took his family back to Arkansas. He returned to camp and within a short time was sent to the Pacific Theater of War and participated in the battles on Leyte and Okinawa. During the battle at Okinawa the fighting was hard with many narrow escapes. Many nights they slept in foxholes filled with water and the rain still pouring down. He often talked about the heavy loads they carried and how hard the war was on the people. During a Jap suicide mission Hughes and about 25 other soldiers were buried alive in a cave. He and about four others survived and were sent to a hospital on New Guinea, Island. Hughes suffered head, spine and back injuries that caused him much suffering the rest of his life.

Hughes told many stories of his war experiences. One time he and a jeep driver were sent with supplies to the troops on the front line. The only way they could start the jeep was to push it. They came across the body of a dead soldier and loaded it in their jeep. They hadn't gone far on their way back to camp when the jeep stalled, then snipers began firing at them. After trying several times, it started up and they got back to camp. Later when they pulled the jeep into the motor pool for repair, the whole bottom came out of it. Hughes called it a miracle that they had made it back.

He liked to tell that while on maneuvers one time, he started to make biscuits and didn't have lard, so he used butter. The Colonel came by, filled his plate and kept bragging on those biscuits. After that, he always complemented Hughes biscuits.

Another day they kept hearing a commotion; it was a group of women yelling and jabbering. They were chasing a Jap officer who had killed their babies.

When the war ended his unit returned to the states and he had advanced in rank to T/Sgt. 4. He received his discharge, December 26, 1945, at Fort Chaffee, AR. and returned home with a handful of medals. Hughes was back home with his family on the farm he loved. When spring came, he bought two white horses and began making plans to start farming all over again. Another joyful time was, August 1948, when their son, Dale was born. Fifteen years later Hughes suffered a heart attack. His doctor advised him to keep his hands in his pocket and a smile on his face, because his fanning days were over.

In 1969, Hughes and Jewell moved to Waynesboro, TN and for the next few years, he suffered many episodes with his heart, a malignant spot on his lung, lung surgery and then osteo-arthritis. Twenty years later, in 1989, they moved to their present home near Waynesboro, where they could raise calves as a hobby. Hughes health became worse; the osteo had worsened, he had two back surgeries and finally a severe stroke. His life ended March 3, 2000. He is buried at Highland Cemetery near the Lawrence County line. Hughes and Jewell were married over 60 years. They have three grand - children, Caprice Poag, Tina Poag (McMechan) and Paul Scott Poag; two great-grandchildren, Codi Jewell Scipper and Lillie Rose Moore.

POINTER, BOB, JR., Serial Number 34 521 837, was a Private First Class in 873rd Aviation Squadron in the Army of the United States. His permanent mailing address was 441 Douglas Avenue, Macon, Bibb County, Georgia. He was born 31 January 1917 in Waynesboro, Tennessee. His race was Negro. He was registered with Selective Service Board in Wayne County, Tennessee. His Civilian Occupation was Porter. He was married when he was inducted 27 November 1942 and entered into active service 5 December 1942 at Camp Forrest, Tennessee. His Military Occupational Specialty was Duty Soldier. His Military Qualifications included Marksman Rifle. He was not in any battles. The following decorations were awarded to Pointer: World War II Victory Medal, Good Conduct Ribbon, American Theater Medal, and Asiatic Pacific Theater Ribbon. He left the USA 27 June 1945 for the Asiatic Pacific Theater Operation, and returned to USA 2 February 1946. He was discharged 10 February 1946 at Camp Chaffee, Arkansas.

POLLACK, JACK, went to the US Army from Wayne County and was inducted into service at Ft. Oglethorpe, GA. He was

the son of Pleasant and Etta Hoover Pollock. He had one sister Ruby. Jack never married.

POPE, CLYDE L., Serial Number 34 361 750, was a Staff Sergeant in Company I, 22nd Infantry 4th Division in the Army

of the United States. His permanent mailing address was Route 6, Waynesboro, Tennessee. He was born 8 September 1919 in Clifton, Tennessee. He was registered with Selective Service Board in Wayne County, Tennessee. His Civilian Occupation was General Farmer. He was inducted 25 July 1942 and entered into active service 8 August 1942 at Fort Oglethorpe, Georgia. His Military Occupational Specialty was Squad Leader. His Military Qualifications included Rifle Marksman. He attended the Agricultural School in Daytona Beach, Florida for one month in July 1945. He was in the battles of Normandy, Northern France and Germany. The following decorations were awarded to Pope: European-African Middle Eastern Campaign Ribbon with 3 Bronze Battle Stars, Purple Heart with one Oak Leaf Cluster, One Bronze Arrowhead, World

War II Victory Medal, American Theater Medal, Good Conduct Ribbon, Combat Infantryman Badge and Distinguished Unit Badge. He was wounded in action 30 November 1944 in the European Theater. He left the USA 18 January 1944 for England, left there 5 June 1944 for France, Left 8 September 1944 for Belgium. Left 12 September 1944 for Germany, left 6 October 1944 for Belgium, left 11 November 1944 for Germany, and returned to USA 10 March 1945. He had a seventh grade education. He was discharged 4 April 1946 from Kennedy General Hospital in Memphis, Tennessee.

Clyde was the son of George Thomas and Argie Elizabeth (Don) Bunch Pope. His brothers were: Ernie, Ruby (Red), Harvey, I.V., Willard and Dallas Pope. He had one sister, Lela Pope Davis. Clyde married Cordelia Marie White on July 6, 1946, in Corinth, MS. They made their home in Waynesboro on Highway 13 North. Clyde and Marie were the parents of five children: N.J., Linda Pope Blackwell, Donald Ray, Ronnie Lee and Carol Pope Warren.

Clyde died on April 23, 1996, and was buried in Memorial Gardens of Wayne County, Waynesboro, TN.

POPE, HILUARD ALVIS, was born and raised in Wayne County, Tennessee in 1912. He was one of eleven children of

Will and Ethel Pope. After his marriage to Geneva Haynes Pope, the couple moved to Miami, FL where he worked for the City of Miami. When the war broke out, Hiluard, along with two of his brothers, volunteered to serve.

Hiluard joined the Navy, and because of his experience with heavy equipment, enlisted in the Cee Bees. Throughout the war, he served in the South Pacific. The Cee Bees immediately followed the Marines on to the many islands that were taken from the Japanese. Their responsibility was the task of building airstrips, unloading cargo ships, etc.

While serving his country, the first child of Hiluard and Geneva was born. Hilda Jo Pope (now Reed) was born in 1942 and was approximately three years old before Hiluard was able to see her. In 1946, their second child, James (Jim) William Pope was born. While living in Lawrenceburg, TN, Hiluard was a millwright and a carpenter.

In 1950 the family moved back to Waynesboro. Hiluard worked as a car salesman for the next nine years, then he became an independent insurance agent. He remained in the insurance business in Lawrenceburg, TN until he retired.

In 1974, Hiluard's beloved and beautiful wife, Geneva, died at the age of 56. Prior to Geneva's death, the couple lovingly provided Christian influence and support to their two children. They were able to see both graduate from college and begin, what would be, successful careers.

In 1977, Hiluard married Pauline Warren. They still reside in Waynesboro, TN. During their retirement years, Hiluard and Pauline have enjoyed camping and fishing.

POPE, I.V., Serial Number 34 920 928, was a Technician Third Grade in Medical Detachment 184th Infantry in the Army of

the United States. His permanent mailing address was Route 6, Waynesboro, Tennessee. He was born 18 March 1924 in Waynesboro, Tennessee. He was registered with Selective Service Board in Wayne County, Tennessee. His Civilian Occupation was General Farmer. He was inducted 15 December 1943 and entered into active service 5 January 1944 at Fort Oglethorpe, Georgia. His Military Occupational Specialty was Surgical Technician. His Military Qualifications included Medical Badge. He was in the battles of Southern Philippines, and Western Pacific. The following decorations were awarded to Pope: World War II Victory Medal, Good Conduct Ribbon, Asiatic Pacific Theater Ribbon with 2 Bronze Service Stars and one Bronze Arrowhead, Philippine Liberation

Ribbon, Purple Heart and a Lapel Button. He left the USA 8 August 1944 for the Asiatic Pacific Theater Operation, and returned to USA 11 February 1946. He was wounded in the Asiatic Pacific Theater in April 1945. He was discharged 18 February 1946 at Camp Chaffee, Arkansas.

POPE, JAMES RAY, son of Bentley and Florence (Blasingim) Pope, was born 28 August 1920, and died 1 May 1989. He graduated from the eighth grade on 17 May 1935 at Frank Hughes Elementary school in Clifton. He joined the Civilian Conservation Corps 10 April 1939 where he was employed as a truck driver under the War Department at TVA in Kingston, Tennessee. He was discharged 11 May 1940 to accept other employment. He was inducted into the Marine Corps 3 June 1941 and completed boot training in North Carolina. He was then transferred to the Marine Detachment aboard the USS ALCOR and was promoted to Private First Class 21 Feb 1942. Later, he was transferred to Hawaii and then to Guam where he spent 2 1/2 years as a truck driver. He was discharged 1 June 1947 in San Diego, California with the rank of Corporal.

He married Josephine Goodrich, 18 April 1943 in South Mills, North Carolina. They lived in Portsmouth and had four children, two boys and two girls. James was employed as a truck driver and retired from Virginia Chemicals with over twenty years of service.

POPE, JOHN MACK, Serial Number 34 185 296, was a Private First Class in Company F, 147th Infantry in the Army of

the United States. His permanent mailing address was Route 3, Waynesboro, Tennessee. He was registered with Selective Service Board in Gibson County, Tennessee. His Civilian Occupation was Highway Maintenance. He was inducted 10 January 1942 at Fort Oglethorpe, Georgia. His Military Occupational Specialty was Rifle-

man. His Military Qualifications included Expert Infantryman Badge for Sharpshooter Carbine and Marksman M 1 Rifle. He was in the battles of Guadalcanal. The following decorations were awarded to Pope: Good Conduct Ribbon, and Asiatic Pacific Theater Service Ribbon. He left the USA 20 May 1942 for the Fiji Islands, and returned to USA 22 February 1944. He had an eighth grade education. He was discharged 26 October 1945 at Fort George Meade, Maryland.

He received a certificate of appreciation in grateful recognition of valuable service contributed to the nation and to the Selective Service System in the administration of the universal military training and service act as amended signed by Lyndon B. Johnson, President of the United States.

John Mack was the son of William James and Nora E. (Tharpe) Pope. His siblings are Lester James "Jim", a WW II Veteran, Marvin, Reba Bray, Willie Pope, Betsy Pope, Grace Fisher, Inez Freeze and Ruth Ashmore. Betsy Pope and Grace Fisher are deceased.

He died August 1969 and was buried in Bell Cemetery.

POPE, LESTER JAMES, Serial Number 34 886 063, was a Technician Fifth Grade in Headquarters Company, 2nd

Battalion, 9th Infantry in the Army of the United States. His permanent mailing address was Route 3, Waynesboro, Tennessee. He was registered with Selective Service Board in Wayne County, Tennessee. His Civilian Occupation was Farmer. He was single when he was inducted into active service. His Military Occupational Specialty was Cook. His Military Qualifications included Combat Infantry Badge. He was in the battles of Northern France, Rhineland, and Central Europe. The following decorations were awarded to Pope: European-African Middle Eastern Campaign Medal with 3 Bronze Stars, Good Conduct Ribbon, and Purple Heart with one Oak Leaf Cluster. He was wounded in action in the European-African Middle Eastern Theater of Operations 17 September 1944 and 23 February 1945. He left the USA 16 July 1944 for the European-African Middle Eastern Theater Operation, and returned to USA 19 July 1945. He had a high school education. He was discharged 29 October 1945 at Camp Fannin, Texas.

Jim, the son of William James and Nora E. (Tharpe) Pope, was born 12 March 1918 in Waynesboro, died 16 June 1998 and was buried in Bell Cemetery. His siblings are John Malcolm "Mack", a WW II Veteran, Marvin, Reba Bray, Willie Pope, Betsy Pope, Grace Fisher, Inez Freeze and Ruth Ashmore. Betsy Pope and Grace Fisher are deceased. Jim married Willodean Patton and they had one son, James Morris Pope.

POPE, TALMADGE RAY, He had the grade of Aviation Machinist's Mate Third Class in the United States Navy. He was

discharged 30 December 1945 from the United States Naval Personnel Separation Center in Memphis, Tennessee.

POPE, THOMAS JOHN "T.J.", was a native of Wayne County, Tennessee. He

was the son of Wilburn Anderson and Daisy Pearl Treadwell Pope.

He served in the United States Army during World War II.

He was a retired postal clerk and was of the Baptist faith. T. J. died on November 25, 1995, at his home near Waynesboro, Tennessee, and was buried in the Oak Ridge Cemetery. He was survived by his wife, Lenora H. Pope, and sons, Mark, Ross and Craig, and one daughter, Holly.

POPE, WILLARD L., Serial Number 34 022 605, was a First Sergeant in Company B, 509th Military Police Battalion in

the Army of the United States. His permanent mailing address was Route 3, Waynesboro, Tennessee. He was born 15 June 1918 in Wayne County, Tennessee. He was registered with Selective Service Board in Wayne County, Tennessee. His Civilian Occupation was Belt Worker at the Handle Factory. He was married when he was inducted into active service 25 February 1941 at Fort Oglethorpe, Georgia. His Military Occupational Specialty was Military Policeman. He was in the battles of Normandy, Northern France, Rhineland, Central Europe and Ardennes. The following decorations were awarded to Pope: European-African Middle Eastern Theater Ribbon with 5 Bronze Stars, Good Conduct Ribbon, and a Bronze Star Medal. He left the USA 17 July 1943 for the European Theater Operation, and returned to USA 18 September 1945. He had a high school education. He was discharged 21 September 1945 at Camp Atterbury, Indiana.

POPE, WILLIAM A., Serial Number 34 494 876, was a Technician Fifth Grade in Company A, 1339th Engineer Construction Battalion in the Army of the United States. His permanent mailing address was Route 3, Waynesboro, Tennessee. He was born 12 June 1921 in Waynesboro. He was registered with Selective Service Board in Wayne County, Tennessee. His Civilian

Occupation was Light Truck Driver. He was single when he was inducted into active service. His Military Occupational Specialty was Construction Machine Operator. His Military Qualifications included Marksman Rifle. He was in the battles of Eastern Mandates, and Ryukyus. The following decorations were awarded to Pope: World War II Victory Medal, Good Conduct Ribbon, Asiatic Pacific Theater Ribbon with 2 Bronze Service Stars and Meritorious Service Unit Award. He left the USA 4 April 1944 for the Asiatic Pacific Theater Operation, and returned to USA 11 January 1946. He had a high school education. He was discharged 18 January 1946 at Camp Chaffee, Arkansas.

PORTER, CLEMMON A., served in the United States Army. He was stationed in Meridan, Mississippi.

He was born on June 5, 1921, in Collinwood, Tennessee, the son of Joe and Ann Porter. His father was killed when he was 2 years old. He was married to Hilda Newcomb. They had five children: Levon, Daniel Lee, Le Lennon, Peggy Ann and Louella Mae Porter. He had one brother, Le Lennon, and two sisters, Josephine and Alzona. Clemmon grew up in Clifton, Tennessee. He attended school in Clifton, and he attended St. James Methodist Church in Clifton.

He died on December 31, 1990, and is buried in Clifton in Wayne County, Tennessee.
Source: Wife, Hilda Porter.

POWELL, DEWEY, Pfc, son of Robert and Clara Powell of Clifton recently graduated from the AAF Training Command School in Harlengen Army Air Field in Harlengen, Texas. At class exercises for the graduates a pair of silver wings and a promotion in rank was issued each Aerial Gunner who is expected to join combat crews in the near future.
Source: Wayne County News.

PRATER, CONNIE H., Serial Number 34 494 856, was a Sergeant in 292nd Joint Assault Signal Company in the Army

of the United States. His permanent mailing address was Clifton, Tennessee. He was registered with Selective Service Board in Wayne County, Tennessee. His Civilian Occupation was Radio Repairman. He was inducted 21 November 1942 and entered into active service 29 November 1942 at Fort Oglethorpe, Georgia. His Military Occupational Specialty was Radio Operator. His Military Qualifications included Marksman -M1, 45 Caliber Pistol, and Sharpshooter Caliber Machine Gun. He was in the battles of Philippine Islands, Eastern Mandates, Luzon and Ryukyus. The following decorations were awarded to Prater: Good Conduct Ribbon, Philippines Liberation Ribbon with one Bronze Star, American Theater Service Medal, Asiatic Pacific Theater Service Medal with four Bronze Stars, and World War II Victory Medal. He left the USA 11 April 1944 for the Asiatic Pacific Theater Operation, and returned to USA 15 November 1945. He had a high school education. He was discharged 27 November 1945 at Indaintown Gap, Military Reservation, Pennsylvania.

Connie Howe Prater was born 17 October 1920 in Clifton, Tennessee, died 27 July 1994 in the Veterans Hospital in Nashville and was laid to rest in the Prater's Chapel Cemetery, on land donated by his forbearers for the church and cemetery. . He was the son of Olison Sloan and Elvis Mae (Conway) Prater, Elvis Mae was the daughter of William Sherman and Viola Zanonia (Jeter) Conway. Olison was the son of Todd and Lucy (Battles) Prater. Connie's brothers are James J. died as an infant, and Dennis Sherman Prater. His sisters are, Marjorie Viola, Mae Olison, Billie Jean died young, Dorothy Jane, Lucy Ann, Elizabeth Sue, and Patricia Ellen Prater.

Connie was married 10 April 1937 to Martha Pearl Loyd Foster in Corinth, Mississippi. Their children are, Martha Jane Foster, Timothy Dewayne Prater, Connie Howe Prater, Jr., and Alle Kirk Prater. Connie was married secondly, on June 28, 1947 in Corinth, Mississippi to Helen Ruth Turnbo, daughter of Curtis and Hester (Pevahouse) Turnbo. They had one daughter Glenda Faye Prater.

Connie, a honor student, graduated from Frank Hughes High School in 1939. He worked on the farm and as a radio repairman before entering service. After the war he was a farmer and river boat Captain. He was a member of the Masonic Lodge, the American Legion and the Clifton Church of Christ. He was a leader in the AA in Wayne and surrounding counties.

PRATER, JAMES F., son of Mrs. Charlotte (Prater) Capps of Collinwood, TN was discharged March 27, 1944 from the US Service during WWII.

PRATER, JOHN WESLEY, Serial Number 34 983 730, was a Private First Class in Battery A, 748th Field Artillery Battalion in the Army of the United States. His permanent mailing address was Route 2, Clifton, Tennessee. He was registered with Selective Service Board in Wayne County, Tennessee. His Civilian Occupation was General Farm Hand. He was married when he was inducted 18 March 1944 at Camp Shelby, Mississippi. His Military Occupational Specialty was Cook. His Military Qualifications included Sharpshooter M-1 Rifle. He was in the battles of Rhineland, and Central Europe. The following decorations were awarded to Prater: Good Conduct Medal, World War II Victory Medal, British-French- German Star, and European-African-Middle Eastern Theater Ribbon with 2 Bronze Service Stars. He left the USA 17 December 1944 for the European-African Middle Eastern Theater Operation, and returned to USA 21 December 1945. He was discharged 27 December 1945 at Fort Knox, Kentucky.

John W. was born 3 January 1912 in Clifton, Tennessee, died 12 January 1959 and was entombed in Prater's Chapel Cemetery. He was the son of John and Pricilla (Queen) Prater. His only sibling was a sister, Oda Belle Prater. John married Alice Jane Graham. Their children are, Oda Mae Pevahouse, Leon deceased, Joe Wayne, Mary Ellen Pope, James Faye, Jane Evelyn deceased, and Betty Jean Ray, He had 11 grandchildren and one great grandchild. John Wesley worked in an automobile plant in Detroit until he returned to Wayne County and settled in the Upper Beech Creek Community. He worked at a sawmill and did farm work.

PRATER, MILLARD D., was born on

February 25, 1915. He died on February 10, 1988. He was buried in Prater's Chapel Cemetery near Clifton, Tennessee.

He was born the son of William B. Prater and Lou Griffin Prater. He attended school, church, and worked in the same area he was born and died in. He also married Ida Jeter, daughter of John and Mary Jane (Molly) Pevahouse Jeter, who lived in the same area also, on December 1, 1945.

Millard served in the United States Army. He was sent to Europe during World War II. He stayed there until the war was over. His life work was with timber and Vulcan Materials. He retired from Vulcan. His children were Laura Jane, Jerry Millard, Nancy Lou and Mark Anthony. His siblings were Hollie Houston, Griffin (Tennie), Collins (Blue), Roxie, Pauline, Elva, Minnie, Mary Alice and Nellie.

Submitted by Millard D. Prater.

PRATER, SAM LAVERN, enlisted in 1942 and was a Private in the United States Army. He was stationed in Fort Wayne, Indiana and was discharge there in 1945. Sam was born 9 May 1923. His parents were Sam and Charlotte (Dicus) Prater. They were married 16 June 1916. Sam's siblings are, James and Harold Prater and Louise Blalock. Sam married (1) Mary Christine Cole. Their children are: Elizabeth Nelle Prater Harner, born 17 June 1939, Mary Caroline Prater Richter, born 4 Sept 1942, and Brenda Gayle Prater Sisson, born 8 Feb 1946. Sam married (2) Maxine. They have one daughter, Susan Prater. Sam lived in Collinwood when he enlisted in the army but he lives in California now.

PRATER, W.L. "DUGGAN", Serial Number 34 920 935, was a Private First Class in Company B, 209th Infantry in the Army of the United States. His permanent mailing address was Route 2, Kenton, Obion County, Tennessee. He was born 2 September 1925 in Clifton, son of William McKinley and Lella Hurley Prater. He

was registered with Selective Service Board in Wayne County, Tennessee. His Civilian Occupation was General Farmer. He was inducted 15 December 1943 and entered into active service 6 January 1944 at Fort Oglethorpe, Georgia. His Military Occupational Specialty was Military Policeman. His Military Qualifications included Combat Infantry Badge and SS Rifle. He was in the battles of Ardennes and Rhineland. The following decorations were awarded to Prater: World War II Victory Medal, American Service Medal, Good Conduct Ribbon, Purple Heart and European-African Middle Eastern Theater Ribbon with 2 Bronze Stars. He was wounded in Belgium 28 December 1944. He left the USA 22 October 1944 for the European Theater Operation, and returned to USA 13 May 1945. He finished one year of high school at Frank Hughes in Clifton.

W. L. was a Military Policeman, serving with the 289th Infantry, 75th Division in England France, Belgium and Germany. He assisted in enforcement of military laws and regulations; maintained order and apprehended absentees; and made arrests and assisted civilian police enforcing civil laws pertaining to military personnel. When working as desk clerk, he made records of arrests, and had knowledge of use and care of hand weapons, pistol, riot gun and submarine gun. He was discharged 29 April 1946 at Fort McPherson, Georgia.

W. L. married Loyce Lelia Bell Conner on August 24, 1946. She is the daughter of Ruford Allen Conner and Lona Maybell Turnbo Conner of Hohenwald, Tennessee. They had two daughters, Hilda and Mary Beth. Duggan is a prominent businessman of Waynesboro, Tennessee. He went into business on the public square in 1950 and retired in 1987. He is a member of Green River Baptist Church and the American Legion. Duggan spends much time traveling. He enjoys being involved in the Republican Political Party.

PRATER, WILLIAM BRUCE, Serial Number 34 373 024, was a Private First Class in S V Company, 124th Infantry in the Army of the United States. His permanent mailing address was General Delivery, Clifton, Tennessee. His Civilian Occupation was Horseshoer. He was single when he was inducted 24 September 1942 and entered into active service 8 October 1942 at Fort Oglethorpe, Georgia. His Military Occupational Specialty was Light Truck Driver. His Military Qualifications included Combat Infantryman. He was in the battles of New Guinea and Southern Philippines. The following decorations were awarded to Prater: World War II Victory Medal, Good Conduct Ribbon, American Theater Ribbon, Asiatic-Pacific Theater Ribbon with 2 Bronze Service Stars, Philippine Liberation Ribbon and one Bronze Star, and Meritorious Service Unit Award. He left the USA 16 Jan 1944 for the Asiatic-Pacific Theater Operation, and returned to USA 14 December 1945.

He served with the 124th Infantry in the Asiatic-Pacific Theater of operations as a truck driver. William Bruce drove a two and a half-ton truck hauling equipment, supplies and personnel. He drove day or night over all types of roads. He serviced trucks, making all minor mechanical repairs on the truck. He held an Army motor vehicle operator's license. He was also assigned three months as Private Cavalry Basic Training and 18 months P. F. C. Cook (060) at Fort Oglethorpe, Georgia. William Bruce Prater left the East Coast for Europe. The German U-boats were so thick the troops were rerouted to South America to await further orders. These orders carried them to the South Pacific. In New Guinea, Bruce came down with malaria, which seemed never to quite leave him. He was discharged December 26, 1945, at Camp Chaffee, Arkansas.

William Bruce was the son of William B. Prater and Lou Griffin Prater. He was born on February 15, 1922, in Clifton. He died on February 14, 1951, and was buried in the Prater's Chapel Cemetery near Clifton, Tennessee, where he grew up.

He was a farmer by trade; he also shoed horses. He married Myrtle Burns, daughter of Archie and Ollie Adkisson Burns. He and Myrtle had two daughters, Barbara and Carolyn.

His siblings are Hallie Houston (Dick), Griffin (Tennie), Collins (Blue), Roxie Prater Conoway, Elva Prater Conoway Adams, Pauline Prater Free Pope, Minnie Prater Tatum, Mary Alice Prater Milligan, Nellie Prater Steele and Millard Prater.

Submitted by William Bruce Prater.

PRATER, W.S., was born on December 15, 1924, son of Pink and Willie Ricketts Prater. Willie was the daughter of Will and Roseanna Newborn Ricketts.

W. S. was born and reared in Clifton. He entered the United States Air Force on November 11, 1944 as 808 Aviation Engineer. He served in the South Pacific area of war and was in Japan when the war ended. W. S. was discharged in October 1946. He went into the National Guard in Savannah, Tennessee.

He was married to Mamie Seltzer on April 20, 1945. She was the daughter of Tom and Elter Kyle Seltzer. W. S. and Mamie had two sons, Sammy and Melvin.

W. S. has worked for T. S. Hassell in Clifton for many years. Even after his retirement, he still holds employment there.

PRICE, ELBERT, son of Roxie York Martin, was born on January 31, 1926, in Dover, Ohio. He was living in Waynesboro

at the time he was inducted into the United States Army on February 21, 1944, at Camp Shelby, Mississippi. Elbert served with the 160th Field Artillery Battalion in the Central Europe Campaign. He was awarded the EAME Theater Ribbon with one Bronze Star.

Elbert married Videll Pope, daughter of Guy Pope and Opal Pulley Pope. Soon after he married on November 15, 1951, he entered into Service in the Korean Conflict and was discharged in 1952. They moved to Florida where they were employed for the next few years. In 1964, they returned to Waynesboro and have owned and operated Ray's Blossom Shop in Waynesboro.

Their children are Elbert Jr., Dennis Ray and Conda Price Griffin.

PRICE, HARLEY, Serial Number 34 189 102, was a Private First Class in 937th Engineer Battalion in the Army of the United States. His permanent mailing address was Olive Hill, Hardin County, Tennessee. He was born 15 April 1920 in Lutts, Tennessee. He was registered with Selective Service Board in Wayne County, Tennessee. His Civilian Occupation was General Farm Hand. He was married with two dependents when he was inducted 18 February 1942 and entered into active service 18 July 1942. His home address at time of entry was Lutts, Tennessee. His Military Occupational Specialty was General Carpenter. His Military Qualifications included Marksman Rifle and MM Carbine. He was in the battles of Normandy, Ardennes, Rhineland, and Northern France. The following decorations were awarded to Price: American Theater Medal, Good Conduct Ribbon, World War II Victory Medal, and European-African Middle Eastern Theater Ribbon with 4 Bronze Stars. He left the USA 27 February 1944 for the European-African Middle Eastern Theater Operation, and returned to USA 25 November 1945. He was discharged 30 November 1945 at Fort Knox, Kentucky.

PRINCE, JESSIE W., Serial Number 34 713 888, was a Private in the Army of the United States. He was born in Waynesboro, Tennessee. His Civilian Occupation was Farmer. He was married, had blue eyes, brown hair, fair complexion, was 5'7" tall and 25 years old, when inducted into active service 23 April 1943 at Camp Forrest, Tennessee. He completed four months and twenty-one days in service before he was discharged.

PRINCE, WILLIAM, was born on November 27, 1916, in Iron City, Tennessee. He lived in Iron City and worked as a light truck driver when he entered the United States Army on September 16, 1941, at Camp Oglethorpe, Georgia. William T. served with Headquarters Company 2nd Battalion, 118th Infantry and participated in the battles of Normandy, Northern France, Rhineland, Central Europe and Ardennes. He received the American Defense Service Medal, Good Conduct Ribbon, EAME Theater Ribbon with five

Bronze Stars and the Purple Heart. He was wounded in Belgium on September 29, 1944, and was discharged on August 28, 1945, at Camp Atterbury, Indiana.

PRICE, WILLIAM HASKEL, age 73, son of James William and Elizabeth (Hunt) Price, died 31 March 1994 and was buried in Cromwell Crossroads Cemetery in Wayne County He was survived by three sons, William Ray, Jimmy Ray and James David Price, three daughters, Reba McAlister, Eva Downie, and Mary Price. He had six sisters, Ollie Newborn, Mollie Horton, Irene Stricklin, Louise Cooper, Imogene Wright, and Dorothy Robbins.

Price was of the Baptist faith, a U. S. Veteran of World War II, and a retired employee of Burkley Machine Shop in Garden City, Michigan. He lived in Taylor Michigan for about thirty years before he moved to Decatur, Alabama shortly before his death.

Source: Obituary in Wayne County News.

PUGH, WALTER BRUCE, Serial Number 640 38 42, was a Boatswain's Mate First Class. He entered the United States Navy as a Quartermaster First Class, 4 June 1942 in Pulaski, Tennessee. He was born 2 February 1917 in Clifton, Tennessee. The vessels and Stations served on: NRS, Nashville, Tennessee; Constitution Battalion, USN CTC, NOB, Norfolk, Virginia; 18th Naval Construction Battalion; Rec Ship at San Francisco, California; NCTC, Davisville, Rhode Island; Naval Training Center, Gulfport, Mississippi; and RS, NRB, New Orleans, Louisiana. Walter was discharge 3 October 1945 in New Orleans, Louisiana.

Bruce was born on February 2, 1917, son of Gus and Ada Lyles Pugh. He married a girl from his hometown of Clifton, Tennessee. She was Marie Snodgrass, daughter of James (Jim) and Merle Roberts Snodgrass. Bruce worked on the towboats that navigated the Tennessee, Ohio and Mississippi Rivers. He and Marie had two daughters, Judy and Ginger. Bruce died May 25, 1980, and was buried in the Clifton City Cemetery. His siblings are Roy, Hattie, Cora, Tom, Marie (Dude) and Paul.

PULLEY, ALBERT C., Serial Number 44 040 730, was a Private in Battery A, 776th Field Artillery Battalion in the Army of the United States. His permanent mailing address was Route 1, Waynesboro, Tennessee. He was registered with Selective Service Board in Wayne County, Tennessee. He was born 11 July 1918 in Waynesboro. His Civilian Occupation was General Farm Hand. He was married with four dependents when he was inducted 31

August 1944 at Fort Oglethorpe, Georgia. His Military Occupational Specialty was Field Lineman. His Military Qualifications included Marksman Rifle. He was in the battles of Central Europe. The following decorations were awarded to Pulley: European-African Middle Eastern Theater Ribbon with one Bronze Star, Good Conduct Ribbon, and World War II Victory Medal. He left the USA 23 March 1945 for the European Theater Operation, and returned to USA 22 January 1946. He was discharged 27 January 1946 at Camp Atterbury, Indiana.

PULLEY, ARTHUR HUSTON, Serial Number 966 28 55, enlisted as Apprentice Seaman in the United States Navy on 31 December 1943 in Chattanooga, Tennessee for two years. He was born 22 June 1917 in Waynesboro, Tennessee. He was married, 6' 0" tall, weight 168 lbs, brown eyes, brown hair, and ruddy complexion when he enlisted. He did not complete period of recruit training and was honorably discharged 5 February 1944 at the United States Naval Training Station, Farragut, Idaho.

PULLEY, CHARLES, age 60, son of William Elihue and Dena Irene (Devers) Pulley, died Thursday, April 14, 19?? in his home. Burial was in Griggs Cemetery, near Waynesboro. He was a Veteran of the U. S. Navy, a retired truck driver with Pamex Corporation in Forth Worth, Texas, and had worked with the Fort Worth Police Department for approximately 36 years. Survivors include his wife, Mabel Christian Pulley of Waynesboro, two daughters, Sherrie West and Dena Wright, both of Waynesboro, Three sisters, Ruby Donegan and Ailene Clayton, both of Waynesboro and Kathleen Miller of Fort Worth, Texas; two brothers, Billy and Johnny Pulley, both of Waynesboro and four granddaughters and several nieces and nephews.

PULLEY, CHARLES V., Serial Number 34 494 881, Active service as a rifle-

man, served overseas with 517th Parachute combat team in Africa, Italy, Sicily, France, Belgium, England and Germany. Served over seas 20 months. Discharged December 24, 1945. WWII he was awarded 4 - Bronze Service Stars, Good Conduct Medal, Purple Heart, Victory Medal.

As a trainer and Par 80 Sq. 178 Hq Fort Jackson South Carolina, he was discharged on August 18, 1951. He was born January 29, 1921, and one of ten children. He had five sisters and four brothers. His parents were Walter Woods Pulley and Annie Eura Kelso Puley. His siblings were; Thomas Pulley, 11-13-25; Richard Pulley, 04-30-28; Joe Pulley, 11-22-42; Royce Pulley, 08-05-45; Francis Pulley Morrison, 01-18-23; Doris Imogene Pulley Prater, 05-10-30; Charlene Pulley Overton, 01-19-35; Loudene Pulley Gammons, 05-27-37; Nell Pulley Todd, 08-22-40

Charles lived in Wayne County his young life and served in CC during the '30s. He married Della Christine Turnbo on February 26, 1944. They lived in Mishawaka, Indiana. September 1951 they moved back to Hohenwall, Tn. Sept 1957. They settled in Florence, AL. in January of 1959.

He spent four years and one day in the military service, three years and 27 days in WWII, 11 months and five days in Korean War.

Charles Vernon Pulley passed away May 26, 1984.

PULLEY, ERNEST CLAYTON "DOCK", Serial Number 641 04 66, was a Seaman First Class in the Navy of the United States. He was registered with Selective Service Board in Wayne County, Tennessee. His Civilian Occupation was Machinist. His last employer was Dave Anderson Lumber Company, Waynesboro, 1 August 1942. He was married when he entered into active service 5 October 1942 at Memphis, Tennessee. His Military Qualifications included Boat Cox. He served on the following Vessels, Air Trans-

port Squadron. The following decoration was awarded to Pulley: the Point System and Asiatic-Pacific Area Ribbon. He attended Wayne County schools and had an eighth grade education. He was discharged 7 October 1945 in Shoemaker, California.

Dock was born on January 4, 1911, in Wayne County, son of Willie and Sally (Warren) Pulley. He was married to Esteele Worley and they have a daughter, Glynda Rose Aderhold. He later married Ada Casteel. He was a machinist and enjoyed fishing in his free time. On April 20, 1985, he died and is buried in the Warren Cemetery on Beech Creek. His siblings are Opal and Lark Pulley.

PULLEY, HERBERT, was born April 18, 1921. He entered the Army in 1942 and received a medical discharge very soon thereafter. He was making billets at the time he was called to service and returned to that enterprise upon his discharge.

Herbert married Estelle Collins Thompson in the 1960s and they were later divorced. He went to work at Murry Ohio Plant in 1965 and retired in 1985.

Herbert remarried in July of 1974 to Brenda Gist Toms Haddock, Herbert and Brenda had one son, Herbert's only child. He did have two stepdaughters; Dawana K. Toms Stults and Monica L. Haddock Steele.

Herbert passed away December 31, 1995 at Wayne Medical Center after an extended illness. He had three sisters and three brothers. Charles Pulley and J.C. Pulley are the only surviving brothers. Herbert's son, Johnathan H. Pulley, is now married to Amber Kiddy Pulley and they have a daughter, MaKaela Rayne. Dawana has two sons and a daughter. Monica has two sons.

PULLEY, HIRAM STERLING, Serial Number 34 987 509, was a Private First Class in Company A, 363rd Infantry Regiment in the Army of the United States. His permanent mailing address was Route 2,

Clifton, Tennessee. He was born 8 May 1924 in Wayne County, Tennessee. He was registered with Selective Service Board in Wayne County, Tennessee. His Civilian Occupation was Farmer. He was inducted 11 April 1944 at Camp Shelby, Mississippi. His Military Occupational Specialty was Rifleman. His Military Qualifications included Combat Infantryman Badge and SS Rifle. He was in the battles of Northern France, Apennines, and Po Valley. The following decorations were awarded to Pulley: World War II Victory Medal, Good Conduct Ribbon, Bronze Star Medal and European African Middle Eastern Theater Service Medal with two Bronze Stars. He left the USA 27 September 1944 for the European Theater Operation, and returned to USA 30 August 1945. He had a seventh grade education. He was discharged 17 May 1946 at Fort McPherson, Georgia.

Hiram S. Pulley, age 21, of Clifton, was trained at Fort Blanding, Florida and sailed from Camp Meade, Maryland in September 1944. He participated in the Italian Campaign and was awarded the Bronze Star Medal for his heroic achievement in action. The citation reads as follows: "Hiram S. Pulley (34 987 509) Private, Infantry United States Army. For heroic achievement in action on 17 April 1945, near Barchetta, Italy. Five men were killed and four men seriously wounded by a mortar shell that exploded in the midst of a ration detail of 50 men. Mortar and machine guns fired in the area added to the confusion. The men bunched up on the narrow trail. Private Pulley hurriedly unloaded his pack board, and on the way down the trail, checked to see if the men that were wounded were evacuated. He found one seriously wounded man, and carried him to the foot of the hill.

Private Pulley, then, organized a litter team. He led the teams and the wounded men over the rugged trail under mortar and machine gun fire to the aid station 700 yards away. Private Pulley's initiative and heroism reflects the highest traditions of the Infantry of the United States Army. " signed: William G. Livesay, Major General, U. S. Commanding

Pulley, son of Mrs. Susan Pulley had the following siblings: Alfred Paul, Gavin, Reuben, Joseph Leonard, and Naomi Pulley and Ione C. Denton. He married Myrtle Christine Culp and they had a son and a daughter.

PULLEY, JAMES T., Serial Number 34 043 458, was a Private First Class in Company 1, 4th Infantry in the Army of the United States. His permanent mailing address was Waynesboro, Tennessee. He was registered with Selective Service Board in Wayne County, Tennessee. He was born 7 August 1926 in Waynesboro. His Civilian Occupation was General Farm Hand. He was inducted 26 November 1944 at Fort Oglethorpe, Georgia. His Military Occupational Specialty was Rifleman. His Military Qualifications included Expert with M-1 Rifle. He was not in any battles. The following decorations were awarded to Pulley: Asiatic-Pacific Theater Ribbon, World War II Victory Medal, Good Conduct Ribbon, and Army of Occupation Medal - Japan. He left the USA 6 June 1945 for the Pacific Theater Operation, and returned to USA 23 September 1946. He was discharged 15 November 1946 at Fort Sheridan, Illinois.

PULLEY, OLLIE LARKIN, Serial Number 845 26 13 entered the United States Navy 12 January 1943 and was a Cox (T). He was born 7 August 1923 in Wayne County, Tennessee. The vessels and Stations served on: NTS, Great Lakes, Illinois; NTS NOB, Norfolk, Virginia; and USS POPE. He was discharged 28 January 1946 in Memphis, Tennessee.

PULLEY, RICHARD FERRELL, entered the Army Air Force 11 April 1942 and was discharged 2 May 1946. He was a

Corporal. He received his basic training at Camp Shelby, Biloxi, Mississippi. Next he went to Las Vegas, Nevada, and then to Bellville, Illinois to communications school. He became a teletype operator and later was sent to Headquarters in Kansas City, Kansas, to open a teletype station. Before entering service, he worked in an aircraft plant in Baltimore, Maryland.

He graduated from Frank Hughes High School in Clifton. After his discharge, he farmed, and worked as Welt Room Foreman in the Genesco Shoe Factory for many years. He then operated a grocery store from which he retired. He married Dorothy Turnbo and their children are June Warren, Larry Turnbo, and Ronnie Pulley. He was the son of Richard Escoe and Rebecca

Eva (Sims) Pulley. His sisters are, Bertie Flippo, Iva Della Adcock, and Violet Riley.

PULLEY, REUBIN, Serial Number 34 284 234, was a Private First Class in Service Company, 7th Armored Division in the Army of the United States. His permanent mailing address was Route 2, Clifton, Tennessee. He was registered with Selective Service Board in Wayne County, Tennessee. His Civilian Occupation was Auto Service Station Attendant. He was married with two dependents when he was inducted 23 May 1942 at Fort Oglethorpe, Georgia. His Military Occupational Specialty was Light Truck Driver. His Military Qualifications included Combat Infantryman Badge and Rifle Expert. He was in the battles of Northern France, Ardennes, Rhineland, and Central Europe. The following decorations were awarded to Pulley: European-African Middle Eastern Theater Ribbon with 4 Bronze Stars and Good Conduct Ribbon. He left the USA 7 June 1944 for the European Theater Operation, and returned to USA 12 October 1945. He was discharged 18 October 1945 at Camp Atterbury, Indiana.

Pulley, son of Johnny Bell and Susan (Sanderson) Pulley, was born 15 September 1919 in Clifton, died 19 November 1993 in Baptist Hospital in Nashville and was buried in Balculm Cemetery. He had the following siblings: Hiram, Alfred Paul, Gavin, Joseph Leonard, and Naomi Pulley and Ione C. Denton. His children, James Walter Pulley of Waynesboro, Leola Monroe and Alice Marie Pulley, both of Linden and a stepson, Clayton Howard Mangrum of Waynesboro. He was a farmer and construction worker.

PULLEY, THOMAS O., Serial Number 34 886 112, was a Technician Fifth Grade in 91st Infantry Regiment in the Army of the United States. His permanent mailing address was Route 2, Clifton, Tennessee. He was registered with Selective Service Board in Wayne County, Tennessee. He was born 13 November 1924 in Clifton. His Civilian Occupation was General Farm Hand. He was married when he was inducted 24 November 1945 in Luzon in the Pacific. He was not in any battles. The following decorations were awarded to Pulley: Pacific Campaign Medal, World War II Victory Medal, and Philippine Independence Ribbon. He enlisted in the Asiatic-Pacific Theater and returned to the USA 17 January 1946. He left the USA again 25 May 1946 for the Asiatic-Pacific Theater Operation, and returned to USA 15 March 1947. He was discharged 16 April 1947 at Camp Beale, California. His prior service in the Army lasted for two years, one month and nineteen days.

QUEEN, DOUGLAS EARL, Doug, son of Briley and Pauline (Edwards) Queen, was born 22 November 1926 in

Waynesboro, Tennessee, died November 1949 and is buried in Boyd (Greenwood) Cemetery in Waynesboro. His siblings are Charles Edward, deceased, Briley Imogene Adcock and Robert Glendon Queen. He was married in October 1946 to Helen Graves, daughter of Fred and Mamie (Hickerson) Graves. They had one daughter, Paula Queen born 1948. He attended Waynesboro Elementary school and graduated from Wayne County High in 1944. While a student, he joined Tennessee State Guard at age 16 and was a Private First Class in Company C, 10th Infantry Regiment. He was discharged in April 1944 to volunteer for the United States Navy as a Signalman and 2nd Class Petty Officer. He was discharged again in 1946.

QUILLEN, CHESTER H., Pfc, son of Mr. and Mrs. John Quillen of Route 3, Iron City, Tennessee, was honorably discharged from the United States Army, through the Separation Center in Fort McPherson, Georgia. His release was granted 16 November 1945. PFC Quillen entered the service 26 December 1942. He spent thirteen months in the European Theater of Operations. Before enlisting, he was an employee of the Tennessee Valley Authority. He married Lenice McMurtry.

Source: Wayne County News, Friday 14 December 1945.

QUILLEN, HERBERT, Private First Class, son of Mr. and Mrs. John Quillen of Route 3, Iron City, Tennessee, served in the European Theater of War. PFC Quillen entered the service 27 July 1944. He served in France, Belgium, Czechoslovakia, Poland and Germany. He received the European Theater of Operations Ribbon with three battle stars, Combat Infantry Badge, World War II Victory Medal, Presidential

Unit Citation Bar with Cluster and Good Conduct Medal.

Source: Wayne County News, Friday 18 January 1946.

QUILLEN, WILLIAM H., Serial Number 34 185 121, was a Private First Class in 475th Collecting Company in the Army of the United States. His permanent mailing address was Route 3, Iron City, Tennessee. The son of Mr. and Mrs. John Quillen, of Route 3, Iron City, he was born 19 February 1920 in Wayne County. He was registered with Selective Service Board in Wayne County, Tennessee. His Civilian Occupation was General Farm Hand. He was inducted 7 January 1942 at Fort Oglethorpe, Georgia. His Military Occupational Specialty was Hospital Orderly. His Military Qualifications included MKM Rifle. He was in the battles of Rhineland, Central Europe, England, France, Belgium and Germany. The following decorations were awarded to Quillen: American Theater Medal, European African Middle Eastern Theater Ribbon with 2 Bronze Stars, Good Conduct Ribbon, and World War II Victory Medal. He left the USA 3 November 1944 for the European Theater Operation, and returned to USA 1 July 1945. He was discharged 6 November 1945 at Fort Benning, Georgia.

RAINEY, WALKER, He and Leonard were the sons of Bird Rainey. They lived in Clifton before entering the service. Walker served in the Army of the United States and was engaged in the campaigns in the European Theater.

RAMAGE, HARVEY M., of Wayne County, TN served as T/Sgt with Battery B. 68th Armored Division in Italy during August 1944.

RASBURY, JAMES WALKER, son of Lovick Timothy and Sallie Ann (Luna) Rasbury, was born 2 May 1926 in the Topsy community of Wayne County, Tennessee. He was the grandson of William Lovick "Billie" and Sallie (Walker) Rasbury. His maternal grandparents were John Thomas and Winnie (Dyer) Luna. He was of a family of ten children, four of whom died in infancy. Brothers and sisters are Ara Catherine married Lee Grady Skelton, William Thomas married Vesta Irene Nutt, Edith Robena married Augusta McLemore "Mack" Wisdom, and after his death married Carlos Gunter, Luna Timothy "L.T." married Martha Angie Lipscomb, and Victor Stewart married Joy Petty. From the time of his birth he was called by his middle name and it is known to most everyone as Walker. He was born in the house built by his great grandfather, Lot Groom Rasbury. While growing up he worked the fields that were cleared by his great grandfather and attended school at Topsy. At age sixteen he went to Detroit Michigan and worked in a plant making airplane parts. He worked there until he was eighteen and drafted into the army.

From Waynesboro, his group went by bus to Fort Oglethorpe, Georgia and there were sworn into the army. He said, "They gave us clothes, pants to fit or not to fit, usually way to big. We could keep our hair but must keep it short. " Of those who went in the same call, he remembers only Thomas Schmittou. They were at Fort McPherson for a short time.

Next, his group were sent to Fort Hood, Texas. He described the last day of boot training as "crawling on my back, under barb wire through the mud and cold rain. The machine gun tracers were passing just above the ground. The mud came up to my ears as I pressed my head close to the ground. When we were across the field there was a big log fire. We changed into dry clothes. When we were back at camp, each of us received a ticket to Fort Meade, Maryland with a four day delay enroute. My four days were scheduled in Memphis. In Memphis I found a barber shop and got the rest of the Texas Mud washed out of my hair. It was New Year's Eve. I remember hearing the horns blowing. I spent the four days going home to see my parents in Wayne County. Ernest Brown, of the Topsy community, was home from the Air Force and we returned to Memphis together. "

From Fort Meade, Maryland, Walker went by train to a camp in New York. On January 24, 1945 about midnight, he and several thousand others boarded the Queen Mary. He said, "Before all were on board someone stole my life jacket but I didn't go to bed till I got one. " The Queen Mary was fast and did not have an escort. He said, "The seas were rough and the waves rolled over the stern of the ship. " The crossing of the ocean took five days.

Landing in Scotland January 31, 1945, they boarded cars on a narrow gauge railroad. A woman from the Red Cross brought doughnuts and coffee. "We were so hungry that we ate all of them. She called us a bunch of hogs. " The train carried them south across England to the English Channel. On the way to the channel boats he remembers, "We met an old gentleman with a high top (stove Pipe) hat and he tipped the hat to us. "

Walker says, "We crossed the channel at night on small ships or channel boats. The boats stood off shore and landing craft called assault craft came out and carried us ashore. We landed on the beach somewhere in France. We were herded into boxcars for a train ride that would last for three days. They stopped twice a day, set up their kitchen on the tracts, and fed us. Sleeping while moving was rough but for those who slept over the wheels, their heads just popped up and down. "

Upon reaching the Maginot Line they were broken up and became replacements for outfits that had suffered casualties. Walker said. "One officer talked to me about being a radio man and spotter for artillery fire. I asked what happened to their last man and he didn't answer. Another talked to me about being a Light Machine Gunner. It probably wasn't any better but I took it. I was put in Company E, 301st Infantry Regiment. They were joined to the 94th Division and were a part of the Third Army under General George S. Patton. We moved up and occupied part of the Siegfried line. It was blown up and bombed out. It was here that I took pneumonia and was sent to a hospital somewhere in France. "

After his recovery, Walker rejoined his company in Germany on the West bank of the Rhine River. "We crossed the Rhine on pontoon bridges at Ludendorff. We had advanced to a little town east of the Rhine when news came of the German surrender. Many of the German soldiers did not surrender. They took off their uniforms and put on civilian clothes. We had quite a job rounding them up. One night I was on guard duty in the town with orders to clear the streets. I heard the sound of hob nailed boots on the pavement and knew someone was coming. When he was straight across the street from me I called to him to "Halt. " He pivoted and came straight toward me. I called again for him to "Halt. " He kept coming. I brought my gun up and loudly told him to "Halt or else. ' He stopped. He spoke good English. He was wearing an arm band, said he was a policeman and had a right to be on the street at night. I said, "My orders are to clear the street, get off." He did.

"The Germans had big fine cavalry

horses. Some were stabled near us. Some of the boys went out and rode them. My buddy and I went out to ride. The man at the barn asked if we wanted gentle horses. My buddy chose a gentle one. I asked for the most frisky and meanest horse in the barn. When the horse was brought out he looked mean and had a muley saddle. When they turned us into the field, I saw right quick that I had made a mistake. We went flying across the field, coming to a ditch that was to big too jump. We just sailed over it. He didn't turn for anything. Whatever got in front, we just sailed over it. Back to the barn I went, I had enough. I would not ride Sampson again. "

From the Rhineland, Walker's outfit went to Blanton in Czechoslovakia. As he remembers it was at Blanton that they stayed in homes. He remembers an old man driving geese with a whip and how the geese "yelled" when he passed the house.

The next move was to Krumlov in Czechoslovakia. He tells of an event that happened here and says he was a little bit scared. "I was on guard duty at the motor pool when I saw a GI working on a jeep. I thought he was supposed to be there and helped him start it. He got in the jeep and drove away. Next day it was reported stolen. It was found in a nearby motor pool. The old boy was going to town and didn't want to walk. "

While at Krumlov, he was sent to Germany for an operation. When he returned the wash woman had given away all of his clothes.

He got a pass to Paris. He said, "When I got to Paris, I met an old boy with a five day pass who had been there for two days and knew his way around. We teamed up and went over the town again. We went up the Eiffel Tower, to the Louvre and other places. "

At Krumlov the 94th was broken up. They were joined to the 1st Division and moved to Nuremberg, Germany. "Two of us were in a jeep and as we went over the mountains we found the roads were covered with ice. We had a two-wheeled trailer behind the jeep. As we went off the mountain, the jeep would slide and almost turn around. We would push it back straight and go on till it happened again. The convoy left us but we caught up in Nuremburg."

In Nuremburg he was assigned to guard duty at the prison where the Nuremburg trials were taking place. Twenty-two German officials were being held and tried here. One of them was General Herman Goering who was second to Adolph Hitler as leader of Nazi Germany, Reich Marshal and commanding General of the Air Force. In describing the prison and his guard duties, Walker said, "We went inside the prison and stayed twenty-four hours. We were on duty four hours and off four hours.

The courtroom was inside the prison walls. The walls were thick enough that one could walk along the top. Guard houses were along the top of the walls. The place was heavy fortified on the outside. At times I was guard for General Goering while he was taking walking exercise. I was in the Court room one time. I left Nuremburg before the trials were over. "

Walker was in Belgium for a Memorial Day parade at the cemetery where General George S. Patton was buried. In June 1946 he was one of the group scheduled to return to the States. "We traveled by truck from Nuremburg to La Harve, France. The ship that we came back on was small and the sea was rough. As we went up the front side of a wave the ship seemed to stop, roll and quiver. As we went down the back of the wave, it seemed to do it again. On the Queen Mary we had watched the big fish roll up. On the way back we didn't see any fish. Everyone was to sick. The only fresh water that we had was drinking water. There was no water for showers or baths. When we tried to wash our hands in the sea water, the soap seemed to melt and disappear. After seven days we arrived in New York. "

They went to Fort Meade, Maryland to be discharged and each one went his separate way home. Walker went by bus to Nashville and caught the late bus to arrive in Hohenwald at night. There were no pay phones. He had a brother and sister who had moved to Hohenwald but he did not know where. He said, "I went to the front of the old hotel (Merriwether Lewis Hotel) and called out but got no answer. There was an old dog on the street that acted as if he wanted to bite me. I was used to rough living so it didn't bother me much. " The next day was a great homecoming.

While Walker was in the service his father sold the old homeplace in Wayne County and moved up Buffalo River to Lewis County. He lived with his parents until 4 October 1947 when he married Monia Peeler, daughter of Grady and Viola (Bates) Peeler. She was born 8 August 1925 in the Indian Creek community of Lewis County. They had one child, Eddie Wayne Rasbury, born 2 March 1951, died 15 January 1994 in Lewis County with a heart attack and was buried in Swiss Cemetery in Hohenwald. Eddie Wayne was married 31 December 1976 in Maryville, Tennessee to Deborah Ann Graves, daughter of Mr. and Mrs. J. B. Graves and they have one daughter, Allison Marie Rasbury born 27 July 1982.

Walker worked for Henry I. Siegel for several years and drove the school bus for several years. He is retired but still operates his farm on Grinders Creek in Lewis County.

RASBURY, LANDON CARUTHERS, Serial Number 34 189 136, was a Technician, Fifth Grade in 644th Tank Destroyer

Battalion in the Army of the United States. His permanent mailing address was Route 6, Waynesboro, Tennessee. He was registered with Selective Service Board in Wayne County, Tennessee. His Civilian Occupation was General Farmer. He entered into active service 18 February 1942 at Fort Oglethorpe, Georgia. His Military Occupational Specialty was Artillery Mechanic, Minor Maintenance. His Military Qualifications included Carbine Sharpshooter. He was in the battles of Rhineland, and Central Europe. The following decorations were awarded to Rasbury: European-African Middle Eastern Theater Ribbon with 2 Bronze Stars, Good Conduct Ribbon, American Theater Ribbon, World War II Victory Medal, and a lapel button was issued. Landon served in the Tank Destroyer Battalion, repairing artillery pieces and small arms, replaced defective parts, using small hand tools. He served eleven months in the European Theater with part of the time in combat. He finished one year of high school at Lewis County High. He was discharged 12 December 1945 at Camp Atterbury, Indiana.

Message from President Harry Truman: "To you who answered the call of your country and served in its Armed Forces to bring about total defeat of the enemy, I extend the heartfelt thanks of a grateful nation. As one of the Nation's finest, you undertook the most severe task one can be called upon to perform. Because you demonstrated the fortitude, resourcefulness and calm judgement necessary to carry out the task, we now look to you for leadership and example in furthering our country in peace."

Landon, son of Alonzo Malone and Dora Nix (Cothran) Rasbury, was born 20 December 1908 in Wayne County, died 25 February 1994 in the Wayne County Hospital and was buried in Memorial Gardens in Waynesboro. His grandparents were Andrew Carouthers and Jane (Voorhies) Rasbury and Ezekiel and Roena (Fite) Cothran. His siblings are Lonnie, Jr., Jane Flippo and Roxie Edwards. Landon married Marguerite Gray, daughter of John and Marcella Gray. There were no children born to this union.

RASBURY, VAN BROWN, Serial Number RA 14 220 296, was a Private First Class in Battery C, 271st FA Battalion,

Regular Army, First Calvary Division in the Army of the United States. He volunteered. His permanent mailing address was Route 6, Waynesboro, Tennessee. His Civilian Occupation was Student. He was single when he entered into active service 1 October 1946 at Fort Oglethorpe, Georgia. His Military Occupational Specialty was Light Truck Driver. His Military Qualifications included Rifle N 1 Marksman. He was not in any battles. The following decorations were awarded to Rasbury: World War II Victory Medal, and Army of Occupation Medal-Japan. He left the USA 13 December 1946 for the Asiatic Pacific Theater Operation, and returned to USA 24 February 1948. He had a high school education. He was discharged 10 March 1948 at Camp Stoneman, California.

Van Brown, the son of Van C. and Florence (Brown) Rasbury, was born 6 July 1928 in the Topsy community, Wayne County, Tennessee and lives on the family farm today. His grandparents were Billy and Sallie (Walker) Rasbury and Ike and Molly (Bastin) Brown. His five sisters are, Monetta Bullion, Sarah Rosetta Shann, Florine Gossset, Nadine Turnbow and Judy Woodruff. He married Charlotte Skelton and they had one daughter, Susan Tucker.

RASBURY, WILLIAM HAROLD, son of William Hyder and Vena Mae (Staggs) Rasbury, was born 1 January 1926 in the Ashland Community of Wayne

County, Tennessee, died 5 March 1993 at the Eliza Coffee Memorial Hospital in Florence, Alabama and was buried 7 March 1993 in Memorial Gardens in Waynesboro. His brothers are Earl Thomas and Douglas Wade Rasbury. His sisters are Erma Ellen Cox, Dorothy Evelyn Edwards, and Esma Lucille Downey. He married Marjorie Colene Shelton. They have two sons, John Lynn and Richard Marvin Rasbury.

Harold entered the United States Navy 24 January 1944 in Waynesboro and was discharged 8 May 1946 in Memphis, Tennessee. His rank was Motor Machinist Mate, 3rd Class. He served on a light destroyer, a PC580 and was stationed in Pearl Harbor, Hawaii.

RAY, BEN HOOPER, C/GM enlisted in the United States Navy in December 1940 for a period of six years, then, later reenlisted for another twenty years.

The following is an account given by Ben H. Ray on 29 September 1992. "When I heard that World War II had been declared, I was aboard a Destroyer in Capetown, South Africa. We received news of the Japanese attack on Pearl Harbor.

We went through the Panama Canal three times during the early part of the war, as we were operating from Africa to the

Arctic Circle in escort duty against German submarines.

Near the end of the war we were in the Pacific Theater. During the Okinawa Campaign, the scene of heavy combat in the war, we were hit by two of the Japanese suicide planes. Our ship was destroyed along with 158 of its members. When the first plane struck, big waves or splashes of water came over the ship, scattering debris containing shrapnel all over the ship. The shrapnel penetrated our skin, causing quite a bit of trouble then and later. The ship got on fire. My gun station was a 5 inch mount. We kept firing ever after going to emergency power. We survived the first attack.

When the second attack from the suicide plane hit, carrying a 1,000 pound bomb, it cut the ship in half and within 90 seconds the USS Drexler DD741 started sinking. The concussion of the explosion blew me through a hatch in the top of the gun mount. From that moment I became unconscious; coming back to consciousness I was aware of the fact that I was floating in a life jacket in the water coated with oil.

I began using my handkerchief trying to rid myself of the oil from my face. I also was aware that the ship was on fire. In a short time within an hour, I suppose, another ship started picking us up out of the ocean. They transported us to a military hospital in Saipan. For several months I had shrapnel (hot metal) from the explosion picked out of my body. I survived with a finger ring and "dog tags" for identification. During all this time we crossed the meridian line and lost a day. We were months in and out of the hospital. I received the Purple Heart, Navy International Waters Ribbon, Bronze Star, and 8 Battle Ribbons.

We made all ports in the Atlantic Ocean. We flew the first American flag through the Suez Canal, laid the "groundwork" for what was later to be called "Desert Storm."

During my last twenty years we made more foreign country ports than we have states. During my time in service I never looked through a gun sight at any live personal enemy. However, ships, planes and beaches, yes, I did at times. We spent a lot of time at sea. Sometimes, we stayed out several months without seeing land. I spent 16 years at sea, 100,000 miles a year, and four years in Memphis on shore duty before retiring from the Navy in Memphis in 1960. I traveled the world over and over and returned to Wayne County to live.

I was born 29 August 1921 to William Henry and Lily Mae (Conway) Ray. My brothers and sisters include Matt Ray, Elma Wilson, Delphia Brany, Zula Gathergood, Kate McCullough, and Opal Goodman. I married Gloria Brown and our children are Dolly, David and Ben Harris Ray. I am a

member of the Primitive Baptist Church, of the Forrest Land Owners Association, American Legion and an ASCS Office Community Committeeman. I am a farmer and I help to feed America."
Submitted by Ben Ray.

RAY, HERBERT, was born in LaGrange, AR on January 4, 1925, the oldest son of George Nathanal and Lois

(DeShazo) Ray. I attended high school in Marianna, AR and Fresno, CA and college at Fresno State College.

I enlisted in the U. S. Navy in December 1942 and retired with twenty years service as chief petty officer in the Hospital Corp. I attended the following schools in the navy: Hospital Corp School, Clinical Labratory School, X-ray School, Venereal Disease Control, Supervisors Training, Advanced Military Etiquette and Atomic, Biological and Chemical Welfare School.

I worked three years in ward nursing; one year in eye, ear, nose and throat surgery; three years in clinical laboratory; pharmacy work; morgue work and twenty years of x-ray, radiation therapy and abdominal ultrasound work. I served as chief hospital-man on small naval vessels and was an instructor in atomic, biological and chemical warfare.

My foreign service was two years in the Aleutian Islands; one year on Kwajalein, Marshall Island; one year at Pearl Harbor, Hawaii; six months in Korea on the battleship, New Jersey and six months in the Mediterranean on a destroyer. I served on two repair ships, an oceans graphic survey ship, a destroyer and a battleship.

Following retirement from the navy, I worked two and one half years in South Viet Nam with a U. S. Public Health Service Outpatient Clinic in St. Louis, MO. and twelve years in the VA Hospital in Memphis, TN.

On June 17, 1976, Josephine Davis and I were married. In February 1980, I retired after thirty five years of time in the U. S.

Navy and U. S. Civil Service. Josephine and I live at 1030 Collinwood Hwy, Waynesboro, TN and spend our time gardening and fishing.

RAY, JAMES MORRIS, Serial Number 845 48 79, was a Radioman Third Class in the United States Navy. He entered ac-

tive service 10 June 1943. He served on the following vessels and stations: NRS Chattanooga, Tennessee; NTS, Bainbridge, MD; ATB Camp Bradford, North Carolina; ATB Fort Pierce, Florida; 10th Beach Battalion; NTS New Port, Rhode Island; and USS MONTOUR. His main civilian occupation was student before the war and after he was an accountant for fifteen years and a merchant for twenty-five years. He had a high school education. He was awarded the American Theater Medal and the Asiatic-Pacific Medal. He was honorably discharged 21 March 1946. His home address was Route 1, Waynesboro, Tennessee.

Morris, son of Frank and Georgia (Morris) Ray, was born 7 June 1923 in Wayne County, Tennessee, died 15 April 1996 in Waynesboro and was buried in Memorial Gardens in Waynesboro. He has one brother, Bobby Copeland Ray. Morris married Betty Jean Turman and they had two children, Martha Jean (Ray) Belew and Jimmy Ray. They also have two grandchildren, Jon and Amy Gobbell of Lawrenceburg.

RAY, JOHN W., Serial Number 34 366 637, was a Private First Class in Company G, 422nd Infantry in the Army of the United States. He was registered with Selective Service Board in Wayne County, Tennessee. He was born 28 February 1921 in Waynesboro, Tennessee. His Civilian Occupation was Farmer. He was inducted 26 August 1942 and entered into active service 26 August 1942 at Fort Oglethorpe, Georgia. His Military Occupational Specialty was Duty Soldier. He was in the battles of Naples-Foggia, Rome-Arno,

Central Europe and Southern France. The following decorations were awarded to Ray: Good Conduct Ribbon, and European-African Middle Eastern Theater Ribbon with 5 Bronze Stars. He left the USA 2 April 1943 for the European Theater Operation, and returned to USA 29 September 1945. He had a seventh grade education. He was discharged, date unknown.

RAY, MORRIS GILFORD, Serial Number unknown, was a Seaman, First Class, in the United States Navy. He was registered 8 July 1943 in Waynesboro for two years. He held the following ratings: S1/C, V6, 3V, USNR. He served on the following stations and vessels: US NTS, San Diego, California; Landing Craft School LCS, PAC; USS Prince George (Ap 165); USN Base Hospital No. 8; Navy Air Base Dispensary Number 3237, USNH, Navy Number 10; US Navy Base, Navy Number 4245, USNH Cahu; TH USNH, Navy 10; and USNH, Portsmouth, Virginia. He was discharged 7 September 1945 in Portsmouth, Virginia with excellent character and received a Discharge Button and Honorable Service Emblem. He was born 9 October 1914 in Lutts, Tennessee.

RAY, ROBERT HOWARD, Serial Number 34 920 942, was a Staff Sergeant in Company L, 30th Infantry Regiment,

3rd Infantry Division in the Army of the United States. His permanent mailing address was Route 3, Waynesboro, Tennessee. He was registered with Selective Service Board in Wayne County, Tennessee. His Civilian Occupation was General Farmer. He was inducted 15 December 1943 and entered into active service 6 January 1944 at Fort Oglethorpe, Georgia. He was sent to Camp Wheeler, Georgia for basic training. His Military Occupational Specialty was Motor Transportation. His Military Qualifications included SS Rifle M-1 and Combat Infantryman Badge. He was in the battle of Rhineland. His attachment took part in the invasion of Southern France. The following decorations were awarded to Ray: Good Conduct Ribbon, European-African Middle Eastern Theater Ribbon, World War II Victory Medal, One Battle Star, and Army of Occupation Medal - Japan. He left the USA 1 July 1944 for Italy, and returned to USA 4 September 1946. He had an eighth grade education. He was discharged 8 November 1946 at Fort George G. Meade, Maryland. Then he served in the Tennessee National Guard in order to have a total of twenty years service, which entitle him to service retirement. He was promoted to Master Sergeant in the National Guard and retired 13 January 1984. In later years he worked for Genesco Shoe Company in Waynesboro.

Robert, son of Grady Homer and Lettie Gertrude (Simmons) Ray, was born 13 January 1923 in Waynesboro, Tennessee. He has two brothers, Homer and Howard Ray and a sister, Wilton Ray. He married Elise Turnbo and they have one daughter, Teresa Ray, who married David McDaniel. They have two children, Clare and John Russell McDaniel.

RAY, WILL, Serial Number 966 28 45, was a Seaman, Second Class, V-6 in the United States Navy. He enlisted 31 December 1943 at Chattanooga, Tennessee for two years as an AS. He held the following ratings: AS, USN-1 and S2/C V-6 USNR. He served on the following stations and vessels: US Naval Recruiting Station, Chattanooga, Tennessee; US NTS, Great Lakes, Illinois; US Naval Construction Training Center, Camp Peary, Williamsburg, Virginia; and US Naval Hospital, Memphis, Tennessee. His main civilian occupation was farming for himself. He had a 7th grade education. He was discharged 28 August 1944 from a U. S. Naval Hospital in Memphis, Tennessee with a physical disability. He was born 14 November 1913 in Clifton, Tennessee.

Will Ray, son of John Anderson and Mary Ada (Turnbo) Ray, born 14 November 1913 in Clifton, Tennessee, died 9 March 1994 and was buried in Prater's Chapel Cemetery. His siblings are: Earl Ray, Jewell Ray married Jessie Prater, Pauline Ray married Marvin Churchwell and Grace Ray married Roy Tate. Will married (1) Nannie Lee Inman and their children are: J. W. Ray of McKena, IL; W. S., Thomas, James Ray and Brenda Ray Hill of Beech Creek, Jerry of Waynesboro, Donnie of Savannah, and Jean Ray Warren of Clifton. Will married (2) Flossie Hickerson. They did not have any children. Will accumulated several acres of land on Beech Creek. He and his sons worked hard at farming and raising live stock. He was a good manager and provided for his fam-

ily. He was 80 years old when he died and left a home on Route 6, Savannah, Tennessee. He was a Methodist.

RAY, WILLIAM CURTIS, Serial Number 34 884 600, was a Private in the Medical Detachment 361st Infantry in the

Army of the United States. His permanent mailing address was Route 2, Clifton, Tennessee. He was registered with Selective Service Board in Wayne County, Tennessee. His Civilian Occupation was General Farmer. He was married when he was inducted 3 September 1943 and entered into active service 24 September 1943 at Fort Oglethorpe, Georgia. His Military Occupational Specialty was Litter Bearer. His Military Qualifications included Combat Infantry Badge and Medical Badge. He was in the battles of Naples and Foggia. The following decorations were awarded to Ray: European-African Middle Eastern Theater Ribbon with 1 Battle Star and a Distinguished Unit Badge. He left the USA 16 May 1944 for the European Theater Operation, and returned to USA 3 March 1945. He was discharged 18 September 1945 at Camp Atterbury, Indiana with a Certificate of Disability.

William Curtis, son of Earl and Gnetta (Culp) Ray, was born 12 June 1924 in Dyersburg, Tennessee. His parents were natives of Wayne County and returned here to raise their children on Beech Creek. William Curtis attended the local schools and was of the Baptist faith. After his return from military service he married Ruth Briley of Perry County, Tennessee and they lived on Beech Creek for a while and he worked for TVA. In July 1964 they moved to Smithland, Kentucky. He worked for a crushed stone company in Smithland. He also worked with Airco Alloys Steel Mill in Calvert City, Kentucky. He retired as a heavy duty machinery mechanic. His home is located at 191 Lakeview Drive, Ledbetter, Kentucky. William and Ruth had nine children, Gayle, Rhetta, Barbara,

Michael, Pat, Carol, Robin, Chris, and Kim Ray. The last three were born in Kentucky. William married Louise Ray after the death of his first wife, Ruth. The siblings of Mr. Ray are Blondel, Willie Dee and W.E. Ray.

RAY, WINFRED, Serial Number 44 126 820, was a Private First Class in 3373rd Signal Service Company, 85th Signal Battalion in the Army of the United States. His permanent mailing address was Route 2, Clifton, Tennessee. He was registered with Selective Service Board in Wayne County, Tennessee. His Civilian Occupation was Group Leader. He was inducted 1 November 1945 at Fort Oglethorpe, Georgia. His Military Occupational Specialty was Teletype Mechanic. He was not in any battles. The following decorations were awarded to Ray: World War II Victory Medal, Army of Occupation Medal - Japan. He left the USA 26 March 1946 for the Pacific Theater Operation, and returned to USA 12 January 1947 He finished two years of high school. He was discharged 7 February 1947 at Fort Sheridan, Illinois.

Winfred, son of Alvy W. and Sally (Anderson) Ray, was born 14 February 1924 in Clifton, Tennessee. He attended school in the Clifton area. He went to Oak Ridge, Tennessee to work in the Atomic Plant before and up till the time he was drafted into the World War II conflict. After his discharge, he returned to Oak Ridge to work until he retired in 1993. He married Martha Reece from Fulton, Kentucky. They have one son, Bob Ray. Winfred's siblings are Vogal, Herbert and Gilbert Ray. His hobby is genealogy.

REATHERFORD, ERNEST CLYDE, was born on January 1, 1923, in Lutts, Tennessee, to Thomas Marvin and Ollie Belle

Melson Reatherford. He worked at a sawmill and farmed, until he was inducted into the United States Army on January 18, 1943, at Ft. Oglethorpe, Georgia. He was

stationed at the Harbor Defenses of Boston and worked as a medic at the 16th General Hospital at Ft. Devens, Massachusetts, where he was discharged on September 22, 1943, due to ill health.

Ernest and Opal Hanback were married on October 27, 1943, and lived in the Lutts community a short time. They moved to Michigan where he was employed at Barr Steel until he retired in 1972. A few years after returning to Wayne County, Ernest entered a nursing home in Hardin County, Tennessee, and died on January 18, 1998, at Hardin County Hospital from pneumonia. He is buried in Cromwell Cross Roads Cemetery. He and Opal have three children: Patricia Ann Thompson of Savannah, Tennessee; Larry Van of Clarkston, Michigan; and Dale, who drowned in Honolulu, while on rest and recreation from Vietnam.

Earnest was a member of the Collinwood Freewill Baptist Church and had taught Sunday school for over 35 years in Michigan and Tennessee. He had one brother, Thomas Reatherford, one sister Mary Ruth White, both of Waynesboro, and four grandchildren.

Submitted by Ernest Clyde Reatherford.

REATHERFORD, RAYMON R., Serial Number 34 888 802, was a Private First Class in 17th Infantry in the Army of the

United States. His permanent mailing address was Route 2, Waynesboro, Tennessee. He was born 30 November 1924 in Waynesboro, Tennessee. He was registered with Selective Service Board in Wayne County, Tennessee. His Civilian Occupation was General Farm Hand. He was inducted 13 November 1942 and entered into active service 5 December 1942 at Fort Oglethorpe, Georgia. His Military Occupational Specialty was Rifleman. His Military Qualifications included Combat Infantryman Badge, and Rifle M1 Marksman. He was in the battles of Southern Philippines and Ryukyus. The following decorations were awarded to Reatherford:

REATHERFORD, THOMAS E., Serial Number 44 121 852, was a Private First Class in Headquarters and Headquarters

Detachment, Section No. 1 Army Service Unit Station Complement in the Army of the United States. His permanent mailing address was Route 2, Waynesboro, Tennessee. He was born 19 March 1927 in Wayne County. He was registered with Unknown. His Civilian Occupation was Farmer. He was single when he was inducted. His Military Occupational Specialty was Military Police. His Military Qualifications included MM Rifle. He was not in any battles. The following decorations were awarded to Reatherford: World War II Victory Medal, and Good Conduct Medal. He was discharged 3 December 1946 at Fort McClellan, Alabama. His prior army service was for 6 months and 8 days.

REAVES, EVERETT W., Serial Number 34 501 228, was a Private First Class in 612th Tank Destroyer Battalion in the Army of the United States. His permanent mailing address was Waynesboro, Tennessee. He was born 3 July 1922 in Waynesboro. He was registered with Selective Service Board in Wayne County, Tennessee. His Civilian Occupation was Truck Driver. He was married when he enlisted 20 December 1942 at Fort Oglethorpe, Georgia. His Military Occupational Specialty was Truck Driver. He was in the battles of Normandy, Rhineland, and Northern France. The following decorations were awarded to Reaves: European-

World War II Victory Medal, American Service Medal, Asiatic-Pacific Medal and Philippine Liberation Ribbon. He left the USA 27 December 1944 for the Asiatic-Pacific Theater Operation, and returned to USA 24 October 1945. He had an eighth grade education. He was discharged 23 February 1946 at Welch Convalescent Hospital, Daytona Beech, Florida with a Certificate of Disability.

REATHERFORD, THOMAS E., Serial Number 44 121 852, was a Private First Class in Headquarters and Headquarters

African Middle Eastern Theater Ribbon with 3 Battle Stars. He left the USA 2 April 1944 for the European Theater Operation, and returned to USA 12 March 1945. He was discharged 16 November 1945 at Crile General Hospital in Cleveland, Ohio with a Certificate od Disability.

RECTOR, CHARLIE EDGAR, Serial Number 976 82 45, was a Coxswain in the United States Navy. He was born 1 October 1926 in Benton County, Tennessee. He was inducted 1 February 1945. He served on the following stations and vessels: US NTC, Great Lakes, Illinois; SCOLS and TRNG COMD, Williamsburg, Virginia, and USS LCT (L) 606. He was discharged 1 May 1946 in Memphis, Tennessee. Under Remarks are: Coxswain, American Area, Asiatic Pacific Area and Victory Medal.

REEVES, FLOYD HAROLD, SR., was born 21 September 1925 in Wayne County, Tennessee, to Percy and Eula

(Rose) Reeves. The only son, his sisters include: Betty and Peggy Jean Reeves, both deceased and Rachel Skelton, all of Waynesboro and Jo Bomar of Florence, Alabama. His grandparents were Mr. and Mrs. Alvin C. Reeves and Mr. and Mrs. John Rose all of Wayne County. Floyd married Esther M. Matlock on 30 October 1943, just prior to entering the U. S. Navy. They are the parents of seven children: Floyd H. Jr., and Johnny E. Reeves of Portland, Tennessee; Joe D. Reeves, Geraldine Thrasher, Betty J. Risner, Mary A. Butler, all of Waynesboro and Barbara S. Davis of Savannah.

Upon entering the US Navy on 27 December 1943, he took Basic Training at the US Naval Training Station in San Diego, California. After Completion of basic, he went to sea aboard the USS Torrence from Hoboken, New Jersey. He served in the South Pacific Theater until V-Day, 8 May 1945, where he was awarded three Battle

Stars. Seaman First Class Reeves was promoted to Petty Officer Third Class as well as Gunner's Mate 3rd Class on 20 November 1945. He also served as a S. P. He completed his tour of duty and was discharged 24 January 1946. Luckily, he was never wounded. Mr. Reeves lived in Wayne County and worked as a carpenter until his death from lung cancer on 20 October 1981. He was buried in Shields Cemetery near Waynesboro.

REEVES, OSCAR DOUGLAS "DOUG", Serial Number 845 30 63, was a Coxswain in the United States Navy. His

permanent mailing address was Box 37, Collinwood, Tennessee. He enlisted 13 December 1945 in San Francisco, California. He served on the following stations and vessels: R/S, San Francisco, Headquarters 12th ND T. I. Shipyard in San Pedro; and USS Loftberg. His main civilian occupation was student. He was discharged 18 October 1947 in San Pedro, California. Reeves was awarded the following decorations: Good Conduct Medal, Asiatic-Pacific Medal with one Star, American Area Medal, Philippine Liberation with two Stars and World War II Victory Medal.

Doug was born on August 15, 1923, in Lutts, Tennessee, the son of Willie (Bill) Reeves and Etta Mae Melson Reeves. He graduated from high school in Collinwood, Tennessee, in 1942 and volunteered for service in the United States Navy the same year. He was sent to the Great Lakes Training Center for boot training. After completing here, he was sent to Corpus Christi, Texas, and was assigned to the Tianglum, a cargo ship, then the USS Loftburg, a destroyer. This destroyer was sent to the Pacific War Zone. Doug spent his time here until he was discharged at the war's end.

He was married to Jimmie Juanita Jones on September 4, 1948. They are parents of three children: Glenda Gail, Cynthia Lynn and Joseph Douglas. After his discharge he worked as a millwright in Memphis, and

Florida for Armour and Company and U. S. Steel, retiring from U. S. Steel. He and his wife live in Cherokee, Alabama. He is a member of the V. F. W. and the American Legion and is an avid golfer.

REEVES, STERLIN J., Serial Number 34 284 227, was a Corporal in Headquarters Squadron Far East Air Force APO 925 in the Army of the United States. His permanent mailing address was Route 3, Iron City, Tennessee. He was born 22 August 1909 in Wayne County. He was registered with Selective Service Board in Wayne County, Tennessee. His Civilian Occupation was Circular Ripsaw Operator. He was Single when he entered into active service 23 May 1942 at Fort Oglethorpe, Georgia. His Military Occupational Specialty was Duty Soldier III. His Military Qualifications included Sharpshooter Carbine. He was in the battle of Luzon. The following decorations were awarded to Reeves: Good Conduct Ribbon, Philippines Liberation Ribbon, World War II Victory Medal, American Theater Medal, and AF Theater Ribbon with 1 Bronze Service Star. He left the USA 18 May 1945 for the AF Theater Operation, and returned to USA 3 December 1945. He had a seventh grade education. He was discharged 14 December 1945 at Camp Chaffee, Arkansas.

RICH, CEMON D., Serial Number 44 042 127, was a Private First Class in Company D, 27th Infantry in the Army of the

United States. His permanent mailing address was Route 1, Cypress Inn, Tennessee. He was born 22 January 1926 in Cypress Inn. He was registered with Selective Service Board in Wayne County, Tennessee. His Civilian Occupation was General Farmer. He was inducted 18 October 1944 at Fort Oglethorpe, Georgia. His Military Occupational Specialty was Heavy Weapons Crewman. His Military Qualifications included 1 CL GNR Cal 30 HMG. He was in the battle of Luzon. The

following decorations were awarded to Rich: Asiatic-Pacific Theater Ribbon with one Bronze Battle Star, Philippines Liberation Ribbon with one Bronze Battle Star, World War II Victory Medal, and Good Conduct Medal. He left the USA 28 April 1945 for the Pacific Theater Operation, and returned to USA 21 September 1946. He was discharged 20 November 1946 at Fort Sheridan, Illinois.

He married Emmo Jean Risner Oct. 20, 1946. She is the daughter of the late Charlie and Dora Risner. All four of her brothers, Rex, Lloyd "Bugg", Charles, and Carl are deceased.

Cemon and Emmo Jean were blessed with nine children, three daughters and six sons. Their daughters are Betty Tatum, Brenda Rich, and Vickie Butler. Their sons are Larry, David, Gary, Randy (deceased) Harlan and Ricky

They have also been blessed with twenty-one grandchildren and fourteen great-grandchildren.

Cemon said "I am proud to say I served our country and am glad I lived to tell about it, because so many didn't."

RICH, DENSIE ARVIL, Serial Number 34 727 059, was a Technician Fifth Grade in 1582nd Ordnance Supply and Maintenance Company (Aviation) in the Army of the United States. His permanent mailing address was Route 1, Lutts, Tennessee. He was born 14 February 1924 in Lutts. He was registered with Selective Service Board in Wayne County, Tennessee. His Civilian Occupation was General Farmer. He was inducted 20 March 1943 and entered into active service 27 March 1943 at Fort Oglethorpe, Georgia. His Military Occupational Specialty was Munitions Worker. He was in the battles of Central Burma and India-Burma. The following decorations were awarded to Rich: World War II Victory Medal, American Theater Medal, Good Conduct Ribbon, Asiatic-Pacific Theater Ribbon with 2 Bronze Service Stars and Distinguished Unit Badge. He left the USA 26 September 1944 for the Asiatic-Pacific Theater Operation, and returned to USA 6 March 1946. He had an eighth grade education. He was discharged 13 March 1946 at Camp Chaffee, Arkansas.

He was the son of Mr. and Mrs. Harrison Rich of Lutts. He had two brothers, T. F. Rich and Ordie F. Rich, both of whom were in World War II.

RICH, ERNEST FRED, Serial Number NA, was a Private First Class in Company F, 10th Infantry Regiment in the Army of the United States. His permanent mailing address was Route 2, Collinwood, Tennessee. He was in battles in France,

Luxembourg, Germany, Czechoslovakia, and Austria.

Ernest, son of Chester C. and Virgie (Whitten) Rich, was born about 1926. His siblings are Glen and Everette Rich and Pauline (Rich) Kelly. He married (1) Earline Stooksberry and (2) Lois Moore Holt. His children are Dean Holt, Delia Roberson and Larry Fred Rich. Ernest retired from Monarch Ceramic Tile Company the 30 April 1991 and has been a Free Will Baptist minister since 1959.

One part about his service unit states, "… The Civilians in Frankfurt caused us more trouble than the Germans soldiers. We had lost several men and sweated-out several amazingly accurate barrages before we discovered that the civilians were directing the fire and observing from windows.… Some of those people had regular army binoculars and all the observing paraphernalia. If they wanted to play soldier, it was all right with us once we knew the score, but they couldn't seem to make up their minds. They'd cause a lot of trouble and then, when we caught them, they'd start crying and showing us pictures of their wives or husbands or children. The only picture we could see were buddies lying in the street killed by the artillery that the civilians had directed. We didn't waste much time with them"…. Corporal, 10th Infantry.

RICH, JAMES E., Serial Number 34 882 251, was a Private First Class in 358th Cannon Company, 90th Division in the Army of the United States. His permanent mailing address was Cypress Inn, Tennessee. He was born 20 November 1923 in Cypress Inn. He was registered with Selective Service Board in Wayne County, Tennessee. His Civilian Occupation was General Farmer. He was inducted 3 August 1943 and entered into active service 24 August 1943 at Fort Oglethorpe, Georgia. His Military Occupational Specialty was Light Machine Gunner. His Military Qualifications included Combat Infantryman Badge. He was in the battles of Normandy, Northern France, Ardennes, Rhineland, and Central Europe. The following decorations were awarded to Rich:

European-African Middle Eastern Theater Ribbon with 5 Bronze Service Stars, Good Conduct Ribbon, World War II Victory Medal, and Purple Heart Medal while he was with the 358th Infantry. He was wounded in action in Germany 13 December 1944. He left the USA 12 May 1944 for the European-African Middle Eastern Theater Operation, and returned to USA 28 November 1945. Date he was discharged not available.

RICH, JOSEPH R., Serial Number 44 121 850, was a Private First Class in Headquarters Base Service Squadron, 582nd Air Service Group in Canal Zone in the Army of the United States. His permanent mailing address was Route 2, Collinwood, Tennessee. He was born 16 February 1927 in Lutts, Tennessee. He was registered with Selective Service Board in Wayne County, Tennessee. His Civilian Occupation was Farmer. He enlisted 5 February 1946 at Kessler Field, Mississippi. His Military Occupational Specialty was Auto Equipment Mechanic. He was not in any battles. The following decorations were awarded to Rich: World War II Victory Medal, American Campaign Medal, and Good Conduct Ribbon. He left the USA 20 May 1946 for the American Theater Operation, and returned to USA 7 January 1947. He had an eighth grade education. He was discharged, date not given, at New Orleans Personnel Center, New Orleans, Louisiana.

RICH, ORBIE FRANKLIN and LOYAL SMITH RICH, Orbie was born February 27, 1914, at Lutts, TN. His father

was Marion Harrison Rich, his mother was Lydia Pearl Gillis. His early years were spent on his father's farm. He finished the grade at Cheatham School in Lutts. He continued farm work until he was drafted in March of 1942. He took Infantry training at Camp Polk, LA. He was then transferred to Camp Howze, TX, and trained as a medical technician. It was here that he met the nurse who would later become his wife.

He remained in TX until November of

1945 being upgraded from Private to Technical Sergeant with the 1885 SCU Medical Detachment. He was discharged November 1945. He reenlisted at once and was sent to Mason General Hospital at Brentwood, NY. He was assigned as a medical aid man in Neuropsychiatry where he stayed until his honorable discharge December 28, 1946. He was authorized to wear the World War 11 Victory Medal and the American Theater Service Medal. Orbie was proud of his Army Service and his Army record.

Orbie married Loyal Smith of Chatham, LA, on February 28, 1948, They had four daughters and three sons. His children and grandchildren were his greatest love. He died of a heart attack on February 19, 1991, He left many friends.

Loyal Caroline Smith Rich was born September 28, 1920, at Chatham (Jackson Parrish) LA. Her parents were Floyd Franklin and

Frances Josephine McKaskle Smith. Loyal graduated from Chatham High School in 1937 as Valedictorian. From September 1, 1940 to September 1, 1943, she took nurses training at Shreveport Charity Hospital finishing the three-year course as a Registered Nurse. She continued work at the same hospital until December 1, 1943, when she enlisted in the Army Nurses Corp. with the grade of Second Lieutenant. Her basic military training was at Ft. Sam Houston in San Antonio, TX She was transferred to Regional Hospital, Camp Barkeley, TY., which is in, Abilene, then to 1871 Service Unit POW Camp at McLean TX From there to Camp Howze, TX She then went to Manila in the Philippines arriving during the Battle for Manila. She served with the 5th Field Hospital until Japan surrendered. Then she was assigned to the 248th General Hospital until she was shipped back to Ft. Sam Houston, TX She honorably discharged February 19, 1946. She is authorized to wear the Asiatic Pacific Theater Ribbon with one Bronze Star, American Theater Ribbon, Philippine Liberation Ribbon and the World War II Victory Medal.

Loyal continued working as RN until her marriage in 1948. She came to Tennessee with her husband where she has lived ever since. She did not return to Nursing until 1964 when she worked as RN at Coffee Hospital. She retired in 1982.

RICH, RAYMOND EUGENE, was the son of the late John L. and Winnie Rich. The family lived in the Cypress Inn community when Raymond went into the Army. Raymond's brothers were: Gaynes (deceased), Granville (deceased), Ralph, J.W., and Norman. Raymond's sisters were: Ocie Richerson, Hazel Holt Kelley, Genevive Horton and Winnie Mae Grimes.

Raymond went in the Army March 18, 1944. He was in the H/S Battery, 611" Battalion at the time he was discharged. He was a radio technician, 4th grade. He had enlisted for the last year he was in the Army. His last unit was different from his previous assignment. He didn't enjoy that duty because they used mules for many of their needs. Raymond felt that the mule's welfare came before those of the men. He was discharged December 13, 1946 at Camp Carson, CO.

Raymond married Josie Earline Robbins January 12, 1947. She is the daughter of the late Jasper and Stella Horton Robbins. Earline's family consists of Jaunita Berry, Lady Ruth Keeton and Jasper Robbins, Jr. (deceased) Raymond and Earline have the following children: Connie Jean Married Marvin Morrow; Dannie Joe (deceased) married Brenda Rich; Earl Dwain married Gwen Holcomb; and Jasper Eugene married Sherry Morgan. Dannie Joe died May 4, 1983 with a heart attack at 31 years of age.

Raymond was diagnosed with cancer in July of 1987. He lived until January 9, 1988. He was 64 years of age.

He and Earline had a good fife together and their family has produced good citizens for their communities. They have nine grandchildren and five great-grandchildren. Earline is very proud of her family and cherish the memories of Raymond and Dannie Joe.

RICH, ROY E., Serial Number 34 886 062, was a Technician Fourth Grade in Company C, 1778th Engineer Construction Battalion in the Army of the United States. His permanent mailing address was General Delivery, Collinwood, Tennessee. Roy, son of Mr. and Mrs. Cile Rich of Collinwood, was born 15 September 1923 in Iron City, Tennessee. He was registered with Selective Service Board in Wayne County, Tennessee. His Civilian Occupation was Surface Grinder Operator. He was married when he was inducted 5 October 1943 and entered into active service 27 October 1943 at Fort Oglethorpe, Georgia. His Military Occupational Specialty was Burner Acetylene. His Military Qualifications included MM Rifle. He was not in any battles. The following decorations were awarded to Rich: World

War II Victory Medal, American Theater Ribbon, Good Conduct Medal, and Asiatic-Pacific Theater Ribbon. He left the USA 25 June 1945 for the Asiatic-Pacific Theater Operation, and returned to USA 14 February 1946. He finished two years of high school. He was discharged 22 February 1946 at Camp Chaffee, Arkansas.

RICH, T.F., Serial Number 34 987 516, was a Private in Company A, 198th Infantry Training Battalion in the Army of the United States. He was born in Lutts, Tennessee. His Civilian Occupation was General Farm Hand. He was 18 years and 3 months old when he enlisted. His Military Occupational Specialty was Duty Soldier III. His Military Qualifications included MM Rifle. He was not in any battles. He was discharged 20 December 1944 at Fort McPherson, Georgia.

T. F. was the son of Harrison and Pearl (Gillis) Rich of Lutts. His brothers, Orbie F. and Denzie Arvil Rich also were veterans of World War II.

RICH, WARREN G., was born March 10, 1922, being the oldest of six children to Dave M. Rich and Gertie V. Holt Rich.

Brothers consists of Cemon D. Rich of Cypress In, TN; Harl Rich of Florence, AL; Hoover Rich (deceased) whose home was also Cypress Inn, and Ross who passed away at the age of nine. Two sisters consists of Lorene McFall of Collinwood, TN, and Evelyn Vickery of Lutts, TN. All of his brothers are veterans of the U.S. Army except Ross.

He was inducted into the army at Fort Oglethorpe, Georgia on November 22, 1942/ From there to Fort Ontario, New York and then on to Fort Pine Camp, New York. He left the United States from Fort Patrick Henry, VA in July, 1943, and he landed in Africa on July 30, 1943. In December of 1943 he landed in Italy where he served in different cities such as Naples, Florence, and Rome. For a short time he

was stationed in Greece and then back to Italy in October 1945. On December 3, 1945 he landed back in the good old USA at Fort Patrick Henry, VA. He received his discharge at Fort Knox, Kentucky on December 23, 1945.

Decorations received were the European Middle Eastern Theatre Ribbon with two bronze service stars, the Good Conduct Medal, and the World War 11 Victory Medal. One furlough to remember was in June 1943.

On January 4, 1951 he married Martha Nell Hensley. They have two daughters, Judy Ray and Donna Ray of Clifton, TN, and two sons, Lee, and Kenneth of Cypress Inn. They are blessed with three granddaughters: Kelly Ray, Chelsea and Cassie Rich; and one grandson, Jamie Ray.

Other than his army career and a few months in Michigan he has always lived at Cypress Inn at almost the same location. After getting out of the army, he farmed a few years and them went to work for Hassell & Hughes Lumber Company and worked for 33 years before retiring.

He is very proud to have served his country. The army experiences and the places he saw have been something to remember and tell his family.

Written by the children.

RICKETTS, EDWARD A., Serial Number 34 366 659, was a Technician Fifth Grade in 832nd Amphibians Truck Company in the Army of the United States. His permanent mailing address was Route 4, Waynesboro, Tennessee. He was born 18 April 1921 in Wayne County. He was registered with Selective Service Board in Wayne County, Tennessee. His Civilian Occupation was General Farm Hand. He was single when he was inducted 26 August 1942 and entered into active service 9 September 1942 at Fort Oglethorpe, Georgia. His Military Occupational Specialty was Amphibian Truck Driver. His Military Qualifications included MM Rifle. He was in the battles of Southern France, Rome-Arno, Rhineland, and Central Europe. The following decorations were awarded to Ricketts: World War II Victory Medal, Asiatic-Pacific Theater Ribbon, Good Conduct Medal, Philippine Liberation Ribbon and European-African Middle Eastern Theater Ribbon with 4 Bronze Service Stars and one Bronze Arrowhead. He left the USA 5 March 1943 for the European-African Middle Eastern Theater Operation, left there 2 June 1945 for the Asiatic-Pacific Theater Operation, and returned to USA 23 November 1945. He had an eighth grade education. He was discharged 5 December 1945 at Camp Chaffee, Arkansas.

RICKETTS, ELBERT LEE, was

born on May 26, 1909. He died on February 10, 1958 and is buried in the Prater's Chapel Cemetery near Clifton, Tennessee, in Wayne County. Elbert served his country in TN SC2 United States Navy during World War II. He was the son of William (Bill) and Virginia Hodge Ricketts. He married Carrie Prater, daughter of Allen and Alzona Stricklin Prater. He and Carrie had four children: Billy Joe, James Malcolm, De Vaughn and Madelin. His siblings are Viola, Robert and Claude.

RICKETTS, LESTER MELVIN, Serial Number 34 495 067, was a Private in Headquarters Company Northern California Sector, Western Defense Command in the Army of the United States. He was born in Clifton, Tennessee. His Civilian Occupation was Laborer. He was 22 1/2 years old when he enlisted. His Military Occupational Specialty was Basic. His Military Qualifications included MM M-1 Rifle. He was not in any battles. He was discharged 11 October 1943 at Fort Winfield Scott, California.

Lester, son of James A. and Sara Ricketts, was born 15 October 1920, was killed on a boat in Nashville 8 December 1956 and was buried in the Clifton City Cemetery. He was working as a deck hand on the boat at the time of his death. He married Jonada Ricketts. They had a son, Jimmy, and an infant daughter, Melodee Jeanne who died two days after birth and was buried with him in the Clifton Cemetery. Lester's siblings are George H., Clarence, Raymond, Guy, and Dorothy Jean "Tincy" Ricketts and Vera (Ricketts) McMahan. Lester has a half brother, Roy Ricketts, and a half sister, Bertha (Ricketts) Woodfield.

RICKETTS, RAYMOND B., was born in 1915, the son of James A. (Jim) and Sara H. Ricketts.

He grew up in the Clifton area. He was a button cutter and migrated to Muscatine, Iowa, on this job.

Raymond served his country during World War II.

His siblings are Berta, George H., Vera, Lester, Clarence, Guy and Dorothy Jean (Tinee).

RICKETTS, TOM FRANK, was born, May 11, 1925, at Olive Hill and worked as a farmer until he entered the U. S. Navy, September 17, 1943, at Chattanooga, TN. He served as Seaman First Class on the following vessels or stations; NTS Great Lakes, 11; R/S San Francisco, Co. and USS Harry Lee APA- 10 He received the following citations; Philippine Oper. medal with one Bronze Star, Victory Medal, Asiatic Pacific Medal with one Sil-

ver Star. He was discharged, March 23, 1946 at Memphis, Tn.

RILEY, CHARLES E., Serial Number 44 173 947, was a Private in Company B, 5th Infantry Battalion, TNG Regiment in the Army of the United States. His permanent mailing address was Route 5, Waynesboro, Tennessee. He was registered with Selective Service Board in Wayne County, Tennessee. His Civilian Occupation was Truck Driver. He enlisted 11 September 1946 at Fort Oglethorpe, Georgia. His Military Occupational Specialty was Basic. He was not in any battles. He was discharged 3 January 1947 at Fort Knox, Kentucky.

Charles, son of Elmer and Bertha Jane (Stutts) Riley, was born 1 April 1927 in Waynesboro, died 28 December 1993 in Williamson County Medical Center in Franklin, Tennessee, and was buried in Whitehead Cemetery in Topsy. He married Jean Mathis of 1169 Centerville Highway in Hohenwald. They had three children, Susan Tilley of Morrilton, Arkansas, Cynthia Parker of Hohenwald and Larry L. Riley of Smyrna, Tennessee. His siblings are: James Riley, Jacqueline Holt, Pat Baer and Betty Edwards all of Waynesboro, and Peggy Kelley of Fort Worth, Texas and five grandchildren. He was a construction worker.

RILEY, CLOVIS WILSON, was a native of Wayne County and the son of Wesley Gant and Ida Belle (Holt) Riley. He died 27 September 1994 at the age of 75 in the St. Thomas Hospital in Nashville. He was buried in Memorial Gardens in Waynesboro. His siblings are, Howard and Dewey Riley, Thelma Lineberry and Elsie Skelton. He married Imogene Bundrant. His children are Betty Rich and James "Pete" Turnbow.

He was a World War II Veteran, serving in the United States Army from 1941 to 1949. He was a member of the Masonic Blue Lodge, the Tennessee Lodge of Research and was of the Protestant Faith. He was a retired factory worker.

RILEY, GRADY EDWARD, Serial Number 34 936 459, was a Private First Class in Company B, 346th Regiment, 87th Infantry in the Army of the United States. His permanent mailing address was Route 2, Clifton, Tennessee. He was born 7 January 1926 in Clifton. He was registered with Selective Service Board in Wayne County, Tennessee. He enlisted 28 July 1944 at Camp Forrest, Tennessee. He left the USA 3 January 1945 for France and returned to USA 11 November 1945. He was discharged 18 December 1945 at Kennedy General Hospital, Memphis, Tennessee.

Pvt. Grady Edward Riley, son of Grady and Lois (Conway) Riley of Route 2, Clifton, Tennessee, was wounded in action in Belgium on January 30, 1945, while serving in the Infantry of the Third Army according to word received from the War Department by his parents. He was sent to a hospital in England. Pvt Riley, a graduate of Frank Hughes High School in Clifton, entered the armed services in July 1944. He took his basic training at Camp Wheeler, Georgia. He was in the Battle of The Bulge and received the Purple Heart.

He was born and reared in the Beech Creek community in Wayne County, Tennessee. Edward married Lorene Skelton and they had four children, Sue Brashier, Herschel Edward Riley, Billy Joe Riley and Gene Riley. He also had one brother, Johnny N. Riley (Johnny). He was buried in Prater's Chapel Cemetery near Clifton, Tennessee.

RILEY, FLOYD E., Serial Number 34 013 668, was a Private First Class in Company C, 1629th Engineer Construction Battalion in the Army of the United States. His permanent mailing address was General Delivery, Waynesboro, Tennessee. He was born 15 June 1913 in Waynesboro. He was registered with Selective Service Board in Wayne County, Tennessee. His Civilian Occupation was General Farm Hand. He was married when he enlisted 22 January 1941 at Fort Oglethorpe, Georgia. His Military Occupational Specialty was Duty Soldier III. His Military Qualifications included Sharpshooter Rifle. He was in the battle of Luzon. The following decorations were awarded to Riley: World War II Victory Medal, Good Conduct Medal, American Theater Medal, American Defense Service Ribbon, Asiatic-Pacific Theater Ribbon with one Bronze Service Star, Philippine Liberation Ribbon and one Bronze Star. He left the USA 26 April 1945 for the Asiatic-Pacific Theater Operation, and returned to USA 30 December 1945. He had a seventh grade education. He was discharged 8 January 1946 at Camp Chaffee, Arkansas.

RILEY, JAMES CALVIN, Serial Number 845 64 92, was a Ship's Cook Third Class in the Navy of the United States. His permanent mailing address was Route 5, Waynesboro, Tennessee. He was registered with Selective Service Board in Wayne County, Tennessee. He was born 28 October 1924 in Waynesboro. He was inducted 3 July 1943 and entered into service 10 July 1943 in Waynesboro. He held the following ratings: A3, S2/C and SC3C. He served on the following stations and vessels: San Diego, California, LCS (PAC); USS DeGRASSE; Com Ser PAC

ADV Base, Adm Pool; Navy #825 Com Ser Pac Adv Base; Adm Boat Pool #3234 Heavy. His last employer was Elmer Riley Lumber Company, Waynesboro from February 1941 to July 1943 as a Truck Driver. His Government Vocational Education course was in Automobile Education. He was discharge 11 December 1945 in Memphis, Tennessee.

RILEY, JAMES LAWRENCE, served in the United States Army. He was the son of Bud and Lily Hortense (Morgan) Riley.

gan) Riley. He married Minnie Youst and had two children, Paul Stephen and Mary Ann Riley. They moved to Toledo, Ohio, where they lived the rest of their lives and were buried there. His half brother and siblings are, Raymond, and Ruby Dixon, Pearl McGee and Naomi Matthews.

RILEY, MALCOLM RANDOLPH, was born 12 January 1911 near Clifton, Tennessee, died 11 May 1982 and was entombed in the Shiloh National Park Cemetery. He was the son of Eunis and Argent (Culp) Riley. He had two brothers, J. Erving and Forrest Riley. He never married. He attended school in Wayne County, mostly at Frank Hughes in Clifton. He was good in sports and added much to the basketball team at F. H. He belonged to the David Crockett Post of the Veterans of Foreign Wars.

His Honorable Discharge certifies that Randolph, had Serial Number 37 378 362, and was a Staff Sergeant in Company F, 360th Engineers (General Service) Regiment. He was discharged 6 December 1945 in Fort Knox, Kentucky. He had blue eyes, brown hair, 6' 1" tall, 190 lbs, and farmer. He was inducted 17 August 1942 and entered active service 31 August 1942. His Military Qualifications included MM M-1 Rifle. He was in the battles of Northern France, and Rhineland. He was decorated with European-African Middle Eastern Theater Ribbon with 2 Bronze Service

Stars, Good Conduct Medal, and World War II Victory Medal.

RILEY, SAMUEL D., was born 27 April 1921 in Wayne County to Daniel and Mary (Grooms) Riley. An only son, he had

two sisters, Erma Lee Kelly and Verna Lineberry. "S. D." as most of his friends called him, married Violet Pulley in 1942. Two sons were born from this marriage, S. D. Riley, Jr., of Waynesboro and B. J. Riley of Hendersonville. Violet died in 1973 and in 1977 S. D. married Frances Hughes Robinson of Clifton.

S. D. was inducted into the United States Army in October 1943 and was discharged in January 1946. He served as a Military Police in the European Theater, mostly in Germany and Austria. He was involved in the liberation of the German concentration camp, Dachau. He was wounded in action twice and received two Purple Hearts. When a shell exploded very close to him, he was knocked unconscious and sent to a hospital. He was separated from his unit, and, for this reason, his family was notified that he was missing in action until he was identified and returned to his unit. He spent the rest of his time guarding German prisoners and overseeing the confiscation of arms of the German civilian population.

RILEY, SAMUEL DEWEY, was a Private First Class in the Army of the United States. He was registered with Selective Service Board in Wayne County, Tennessee. His Civilian Occupation was General Farmer. He was single when he was inducted in the Army at Fort Oglethorpe, Georgia. He saw foreign as well as continental service.

Riley was born in Wayne County on 1 March 1908, died 13 October 1968 in Waynesboro and is buried in the Riley Cemetery on Little Beech Creek. He was a son of Wesley G. (1881-1934) and Ida Bell (Holt) Riley (1887-1970). His broth-

ers included Clovis and Howard Riley of Waynesboro. Other brothers, Andy, Wesley and Barney died young. His sisters were Thelma Lineberry and Elsie Shelton. He never married. He bought the well-known "Railroad" George Johnson farm on upper Green River where he farmed before and after the war.

RIPPY, CLINTON F., son of Jack and Irene Rippy, was born about, 1904, at Clifton, Tn. His father, Jack, drown when Clint was a small boy, so he started working early in life, doing small, odd jobs to help his mother pay the bills. As he became older, he did various jobs such as fanning, sawmill work, a Coca-Cola Bottling Co. and as a fireman. He and Nannie Fraley were married and lived near Clifton; divorced. They have three children, Shelby Jean, Buddy and Kenneth.

March 15, 1942, at the age of 38, Clint was inducted into the U. S. Army at Ft. Oglethorpe, GA. He took his training in the states, then was discharged, March 23, 1943. March 20, 1980, he died and is buried at Forty-Eight Creek Freewill Baptist Church Cemetery near Waynesboro, Tn. His siblings are Ethel and Clyde Rippy.

RISNER, ALEX L., Serial Number 34 361 753, was a Corporal in Company A, 141st Infantry in the Army of the United States. His permanent mailing address was Route 2, Iron City, Tennessee. He was born 12 August 1916 in Iron City. He was registered with Selective Service Board in Wayne County, Tennessee. His Civilian Occupation was General Farm Hand. He was inducted 25 July 1942 and entered into active service 8 August 1942 at Fort Oglethorpe, Georgia. His Military Qualifications included Combat Infantry Badge. He was in the battles of Naples-Foggia. The following decorations were awarded to Risner: European-African Middle Eastern Theater Ribbon, and Purple Heart. He was wounded in Italy 17 November 1943. He left the USA 2 April 1943 for the European-African Middle Eastern Theater Operation, and returned to USA 12 May 1945. He was discharged 7 October 1945 at Camp Blanding, Florida.

RISNER, APRIL DALLAS, son of Aurthur Walter and Myrtle W. (Casteel) Risner, was born, April 8, 1920, on Double Branches Creek in Wayne County. Since his father followed the timber and sawmill business, they lived in several different communities in Wayne and Lawrence Counties and North Alabama. Dallas entered the U. S. Army, October 13, 1942 at Ft. Oglethorpe, Ga. and got his training at Ft. McClellan, Al. with the 300th Infantry. They had been assigned to the 98th Division and were headed for the Pacific Islands, but when they arrived the fighting had ended. January, 1946, he received his discharged and returned to Wayne County.

Dallas and Katherine Aldridge were married, January 11, 1944, and lived in Wayne County a short time. They worked in Ohio for some time, then went to Nashville, where Dallas worked until he retired. They live at Waynesboro, attend Green River Baptist Church and their hobby is bowling. They have a daughter, Martha Nell.

RISNER, EDGAR, Serial Number 34 723 012, was a Sergeant in Battery A, 483rd Antiaircraft Artillery A W Battalion

in the Army of the United States. His permanent mailing address was Route 4, Waynesboro, Tennessee. He was registered with Selective Service Board in Wayne County, Tennessee. His Civilian Occupation was Sorter. He was inducted 20 February 1943 and entered into active service 27 February 1943 at Fort Oglethorpe, Georgia. His Military Occupational Specialty was Automatic Weapons. His Military Qualifications included Expert Rifle. He fought in Ground Combat in Eastern Mandates, and Iwo Jima. The following decorations were awarded to Risner: World War II Victory Medal, Good Conduct Ribbon, American Theater Ribbon, and Asiatic-Pacific Theater Ribbon with 2 Bronze Stars. He left the USA 16 June 1944 for the Asiatic-Pacific Theater Operation, and returned to USA 20 December 1945. He had an eighth grade education. He was discharged 31 December 1945 at Camp Chaffee, Arkansas.

Edgar, son of Mr. and Mrs. Roy Risner, was born 9 December 1923 in Waynesboro. His sisters are Opal and Geneva Skelton.

RISNER, JOE C., Serial Number 34 884 703, was a Private in unassigned, attached, Special Training Unit in the Army of the United States. His permanent mail-

ing address was Waynesboro, Tennessee. He was born in Lawrenceburg, Tennessee. His Civilian Occupation was Welder. He was 32 and 4/12 years old and married when he was inducted 7 September 1943 at Fort Oglethorpe, Georgia. Under Remarks, "Soldier transferred to ERC on date of induction and called to active duty 28 September 1943. " He was discharged 2 December 1943 at Fort McPherson, Georgia in poor physical condition but with excellent character.

RISNER, J.P., Serial Number 605 07 73, was a Ship's Cook, First Class in the United States Navy. He was born 12 July 1922 in Iron City, Tennessee. His home address was Route 3, Iron City. He enlisted 7 October 1942 in Florence, Alabama. He held the following ratings: AS, S2C, SC3C, SC2C(T) and SC1C(T). He served on the following vessels and Stations: USNTS, San Diego, California; USNH Corona, California; and USS LSM 320. His main civilian occupation was farm hand for his brother, C. M. Risner, in Iron City from January 1938 to October 1942. He was discharge 27 November 1945 in Norman, Oklahoma. He completed a Service School Class A, Cooks and Bakers School in San Diego. Under remarks, "Good Conduct, U. S. Reserve, Honorable Discharge Button and Service Lapel Button. "

The following poem was sent to the Wayne County News office by J. P. Risner, 2/C and was published in the Friday, December 14, 1945 edition of the paper. This poem expressed J. P.'s sentiment at that time.
"That Great Glad Day
Some glad day when the sun shines brightly
When those clouds drift away.
And we sail in to Fresno Harbor,
It will be a great glad day.
Then our work over here is ended.
God speed the time I pray;
When the enemy is defeated
That will be a great glad day.
No more rolling on the ocean.
No more getting on the way;
When our feet shall tread upon the land
What a glorious great glad day.
Then at home again with love ones
Forever more to stay;
Then we start our life new again
What a wondrous great glad day.
God bless our dear old country
The good old U. S. A.
We will never cease our struggle
Until we reach that great glad day.
From your sailors on the dark blue sea.
To our beloved at home we say;
Unite your hearts in prayer to God.
To spend that great glad day.
We leave these few words to you
Go pray to God each day;

To do his will the best toward us
Until we reach that great glad day
To be home to stay. ".

RISNER, RALEIGH, Serial Number 34 921 956, was a Private in 577th AAA AW Battalion in the Army of the United States. He was born in Lawrence County, Tennessee. His Civilian Occupation was Truck Driver. He was 33 4/12 years old when he was inducted into active service. His Military Occupational Specialty was 40 MM Gun Section Crewman. His Military Qualifications included Rifle M1 Caliber 30. He was discharged 26 October 1944 at William Beaumont General Hospital in El Paso, Texas in poor physical condition.

RISNER, REX, Serial Number 34 494 882, was a Private in Headquarters and Headquarters Battery, 130th Coast Artillery in the Army of the United States. He was born in Collinwood, Tennessee. His Civilian Occupation was Laborer. He was 21 and 8/12 years old when he was inducted 22 November 1942 at Fort Oglethorpe, Georgia. He was not in any battles. He was discharged 14 August 1943 in fair physical condition.

RISNER, ROBERT EZELL, Serial Number 845 64 95, was a Seaman First Class in the Navy of the United States. His

permanent mailing address was Box 234, Waynesboro, Tennessee. He was born 19 November 1924 in Lawrenceburg, Tennessee. He was registered with Selective Service Board in Wayne County, Tennessee. His Civilian Occupation was Welding-Shipyard Training in Savannah, Georgia. He was inducted 3 July 1943 and entered into active service 10 July 1943 at Chattanooga, Tennessee. The Stations and Vessels that he served on were: USNTS, San Diego, California; Landing Craft School (PAC); USS DeGRASSE (AP 164); US Naval Recreation Base, San Pedro, California; RS, NYD, Philadelphia, Pennsylvania; USN Asiatic-Pacific PD, San Bruno, California; and Overseas; Acorn 51, NAB Navy; and 3858 Mactan, Philippines. He had a seventh grade education. He was discharged 4 February 1946 at Memphis, Tennessee.

Robert was married 9 February 1946 to Neva Jane Skelton. Their children are, Roger Louie, born 25 September 1947, and Timothy Wayne born 12 January 1954. Both children are deceased. They have three grandchildren and four great grandchildren.

ROBBINS, BARNEY, was born, May 13, 1912, in Wayne County and worked as a fanner until he was inducted into the U. S. Army, April 17, 1943, at Ft. McClellan, Al. He served with Hdq. Co. 3rd Engineers Special Brigade as a light truck driver. Barney received his training in the states and arrived in the Pacific Theater, January 22, 1944, and stayed a year and three months. He was in the battle of New Guinea and received the following citations; Asiatic-Pacific Theater Ribbon with one Bronze Star and Good Conduct Medal. He arrived in the states, April 23, 1945, and was discharged, July 19, 1945, at Ft. McPherson, GA.

ROBBINS, COVA M., Serial Number 34 987 510, was a Private First Class in Company I, 106th Infantry in the Army of the United States. His permanent mailing address was General Delivery, Lutts, Tennessee. He was born 11 December 1923 in Lutts. He was registered with Selective Service Board in Wayne County, Tennessee. His Civilian Occupation was General Farm Hand. He was married when he enlisted 11 April 1944 at Camp Shelby, Mississippi. His Military Occupational Specialty was Light Truck Driver. His Military Qualifications included Sharpshooter Rifle. He was not in any battles. The following decorations were awarded to Robbins: World War II Victory Medal, Good Conduct Ribbon, American Theater Ribbon, and Asiatic-Pacific Theater Ribbon. He left the USA 30 June 1945 for the Asiatic-Pacific Theater Operation, and returned to USA 28 April 1946. He was discharged 6 May 1946 at Camp Chaffee, Arkansas.

Cova is a farmer and a Church of God minister for the Revival Center Church in Clifton. He is a very knowledgeable person and a good leader. He married Gladys Stricklin and they have one daughter, Joyce Marie. Joyce married Norman Neal Riley and they have two sons, Shane Neil and Jason Mark Riley. Jason married Lori Michelle Long and they have one son, Brice Willard Riley.

ROBBINS, FRED, Serial Number 34

375 299, was a Private First Class in Company D, called "Blue Devils", 351st Infantry in the Army of the United States. His permanent mailing address was Route 2, Lutts, Tennessee. He was born 7 October 1914 in Lutts. He was registered with Selective Service Board in Wayne County, Tennessee. His Civilian Occupation was General Farmer. He enlisted 3 October 1942 and entered into active service 17 October 1942 at Fort Oglethorpe, Georgia. His Military Occupational Specialty was Ammunition Bearer. His Military Qualifications included MM Rifle and Combat Infantryman Badge. He was in the battles of Rome-Arno, Northern Apennines and Po Valley. The following decorations were awarded to Robbins: European-African Middle Eastern Theater Ribbon with 3 Bronze Stars, American Service Medal, Good Conduct Medal, and World War II Victory Medal. He left the USA 22 November 1943 for the European Theater Operation, and returned to USA 10 November 1945. He had an eighth grade education. He was discharged 16 November 1945 at Fort McPherson, Georgia.

Fred married 21 April 1946, Estelle Warrington. Their daughters are, Peggy Monroe of Collinwood and Frances Boyd of Linden.

Fred was the son of Henry and Flora Rebecca Holt Robbins of Lutts, Tennessee He had three brothers, William, Cecil, and H. B., two sisters, Mearl Robbins Sherrill, and Mazy Bell Robbins Melson. Fred was a member of the Lutts Methodist Church, he was also a member of the American Legion. He enjoyed hunting as long as he was able to walk. After he came out of W. W. II, he farmed on his farm which he had saved the money during his service in the war and bought. He continued to be a farmer until he became disabled. He also was a part time surveyor with Mr. Jim Hurst from Collinwood. Fred died May 23, 1996. He was buried at the Lutts Cemetery He loved America, and what it stood for. He would tell us of lay-

ing in fox holes with snow during the war. He never regretted it because of his strong patriotism for his country. Amelia Marie Monroe, Johnathan Gary Monroe, Sabrina Boyd and Erica Boyd.

ROBBINS, GAINES, was a Captain in an Army Regiment in the Army of the United States. He was born 8 March 1924, died 7 July 1944 and was buried in the Cromwell Crossroads Cemetery, Southwest of Collinwood on Bear Creek Road in Wayne County.

ROBBINS, WILLIAM T., Serial Number 34 284 291, was a Private First Class in Company B, 470th Infantry Battalion in the Army of the United States. His permanent mailing address was Route 2, Lutts, Tennessee. He was born 30 March 1918 in Lutts. He was registered with Selective Service Board in Wayne County, Tennessee. His Civilian Occupation was General Farm Hand. He was Single when he was inducted into active service. His Military Occupational Specialty was Dog Trainer. His Military Qualifications included Expert Infantry Badge and Expert Rifle M-1. He was not in any battles. The following decorations were awarded to Robbins: American Theater Service Medal and Good Conduct Medal. He left the USA 30 September 1942 for the American Theater Operation, and returned to USA 9 Oct 1942. He left the USA again 5 March 1944 for the American Theater Operation, and returned to USA 6 March 1944 and the third time he left the USA 19 August 1945 for the American Theater Operation, and returned to USA 20 August 1945. He had a seventh grade education. He was discharged 23 October 1945 at Camp Gordon, Georgia.

William was retired from Murray Ohio Manufacturing Company in Lawrenceburg. He died in his home at Route 1, Ethridge, Tennessee and was buried in Cromwell Crossroads Church Cemetery. He was the son of the late John Henry and Flora Rebecca (Holt) Robbins. His survivors include, his wife Peggy (Riser) Robbins, daughter, Katheryn Griggs of Waynesboro and Karen Long of Charleston, South Carolina; a son, Billy W. Robbins of Lewisburg; a stepson, Kenny Haddock of Lawrenceburg; two sisters, Merl Sherrill of Clifton, and Marybelle Melson of Collinwood; two brothers, Fred and Cecil Robbins of Collinwood; two grand children, one step-grandson and two great-grandchildren.

ROBERSON, BOONE, son of Nathan Carroll and Mary Emaline Holt (Lawson), was born , April 11, 1923. He served in the United States Services during WWII.

Boone and Peggy Waller were married, July 1, 1944, and made South Bend, Indiana their home. March 6, 1984, Boone died and is buried at Chapel Hill Cemetery at South Bend.

ROBERSON, ELVIS HUBERT, was born on October 2, 1926, in Wayne County, Tennessee. On October 2, 1944, he entered the United States Navy and served as Seaman Second Class on the USNTS, Great Lakes, Illinois; USNCTC, Davisville, Rhode Island; 36th Special USNCB; and USS Gurke (DD783). He was awarded the following citations: Asiatic-Pacific Campaign Ribbon with one Star, World War II Victory Medal, American Area Ribbon and was commended for performance of duty on April 20, 1945, by Lieutenant G. H. Granger. He received his discharge on June 20, 1946, in New Orleans, Louisiana.

ROBERSON, GRADY EUGENE, was born, May 13, 1920, in Wayne County, TN. to Nathan Carroll and Mary Emaline Holt (Lawson). He served in WWII, then moved to South Bend, Indiana, where he worked until his retirement. He still resides at his home in South Bend.

ROBERSON, JAMES C., Serial Number 34 723 007, was a Private First Class in Battery C, 483rd Antiaircraft Artillery AW Battalion in the Army of the United States. His permanent mailing address was Route 2, Iron City, Tennessee. He was born 4 July 1923 in Iron City. He was registered with Selective Service Board in Wayne County, Tennessee. His Civilian Occupation was General Farm Hand. He was single when he was inducted 20 February 1943 and entered into active service 27 February 1943 at Fort Oglethorpe, Georgia. His Military Occupational Specialty was Cannoneer. His Military Qualifications included MM Rifle. He was in the battles of Western Pacific Ground Combat and Iwo Jima. The following decorations were awarded to Roberson: World War II Victory Medal, Good Conduct Medal, American Theater Ribbon, and Asiatic-Pacific Theater Ribbon with 2 Bronze Service Stars. He left the USA 16 June 1944 for the Asiatic Pacific Theater Operation, and returned to USA 20 December 1945. He had a seventh grade education. He was discharged 31 December 1945 at Camp Chaffee, Arkansas.

ROBERSON, JAMES WILEY, was born, May 10, 1924, at Collinwood, TN. He joined the U. S. Navy, May 2, 1943 and served as a motor machinist mate second class at the following stations or ships~ NRS Nashville, TN., NTS. Bainbridge,

NO., USS Prometheus. January 17, 1946, he was discharged at Memphis, TN.

ROBERSON, JOHN FRANK, served his country during World War II in the United States Navy. He was a farmer and a member of the Mt. Pleasant Methodist Church.

John Frank was 92 years old when he died 7 February 1994 at Rolling Acres Nursing Home in Florence, Alabama. His funeral was conducted in Collinwood and burial was in Mt. Pleasant Cemetery in Cypress Inn on home grounds. He was the son of John Wesley and Laura Roberson. His surviving children were: David, Eugene and Quinten Roberson of Florence, Larry Roberson of Cypress Inn, Faye Cromwell of Florence and Ruth Ann McGee of Okolona, Mississippi.

ROBERSON, RANDLE, Serial Number 34 723 049, was a Private First Class in Battery A, 483rd Antiaircraft Artillery, Automatic Weapon Battalion in the Army of the United States. His permanent mailing address was Route 3, Florence, Alabama. He was born 26 August 1923 in Wayne County, Tennessee. He was registered with Selective Service Board in Wayne County, Tennessee. His Civilian Occupation was High School Student. He was inducted 20 February 1943 and entered into active service 27 February 1943 at Fort Oglethorpe, Georgia. His Military Occupational Specialty was Antiaircraft AW Crewman. His Military Qualifications included S R BEB. He was in the battles of Eastern Mandates, Ground Combat. The following decorations were awarded to Roberson: Atlantic Theater Operation Medal, Asiatic-Pacific Theater Operation Medal, World War II Victory Medal, and Good Conduct Medal. He left the USA 16 June 1944 for the Asiatic Pacific Theater Operation, and returned to USA 19 December 1945. He finished two years of high school. He was discharged 31 December 1945 at Camp Shelby, Mississippi.

He was the son of Luther and Minnie Lee (Wright) Roberson. He has one brother, Ernest Roberson. He married Pauline Morris and they had four children, Randy, Linda, Ricky and Doug who died young. He is a retired sheet metal worker. He lives at 2126 Cloverdale Road in North Florence, Alabama.

ROBERSON, WALTER, was born July 27, 1922, to Henry and Viola Linville Roberson. He was inducted into the U.S. Army November 22, 1942 and took his basic training at Ft. Oglethorpe, GA, and was assigned to the 7th Army. He served in the Aleutian Islands in 1943, the Marshall Islands in 1943, the Philippine

Islands in 1944 and Okinawa in 1945. He was honorably discharged from active service at Ft. McPherson, GA, in 1945. His total overseas time was from February of 1943 to September of 1945.

After his stay in the military, Walter returned to Wayne County and began a career with TVA. He retired in 1984 and took a temporary job with the Wayne County Highway Department for eight years before retiring again.

Walter married Nell Kilburn in 1948 and they have two children; Kevin and Kim.

ROBERSON, WAYLAND L., Serial Number 34 886 064, was a Private First Class in Postal Detachment Transportation Corps in the Army of the United States. His permanent mailing address was Route 3, Iron City, Tennessee. He was born 11 February 1925 in Iron City. He was registered with Selective Service Board in Wayne County, Tennessee. His Civilian Occupation was General Farm Hand. He was inducted 5 October 1943 and entered into active service 27 October 1943. His Military Occupational Specialty was Antiaircraft Gunner. His Military Qualifications included MMS Rifle. He was not in any battles. The following decorations were awarded to Roberson: World War II Victory Medal, European-African-Middle Eastern Service Medal, and American Service Medal. He left the USA 21 March 1944 for Sea Duty (ET), and returned to USA 20 April 1945. He had an eighth grade education. He was discharged 9 March 1946 at Fort McPherson, Georgia.

ROBERTS, JOHN N., Serial Number 14 022 199, was a Sergeant in 2138 Army Air Force Base Unit in the Army of the United States. His permanent mailing address was Clifton, Tennessee. He was born 13 March 1919 in Clifton. His Civilian Occupation was Meat Cutter. He was married with two dependents when he was inducted 18 September 1940 at Montgomery, Alabama. His Military Occupational Specialty was Meat Cutter. He was not in any battles. The following decorations were awarded to Roberts: American Defense Ribbon, Good Conduct Medal, and Soldier's Affidavit. He had a high school education. He was discharged 14 October 1945 at Maxwell Field, Alabama.

J. N. was reared in Clifton by a hard working mother and dad, George W. and Ida (Riley) Roberts. He was taught how to work at an early age. His father kept Jersey Cows, ran a grocery store, sold hamburgers and ice cream in the store. J. N. was kept busy with milking the cows, delivering good rich milk, sold in pint and quart milk bottles in the Clifton area. At all socials and benefit functions "Mr. George" was always there with hamburgers and ice cream with J. N. as his helper.

He joined the Clifton Church of Christ at an early age. He has been a faithful and loyal member. In 1936 he graduated from Frank Hughes High School with his twin sister Dorothy. After his discharge from the Army, he returned to Clifton to become a meat cutter in his father's store, then in his brother Jimmy's store for many years. Later he opened his own business of Electrical and Refrigeration Repair. He was very good in this line of work. Here again, the Clifton and Waynesboro area folks have found J. N. to be very dependable and fair in pricing his work. He is well known in this area. Recently his health problems have forced him to retire. A few years ago, the Clifton Rotary Club voted him Clifton's Man of the Year. He received an award.

He married Raye Grimes from the edge of Hardin County, Tennessee. They have three children, William and Mary Jo Roberts and Dorothy Lynn Holt. His siblings are, Jimmy Riley Roberts, Margaret Martin and Dorothy Dorsey.

ROBERTSON, ANDY W., Serial Number 34 936 465, was a Sergeant in 2114th Service Unit in the Army of the United States. His permanent mailing address was Route 2, Iron City, Tennessee. He was born 7 February 1926 in Iron City. He was registered with Selective Service Board in Wayne County, Tennessee. His Civilian Occupation was General Farm Hand. He enlisted 24 July 1944 at Camp Forest, Tennessee. His Military Occupational Specialty was Special Vehicle Operator. His Military Qualifications included MM 30 Cal Carbine and AAF Air Crew Member Badge. He was not in any battles. The following decorations were awarded to Robertson: American Theater Service Medal, Good Conduct Medal and World War II Victory Medal. He left the USA 29 November 1945 for the American Theater Operation, and returned to USA 25 June 1946. He had an eighth grade education. He was discharged 3 July 1946 at Fort Bragg, North Carolina.

PFC Robertson, son of Mr. and Mrs. J. M. Robertson of Route 2, Iron City, was graduated from the Army Air Force Flexible Gunnery School at Loredo Air Field in Loredo, Texas and was a member of the AAF Training Command. He is now qualified to take his place as a member of a Bomber Combat Crew. Along with his diploma, he received a pair of Aerial Gunner's Silver wings and a promotion in grade at a brief graduation exercise. He was prepared for his place in America's stepped-up air offensive by a comprehensive six week course in every phase of aerial gunnery warfare.

ROBERTSON, HARVEY B., Serial Number 44 069 648 was a Technician Fifth Grade in Company C, 110th Engineer Combat Battalion in the Army of the United States. His permanent mailing address was Route 2, Iron City, Tennessee. He was born 13 February 1921 in Iron City. He was registered with Selective Service Board in Wayne County, Tennessee. His Civilian Occupation was General Farmer. He was married when he was inducted 31 January 1945 at Fort Oglethorpe, Georgia. His Military Occupational Specialty was Cook. His Military Qualifications included MM Rifle. He was not in any battles. The following decorations were awarded to Robertson: World War II Victory Medal, Good Conduct Medal, and Asiatic-Pacific Theater Medal. He left the USA 6 August 1945 for the Asiatic-Pacific Theater Operation, and returned to USA 10 January 1946. He had an eighth grade education. He was discharged 19 January 1946 at Camp Chaffee, Arkansas.

ROBERTSON, RICHARD T., was born August 12,1924 at McGlainery Stand in Collinwood, TN. His parents were William Edgar and Lillie Pearl Holt Robertson.

He has one brother, Norman Robertson, of Cypress Inn, TN, who served in the Korean Conflict.

On May 8, 1947 Richard married Callie Elizabeth Olive of Florence, AL. They have three children: (1) Shelia Wright, Muscle Shoals, AL; (2) Ronald Robertson of Florence, AL; and (3) Nancy Brooks of Collinwood, TN. Richard and Callie have four grandchildren; two boys and two girls. They also have two great-grandchildren; one girl and one boy.

Richard entered the Army July 2, 1943 and he was sent to Camp Haan (Riverside) California for basic training in Anti-Aircraft Artillery. He was shipped overseas March 20, 1944, landing in the Southwest Pacific Area. He served in Battery "D", 104th Antiaircraft Artillery.

Richard was in two major battles; New Guinea and Luzon in the Philippines He received the following decorations: WWII Victory Ribbon, Good Conduct Medal, . AP Theater Ribbon 2 Bronze Stars and the Philippine Liberation Ribbon.

When the war ended, He was shipped to Japan on occupation duty. He received his discharge from the Army January 23, 1946, at Camp Chaffee. AR.

ROSE, ARTHUR ABNER, Serial Number 34 713 913, was inducted into the Army of the United States prior to 30 April 1943, and was released from active duty, and transferred to the Enlisted Reserve Corps, and returned to Waynesboro, Tennessee. On 30 April 1943, he was called to active duty and reported to Fort Oglethorpe, Georgia.

ROSE, H.B., Serial Number 34 713 896, was inducted into the Army of the United States prior to 30 April 1943, and was released from active duty, and transferred to the Enlisted Reserve Corps, and returned to Waynesboro, Tennessee. On 30 April 1943, he was called to active duty and reported to Fort Oglethorpe, Georgia.

ROSE, TALMADGE, Serial Number 34 375 247, was a Private First Class in HQ Company, 1st Battalion, 350th Infantry in the Army of the United States. His permanent mailing address was Route 5, Waynesboro, Tennessee. He was born 14 January 1912 in Waynesboro. He was registered with Selective Service Board in Wayne County, Tennessee. His Civilian Occupation was Lumber Mill Worker. He was single when he was inducted 3 October 1942 and entered into active service 17 October 1942 at Fort Oglethorpe, Georgia. His Military Occupational Specialty was Ammo Carrier. His Military Qualifications included Combat Infantryman Badge. He was in the battles of North

Apennines and Po Valley. The following decorations were awarded to Rose: Good Conduct Medal, and European-African Middle Eastern Theater Ribbon with 2 Bronze Stars. He left the USA 4 December 1943 for the European Theater Operation, and returned to USA 18 August 1945. He had a seventh grade education. He was discharged 8 October 1945 at Camp Atterbury, Indiana.

ROSS, LEVELLE, was born on May 30, 1915, in Waynesboro. He worked as a porter until March 18, 1943, when he was inducted into the United States Army at Ft. Benning, Georgia. He served as a mail clerk and was a T/4 with the 547th Quartermaster Supply Depot Company. He was in the battles of Central Burma and China Offensive and received the following citations: World War II Victory Medal, American Theater Ribbon, Good Conduct Medal and Asiatic-Pacific Theater with two Bronze Stars. On December 24, 1945, Levelle was discharged at Camp Atterbury, Indiana.

He was the son of Lem and Mary Ross. He married Mary Elizabeth Harbell. He had one sister, Edith Ross Richardson. He attended school in Wayne County and graduated from the eighth grade. He was of Methodist faith. Levelle worked for Shull Truck Line for 30 years.

Levelle died in July 1990 and is buried in Ross Cemetery in Waynesboro, Tennessee.

ROWDEN, WILLIAM DARNELL, Serial Number 977 28 95, enlisted as a V-6 in the USNR SV, 29 July 1944 for two years. He was born 1 April 1926 in Collinwood, Tennessee. He served on the following vessels and stations: NRS Nashville, Tennessee; STC & USN TADC WIM A; 27th USNCB ADC NRS Nashville, Tennessee; PERS and JRACOM (RS) NRD, New Orleans, Louisiana and USNH in New Orleans. He was discharged 21 August 1945 from the USNH in New Orleans, Louisiana with an excellent service record.

RUMBAUGH, JAMES, Serial Number 34 377 043, was a Private First Class in Company D, 794 Military Police Battalion in the Army of the United States. His permanent mailing address was Box 58, Collinwood, Tennessee. He was born 25 September 1921 in Wayne County. He was registered with Selective Service Board in Wayne County, Tennessee. His Civilian Occupation was Off-Bearer. He was married with two dependents when he was inducted 13 October 1942 and entered into active service 27 October 1942 at Fort Oglethorpe, Georgia. His Military Occupational Specialty was Light Truck Driver. His Military Qualifications included MM MI Rifle. He was in the battles of Normandy and Northern France. The following decorations were awarded to Rumbaugh: Purple Heart Medal, World War II Victory Medal, American Theater Ribbon, and European-African Middle Eastern Theater Ribbon with 2 Bronze Stars. He was wounded in action in France 27 July 1944. He left the USA 23 March 1944 for the European Theater Operation, and returned to USA 5 December 1945. He was discharged 14 December 1945 at Fort Knox, Kentucky.

RUSS, NIGLE E., Serial Number 34 284 232, was a Private First Class in Battery B, 376th Antiaircraft Artillery Battalion in the Army of the United States. His permanent mailing address was Route 2, Iron City, Tennessee. He was born 1 June 1920 in Wayne County, Tennessee. He was registered with Selective Service Board in Wayne County, Tennessee. His Civilian Occupation was General Farm Hand. He was married with two dependents when he was inducted 23 May 1942 at Fort Oglethorpe, Georgia. His Military Occupational Specialty was Machine Gunner. He was in the battles of Ardennes, Rhineland, and Central Europe. The following decorations were awarded to Russ: American Theater Medal, European-African Middle Eastern Theater Ribbon with 5 Bronze Stars and Good Conduct Ribbon. He left the USA 5 September 1943 for the European Theater Operation, and returned to USA 2 November 1945. He was discharged 6 November 1945 at Camp Atterbury, Indiana.

RYAN, THORTON L., Serial Number 34 924 073, was a Staff Sergeant in 376th Bombardment Group, Army Air Force in the Army of the United States. His permanent mailing address was Collinwood, Tennessee. He was born 1 July 1925 in Hartselle, Alabama. He was registered with Selective Service Board in Wayne County, Tennessee. His Civilian Occupation was Student. He enlisted 13 April 1944 at Fort Oglethorpe, Georgia. His Military Occupational Specialty was Clerk Non-typist. His Military Qualifications included MM Pistol. He was in the battles of Rome-Arno, Northern Apennines, Po Valley and Rhineland. The following decorations were awarded to Ryan: World War II Victory Medal, American Service Medal, Air Medal and European-African Middle Eastern Theater Ribbon with 4 Bronze Stars. He left the USA 31 January 1945 for the European Theater Operation, and returned to USA 29 April 1945. He had a high school education. Service schools that he attended were: AAF Tech School in Tyndall Field, Panama City, Florida and Flexible Gunnery. He was discharged 17 March 1946 at Fort McPherson, Georgia.

Thorton died 20 February 1998 and was buried in Memorial Gardens. He was the son of Lee Thorton and Bessie Goodman Ryan. He was a superintendent of Hassell and Hughes Lumber Company, a member of Collinwood Methodist Church. Survivors include his wife, Lenice Daniel Ryan of Collinwood; one son, Thomas Thorton Ryan of Collinwood; one daughter, Janice Lee Franks of Lutts; two sisters, Margaret Martin of Cookeville and Delia Bryson of Daytona Beach, Florida; nine grandchildren and one great-grandchild.

SANDUSKEY, J.C., entered the Army August 26, 1942. He saw action in New Guinea, Leyte and Luzon. J.C. received the following citation: For meritorious achievement in connection with military operations against the enemy in the Philippine Islands from 16 November 1944 to 4 June 1945. Sergeant Sandusky rendered outstanding service throughout the above period as a gunner of a mortar squad, Squad Leader, and finally as Mortar Section Leader of Company F, 128th Infantry of the 32nd Infantry Division. Throughout the Leyte and Luzon campaigns Sergeant Sandusky's actions were of the highest standards. During the battle of the Villa Verde Trail, he repeatedly went out to for-

ward observation points in enemy held territory, frequently under enemy fire. By his accurate control and direction of the mortars he was highly instrumental in the destruction of hostile positions and the disruption of enemy supply lines. Sergeant Sandusky's skill and initiative in these campaigns aided greatly in the successful completion of his company's combat missions. For these efforts he was awarded the Bronze Star Medal. He was honorably discharged on November 27, 1945.

J.C. was born February 24, 1918. His parents were Carter and Lona Franks Sandusky. He has two sisters; Inez Warren and Wylodean Reynolds. He married Nona Rich on May 22, 1948. She was the daughter of Harrison and Pearl Gillis Rich.

J.C. and Nona have two sons, Danny and Teddy, and one daughter, Judy Sandusky Mathis. They have three grandsons, two granddaughters, one great-grandson, three step grandsons, two step granddaughters, four step great-grandsons, and one step great-granddaughter.

SCHMITTOU, THOMAS W., I am the oldest son of Albert F. and Gladys W. Schmittou, born 29 October 1923 on the Sam Bell farm in a log cabin situated on the banks of Moccasin Creek and Buffalo River. I was educated in the Wayne County School System and attended high school in Waynesboro. I volunteered for service in the U. S. Merchant Marine in May of 1942 and entered duty in August. Firstly, I was assigned to a training station at Sheepshead Bay in Brooklyn, NY; graduated in December 1942 as a Fireman, Steam Boilers and also with a Life Boatman certificate. My first shipboard assignment was on H. F. Alexander, a troop ship loading for a trip to North Africa with troops to take North Africa back from the German Army led by Field Marshall Rommel. We landed in Oran, Algeria, January 1943, off loaded and returned to the States and was assigned to duty aboard an oil tanker working out of West Indies up the U. S. coast,

carrying oil into New York and New Jersey, then, duty on a freighter back to the Mediterranean making a stop in Sicily and Sardinia with supplies being left in Palarmo and Caglaria. On returning to the States, I was assigned to a crew that was taking a new type of freighter out of Newport News, Virginia, shipyard on a maiden shakedown cruise and then, we were loaded with supplies in Norfolk to take through the Panama Canal to the Pacific. We were to discharge cargo in Hawaii and proceed on to the loading of support troops and equipment for the Saipan invasion. For reasons not known to me, the ship was pulled out of the invasion fleet and returned to San Francisco. I left the ship for a visit home. After returning to Tennessee, I decided that I would like to see some service in the Army and in August 1944, I volunteered for service in the army. I was sent to Camp Fanning, Texas, for basic training as an infantry replacement. The basic Training schedule was set up on a seventeen week training period to take a soldier through the required phase for combat. In late 1944, the "Battle of the Bulge" action was so fierce that my class was pulled out of training with only thirteen weeks completed and sent to Europe as replacements that were badly needed in December 1944. I was assigned to C Company, 114th Infantry, 44th Infantry Division as an Automatic Rifleman to carry the Browning automatic rifle in the BAR team. The BAR team was made up of an Automatic Rifleman, assistant rifleman and an ammo carrier. I joined the division in France and served through France, Germany and was up in the Alps Mountains of Austria when the war in Europe ended. I earned two campaign stars, combat infantry badge, bronze star, and European Theater of Operation medal. After the War in Europe ended, my division returned to Fort Smith, Arkansas, for further training to go into combat in the Pacific Theater. During our leave home, the war in the Pacific area terminated and that made it possible for many troops from the European Theater to be discharged, I enlisted in the regular army after I was discharged from the "Army of U. S. " as the drafted soldier was called. Then, was assigned to return to Germany in the Army of Occupation. I arrived in Germany in December 1945 and volunteered for Paratroop training in the 82nd Airborne Division that was the Headquarter Guards in Frankfurt. While in training, I was hurt and was sent to the 97th General Hospital in Frankfurt. Due to my injury, I was transferred out of jump school and assigned to an Engineering Battalion. I performed duties there as a Carpenter Shop Foreman, working German prisoners of war to rebuild and refurbish housing for U. S. Army

Occupation Forces. I returned to the U. S. in January 1947 for discharge. In August 1947, volunteered for four years tour of duty in the U. S. Coast Guard. I completed basic training in Mayport, Florida, and was transferred to New London, Connecticut, to study Marine Gas and Diesel Engineering. This school earned me a position of Lifeboat Station in Puget Sound, Washington. I was there when the Korean Conflict started. His main duties were to keep all our assigned boat engines, diesel and gas, operational. With the help of two personnel, we managed to keep our boats operational and patrol the beaches at night. The station at Neah Bay was manned with a nine man crew normally and we performed all duties, to man lookout tower with radar and telephone switchboard, operate lifeboats, patrol boats as needed and was on duty 24 hours per day for seven days and then, off one day. This station was isolated duty. I was discharged from the U. S. Coast Guard in August 1951. The threat of the cold war spreading to Europe with a major threat of a hot war decided the U. S. to rebuild its dismantled military. The rebuilding of the USAF, offered an opportunity to join the expansion. I enlisted in the Air Force in March 1952, and joined the 20th Fighter Bomber Wing that was programmed to go to England. We arrived in Wethersfield, England, in May 1952. The "Russian Threat" to enslave Europe was great at that time and the 20th Fighter Bomber Wing's mission was to deter that possibility. The normal tour there for a single person was three years. During my duty there, I met an English girl and later, we were married. I returned to the States in 1956 and was stationed at Stewart Air Force Base near Nashville, Tennessee. The English girl, Bernardine Smith, came to the U. S. in September 1956 and we were married 22 September 1956 in Waynesboro, Tennessee. In 1960 I was transferred to a missile training base in Orlando, Florida. Then, in 1963 an Air Force division was formed in Tampa at McDill Air Force to prepare and train for combat duty in Vietnam. I was assigned to the division to help develop and prove the Ground Support Equipment for the new Air Force Fighter, F4C aircraft. The fighter division was deployed to Vietnam in December 1965 and I was left behind to retire from service effect 1 February 1966, and was placed on the Reserve Register. His military service consisted of a total of 34 years active and reserve time from August 1942 to 1 February 1976, and I performed duty with the U. S. Merchant Marine, Army, Coast Guard and Air Force. I have three sisters and one brother living as of this writing; Bettye, Celia, Carolyn and Albert Cordell, and one sister, Ida

Newell, deceased. I have six children; Lorna, Michael Neil, Sonia, Tania and Gloria and Stephen Craig in that order. All of my children attended college. Two work in Dallas, one in Nashville, one in Knoxville and the two boys work in Columbia. I have four grandchildren as of this writing, 21 February 1995.

Submitted by Thomas Schmittou, 250 T. Schmittou Road, Hohenwald, TN 38462.

SCOTT, ALF, enlisted with the 83rd and served in the European Theater. He was wounded in Belgium. Alf Scott is the son of John Harrison and Flora Bryant Scott, His siblings are John Harrison, Jr., Ray of New Albany, Indiana, Charles Edward of Waynesboro, Mary Boaz of Sebring, Florida and Myrtle Bratcher of Waynesboro. He married June Lindsey and they have two children; Alfred and Ann Scott. Alf is deceased. June still resides in Wayne County.

SCOTT, CARL E., was born on February 23, 1922, in Napier, Tennessee. He lived in Collinwood, Tennessee, and worked for the Railroad Company when he entered the United States Army Air Force on June 8, 1943, at Ft. Oglethorpe, Georgia. He served in the Rome-Arno Battle and was awarded the World War II Victory Medal, American Theater Ribbon, EAMET with one Bronze Star and Good Conduct Ribbon. He was discharged on November 23, 1945, in Maxwell Field, Alabama. He was with the 544th Army Air Force Base working as an auto equipment operator.

SCOTT, CHARLIE E., Serial Number 34 361 787, was a Technician Fourth Grade in Company C, 306th Infantry Battalion Engineer of the United States Army. When inducted 25 July 1942 in Fort Oglethorpe, Georgia, his permanent address was Cypress Inn, Tennessee. Civilian occupation was automobile repairman. His education consisted of 8 years in grammar school. He was registered with the Local Selective Service Board in Waynesboro, Wayne County, Tennessee. His Military occupation Specialty was Construction Carpenter. Military Qualifications - Sharpshooter. His battles and campaigns included Southern Philippine and Western Pacific Islands. His decorations included American Theater Ribbon, Asiatic Pacific Theater Ribbon, Philippine Liberation Ribbon, Good Conduct Medal, and Victory Medal. He left the USA 2 June 1944 for the South West Pacific Area and returned 1 December 1945. He was discharged on 16 December 1945 at Fort Bliss, Texas. Sergeant Scott was a member of Major General Paul J Mueller's 71st

Infantry, "Wildcat: Division, which occupied Aomori, Prefecture Northern Honshu. Charlie, son of Velma Scott of Cypress Inn, was born 6 November 1911 in Cypress Inn.

SCOTT, JAKE E., Serial Number 34 373 151, was a Technician Fifth Grade in 825th Engineer Aviation Battalion in the Army of the United States. His permanent mailing address was Route 3, Iron City, Tennessee. He was born 14 October 1911 in Nixon, Tennessee. He was married with one dependent when he entered service. He was registered with the Selective Service Board in Wayne County, Tennessee. His Civilian Occupation was Sheet Metal Worker. His Military Occupational Specialty was Pioneer 729. He was not in any battles. The following decorations were awarded to Scott: American Theater Ribbon, European-African Middle Eastern Theater Ribbon. Good Conduct Medal, and World War II Victory Medal. He left the USA 5 May 1943 for the European-African Middle Eastern Theater Operation, and returned to USA 27 December 1945. His education consisted of 8 years in grammar school and one sixth year of college. He was discharged 4 January 1946 at Fort Knox, Kentucky.

SCOTT, JOHN HARRISON, JR., was born on Indian Creek in Wayne County TN to John Harrison Scott and Flora Emmeline Bryant on 6 May 1923. He was raised on Indian Creek and attended school in the Three Churches Community. He then attended Collinwood High School, graduating 02 April 1943. He worked on the family farm throughout the time he attended school.

He joined the service on 12 March 1944 and was assigned to Camp Fanning, TX for a seventeen week basic training period. Soon after his induction into the Army he was sent to Camp Kilmer, NJ and was shipped overseas in August 1944. As a Staff Sergeant, he served with the Company L lOth Infantry Regiment, 5th Division in Scotland, England, France, Germany, Luxemburg, Austria, and Czechoslovakia.

Landing at Glasgow, Scotland, he was sent by train to England where he remained for two weeks in a replacement center. Sent to France in September, he joined the 5th Infantry Division who were waiting for replacements after having just crossed the Moselle River. The attack on the heavily fortified Metz followed. The conquering armies had taken a city that had never known defeat.

Sent to the Bulge to stem the German December counteroffensive, Staff Sergeant Scott participated in the hazardous crossing of the Sauer River. The crossing was effective only after assault boats had run

through a hail of mortar, machine gun, and artillery fire. Staff Sergeant Scott received many medals during his time in the service.

He received the Award of the Bronze Star:

'For distinctive heroism in connection with military operations against the enemy on 9 January 1945 near Bettendort Germany. As a member of a raiding party that was detailed to gather enemy information and capture enemy personnel for interrogation purposes, Sergeant Scott, a squad leader, displayed supreme courage and initiative in the face of enemy automatic and small arms fire. By his utter fearlessness, individual heroic actions and alert attention to coordination with his leaders and comrades, the patrol was enabled to complete its mission and return to its own lines without suffering loss or injury of a single man. Sergeant Scott's dauntless determination during this daringly executed mission was vitally important in securing of invaluable information which was subsequently utilized in a successful large-scale attack."

John was finally discharged on 24 January 1946 at Fort Knox, KY. He returned home to spend time with his family before going into the service again from 01 October 1946 to 16 September 1949. During that time, he resided in Anchorage, Alaska where he met a future business associate from Memphis TN. John left the service in 1949 to find work in the private sector.

He met and married Lena Kriegisch while in Pennsylvania. They were married on 26 February 1953 in luka, MS. They resided in Savannah, TN where he worked for Hassell Lumber Company with his father, John Sr. Their first child, John Harrison Scott III was born on 06 July 1954.

After moving to Memphis and working with his friend from Alaska until 1959, the family moved to Johnsonburg, PA. On 25 February 1961, their daughter Mary Ann Scott, was born- John and his family lived there from 1959 to 1966, when they decided to move to Dallas, TX and he went to work again with his friend from Alaska.

John retired in 1975 and enjoyed great times fishing, the outdoors, sports, traveling, and so on. He returned to Waynesboro often to visit his family and friends who resided in the area. He spoke often of his adventures during WWII and Alaska. After many years battling arthritis and problems with his leg, John passed away in his home on 07 May 1995, one day after his 72nd birthday. He was laid to rest in Calvary Hill Mausoleum in Dallas, TX He has been solely missed by his family and friends over the years.

SCOTT, LEANDER, Serial Number 34 022 581, was a Private First Class with Battery D, 101st Antiaircraft Artillery Automatic Weapons Battalion in the United

States Army. His permanent mailing address was Collinwood, Tennessee. He was born 12 August 1917 in Wayne County, Tennessee. His Civilian Occupation was General Farm Hand. He was registered with the Selective Service Board No. 1, Waynesboro, Tennessee. He was inducted 25 February 1941 at Fort Oglethorpe, Georgia. His Military Occupational Specialty was Heavy Machine Gunner. His Military Qualifications were MM Rifle, 2nd C1 Gunner. He was in battles in Papua, East Indies and New Guinea Campaign. His decorations included the Good Conduct Ribbon, American Defense Service Ribbon, Philippine Liberation Ribbon, Unit Citation, Asiatic-Pacific Service Ribbon with four Bronze Stars, and American Theater Ribbon. He left the USA 18 February 1942 for the Asiatic Pacific Theater and returned home 21 January 1945. He was honorably discharged 29 June 1945 at Fort McPherson, Georgia.

SCOTT, RICHARD L., was born on December 24, 1927, in Allens Creek, Tennessee. He lived in Collinwood, Tennessee, and worked as a detail assembler, when he received his notice for induction into the United States Army on June 16, 1943, at Ft. Oglethorpe, Georgia. He served with the 1442nd Ordinance Service and Maintenance Company and attended Automotive Mechanics Schools. He was in the battle at Rome Arno and received the following citations: World War II Victory Medal, European African Middle Eastern Theater Ribbon with one Bronze Service Star and Good Conduct Medal.

SCOTT, ROY, was born March 3, 1916 on Indian Creek in Wayne County, TN. His parents were John Harrison and Flom

Bryant Scott. His siblings were: Alf Scott, John H. Scott, Jr., Bill Ray Scott, Charles E. (Hoover) Scott, Myrtle Scott Bratcher, Mary Scott Boaz (deceased.)

Roy attended schools at Indian Creek, Three Churches and Collinwood High School graduating in 1936.

Roy entered military service on December 14, 1940, at Ft. McPherson, GA. After three months of basic training he was assigned duty in the Army Air Corp at MacDill Field in Tampa, FL. He attended six months training in aircraft engine mechanics at Long Island, NY, and one month training at Merlin Roll Royce Engines.

He departed the states August 6, 1942 for England where he was assigned to Bovington Air Base, 8th Air Force and other Air Bases in England. He performed service on B-17s, B-24s, Cargo Planes, etc. He returned to the states on September 26, 1944 and was stationed at Bowman Field, Louisville, KY. He met Mary M. Landers on November of 1944 in Louisville. They married April 21, 1945.

His military service includes: Air Offensive in Europe and the Middle East. He was honorably discharged at Maxwell Field, AL, on October 13, 1945

Roy received the following medals: Good Conduct Medal, two Bronze Stars, Meritorious Service Award.

Roy and Mary had a daughter, Peggy Sue Scott Canter. Peggy's children consist of one daughter, Lisa Michelle Canter who married Jeffrey Lopp. They have the following children: Kristen Nicole and Erika Danielle Lopp. Peggy's son, Kevin Scott Canter married Heather Stouffer.

Roy and Mary also have a son, James Ray Scott who married Connie Joe Carter. They have a son, James Carter Scott, Jr. He married Jennifer Chesser. They have two children - Christopher Carter Scott and Cara Nicole Scott.

SEALS, THOMAS J., Serial Number 44 040 726, was a Private First Class with the 397th Infantry Regiment in the Army of the United States. His permanent mailing address was Waynesboro, Tennessee. He was born 22 August 1920 in Wayne County, Tennessee. He was married when he was inducted 31 August 1944 at Fort Oglethorpe, Georgia. He was registered with the Selective Service Board in Wayne County, Tennessee. His Civilian Occupation was Planner Operator. His Military Occupational Specialty was Packing Case Maker. His Military Qualification was Combat Infantryman Badge and Rifle Sharpshooter. The battles and campaigns that he participated in were: Rhineland, and Central Europe. Decorations and citations were: European-African Middle Eastern Theater Ribbon W/2 Bronze Stars, Good Conduct Medal, Purple Heart, and World War II Victory Medal. He was wounded in action in Germany 14 April 1945. He left the USA 24 January 1945 for the European-African Middle Eastern Theater Op-

eration, and returned to USA 26 Mar 1946. His education consisted of 7 years in grammar school. He was discharged 31 March 1946 at Camp Atterbury, Indiana.

SELPH, EDWARD ABE, Private First Class, of Clifton is with Company L, 393rd Infantry, 99th Infantry Division, 3rd United States Army in Germany. He and his buddies of the Checkerboard Division played leading roles in toppling Hitler's Fortress Germany. While with General Courtney Hodges' First U. S. Army, the soldiers of the 99th helped storm through the Seigfried Line, then across the Cologne Plain, and were the first infantry division of the First Army to bring its forces up to the Rhine. After crossing the famed river, and participating in cleaning out the Ruhr pocket, the 99th was transferred to General George Patton's Third Army and assisted in the final grand-slam drive across the Danube to the heart of Bavaria. Private First Class Selph married Clara Bell Snodgrass of Clifton. They had one daughter, Peggy Sue Selph Lay and one grandson, Joe Edward Lay.

SELTZER, JOEL B. "JACK", P. F. C., served in Patton's 3rd Army. He was sent to England, France and Germany, serving as combat engineer. He was born on February 14, 1914, the son of William Lewis and Fannie McCoy Seltzer. William Lewis was a son of a German immigrant. Jack could speak the German language, which was a helpful tool to carry with him over there. He remained "over there" until the war was over. On his return home, he worked with Kloss Lumber Business. He enjoyed making articles out of wood. Rearing his family, he made a small wagon, which his boys enjoyed very much. Jack married Mary Lillian Northcutt, daughter of Will Northcutt and Sarah Lee Prater Northcutt. They had five children: Joel, James, Tommy, William Lewis (Louie) and Brenda. His siblings are Robert, Tom, Mathie, Aaron and Arthur.

SEVIER, JOE H., JR., son of J. H. and Inez Deford Sevier, was born in 1923. He was a native of Savannah and was educated in the public schools in Savannah. He furthered his education at the University of Tennessee at Knoxville. Joe served his country during World War II with the United States Air Corp and OSS in China. After the war he and his wife, Jane, moved to Waynesboro as owners and operators of the Western Auto Store. Their only child, Betsy, grew up in Waynesboro. Immediately, Joe became involved in the civic, school and community activities of Waynesboro. He was a key figure in the development of Lions Field, served as mayor for five years, was instrumental in

bringing several new industries to the community, and helped create Hurricane Hills subdivision. Jane Vaughn Sevier died in an automobile accident while Betsy was still a small child. Several years later in the early 1970s, Joe and Ruby Beckham Watson were married. Joe died suddenly on October 13, 1996, the victim of an apparent heart attack and is buried in Wayne County Memorial Garden.

SHARP, JAMES K., Serial Number 34 936 455, was a Technician Fifth Grade in 13th Ordnance Maintenance Company in the Army of the United States. His permanent mailing address was Route 6, Waynesboro, Tennessee. He was born 20 February 1926 in Wayne County. He was registered with the Selective Service Board in Wayne County, Tennessee. His Civilian Occupation was General Farmer. He was inducted 28 July 1944 at Camp Forrest, Tennessee. His Military Occupational Specialty was Light Truck Driver. His Military Qualifications included Rifle MKM, and Combat Infantry Badge. He was in the battles of Rhineland, and Central Europe. The following decorations were awarded to Sharp: European-African Middle Eastern Theater Ribbon with 2 Bronze Stars, Good Conduct Ribbon, World War II Victory Medal and Army of Occupation Medal. He left the USA 31 January 1945 for the European Theater Operation, and returned to USA 20 January 1946. He was discharged 25 June 1946 at Camp Atterbury, Indiana.

SHARPE, WILLIAM T., was a member of the U. S. S. St. Louis crew. He was a Seaman First Class, U. S. N. R. from Waynesboro, Tennessee.
Source: Wayne County News, 14 December 1945.

SHARPE, WILSON, Serial Number 34 936 646, was a Private First Class in Company F, 203rd ITB in the Army of the United States. His original unit was Head-

quarters 15th Infantry. His permanent mailing address was Route 6, Waynesboro, Tennessee. He was registered with the Selective Service Board in Wayne County, Tennessee. His Civilian Occupation was General Farmer. He was inducted 7 August 1944 at Fort Oglethorpe, Georgia. He was in the battles of Nurenberg, Augsberg, Munich, Salzburg, Rhineland, and Central Europe. He left the USA from New York 24 January 1945 for the European Theater Operation, and returned to USA as Military Police 28 June 1946. He was discharged 3 July 1946 at Fort George C. Meade in Maryland. After his discharge, Wilson worked in manufacturing plants in Nashville for five years. Then, he moved to Hohenwald and operated his own business in furniture, upholstery, selling appliances, doing automobile repair as well as operating a filling station. He continued in that business until he retired 35 years later. Wilson, son of Crowell and Pauline McCurry Sharpe, was born 10 May 1923 in Wayne County. His grandparents were James L. and Martha D. Whitwell Sharpe and Columbus Mills and Mary Elizabeth Fox McCurry. His sisters: Martha Delila Sharpe Turnbow and Eloise Sharpe, deceased. Wilson married 27 February 1944, Dorothy Sue Robnett. Their children are: David Wilson Sharpe, plant manager of Lincoln Brass Works in Waynesboro and Nancy Robnett Sharpe Strawbridge, a member of the Macon, Georgia Symphony and a music teacher in Atlanta, Georgia.

SHAW, BOB, son of Joe Denton and Mary Lizzie Warren Shaw was born 27 June 1912. He entered active service 23

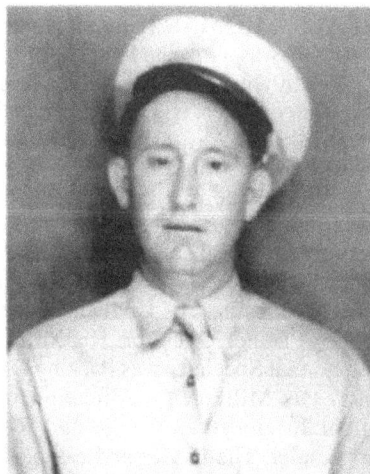

May 1942. He served in Battery D, 634th Antiaircraft Automatic Battalion in the Army of the United States as a machine gunman under General Patton. His first active service was the invasion of North Africa, then, later serving in Algeria-French Morocco, Tunisia, Sicily, Naples-Foggia, Rome-Arno, Rhineland, Southern

France and Central Europe. He completed his service in Austria. The following decorations were awarded to Shaw: European-African Middle Eastern Theater Ribbon with 8 Bronze Stars and Bronze Arrowhead, and Good Conduct Ribbon. His length of service was 3 years, 4 months and 16 days with 2 years, 11 months and 20 days being foreign service. He was discharged 8 October 1946. Bob died 29 January 1997 in Lawrenceburg and was buried in Warren Cemetery. He was survived by two nieces.

SHAW, WALTER J., "I was born 10 November 1919, to William Walter and Elizabeth Shaw. We lived in the Eagle

Creek Community of Wayne County. I have one sister, Hazel Cole. I was married to Mary Nell Phillips, deceased, and I have two children, Janelle and Ronald Shaw. I have seven grandchildren and one great grandchild. I am presently married to Dorothy Berry Lee of Collinwood. Dorothy has two children, Dianna McWilliams and Jimmy Lee. She has four grandchildren. I volunteered for the army on 11 July 1944. I took basic training at Camp Blanding, Florida. From there I was shipped out of New York harbor, to Scotland, England on the Queen Elizabeth, then, on to the front lines in Germany as a replacement soldier. I was wounded in the Battle of the Bulge in the Ardennes Forrest I received a battle star and Purple Heart. I was discharged in July 1945. I served with the 94th Division of the 3rd Army with General George Patton."
Submitted by W. J. Shaw.

SHELBY, JAMES C., He was born 4 December 1906, died 2 January 1966 and is buried in Pinhook Cemetery in Lutts. He was a Private First Class with Company B, 21st England ABN in the Army of the United States during World War II.

SHELBY, LEONARD W., son of Mrs.

Mary I Shelby of R#2, Lutts, TN, was wounded in the Pacific Theater of Operations, according to the, May 25, 1945, issue of The Wayne County News.

SHELTON, JAMES M., of Collinwood,, TN, enlisted in the U. S. Navy and served as, radioman, second class. Shelton was one of the crew who helped 'with the surrender of the Japanese submarine J- 14 and brought her into Tokyo Bay.

SHEPHERD, CLIFFORD, Cpl., son of Mr. and Mrs. C. E. Shepherd of Cypress Inn, entered the service 14 April 1941. He was stationed for two and one-half years in Mississippi before being ordered overseas.

SHEPHERD, C.J., Private First Class, son of Mr. and Mrs. C. E. Shepherd of Cypress Inn, entered the service 20 March 1943. He received his basic training at Fort Bragg, North Carolina, before being transferred to overseas duty in 1944. He was active in France, Holland and Belgium, as a member of the 9th Army.

SHEPHERD, EUGENE, son of Mr. and Mrs. C. E. Shepherd of Cypress Inn, of the U. S. Navy entered the service 18 August 1943. He received his basic training at Great Lakes Illinois and was assigned to overseas duty in November 1944. He was stationed for a time in Australia and then, was transferred to New Guinea.

SHEPHERD, IRA B., Sgt., Waynesboro, was with the 15th AAF in Italy B-24 Liberator Bombardment Group. He helped build a winter home for his group with the aid of the Italian civilian labor.

SHERRILL, EDWARD, Private, entered the service 24 November 1944 and took his training at Camp Blanding,

Florida. He served in the 9th Infantry Division, 34th Field Artillery. He was awarded the Expert Rifleman Badge. Ed-

ward Sherrill, son of Clay Henry and Effie Foster Sherrill, died 22 April 1993 in St. Thomas Hospital in Nashville, and was buried in the Cromwell Crossroads Church Cemetery. His siblings include: Lonzo and Paul, both of Collinwood, Will, Reacel and Clay Sherrill, Jr., all of Waynesboro. He married Mae Tilly and they had two sons, Charles of Waynesboro and Kenneth of Collinwood.

SHERRILL, ELZO, was in the Army of the United States during World War II. He was registered with the Selective Ser-

vice Board in Wayne County, Tennessee. He was inducted September 1942 and had his army training in Camp Wheeler, Georgia, Battle Creek, Michigan, and San Francisco, California. He served in the South Pacific as a Military Police. His occupation after his discharge was heavy equipment operator. Elzo Sherrill, son of Clay Henry and Effie Foster Sherrill, was born in 1921 in South Wayne County, died 2 April 1993 in St. Thomas Hospital in Nashville, and was buried in the Overton Memorial Gardens in Livingston, Tennessee. His siblings include: Edward, Lonzo and Paul, of Collinwood, Will, and Reacel Sherrill, both of Waynesboro, and Clay Sherrill, Jr., of Clifton. He married Merl Sherrill and they had one daughter, Carolyn Sherrill Lineberry of Clifton and three grandchildren and two great-grandchildren.

SHERRILL, GEORGIA S., Serial Number 34 983 727, was a Technician Fifth Grade in 728th Engineer Depot Company in the Army of the United States. His permanent mailing address was Route 1, Lutts, Tennessee. He was born 28 November 1909 in Florence, Alabama. He was registered with the Selective Service Board in Wayne County, Tennessee. His Civilian Occupation was General Farmer. He was married with two dependents when he was inducted 18 Mar 1944 in Camp Shelby, Mississippi. His Military Occupational

Specialty was Cook. His Military Qualifications included Marksman Carbine. He was not in any battles. The following decorations were awarded to Sherrill: World War II Victory Medal, Good Conduct Ribbon and Philippine Liberation Ribbon. He left the USA 25 October 1944 for the American Field and returned to USA 28 March 1946. He was discharged 12 April 1946 at Camp Chaffee Arkansas.

SHERRILL, LONZO, Serial Number 34 713 891, was drafted 30 April 1943 and served in the Third Army, 565 Anti-Air-

craft Artillery Automatic Weapons Battalion of the United States in Europe during World War II. He was registered with the Selective Service Board in Wayne County, Tennessee. Lonzo Sherrill, son of Clay Henry and Effie Foster Sherrill, was born in the South Wayne County. His siblings include: Edward, and Paul, of Collinwood, Will, and Reacel Sherrill, both of Waynesboro, Clay Sherrill, Jr., of Clifton and Elzo, deceased.

SHERRILL, ROY D., Serial Number 34 886 113, was a Private First Class in Company R, 231 Armored Infantry Battalion in the Army of the United States. His

permanent mailing address was Waynesboro, Tennessee. He was registered with the Selective Service Board in Wayne County, Tennessee. His Civilian Occupation was Farmer. He was married with three dependents when he entered into active service 26 October 1943. His Military Occupational Specialty was Light Mortar Crewman. He was in the battles of Northern France, Rhineland, and Central Europe. The following decorations were awarded to Sherrill: European-African Middle Eastern Theater Ribbon with 3 Bronze Stars, Good Conduct Ribbon and Purple Heart. He was wounded in action in Germany 2 November 1944. He left the USA 16 July 1944 for the European Theater Operation, and returned to USA 10 October 1945. He had a high school education. He was discharged 15 October 1945 at Camp Atterbury, Indiana. Roy, son of Mr. and Mrs. Jessie Sherrill of Lutts, was born 6 July 1916 in Waynesboro. He married Bonnie Haddock and they had two daughters who live in Waynesboro.

SHULL, DON, Private First Class, son of Mrs. Virgie T. Shull, Route 1, Waynesboro, was awarded the order of the Purple

Heart for wounds received in action on Luzon Island. He has now returned to duty with his unit. He had served overseas several months before he was wounded. Shull was engaged in farming before entering the service.

Source: Wayne County News.

SHULL, WILLIAM LEO, son of Jack and Virgie Shull, was born on November 5, 1912, in the Hardin Creek community and grew up there. He attended school in Waynesboro, and then married Della Devers. They moved to Kannapolis, North Carolina, where he worked as a pipefitter. They have two children, Ronnie and Cynthia. Leo was inducted into the United States Army on August 7, 1943, at Ft. Bragg, North Carolina. The first few

months he served as a cook, and then transferred to Company L, 116th Infantry and sent to the European Theatre where he was wounded on August 5, 1944, in the Battle of Normandy. After several months in the hospital, he was discharged on April 20, 1945, at Welch Convalescent Hospital at Daytona Beach, Florida, and returned to his home in North Carolina. He was awarded the European African Middle Eastern Theater Medal, Good Conduct Ribbon and Purple Heart. Leo died on November 3, 1989, and is buried in Kannapolis.

SIMMONS, BUFORD, was born 30 Mar 1919, died 21 January 1960 and is buried in Railroad Cemetery located at the Northeast corner of the intersection of Tennessee Highway 227 and 13 South in the Fairview Community. He was a S2 in the USNR during World War II.

SIMMONS, CLIFFORD D., served in the Army during World War II and was in the Invasion of Normandy. He was wounded in service. He married Mauveline Hays. Clifford's siblings are: Wayne Simmons, Ruby Martin, Della Mills, Gertie Faires, Kathleen Holt and Earline Hinton.

SIMMONS, DOIL W., Serial Number 34 886 121, was a Private First Class in the 380th Ordnance Medium Automatic Maintenance Company in the Army of the United States. His permanent mailing address was Route 2, Collinwood, Tennessee. He was born 2 July 1923 in Cypress Inn, Tennessee. He was registered with the Selective Service Board in Wayne County, Tennessee. His Civilian Occupation was General Farmer. He was inducted 5 October 1943 and entered into active service 26 October 1943 at Fort Oglethorpe, Georgia. His Military Occupational Specialty was Light Truck Driver. His Military Qualifications included Marksman Rifle. He was in the battles of Luzon. The following decorations were awarded to Sim-

mons: World War II Victory Medal, American Theater Ribbon, Asiatic-Pacific Theater Ribbon with 1 Bronze Service Star, and Philippine Liberation Ribbon. He left the USA 28 February 1945 for the Asiatic-Pacific Theater Operation, and returned to USA 28 March 1946. He was discharged 4 April 1946 at Camp Chaffee, Arkansas.

SIMMONS, JAMES H., Serial Number 34 495 061, was a Private First Class in 136th Station Hospital in the Army of

the United States. His permanent mailing address was Route 2, Iron City, Tennessee. He was registered with the Selective Service Board in Wayne County, Tennessee. His Civilian Occupation was General Farmer. He was married when he was inducted 22 November 1942 and entered into active service 29 November 1942 at Fort Oglethorpe, Georgia. His Military Occupational Specialty was Military Policeman. He was not in any battles. The following decorations were awarded to Simmons: American Theater Ribbon, European-African Middle Eastern Theater Ribbon, Good Conduct Ribbon and World War II Victory Medal. He left the USA 9 March 1945 for the European Theater Operation, and returned to

USA 19 February 1946. He was discharged 24 February 1946 at Camp Atterbury, Indiana. James, son of Mr. and Mrs. H. T. Simmons, was born 18 June 1921 in Wayne County. He married Bernice Simmons.

SIMS, MILBURN KING, was born in Wayne County on October 13, 1919, to Lester and Lela Nowlin Sims. Milburn attended school in Waynesboro where he met Frankie Beckham who later became his wife.

From June 1937 to April 1943, he assisted in the management of Sims Cafe on the square in Waynesboro. Also, he worked as a local land surveyor.

With the advent of World War 11, he was inducted into the Army Air Force on April 23, 1943. He received his basic training in Miami Beach and then transferred to Camp Lee, VA where he attended ASF Technical School to receive training in Kitchen Management.

After this assignment, he went to Jefferson Barracks in St., Louis, MO, for additional training. In January of 1944, he received his final assignment to Puerto Rico. Here, he performed duties with Army Airborne Squadron. A supervised a mess hall serving approximately 800 men per meal as well as a transient personnel facility serving over 900 men per meal. On March 19, 1946, at Fort McPherson, GA, Milburn received an honorable discharge from the armed services.

He returned to Waynesboro where he and his wife took over the family business. They soon opened a new restaurant and motel on Highway 64 west and called it Sims Motor Lodge. They operated this business until their retirement. The couple had one daughter, Janice Sims Cole.

Milburn passed away November 2, 1993.

SINCLAIR, GEORGE GRADY, Serial Number 34 723 008, entered the service 27 February 1943 in Fort Oglethorpe, Georgia, and took his basic training at Fort Bliss, Texas. He was assigned to the Unit Battery B 483rd Anti-Aircraft Artillery Automatic Weapons Battalion. The 483rd Anti-Aircraft Artillery left the United States from Fort Lewis, Washington 16 January 1944 on the "USS GRANT" and arrived in Hawaii, 24 June 1944. We were constantly on the move, on 24 August 1944, our destination was the Guadalcanal. After a few days, we moved on to destination unknown on the "USS LaSALLE" and arrived on Anguar 17 September 1944 for our first combat mission. We left here 20 October 1944 for the Island of Ulithie for a period of rest and relaxation. Leaving here on the USS LST 121 for our second combat mission 7 February 1945, we arrived on Saipan and moved on and around the waters of Iwo Jima on 14 February 1945. The Marines invaded the Island 19 February 1945. The 483rd moved in on the 25th to complete the attack. We left Iwo Jima to return to the State on 26 November 1945 and landed at Long Beach, California. I was discharged 31 December 1945 at Camp Chaffee, Arkansas with the rank of Private First Class. I received the following decorations: World War II Victory Medal, Good Conduct Ribbon, American Theater Ribbon, Asiatic-Pacific Theater Ribbon, and two Bronze Stars. The 483rd has remained in close touch. The men who served this unit, from all over the US have met every year since 1958 for a reunion on the last full weekend in June. The wives join their husbands and enjoy the reunion each year. At present the group meets each year at Henry Horton State Park in Chapel Hill, Tennessee. Grady, son of John Marshall and Bennie Elizabeth Hardin Sinclair, was born 4 June 1923 in Lutts, Tennessee. His brothers were, Hardin Stockard, Louis and Marshall Robert Sinclair. He has one sister, Mary E. Sinclair Beckham. Grady married Imogene Weatherford 9 May 1947, and to this union were born three sons: Bobby Weatherford 6 August 1949, Johnny Malone 25 May 1952 and William Marshall 17 August 1959.

SINCLAIR, LOUIS L., Serial Number 34 040 694, was a Technician Fifth Grade in 168th Military Police Company in the Army of the United States. His permanent mailing address was Route 2, Lutts, Tennessee. He was born 26 December 1911 . He was registered with the Selective Service Board in Wayne County, Tennessee. His Civilian Occupation was General Farmer, where he worked with his father on the family farm, plowed and cultivated the soil and harvested such crops as cotton, corn, wheat, rye, oats and vegetables products. He also tended the animals: cattle, horses, sheep and hogs. He was inducted 3 April 1941. The following decorations were awarded to Sinclair: European-African Middle Eastern Theater Ribbon, Good Conduct Ribbon and Distinguished Unit Badge. He left the USA 21 September 1942 for the European Theater Operation, and returned to USA 27 January 1945. He was discharged 8 October 1945 at Fort Sam Houston, Texas. Louis summarizes his duties as a Military Policeman in the European Theater as follows: "Kept law and order between civilian and military personnel. Saw that only authorized personnel were allowed out in the city and that they stayed away from restricted zones. Saw that military courtesy was complied with. Arrested offenders and wrote up reports. Guarded prisoners of war in their work and in their movements from front to rear positions. Was guard on military installations protecting valuable government property from sabotage."

SINCLAIR, MARSHALL ROBERT, son of John Marshall and Bennie Elizabeth Hardin Sinclair, he was born 22 June 1914 in Lutts, Tennessee, died 12 January 1959 and is buried in Lutts Cemetery. He had four brothers, Hardin, Stockard, Louis and George Grady Sinclair and one sister, Mary

E. Sinclair Beckham. Marshall married Grace Parrish 30 November 1944, and there were no children. Sinclair enlisted in the US Army, on 15 May 1941 in Savannah, Tennessee and was inducted at Fort Oglethorpe, Georgia. He took his basic training in the Air Force at Maxwell Air Force Base in Alabama. Then, later he was stationed at Shaw Field, Sumter, SC, where he was a cook. His rank was Sgt when he was discharged 13 December 1945 at Camp Joseph T. Robinson, Arkansas.

SINER, KENNIE, was born on March 15, 1905, in Wayne County and was a truck driver living at Clifton, Tennessee, when he entered the Army Air Force on May 22, 1942, at Camp Forrest, Tennessee. He served as Corporal with the Detachment of Patients, AAF Regional Hospital in Scott Field, Illinois. Kennie was in the battle at New Guinea and was discharged on April 9, 1945, in Scott Field, Illinois.

SIZEMORE, OTIS H., Serial Number 34 501 376, was a Private First Class in Battery C 476th Antiaircraft Artillery Automatic Weapons Battalion in the Army of the United States. His permanent mailing address was Route 1, Waynesboro, Tennessee. He was registered with the Selective Service Board in Wayne County, Tennessee. His Civilian Occupation was General Farm Hand. His Military Occupational Specialty was Antiaircraft Artillery Automatic Weapons Crewman. His Military Qualifications included Marksman Rifle. He was in the battles of New Guinea and Southern Philippines. The following decorations were awarded to Sizemore: Distinguished Unit Badge, World War II Victory Medal, Good Conduct Ribbon, Asiatic-Pacific Theater Ribbon with 2 Bronze Service Stars, and one Bronze Arrowhead, Philippine Liberation Ribbon and Purple Heart. He was wounded in action in the Asiatic-Pacific Theater 2 June 1944. He left the USA 27 October 1943 for the Asiatic-Pacific Theater Op-

eration, and returned to USA 20 January 1946. He was discharged 5 February 1946 at Camp Chaffee, Arkansas. Otis, son of Robert L. and Hester Sizemore, was born 12 March 1922 in Clifton, Wayne County. He has three sisters: Lela Cody, Lola Collum, and Bernice Gates all of Memphis, Tennessee. He is married to Christine D. Sizemore and has two stepchildren: Mary E Skelton of Omaha, Nebraska, and Hubert McClain of Waynesboro.

SKELTON, CHARLES COOLIDGE, was born on November 24, 1924, in Waynesboro, Tennessee. He was self-employed when he enlisted in the United States Navy on September 2, 1942, in Pulaski, Tennessee. He served as Aviation Machinist Mate Third Class, V6 USNR at USNTC, San Diego, California; USS Cape ESPEVANCE; NAS Alameda-Carrier Aircraft Service Scouting Squadron 58; Flight Air Noumea Pool, New Calejonia; and Acorn. He received the following citations: American Theater, Asiatic-Pacific with three Bronze Stars, Philippine's Liberation with two Bronze Stars and Good Conduct Ribbon.

SKELTON, CHARLIE HENDRIX, was born 17 May 1926, died 4 March 1984, and was buried in Salem Primitive Baptist Church Cemetery in Northern Wayne County. He is the son of Elmer and Fannie Skelton, who are buried in the Skelton Family Cemetery on Moccasin Creek. Charlie married Senia Flippo and to them were born five children: Larry, Randy, Allen, Douglas, and Glenda Skelton. He entered the United States Army on 13 November 1945 with Serial Number 44 040 711 and served until the end of World War II. His main fields of active duty were in Germany and the Philippines. When he was discharged 31 December 1946 at Fort Lewis, Washington, his grade was Technician Fifth Grade in the H/S Det 1907 ASU. After his discharge he worked in Michigan where he retired not to long before he passed away.

SKELTON, DELL, Serial Number 34 501 393, was a Private First Class in Battery C 476th Antiaircraft Artillery Automatic Weapons Battalion in the Army of the United States. His permanent mailing address was Route 4, Waynesboro, Tennessee. He was born 30 August 1922 in Waynesboro. He was registered with the Selective Service Board in Wayne County, Tennessee. His Civilian Occupation was General Farm Hand. He was inducted 20 December 1942 and entered into active service 27 December 1942 at Fort Oglethorpe, Georgia. His Military Occupational Specialty was AA Fire Control Observer.

His Military Qualifications included Marksman Rifle. He was in the battles of New Guinea and Southern Philippines. The following decorations were awarded to Skelton: World War II Victory Medal, Good Conduct Medal, Asiatic-Pacific Theater Ribbon with 2 Bronze Service Stars and one Bronze Arrowhead, Philippine Liberation Ribbon and one Bronze Star and a Distinguished Unit Badge. He left the USA 27 October 1943 for the Asiatic-Pacific Theater Operation, and returned to USA 21 January 1946. He was discharged 28 January 1946 at Camp Chaffee, Arkansas.

SKELTON, EUNICE EMMETT, left Waynesboro on a bus on 15 Mar 1942 for Fort Oglethorpe, Georgia where he entered

the 907 Glider Field Artillery, 101st Airborne Division of the Army of the United States. He served with them for three years. He went to many places such as Normandy, Ardennes, Rhineland, Central Europe. European Africa, France, Holland, Belgium and Germany. While he was here he was in several battles and campaigns and won ribbons, Victory Medals and a Bronze Star. He received an Honorable Discharge 3 December 1945. Eunice, son of Harrison and Zula Copeland Skelton, was born 2

January 1916, and died 18 February 1987 at the age of 71. He has four brothers, Gilbert, Otto, Harlin and Osteen and three sisters, Irene Skelton, Eva Grannas, and Neva Jane Risner. He married Dorothy Mathis and has two sons, Leo and Waymon Skelton. He also has four grandchildren.

SKELTON, GEORGE CLEVELAND, Serial Number 34 194 610, was a Private First Class in Company A, 53rd

Signal Battalion in the Army of the United States. His permanent mailing address was Waynesboro, Tennessee. He was born 12 December 1919. He was registered with the Selective Service Board in Wayne County, Tennessee. His Civilian Occupation was General Farmer. He was single when he was inducted 4 April 1942. His Military Occupational Specialty was Light Truck Driver. He was in the battles of Algeria-French Morocco, Tunisia, Sicily, Po Valley, Naples-Foggia, Rome-Arno, and North Apennines. The following decorations were awarded to Skelton: European-African Middle Eastern Theater Ribbon with 7 Bronze Stars and Good Conduct Ribbon. He left the USA 21 July 1943 for the European Theater Operation, and returned to USA 26 August 1945. He was discharged 30 August 1945 at Camp Atterbury, Indiana. George, son of Wiley and Jennie Skelton, was born 12 December 1919 in Wayne County, died at Veterans Hospital in Nashville on 10 February 1981 and is buried in Memorial Gardens in Waynesboro. He had six brothers and eight sisters. He married Christine Staggs and they had one daughter, Judy Gail.

SKELTON, HOWARD THOMAS, Serial Number 832-68-16, was a Seaman Second Class in the Navy of the United States. His permanent mailing address was Route 3, Waynesboro, Tennessee. He was born 18 May 1924 in Waynesboro. He was registered with the Selective Service Board in Wayne County, Tennessee. His main

Civilian Occupation was Truck Driver. He was inducted 31 March 1943 and entered into active service 7 April 1943 at Waynesboro, Tennessee. He held the ratings of AS and S2C. He completed the following Service Schools: Armed Guard School Shelton, Norfolk, Virginia, and Armed Guard School refresher course. Vessels that he served on were: USNTS Bainbridge in Maryland; Armed Guard Center in Brooklyn, NY, Armed Guard Center in Norfolk, and Armed Guard Center in the Pacific. His last employer before he entered service was C. A. Thompson Construction Clarksville, Tennessee from April to December 1942. He was discharged 12 December 1945 in Memphis, Tennessee.

SKELTON, HOUSTON L., First Sergeant, a 51 year old professional soldier, spent his career mostly at the Chemical Warfare Center at Edgewood Arsenal, Maryland. He was transferred from the infantry to the Chemical Warfare Service in 1920 when it was a new branch of the Army. As a pioneer in that service, he came to Edgewood Arsenal in 1921 and remained there until 1937. He was a native of Tennessee, born at Hohenwald. His many relatives live on Moccasin Creek which runs into Buffalo River in Wayne County, Tennessee. He began his army career with the 7th Division of the 56th Infantry which served overseas in the first World War. He received his first discharge certificate during the demobilization program in 1919. He reenlisted immediately. After leaving Edgewood Arsenal in 1937 he served the CWS in the Panama Canal Department until 1939. He was then assigned to Fort Benning, Georgia. He was there when he enlisted for the ninth time in July 1941. At the beginning of the Second World War, Sergeant Skelton was back at Edgewood Arsenal assigned as First Sergeant to Headquarters Company and this is where he stayed. *"(Source: EVENING SUN, Baltimore, Maryland)*

The following decorations were

awarded to Skelton: nine hash marks adorn his left sleeve, each one signifying three years in the service, two v-shaped overseas chevrons signifying foreign service in World War I. His Military Occupational Specialty was Expert Gunner's Medal for all the Chemical Warfare Center weapons and the Expert Rifleman Medal. Houston married Lucy Nugent in March 1922 in Maryland. They had two children: Dara May lives in Maryland and Huston, Jr., who had a career in the Navy. Huston is the son of Sam M. Skelton (29 August 1860-6 May 1928) and Annie Mathis Skelton (9 January 1865-1945). Huston was born June 1894 in Lewis County, Tennessee, died in Maryland and was buried at Edgewood Arsenal. His siblings are: Barney Skelton (Sgt US Army WWII, 23 December 1892-10 January 1974); Commodore, Arthur, Martha Skelton Whitehead (2 January 1904-14 February 1958), Stella Frazier and Mae Dickey.

SKELTON, JAMES TAYLOR "JIM", celebrated his nineteenth birthday in basic training in the Navy in 1942. Then,

he had duty in the South Pacific. Later he was in the US Regular Army during the Korean Conflict as a Sergeant First Class. He also trained recruits at Fort Knox, KY for two years. Jim was born 21 September 1923 in Wayne County. He is the son of Olien Skelton (b. 2 January 1904) and Dovie McLean Skelton (b. 18 September 1907). Both are buried in the Skelton Family Cemetery on Moccasin Creek, tributary of the Buffalo River. He is now retired and lives in North Las Vegas, Nevada.

SKELTON, KENNIE, Serial Number 34 194 624, was a Private in 186th Quartermaster Depot Company in the Army of the United States. He was born in Barnsville, Mississippi. His Civilian Occupation was Heavy Truck Driver. He was inducted 4 April 1942 at Fort Oglethorpe,

Georgia. His Military Occupational Specialty was Light Truck Driver. He was not in any battles. The following decorations were awarded to Skelton: European-African Middle Eastern Theater Ribbon and Good Conduct Ribbon. He was discharged 16 November 1944 at Fort McPherson, Georgia.

SKELTON, LANDON LEE, son of Amos and Ada Blackwell Skelton, he was born 22 March 1920 in Wayne County, Tennessee. His family included sisters, Esther Mathis, Era Skelton, Adell Bostic, Delia Ray and Hazel Phalen and brothers, Herman, Therman, Sherman and Roland Skelton. Landon was married on 5 October 1946 to Edith Nell Brewer and to them were born three children, Larry Lee, Donald Keith and Ralanda Kay. Ralanda married Edward Toland and they have three children, Jesse Ryan, Kristina Kay and Jennifer Alayne Toland. Prior to going into service Landon was employed doing saw mill and farm work. After he was discharged from service, he went to a trade school on the G. I. Bill. On 26 January 1948, he went to work for the Bureau of Public Roads and was employed by the bureau until their work ceased in 1952. Like so many other men of the time, Landon went to Detroit in search of work and for a few months worked for Detroit Transmissions, but came home stating that he would rather starve at home than work up north. Then he worked for three different construction companies. When the Bureau of Public Works resumed work on the Natchez Trace Parkway, Landon returned to that position and remained with them until his death in November 1962. Landon was inducted into the army on 3 October 1942 at Fort Oglethorpe, Georgia. His Army serial number was 34 375 253. His date of separation was 21 April 1946 at Fort McPherson, Georgia. His Military Qualifications included Expert Rifleman, Carbine Marksman and 2nd class Antitank Gunner. He was awarded the American

Service Medal, World War II Victory Medal, European-African Middle Eastern Theater Ribbon with 1 Bronze Stars, Philippine Liberation Medal, and the Purple Heart for wounds received 2 June 1945 in the Philippine Islands. He served with the 21st Infantry Regiment, 24th Division in the Asiatic Pacific Theater of Operations, as a member of a Rifle Squad. He loaded, aimed and fired a Thompson submachine gun. He concentrated fire upon fixed targets or moving personnel, acted as a foil to draw fire from the enemy and thus to determine their position, worked in advance of troops, always changing position to avoid gunfire. This responsibility required skill at entrenchment and self concealment and the ability to field strip, oil and clean weapons to keep them in first class firing condition. Landon Lee Skelton was a proud soldier, a proud husband and father and proud to be from Wayne County and the great state of Tennessee.

SKELTON, LUTHER W., Serial Number 34 377 054, was a Private First Class in 887th Military Police Company in the Army of the United States. His permanent mailing address was Route 6, Waynesboro, Tennessee. He was born 15 June 1921 in Wayne County. He was registered with the Selective Service Board in Wayne County, Tennessee. His Civilian Occupation was General Farm Hand. He was inducted 13 October 1942 and entered into active service 27 October 1942 at Fort Oglethorpe, Georgia. His Military Occupational Specialty was Cook. He was not in any battles. The following decorations were awarded to Skelton: World War II Victory Medal, European-African Middle Eastern Theater Ribbon, and Good Conduct Ribbon. He left the USA 8 July 1943 for the European-African Middle Eastern Theater Operation, and returned to USA 29 November 1945. He was discharged 7 December 1946 at Fort Knox, Kentucky.

SKELTON, OBIE KIRK, was the sixth child born to Elmer H and Fannie L. Sharp Skelton. He was born in Wayne County on 6 December 1918. He had four brothers: Hooper, Edward "Ed", Charlie and Herbert. He also had five sisters: Irene Frazier, Inez Mathis, Edna Mathis, Jenny Meredith, and Ethel Mae Whitehead. Obie married Bessie Mae Whitehead on 25 December 1937. They had six children: Virgil Kirk, Jimmy Cleveland, Mable Joyce Tuverson, Fannie Loretta Bridges, Nancy Gertrude Langford and Gerald Travis Skelton, all of which were reared in Wayne County. He has fourteen grandchildren. Obie was a farmer before he entered the armed forces. He was inducted into active service on 28 July 1944 at Camp Forrest,

Tennessee. His army serial number is 34 936 450. He served as a Private First Class in Company B, 52nd Armored Infantry Battalion. He served in the European Theater of Operations from 15 January 1945 until 13 October 1945, primarily in Northern France and Germany. He fought in the battles of Ardennes and Rhineland and the Central European Campaign. He received a Combat Infantryman Badge, Rifle Marksman, and European-African Middle Eastern Theater Ribbon with 3 Bronze Stars. Obie sent his wife a letter on 17 July 1945 from Ansback, Germany. From this date until he came home late in October 1945, his family and friends did not know if he were dead or alive. The only information that they had was from a newspaper article they had read which said Obie's unit, 52nd Battalion, had almost been completely wiped out at the crossing of the Rhine River in Germany. After returning home, Obie told of how he probably would have been killed but his feet and legs became so frost bitten that he couldn't walk and he was taken back to the base hospital. He said the frost bite occurred because he was on his knees praying for the good Lord to spare his life. He said after he got out of the hospital, he didn't know anyone because all of the men he served with were killed or wound at the Rhine River. Obie was honorably discharged 19 October 1945 at Camp Atterbury, Indiana. On his way home to his family four months of mail caught up with him and he learned that he had a new baby girl. Obie worked at Genesco for eight years and continued to farm until his death 3 October 1967 with lung cancer. He was buried in the Skelton Family Cemetery in Wayne County. He worked very hard all of his life. He was a good husband and father and we all loved and respected him very much.

SKELTON, ROBERT, oldest son of Henry and Clatey (Morgan) Skelton, was born, February 28, 1926, in Wayne County and attended Wayne County Schools. He was inducted into the U. S. Army and sta-

tioned in Mississippi for his basic training. After his discharge, he went to Michigan to work.

Bob and Louise Keeton, daughter of Floyd and Pearl (Risner) Keeton, were married. They lived in Michigan, where they were both employed, until Bob retired, then they came back to Wayne County and built a home near, Collinwood, TN. They have four daughters, Sandra Sue (Benedict) and Patsy (Stark) of Michigan, Glenda (Moore) and Donna (Daniel) of Collinwood, TN. Bob's siblings are Belle (Folger) Waynesboro, Irene (Smith) Lawrenceburg, TN, Goldie (McLane) 11, Jean (Pollock) and Howard Skelton, Waynesboro and Helen (Terlecki) Michigan.

SKELTON, ROLAND C., Serial Number 34 904 008, was a Private in Company C, 190th Infantry Training Battalion in the Army of the United States. He was born in Wayne County. His Civilian Occupation was Farmer. He was 27 years of age and married when he was inducted. His Military Occupational Specialty was Rifleman. He was not in any battles. He was honorably discharged 23 September 1944 at Camp Blanding, Florida.

SKELTON, SAMUEL H., Serial Number 44 120 525, was a Private in 38th Ordnance Motor Maintenance Company in the Army of the United States. His permanent mailing address was Waynesboro, Tennessee. He was registered with the Selective Service Board in Wayne County, Tennessee. His Civilian Occupation was Ship Electrician. He was inducted 29 May 1945 at Fort Oglethorpe, Georgia. His Military Occupational Specialty was Automotive Mechanic. His Military Qualifications included Expert M-1 Rifle. He was not in any battles. The following decorations were awarded to Skelton: Good Conduct Ribbon, Army Occupation Medal (Italy), European-African Middle Eastern Theater Ribbon, and World War II Victory Medal. He left the USA 29 November 1945 for Italy and returned to USA 26 June 1946. He was discharged 2

July 1946 at Fort George C. Meade in Maryland. Samuel H. Skelton, was born 24 June 1922 in Waynesboro, died 5 March 1980 and was buried in the Skelton Cemetery. His wife was Emma Mae.

SKELTON, SHERMAN F., Serial Number 34 361 757, was a Private in Battery A 745th Field Artillery Battalion in the Army of the United States. He was born 26 January 1914 in Waynesboro. His Civilian Occupation was General Farm Hand. He was 28 years, 6 months of age when he was inducted, His Military Occupational Specialty was Duty Soldier. His Military Qualifications included Rifle MM Carbine. He was not in any battles. He served on active duty from 8 August 1942 until 31 October 1944. He was discharged 31 October 1944 at Fort McPherson, Georgia. He is buried in Swiss Cemetery in Hohenwald where his wife, Geneva, was buried 22 January 1969.

SKELTON, WILLIAM GILBERT, son of William Thomas Harrison and Zeda Belle (Copeland) Skelton, was born in Wayne County, Tennessee on August 26, 1924. He grew up in the Mt. Hope community, along with four brothers (Emmett, Otto, Harlin and Osteen Skelton) and three sisters (Irene Skelton, Eva Skelton Granaas and Neva Jane Skelton Risner). He finished 8th grade at Mt. Hope School. Then graduated High School from Wayne County High in Waynesboro, Tennessee, where he played on the basketball team for four years. He graduated in 1943. He then went into the service in the Coast Guard for four years, and then spent four years in the Navy, stationed in Norfolk, Virginia. He came home from Navy in 1951 and married Ritha Mae Ray. They had five children. He moved to Tullalah, Louisiana, where he was superintendent of a Lumber Mill at the time of his death in 1990. He is buried in Tullalah, Louisiana.

SKILLERN, HARRY A., Serial Number 34 194 613, was a Technician Fifth

Grade in Headquarters and Service Company, 131st Engineer Combat Battalion in the Army of the United States. His permanent mailing address was General Delivery, Collinwood, Tennessee. He was born 13 September 1906 in Waynesboro. He was registered with the Selective Service Board in Wayne County, Tennessee. His Civilian Occupation was Grocery Clerk. He was inducted 4 April 1942 at Fort Oglethorpe, Georgia. His Military Occupational Specialty was Water Supply Technician. He was in the battles of Northern Solomons, and Luzon. The following decorations were awarded to Skillern: Good Conduct Ribbon, Philippine Liberation Ribbon, and one Bronze Star, Asiatic-Pacific Service Ribbon and two Bronze Service Stars. He left the USA 20 October 1942 for the Asiatic-Pacific Theater Operation, and returned to USA 24 September 1945. He was discharged 2 October 1945 at Camp Chaffee, Arkansas. Private First Class Harry Skillern, son of Mr. and Mrs. T. A. Skillern of Collinwood, entered the service 3 April 1942 and took his basic training at Camp Shelby, Mississippi and Fort Ord, California. Private First Class Skillern has served in New Guinea, New Caledonia, Boganville, and in the Philippines serving as an engineer. Before entering service he was employed by the Vultee Aircraft Company in Nashville. He is a brother of Pvt. Paul Skillern recently liberated from a Japanese prison camp.

SMELSER, LESLIE C., was born on January 7, 1925, in Alabama and was living near Waynesboro, Tennessee, farming when he received his notice for induction into the United States Army on August 31, 1944, at Ft. Oglethorpe, Georgia. He served with Company K, 406th Infantry Regiment in England, France, Belgium, Holland and Germany. He participated in battles of the Rhineland and Central Europe with Bronze and Silver Stars. He received the World War II Victory Ribbon and EAMET Ribbon. He was discharged on November 16, 1945, in New York. He reenlisted on November 17, 1945, in Germany. He was a Corporal with the 1600th Motor Vehicle Squadron and worked as an automotive mechanic. Three years later, on November 16, 1948, he was discharged at Westover Air Force Base, Massachusetts. He was awarded the Army of Occupation Medal (Germany).

SMITH, ARTHUR WILSON, Serial Number 34 987 501, was a Private First Class in Company L, 335th Infantry in the Army of the United States. His permanent mailing address was Route 3, Lutts, Tennessee. He was registered with the Selective Service Board in Wayne County, Tennessee. His Civilian Occupation was circular saw operator at a sawmill. He was

inducted 11 April 1943 at Camp Shelby, Mississippi. His Military Occupational Specialty was Rifleman. His Military Qualifications included MM Rifle. He was in the battle of Ardennes. The following decoration were awarded to Smith: European-African Middle Eastern Theater Ribbon with 1 Bronze Star. He left the USA 12 December 1944 for the European Theater Operation, and returned to USA 9 March 1945. While serving overseas, his feet froze. He was discharged 26 August 1945 at Fort McPherson, Georgia. Arthur W. Smith, son of Lewis Franklin and Ruthie Tittle Smith, was born 21 September 1919 in Collinwood, and died 10 September 1988 at St. Thomas Hospital in Nashville and was buried in Lutts Cemetery, Lutts, Tennessee. He married Velma Robbins and they had three children: Thomas, Smitty and Janette and six grandchildren: Patrick, Penny, Brian, Michelle, T H. and Eric. He attended school in Collinwood. After leaving service, he returned to Collinwood where he worked at a sawmill until he retired in 1981.

(Editor's Note: This was a very bad xerox copy and may have errors.).

SMITH, CARNELL "RABBIT", . son of Ed and Eddie Pearl White Smith, was born on May 8, 1926, near Collinwood, Tennessee. He is married and has three children: Randy, Rhonda and Mike. Carnell was inducted into the United States Army on July 27, 1944, in Tullahoma, Tennessee, and served as a light truck driver. In December 1945, he was discharged and continued truck driving as his occupation. He is now semi-retired living in Savannah.

SMITH, CECIL EDWARD, son of William Louis and Myrtle Fitzpatrick Smith, was born 30 October 1919. He was inducted into the United States Horse Calvary at Fort Riley, Kansas, 4 October 1941. After a few months the Horse Calvary was being phased out, so he transferred to the Eight Air Force in Tacoma, Washington.

Most of his two years in the States were spent at Drew Field Air Force Base near Tampa, Florida with the Ninth Air Force. In October 1943 he was transferred to England and spent the next two years in the European Theater of Operations. He was discharged from the Ninth Air Force on 12 November 1945. Cecil married Frances Devers in 1943 and they have two sons and a daughter. He continued living in Wayne County.

SMITH, C.W., JR., son of Clinton W. Smith, Sr., and Gladys Irene Bell Smith, was born 2 June 1922. One younger brother, Hoyt O. Smith, was a Navy Veteran of the Korean War. C. W., Jr., married Norma Gallaher of Collinwood, in April 1950. He has one stepdaughter, Sara. C. W., Jr., also had four uncles who were in the U. S. Navy in World War II: Gaston Bell, Raymond Bell, James White Bell and Dwight Bell. C. W., Jr., graduated from Collinwood High School in 1939, Vanderbilt University with a BA in 1950 and a MA in 1951. He also attended UCI, UCLA, Whittier College, USC, Cal State in Fullerton and Cal State in Long Beach. Smith, another Tennessee Volunteer, joined the Navy 11 June 1940 and was honorably discharged 10 June 1946 with the Rate of Gunner's Mate First Class. The following decorations were awarded to Smith: American Campaign with 1 Battle Star, European-African Middle Eastern Theater Ribbon, American Defense, Asiatic Pacific Campaign with 4 Battle Stars (Guadalcanal-Rendova Area) 2, Good Conduct Ribbon, Purple Heart (Air raid shrapnel in left knee, Rendova Island), Navy Medal, Navy Achievement Medal (Gunnery Instructor of the Year, 1944), Navy Expert Rifle Shot, Navy Expert Pistol Shot, Navy Distinguished Pistol Shot, Naval Reserve Medal, Naval Reserve Meritorious Service Medal, UDC Cross of Military Combat WWII, and World War II Victory Medal. C. W. Jr., states, "I do humbly appreciate the awards that I received for my Naval service in WWII, but like

most WWII Veterans, I simply did what I could to help and tried my best to stay alive. However, I did make one great sacrifice for which I feel I deserve a medal that I did not get. On V-J night in San Francisco in August 1945, an estimated one million people jammed Market Street to celebrate the Japanese surrender and the end of WWII. Market Street was carpeted with wall to wall people - all the way to the Ferry Building. Four and a half years of pent up frustrated adrenaline was beginning to flow and I knew it was my patriotic duty to help the excited, screaming citizens celebrate our long awaited victory, so I fervently threw myself into the now famous Battle of Market Street. Like many Sailors, I hugged and kissed thousands of happy, joyous, beautiful women. IT WAS AWFUL! My clothing was tattered and torn, even my head was covered with lipstick. My lips were swollen and bleeding, but even such obvious terrible pain did not stop me. I kept summoning more courage from somewhere to hug the next tired beautiful girl. And ... somehow I survived the night... and didn't miss a single kiss. Wounded, bleeding and completely devoid of energy, I finally understood the true meaning of WAR IS HELL! As they carried my exhausted body off the battlefield, I had a smile on my face and I actually regretted that I only had one life to sacrifice for my country. But, I did not get another medal! I guess it's like Uncle Charlie Belew used to say, "Some days it just doesn't pay to get out of bed. "C. W also states that he has six ancestors who fought in the Revolutionary War: James Bell, David Douglas, Frederick Tillman, Claiborn Harris, Benjamin Harris and George Daugherty; two fought in War of 1812: Jones Douglas and General George Daugherty; one in the Creek and Indian War: Lemuel Douglas; two with the Confederate Army: Andrew Smith and Inman Leath; one ancestor and eight GG uncle's in the Union: White Logan (great-grandfather) and seven of his brothers plus GG uncle General John Alexander Logan; one G Uncle in WWI, Nick Logan, plus more relatives in WWII than there are Brewer's in Wayne County.

SMITH, CHARLES H., son of Roy and Effie Smith, was born, February 28, 1926, and spent most of his life in Wayne County. He served three years with the U. S. Army during World War II. Several months of that time was spent in the European Theater of War.

After he was discharged from the army, he returned to Wayne County and married Christine Mitchell, daughter of Charlie and Pearl (Matlock) Mitchell and made their home at Waynesboro. Charles was employed as maintamce foreman during the building

of the Natchez Trace and received a citation 16'r thirty years service at his retirement. He and Christine have both died from cancer; Christine died, July 12, 1986, and Charles died January 9, 1997. They are buried at lEghland Cemetery near the Lawrence county line. They have five sons, Larry, Gary (deceased), Jerry, Steve and Jasper.

SMITH, EUNICE C., JR., Serial Number 34142893, Private First Class, served in the United States Army in Cannon Company, 12th Infantry. He was inducted at Fort Oglethorpe, Georgia, on July 10, 1941, and was assigned as Light Truck Driver. His permanent mailing address was Waynesboro, Tennessee. He was registered with the Selective Service Board in Wayne County, Tennessee. His Civilian Occupation was Mill Man. He left the United States on January 18, 1944, and arrived in Europe on January 29, 1944. He returned to the United States on July 5, 1945. He was awarded the European African Middle Eastern Theater Ribbon, Good Conduct Medal, four Bronze Stars, one Bronze Arrowhead, the Purple Heart and the American Defense Service Ribbon. He received his honorable discharge on July 10, 1945, at Fort McPherson, Georgia. His military qualifications included: Combat Infantry Badge, Expert Rifle, Expert Carbine, S. S. Bar. He was active in the Normandy, Northern France, Rhineland and Central Europe battles. He was wounded in action on August 8, 1944, and August 11, 1944, both times in France. Eunice C. Jr. was born on May 30, 1917, in Waynesboro, Tennessee, the son of Eunice C. Sr. and Ada Helton Smith. He died on October 18, 1990, and is entombed in Memory Gardens in Waynesboro, Tennessee. He finished his third year in high school and was a star player on the Waynesboro football team before entering the service. He became an avid football fan for the Tennessee Vols. He was an outdoorsman and loved to hunt and fish. He enjoyed going on a deer hunt. He was a man who enjoyed giving of himself, doing for others, and doing worthwhile activities. He belonged to the First Christian Church in Waynesboro, the V. F. W. and the American Legion. He was married to (1) Equilla Crews and (2) Earline Norton. He had three children: June Smith Walker, Margo Smith Sharpe and Eunice Smith III (Sonny). He also had seven grandchildren. His has two sisters, Carline and Nadine.

SMITH, JOHN ANDERSON, was born 25 October 1913, died 8 December 1971 and is buried in McGlamery Cemetery in Collinwood. His parents were William Louis and Florence Skillern Smith. He married Eva Burns and they had five children: Carolyn Smith Warrington lives in Mechanicsburg, Pennsylvania, Judith Smith Carroll and John Thomas Smith, both of Knoxville, Tennessee, Paul Herschel Smith of Russellville, Alabama, and William Lewis Smith of Stone Mountain, Georgia. John was inducted into the US Navy on 31 December 1943 at Chattanooga, Tennessee. He was sent to Great Lakes, Illinois for his basic training and then, sent to NAS at Newport, Rhode Island for Gunners Mate School. He had a severe heart attack while he was there and was hospitalized for five months. He was discharged with a Service Connected Disability on 8 August 1944 at Newport, Rhode Island.

SMITH, JOHN TOM, son of John Tom Smith, Sr., and Laura Hughes Smith, he was born in Abilene, Texas. After his father died in 1930, his mother returned to her hometown, Clifton, Tennessee to rear and educate her three children. John Tom entered Frank Hughes and graduated there. In 1942 he enlisted in the United States Marine Corps at the age of 18. He was sent to Hawaii, and there he took advantage of the V-12 program. He returned to the States to settle in California. He entered the University of Southern California and graduated in the V-12 program. He was a self-employed commercial developer for 30 years before his death on 9 December 1992 in Redlands Community Hospital in Redlands, California. His funeral was conducted at the Beaumont Presbyterian Church and he was buried in Mt. View Cemetery in Beaumont, California. At the time of his death, he lived in Cherry Valley, California. He was survived by his wife, Karoline V. Smith, son, Steven S. Smith of Carlsbad and daughter, Jacqueline Smith of Cherry Valley and two grandsons. He also has a sister, Lillian Ida Chaffee of Sunnyvale, California. His brother, William Smith preceded him in death.

SMITH, LONNIE D., son of George and Ollie Smith, was born on January 31, 1913. He enlisted in the United States Navy and served until the end of the war. He married and has four children; divorced. On June 21, 1954, Lonnie and Minnie Warren were married. They made their home in Waynesboro. Lonnie was employed as an engineer with Wayne County General Hospital until his death from a heart attack on October 27, 1982. He is buried in Warren Cemetery on Beech Creek. *(See page 234 for photo.)*

SMITH, LYNDON E., 75, of Route 1, Collinwood, died April 6, 1997, at Eliza Coffee Memorial Hospital in Florence and was buried in Memorial Gardens. A native

Lonnie D. Smith

of Carroll County, VA, he was the son of Ruff and Viola Worrell Smith. A veteran of WWII serving in the US Army as a truck driver and carpenter, a member of Veterans of Foreign Wars, American Legion and attended the Collinwood Church of God. Survivors include his wife, Helen Smith, Three sons: Bernard C. of Groveland, FL; Larry Cambell of Apopka, FL and Jimmy Smith of Monticello, FL; two daughters, Patsy D. Hill of Collinwood and Linda Carol Turner of Sorrento, FL; two brothers, Clytus A. Smith and Ivan R. Smith of Berkley, WV; two sisters, Glada Bloom of Estill Springs and Laura Bloom of Berkley, WV; 16 grandchildren and 11 great-grandchildren.

Source: Wayne County News, April 9, 1997.

SMITH, ROBERT W., Serial Number 34 987 506, was a Private First Class in Headquarters Company, 935 Engineer Aviation Regiment in the Army of the United States. His permanent mailing address was Route 2, Clifton, Tennessee. He was born 25 April 1923 in Clifton, Wayne County. He was registered with the Selective Service Board in Wayne County, Tennessee. His Civilian Occupation was General Farmer. He was married when he was inducted 11 April 1944 at Camp Shelby, Mississippi. His Military Occupational Specialty was Light Truck Driver. His Military Qualifications included Rifle Marksman. He was in the battles of Ryukyu. The following decorations were awarded to Smith: World War II Victory Medal, Good Conduct Ribbon, American Theater Ribbon, Asiatic-Pacific Theater Ribbon with 1 Bronze Star. He left the USA 18 February 1945 for the Asiatic Pacific Theater Operation, and returned to USA 18 January 1946. He was discharged 27 January 1946 at Camp Chaffee, Arkansas. Robert was the son of Mr. and Mrs. L. C. Smith. He married Frances Adams. They had three children: Robbie Smith married Joe Jones, Doris Smith married Adolph

Halford, Jr., and Terry Smith married Joe Warrington. Robert's siblings were: Alfred, John Ed, Hester Kyle and Tilda M. Turnbo.

SMITH, WALKER G., was born on April 23, 1919, in Wayne County, Tennessee. He was a farmer living near Collinwood when he entered the United States Army on January 25, 1943, at Ft. Oglethorpe, Georgia. Walker served as T/5 with the 1524th Quartermaster Laundry Company and worked as a Laundry Machine Operator. He was awarded the American Theater Ribbon, Asiatic-Pacific Theater Ribbon, World War II Victory Ribbon and Good Conduct Ribbon. He was discharged on February 22, 1946, at Camp Chaffee, Arkansas.

SMITH, WALTER BROWN, Serial Number 34 987 512, was a Corporal in 1560th Service Command Unit (Separation Center) in the Army of the United States. His permanent mailing address was Route 2, Clifton, Tennessee. He was born 4 May 1925 in Clifton, Tennessee. He was registered with the Selective Service Board in Wayne County, Tennessee. His Civilian Occupation was General Farmer. He was inducted 11 April 1944 at Camp Shelby, Mississippi. His Military Occupational Specialty was General Clerk. His Military Qualifications included Combat Infantry Badge and Rifle MKM. He was in the battle of Rhineland. The following decorations were awarded to Smith: American Theater Ribbon, European-African Middle Eastern Theater Ribbon with 1 Bronze Star, Good Conduct Ribbon, Purple Heart and World War II Victory Medal. He left the USA 22 October 1944 for the European Theater Operation. Cpl. Walter Brown Smith is the son of Alfred and Rixie Gordon Smith of near Clifton, Tennessee. His siblings are Jack, Carmack, Claude, Fay, Glenn, Bobby Gene, Edith and Bill Smith. He landed in France 4 November 1944 and was in active duty there and in Germany. He was slightly wounded on December 10, 1944, was sent to the field hospital for some time, sent back to the front and then sent back to convalescence hospital in England. He was given a seven day furlough in London. He remembers seeing much destruction here. He was then sent to France to rejoin the 95th Division. This division was sent to the States and was scheduled to go to the Pacific. While on a thirty day leave the Japanese surrendered. Smith was sent to Camp Atterbury, Indiana, and worked as a clerk in the Separation Center until he was discharged 29 April 1946. He was privileged to have his wife with him at Camp Atterbury.

SMITH, WARREN H., I was born, March 5,1926, near Alamo, TN to David and Esther Smith. I attended Halls High

School through the tenth grade. March 3, 1944, 1 joined the U. S. Navy and was inducted at Memphis, TN. I was a Seaman First Class and served with the following listed vessels and stations; NRS Memphis, TN; NTS San Diego, CA; Const. Batt USNCTC Williamsburg, VA; USNTADC Williamsburg, VA; Ship's Co. Camp Peary Williamsburg, VA; ATB Camp Bradford, Norfolk, VA; USN Barracks Houston, TX; NAS Memphis, TN. and the USS LST 284.

I spent fifteen months on the USS LST 284. It was an ammunition supply ship, so we supplied ammunition during the Okinawa Campaign. We also supplied ammo to destroyers, de's and the battleship, "Tennessee". We had off loaded the ammo and sailed to Leyte Gulf in the Philippines and were still there when the war ended. We then began transporting occupation troops to Yokohama, Japan. We made three loads, one from Battan and two from Okinawa.

May 20, 1946, 1 was discharged from the Navy at the U. S. Naval Personnel Separation Center at Memphis, TN. with the following citations, Asiatic Pacific Ribbon with one star, American Area Ribbon, Victory Medal and the Philippine Liberation Medal.

Four years later, May 20, 1950, Lillie-Mathis and I were married; she is the daughter of Dave and Duffle Mathis of the Topsy Community in Wayne Co. For more than a year we have lived in retirement at 1191 Natural Bridge

SMITH, WILLIAM, "BILLY", son of John Tom Smith, Sr., and Laura Hughes Smith, was born 9 January 1927 in Abilene, Texas. After his father died in 1930, his mother returned to her hometown, Clifton, Tennessee to rear and educate her three small children. Billy went to Frank Hughes School and graduated there. He enlisted in the United States Army Air Force in July 1945. He was in the Philippines and was discharged in January 1947 as a Private First Class. After his discharge, Billy returned to California where his family lived.

He was working for his brother on heavy duty machinery when he met an early death. He was survived by his mother, his brother, John Tom Smith and sister, Lillian Ida Smith Chaffee.

SMITH, WILLIAM CHARLES, son of Otha "Tobe" and Mary Shipman Smith of Collinwood, was born 19 June 1925. He

married Betty Jean Martin, 17 October 1947. They had three sons, William Steven, Robert Stanley and Richard Dennis Smith and two granddaughters, Jillian Leigh and Tonya Leanne Smith. There are three grandsons, Christopher Steven, Dustin Vance and Dakota Smith. Smith entered service 4 September 1943 with the United States Navy and received his boot training at San Diego, California. His rank was Radioman Third Class. The Service Vessels and Stations that he served on were: NRS Chattanooga, Tennessee, USNTS San Diego, California, USS CLYDE and USS MARIVELES. The following decorations were awarded to Smith: Asiatic-Pacific Theater Ribbon, Philippines Liberation Ribbon and World War II Victory Medal. He was honorably discharged 13 April 1946 in Memphis, Tennessee. He now lives in Collinwood and served as a Rural Mail Carried for Route 2, Collinwood.

Siblings: Ruth Smith Hanback, Otha Smith, Jr., Margaret Smith Daniels, David Smith, and Melvin Smith.

W.C. died October 25, 1995, and is buried in the McGlamery Cemetery near Collinwood.

SMITH, WILLIAM CLYDE, is the seventh child of William Louis and Myrtle (Fitzpatrick) Smith. He was born, April 7,

1923, at Collinwood, TN and attended different schools in Wayne County. Since his father followed timber work, they lived in different sections of the county, but most of his growing up days were spent in the Hardin Creek Community. Clyde's first job as a teenager was working at a sawmill.

January 25, 1943, Clyde was inducted into the U. S. Army at Ft. Oglethorpe, GA. and assigned to the 243rd Field Artillery Bn. About six months later he was shipped to the European-African Theater and landed, August 11, 1943. He participated in the battles at Normandy, Northern France, Ardennes and Rhineland and received the following citations; Service Medal with Service Stars, Good Conduct Medal, WWII Victory Medal, American Theater Ribbon, European-African Middle Eastern Service Medal with four Bronze Stars. Also, he had served with the 2nd Battalion 329th Infantry, 1539th Engineer Survey Co. and 660th Topo. Engineers Bn. After serving two years and two months in Europe, he returned to the States and received his discharge, October 30, 1945 at Ft. Knox, Ky.

He returned to Hardin Creek then a few months after his discharge he was employed at Champion Sparkplug Co. at Toledo, Ohio. He met Vem Mae Troxel; several months later they were married and made their home at Toledo. Vera was born, July 25, 1929, at Toledo to Mr. and Mrs. Martin Troxel. Clyde and Vera are both refired; he spent 33 years at Champion, Inc. The first few years of their retirement, they spent a lot of time traveling through the states. Vera's hobby is bowling and Clyde's

pride and joy is his replica of a 1929 Model A Ford Roadster.

Their two children grew up in Toledo. William Lawrence (Larry), who was born, May 8, 1952, is employed with Mogul Industries at Burlington, Iowa. He is single and a motorcycle enthusiast; he spends his spare time traveling around the country on his bike. Debbie Ann was born, December 23, 1954. She is a nail tech and married to Barry Smith. They and their four children live at Toledo.

Clyde's siblings are Louis Allen (deceased), Ruby Irwin Keeton, Pearl Griggs Wallace, Guy W. (deceased), Cecil E., Walter D., Maynard R. and Mary Nell Pierce. Both of his parents are deceased.

SMITH, WILLIAM J., Serial Number 44 069 672, was a Private First Class in Company B, 4th Infantry in the Army of the United States. His permanent mailing address was Route 1, Collinwood, Tennessee. He was born 23 October 1921 in Iron City, Tennessee. He was registered with the Selective Service Board in Wayne County, Tennessee. His Civilian Occupation was General Farmer. He was married when he was inducted 31 January 1945 at Fort Oglethorpe, Georgia. His Military Occupational Specialty was Rifleman. He was not in any battles, The following decorations were awarded to Smith: World War II Victory Medal, Asiatic-Pacific Theater Ribbon with 1 overseas Service Bar, Army of Occupation Medal - Japan and Good Conduct Ribbon. He left the USA 8 August 1945 for the Pacific Theater Operation, and returned to USA 16 August 1946. He was discharged 23 August 1946 at Fort Sheridan, Illinois.

SMOTHERMAN, ELZIE A., Cpl. in the United States Army, entered the service 4 October 1941 and spent seventeen months with the Calvary Division. He was sent to Fort Benning, Georgia, then he went to parachute training in August 1942. He served in Africa and Italy. Then he went to England and was wounded in August 1944. He was hospitalized for eleven months before he was discharged in late July 1945. He was then employed by TVA until he retired.

SMOTHERMAN, WILBURN F., was born on February 7, 1920, in Arkansas and was working as a farmhand in Collinwood, Tennessee, at the time he was inducted into the United States Army on April 4, 1942, at Ft. Oglethorpe, Georgia. He served with the 232nd Station Hospital in Europe and was awarded the following citations: Good Conduct Medal, World War II Victory, European-African Middle Eastern Theater and American Theater Ribbon. He was discharged on January 7, 1946, at Ft. Knox, Kentucky.

SNODGRASS, J. HUGH "DICK", Machinist, entered the US Navy in January. 1943. He was sent to Great Lakes for his basic training. He was assigned to the USS AIRCRAFT CARRIER, INTREPID. He was involved in numerous battles in the Pacific area of war. He received the President's Citation Medal and numerous Battle Stars. He was discharged in 1945 and joined the US Air Force almost immediately. He served until 1956. Before entering service, he attended school at Frank Hughes in Clifton. Later he worked on the river boat. After service he returned to Clifton and once again worked on the river as a boat pilot until retirement. Snodgrass is the son of James and Mearl Roberts Snodgrass. His siblings are: Clara Bell Selph, Marie Pugh, Mary Frances Snodgrass, Jimmie Snodgrass and John Robert who died young. His children are, Wanda, Linda, Michael and Ricky Snodgrass.

SOUTHERLAND, FREDERICK H., Serial Number 14 211 165, was a Private in 610 AAF Base Unit in the Army of the United States. His permanent mailing address was Route 1, Cypress Inn, Tennessee. He was born 10 December 1928 in Cypress Inn. His Civilian Occupation was Farmer. He enlisted 9 February 1946 at Fort Oglethorpe, Georgia. His Military Occupational Specialty was Duty Soldier. His Military Qualifications included Carbine MKM. He was not in any battles. The following decorations were awarded to Southerland: World War II Victory Medal. He was discharged 20 December 1946 at Eglin Field, Florida.

SOUTHERLAND, OLEN EUGENE, Serial Number 34 713 887, was a Technician Fourth Grade in 565th Antiaircraft Artillery Automatic Weapons Battalion in the Army of the United States. His permanent mailing address was Route 1, Cypress Inn, Tennessee. He was born 1 January 1923 in Lutts, Tennessee. He was registered with the Selective Service Board in Wayne County, Tennessee. His Civilian Occupation was General Farmer. He was married with two dependents when he was inducted 23 April 1943 and entered into active service 30 April 1943 at Camp Forrest, Georgia. His Military Occupational Specialty was Light Truck Driver. His Military Qualifications included SS Rifle. He was in the battles of Ardennes, Rhineland, and Central Europe. The following decorations were awarded to Southerland: European-African Middle Eastern Theater Ribbon with 3 Bronze Stars, Good Conduct Ribbon, World War II Victory Medal and Army of Occupation Medal - Germany. He left the USA 6 Oc-

tober 1944 for the European Theater Operation, and returned to USA 19 June 1946. He was discharged 24 June 1946 at Camp Atterbury, Indiana. Private First Class Olen E. Southerland, son of Mr. and Mrs. G. O. Southerland of the Cypress Inn community, received his basic training at Camp Forrest, Tennessee, and Camp Stewart, Georgia, before he was assigned to overseas duty September 1944. He was in service in England, France, Luxembourg and Germany. He was with the 3rd Army. His wife is Inez Sandusky Southerland, daughter of Mr. and Mrs. Carter Sandusky of Cypress Inn.

STAGGS, BONNIE C., Serial Number 34 185 053, was a Corporal in Company D, 716th Military Police Battalion in the Army of the United States. His permanent mailing address was Route 4, Waynesboro, Tennessee. He was born 19 June 1920 in Madison, Tennessee. He was registered with the Selective Service Board in Wayne County, Tennessee. He was married with three dependents when he enlisted 20 October 1945 at Stark General Hospital, Charleston, South Carolina. His Military Occupational Specialty was Military Police. His prior service was 3 years, 9 months and 12 days in the Regular Army. He was not in any battles. The World War II Victory Medal was awarded to Staggs. He was discharged 11 June 1946 at Fort Bragg, North Carolina.

STAGGS, CLARENCE D., was born in Waynesboro, Tennessee, in 1916 and worked as an automobile mechanic until he was inducted into the United States Army on October 8, 1942, at Camp Forrest, Tennessee. He served with a Detachment of Patients and was discharged on October 7, 1943, in Nashville, Tennessee.

STAGGS, HORACE FRANKLIN, was born 26 December 1919 in Lawrence County, Tennessee. He was the second son

of James I. and Willie Gobble Staggs. He had two brothers and two sisters: Henry Farce, Louise R., Lewis E. and Bertha M. Staggs. His schooling was in Lawrence County, Lauderdale County, Alabama and Wayne County. He worked locally until he joined the army in 1942. He was stationed at Fort Oglethorpe, Georgia and Fort Eustis, Virginia, until the war ended. His rank was Sergeant. While at Fort Eustis, he met and married Sarah Marie McEnerney in 1944. They had one daughter, Nancy L. Staggs. After the war he made his home in Smithfield, Virginia, until his death in 1970. He was area manager for Combined Insurance Company.

He was forced to retire after a serious heart attack. May 9, 1970, died in his sleep. He is buried at Smithville, VA. His siblings are Farce, Louise, and Bertha.

STAGGS, LEONARD, Serial Number 34 146 101, was a Private First Class in Company F, 106th Infantry in the Army of the United States. His permanent mailing address was Route 3, Waynesboro, Tennessee. He was born 27 February 1919 in Wayne County. He was registered with the Selective Service Board in Wayne County, Tennessee. His Civilian Occupation was General Farm Hand. He was inducted 16 September 1941 at Fort Oglethorpe, Georgia. His Military Occupational Specialty was Light Mortar Crewman. His Military Qualifications included Combat Infantryman Badge and SS Rifle. He was in the battles of Eastern Mandates, Western Pacific and Ryukyu. The following decorations were awarded to Staggs: American Defense Service Medal, Asiatic-Pacific Service Medal with 3 Bronze Stars, and Good Conduct Medal. He left the USA 10 March 1942 for the Pacific Theater Operation, and returned to USA 8 October 1945. He was discharged 17 October 1946 at Fort McPherson, Georgia.

STAGGS, LEWIS EVANS, Serial Number 34 738 878, was a Private in Battery C, 380th Antiaircraft Artillery Automatic Weapons Battalion in the Army of the United States. He was born in Florence, Alabama. His Civilian Occupation was Truck Driver. He was 18 years and 11 months of age and single when he was inducted 2 July 1943 at Waynesboro, Tennessee. His Military Occupational Specialty was Instrument Operator and Fire Control. His Military Qualifications included 2nd Class Gunner. He was not in any battles. He was discharged 24 June 1943 at Camp Haan, California.

He is the son of James Icam and Willie Belle (Gobble) Staggs. He was born, August 25, 1925, in Wayne County. TN. and attended Wayne County schools. He entered the U. S. Army during the early days of the war and was stationed in California. One day a gas stove blew up, while the troops were training out in the field: Louis was injured and served the balance of the, war in California.

He married Roberta Gannon and lived at Waynesboro, where he worked as a truck driver. They have two daughters, Linda and Brenda. August 28. 1989, Louis died from lung cancer and is buried at Wayne County Memory Garden. His siblings are Horace, Louis and Bertha.

STAGGS, LONNIE S., Serial Number 44 040 709, served in the Army of the United States. His Civilian Occupation was

General Farmer. He was drafted 30 August 1944, examined at Camp Forrest, Tennessee and inducted at Fort Oglethorpe, Georgia. He received his basic training at Camp Blanding, Florida and left New York Harbor for European Theater Operation in November 1944. He was in Combat with the 99th Division, then with the 2nd Division, 23rd Regular 4th Battalion Company D. He served in England, France, Germany and Czechoslovakia. After the war was over in Europe, he returned to the States with the 2nd Division in August 1945 and was stationed in Ft. Lewis, Washington where he worked as an auto mechanic. After his discharge 21 March 1947 at Fort Lewis Washington, he was engaged in construction and farming. Then, he went to work for Genesco in 1954 and retired in 1988. Lonnie, son of Clarence and Dealie Gobbell Staggs, was born 30 May 1926. His brothers are: Mack, Marvin, and Lawrence. His sisters are: Lois Crews, Sue Pope, and Carol Thompson. He married Freddy June Bromley and they have three children: Teresa Wilson, Myra B. Staggs and Gerald L. Staggs and one grandson, Michael Thomas Wilson.

STAGGS, PAUL G., Serial Number 34 884 601, was a Private First Class in Headquarters and Service Company, 160th Engineer Combat Battalion in the Army of the United States. His permanent mailing address was Waynesboro, Tennessee. He was born 15 September 1923 in Wayne County. He was registered with the Selective Service Board in Wayne County, Tennessee. His Civilian Occupation was Barber. He was married with one dependent when he was inducted 3 September 1943 and entered into active service 24 September 1943 at Fort Oglethorpe, Georgia. His Military Occupational Specialty was Rifleman. His Military Qualifications included Rifle. He was in the battles of Ardennes, Rhineland, and Central Europe. The following decorations were awarded to Staggs: European-African Middle Eastern Theater Ribbon with 3 Bronze Stars, Good Conduct Ribbon and World War II Victory Medal. He left the USA 16 August 1944 for the European Theater Operation, and returned to USA 20 March 1946. He was discharged 24 March 1946 at Camp Atterbury, Indiana.

STAGGS, RALPH B., Serial Number 34 501 372, was a Technician Fifth Grade in Company B, 808th Tank Destroyer Battalion in the Army of the United States. His permanent mailing address was 2126 - 11th Avenue North, Nashville, Tennessee. Address from which employment will be sought, 1001 Union Street, Indianapolis, Indiana. He was born 15 September 1922 in Waynesboro. He was registered with the Selective Service Board in Wayne County, Tennessee. His Civilian Occupation was Trucking. He was inducted 20 December 1944 and entered into active service 27 December 1944 at Fort Oglethorpe, Georgia. His Military Occupational Specialty was Tank Driver. His Military Qualifications included Rifle M-1 (MKM) and Carbine, MKM. He was in the battles of Rhineland, and Central Europe. The following decorations were awarded to Staggs: European-African Middle Eastern Theater Ribbon with 1 Battle Stars. He left the USA 11 August 1944 for the European Theater Operation, and returned to USA 2 July 1945. He was discharged 10 November 1945 at Camp Atterbury, Indiana, with a Certificate of Disability.

STAGGS, WILLIE L., Serial Number 34 494 854, was a Private First Class in 13th Troop Carrier Squadron in the Army of the United States. His permanent mailing address was Route 4, Waynesboro, Tennessee. He was born 20 December 1921 in Waynesboro, Wayne County. He was registered with the Selective Service Board in Wayne County, Tennessee. His Civilian Occupation was Tractor Mechanic. He was inducted 22 November 1942 and entered into active service 29 November 1942 at Fort Oglethorpe, Georgia. His Military Occupational Specialty was Automotive Mechanic. He was in the battles of Bismarck-Archipelago, New Guinea, North Solomons, Southern Philippines, Luzon and Western Pacific. The following decorations were awarded to Staggs: World War II Victory Medal, Good Conduct Ribbon, and Asiatic-Pacific Theater Ribbon with one Silver Star and one Bronze Star. He left the USA 18 May 1943 for the Asiatic-Pacific Theater Operation, and returned to USA 10 December 1945. He had an eighth grade education. He was discharged 21 December 1945 at Camp Chaffee, Arkansas.

STANFIELD, OTIS A., Serial Number 34 903 992, was a Technician Fourth Grade in Detachment 1, 3169th Signal Service Battalion in the Army of the United States. His permanent mailing address was Box 5, Waynesboro, Tennessee. He was born 27 February 1908 in Savannah, Tennessee. He was registered with the Selective Service Board in Wayne County, Tennessee. His Civilian Occupation was Manager Service Establishment. He was married with four dependents when he was inducted 22 January 1944 and entered into active service 13 February 1944 at Camp Forrest, Tennessee. His Military Occupational Specialty was Radio Repairman. His Military Qualifications included Sharp Shooter Rifle. He was in the battles of New Guinea, Southern Philippines, and Luzon. The following decorations were awarded to Stanfield: World War II Victory Medal, Good Conduct Ribbon, Asiatic-Pacific Theater Ribbon with 3 Bronze Service Stars, and Philippine Liberation Ribbon. He left the USA 10 October 1944 for the Asiatic-Pacific Theater Operation, and returned to USA 13 December 1945. He had a high school education. He was discharged 24 December 1946 at Camp Chaffee, Arkansas. He had over 8 years prior service with the National Guard.

STEELE, HENRY ARNOLD, was the son of Henry and Julia Sewell Steele. He came to the Clifton area from Union City, Tennessee, as a young teen after his mother's death. He graduated from Frank Hughes High School in 1942. He served his country during World War II in the United States Navy, located in the Air Station in Jacksonville, Florida, and perhaps other locations during the conflict. After his service release, he continued his education, graduating from University of Tennessee in Knoxville, with a degree in electrical engineering. He worked in different locations in this field of work and retired from Meriwether Lewis Electric Cooperative in Centerville, Tennessee as manager.

His siblings are Estelle, Jimmie Pearigen and Edgar Steele. Henry married Frances Moore and they have a son and a daughter. He has a home in Florida where they live part time.

STEELE, MARVIN TENNIE, JR., Serial Number 44 044 581, was a Sergeant in NAGONA Military Government Team

in the Army of the United States. His permanent mailing address was Route 2, Clifton, Tennessee. He was registered with the Selective Service Board in Wayne County, Tennessee. His Civilian Occupation was General Farmer. He was inducted 19 December 1944 and entered into active service 19 December 1944 at Fort Oglethorpe, Georgia. His Military Occupational Specialty was Heavy Truck Driver. His Military Qualifications included SS M-1 Rifle and Expert Infantry Badge. He was not in any battles. The following decorations were awarded to Steele: Philippine Liberation Medal, Asiatic-Pacific Service Medal, Good Conduct Ribbon, World War II Victory Medal and Army of Occupation Medal (Japan). He left the USA 4 June 1945 for the Asiatic-Pacific Theater Operation, and returned to USA 30 September 1946. He was discharged 28 November 1946 at Fort Lewis, Washington. Marvin, Jr. son of

Marvin Tennie Steele, Sr., and Fannie Rinehart Steele, He had one sister, Tennie Steele Ruble. He was born 18 January 1925 in Clifton, Tennessee and died 17 September 1987.

STEELE, RALPH E., Serial Number 34 738 844, was a Technician Fourth Grade in Company A, 1891st Engineer Aviation Battalion in the Army of the United States. His permanent mailing address was Peters Landing, Tennessee. He was born 2 January 1924 in Clifton. Tennessee. He was registered with the Selective Service Board in Wayne County. His Civilian Occupation was High School Student. He was inducted 2 July 1943 and entered into active service 16 July 1943 at Fort Oglethorpe, Georgia. His Military Occupational Specialty was Construction Machine Operator. His Military Qualifications included MM Rifle. He was in the battles of China Defensive, China Offensive, Central Burma, and India Burma. The following decorations were awarded to Steele: Asiatic Pacific Service Medal with 4 Bronze Stars, American Service Medal, Good Conduct Ribbon and World War II Victory Medal. He left the USA 29 August 1944 for the Pacific Theater Operation, and returned to USA 28 December 1945. He had a high school education. He was discharged -date not given.

Ralph was the son of Lloyd and Lena Holder Steele, Clifton, Tennessee. He was the grandson of Arch and Lissie Steele, and John I and Betty Turnbo Holder. Ralph married Ann from Luka, MS., they had one daughter, Sheryl, two sons, Tim and Patrick. Siblings: Russell Forrest, Rex Holder, Eula Marion, and Deanna Jean.

STEELE, RUSSELL FORREST, served his Country during W.W. II in the United States Army. He was born Sept. 25,1927 in Wayne County, Tennessee.

He was the son of Lloyd and Lena Holder Steele. Grandson of Archie and Lissie Steele and John J. and Betty Turnbo Holder, all the family lived near Clifton, TN. Forrest married Bessie Horton from Lutts, TN. They had one son, Archie, two daughters, Tina, and Rita. Siblings: Ralph Edward, Rex, Eula Marion, and Deanna Jean.

STEELE, WILLIAM EDGAR, T5, United States Army was born Sept. 26, 1908 and died April 23 1983. He was buried at Prater's Chapel Cemetery near Clifton, TN. He was the son of Henry and Julia Sewell Steele, grandson of Jessie Briley and Eliza Frances (Grimes) Steele. His siblings were Henry Arnold Steele, Jimmie Steele Pearigen and Estelle Steele White.

Edgar had two children: Gene Edgar Steele and Pattie Steele Young and two

grandchildren: Jason Steele and Peyton Young. He served his country during WWII.

STEVENS, THOMAS MILES, was drafted from Wayne County, Tennessee in the Spring of 1943 and served in the United

States Navy on a Destroyer Ship in the Pacific Area during World War II. After the war was over he returned to Copperfield Steel in Warren, Ohio and worked there for 37 years. Thomas, son of Isaac Black, Sr., and Bertha Harder Stevens, was born 6 July 1924, died 18 March 1985 with cancer and was buried in Milan Cemetery in Hickman County at the intersection of Highways 48 and 100. His brothers were: Isaac Black, Jr., Gerald, James, Robert and Willie Stevens and sister, Ramona Farris.

STOCKARD, EDMOND J., Serial Number 34 501 375, was a Private First Class in 63rd Division, Military Police Platoon in the Army of the United States. His permanent mailing address was Route 5, Waynesboro, Tennessee. He was born 18 September 1922 in Waynesboro. He was registered with the Selective Service Board in Wayne County, Tennessee. His Civilian Occupation was General Farm Hand. He was inducted 20 December 1942 and entered into active service 27 December 1942 at Fort Oglethorpe, Georgia. His Military Occupational Specialty was Military Policeman. His Military Qualifications included MKM M-1 Rifle and MKM 1917 Rifle. He was in the battles of Rhineland, and Central Europe. The following decorations were awarded to Stockard: Good Conduct Medal, American Theater Ribbon, European-African Middle Eastern Theater Ribbon, and World War II Victory Medal. He left the USA 5 January 1945 for the France, and returned to USA 11 September 1945. He was discharged 14 January 1946 at Fort George Meade, Maryland. Edmond and his brother, Robert, met in Germany on May 30 after having not seen each other for almost two years. They had both been on active duty in the European Theater of Operations, stationed at Army bases inside Germany. Their parents were Clifford and Ima Lay Stockard of the Factory Community in Wayne County.

STOCKARD, HERMAN W., Serial Number 36 897 673, was a Private assigned to Battery A, 881st Field Artillery Battalion in the Army of the United States. He was born August 1913 in Waynesboro. His Civilian Occupation was Riveter. He was inducted 13 January 1944 at Detroit, Michigan, at the age of 30 years and 5 months. He had blue eyes, brown hair, ruddy complexion and was 5' 11 & 1/2 " tall. He was discharged 27 October 1944 at Fort McPherson, Georgia. He was the son of Eules and Lizzie Copeland Stockard. His siblings were: Hattie Brown, Clifford, Jessie, Eula Kelley, Lola, Velma Lands, Eliotte, Clinton, Clemon, and Hazel Stockard.

STOCKARD, ROBERT S., Serial Number 34 886 105, was a Technician Fifth Grade in 597th Bombardment Squadron, 397th Bomb Group in the Army of the United States. His permanent mailing address was Route 5, Waynesboro, Tennessee. He was born 18 May 1924 in Wayne County. He was registered with the Selective Service Board in Wayne County, Tennessee. His Civilian Occupation was High School Student. He was inducted 5 October 1943 and entered into active service 26 October 1943 at Fort Oglethorpe, Georgia. His Military Occupational Specialty was Telephone and Telegraph Lineman. His Military Qualifications included Combat Infantryman Badge. He was in the battles of Normandy, North France, Rhineland, and Central Europe. The following decorations were awarded to Stockard: European-African Middle Eastern Theater Ribbon with 4 Bronze Service Stars, Good Conduct Ribbon, World War II Victory Medal and Distinguished Unit Badge. He left the USA 5 April 1944 for the European African Middle Eastern Theater Operation, and returned to USA 4 January 1946. He was discharged 12 January 1946 at Fort Knox, Kentucky. Robert and his brother, Edmond, met in Germany on May 30 after having not seen each other for almost two years. Their parents were Clifford and Ima Lay Stockard of the Factory Community in Wayne County. They had a sister Mamie and other siblings.

STOCKARD, WILLIAM, Serial Number 34 936 441, was a Technician Fourth Grade in Company C, 51st Armored Infantry Battalion, 4th Armored Division in the Army of the United States. His per-manent mailing address was Waynesboro, Tennessee. He was born 16 June 1919 in Collinwood. He was registered with the Selective Service Board in Wayne County, Tennessee. His Civilian Occupation was Aircraft Riveter. He was married with two dependents when he was inducted 28 July 1944 at Camp Forrest, Tennessee. His Military Occupational Specialty was Cook. His Military Qualifications included Rifle MKM and Combat Infantry Badge. He was in the battles of Central Europe. The following decorations were awarded to Stockard: European-African Middle Eastern Theater Ribbon with 1 Bronze Stars, World War II Victory Medal and Army of Occupation Medal (Germany). He left the USA 15 March 1945 for the European Theater Operation, and returned to USA 14 June 1946. He was discharged 20 June 1946 at Camp Atterbury, Indiana.

STOOKSBERRY, HERSHEL W. "JINK", was born on Oct. 11, 1920 in Wayne Co., TN and died on Oct. 9, 1977

in Lawrenceburg, Lawrence Co., TN. He is buried in the Collinwood Memorial Gardens in Wayne Co., TN. He was the son of William Carver "Will" & Flora Bell (Martin) Stooksberry. He was the great, great, great grandson of the Revolutionary war soldiers Jacob Stooksberry and Isaac Horton.

He was drafted into the Army on Nov. 29, 1942 during WWII. His Serial No. was 34495076. He received the Expert Infantrymans Badge on Apr. 8, 1944 and the Good Conduct Medal on May 27, 1944 in Company B 409th Infantry, Camp Howze, TX. He served in Germany and France. He was wounded twice during his stay. He received the Purple Heart medal for being wounded on Oct. 17, 1944 in the Replacement Co., 143rd Infantry in Eastern FRANCE. He was shot in the wrist. He received a 10%, disability check for the remainder of his life. He received the Bronze Star Medal for Heroic Achievement in combat on Mar. 17, 1945 in Gunstett, France on Aug. 9, 1945 in Company C 143rd Infantry Regiment, 36th Infantry Division.

After returning from the army, he married Edith Pauline Butler on Apr. 7, 1946. She was the daughter of Harve Lucas "Harve" & Luanner Jane (Daniel) Butler. They had 3 children: Wayne "Gomer" was born on Jan. 20, 1947 and James Lee was born on May 13, 1948 in the Woods hospital in Waynesboro, Wayne Co., TN; Willis Ray was born on Feb. 19, 1950 on the family farm on First Butler Creek in Wayne Co., TN.

He farmed all of his life. After returning from the army, he returned to the family farm. After marriage he row cropped for a while and lived on the Clyde Robertson farm on the head of First Butler creek. He then helped to farm and lived on the Zeno Lindsey farm on Indian creek. We purchased the family farm in Dec. of 1949. It was the old Marion Rich farm on the head of First Butler creek. We farmed and pedaled farm products to the people in Florence, AL exclusively until 1953 when he went to work for the Hassell & Hughes Lumber Co. in Collinwood, TN- He worked here as a supervisor for the flooring mill until 1969 when he had a stroke. After this, he was encouraged to return to work as supervisor. After returning to work he was demoted and shortly after that he was laid off. He then worked for a while for the Iron City Stamping Co. in Iron City, TN. He eventually returned to work for Hassell & Hughes but was routed to the outside in the cold winter. He would not quit and they gave him a permanent layoff and canceled his retirement. After this he went to work for TVA in Florence as janitor and worked until he was involved in a vehicle accident which resulted in his death.

STOOKSBERRY, JAMES ELI, son of Mr. and Mrs. W.H. Stooksberry of Rt 3, Iron City, TN, enlisted in the US Navy in March 1945.

STOOKSBERRY, ROBERT DEWITT, My parents are Sam and Mary Belle Stooksberry. I was born March 21, 1924 in Lawrence Co. Tennessee, I was raised on the Stooksberry farm at McCalls.

I was inducted into service March 27, 1943 just after my 19 birthday. I was loaded on a bus and sent to Ft. Oglethorpe, Georgia and was sent by train to Camp Haan just outside of Riverside, California. I trained with Battery D-782nd, which was later deactivated. After two months of training there, I was sent to Camp Irvin in the Mojava dessert. We were an experiment to see how troops managed in the hot desert during the months of June, July, August

and September. I can tell you it was extremely hot at times it would reach 115 degrees. We were training on a 40 mm-cannon and a 50-caliber machine gun used to shoot down enemy aircraft. After completion of this training, A few of us were shipped out and the rest were retrained for the infantry. We were shipped oversees to replace prior casualties,

We left the U.S. on 10th of October 1943 and arrived at our destination the I 6th of October 1943. Our stopping point was Hickman Field on the island of Oahu. My new outfit was Battery B-864-AAA-AW Battalion, which had seen action at the battle of Pearl Harbor. After staying at Hickem Field for seven or eight months we were put on alert to be shipped out on a mission as a support group for the 4th Marine Division. On the last week in May we left Pearl Harbor, and traveled west in convoys for 24 days. Our designation turned out to be Saipan in the Mariana Island chain. We started suffering heavy casualties on the 15th of June (our D-Day). The 2nd Marine Division and the 27th Army division assisted the 4th Marine Division. My unit did not go ashore for about three days; we had to wait for the beaches to be cleared. On the 5 day we finally got to our designation, the Airsalito Air Field.

The marines were having trouble getting the Japanese out of the caves about a mile or so away from the airfield. They requested that the Navy ship fire in the caves to assist them. This didn't work because some of the shots missed their targets and struck some of the marines, causing several casualties. It was decided that they would take some of our antiaircraft guns up and fire into the caves. After two days of firing the caves were taken. The Island of Tinian, where the Anola Gay took off from in 1945, was only about, seven miles away. But at this time it was still occupied by the Japanese and we were shelled from their location on several different occasions.

During our invasion of Saipan, the Japanese Navy intended to attach the U.S. Naval forces and destroy the landing field on Saipan. But the American Navy discovered their plans and set a trap for them. This was the prelude to the Marianna Turkey shoot. Some of our Navy planes ran low of fuel and landed on our airstrip instead of reaching their aircraft carriers. At this same time, there was a cliff next to the ocean named the Banzai Cliffs, about a mile away still under the control of the Japanese. The Japanese were committing suicide from this cliff to the rocks about 100 feet below. Some were forced to jump; others were convinced that this death was better than being captured by the Americans. After about thirty days of fighting the island was secure. The Airsaleto airfield was renamed Isley and they started working 24 hours a day, seven days a week, and had it completed by Sept., 44.

Thanksgiving Day of 1944 was the largest air attack on the airfield. By that time the B-29s were on the field. All of the attacking plains were finally shot down, they would continue circling and firing until we managed to down them. One of the planes that my gun crew hit circled and tried to fly into the gun crew with us. It missed by only a short distance. Sometime later in another air raid, a plane attempted to come in. The aircraft gunners seemed to have hit the plane, but it was later discovered that it had launched a baka bomb, which landed a short distance away on the runway.

Things begin to quieten down and after the atomic bomb was dropped, the war started to end. I was assigned to Military Police who were in charge of the separation center. I was processed out to come home the 25th of November in 1945. 1 arrived in the states the 9th day of December in 1945 on the West Coast. I went from the West Coast to Ft. Bliss, TX Where on December 14th, 1945 1 was handed my discharge papers by General Wainright, who had replaced MacArthur in the Philippines at the start of the war and had been a prisoner of war for over four years. A few months later General Wainright died from malnutrition.

From Saipan, I had traveled by boat, train, bus and taxi to return home. I arrived home a day earlier than expected to find an empty house with three stars in the window. These stars represented me and my two brothers, Samuel Davis, stationed in Italy and Walter Wade station in France serving under Governor Gordon Browning.

Several years later I met and married Ruth Edwards. We had four children. Patricia Walker, a nurse, Elizabeth Richardson, housewife and painter, and Cindy Kephart, bookkeeper at the County Executive Office, are our daughters. Robert Michael Stooksberry is our son.

Michael is a Major in the Tennessee National Guard. After 35 years of marriage, Ruth passed away. I later married Janice (Mathis) Odle. She has three children, Harold Wayne Gipson, Jr. Gwen (Gipson) Wilbanks, and Kimberly (Odle) Sherrill. Between the two of us we have fifteen grandchildren and three great-grandchildren.

I am member of the American Legion and Veterans of Foreign Wars and am of the Baptist faith. I worked for Genesco for 34 years before retirement. I now enjoy tending my yard and garden and watching the Chicago Cubs play ball.

STOOKSBERRY, SAM D., Serial Number 01 577 911, was a First Lieutenant in 4511th, AAF Base Unit, Quarter

Master Corp in the Army of the United States. He was born 3 September 1922 in Collinwood and was the son of Sam and Belle Davis Stooksberry. His Civilian Occupation was Farm Manager. He volunteered and entered into active service 14 August 1942. His Military Occupational Specialty was QM Staff Officer. He was in the battles of Tunisia, Naples-Foggia, and Rome-Arno. The following decorations were awarded to Stooksberry: American Defense Service Medal, and European-African Middle Eastern Theater Medal. He left the USA 12 December 1942 for the European-African Middle Eastern Theater Operation, and returned to USA 28 May 1945. He had a high school education. He was discharged 28 January 1946 at Baer Field, Fort Wayne, Indiana. He was married and had two dependents.

STORY, HOLLIS BOYD, was the only son of Roy and Minnie Bell Hollis Story, was born 5 July 1922 in Wayne County, in the area of Factory Creek and Bethlehem Church. Hollis was inducted into the United States Army on 22 November 1942 and entered active service seven days later at Fort Oglethorpe, Georgia. He was trained as a rifleman and served with Company C, 185th Infantry Division. He was listed as a "Combat Infantryman" and he saw more than his share of combat. He fought in the battle of Bismarck Archipelago, the Southern Philippine Campaign, and Luzon. He was decorated with Good Conduct Medal, a Philippine Liberation Ribbon and one Bronze star, Asiatic-Pacific Theater Ribbon with 4 Bronze Service Stars and one Bronze Arrowhead and World War II Victory Medal. He was honorably discharged 13 December 1945 at Camp Chaffee, Arkansas. Upon his return to civilian life, Hollis was married to Neva Dixon, daughter of Rube Allen and Alva Lois Todd Dixon. Hollis and Neva had four children: Varble Boyd Story, Rosetta Robertson Sisson, Randy Roy Story and Stacy Story. Hollis died July 1987 after waging a valiant fight against lung cancer. He was buried in Bethlehem Baptist Church Cemetery on Factory Creek. Hollis served his country with bravery and valor. Let us hope that he has been duly rewarded and that he will be remembered in that light for many years to come. *Submitted by Shirley Hollis Rice* .

STORY, J.F., a native of Wayne County, he was a World War II Veteran. He was a retired machine operator for Genesco shoe plant in Waynesboro. He was a member of the Bethlehem Baptist Church and the son of William and Lona Cannon Story. He died at his home at Route 1, West Point, Tennessee, on 8 June 1994, age 71 and was buried in Bethlehem Baptist Church Cemetery. His survivors include: wife, Carlene Caperton Story, two daughters, Doris Hall of Lexington, Alabama, and Wanda Carter of Killen, Alabama, one son, Mike Story of West Point, one sister, Mary Jo Weaver of West Point, two granddaughters and one great granddaughter.
Source: Obit.

STORY, J.T., Serial Number 44 070 843, was a Private First Class in 627th QM Refrigeration Company in the Army of the United States. His permanent mailing address was Route 1, West Point, Tennessee. He was born 2 May 1922 in West Point. He was registered with the Selective Service Board in Wayne County, Tennessee. His Civilian Occupation was General Farmer. He was inducted 23 February 1945 at Fort Oglethorpe, Georgia. His Military Occupational Specialty was Rifleman. His Military Qualifications included MM M-1 Rifle. He was not in any battles. The following decorations were awarded to Story: Meritorious Unit Award, World War II Victory Medal, Asiatic-Pacific Theater Ribbon with 1 Overseas Service Bar, Army of

Occupation Medal-Japan and Good Conduct Ribbon. He left the USA 6 October 1945 for the Pacific Theater Operation, and returned to USA 24 July 1946. He had an eighth grade education. He was discharged 3 August 1946 at Fort Sheridan, Illinois.

STORY, T.C., JR., was a veteran of the Army of the United States. He taught Vocational Agriculture at Collinwood High School for approximately thirty years. He was also Wayne County Production Credit office manager, a position he held until he retired in 1978. He was a member of the Collinwood Masonic Lodge and the Collinwood Methodist Church. T. C. was born in 1923 in Wayne County, died 3 July 1993 in Parkview Hospital in Nashville and was buried in Memorial Gardens Cemetery in Collinwood. He was the son of Tom C. Story, Sr., and Villie Nelson Story. His two brothers are Lonnie Story of Collinwood and Jack Story of Lawrenceburg. His two sisters are Waymon Dixon of West Point and Gertie Boatwright of Indiana. His two sons are Ricky Story of Overland Park, Kansas, and Randy M. Story of Collinwood. He also has three grandchildren.

STRAIT, HOMER C., Serial Number 34 189 093, was a Private in 338th Military Police Escort Guard Company in the Army of the United States. He was born in Wayne County. His Civilian Occupation was Wood Cutter. He was 31 years of age and single when he was inducted 18 February 1942 at Fort Oglethorpe, Georgia. He was not in any battles. He was discharged 10 December 1943 in Huntsville, Texas, after serving 1 year, 9 months and 23 days.

STRICKLIN, BILLIE C., was born, January 19, 1925, near Lutts, TN to William Tom and Mattie Mae (Brown)

Stricklin. He was the oldest son of five children. His first school was Martin's Mill. He had to help his dad on the farm, so he only completed the second grade.

July 28, 1944, Billy was inducted into the United States Army at Camp Forrest, TN. He sailed for Hawaii, May 27, 1945 and remained there until September 7, 1945. When he arrived in Japan, September 27, 1945, his Military Occupational Specialty was Light Artillery Gun Crewman. While there he was awarded the Asiatic-Pacific Campaign Ribbon and WWII Victory Medals. He was stationed at Nara, Honshu, SW, Japan, when he reenlisted. A short time later he was sent to Ft. Jackson, S. C., as a corporal and rifle instructor, where he remained until, April 23, 1947, when he was discharged.

Billy returned home to work on the farm and in timber. December 26, 1946, he married Jewel Melson, the daughter of Jay and Pearle (Bums) Melson. Billy and Jewel made their home in the Rayborn Creek Community raised their children there. They have six children, Margaret, Frances, Billie Ann, Larry, Bobby and Lisa, but unfortunately the three youngest died shortly after their birth. Their daughters helped on the farm and attended Pinhook School through the eighth grade, then Collinwood High School.

In, 1965, Billy gave up working in the woods. He continued to farm and was employed at Collinwood Mfg., Co. until he became ill and died, April 22, 1969. He is buried at Cromwell Crossroads Cemetery, Southwest of Collinwood on Bear Creek Road.

He was a good, hard working husband and daddy. His family is very proud of him for serving his country and helping make this land a better place to live. His seven grandchildren, Steve, Marcia, Lance, Jason, Jonathan, Luke and Lindsey; his three great-grandchildren, Erica, Nathan and Christopher loved and miss him very much, as we do.

STRICKLIN, CLARENCE DEE, Serial Number 14 133 875 was a Technician Fourth Grade in the Army of the United

States. His permanent mailing address was 209 King Street, Smyrna, Georgia. He was registered with the Selective Service Board in Wayne County, Tennessee. He enlisted 23 July 1942 at Camp Forrest, Tennessee. He received his basic training at Fort McClellan, Alabama. He was injured in 1942 and was transferred to Lawson General Hospital at Fort McPherson, Georgia and was in limited service for the duration. He was stationed at Camp Shelby, Mississippi, a Rehabilitation Service in Miami, Florida, and at Fort McPherson before he was transferred overseas in December 1942. He served in South Hampton, England, LeHarve, Etempe and Bapaume, France, and Antwerp, Mons, and Liege, Belgium. He returned to the States in December 1944. He was in the battles of Rhineland. The following decorations were awarded to Stricklin: American Theater Ribbon, European-African Middle Eastern Theater Service Medal, Good Conduct Ribbon and World War II Victory Medal. He had four years of college education. He was discharged 31 December 1944 at Camp Gordon, Georgia. Clarence Dee, son of George and Lizzie Stricklin, was born 10 April 1911 in Lutts, died in Palatka, Florida and is buried in Palatka Memorial Gardens. He lived in Palatka, Florida, for 26 years, coming from Marietta, Georgia. He was a retired school teacher with Putman County School System. He had also taught in Wayne County and Luka, Mississippi. He is survived by his wife, Kathryn, sons, Dr. George P. Stricklin of Nashville, David Eugene of Micanopy, Florida, and John F. of Interlachan, Florida; daughters, Nancy L. Huff of San Antonio, Texas, and Ann Will of Archer, Florida. His brothers are James of Waynesboro and Fred of Lutts and sister, Estelle McFall of Savannah.

STRICKLIN, FRED, Serial Number 967 13 61, was in the Navy of the United States. He registered 1 July 1941 with the Selective Service Board in Wayne County,

Tennessee. His Civilian Occupation was General Farmer. He entered into active service 10 April 1944 and served in Navy reserve in the South Pacific on the USS BURLEIGH APA 95. He was discharged 23 January 1946 at Memphis, Tennessee. Fred, son of George Washington and Lizzie Virginia Perry Stricklin, was born 21 June 1920 in Lutts, died in Lutts and is buried in Lutts. He was married 16 March 1951 to Edith Edwinna Gallaher, daughter of Robert Taylor and Anne Cole Gallaher. They did not have any children. His half brothers were: Charlie R. and Arthur. His full brothers were: Elbert Lee, James Frank, Clarence Dee and Jay William. He had one sister, Estelle who married Robert McFall.

STRICKLIN, HERMAN LINDSEY, was inducted 23 November 1942 at Fort Oglethorpe, Georgia and served there in

the Reception Center on Special Duty. His basic training was at Camp Sibert, Alabama. He spent some time with the Military Hospital in Rome, Georgia. His overseas duty was in Northern Solomons, Southern Philippines and Japan with the 121st Medical Battalion, American Division in the Army of the United States. He was honorably discharged 14 January 1946 at Camp Chaffee, Arkansas with the rank of Technician Third Grade. The following decorations were awarded to Stricklin: World War II Victory Ribbon, American Theater Ribbon, Asiatic-Pacific Theater Ribbon with 2 Bronze Stars, Philippine Liberation Ribbon and one Bronze Star. Lindsey, son of Herman A. and Dola Lindsey Stricklin, was born 17 August 1921 in Waynesboro, Tennessee. He attended Pinhook Elementary, Wayne County High, Florence State College and the University of North Carolina where he received his AB and MA Degrees. He chose to be an educator and has been both teacher and principal at Pinhook Elementary School in Lutts, He retired in 1986 as

Associate Professor of English at the University of North Alabama. He is now Professor Emeritus, living in Florence, Alabama and teaching part time.

STRICKLIN, JESSIE A., spent twenty years in the Navy of the United States from 1942 to 1962. He was born 15 September 1921, died 31 January 1989 and is buried in Lone Chestnut Cemetery in Decatur County, Tennessee. He is the son of Henry and Elma Steele Stricklin. He married Louise Gordon, daughter of Pete and Velt Walker Stricklin. His siblings are Verl Waters, Stella Lee Prater, Lela Marie Bowlen, Hubert and Elred B. Stricklin.

STRICKLIN, THOMAS EARL, was inducted September 1946 at Fort Oglethorpe, Georgia and was assigned to Service

Troop, 4th Constabulary Regiment in the Army of the United States. His overseas duty was in Germany from February to April 1947. He was honorably discharged May 1947 with the rank of Private First Class. The following decorations were awarded to Stricklin: World War II Victory Ribbon, and Army occupation Medal. Thomas Earl, son of Herman A. and Dola Lindsey Stricklin, was born 8 December 1925 in Lutts, Tennessee, died 13 March 1972 in Washington, DC and is buried in Lutts Cemetery. He attended Pinhook Elementary, Collinwood High, and Florence State College. His civilian career was spent as a civilian attached to the US Air Force at the Pentagon in Washington. In October 1957, he received a Distinguished Award, Directorate of Installations, Real Estate Division, USAF, Pentagon, Washington, D. C.

STRICKLIN, WILEY AMOS "TED", left Tennessee in 1937 and was drafted while living in Muscatine, Iowa. On 11 November 1943, he was sworn into the United States Navy in Des Moines, Iowa and went through boot camp at Farragut, Idaho. After boot camp he at-

tended the following schools: Diesel Engineers course at Iowa State College in Ames, Fairbanks Morse Diesel school at Beloit, Wisconsin where he specialized in 11 cylinder opposed piston engines, Navy Diesel School at Naval Operating base in Norfolk, Virginia, and Naval Firefighters School at Little Creek, Virginia. After completing school he was sent to a shipyard in Houston, Texas, to board a LSM. While on board the LSM in Galveston, Texas, undergoing demagnetization of the ships hull, he contracted chronic bronchitis and was sent to the Naval Hospital in Camp Wallace, Texas for treatment. He was honorably discharged 4 October 1944 and returned to Iowa. In 1946 he returned to Tennessee. He has been a member of Plumbers and Steamfitters Local 572 in Nashville for 40 years. As a steamfitter and draftsman, he worked throughout Tennessee, Alabama and Kentucky until he retired in July 1978. Ted, son of Iley Amos and Flora Ethel Brewer Stricklin, was born 21 January 1918 in Clifton, Tennessee. He is the grandson of Amos Furgerson and Sarah Hendrix Stricklin and Wiley Valentine and Frances Smith Brewer. On 22 March 1947 Ted married Marie Greeson. They have one son, Ted Alan Stricklin. Ted Alan also served in the Navy, retiring with the rank of Commander. Ted Alan married Phyllis Dianne Townes of Hermitage, Tennessee, and they have three sons, Todd Alan, William Arthur and Jason Edward. The family resides in Waynesboro.

STRICKLIN, WILLIAM ELLIS, "BILL", was inducted March 1943 at Fort Oglethorpe, Georgia. He was stationed in Camp Haan and Camp Irwin (Mojava Desert), California and Granda, Mississippi. His overseas duty was in the European Theater with the 26th Infantry, 1st Army Division in the Army of the United States. He was wounded in action in the battle of Hurtgen Forrest in Germany in November 1944. The following decorations were awarded to Stricklin: Purple

Heart and one Bronze Star Medal. He was honorably discharged June 1945. Bill, son of Herman A. and Dola Lindsey Stricklin, was born 7 February 1924 in Lutts, Tennessee. He attended Lutts Elementary, Lutts Junior High and Collinwood High and was awarded the Bachelor of Fine Arts Degree from the University Of Alabama in Tuscaloosa in 1949. He was a member of the Delta Chi Fraternity. Bill married Edith Webster in 1957 and they have one son, William Sam Stricklin, who is married to Connie Blackwell. They have two sons, Adrien and Hunter Stricklin. He has one brother, Lindsey. Bill began his civilian career in advertising, first with the Reuben H. Donnelly Corporation in Washington, DC , and then in Nashville with a newspaper printing corporation, at one time the publisher of both the Tennessean and the Nashville Banner. From there he became a partner in a Nashville Advertising firm, leaving after several years to form his own agency, Bill Stricklin and Associates in Hendersonville, which was an advertising, print and broadcast production. Continuing in this capacity up until the time of his illness, which took his life. He died in October 1993 and was buried in Woodlawn Cemetery in Hendersonville.

STULTS, HARDIN C., Sergeant, was awarded the Bronze Star Medal for heroic achievement in action. The Citation is as

follows. "Hardin C. Stults (34 378 439) Sergeant, Infantry, United States Army, for heroic achievement in action 19 October 1944 near Canovette, Italy. In his action in repairing, without tools, a vital communication line in the midst of enemy artillery fire, Sergeant Stutts demonstrated the high courage of the American Soldier. He volunteered for a dangerous task above the call of duty, repairing of the line with no tools but his hands and teeth. Sergeant Stults prompt and heroic action saved a number of his platoon from being wounded or killed. His accomplishment

was even made more exceptional in that it was made by an individual facing enemy fire alone, necessarily without the close presence of comrades to aid him. Sergeant Stults actions are of great credit to himself and the Armed Forces of the United States. He entered Service from Iron City, Tennessee. Signed: R. E. S. Williamson, Brigadier General, USA, commanding.

STULTS, RAY ALTON, Serial Number 90 25 84, was a Corporal (TW) in the Marine Corps of the United States. He en-

listed 7 October 1943 at Nashville, Tennessee to serve during the National emergency years. His Military Occupational Specialty was Telephone Man. His Military Qualifications included Rifle Sharpshooter. He was in the battles at Okinawa, Ryukyu Islands from 14 April 1946 to 21 June 1946 and served in the occupation of China from 10 October 1945 to 3 Apr 1946. The following decorations were awarded to Stults: Serlap Button, and Good Conduct Ribbon and World War II Victory Medal. He was discharged 6 May 1946 at Camp LeJeune, North Carolina and from United States Marine Corps Reserve. Ray Alton, son of Mathney and Nettie Leigh (Victory) Stults, was born 17 June 1923 at Cypress Inn in Wayne County, passed away 17 March 1987 and was buried in Memorial Gardens in Collinwood. He had six brothers and one sister. Living brothers are: Aaron, Clifford and Therman. Deceased siblings are: Raymond, Arlie, Doyle and Erma. He married Effie Irene Pigg on 27 October 1946. They had three children: Jimmy Ray and Jerrol Stults and Judy Elaine Stults Hays, Nine grandchildren and two great-grandchildren.

STULTS, RAYMOND CHARLIE, Serial Number 967 13 69, was a Ship's Cook Third Class in the Navy of the United States. He was born 11 October 1924 at

Cypress Inn in Wayne County. He entered into active service 11 April 1944. He served on the following vessels and stations: Constitution Battalion USNCTC in Williamsburg, Virginia, US Naval Training Station, Newport, Rhode Island, and the USS Burleigh (APA 95). The following decorations were awarded to Stults: American Campaign Ribbon, Asiatic-Pacific Theater Ribbon with 1 Bronze Stars, and World War II Victory Medal. He was discharged 11 March 1946 at Memphis, Tennessee.

STULTS, WILLIAM H., Serial Number 34 987 508, was a Private First Class in Company F, 8th Infantry Regiment in the Army of the United States. His permanent mailing address was Route 1, Waynesboro, Tennessee. He was born 6 March 1924 in Iron City, Tennessee. He was registered with the Selective Service Board in Wayne County, Tennessee. His Civilian Occupation was General Farmer. He was inducted 11 April 1944 at Camp Shelby, Mississippi. His Military Occupational Specialty was Light Mortar Crewman. His Military Qualifications included MM Rifle. He was in the battles of Ardennes, and Rhineland. The following decorations were awarded to Stults: Good Conduct Ribbon, World War Victory Medal, Purple Heart with 1 Bronze Oak Leaf Cluster, American Service Ribbon, and European-African Middle Eastern Theater Ribbon with 2 Bronze Stars. He was wounded in action in the European Theater 18 January 1945 and 28 February 1945. He left the USA 10 December 1944 for the European Theater Operation, and returned to USA 10 July 1945. He was discharged 28 January 1945 at Fort McPherson, Georgia.

STUTTS, CLIFFORD C., Serial Number 34 377 046, was a Technician Fourth Grade in Company H, 289th Infantry in the Army of the United States. His permanent mailing address was Route 4, Waynesboro, Tennessee. He was born 14 February 1908 in Waynesboro. He was registered with the Selective Service Board in Wayne County, Tennessee. His Civilian Occupation was Auto Mechanic. He was inducted 13 October 1942 and entered into active service 27 October 1942 at Fort Oglethorpe, Georgia. His Military Occupational Specialty was Auto Mechanic. His Military Qualifications included Combat Infantryman Badge. He was in the battles of Ardennes, Rhineland, and Central Europe. The following decorations were awarded to Stutts: European-African Middle Eastern Theater Ribbon with 3 Bronze Stars, American Theater Ribbon, Good Conduct Ribbon and Bronze Star Medal. He left the USA 22 October 1944 for the European Theater Operation, and returned to USA 23 October 1945. He was discharged 28 October 1945 at Camp Atterbury, Indiana. "Under the provisions of AR 6000-45, 22 September 1943, as amended, the Bronze star Medal was awarded to Technician Fourth Grade Clifford C. Stutts for heroic achievement in connection with military operations against the enemy on 10 April 1945 in Germany. Technician Stutts volunteered to recover a medical Vehicle taken by the enemy on the previous night. He and two other men arrived in an area where intermittent sniper and automatic weapons fire was placed upon them from short range. Despite the persistent aimed fire he and his comrades towed the vehicle back to our lines. His courage and cool actions under fire reflect great credit upon himself and his unit. Technician Stutts is the husband of Mrs. Mildred Hampton Stutts. He is the son of Mr. and Mrs. H. A. Stutts. He has a daughter, Luquetta Ann. They are natives of Waynesboro, Tennessee. "Clifford C. Stutts died 16 December 1961. He was buried in Old Town Cemetery, located across Green River and one mile East of the Courthouse Square.

STUTTS, CLIFTON, served in the Army of the United States during World War II. He married Betty Jo Inman Davis. Their three children are: Timmy, Rhonda Kay and Steven Stutts. He has a brother, Rawleigh Stutts.

STUTTS, COMMODORE, was born 28 December 1920 in Wayne County, Tennessee. He was the seventh son of H. A and Leslie Beckham Stutts. After graduating from the public schools of Wayne County, he worked locally until joining the United States Marine Corps in January 1942. During a military career spanning twenty-two years, Commodore saw service in the South Pacific during World War II, Korea, China and Japan. During peacetime, he was stationed such places as Virginia, North Carolina, Hawaii and Georgia. He retired from the service as Chief Warrant Officer III (First Lieutenant) on 1 September 1964, while stationed in Albany, Georgia. Decorations received include the World War II Victory Medal, the China Service Medal, the United Nations Korea Medal, and the National Defense Medal. Upon returning home to Waynesboro, Commodore was employed as a service station owner/operator and with W. J. Schoenberger Company (now Lincoln Brass). He also served a four year term as mayor of Waynesboro prior to his death on 15 April 1974. He was married 30 April 1949 to Bertha Staggs. They had three children: Barbara Jean Risner and James Harvey and Charles Jay Stutts. Semper Fidelis!.

STUTTS, ELVIN, served in the U.S. Army during World War 11. Like his four brothers he was honorably discharged from military service after the war was over. He was the son of Harvey (Todd) and Leslie Bell Beckham Stutts. His siblings were Clifford, Jim Neal, Woodrow, Commodore and Mildred.

After he was discharged from the Army he went to Indiana to find employment with an auto maker. After he retired from

this career he moved with his family to Linden Tennessee. He had married Verna Tucker and they had one son, Wayne who lives in Nashville. He ran a grocery business in Linden until he became disabled with Arthritis. He died in the Veterans Hospital from complication stemming from his Arthritis.

STUTTS, JAMES NEAL, was born 28 March 1915 in Wayne County to Harvey Annanias (Todd) and Leslie Belle

(Beckham) Stutts. He had five brothers: Lonnie, Elvin, Clifford, Woodrow and Commodore, and one sister, Mildred Phillips. Jim Neal attended school in Wayne County, graduating from Wayne County College in 1933. He attended the University of Tennessee in Martin, then taught school in the southern part of Wayne County for four years. Upon the outbreak of World War II, Jim Neal enlisted in the United States Marine Corps on 29 June 1940. At one time Jim Neal and four of his brothers were in the armed forces: Jim Neal, Elvin, and Commodore in the Marines, Clifford in the Army and Woodrow in the Navy. Jim Neal received his training at Parris Island in South Carolina. He qualified as a Pistol Marksman on 15 August 1940, and was promoted to Private

First Class on 20 January 1941. He worked as a wire repairman, being trained as a technician in the use, installation, repair and maintenance of all types of the Marine Corps telephone equipment. Jim Neal was at Pearl Harbor when the Japanese attacked early on Sunday Morning, 7 December 1941. He always vividly remembered riding in a truck down the streets of Pearl Harbor with bullets whizzing all around him, stopping to help pull men from water who had been on ships in the harbor when the attack came. After the attack Jim Neal was stationed on various islands in the Pacific. While there, Jim Neal contracted malaria, as many of the troops did. The medical unit had run out of quinine and he, along with many of his friends, came near to death before a supply was received from the States. He suffered with bouts of Malaria for the rest of his life. He married Sue Davis of Hohenwald on 9 June 1944 while on leave, He had to return immediately to Camp LeJeune in North Carolina where Sue was able to go and stay with him for about a month before he had to return to Camp Pendleton, California, where he was stationed as an instructor. He was only there for a short time before he had to go to Guam. The following is a list of some of the ships that he was on during the war and their destinations: The Wharton to Cuba, the Nitro to San Diego, the Henderson to Pearl Harbor, the Crescent City to Efate (an island in the Pacific), The Henry T. Allen to New Zealand, the Del Brazil to Guadalcanal, the LCT #67 to Vella LeVella, the Afoundria to San Francisco, the Stewart to Pearl Harbor, Pickaway to Guam, the Neville to Truk, the LST 288 to Guam, and the Neshoba to San Francisco. When the Atomic bomb was dropped on Nagasaki and Hiroshima, Jim Neal's unit had already received their orders to go to Japan. They would have been some of the first troops to land on the island to try to force their surrender, After the war ended, Jim Neal was stationed on Truk Island in the Pacific, where his unit was in charge of rounding up the remaining Japanese from the island. When his unit was getting ready to leave Truk Island, the military lost his assignment papers. At the last minute one of the men came hurrying up on a jeep and told him he was supposed to be on the ship. He had to jump in the jeep and run for the ship as it was pulling out. He didn't have time to get his personal belongings, but needless to say, he was glad to be on his way home. He was honorably discharged 28 June 1946 at Camp LeJeune, North Carolina with the rank of Sergeant. He was awarded lapel button, Good Conduct Medal, and good conduct Medal Bars. His monthly rate of pay was

$81. 90 per month. He returned to Waynesboro to make his home, where he worked as a lineman for the telephone company for about four years. In 1950 the Stutts family moved to Old Hickory, where Jim Neal worked for DuPont. Their daughter Wanda was born while they lived here. About 1959 the family moved back to Waynesboro. Jim Neal worked as a plumber and electrician in Wayne and adjoining counties. He was a member of Highland Methodist Church and was employed by Mallory when he died on 26 May 1975.

STUTTS, JOHN LEMUEL, Serial Number 783 82 96, was a Seaman First Class in the Navy of the United States. He was born 15 June 1927 in Decatur, Alabama. He entered into service 16 November 1944. The Vessels and Stations he served on were: NTC, Great Lakes Illinois; NATTC, Memphis, Tennessee; NATTC, Jacksonville, Florida; and Cub 17 ABATU, Lido Beach, Long Island, New York. He was discharged 25 April 1946 in Memphis, Tennessee.

STUTTS, LAWRENCE FREEMAN, was born and grew up in Wayne County, TN- He is the son of George and Ella Ann Stutts. Lawrence Freeman attended school at Waynesboro, then volunteered for the United States Marines, January 8, 1942. He received his training at a marine base in San Diego, CA. and went on to the Solomon Islands, where he spent many months during WWII. In 1943 he was involved in an accident on ship that almost took his life, when he fell several feet while on duty.

He remained in the marines until retirement age, then settled in Arizona with his wife, Mary, and their children. His brothers are Harry Lee, Raliegh, John and Clifton. Lawrence died in Arizona from a heart attack and is buried there.

STUTTS, RALEIGH B., Serial Number 36 864 362, was a Private First Class in Company B, 3rd Battalion, Armored Replacement Training Center in the Army of the United States. He was born in Wayne County. His Civilian Occupation was Arc Welder. He was 23 2/12 years old and married when he was inducted. His Military Occupational Specialty was Basic. His Military Qualifications included Marksman - Rifle. He was not in any battles. The following decorations were awarded to Stults: Lapel Button. He was discharged 3 November 1943 at Fort Knox, Kentucky.

STUTTS, WOODROW DONALD, was a native of Waynesboro and the son

of H. A. and Leslie Bell Beckham Stutts. He was a United States Navy Veteran of World War II and a lifetime member of Disabled Veterans. He was in the air conditioning and refrigeration business. He died 27 November 1992 at Wilson N. Jones Hospital in Sherman, Texas and was buried in Sadler Cemetery in Sadler, Texas, the place where he lived at the time of his death. Survivors included a daughter, Sharon Joyce Moore of Pascagoula, Mississippi and a sister, Mildred Phillips of Waynesboro.

TATE, JESSIE ROY, Serial Number 44 120 698, was a Private in Company A, 4th IT (Infantry) Battalion in the Army of

the United States. His permanent mailing address was Route 1, Clifton, Tennessee. He was born 11 June 1919 at Route 1, Peters Landing, Tennessee. His Civilian Occupation was Farmer. He was inducted 31 May 1945 at Fort Oglethorpe, Georgia. His Military Occupational Specialty was Infantry Basic. He was not in any battles. The following decorations were awarded to Tate: World War II Victory Medal and a Lapel Button. He was discharged 17 November 1945 at Fort Oglethorpe, Georgia. Jessie Roy Tate was the son of Spence and Cora Walker Tate. His brother is Plase

"Bud" Tate and his sisters are Aline, Willie and Lois Tate. He married Grace Ray. They have three children: Ellen Nix, Sue Battles and Dorothy Imogene Tate.

TATUM, CHARLES WALTON "WALT", was born on August 7, 1922, in Wayne County, Tennessee. He was the son

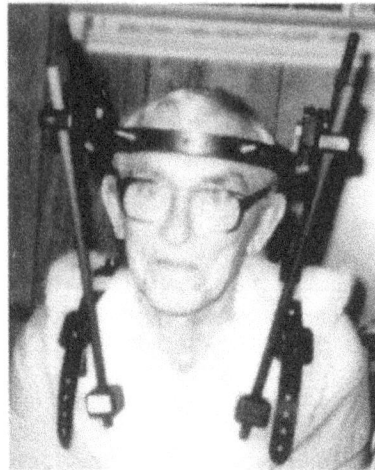

of William "Bill" Tatum and Ada Sharp. "Walt" served the Army in World War II. He didn't go overseas, but he served his tour of duty in the states. He married Mae Edith Holt on July 3, 1946, in Wayne County, Tennessee. She is the daughter of Harvey Dixon Holt (December 7, 1893-April 28, 1993) and Bessie Sally Holder (July 31, 1900-June 17, 1945). Walt and Mae had the following children: Carolyn Fay, Charles Wayne and Donna Kay Tatum. His siblings are Bob, Hollis, Hunter, John, Malcolm, Howard, Minnie, Royie, Clemmie, Nancy and Martha.

TATUM, JOHN DEWITT, was born on December 17, 1915, in Perry County, Tennessee, and worked as a farmhand in

Flat Woods, Tennessee, when he entered the United States Army on March 15, 1941, at Ft. Oglethorpe, Georgia. He served with Company M, 117th Infantry as a light truck

driver. DeWhitt served in the battles of Normandy, Northern France, Central Europe, Ardennes and Rhineland. He was awarded the EAME Theater Ribbon with five Bronze Stars, American Defense Service Medal and Good Conduct Ribbon. He was discharged on June 29, 1945, at Camp Atterbury, Indiana.

TATUM, JOHN "JOHNNIE", was born on November 14, 1920, in Wayne County, Tennessee, the son of William

(Bill) Tatum and Ada Sharp Tatum. He served in the United States Army during World War II, but he did not have overseas duty. He served in the States. He was killed in a truck wreck accident soon after he came home from the Service in Hohenwald, Tennessee.

TATUM, MALCOLM, (P.F.C. so 16 394th Infantry Aus.) was inducted into service on November 22, 1942, at Fort

Oglethorpe, Georgia, for World War II. He was sent to the European, African and Middle East Theatre of War. He was awarded an EAME Combat Medal, a Good Conduct Medal and the Expert Infantryman Badge for marksmanship for the cal. 30 carbine. He received a Certificate of

Disability for discharge on November 4, 1944, and was discharged on July 20, 1945, at Brooks Convalescent Hospital FSHTex. He was in Foreign Service for five months and 25 days. Malcolm was born on December 4, 1918, the son of William (Bill) and Ada Sharp Tatum in Linden, Tennessee. He is an avid hunter. For a livelihood he worked with timber, lumber and Vulcan Materials. He married Minnie Prater, daughter of William B. and Lou Griffin Prater. They have a daughter, Debra. They live near Waynesboro, Tennessee. His siblings are Bob, Hollis, Walton, Hunter, John, Howard, Minnie, Roxie, Clemmie, Nancy and Martha.

TEMPLETON, CURT, JR., served as a gunner in an 81 MM Mortar Squad. He was assigned to an Eight Air Force P-51 Mustang Station. He was trained in welding with the 78th Fighter Group commanded by Lieutenant Colonel John D. Landers from Joshua, Texas. Private First Class Templeton landed in France in December 1944, and was in action during the German break through in the Ardennes Forest. He was wounded in Europe and was sent to England to a hospital for recuperation. He graduated from Frank Hughes High School in Clifton in 1943, just before he entered the Army in June 1943. Curt, Jr., is the son of Curt, Sr., and Roxie Garrard Templeton, Clifton, Tennessee. His siblings are: Marietta Cole and Eugene T. (Bill) Templeton. He married Martha Jack Lynch from Clifton. They have two children: Leslie and Mary Beth Templeton. After his discharge, he became part owner and operator of a storage company in Nashville, Tennessee.

TEMPLETON, EUGENE F. "BILL", Serial Number 44 121 845, was a Technician Third Grade in the 977th Signal Service Company in the Army of the United States. He was born 13 December 1926 in Clifton, Tennessee. He had blue eyes, black hair, was 5' 11 1/2" in height and weighed 174 lbs. He was inducted 20 June 1945 and entered into active service 20 June 1945 at Fort Oglethorpe, Georgia. His Military Occupational Specialty was Teletype Operator 237. His Military Qualifications included MI Rifle 55167 on August 4, 1945. He spent seven months at the Clerks School Camp in Plauche, Louisiana. He was not in any battles. The following decorations were awarded to Templeton: Army of Occupation Medal and World War II Victory Medal. Lapel Button Issued: No days lost under AW 107 ASR Score 2 September 1945. He left the USA 13 December 1945 for the MT Operation, and returned to USA 26 December 1946. His total foreign service was one

year and two days. He was honorably discharged from the Military Services of the United States of America of Honest and Faithful Service to this country on 21 January 1947 at Fort Dix, New Jersey. Bill, is the son of Curt, Sr., and Roxie Garrard Templeton, Clifton, Tennessee. He graduated from Frank Hughes High School in 1945 in Clifton, Tennessee. His siblings are: Marietta Cole and Curt Templeton, Jr. He married Kay Welch from Savannah. They have two children: Pattie and Rennie Templeton. After his discharge, Bill worked for TVA and later for the Clifton Towing Company. The Crounse Towing Company hired him as boat pilot, port captain and promoted him to operations office manager in Paducah, Kentucky. He retired from Crounse in March 1986 and resides in Paducah where he enjoys golf and boating.

THARPE, AUSTIN C., Serial Number 34 920 982, was a Technician Fifth Grade in 205th Hospital Ship Complement in the Army of the United States. His permanent mailing address was Route 3, Waynesboro, Tennessee. He was born 10 April 1914 in Wayne County. He was registered with the Selective Service Board in Wayne County, Tennessee. His Civilian Occupation was General Farmer. He was married with one dependent when he was inducted 15 December 1943 and entered into active service 16 January 1944 at Fort Oglethorpe, Georgia. His Military Occupational Specialty was Surgical Technician. His Military Qualifications included Rifle Marksman. The following decorations were awarded to Tharpe: American Service Medal, Asiatic-Pacific Medal, World War II Victory Medal, and the Good Conduct Medal. He left the USA 20 August 1945 for the Pacific Theater Operation, and returned to USA 11 December 1945. He left again for the same assignment 1 January 1946 and returned 5 March 1946. He was discharged 23 May 1946 at Fort McPherson, Georgia. The USS COMFORT was commissioned 5 May 1944, and attached to the 7th Fleet. It was a hospital ship hit by a suicide plane in the Battle of Okinawa. The operating room was hit and sixteen people were killed. The ship was brought back to the United States for repairs. Austin was assigned to this ship when it set sail again for overseas. Surgical Technician Tharpe performed duties at a general hospital in the Continental United States; assisted medical officers in rendering surgical care and treatment to patients; prepared operating room and surgical equipment for use; cleaned and washed equipment and instruments; assisted in preparing patients for operations and administering hypodermic injections; assisted in

transporting patients to and from operation room; changed bandages and dressings; treated minor injuries; served as medical technician on hospital ship returning sick and wounded from the Asiatic-Pacific Theater. The following report was given to the Army when Tharpe enlisted: He owned and operated a 70 acre farm along Buffalo River near Waynesboro, Tennessee where he planted cultivated and harvested crops of corn and peanuts for market, raised garden vegetables, hogs and poultry for domestic consumption, drove a Farmall-20 tractor in the farming operations, tended ten beef cattle for market, used mules for some farm work, and employed one man to assist him in farm work. Austin was the son of J. M. Tharpe (1878-1925) and Jennie Warren Tharpe (1880-1965). He was born 10 April 1914 in Wayne County. Austin married Ruth Ray and they have one daughter, Mary Ann Inman. He has one brother, Ottie Tharpe of Hohenwald. The home address of Austin and Ruth is 102 Southern Drive, Hendersonville, Tennessee 37075.

THOMPSON, BOYD, was born in Wayne County in the year 1915. He was the son of James and Sarah Thompson. He

spent his military time with the U.S. Army and received an honorable discharge.

Boyd's children were; Rhonda, Steve, Therian, Tim and Melissa. His siblings were; Maudie Melton, Bertha Daniel, Bessie Brewer, Lydia Brewer, Nell Simmons, Floyd, Lloyd, Maynard and Nable.

Boyd died in 1978 and is buried at McGlamery Cemetery.

THOMPSON, CHARLES LEON, Serial Number 34 723 009, was a Private First Class in Company A, 319th Engineer Battalion, 94th Infantry Division in the Army of the United States. His permanent mailing address was Route 3, Iron City, Tennessee. He was born 28 October 1923 in Iron City, Tennessee. He was registered

with the Selective Service Board in Wayne County, Tennessee. His Civilian Occupation was Light Truck Driver. His Military Occupational Specialty was Light Truck Driver. His Military Qualifications included Marksman Rifle. He was in the battles of Northern France, Ardennes, Rhineland, and Central Europe. The following decorations were awarded to Thompson: American Theater Ribbon, European-African Middle Eastern Theater Ribbon with 4 Bronze Stars, Good Conduct Medal, World War II Victory Medal and Lapel Button. He left the USA 6 August 1944 for the European-African Middle Eastern Theater Operation, and returned to USA 30 December 1945. He was discharged 6 January 1946 Fort Knox, Kentucky. Charlie Leon Thompson, son of Jahue and Nancy Daniel Thompson, died 15 March 1994 at ECM Hospital in Florence, Alabama and was buried in Butler Grove Cemetery with military rites at the grave side. He was survived by his wife, Mary Thompson and sons: Danny, Anthony and Charles, Jr. and daughters, Judy Franks, Pat Staggs and Susan Weichselbaum. His siblings are Talmadge and Leonard Thompson, Lizzie Jackson, Lorene Melton, and half- siblings: Carter and Ed Holt, Eurlene Hollander, Iva Dean Daniel, and Thelma Williams. Mr. Thompson was a retired auto repairman and painter with the Chrysler Corporation and a member of the Butler Grove Freewill Baptist Church.

THOMPSON, EUNIS C., Serial Number 34 361 754, was a Private in Company G, 135th Infantry in the Army of the United States. He was born Nov 1920 in Wayne County. His Civilian Occupation was General Farmer. He was inducted 25 July 1942 at Fort Oglethorpe, Georgia. He had hazel eyes, brown hair, ruddy complexion, and was 5' 10" in height. His Military Occupational Specialty was Rifleman. The following decorations were awarded to Thompson: Purple Heart and, European-African

Middle Eastern Theater Medal. He left the USA 5 March 1943 for North Africa Theater of Operations and returned to USA 25 June 1943. He was honorably discharged 20 October 1943 at Kennedy General Hospital in Memphis, Tennessee. Eunis was the son of Louish B. and Ena Howell Thompson. His siblings are: Elbert Thompson, and Jessie Mae Tatum. He married Frances McMahan and their children are: Glenda, Brenda, Linda, Fay, Ronnie and Benjamin Thompson.

THOMPSON, HERMAN CLYDE, Serial Number 966 28 46, was a Seaman Second Class was in the Navy of the United

States. He was born 26 May 1917 in Iron City, Tennessee. His Civilian Occupation was working for Hassell and Hughes Lumber Company in Collinwood. He entered into active service 6 January 1944 and was sent to Great Lakes, Illinois for his boot training. Then he was assigned to a ship and sent to the Pacific Theater of war. Here is a list of the vessels and stations where he served: NTS, Great Lakes, Illinois; NRS San Francisco, California; NRB Portland, Oregon and USS PONAZANSET. The following decorations were awarded to Thompson: American Theater Medal, Asiatic-Pacific Theater Medal with 2 Stars,

Philippine Liberation Medal and World War II Victory Medal. He was discharged 14 January 1946 at US Naval Personnel Separation Center in Nashville, Tennessee.

Herman's parents were S.R. and Polly Ann Daniel Thompson. Herman married Sarah Ruth Brewer and they had the following children: Mary M. Thompson Jackson, Herman C, Thompson, Jr., Martha A. Thompson Pulley, Travis W. Thompson, Palma J. Thompson Caperton, Dennis R-Thompson.

Herman's siblings are: Mamie E. Thompson Martin Melson, Annie E. Thompson Daniel, Herschel H. Thompson, Willie E. Thompson, Jesse F. Thompson, Hubert P. Thompson, Richard L. Thompson, Walter H. Thompson, James M. Thompson.

Herman died March 3, 1999, and he is buried at McGlamery Cemetery in Collinwood, TN. His family received a letter honoring the memory of Herman for having served his country from President William Clinton.

THOMPSON, HUBERT P., was inducted into the U.S. Army 1 November 1942 from Wayne County Tennessee and

discharged 29 November 1945. 1 took my basic training at Camp White Oregon and the rest of my time was spent in the Pacific Theaters of operation. I was in the 7th Infantry Division and was sent to the Aleutian Islands first then the Marshal Islands and in between battles was spent on Oahu, Hawaii. I had three brothers drafted from Wayne county, Jessie F. Thompson, Herman C. Thompson, and Richard L. Thompson and at one time three of us met in Hawaii. The next battle was Leyte Island in the Philippine, after the battle I was sent to Okinawa 350 miles from Japan. I was there when the Atomic bomb was dropped on Hiroshima Japan. When the war was over, I was sent to Korea to help with the occupation of South Korea. World war two was a war not only for the military but everyone was working to furnish material and supplies

without which we could not have completed the job of securing peace, after December 7, 1941 we did not have enough ships, airplanes, tanks or even small arms. The American public went into the factories working for small wages to build the material needed, and many of them had never worked in an industrial job of any kind.

THOMPSON, JAMES H. "DICK", was sent to the European Theater of Operations. He had two brothers in service too during World War II: Lewis Clay, who fought in the European Theater and Loyal Waco who served in the Pacific. His parents were Cary and Vada Thompson.

THOMPSON, JESSE FRANKLIN, Serial number 845 38 15, PFC Thompson, entered the Navy 24 April 1943. He received his boot training at Norfolk, Virginia. He served four months in the Atlantic and participated in the Invasion of Sicily for which he received two stars. Prior to entering service, he was employed at the Naval Base in Memphis. He served on the following Vessels and Stations: NTS Bainbridge, Maryland; NTS Norfolk, Virginia, and USS MURPHY. He was registered with the Selective Service Board in Wayne County, Tennessee with his home address as Cypress Inn, Tennessee. He was discharged 16 December 1945 at US Naval Personnel Separation Center in Nashville, Tennessee. Remarks made by C. V. Lynch, Lieutenant (D) USNR included: "Commended by the President of the USA while a crewman of the USS MURPHY Authority". The American Area Victory Medal, and European-African Middle Eastern Theater Medal are some of the honors he received. PFC Thompson, son of Mr. and Mrs. H. R. Thompson of Collinwood, was born 10 March 1907 in Iron City, Tennessee. He married Maethel Brewer.

THOMPSON, JOE WILBUR, son of Henry and Elvie Thompson, was born on Eagle Creek on November 19, 1925. He attended Lone Ceder School and worked as a farmhand when he was inducted into the United States Army on January 22, 1944, at Camp Forrest, Tennessee. He was assigned to C. E. 194th Infantry Training Battalion and was discharged on October 18, 1944, for health reasons at Ft. McPherson, Georgia. Wilbur married his wife, Estelle, and lived on Eagle Creek. They had two children, Joe Henry and a daughter. He died on July 31, 1968, and was buried in Walker Cemetery on Eagle Creek in Wayne County, Tennessee.

THOMPSON, JOHNNIE NOBLE, Serial Number 34 375 238, was a Private in Station Complement at Camp Forrest, Tennessee, in the Army of the United States. His Civilian Occupation was Farmer. He was 23 years old when he was inducted 3 October 1942 at Fort Oglethorpe, Georgia. He was not in any battles. He was discharged 15 September 1943 at Camp Forrest, Tennessee with poor physical condition. Johnnie, son of James Monroe and Sarah Malinda Daniels Thompson, was born in Iron City, Wayne County, Tennessee, died 4 August 1993 in Wayne County General Hospital and was buried in Butler Grove Cemetery. He resided on Route 1, Box 53, Collinwood. His siblings are: Maynard and Floyd Thompson and Bessie and Lynda Brewer all of Collinwood and Nell Simmons of Waynesboro.

THOMPSON, LEWIS CLAY, Sergeant, volunteered for service in the Armed Forces in September 1942. He was trained for operating in a tank destroyer unit. He was sent to the European Theater of War and served in England. He was hospitalized for four months and separated from his company. He is the son of Cary and Vada Thompson. He married Iva Dell Risner, and they had one daughter when this clipping appeared in the Wayne County News.

THOMPSON, LOYAL WACO, was the son of Cary and Vada Thompson. He served in the Pacific Area during World War II. He also had two brothers in service during this time, Lewis Clay and James H. Thompson.

THOMPSON, MAYNARD, Serial Number 967 13 51, Seaman First Class Thompson entered the Navy 10 April 1944. He was born 5 March 1923 at Collinwood, Tennessee. He served on the following Vessels and Stations: Constitution Batts USNCTC, Williamsburg, Virginia; Com Ser 7th Fleet, R/B edur; Com MTB Rone 7th Fleet (PT1); and Advance Unit No. 4; and USS Crux (AK-115). He was dis-

charged 12 January 1946 at US Naval Personnel Separation Center.

THOMPSON, RAYMOND L., was a Corporal in Battery A 15th Field Artillery Battalion, 2nd Division in the Army of the United States. His permanent mailing address was Route 2, Iron City, Tennessee. Raymond, son of Mr. and Mrs. L. H. Thompson, was born 28 June 1922 in Iron City. His Civilian Occupation was Farming. He was inducted 29 November 1942 at Fort Oglethorpe, Georgia. He took training at Van Dorn, Mississippi, Maxey, Texas and Fort Sill, Oklahoma. While he was overseas, he served in England, Belgium, and Germany. His Military Occupational Specialty was Field Lineman. His Military Qualifications included SS Carbine. He was engaged in the battles of Ardennes, Rhineland, and the Central Europe Campaign. The following decorations were awarded to Thompson: American Theater Medal, European-African Middle Eastern Theater Medal with 3 Bronze Service Stars, Good Conduct Medal, one Overseas Service Bar and a Lapel Button. He left the USA 29 September 1944 for the European-African Middle Eastern Theater Operation, and returned to USA 19 July 1945. He was discharged 26 November 1945 at McCloskey General Hospital in Temple, Texas.

THOMPSON, RICHARD L., Private, son of Mr. and Mrs. H. R. Thompson, entered the service February 1943. He took his basic training at Fort Bliss, Texas and San Luis Obispo, California. He was transferred overseas in June 1944 and served with an AAA Battalion in the Southwest Pacific. Before going into the Army, Private Thompson was employed with a construction company in Clarksville, Tennessee.
Source: Wayne County News.

THOMPSON, WILLIAM EDD, Serial Number 34 377 045, was inducted into the United States Army 27 October 1942. Private First Class Thompson served with

the 331st Infantry, Company F of the 83rd Division. He spent 20 months in England, France, Belgium, Holland, Luxembourg and Germany. He served as 2nd cook and baker. He cooked meals for 180 service men near the front lines. He also did barber work while near the front line. He was awarded the Certificate of Merit in the European Theater of Operations. This citation covered activities from 2 November 1944 to 20 February 1945 while in the campaign in Luxembourg, Germany and Belgium. He received the Good Conduct Medal. He also served in the Army of Occupation. After the war ended, he organized a country western band in Germany. They were known as the "Stump Jumpers". The band was made up of six men, two guitars, an accordion, a mandolin and two violins/fiddles. They entertained the service men until he was honorably discharged 6 December 1945 at Fort Knox, Kentucky. Edd, son of Charlie Cicero and Maggie Emily Huckaba Thompson of the Eagle Creek Community in Wayne County, was born 2 January 1921 in Waynesboro, Tennessee. His siblings are: Oscar, Earl, John, Shields, Fred, Gladys and Pearl. He married Thelma Jewell McGhee from the Double Branches Community in Wayne County. Their children are: Brenda Jane, Eddie Wayne, Daniel Alan, Phyllis Elaine and Marcus Wendell Thompson.

THOMPSON, WILLIE M., Serial Number not available, was a Private First Class in Headquarters Company, 701st Tank Destroyer Battalion in the Army of the United States. His permanent mailing address was Route 2, Iron City, Tennessee. He was born 29 September 1921 in Wayne County. He was registered with the Selective Service Board in Wayne County, Tennessee. His Civilian Occupation was General Farmer. His Military Occupational Specialty was Light Machine Gunner. His Military Qualifications included Marksman Rifle. He was in the battles of Rome-Arno, North Apennines, and Po Valley. The fol-

lowing decorations were awarded to Thompson: European-African Middle Eastern Theater Medal, Good Conduct Medal, Croix De Guerre, Bronze Arrowhead and a Lapel Button. He left the USA 8 February 1943 for the European-African Middle Eastern Theater Operation, and returned to USA 23 August 1945. He was discharged 16 October 1945 at Camp Blanding, Florida.

THOMPSON, VERNIE L., age 79, died 30 December 1994 in Hohenwald Tennessee. He was buried in Fallbrook Masonic Cemetery in Fallbrook, California. Survivors included: two daughters, Mary L. West and Rebecca A. Eckles and three sisters: Elease Parker, Vergie Berry and Birdie Heard. He was a native of Iron City, Tennessee and a World War II Veteran of the United State Army. He worked for H. B. McCarmac as a rancher for 38 years before he retired.

TIDWELL, ERNEST HUGH, was a World War II Army veteran. He was the son of Willie Wyld and Jessie Mae Tidwell. He was a member of the Iron City Masonic Lodge and Hollis Chapel Church. He retired from Murray Ohio Manufacturing Company. He died on Monday, April 14, 1997. Burial was in the Hollis Cemetery with full military honors. Masonic services were held on the night previous to the funeral service. He was survived by his wife, Vernon Kelley Tidwell; two sons, Lister Allen and Paul Nolan; and one daughter, Pat, all of Iron City, Tennessee. His siblings are Ed, Glen, Billy, Rex, Charlsie, Bonnie and Beverly.

TININ, JAMES HUBERT, Serial Number 34 888 744, was a Sergeant in Company F 148th Infantry in the Army of

the United States. His permanent mailing address was Route 2, Clifton, Tennessee. He was born 17 August 1924 in Clifton. His Civilian Occupation was General Farmer. He was inducted 13 November

1943 and entered into active service 5 December 1943 at Fort Oglethorpe, Georgia. His Military Occupational Specialty was Assistant Squad Leader. He was in the battles of Northern Solomons and Luzon. The following decorations were awarded to Tinin: World War II Victory Medal, Good Conduct Medal, Asiatic-Pacific Theater Ribbon with 2 Bronze Service Stars, and 1 Bronze Arrowhead, Philippines Liberation Ribbon and 1 Bronze Star, a Purple Heart and a Lapel Button. He left the USA 3 April 1944 for the Asiatic-Pacific Theater Operation, and returned to USA 9 January 1946. He was discharged 18 January 1946 at Camp Chaffee, Arkansas. James H., son of Ralph Willard and Nona Delphia Battles Tinin, was a life time resident of Clifton. His siblings are: Willodean Neal, Jewel Holt, and Elizabeth Ann Templeton. He married Virginia Graham. Their two children are: Patricia married Jimmy Borroughs, and Tommy married Sybil Davis. James attended Frank Hughes School. He has continued his farming career and drives a school bus for the Wayne County School System.

TIPTON, CLARENCE H., Serial Number 34 363 109, was a Private in 215th General Hospital in the Army of the United States. He was born in Madison, Arkansas. His Civilian Occupation was Fish Man. He was 37 7/12 years old and married when he was inducted 5 August 1942 at Fort Oglethorpe, Georgia. He had blue eyes, brown hair, ruddy complexion, and was 5'6" in height. He was discharged 26 February 1943 at Camp McCoy, Wisconsin. (Discharge Book 1, page 414.).

TODD, GENTRY, Serial Number 976 60 98, was a Seaman First Class in the Navy of the United States. His permanent mailing address was Route 1, West Point, Tennessee. He was born 19 May 1926 in West Point. He was registered with the Selective Service Board in Wayne County, Tennessee. His last employer was the Gable Saw Mill in West Point. His Civilian Occupation was Farmer. He was inducted into active service 31 August 1944 at Chattanooga, Tennessee. He served on the following Vessels/Stations: Rec Trg Com and USNTADC, Williamsburg, Virginia and USS Alkaid. The following decorations were awarded to Todd: Asiatic-Pacific Theater Ribbon with 1 Star, World War II Victory Medal and American Theater Ribbon. He was discharged 11 March 1946 at Personnel Separation Center in Memphis, Tennessee. Gentry was the son of Broadus and Bertha Andrews Todd. His siblings are: J. D. Todd, Roberta Weaver, Dorothy Jean Robertson, and Joel Todd. He married Mary Jo Robertson.

Their children are Ricky and Tony Todd.

TODD, JACK D., Serial Number 34 146 869, was a Technical Sergeant in 3560th Service Command Unit in the Army of the United States. His permanent mailing address was Box 42, Collinwood, Tennessee. He was born 7 July 1918 in Collinwood. His Civilian Occupation was Wholesaler. He was married when he entered into active service 9 October 1941 at Fort Oglethorpe, Georgia. His Military Occupational Specialty was Administrative NCO. His Military Qualifications included Sharpshooter Rifle. He was not in any battles. The following decorations were awarded to Todd: American Defense Ribbon, American Theater Ribbon, Good Conduct Medal, Lapel Button and World War II Victory Medal. He graduated from high school and had a half year of college. He was discharged 20 November 1945 at Fort Knox, Kentucky.

TOWNSEND, JEFFERSON R., Serial Number 34 366 655, was a Private in Company B, 111th Engineer (C) Battalion in the Army of the United States. He was born in Wayne County. His Civilian Occupation was Service Station Attendant. He was 41 7/12 years of age when he was inducted 26 August 1942 at Fort Oglethorpe, Georgia. His Military Qualifications in arms included Marksman, Caliber 30 Rifle. The following decorations were awarded to Townsend: a Lapel Button issued 12 February 1944 in Detroit, Michigan. He was discharged at Camp Edwards, Massachusetts.

TOWNSEND, JOSEPH W., Serial Number 34 361 756, was a Private First Class in Service Company, 739th Medium Tank Battalion Special in the Army of the United States. His permanent mailing address was Collinwood, Tennessee. He was registered with the Selective Service Board in Wayne County, Tennessee. His Civilian Occupation was Light Truck Driver. He was single when he was inducted 25 June 1942 and entered into active service 8 August 1942 at Fort Oglethorpe, Georgia. He was in the battles of Ardennes, Rhineland, and Central Europe. The following decorations were awarded to Townsend: American Theater Ribbon, European-African Middle Eastern Theater Ribbon with 3 Bronze Stars, Good Conduct Medal, Lapel Button and World War II Victory Medal. He left the USA 26 July 1944 for the European-African Middle Eastern Theater Operation, and returned to USA 5 January 1946. He finished two years of high school. He was discharged 14 January 1946 at Fort Knox, Kentucky. He was the son of Dr. James and

Nipsie Townsend. He was born 15 June 1912 in Wayne County.

TREADWELL, JAMES GRANVILLE, Serial Number 965 96 56, was a Gunners Mate Third Class in the Navy of the United

States. He was born 30 May 1924 in Waynesboro, Tennessee. He entered into service 22 November 1943. He served on the following Vessels and Stations: USNTS Great Lakes, Illinois, AGC SO Brooklyn, New York, SS BUTTON GEVINNETT and SS MONOCACY. His campaign areas were: European-African Middle Eastern Theater Ribbon with 1 Star, American Theater Ribbon, and Asiatic-Pacific Theater Ribbon. He had a high school education and after the war graduated from Martin Methodist College in Pulaski, Tennessee. He was discharged 18 May 1946 at US Naval Personnel Separation Center in Memphis, Tennessee. Granville is the son of Samuel Grady Treadwell (1892-1979) and Josie Brown (1896-1986). His siblings are Charlene, Dorothy Dell, Sarah Jane and Thomas Hugh Treadwell and Fayetta Delk. He married 30 May 1948 Jeannette Harris. He met her while he was attending Martin College. Their children are James Harvey (1953-1981), Thomas Grady, born 1957 and John Michael, born 1960. Granville and Jeannette reside on his father's home place in the Mt. Hope community.

TREADWELL, WEMAN EDWARD "BILL", the third child of Maggie Chumney and John Treadwell, was born 21 October 1923 in Flatwoods, Perry County, Tennessee. He had just turned eleven when his mother died. The country was in the middle of the Great Depression and his father found it impossible to keep his large family together. Four of his sisters were sent to school in Nashville while his older brother and sister, Walter and Lois, went to live with their maternal grandparents, Mr. and Mrs. Edward Chumney, near Hohenwald. It was during

the spring of 1938, that a young boy appeared at the home of Mr. and Mrs. W. B. Culp, who were still newlyweds, asking if they had any work for him. He tried to stand tall, as he assured them that he was a hard worker and had experience ploughing the fields. If W. B. and Montie had any reservations about this young man, they did not hesitate long. They showed great compassion for Weman and soon Mrs. Culp sat him down and told him that if he stayed with them, he would have to go to school. That must have pleased Weman for he was a quiet, serious and studious person. The few years that Weman stayed with them were very positive and rewarding for him. His sister, Wilton Scott, remembers Weman talking about the Culps in a fond and loving way. He truly felt that he was part of the family in Clifton, Tennessee. As part of Roosevelt's New Deal, the Civilian Conservation Corps (CCC) was created and young men were recruited from across the country. Weman found himself on a train headed for Oregon. He worked on reforestation and the fisheries, supplying the lakes with minnows. In 1942-1943 Weman was employed by Boeing Aircraft Company in Seattle and attending night school. On 15 May 1943 Weman enlisted in the Navy and served on the USS ARGUS Unit # 17 in the Asiatic-Pacific area. He was honorably discharged in March 1946, having received medals for Military Merit, The American Campaign, Asiatic-Pacific Campaign, Freedom Medal, and Good Conduct Medal. Once he had a taste of life at sea, he was not content with civilian life. He, therefore, reenlisted and served twenty years. Again he was given an honorable discharge. Weman took a job as manager of a golf course in Oakland, California. He took up golf and became an excellent player. Some years later he was written up in one of the Seattle papers for getting a hole in one. However, the sea lured him back again, this time as a Merchant Marine. During his many years of service, he served on a number of vessels: Fleet Air Wing Two, U. S. Naval Air Station-North Island-San Diego, USS HUNTINGTON, USS ENGLISH DD696, USS WINSTON AKA-94 and USS TERRELL COUNTY LST-1157. Always eager to learn, Weman completed numerous courses, specializing in Radar Observation. He retired 16 July 1982 as a Merchant Marine Officer Second Class after a total of 36 years of service and prepared to enjoy retirement in his new home in Kirkland, Washington. He continued to enjoy his golf game. Over the years he developed an interest in the stock market and invested with considerable success. In 1983, Weman's health began to deteriorate and he required a triple-by-pass. He recuperated very well. However, in 1985 he suffered a stroke which left him unable to communicate. He spent the last five years of his life in a nursing home. He passed away 14 September 1990 A grateful nation honored him by allowing him to be buried in Willamette National Cemetery in Portland, Oregon. The cemetery is truly a national shrine, with it's boulevard of flags which are displayed on Memorial Day and Remembrance Day. Officer Treadwell is a credit to his country, and is lovingly remembered in the hearts of all those he touched during his voyage through life.

TREADWELL, WALTER D., of Clifton Tn., enlisted in the US Navy and served as machinist mate third class on the USS India, when she along with the victorious third fleet dropped anchor in Toyko Bay.

TRIMMER, JAMES L., Serial Number 34 142 895, was a Sergeant in 919th Air Engineer Squadron, 501st Air Service Group in the Army of the United States. His permanent mailing address was West Point, Tennessee. He was born 7 June 1918 in Wayne County. He was registered with the Selective Service Board in Wayne County, Tennessee. His Civilian Occupation was Farm Hand. He was single when he was inducted 10 July 1941 at Fort Oglethorpe, Georgia. His Military Occupational Specialty was Automatic Mechanic. His Military Qualifications included Rifle Marksman. He was in the battles of Tunisia, Sicily, Naples-Foggia, Rome-Arno, North Apennines, and Rhineland. The following decorations were awarded to Trimmer: American Certificate of Merit for Heroism, Defense Service Medal, Good Conduct Medal, European-African Middle Eastern Theater Ribbon with 7 Bronze Stars, and a Lapel Button. He left the USA 14 January 1943 for the European-African Middle Eastern Theater Operation, and returned to USA 19 September 1945. He was discharged 24 September 1945 at Camp Atterbury, Indiana.

J. B. Trimmer, 79, of 203 Railroad Street, West Point, Tennessee, died 20 April 1998 in his home. He was buried in Blair Cemetery. He was a member of the West Point Baptist Church, a World War II Army Veteran, a son of Will and Emma Ezell Trimmer and a retired electrician at Brown's Ferry. Survivors include his wife, Dorothy Russ Trimmer, one son, Wade Trimmer of Augusta, Georgia; one daughter, Patsy Story of West Point; one sister, Mattie Turner of Opoka, Florida and five grandchildren.
Source: Wayne County News, 22 April 1998.

TRIPP, FLOYD R., Serial Number 44 070 825, was a Private in Company C, 3rd Infantry in the Army of the United States. His permanent mailing address was % Postmaster, Waynesboro, Tennessee. He was born 19 November 1926 in Lawrenceburg, Tennessee. He was registered with the Selective Service Board in Wayne County, Tennessee. His Civilian Occupation was Edger Man. He was inducted 24 February 1945 at Fort Oglethorpe, Georgia. His Military Occupational Specialty was Guard Patrolman. He was not in any battles. The following decorations were awarded to Tripp: Good Conduct Medal, Army Occupation Medal (Germany), World War II Victory Medal and Lapel Button. He left the USA 20 December 1945 for the Germany, and returned to USA 16 September 1946. He was discharged 24 October 1946 at Fort George G. Meade, Maryland.

TURMAN, EARL SIMS, enlisted in the United States Navy at Nashville, Tennessee, on 22 April 1943. His home address was 309 Fairfax Avenue, Nashville. He was in the (N) CB's, 140th Battalion. He took his basic training in San Diego, California. Later he was sent to Australia and the Admiralty Islands in the Pacific. His parents were Benjamin Franklin Turman of Wayne County, Tennessee and Emma Kate Spinks of Meade County, Kentucky. They were married 11 April 1895. His grandparents include John Matthew and Dorothy Ann Sims Turman of Wayne County. William Whitsett and Emma Brown Spinks of Meade County, Kentucky. He has one sister Dorothy Eloise Turman, born about 1908 in Wayne County. She married (1) Bill Workman and (2) Lewis Andrews. They lived in Nashville. Dot was a beautician but is now deceased. Earl married (1) Virginia _____, (2) married 29 May 1932 Nona Louise Johnson, and divorced her in 1944. Nona, daughter of John William and Bettie Collins Johnson, was born in 1913 in Clifton. (3) was married 6 February 1946,

to Mary Turner Wolfe. Mary, daughter of Fred Wade and Jennie L. S. Nichol Wolfe, was born 14 September 1918 in Rome, Georgia. Earl's children include: (1) Betty Ann, born 7 April 1933 in Waynesboro, (2) Edna Earl, born 26 September 1934 in Indianapolis, Indiana and died 24 May 1935, (3) Charles Richard, born 17 February 1936 in Lawrence County, Alabama, (4) Earl Sims, Jr., born 2 August 1949 in Madison County, Tennessee, and now lives in San Diego, (5) Mary Jane, born 24 Dec 1953 at Nashville, (6) Benjamin Frederick "Bennie", born 6 April 1955 in Gallatin, Tennessee and now living in Washington State, (7) Robert Edward born 4 July 1956 in Gallatin and lives in Washington. (8) Kenneth Marshall born 21 Sept 1957 at Gallatin and living in Washington. Earl was a carpenter before and after the war. He worked with TVA before his military service, on Wheeler, Ocoee, Hiwassee and Guntersville Dams as a cement finisher. Earl obtained his education in the Waynesboro school system. Earl and Mary bought a farm in Gallatin and lived there until about 1953 when they moved to San Diego. Earl died 29 May 1975 in San Diego, California.
Source: daughter, Betty Ann of Savannah.

TURMAN, HOLLIS, Serial Number 34 723 011, was a Private in 20th Bombardment Squadron in the Army of the

United States. His permanent mailing address was Route 1, Collinwood, Tennessee. He was born 14 August 1923 in Collinwood. He was registered with the Selective Service Board in Wayne County, Tennessee. His Civilian Occupation was Block Setter at Holthouse and Hardup Mill in Waynesboro. He was inducted 20 February 1943 at Fort Oglethorpe, Georgia. His Military Occupational Specialty was Aircraft Sheet Metal Worker. He was in the battles of Po Valley, Rome-Arno, North Apennines, Normandy, Northern France,

Rhineland, Southern France and Air Offensive Europe. The following decorations were awarded to Turman: European-African Middle Eastern Theater Ribbon with 9 Bronze Stars, Good Conduct Ribbon, Distinguished Unit Citation with 1 Oak Leaf Cluster and Lapel Button. He left the USA 13 November 1944 for the European Theater Operation, and returned to USA 4 October 1945. He was discharged 8 October 1945 at Camp Atterbury, Indiana. Private First Class Turman is the son of Mr. and Mrs. Carl Turman of Lutts. He was a member of a B-17 Flying Fortress group awarded the Distinguished Citation in recognition of one of "the outstanding bombing missions of the War. " The group was cited for action on July 18 when 26 Fortress of the unit participated in a mission against the airdrome and installations of Memmingen, Germany. En route to the target the bomber formations were scattered by adverse weather and the Fortresses approached the objective alone and without fighter escort. The unit was attacked by 200 German fighter planes and, after downing 65 of them, continued to target where 35 more parked planes were destroyed. They completed the mission and returned with a loss of 14 fortresses and 143 officers and enlisted men. PFC Turman was a member of the ground crew.

Hollis was stationed at Foggia, Italy until the war ended. He arrived back in the states October 1945. After working at various jobs he was employed by the Army Air Force in Honolulu as a civilian. He passed away there on March 5, 1948.

TURNBO, HOWARD EDSEL, Serial Number 44 127 805, was a Private First Class in 34th Station Hospital in the Army of the United States. He was born 12 June 1926 in Clifton, Tennessee. His Civilian Occupation was Farmer. He was inducted 9 January 1946 at Fort Oglethorpe, Georgia. His Military Occupational Specialty was Laboratory Technician. He was not in any battles. The following decorations were awarded to Turnbo: World War II Victory Medal, Army of Occupation Medal and a Lapel Button. He left the USA 25 June 1946 for the MTO, and returned to USA 27 February 1947. He was honorably discharged 26 May 1947 at Fort Dix, New Jersey. Howard is the son of Curtis and Hester Pevahouse Turnbo. He has a sister, Helen Howell. He married Dorothy Turnbo and they have three children: Jamie and Terry Turnbo and Linda Brown. Howard graduated from Frank Hughes High School. He has worked as a farmer and factory foreman for many years. He is a member of the Beech Creek Church of Christ for which he donated the land.

Howard married Dorothy Turnbo, daughter of Kennie and Mary (Boyd) Turnbo. They lived on a farm, where he farmed on a small scale and worked as a shipping clerk at Clifton, Mfg. Co., until he retired. He was a member of the Beech Creek Church of Christ and the American Legion. He and Dorothy have three children, James Allen (Jamie), Terry Lynn and Linda #ale. November 10, 1996, Howard died and is buried at Memorial Garden at Waynesboro. He has a sister, Helen Virginia.

TURNBO, LESTER LEE "LECK", Serial Number 34 375 248, was a Technician Fifth Grade in Company L, 394th Infantry in the Army of the United States. His permanent mailing address was Clifton, Tennessee. He was registered with the Selective Service Board in Wayne County, Tennessee. His Civilian Occupation was Light Truck Driver. He was inducted 3 October 1942 and entered into active service 17 October 1942 at Fort Oglethorpe, Georgia. He trained in Camp Blanding, Florida and Camp Meade, Kansas. His Military Occupational Specialty was Light Truck Driver. His Military Qualifications included Rifle MM and Combat Infantryman Badge. He was in the battles of Normandy, Northern France, Rhineland, and Central Europe. The following decorations were awarded to Turnbo: European-African Middle Eastern Theater Ribbon with 4 Bronze Stars, Good Conduct Ribbon and Distinguished Unit Citation. He left the USA 7 April 1944 for the European Theater Operation, and returned to USA 29 September 1945. He was discharged 5 October 1945 at Camp Atterbury, Indiana. Four days after D-Day, Leck joined the other men fighting under General Patton and General Eisenhower in the Invasion of Normandy. He served with the 315th Infantry, 79th Division. He was in four major battles. He remarked that there were times while he was in his fox hole that he would have given fifty dollars for a good cup of coffee. Leck was the son of Andrew

"Andy" Chester and Jimmie Annis Stegall Turnbo. He was born 7 August 1917 at Peters Landing, Tennessee, died 5 December 1990 and is entombed in Memorial Garden in Savannah. His sisters are Ermadine Riley, Bernice Evelyn Cromwell and Mary Kathryn Mathis. He was married 2 February 1941 to Hazel Love, daughter of Arthur Brown and Lillie Harville Love of Savannah, Tennessee. They had two sons, Gene Lee and Dennis Love Turnbo. Gene Lee was born 28 February 1942 and married Janice Thomas in Michigan. They have two children Melissa Ann and Thomas Lee. Dennis was born 20 March 1947 and married Linda Steele from Kentucky. They have one son Justin Lee. Both boys are veterans of the Vietnam War. Leck attended Frank Hughes High School and the Methodist Church in Clifton. His first job was driving a truck for the Gem Bottling Company in Clifton. Some of Leck's ancestors who also fought for our freedom are as follows: Revolutionary War are: g-g-g-g-g-grandfathers Ambrose Powell and John Turnbo, g-g-g-g-grandfather Henry William Davis, War of 1812 g-g-g-grandfather Hugh Turnbo, Civil War g-grandfathers John Isom Turnbo and Moses Jones and g-g-grandfather Henry William Davis. After the War, Leck worked for Hassell Oil and Gas in Savannah. Then in 1951 he moved his family to Detroit for economic reasons. Both he and his wife worked for Chrysler Corporation and Leck worked at a second job in a filling station. After retirement in 1977, Leck and Hazel returned to Savannah, Tennessee. They also traveled extensively throughout the United States.

VICKERY, A.C., was inducted into the United States Army and was assigned to Company A, 32nd Signal Construction Battalion. He stayed in this unit until he was discharged. A. C. was the son of Thomas and Lula Vickery. His brothers are: Woody, Reuben, Melvin, Lee and Jack Vickery. His sisters are: Pauline Kilburn, Mauvaline Montgomery, Ava Jean Hearlston and Roseanne Riedout. His half brothers and sisters are: Edd, Charlie, Steve, Carl, and Raymond Vickery, Martha Martin, Stella Hill, and Bessie Vickery. His brothers Reuben, Melvin and Lee are also World War II veterans.

VICKERY, ALVER, was born in South Wayne County about 1919 to Jim and Ada Vickery. He and his brothers, Dural 0. and James Franklin along with other siblings, grew up in different communities in South Wayne County as their father followed different jobs. Dural and James Franklin answered their call to the United States Army and within a short time both had been killed. A short time later

Aver received his call and was sent into battle in the European Theater, also, where he was wounded. Wherever he was sent he was always searching for his brothers graves, which he never found.

After his discharge, he lived in Florida a short time with his wife, Bernice, then began moving across the country. His location has been unknown for several years.

VICKERY, CLAUDIE JAMES "JACK", was a Private in (Tennessee) Company D, 77th Chemical Battalion, MT2 in the Army of the United States. Jack, son of John and Ora Balentine Vickery, was born 9 June 1925, died 2 September 1952 and was buried in Lindsey Chapel Cemetery in Cypress Inn, Tennessee. His parents were James F. and Ada (Handley) Vickery.

VICKERY, CLIFFORD C., Serial Number 34 936 423, was a Private in First Class Headquarters and Headquarters Company, 383rd Infantry in the Army of the United States. His permanent mailing address was Route 1, Cloverdale, Lauderdale County, Alabama. He was born 21 April 1925 in Cloverdale. He was registered with the Selective Service Board in Wayne County, Tennessee. His Civilian Occupation was General Farm Hand. He was single when he was inducted 28 July 1944 at Camp Forrest, Tennessee. His Military Occupational Specialty was Rifleman. His Military Qualifications included Combat Infantryman Badge. He was in the battles of Western Pacific and Ryukyu. He also served in Okinawa with the 96th Infantry Division called "Dead Eye". The following decorations were awarded to Vickery: World War II Victory Medal, 3 Overseas Service Bars, Asiatic-Pacific Theater Ribbon with 2 Bronze Stars, Good Conduct Medal, and Army of Occupation Medal (Japan). He left the USA 12 January 1945 for the Asiatic-Pacific Theater Operation, and returned to USA 11 August 1946. He was discharged

19 August 1946 at Fort Sam Houston, Texas. Clifford was son of Monroe and Callie Creasy Holt Vickery. He married Dorothy Burgess 19 July 1947. They had four children, Ronald, Roland, Ricky and Roger Vickery. After he was discharge he went to Cloverdale to live because his parents lived there. He drove a concrete truck there for thirty-three years before he retired.

VICKERY, LEE, Serial Number 34 494 870, was a Private First Class in Company C, 783rd Military Police Battalion in the Army of the United States. His permanent mailing address was Route 1, Lutts, Tennessee. He was born 1 September 1920 in Winfield, Alabama. He was registered with the Selective Service Board in Wayne County, Tennessee. His Civilian Occupation was Farmer. He was married when he was inducted 22 November 1942 and entered into active service 29 October 1942 at Fort Oglethorpe, Georgia. His Military Occupational Specialty was Military Policeman. He was in the battles of Normandy, Northern France, Rhineland and Ardennes. The following decorations were awarded to Vickery: European-African Middle Eastern Theater Ribbon with 4 Bronze Stars, American Theater Ribbon, Good Conduct Medal and World War II Victory Medal. He left the USA 12 February 1944 for the European Theater Operation, and returned to USA 5 November 1945. He was discharged 9 November 1945 at Camp Atterbury, Indiana. Lee, son of Thomas and Lula Vickery, married Cora Elizabeth Bevis. Their children are: Linda Sue married Linden Balentine and Stephen Lee married Donna Baggett. Lee has one granddaughter, Lorie Lee Balentine. His siblings are: Woody, Reuben, Melvin, A. C., Jack W., Pauline Kilburn, Mauvaline Montgomery, Ava Jean Hearlston and Roseanne Riedout. His half brothers and sisters are: Edd, Charlie, Steve, Carl, and Raymond Vickery, Martha Martin, Stella Hill, and Bessie Vickery.

VICKERY, MELVIN, son of Thomas and Lula Vickery, was inducted 16 January 1943 in the 353rd Engineering in the Army of the United States. He served in the Southwest Pacific Theater of War. He was discharged 3 July 1945 at Camp Gordon from the 1663rd Engineering Utility Attachment as a Corporal. Melvin is the son of Thomas and Lula Vickery. His siblings are: Woody, Reuben, Lee, A. C., Jack W., Pauline Kilburn, Mauvaline Montgomery, Ava Jean Hearlston and Roseanne Riedout. His half brothers and sisters are: Edd, Charlie, Steve, Carl, and Raymond Vickery, Martha Martin, Stella Hill, and Bessie Vickery.

VICKERY, REUBEN E., Serial Number 34 375 352, was a Private in Company G, 339th Infantry, 85th Division in the Army of the United States. His permanent mailing address was Route 1, Cypress Inn, Tennessee. He was born 29 October 1917 in Winfield, Alabama. He was registered with the Selective Service Board in Wayne County, Tennessee. His Civilian Occupation was Farmer. He was married when he was inducted 3 October 1942 and entered into active service 17 October 1942 at Fort Oglethorpe, Georgia. His Military Occupational Specialty was Rifleman. He was in the battles of Rome-Arno. The following decorations were awarded to Vickery: Purple Heart, Distinguished Unit Badge, 1 Bronze Service Star, Combat Infantry Badge, European Theater Ribbon, Good Conduct Ribbon and 2 Overseas Bars. He left the USA 24 December 1943 for the North Africa Theater Operation, and returned to USA 8 June 1945. He was wounded twice. He was discharged 20 September 1945 at Borden General Hospital in Chickasha, Oklahoma. Reuben, son of Thomas and Lula Vickery, married Mamie Hill Wright, They had one son, Robert. His siblings are: Lee, Woody, Melvin, A. C., Jack W., Pauline Kilburn, Mauvaline Montgomery, Ava Jean Hearlston and Roseanne Riedout. His half brothers and sisters are: Edd, Charlie, Steve, Carl, and Raymond Vickery, Martha Martin, Stella Hill, and Bessie Vickery. Reuben retired in Effingham, Illinois.

WALKER, BERT, A selectee, he entered into active service in May 1941. He was in the 8th Medical Battalion and then

transferred to the Air Corps, Jefferson Barracks, Fort Jackson, South Carolina. He served as an airplane mechanic when he reached Rantaul, Illinois. He attended a mechanic school on B-24's in Detroit, Michigan. He was stationed in Salt Lake City with "an Induction Center", in Tucson, Arizona, Colorado and Selina, Kansas. He was assigned to invasion areas in the bomb group during this time, and he was also in a Training Squadron. He was discharged in November 1945. Bert, son of John and Laura Morrison Walker, was born and reared in Wayne County. He has a brother Jean, who was also served in World War II. After he was discharged, Bert lived in Memphis where he worked as an aircraft mechanic. He retired and has lived in Waynesboro since 1983.

WALKER, JEAN, Serial Number 34 713 905, was a Staff Sergeant in 577th Bombardment Squadron, Army Air Force

in the Army of the United States. His permanent mailing address was Waynesboro, Tennessee. He was born 22 June 1917 in Waynesboro, Tennessee. He was registered with the Selective Service Board in Wayne County, Tennessee. His Civilian Occupation was Light Truck Driver. He was married when he was inducted 23 April 1943 and entered into active service 30 April 1943 at Camp Forrest, Tennessee. His Military Occupational Specialty was Airplane Mechanic Gunner. His Military Qualifications included MM Rifle Expert Carbine, MM Pistol and AAF Technical Badge. He was in the battles of Ardennes, Rhineland, and Central Europe. He was stationed in France. The following decorations were awarded to Walker: Air Medal with 1 Silver Oak Cluster, Good Conduct Medal, and European-African Middle Eastern Theater Ribbon with 3 Bronze Stars. He left the USA 12 October 1944 for the European Theater Operation, and returned to USA 18 October 1945 His education consisted of two years in High School. He was discharged 24 October 1945 at Fort McPhearson, Georgia. Jean Walker, son of John and Laura Morrison Walker of Waynesboro, received a letter of Commendation from Congressman Wirt Courtney for excellent performance of duty in the European Theater Operation. He also had a brother, Bert, who was overseas in ac-

tive service. He married Christene Christian. He had three children: Jean, Jr., David and Martha Jo Walker. He is of the Methodist faith and worked at Genesco Shoe Plant in Waynesboro. He retired from Wayne Metal in Waynesboro.

WALKER, JOHN, of Clifton, TN entered the US Army, October 10, 1943 and received his basic training at the Armored Replacement Center, preparing of combat duty with an armored suit.

WALKER, J.W., served in the United States Navy during World War II from 10 April 1944, until his discharge 3 February

1946. He attained the rank of Seaman First Class. His service number was 967 13 54. He was awarded the American Area Camp Medal, Arctic-Pacific Camp Medal, and the Victory Medal. He was a son of Allen and Pearl Bates Walker, and a grandson of Frank and Sarah Frances Rochelle Walker and Jesse and Emma Hughes Bates. He was born 6 April 1923 in Wayne County, Tennessee. He had two brothers, one who died in infancy and Allen, Jr., who died in 1984. He had two sisters, Mable Jean Walker Bush and Ina June Walker Pennington. J.W. attended Walker school in Wayne County, Hohenwald school in Lewis County and Hume-Fogg in Nashville. As he was growing up, he started farming, enjoyed it very much and dreamed of the time when he could farm on his own. But the war was raging overseas, so just past his nineteenth birthday, he volunteered to serve in the Navy. He received his boot training in Williamsburg, Virginia, and then was assigned to the troop transport ship, the USS BURLEIGH, for a tour of duty in the Pacific. Just before sailing, he got a leave to come home and marry his sweetheart, Lessie Creecy. She was teaching in Waverly Central High School and doing volunteer work to help on the home front. While in the Pacific, J.W. developed a great admiration for the Marines,

after transporting so many into the battle area. He was aboard the USS BURLEIGH when they made a landing on Okinawa on Easter Sunday in 1945, on his twentieth birthday. While he was in the Pacific, his ship rammed a tanker and had to return to the West coast for repairs and was in dock for a short while in Bremerton, Washington, in the summer of 1945. He was granted a short leave and came home and soon after came down with malaria that he had contracted while in the Pacific. He was admitted to the Veterans Hospital in Nashville for treatment. He was later moved back to Bremerton. While he was in the hospital, his ship was sent back to the Pacific. He was very disappointed at being separated from his crew, that he had grown close too. When he recovered, he was sent to the Naval Center in Farragut, Idaho. He remained there until he was sent to the USN Separation Center in Charleston, South Carolina, where he was honorably discharged. J.W. came home to Wayne County. He and Lessie bought a farm near Buffalo River in the Topsy Community and built a home. They had one son, James McKinley Walker, who now owns most of the farm and operates all of it. Lessie continued to teach in Wayne County High School and J.W. farmed as he had dreamed of doing. He was always a worker for the advancement of Agriculture and the community. He was a member of the Topsy Church of Christ, where he worshipped the rest of his life. He always showed a love for our flag and wore out several displaying them from the front porch. His health began to fail in 1981 and in 1987 he suffered a severe heart attack. On the 5th of May 1989, at the age of 66, he died after suffering another attack and a stroke. He is buried in Swiss Cemetery in Hohenwald, Tennessee.

WALKER, LOFTIES W., was born on January 22, 1923, in Decatur County, Tennessee, the son of Bud and Lucy Yarbor. He had one brother, Joe Yarbor, and one sister, Gertrude Lofties Walker. He attended school in Hardin County, Tennessee, and attended Mt. Tabor Baptist Church in Clifton, Tennessee. He lived near Clifton working as a cotton farmer when he was inducted into the United States Army on March 22, 1944, at Ft. Benjamin Harrison, Indiana. He served in Okinawa with A. 81st Signal Training Company and received the following citations: American Theater Ribbon, Asiatic-Pacific Theater Ribbon and World War II Victory Ribbon. He was discharged on June 1, 1946, at Camp Atterbury, Indiana. He was married to Juanita Bailey. They had six children, five boys and one girl. He died in August 1989 and is buried in Sandusky, Ohio.

Source: Gertrude L. Walker.

WALLACE, JAMES T., "TOM", age 97, died 15 July 1997 at his home in Florence and was buried in Greenview Memorial Park.

WARD, JAMES EDGAR, Serial Number 34 713 ??4, was inducted into the Army of the United States prior to 30 April 1943, and was released from active duty, and transferred to the Enlisted Reserve Corps, and returned to Waynesboro, Tennessee. On 30 April 1943, he was called to active duty and reported to Fort Oglethorpe, Georgia.

WARHURST, ERNEST, son of Ernest and Mattie Warhurst, was a Seaman in the Navy of the United States. He received his Basic Training in general seamanship, life saving, physical development, mental fitness first aid and fire fighting at St. Petersburg, Florida. His permanent mailing address was Iron City, Tennessee.

WARREN, AUSTIN, was inducted into the Infantry Division of the Army of the United States for less than one year. He trained at Fort Chaffee, Arkansas. His Civilian Occupation was saw mill worker and a cabinet maker. Austin was the son of Harvel and Dora Williams Warren. His siblings are: Urgent, Roy, Cletis, Region V. "Pat", Kenneth and Buddy Warren, Myrtle Howell, Juanita Copeland, and Mavis McDonald. He married (1) Maudie Combs and their children are: Joe Boyd and Austin Warren, Jr. He married (2) Guyeula Overton and their children are: Jack, Karen, Landrel, Darryl, Randy, Guy and Lance Warren.

WARREN, GUY ALVIN, was born on April 15, 1926, son of Hugh Oscar (Red) Warren and Carrie (Bess) Lineberry Warren of the Beech Creek community in Wayne County, Tennessee. Guy went in to the Navy Reserve on July 29, 1944, and was a Seaman First Class (Serial Number 977 28 92). He received his basic training at Camp Perry, Virginia. He served on the following Vessel and Stations: REC TRG COM and USNTADC in Williamsburg, Virginia and NAS in Norfolk, Virginia. The following decorations were awarded to Warren: World War II Victory Medal and American Area Ribbon. He was discharged 9 April 1946 from the U. S. Naval Personnel Separation Center in Memphis, Tennessee. When the war was over, he was shipped to Elizabeth City, North Carolina. In 1953 Guy was hired as a Tennessee State surveyor. He continued in this work until his retirement in 1984. He married Hazel Burgess, daughter of Walter Frank and Audrey Mae Ferguson Burgess. Guy and Hazel had four children: Gary Burgess,

Sandra Geannine, Gerald Alvin and Jerry Dale. Guy is a member of the Masonic Fraternity Lodge No. 173 Scottish Rite Fraternity in Nashville and a member of the AL Menah Temple in Nashville. He enjoys hunting and fishing. Guy and Hazel make their home in Clifton, Tennessee, close to where he was reared and went to school and church. His siblings are Nick, James, Audrey and Edsel.

WARREN, JAMES BARNEY, Serial Number 34 886 464, was a Private First Class in 275th Infantry, 70th Division in the Army of the United States. His permanent mailing address was Route 3, Waynesboro, Tennessee. He was born 27 November 1924 in Clifton, son of Joseph Wesley and Mary Isabelle (Davis) Warren. He was registered with the Selective Service Board in Wayne County, Tennessee. He worked as a farmhand until he was inducted into the United States Army on October 9, 1943. His Military Occupational Specialty was Heavy Machine Gunner. His Military Qualifications included Combat Infantry Badge and Rifle MKM. He was in the battles of Rhineland, and Central Europe. The following decorations were awarded to Warren: American Theater Ribbon, European-African Middle Eastern Theater Ribbon with 2 Bronze Stars, Good Conduct Medal and World War II Victory Medal. He left the USA 6 December 1944 for the European Theater Operation, and returned to USA 24 April 1946. He was discharged 30 April 1946 at Camp Atterbury, Indiana. Barnie returned home and married Sarah Dean Higgins of Decaturville, Tennessee, on May 20, 1947. They lived in Clifton and Barnie began driving the Ladd Bus from Waynesboro to Nashville. Within a few years his route increased to take in most of middle Tennessee and parts of Alabama. By retirement time for Barnie, few people were riding a bus, so his route was greatly reduced. His children are Erma Lee, Brenda Kate, Dennis Barnie, James Steven, Terry Michael, Connie Regina and Myron Randell. Barnie tells this amusing story: Before many people owned automobiles, his granddaddy had never driven, but he bought the first one in his community from his son-in-law's uncle, Stennit Whitehead. Barnie's son-in-law is Jerry Duren, owner and operator of Duren's Healthmart Pharmacy in Waynesboro. Barnie is retired and living in Hickman County near Centerville, Tennessee.

WARREN, KENNETH, Serial Number 3z4 506 512, was a Corporal in 62nd Troop Carrier Squadron in the Army of the United States. His permanent mailing address was Route 3, Waynesboro, Tennes-

see. He was registered with the Selective Service Board in Wayne County, Tennessee. His Civilian Occupation was General Farm Hand and Lumber Industry before service and after service he was a Die Setter for Tennessee Industry. He was inducted 3 January 1943 and entered into active service 25 January 1943 at Fort Oglethorpe, Georgia. His address at time of entry was Route 2, Collinwood, Tennessee. His basic training was at Wilmington, Delaware, Fort Oglethorpe, Georgia and Miami Beach, Florida. His Military Occupational Specialty was Truck Driver. His Military Qualifications included Marksman Carbine, 30 Caliber. He was in the battles of North Apennines, Po Valley and Air Combat in the Balkans. The following decorations were awarded to Warren: Good Conduct Medal, World War II Victory Medal, and European-African Middle Eastern Theater Ribbon with 3 Bronze Stars. He left the USA 24 December 1943 for the European-African Middle Eastern Theater Operation, and returned to USA 26 November 1945. He served in Italy with the 8th Troop Group Squadron. Kenneth, son of Harvel and Dora Williams Warren, was born 26 January 1924 in Lobelville, Tennessee, died 20 July 1994 at Baptist Hospital in Nashville and was buried in Memorial Gardens in Waynesboro. His siblings are: Urgent, Roy, Cletis, Region V. "Pat", Austin and Buddy Warren, Myrtle Howell, Juanita Copeland, and Mavis McDonald. He married (1) Blondell Ray and they had these children: Kenneth, Jr., Samuel Earl, and Judith Ann McFall, David, Danny, and Ronnie Warren, Charlotte Ritter and Sheila Thomas. He married (2) Jewell Murray.

WARREN, REGION VILLES "PAT", Serial Number 295 72 05, enlisted in the Navy of the United States, 6 August 1940 in Jackson, Tennessee but took his oath in Nashville. His rating was Gunner's Mate Second Class. He enlisted as AS, USN for six years. Other ratings held while

he was in service included S2C, and GM3C. His Military Occupational Specialty was Duties of Rating. Vessels and Stations that he served on were: U. S. Naval Recruiting Station in Nashville, Tennessee, U. S. Naval training Station in Norfolk, Virginia. USS MARYLAND, USS RIO GRANDE, US Naval Base Hospital #11, #3, and #15, US Naval Fleet Hospital #108 and US Naval Hospital in Memphis, Tennessee. Pat went aboard the USS MARYLAND in Long Beach, California, and sailed to Pearl Harbor. His crew was in and out of Pearl Harbor for several months, but their ship was anchored in Pearl Harbor at the time of the Japanese attack on 7 December 1941. The following is what Pat distinctly remembers, "I was talking to the mess cook when I heard planes overhead. I went to the top side and saw torpedo planes and bombers flying so low that if I had a pistol, I could have shot the pilot. They sprayed me with machine-gun fire. I rolled back down the ladder and told the mess cook that the Japs were bombing us, sure as hell. Everybody went to their battle station. Mine was in the Chief's quarters. A bomb came through; water came in. I stayed on flood control station as long as I could. The water got too deep; I had to climb out. I went to the top side to help on guns and to help get people out of the Oklahoma Battle Ship. We had to cut men out of the bottom. I was needed in the Handle room to set the fuse on the aircraft shells. I stayed there all night. The SEVENTH of December was OVER!" Pat's duties were in the East and South Pacific after this. He was discharged 8 June 1945 at the US Naval Hospital in Memphis, Tennessee. Pat was awarded the Pearl Harbor Survivors Metal with a Silver Nickel in 1992 during a Democrat Political Rally. Pat was honored for his contribution to the Democratic Party. He has served many years as chairman of the Wayne County Election Board. He used a room of his business establishment as Democratic Headquarters in 1992. This World War II Citation was an award from the party for his loyalty. Pat, son of Harvel and Dora Williams Warren, was born 22 August 1917 in Coble, Tennessee. His siblings are: Urgent, Roy, Cletis, Kenneth, Austin and Buddy Warren, Myrtle Howell, Juanita Copeland, and Mavis McDonald. He married Eva Pauline McDonald and they had two children: Patty Sharon and Donald Gene Warren. Region V. (Pat) Warren.

WARRINGTON, EDWARD YOUNG, Serial Number 14 220 177, was a Staff Sergeant in 1921st AACS in the Air Force in the Army of the United States. His permanent mailing address was Route 2, Lutts, Tennessee. He was born 10 September 1928 in Lutts, Tennessee. He was registered with the Selective Service Board in Wayne County, Tennessee. His Civilian Occupation was Farmer. He was married with one dependent when he was inducted -date and place not available. His Military Occupational Specialty was Teletype Operator. His Military Qualifications included Carbine SS. He was not in any battles. He left the USA 12 May 1947 for the Pacific Theater Operation, and returned to USA 13 December 1948. He had a high school education. He was discharged 24 September 1949 at CAFB Fort Worth, Texas. He reenlisted 24 October 1949 in Gadsden, Alabama, for three years in the Reserve. This time he was discharged 20 February 1953 at Scott Air Force Base, Illinois.

WARRINGTON, JOHN S., was born February 17, 1927, to John Carlos and O'Della Southerland Warrington.

John S. graduated from Collinwood High School in 1945 and was inducted into the service in September of 1945 at Fort Orgelthorpe, GA. He was sent to work in the Post Office at Fort McPherson, then Fort Lee, VA, for training. From there he went to Aberdeen Proving Grounds, MD, for the remainder of his time in the U.S. Army.

He spent 10 years in the Army reserve and was discharged as a Master Sergeant. He then worked in the U.S. Post Office at South Bend, IN. Later John S. managed an automobile dealership, and still later as leasing manager of a Real Estate Corporation. He and another friend started a radio "beeper" service in Las Vegas, Nevada, and he managed it until retirement and sale to Motorola Corp.

He married Theresa Martino of South Bend and has one daughter, Michelle, and two grandchildren.

WATERS, FRED A., Serial Number 34 040 770, was a Private in the Army of the United States. He was born 20 January 1905 in Perry County, Tennessee. He was 36 years of age when he was inducted 3 April 1941 at Fort Oglethorpe, Georgia. His battles were not listed but he returned from the Southwest Pacific 2 February 1943 in poor health. He was discharged 6 March 1943 from the 2nd Indiana CDD Headquarters, Hammond General Hospital, Modesto, California. Fred, son of Amos Wilburn and Susie McKutchen Waters, died 13 March 1979 and was buried in Praters Chapel Cemetery in Wayne County. His wife is Verle Waters Conner, Savannah, Tennessee.

WEATHERSPOON, JOHN TONY, JR., Serial Number 845 82 73, was a Steward's Mate, Third Class in the Navy of the United States. He was born 10 March 1922 in Clifton. He was inducted 26 May 1943 at Nashville, Tennessee. He was discharged 2 July 1943 at Norfolk, Virginia. He was 5' 7" tall, weighed 124 pounds and his complexion was negro. John lived in Sandusky, Ohio for many years. He came to Lompoc from San Diego. He was a self-employed truck driver. He was a member of the Operating Engineer Local 12. John, son of John T. and Madge Witherspoon, died 7 August 19?? at Marian Extended Care Center in Santa Maria, California after a long illness and was buried in Lompoc Evergreen Cemetery in Lompoc, California. Survivors included his wife, Linda, four daughters, Audrey and Cheryl, both of Ohio, Bernita and Pamela both of Lompoc; sons, John T. and John P. both of Lompoc, Lester of Santa Barbara, and Billy of Lima, Ohio, eleven grandchildren, five sisters, Rhea Sinclair and Carrie Siner both of Minneapolis, Nettie Lynum of Nashville, and Elsie Johnson and Bobbie Yarboro both of Sandusky, Ohio, and one brother, Robert of National City.

WEATHERSPOON, RAYMON F., was born on January 25, 1921, in Clifton, Tennessee, and worked as a farmer near Clifton until he was inducted into the United States Army on June 2, 1943, at Camp Forrest, Tennessee. He served with the 396th Quartermasters Truck Company as a mechanic. Raymon participated in the battles of Northern France, Ardennes, Rhineland Central Europe. He received the following citations: American Theater Campaign Medal, EAMET Campaign Medal with four Bronze Stars; Good Conduct Medal and Victory Medal. He was discharged on December 2, 1945, at Ft. Bragg, North Carolina.

WEAVER, EDWARD DOYLE, son of Mr. and Mrs. Calip Weaver of R#2, Iron City inducted into the U. S. Navy, November 11, 1943. He received his training at

Great Lakes, IL, Grosse Isle, MI and San Francisco, CA. During 1945, he served as a S2/C in the South Pacific.

WEAVER, WILLIAM M., Serial Number 34 983 029, was a Private First Class in Company L, 10 Infantry Regiment in the Army of the United States. His permanent mailing address was Route 1, West Point, Tennessee. He was born 28 February 1924 in West Point. He was registered with the Selective Service Board in Lawrence County, Tennessee. His Civilian Occupation was General Farmer. He was inducted 12 March 1944 at Camp Shelby, Mississippi. His Military Occupational Specialty was Rifleman. His Military Qualifications included MM Rifle and Combat Infantryman Badge. He was in the battles of Northern France, Ardennes, Rhineland, and Central Europe, Germany, Luxembourg, Czechoslovakia and Austria. The following decorations were awarded to Weaver: European-African Middle Eastern Service Medal with 4 Bronze Stars, and World War II Victory Medal. He left the USA 16 August 1944 for the European Theater Operation, and returned to USA 18 July 1945. He had two years of High school education. He was discharged 6 February 1946 at Fort McPherson, Georgia. William is the son of Walker Lafayette and Mary Jo Story Weaver. He has two sisters, Doris Geralgean Lipscomb and Elizabeth Sharon Brown. On 23 December 1947 in Corinth, he married Roberta Todd. She was born 12 December 1927. Their children are: (1) Stanley Morris Weaver born 14 February 1952 in Wayne County and (2) Judy Rae born 25 April 1955. She married a Baker and lives at 5661 Ryewyck Drive, Number 2, Toledo, Ohio 43612. William attended Springer and Darnell Elementary schools and Collinwood High School. He has worked for Genesco and retired in 1988 from Libby-Owens-Ford Glass with 35 years of service.

WEEKS, GRADY L., served his country during World War II in the United States Army. He was a recipient of the Purple Heart. He was a son of Wiley and Mary (Motes) Weeks. He died at the age of 75 years on February 22, 1999, at the James E. Vanzandt VA Medical Center in Altoona, Pennsylvania. He was a resident of Jenner Crossroads, Pennsylvania. Burial was in Husband Cemetery in Somerset, Pennsylvania. He was a member of the Greater Johnston Christian Fellowship, Boswell Lions Club and Jennerstown Volunteer Fire Company. He was married to Hazel Sellers Weeks. They had one son, Bobby L. Weeks. He had one stepson, Edward Sellers. He had two sisters, Ruth Barkley and Marie Hays, and four brothers: Ralph, James, Robert and Gene.

WEEKS, W.R., Serial Number 44 042 136, was a Private First Class in 29th Division, 116th Infantry Regiment in the Army of the United States. His permanent mailing address was Route 1, Lutts, Tennessee. He was born 28 June 1926 in Cypress Inn, Wayne County. He was registered with the Selective Service Board in Wayne County, Tennessee. His Civilian Occupation was General Farmer. He was inducted 20 October 1944 at Fort Oglethorpe, Georgia. His Military Occupational Specialty was Warehouseman. His Military Qualifications included M-1 Rifle Sharpshooter. He was not in any battles. The following decorations were awarded to Weeks: Good Conduct Medal, Army Occupation Medal (Germany), European-African Middle Eastern Theater Ribbon, World War II Victory Medal and a Lapel Button. He left the USA 3 April 1945 for France, and returned to USA 2 August 1946. He was discharged 7 August 1946 at Fort George Meade, Maryland.

WEIR, D.J., son of Gus T. and Lou Alice Dodd Weir, he was born 16 June 192-31 in Wayne County. His father, Gus, was born 2 October 1893, died 26 August 1970 and is buried in Mt. Hope Cemetery. His mother, Lou, was born 12 April 1902. His children include: David Jerome, who teaches at New York University, Barbara Of Huntsville and Kyle of Missouri.

D.J. attended Pinhook school and graduated from Collinwood High school in 1940 after which he joined the CCC and spent a year in Washington State. He enlisted in the Army and was sent overseas. When his ship docked in England. He had the measles. He saw combat in Germany and France. After the war, D.J. worked on the Natchez Trace and went to college. He received his doctor's degree in New York.

WEST, JAMES T., Serial Number 34 713 902, was a Private First Class in 469th Ordinance Evacuation Company in the Army of the United States. His permanent mailing address was Route 3, Iron City, Tennessee. He was born 25 December 1924 in Collinwood, Tennessee. He was registered with the Selective Service Board in Wayne County, Tennessee. His Civilian Occupation was General Farmer. He was single with one dependent when he was inducted 23 April 1943 and entered into active service 30 April 1943 at Camp Forrest, Tennessee. His Military Occupational Specialty was Heavy Truck Driver. His Military Qualifications included Rifle 30 Caliber SS. He was in the battles of Northern France, Ardennes, Rhineland, and Central Europe. The following decorations were awarded to West: American Theater Ribbon, European-African Middle Eastern Theater Ribbon with 4 Bronze Stars, Good Conduct Medal and World War II Victory Medal. He left the USA 29 May 1944 for the European-African Middle Eastern Theater Operation, and returned to USA 5 January 1946. He was discharged 14 January 1946 at Fort Knox, Kentucky. A description of his military occupation - he was a heavy truck driver serving with the Evacuation Company for twenty months where he made long day hauls carrying heavy equipment, such as tanks. He averaged about 125 miles per day. He made trip tickets and operated winches to load and unload the trucks. In civilian life before service, James worked for his father, Luther West of Iron City. He planted, cultivated and harvested corn, vegetables, potatoes, cotton and hay with a two-horse team. He built and kept in repair the fences and farm buildings. He raised livestock and poultry.

WEST, WILLIAM FRANKLIN, Serial Number 845 38 17, was a Seaman First Class in the Navy of the United States. He was born 20 February 1925 in Iron City, Tennessee. He entered into active service 2 May 1943. He served on the following Vessels and Stations: NTS Bainbridge, Maryland, RS SO Annex NOB Norfolk, Virginia, USS BILOXI, and USS MINNEAPOLIS. He was discharged 20 February 1946 from the U. S. Naval Personnel Separation Center in Memphis, Tennessee.

WHITE, ILEY, Serial Number 36 893 647, was a Private in 368th General Service Regiment in the Army of the United States. His permanent mailing address was Route 1, Waynesboro, Tennessee. He was born 7 March 1913. He was registered with the Selective Service Board in Michigan. His Civilian Occupation was Inspector. He was married with seven dependents when he was inducted 9 December 1943 and entered into active service 30 December 1943 in Detroit, Michigan. His basic training was at Fort Sill, Oklahoma, and Camp Pickett, Virginia, before he was sent overseas. His Military Occupational Specialty was Heavy Truck Driving. His Military Qualifications included Marksman. He was in the battles of Rhineland, and Central Europe. The following decorations were awarded to White: American Theater Ribbon, European-African Middle Eastern Theater Ribbon with 2 Bronze Service Stars, Good Conduct Medal, Lapel Button and World War II Victory Medal. He left the USA 3 January 1945 for the European-African Middle Eastern Theater Operation, and returned to USA 26 November 1945.

He was discharged 5 December 1945 at Fort Knox, Kentucky. Iley was the son of Mr. and Mrs. Will White of Lower Green River in Wayne County. He married Lavenia Love and they had six children, ages 3 to 11, which explains the seven dependents. He attended school on Indian Creek in Wayne County.

WHITE, JAMES BOYD, Serial Number 783 81 69, was a Seaman Second Class in the Navy of the United States. He was born 26 October 1926 in Lutts, Tennessee. He entered into active service 9 November 1944. He served on the following Vessels and Stations: Naval Training Station, Great Lakes, Illinois, Tadcen Shoemaker, California, Renshaw Navphibbase, Little Creek, Virginia, and USS OKLOOSA. The following decorations were awarded to White: American Area Medal, and World War II Victory Medal. He was discharged 18 April 1946 from the U. S. Naval Personnel Separation Center in Shelton, Virginia.

WHITE, J.T., Serial Number 976 90 22, was a Seaman Second Class in the Navy of the United States. He was born

27 March 1918 in Waynesboro, Tennessee. He entered into active service 15 March 1945. He served on the following Vessels and Stations: United States Naval Training Station, Great Lakes, Illinois, NT SCH (RM) T. I. California, and USS PATAPOSCO. The following decorations were awarded to White: American Campaign Asiatic Pacific Medal, and World War II Victory Medal. He was discharged 26 March 1946 from the U. S. Naval Personnel Separation Center in Memphis, Tennessee.

WHITE, LEE ANDER, Serial Number 34 713 915, was inducted into the Army of the United States prior to 30 April 1943, and was released from active duty, and transferred to the Enlisted Reserve Corps, and returned to Waynesboro, Tennessee. On 30 April 1943, he was called to active

duty and reported to Fort Oglethorpe, Georgia.

WHITE, THOMAS EDISON, Serial Number 34 524 516, was a Private in Battery 251st A, Field Artillery Battalion, 37th

First Hq. Division in the Army of the United States. He was born 29 May 1922 in Hohenwald, Tennessee. He was registered with the Selective Service Board in Lewis County, Tennessee. His Civilian Occupation was Variety Saw Operator. He was inducted 18 December 1942. His Military Occupational Specialty was Field Lineman. His Military Qualifications included Sharpshooter Carbine. He was in the battles of French Haven, New Guinea and Luzon, Philippines. The following decorations were awarded to White: World War II Victory Medal, Lapel Button, Good Conduct Medal, American Theater Ribbon, Atlantic Theater Ribbon with 2 Bronze Clusters, Philippine Liberation Ribbon, one Bronze Star Medal and Sharpshooter Badge. He left the USA 24 March 1944 for the Asiatic-Pacific Theater Operation, and returned to USA 11 December 1945. He was discharged 24 December 1945 at Camp Chaffee, Arkansas. On 6 September 1945 by Command of Major General Beightler to Adjutant General Ralph Westfall, who sent the following announcement to T. E. White is as follows: "For Meritorious achievement in connection with military operations against the enemy at Luzon, Philippine Islands from 15 May 1945 to 15 June 1945, Private White, a lineman for a field artillery battery, ably assisted in the task of maintaining wire communications between the artillery liaison officer, serving with the attack elements and the Battalion Fire Direction Center. On one occasion, when wire communications broke down because of heavy enemy artillery fire, he voluntarily advanced through a draw covered by enemy snipers and machine gun fire to an adjacent forward observation post and obtained bat-

teries necessary for the operation of his party's radio. Vitally needed communications were quickly reestablished due to his courageous act, enabling his Forward Observer to continue to direct effective fire. Private White's efficiency, devotion to duty and coolness under fire contributed materially to the success of his Battalion in the operation against the enemy. "Thomas married Ruby Campbell and they had a daughter, Glenda Rose White Ross.

WHITEHEAD, ALBERT CLARK, Serial Number 976 87 27, was a Seaman First Class in the Navy of the United States.

He was born 24 November 1926 in Wayne County. He entered into active service 24 February 1945. He served on the following Vessels and Stations: United States Naval Training Station, Great Lakes, Illinois; Naval Training Station NOB Norfolk, Virginia, and USS WILTSIE. The following decorations were awarded to Whitehead: American Area Medal, and World War II Victory Medal. He was discharged 28 June 1946 from the U. S. Naval Personnel Separation Center in Memphis, Tennessee.

WHITEHEAD, CARL ARNOLD, was a Private First Class in Company E, 105 Infantry, 27th Infantry Division in the Army of the United States. He was born 30 September 1927 and died 18 January 1955 and is buried in Banks Cemetery, located in North Riverside and split by the road in Lewis County, Tennessee.

WHITEHEAD, EDD ESLICK, Serial Number 846 08 21, volunteered and joined the Navy of the United States. He was born 22 August 1924 in Wayne County. He enlisted 4 September 1943 in San Diego, California. He was discharged 2 November 1943. Edd, son of Tommy and Lillie Mae Adkins Whitehead, married Marjorie Hendrixs, daughter of Jim and Nona Edwards Hendrixs. They have one daughter. Edd's siblings are Charlie Whitehead and Estelee Burke. Edd retired from the lumber business in 1992.

WHITEHEAD, JOE CLEVELAND, Serial Number 34 490 161, was a Private First Class in the Army of the United

States. He was born near Waynesboro in Wayne County. His Civilian Occupation was Farmer. He was 21 and 7/12 years old and married when he was inducted 29 October 1942 at Fort Oglethorpe, Georgia. He was not in any battles. He was discharged 4 September 1943 at Camp Collan, San Diego, California. Joe is the son of Robert and Martha Skelton Whitehead who lived in the Moccasin Community in Wayne County. His siblings are: Carl W., Olin F., Ruth Carroll, Gertrude Frazier, Bessie Potete, Nora Gassman, Rebecca Higgins and Fannie Warren. Joe's children are Delbert, Donald, Jo Bell Hollis and Clara Mae Dixon. Joe died 16 July 1994 at his home on Moccasin and is buried in the Skelton Cemetery.

WHITSETT, TURNER F., of Lutts, Tn. entered the U. S. Army, July 28, 1944, at Camp Forrest and served with the 325th Glider Inf. 82nd Airborne Div. Battles; Central Europe and Rhineland. Citations; EAME Service Medal with three bronze stars, Good Conduct Medal, WWII Victory Medal and ETO Occupation Medal. Discharged, July 2, 1946.

WHITTEN, JULIUS "JESSIE" HOWARD, Serial Number - not available, was a Private First Class in Combat Engineers in the Army of the United States. His permanent mailing address was Route 3, Iron City, Tennessee. He was born 28 June 1925. His Civilian Occupation was General Farmer. He was inducted October 1943. His basic training was at Camp Shelby, Mississippi and Camp Swift, Texas. He was shipped overseas to the European Theater. The ship landed in En-

gland and he went across the English Channel to France and Germany. He drove a truck as they passed through Germany. He also built bridges and dug fox holes. He was discharged April 1946. Julius, son of Jones Thomas and Emma Spires Whitten, married Annie Ruth Montgomery. They have seven children: Kenneth Howard, Margaret Ruth Yarber, Sammy Eugene, Randy Dale, Patsy Ann Gray, Sarah Renee Crittenden, and Mark DeWayne. His siblings are James Albert and Vernon Gilbert Whitten, Hattie Hays, and Ida Geneva Crosslin, Julius had a general merchandise store on Cloverdale Road in Florence, Alabama. Later he went into the Chrysler-Plymouth dealership in Florence but is now retired and lives in Florence.

WHITTEN, WESLEY E., Serial Number 34 494 857, was a Sergeant in 328th Engineers Combat Battalion in the Army of the United States. His permanent mailing address was Route 5, Box 71, Waynesboro, Tennessee. He was born 7 January 1921 in Florence, Alabama. He was registered with the Selective Service Board in Wayne County, Tennessee. His Civilian Occupation was Marker. He was married with two dependents when he was inducted into the Army. His Military Occupational Specialty was Construction Foreman. His Military Qualifications included MM 30 caliber Rifle, MI. He was in the battles of Rhineland, and Central Europe. The following decorations were awarded to Whitten: American Theater Campaign Ribbon, European-African Middle Eastern Theater Campaign Medal with 2 Bronze Service Stars, Good Conduct Medal, Bronze Star Medal, Lapel Button and World War II Victory Medal. He left the USA 6 October 1944 for the European-African Middle Eastern Theater Operation, and returned to USA 10 September 1945. He had a high school education. He was discharged 6 November 1945 at Fort Bragg, North Carolina.

WILLIAMS, FOY, son of John and Florence (Gambrell) Williams, was born, December 20, 1924 and grew up in the Holly Creek Community, attending Holly Creek Elementary School. He entered the U. S. Army in 1941 at the age of eighteen and served two and one -half years. He was classed as an expert rifleman and participated in the battles of Central Europe. Foy was wounded in his right leg and received bums on his body when hit in a foxhole, during a battle in Belgium. He was returned to the states and hospitalized for a while. He was awarded the Purple Heart, then discharged in 1943 from the injuries he had received.

After his discharge, Foy returned to Wayne County. He participated in several business ventures; a grocery store, grain and elevator business and drove a semi-truck several years.

Foy and Becky (Yeiser) Williams were married; Becky, the daughter of Ed and Estoille (Belew) Yeiser is a registered nurse. She has always had a love for antiques. Several years after their marriage, Becky and Foy opened an antique shop; Becky deals in antiques and Foy does picture framing and matting. Their children are Kenny, Carol, Milicent, Megan and Haley.

WILLIAMS, FRANK, Serial Number 34 043 815, was a Private First Class in Headquarters Company, 194th Glider Infantry in the Army of the United States. His permanent mailing address was Waynesboro, Tennessee. He was born 21 August 1918 in Wayne County. He was registered with the Selective Service Board in Wayne County, Tennessee. His Civilian Occupation was Truck Driver. He was inducted 15 May 1941 at Fort Oglethorpe, Georgia. Frank received his military training at Camp Wheeler, Georgia, Fort McCellan, Alabama, and bases in North Carolina and Massachusetts. He served with the 82nd Airborne Division in North Africa, Sicily, Italy, Iceland, England, France, Holland, Germany and Belgium. He participated in the invasion on D-Day. His Military Occupational Specialty was Light Truck Driver. His Military Qualifications included Combat Infantry Badge. He was in the battles of Sicily, Naples-Foggia, Normandy, Ardennes, Rhineland, and Central Europe. The following decorations were awarded to Williams: European-African Middle Eastern Theater Ribbon with 6 Bronze Stars and one Bronze Service Arrowhead,, Good Conduct Medal, and Distinguished Unit Citation per Go Headquarters, 82nd Airborne Division 1944. He left the USA 29 April 1943 for the European Theater Operation, and returned to USA 14 September 1945. He was discharged 19 September 1945 at Camp Atterbury, Indiana. Frank married Jo Shirley.

WILLIAMS, GAYLON S., Serial Number 34 141 774, was a Staff Sergeant in Company E, 2nd Battalion Headquarters and Service Group in the Army of the United States. His permanent mailing address was Route 2, Iron City, Tennessee. He was born 2 March 1917 in Wayne County. He was registered with the Selective Service Board in Wayne County, Tennessee. His Civilian Occupation was Truck Driver. He was inducted 25 June 1941 at Fort Oglethorpe, Georgia. He was in the battles of New Guinea, South Philippines (Liberation), and Luzon. The following decorations were awarded to Williams: American Defense Service Ribbon, Asiatic-Pacific Theater Ribbon, and Good Conduct Medal. He left the USA 1 March 1944 for the Southwest Pacific Theater Operation, and returned to USA 8 October 1945. He was discharged 19 October 1946 at Headquarters, Camp Gruber, Oklahoma. Gaylon was the son of Wiley and Bessie Bromley Williams. He had two brothers, James and Homer. He married Jane Williams.

WILLIAMS, JAMES M., Serial Number 34 193 017, was a Private First Class in 677th Glider Field Artillery Battalion in the Army of the United States. He was born in Wayne County. His Civilian Occupation was Aluminum Worker. He was inducted 15 March 1942 at Fort Oglethorpe, Georgia. His Military Occupational Specialty was Battery Aide. He was not in any battles. He was discharged 29 October 1943 at Stark General Hospital, Charleston, South Carolina, in poor physical condition.

WILLIAMS, RALPH T., Serial Number 34 146 902, was a Private First Class in Company G, 121 Infantry, 8th Division,

2nd Battalion in the Army of the United States. His permanent mailing address was Route 2, Iron City, Tennessee. He was born 28 April 1920 at Route 2, Iron City, Tennessee. He was registered with the Selective Service Board in Wayne County, Tennessee. His Civilian Occupation was Farmer. He was single when he was inducted 4 October 1941 at Fort Oglethorpe, Georgia. His Military Occupational Specialty was Rifleman. His Military Qualifications included Combat Infantry Badge. He was in the battles of Normandy, and Rhineland. The following decorations were awarded to Williams: American Defense Theater Ribbon, American Theater

Ribbon, European-African Middle Eastern Theater Ribbon with 2 Bronze Stars, Good Conduct Medal, and Purple Heart Medal. He was wounded in action in France 9 July 1944. He left the USA 5 December 1943 for the European-African Middle Eastern Theater Operation, and returned to USA 19 November 1945. He was discharged 25 November 1945 at Fort Knox, Kentucky.

WILLIAMS, WILBERT R., son of Mrs. Lilly L. Williams of R#3, Lutts, Tn., entered the U. S. Army, February 1944, and served with the second Infantry Division. February 1945, he was awarded the Combat Infantryman's Badge for his duties in France and Germany.

WILSON, CHARLES W., JR., Serial Number 34 727 057, was a Private First Class in Battery A 272nd Field Artillery Battalion in the Army of the United States. His permanent mailing address was Route 6, Waynesboro, Tennessee. He was born 18 June 1925 in Evansville, Indiana. He was registered with the Selective Service Board in Wayne County, Tennessee. His Civilian Occupation was General Farmer Hand. He was inducted 20 March 1943 and entered into active service 27 March 1943 at Fort Oglethorpe, Georgia. His Military Occupational Specialty was Radio Operator, Low Speed. His Military Qualifications included Marksman Carbine. He was in the battles of Northern France, Ardennes, Rhineland, and Central Europe. The following decorations were awarded to Wilson: American Theater Ribbon, European-African Middle Eastern Theater Ribbon with 4 Bronze Service Stars, Good Conduct Medal and World War II Victory Medal. He left the USA 20 April 1944 for the European-African Middle Eastern Theater Operation, and returned to USA 30 December 1945. He finished two and a half years of high school. He was discharged 6 January 1946 in Fort Knox, Kentucky. Charles was the son of Walter and Esther Skelton Wilson. His siblings are: Tommy Christian, Ellinor Allen, Betty and Richard Wilson. He married Mary Whitehead and they have a son, Michael. His occupation after the war was Chevrolet factory worker in Michigan where he still lives.

WILSON, FLOYD, was a Private First Class in the Army of the United States. He was discharged a short time later because of health problems. He worked in a factory in Lincoln Park, Michigan. He married Nadine Morgan of Wayne County. Their children are: Linda, Wanda and DeWayne Wilson. His parents are Cicero and Addie Sharpe Wilson. His siblings are

Tommy, Ruth, Joe and Walter Wilson and Millie Johnson.

WILSON, FLOYD ALFRED, entered the United States Navy as a Apprentice Seaman 12 January 1943 and was honorably

discharged 22 January 1943. He was born 3 April 1923 in Waynesboro, Tennessee.

WILSON, JOE CICERO, Serial Number 641 87 72 was in the United States Navy. He served on the following

Vessels or Stations: USNTS San Diego, California and NRS Nashville. He was discharged 21 September 1943 in San Diego. He reenlisted in the United States Army Reserve and was inducted 22 March 1951 and transferred to Army Reserves 22 March 1953. He was discharged 5 April 1957. His parents are Cicero and Addie Sharpe Wilson. His siblings are Tommy, Ruth, Floyd and Walter Wilson and Millie Johnson.

WILSON, KENNETH K., son of Mr. and Mrs. Olla Wilson of Collinwood, TN, enlisted in the U. S. Navy and served thirty-one months, seventeen months were, spent at sea in the Pacific area.' He wore 10 battle stars for participating in 12 battles. He was married to Mary Bryant Wilson of Collinwood.

WILSON, ORLIE EARL, Serial Number 273 08 18, was a Radioman Third Class in the Navy of the United States. He was born 21 March 1926 in Wayne County. He entered into active service 13 April 1944. He served on the following Vessels and Stations: Constitution Battalions NCTC, Williamsburg, Virginia and Supp. Radio Station Wahiawa, TH. The following decorations were awarded to Wilson: Asiatic-Pacific Victory Medal, Navy Unit Commendation and American Theater Medal. He was discharged 7 June 1946 from the U. S. Naval Personnel Separation Center in Memphis, Tennessee. He is the son of Mr. and Mrs. Proctor Wilson.

WILSON, TED, Serial Number 34 193 027, was a Technician Fifth Grade in Detachment Quartermaster Section ASF in the

Army of the United States. He was born in Wayne County. His Civilian Occupation was Farmer. He was 27 5/12 years old when he was inducted 15 March 1942 at Fort Oglethorpe, Georgia. His Military Occupational Specialty was Truck Driver. His Military Qualifications included Sharpshooter Rifle Caliber 30. He was not in any battles. The following decorations were awarded to Wilson: Good Conduct Medal. He was discharged 13 October 1944 at Fort McPherson, Georgia. His parents are Ollie and Mildred Keeton Wilson. His siblings are: Marvin, Clarence, and Mary Wilson and Grace Rose. He married Melba Eva Flury. He was a member of the American Legion. Ted died 2 April 1993 and is buried in Memorial Gardens in Waynesboro.

WILSON, TOMMIE A., Serial Number 34 022 568, was a Sergeant in Military Police Detachment A, Section 1, Station Complement, SCU 1458 in the Army of the United States. His permanent mailing

address was Route 6, Waynesboro, Tennessee. He was born 28 January 1919 in Wayne County. He was registered with the Selective Service Board in Wayne County, Tennessee. His Civilian Occupation was Farmer. He was single when he was inducted 25 February 1941 at Fort Oglethorpe, Georgia. His Military Occupational Specialty was Radar Mechanic. His Military Qualifications included Marksman Rifle. He was in the battles of Northern Solomons. The following decorations were awarded to Wilson: American Defense Service Ribbon, Asiatic-Pacific Theater Ribbon with 1 Bronze Stars, Good Conduct Medal and Lapel Button. He left the USA 23 January 1944 for the Pacific Theater Operation, and returned to USA 29 December 1944. He had an eighth grade education. He was discharged 24 August 1945 at Fort McPherson, Georgia. His parents are Cicero and Addie Sharpe Wilson. His siblings are Ruth, Floyd, Joe and Walter Monroe Wilson and Millie Johnson. Tommie married Mildred Noles from McNairy County. Their children are: Terry, Jimmy, Dennis, Robin, Elena and Tommie, Jr., He retired as a machinist in California.

WILSON, WALTER M., Serial Number 44 127 583, was a Private First Class

in 3704th Army Air Force Base Unit in the Army of the United States. His permanent mailing address was Route 6, Waynesboro, Tennessee. He was born 30 August 1927 in Wayne County. He was registered with the Selective Service Board in Wayne County, Tennessee. His Civilian Occupation was Farmer. He was single when he was inducted 11 December 1945 at Fort McPherson, Georgia. His Military Occupational Specialty was Basic 521. He was discharged 8 March 1946 at Keesler Field, Mississippi so that he could reenlist in the Regular Army. He was inducted 9 March 1946 at Keesler Field. His Military Occupational Specialty was Photo Laboratory Technician. He was not in any battles. The following decorations were awarded to Wilson: American Theater Service Medal, and World War II Victory Medal. He was discharged the second time 8 September 1947. His parents are Cicero and Addie Sharpe Wilson. His siblings are Tommy, Ruth, Floyd, Joe Wilson and Millie Johnson. Walter married Ellinor Wilson and they have one daughter, Nancy Wilson. After the War, Walter and his family lived in Detroit where he retired from factory work.

WOODS, DEXTER L., SR., was born in Hico, Texas, 21 April 1900, the only child of Cullen C. and Christine O'Leary

Woods. He received his early education in the public schools of Texas, and during World War I as a student at one of the army training schools in Decatur, Texas. He continued his education at Middle Tennessee State Normal in Murfreesboro, Tennessee, from which he graduated in 1919. Then he studied medicine at Vanderbilt University, graduating from the school of medicine in 1926. He spent the first three years of his career as a physician and surgeon in Fort Worth, Texas. From there he came he came back to Murfreesboro, Tennessee, where he practiced for a short time. In March 1930, he came to Waynesboro where he gave the rest of his life to Wayne County People. During World War II, Dr. Woods was called to the service of his country and was stationed in the European Theater. While there he developed a health problem, was discharged and returned home. He established his own hospital, "The Cullen C. Woods Memorial Hospital." His son, Dr. Dexter L. Woods, Jr., worked with him. They practiced at Wayne County General Hospital later. Other children of Dr. and Mrs. Woods are Cullen, Christine and Jeanette Woods. When Dr. Woods was unable to practice anymore, he and his wife moved to Oklahoma to live near their son, Cullen, a dentist. Dr. Woods passed away in 1973. His body was brought back to Waynesboro for the funeral and he was buried in Murfreesboro.

WOODS, EDDIE I., Serial Number - not available, was a Private First Class in the 14th Tennessee Battalion in the Army of the United States. He was born 28 January 1919, died 28 December 1951 and was buried in Railroad Cemetery, Northeast corner of the intersection of Tennessee Highway 227 and Tennessee Highway 13 South, in the Fairview Community in Wayne County.

WOODS, WILLIAM LAWRENCE, Serial Number 34 377 049, was a Corporal in Company H, 329th Infantry, 83rd Division in the Army of the United States. His permanent mailing address was Route 1, Waynesboro, Tennessee. He was born 15 August 1920 in Lawrenceburg, Tennessee. He was registered with the Selective Service Board in Wayne County, Tennessee. His Civilian Occupation was General Farm Hand. He was single when he was inducted 13 October 1942 and entered into active service 27 October 1942 at Fort Oglethorpe, Georgia. His Military Occupational Specialty was Heavy Mortar Crewman. His Military Qualifications included Combat Infantryman Badge. He was in the battles of Normandy, Northern France, Ardennes, Rhineland, and Central Europe. The following decorations were awarded to Woods: European-African Middle Eastern Theater Ribbon with 1 Silver Star, World War II Victory Medal, Good Conduct Medal and Distinguish Unit Badge. He left the USA 6 April 1944 for the European-African Middle Eastern Theater Operation, and returned to USA 26 November 1945. He was discharged 3 December 1945 at Fort Knox, Kentucky. William, son of William and Zona Walker Woods, was a member of the Veterans of Foreign Wars, American Legion and a member of Evans Chapel United Methodist Church. He was a retired timber worker. He died 23 October 1994, age 74, in the

Veterans Hospital in Nashville and was buried in the Walker Cemetery on Eagle Creek in Wayne County. He married Eva Barkley. They had three children: William David Woods, Debra Mitchell and Cathy Southerland and four grandchildren. He had one sister, Louise Woods Horn.

WRIGHT, ALVIN WASHINGTON, Serial Number 34 373 149, was a Private First Class in Company G, 134 Infantry in

the Army of the United States. His permanent mailing address was Cypress Inn, Tennessee. He was born 22 April 1920 in Cypress Inn in Wayne County. . He was registered with the Selective Service Board in Wayne County, Tennessee. His Civilian Occupation was General Farmer. He was married with three dependents when he was inducted 24 September 1942 and entered into active service 8 October 1942. His Military Occupational Specialty was Light Machine Gunner. His Military Qualifications included Carbine Expert and Combat Infantry Badge. He was in the battles of Northern France and Rhineland. The following decorations were awarded to Wright: American Theater Ribbon, European-African Middle Eastern Theater Ribbon with 2 Bronze Stars, Good Conduct Medal, Purple Heart and World War II Victory Medal. He was wounded in action in France 9 November 1944. He left the USA 25 July 1944 for the European Theater Operation, and returned to USA 13 November 1945. He was discharged 19 November 1945 at Camp Atterbury, Indiana. Alvin also served with Company 398 (Wagon Wheel), 35th Infantry. He remembers, "We had taken the Argonne Forest and were in Metz, France on the 9th of November 1944. It was snowing and the ground was very slushy. We were pushing on toward Belgium and we were being fired on, at first intermittently, then heavier. When this started, we hit the ground crawling, as I was raising my body up to crawl a little further, I was hit in the abdomen. I

was picked up and carried into Metz, France for two days, then I was flown to Poole, England to an old house used as a field Hospital. They operated on me there, and flew me back to Paris and was later sent to the 85th General Hospital in England. I spent five months there before I was sent home. Actually, I was wounded twice, first time shrapnel hit my knee, the second time was a very serious wound. The Germans used 31 caliber guns and we used 30 caliber. Alvin, son of Henry Washington and Ella Panola Montgomery Wright, married (1) Margaret Lorene Vickery. Their children are: Billy Ray, Betty Ann, Carl Washington, and Helen Carolyn Wright. He married (2) Gertrude Allison and they adopted one child, Kathy Renea Allison Wright. He farmed some then worked for TVA for 25 years before he retired.

WRIGHT, CECIL CLAUDE, entered service in 1942, but received a discharge in less than a year from Fort Sill, Okla-

homa. He was born 27 Oct 1917 in Wayne County, Tennessee and died 6 March 1997 in the Wayne County Nursing Home in Waynesboro and was buried in Mt. Pleasant Cemetery in Wayne County. He was a native of Wayne County, a son of the late Henry Washington and Ella Panola (Montgomery) Wright. He made his home in Florida where he was a supervisor in a bakery shop prior to returning to Cypress Inn. He was a Mason and a member of the Holiness Church. Survivors include one brother, Alvin W. Wright of Cypress Inn; four sisters Ethel Balentine of Waynesboro, Wylodean Craig, Ollie Weeks and Rachel Craig all of Cypress Inn and nieces and nephews.
Source: Obit in Wayne County News 12 March 1997.

WRIGHT, CLINTON FREDERICK, Serial Number 44 069 896, was a Private in Military Police Detachment, Section 1, SCU 1447 in the Army of the United States. His permanent mailing address was

Cypress Inn, Tennessee. He was born 14 February 1919 in Cypress Inn. He was registered with the Selective Service Board in Wayne County, Tennessee. His Civilian Occupation was Farmer. He was married with seven dependents when he was inducted 5 February 1945 at Fort Oglethorpe, Georgia. His Military Occupational Specialty was Duty Soldier. He was not in any battles. The following decorations were awarded to Wright: World War II Victory Medal and a Lapel Button. While he was stationed at Jacksonville, Florida, he developed double pneumonia and later received a medical discharge 15 December 1945 at Fort McPherson, Georgia. His parents are Jessie Newton and Mary Emma Holt Wright. He was married 27 October 1940 to Lucy Inez Fowler, who was born 22 April 1920. Their children are: Vida Joyce, Patricia Joan, Robert Joel, Jimmy Lowell, Jason Frederick, Jessie Earl and Jennifer Ann Wright. Clinton died 11 September 1973. Clinton Frederick Wright.

WRIGHT, HAROLD PAUL, Serial Number 34 886 074, entered service 5 October 1943 in Fort Eustis, Virginia. He

was sent overseas and served in England, France, Belgium, Holland, Luxembourg, Germany and Austria. He earned two

Battle Stars. He was discharged 28 April 1946. Harold, son of J. Eddie and Alpha Lucinda Darby Wright, was born 6 February 1925 in Lauderdale, Alabama. He married Mildred Wells and they now live in Huntsville, Alabama.

WRIGHT, JAY F., Serial Number 34 920 969, was a Private First Class in Headquarters Company, 289th Infantry Regiment in the Army of the United States. His permanent mailing address was Route 2, Collinwood, Tennessee. He was born 11 September 1925 in Cypress Inn, Tennessee. He was registered with the Selective Service Board in Wayne County, Tennessee. His Civilian Occupation was General Farm Hand. He was married with three dependents when he was inducted 15 December 1943 and entered into active service 5 January 1944 at Fort Oglethorpe, Georgia. His Military Occupational Specialty was Guard Patrolman. His Military Qualifications included Combat Infantry Badge. He was in the battles of Ardennes, Rhineland, and Central Europe. The following decorations were awarded to Wright: European-African Middle Eastern Theater Ribbon with 3 Bronze Stars, Good Conduct Ribbon, World War II Victory Medal and a Purple Heart. He was wounded in Action in the Belgium breakthrough 26 December 1944. He left the USA 22 October 1944 for the European Theater Operation, and returned to USA 8 March 1946. He was discharged 13 March 1946 at Camp Atterbury, Indiana. Jay is the son of John Henry and Fannie Sherrill Wright. His siblings are: Clayborn, Clifford, Robert D., and Guilford C. Wright, Ruthie Patterson, Ruby Southerland, Ruie Pigg, and Eva Roberson. He married Effie Vickery and they have one son, Larry K. Wright.

WRIGHT, OLIN E., Serial Number 34 506 481, was a Technician Fifth Grade in 3783rd Quartermaster Truck Company in the Army of the United States. His permanent mailing address was Cypress Inn, Tennessee. He was born 18 February 1923 in Lauderdale County, Alabama. He was registered with the Selective Service Board in Wayne County, Tennessee. His Civilian Occupation was General Farmer. He was inducted 18 January 1943 and entered into active service 25 January 1943 at Fort Oglethorpe, Georgia. His Military Occupational Specialty was Light Truck Driver. His Military Qualifications included MM Rifle. He was not in any battles. The following decorations were awarded to Wright: American Service Medal, Good Conduct Medal, Lapel Button and World War II Victory Medal. He had a seventh grade education. He was stationed in New-

port News, Virginia when the war ended. He was discharged 26 February 1946 at Fort McPherson, Georgia. Olin was the son of James Samuel and Mamie Hill Wright. He married Angie B. Holt and they had two children: Terry Wade Wright and Judy Diane DeHart. He worked 37 1/2 years for Florence, Alabama Electric Department before he retired. He is a member of the Sherwood Avenue Church of Christ and enjoys car races.

WRIGHT, RANDELL LANDON, served from 1943 to 1946 in 4th Field Artillery in the Army of the United States.

He was born 5 June 1921 in Lauderdale, Alabama. He was inducted at Fort Custer, Wayne, Michigan. He took his basic training in Camp Adair, Oregon and was sent to the South Pacific. He is the son of J. Eddie and Alpha L. Darby Wright. He married Nettie Hayes 25 October 1941. Their two children are Randell Leon, and Stephen Gregory Wright and they have five grandchildren. He attended school at Cypress Inn, Holts and Collinwood High School. He now lives in Clauson, Michigan.

YARBORO, HERDISE JUNIOR, Serial Number 933 71 80, was a Steward Third Class in the Navy of the United States. He was born 12 January 1925 in Decaturville, Tennessee. He entered the Navy 1 March 1945. He served on the following Vessels and Stations: NTC Bainbridge, Maryland, Tadcen Shoemaker, California and USS ZEILEN. The following decorations were awarded to Wright: American Area Ribbon, Asiatic-Pacific Theater Ribbon and World War II Victory Medal. He was discharged 3 May 1946 from the U. S. Naval Personnel Separation Center in Memphis, Tennessee.

YEISER, ROBERT J., Lieutenant Commander, served on active duty in the Marine Corps in the United States Navy from 16 February 1942 until he was detached 12 October 1945. Dr. Yeiser served in the Dental Corps and was in the Reserve before Pearl Harbor. He served at Parris Island, South Carolina and at the U. S. Navy Section Base in Trinidad, British West Indies, Navy Center at Gulfport, Mississippi, and at the Navy Pre-Flight School, Chapel Hill, North Carolina. Dr. Yeiser was commissioned as Lieutenant Junior Grade and was detached Lieutenant Commander. Dr. Yeiser, son of Jay and Ethel Nowlin Yeiser, was born 28 January 1915 in Waynesboro. He attended Waynesboro Elementary School, Tate School in Shelbyville, Mulligan College in Johnson City, Tennessee, Union University in Jackson, Tennessee and graduated from the University of Tennessee Dental College in Memphis. Dr. Yeiser practiced Dentistry in Savannah, Tennessee, where he joined the Naval Reserve. He is married to Mavis Kerns and is the father of four children. After he was discharged Dr. Yeiser practiced in Johnson City, Tennessee, until his retirement in June 1990 His siblings are Emmett Yeiser of Savannah, Josephine Thompson of Jonesboro, Tennessee and Clara Nell Phillips of Waynesboro.

His Naval Service included the U.S./ Navy Hospital, Paris Island, SC; U.S. Navy Section Base, Trinidad, BWI; U.S. Navy Training Center, Gulfport, MS; U.S. Navy PreA/Flight School, Chapel Hill, NC. He was discharged October 12, 1945, after three years .0 and ten months service with the rank of Lt. Commander.

During his years of practice, he was active in the First District Dental Society where he served as President, Treasurer and a member of various committees. He also was active in the Tennessee Dental Society where he received the Fellowship Award for Distinguished Service to Dentistry. He was also a member of the American Dental Association. Dr. Yeiser was a member of the First Christian Church in Johnson City, TN; Kiwanis Club; the Investment Club and Sons of the Revolution,

He died October 21, 1999, at the Johnson City Medical Center. He is survived by his wife, Mavis; daughter, Judith Y., Ferrell of Knoxville, TN; son, Robert Jay Yeiser of Arlington, VA; son, Thomas Kerns Yeiser of Johnson City, TN; Edwin Sims Yeiser of Knoxville, TN; grandson, Robert Jay Yeiser, Jr. of Nashville, TN; grandson, William Houston Yeiser of Jackson, WY.

YEISER, RUSS, JR., Serial Number 34 366 694, was a Private in Company G, 159th Infantry, 7th Division in the Army of the United States. His permanent mailing address was Route 2, Waynesboro, Tennessee. He was born 22 October 1920 in Waynesboro, Tennessee. He was registered with the Selective Service Board in Wayne County, Tennessee. His Civilian Occupation was Farmer. He was inducted 25 August 1942 at Fort Oglethorpe, Georgia. His Military Occupational Specialty was Duty, NCO. His Military Qualifications included Rifle 21. He was in the battles of the Aleutian Islands Campaign. The following decorations were awarded to Yeiser: Asiatic-Pacific Theater Ribbon with 1 Battle Star, and Good Conduct Ribbon. He left the USA 27 June 1943 for the Asiatic-Pacific Theater Operation, and returned to USA 16 December 1944. He was discharged 6 November 1945 at Camp Joseph T. Robinson, Arkansas.

YOUNGBLOOD, ROSS, Serial Number 34 189 074, was a Corporal in 424th Air Service Group, Army Air Force in the Army of the United States. His permanent mailing address was General Delivery, Collinwood, Tennessee. He was born 29 October 1906 in Collinwood. He was registered with the Selective Service Board in Wayne County, Tennessee. His Civilian Occupation was General Painter. He was single when he was inducted 18 February 1942 at Fort Oglethorpe, Georgia. His Military Occupational Specialty was Military Policeman. He was not in any battles. The following decorations were awarded to Youngblood: European-African Middle Eastern Service Medal. He left the USA 5 December 1943 for the European Theater Operation, and returned to USA 1 August 1945. He was discharged 9 September 1945 at Fort McPherson, Georgia.

WAYNE COUNTY, TENNESSEE VETERANS WITHOUT BIOGRAPHIES

No source is readily available to obtain accurate lists of veterans from ANY war. That information is considered confidential and not available to the public. In addition, any veteran who entered the service from any other place other than Wayne County would not be included on a Wayne County list. As a result, the committee had to rely on registered discharge papers, Wayne County News articles, word of mouth and personal knowledge to gather information.

No biographical information, or photo, was submitted for the following list of WWII veterans. Efforts to contact relatives for information were unsuccessful. They are listed here to assure that they are included as having served.

Anderson, Kenneth Edward	Hall, Elbert Leroy	Martin, John Henry	Rector, Vernon
Anderson, William Robert	Hanback, Grady E.	Martin, Taylor, Jr.	Reeves, Jack C.
Amett, Hollis	Hanback, Vernon	Martin, Willard	Riley, Dewey
Arnold, Claude Willis	Harbin, Lee Ellis	Martin, William D.	Risner, Cleo Earnest
Berry, Charles	Harris, Cecil R.	Mason, Dave Robert	Risner, Floyd D.
Berry, James A.	Harville, Jimmie W.	Mathis, Leslie Loyd	Roberson, Glenn
Brewer, Elliott T.	Harville, Odell	Mathis, Sylvester, Jr.	Rose, Cleo
Brewer, James H.	Hawks, Houston D.	Matney, Edward	Scott, Grayford Reuben
Bromley, Albert L.	Henson, Frank	Matney, Kenneth E.	Shands, Lee A.
Bromley, Carroll Q.	Henson, George, Jr.	Mayberry, Harry R.	Shaneyfelt. Ernest
Brown, Harley L.	Higgins, Willard D.	McCurry, Lee Edward	Shelton, Charles L.
Brown, Oliver E.	Hill,, Edward Wendal	McCurry, John	Sherrill, Howard Russell
Burnett, Edward F.	Henson, Oliver M.	McFall, Oliver J.	Sherrill, Warren Guy
Burns, James Everett	Hinton, Cecil Elbert	McGee, Lawrence W.	Simmons, Johnny D.
Bums, Willie 0.	Holt, Edwin B.	McMahon, Jack	Sims, Lonnie Claude
Butler, Andy J.	Holt, Herbert H.	McWilliams, Fain	Sinclair. Alfred S.
Butler, James W.	Horton, Clyde C.	Miller, Roy W.	Skelton, Elmer D.
Carpenter, Neal	Horton, Herman H.	Montgomery, Aaron Francis	Skelton, Enis T.
Chambers,, Bert, Jr.	Howell, Johnny H.	Montgomery, James Randolph	Skelton, Felix R.
Cherry, Frank Gilbert	Hunt, Davis	Moore, Everett Worth	Skelton, Ray L.
Cherry, Charles R.	Hurst, Robert Welch	Moore, Grady	Skimehorn, J.D.
Churchwell, Calvin W.	Jackson, James 0.	Morgan, Ralph B.	Smith, David
Combs, James R.	Jeter, John Edd	Nelson, Earnest Walker	Smith, Floyd
Cook, Everett Conrad	Jobe, Will T.	Nelson, John W.	Sparks, George E.
Cook Lige A.	Johnson, Ira	Nelson, Nehew W.	Staggs, Clayton
Cornelius, John Garvie	Johnson, James G.	Nelson, Peter E.	Staggs, Fred
Crews, William Leonard, Jr.	Jones, Thomas F.	Nelson, William E.	Staggs, James
Daniel, Johnny	Kelley, Horace, Jr.	Norris, Gilford Ray	Staggs, Obie
Darnell Ira	Kelley, James Clamon	Nutt, William G.	Tatum, Elmer R.
Dixon, John C.	Kelley, Ray F.	Odle, J.C.E.	Thompson, Grayford R.
Dixon, Johnny Rayford	Kelley, Thomas S,. Jr.	Odle, Lovell C.	Thompson, Robert F.
Dixon, William	Kilburn, Albert N.	Odle, William D.	Thompson, William, Jr.
Downing, Jaxie C.	Kilburn, Clemon K.	Olive, James Henry	Walker, James H.
Fowler, Dallas W.	Kilburn, John Dewey	Patterson, Robert H.	Walker, Joseph F.
Fowler,, Frank B.	Kilburn, Roy	Perry, Loyce	Walker, Robert E.
Franks, Roy	Kimbrell, A.J.	Pigg, Richard	Watkins, Noble R.
Gambrell,, Byron S.	Lakey, Copeland E.	Poag, Dudley	Watson, Toland
Gambrell, Harry	Lakey, Jasper Martin	Poag, Stanley	Weatherspoon, Clifford
Gambrell, James N.	Linville, James William	Pollock, Ray	Weatherspoon, Floyd E.
Gobbell, Robert E.	Linville,, Pinkney W.J.	Potts, Jake E.	Weaver, Gifford L.
Gordon, Cazey C.	Long, Leonard George	Powers, Virgie Franklin	White, Ernestean
Gordon, Lawrence	Lopp, George E.C.	Prater, Charles E.	Whitehead, Charlie D.
Gower, Ralph L.	Lopp, Henry M.	Prater, J.D.	Whitehead, James Wimmer
Griggs, Freeman H.	Lucker, Oliver	Prater, Robert E.	Whitehead, Miles
Griggs, James Hubert	Lynch, Jimmy	Pulley, Roy U.	Williams, Joe Weaver
Grimes, Cheslie L.	Lynum., Cecil	Pulley, Wallace	Wilson, Arthur
Grimes, Monroe	Martin, Elihue	Quillen, Floyd C.	Wilson, George L., Sr.

MILITARY ABBREVATIONS

b.	born		Rec.	received
d.	died		RR	Railroad
sp.	spouse		S/O	Son of
ch.	child		D/O	Daughter of
chi.	children		Sp. Amer.	Spanish American
F	farmer		USA	United States of America
Bur.	buried		WIA	Wounded in Action
Enl.	enlisted		Co.	County
Dschg.	discharged		Pul.	Pulaski
Cpl.	Corporal		Indpls.	Indianapolis
Pfc.	Private First Class		Cinn.	Cincinnati
Pvt.	Private		N.	North
Sgt.	Sergeant		S.	South
Sgt/1c	Sergeant First Class		E.	East
A/1c	Airman First Class		W.	West
A/2c	Airman Second Class		C.	Central
T/Sgt	Techanical Sergeant		SAC	Strategic Air Command
M/Sgt	Master Sergeant		CON AC	Continental Air Command
Lt.	Lieutenant		Adm.	Administrator
2nd. Lt.	Second Lieutenant		Prof.	Professor
Capt.	Captain		Ser.	served
Col.	Colonel		Occ.	occupation
Gen.	General		M D	Medical Doctor
Hq.	Headquarters		Bd.	Board
Sq.	Squadron		Ed.	Education
Fld.	Field		Comm.	Community
Tng.	Training		AFB	Air Force Base
Maint.	Maintainence		USAF	United States Air Force
Plt.	Pilot		w/3	with 3
Natl.	National		Art.	Artillery
Cem.	Cemetery		Bn.	Battalion
Dec'd	deceased		Batt.	Battery
Is.	Island		Coll.	College
KIA	Killed in action		Chem.	Chemistry
Mem.	Memorial		EAME	Eastern African Middle
OS	Overseas		Europe	
POW	Prisoner of War			

Silver Star: For gallantry in action against an opposing armed force.

Purple Heart: Awarded for wounds or death as result of an act of any opposing armed force.

Bronze Star Medal: For heroic or mentorious ahcievement of service not involving aerial flight in connection with operations against an opposing armed force Bronze V device worn to denote valor.

Defense Superior Service Medal: Awarded by the Secretary of Defense for superior meritorious service while in a position of significant responsibilty.

Legion of Merit: For exceptionally meritorious conduct in the performance of outstanding services.

World War II Victory Medal: For service in World War II.

Vietnam Service Medal: For service in Vietnam and contiguous waters from 1 July 1958 through 28 March 1973.

Good Conduct Medal (Army): Awarded for exemplory behavior, efficiency and Fidelity while on active duty. A clasp with loops denotes subsequent awards.

Good Conduct Medal (Navy): Based on conduct for four-year periods of continuous active service. Bronze stars denotes subsequent awards.

Good Conduct Medal (Marine Corps): Based on conduct for three-year periods of continuous active service. Bronze stars denote subsequent awards.

Good Conduct Medal (Air Force) Awarded for exemplary behavior efficiency and fidelity. Oak leaf clusters denote subsequent awards.

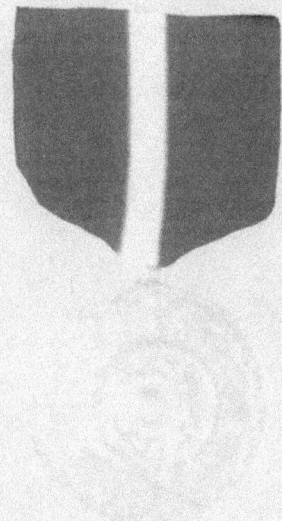

Good Conduct Medal (Coast Guard): Based on conduct for three-year periods (after 1 January 1980) of continuous active service. Bronze stars denote subsequent awards.

Medal of Honor with Service Ribbon (Army): For conspicuous gallantry and intrepidity at the risk of life above and beyond the call of duty in action involving actual conflict with an opposing armed force.

Medal of Honor with Service Ribbon (Navy-Marine-Coast Guard): For conspicuous gallantry and intrepidity at the risk of life above and beyond the call of duty in action involving actual conflict with an opposing armed force.

Medal of Honor with Service Ribbon (Air Force): For conspicuous gallantry and intrepidity at the risk of life above and beyond the call of duty in action involving actual conflict with an opposing armed force.

INDEX

Editor's Note: This index includes those names of listed individuals with full names. Those whose name appears in all capitals are those who have listed biographies.

GIVENS, LOUIS R. 109
Gobbel, Floziada 152
Gobbell, Ada Mozelle 110
Gobbell, Amy 208
Gobbell, Anna Lou 128, 129
Gobbell, Elzadia 109
GOBBELL, FRED M. 109
Gobbell, Georgie 169
Gobbell, Minnie (Hooks) 110
GOBBELL, ODELL 109
Gobbell, Robert E. 266
Gobbell, Rotha Nell (Stricklin) 152
Gobbell, Tessie 59
GOBBELL, WILEY CLAYTON 109
GOBBELL, WILLIAM W., Jr. 110
Gobble, Bettie Rae 178
Gobble, Emily Rebecca 77
Gobble, Pearl 20
Gobble, Ruth 60
Goode, John Monroe 6
Goode, Shirley Lee 175
GOODMAN, ALBERT LOUIS 110
Goodman, Albert Louis 110
Goodman, Bessie L. Davis 110
GOODMAN, EDGAR DANIEL 110
Goodman, Jewell 145
Goodman, Opal 207
Goodman, Ora Parker 189
Goodman, Timothy Shane 110
Goodrich, Josephine 198
GOODWIN, OTIS L. 110
Gordon, Cazey C. 266
Gordon, Lawrence 266
Gordon, Louise 242
Gossset, Florine 207
GOWER, CARMEL E. 110
Gower, Ralph L. 266
Grady, Marvin 11
Graf, Jim 25
Graham, Alice 111
Graham, Alice Jane 200
Graham, Belinda 97
Graham, Bonnie 111
Graham, J. C. 111
GRAHAM, J.C. 110
Graham, James 111
GRAHAM, JAMES EDWARD 111
Graham, Mae 111
Graham, Mary Hill 111
Graham, Mary Jane Hill 125, 126
Graham, Nola 111
Graham, Ora Belle 10
Graham, Virginia 250
GRAMBELL, LOUIS 111
Grandinetti, Peggy 43
Grandinetti, Petty 42
Grannas, Eva 229
Graves, Bess 111
Graves, Deborah Ann 206
Graves, Helen 204
Graves, J. B. 206
Graves, Mamie (Hickerson) 204
Graves, Mattie 111
GRAVES, ROBERT T. 111
Graves, Roy 111
Graves, Wilma (Kitty) 191
Gray, Elizabeth 136
Gray, Marcella 207
Gray, Marguerite 207
Gray, Patsy Ann 260
Gray, Peggy 57
Green, Cora 134
Green, Linda 98
Green, Mable 62
Greer, Janice Davis 83
Greeson, Ada 156, 157, 158
Greeson, Billie Carrol 111
GREESON, BILLY CARROLL 111
GREESON, HERMAN CHARLES 111
Greeson, Jerry Randall 111
Greeson, Larry Carrol 111
GREESON, LEMUEL 111
Greeson, Marie 243
Greeson, Mary Alice 135
Greeson, Mary Victoria Emmaline Parker 111
Greeson, Montie Shipman 111
Greeson, Ronnie Joe 112
GREESON, WILLIAM EDGAR, Jr. 112
Griffin, Conda Price 202
Griggs, Alfred 113
Griggs, Alfred Franklin 113
GRIGGS, ARVIE 112
Griggs, Burnsie Martin 158

Griggs, Cicero 156
GRIGGS, CLAUDE E. 112
GRIGGS, CLIFFORD FRANKLIN 112
Griggs, Edith 22
Griggs, Elmer 112
GRIGGS, FORD 112
Griggs, Ford 112
Griggs, Freeman H. 266
GRIGGS, HOMER LEO 113
Griggs, James Hubert 266
Griggs, James Quinton 113
GRIGGS, JOHN WASHINGTON 113
Griggs, Katheryn 217
Griggs, Lillian Lay 149
Griggs, Louise 169
Griggs, Madge 59
Griggs, Margie Gallaher 101
Griggs, Mary Jane Dixon 113
Griggs, Thelma Lands 113
Griggs, Virginia Cole 113
GRIGGS, WADE 113
Griggs, Wilma 125
Grimes, Anita Neil 114
Grimes, Annie McCain 114
GRIMES, ARVIE 113
Grimes, Barbara Walohager 115
GRIMES, BONNIE JACKSON 113
Grimes, Cheslie L. 266
GRIMES, CLARENCE H. 113
GRIMES, EATHEL IRIS 114
Grimes, Gary L. 114
Grimes, Gladys Crews 115
Grimes, Hazel 113
Grimes, James 113
GRIMES, JAMES C. 114
Grimes, Jean Hassell 113
GRIMES, JOHNNIE FRANK 114
Grimes, Linda 113
Grimes, Martha Collie 114
Grimes, Monroe 266
GRIMES, MONTIE JOHNSON 114
GRIMES, OPHNIE CHARLES 114
Grimes, Raye 209
GRIMES, RAYMOND FOY 115
Grimes, V. C. 113
GRIMES, WALTER W. "BUD" 115
Grimes, Wanda 114
Grimes, Winnie Mae 213
Grinnell, Kathryn 132
GROSSMAN, SIGUARD SANDOR 115
Gunter, Carlos 205
Guttery, Sarah Elizabeth 157

H

HADDOCK, ARDELL JOHN, Jr. 115
Haddock, Arlie (Adkisson) 116
Haddock, Bonnie 226
Haddock, Brenda Gaye 116
Haddock, Brenda Gist Toms 203
HADDOCK, CLARENCE S. 115
Haddock, Clyde 143
HADDOCK, CLYDE D. 116
Haddock, Holli Jan 116
HADDOCK, JAMES H. 116
Haddock, James K. Polk 116
Haddock, Jean (Brewer) 49
Haddock, Jonathan Douglas 116
Haddock, Kenny 217
Haddock, Maedon 177
Haddock, Mollie (Bryson) 115
Haddock, Wynelle 60
Haggard, Anna Lou (Montague) 116
Haggard, Mary Bell 41
HAGGARD, ROBERT ROY, JR. 116
Haggard Sr., R. R 116
Haithcock, Cynthia Rose Overby 116
Haithcock, Doris Harris 116
Haithcock, Earl 117
HAITHCOCK, ROY W. 116
Haithcock, Roy W., Jr. 116
Haley, Maureen 159
Halford, Adolph, Jr. 234
Hall, Doris 241
Hall, Elbert Leroy 266
Hall, Hazel 145
Hall, P. J. 117
HALL, WARREN W. 117
HAMACK, WILLIAM D. 117
Hambree, Sherrye Lee Dixon 86
Hamilton, Clyde 12
Hamilton, Ernest 12
Hamilton, Essa Kate 43
HAMILTON, J.W. 12

Hamilton, Kate 42
Hamilton, Leonard 12
Hamilton, Louise Davis 83
Hamilton, Mattie Bell 12
Hamm, Essie Mae Hickerson 117
HAMM, JOHNNY B. 117
Hamm, Myrtle Lois 117
Hammack, Alta Barkley 37
Hammond, Sandra 81
Hampton, Allen Wade 117
Hampton, Anthony 117
Hampton, Chadwick 117
Hampton, Charlie 117
Hampton, Christi 117
Hampton, Christopher Thomas 117
Hampton, John Robert 117
Hampton, Ruth Ella 165
Hampton, Talmage Allen 117
HAMPTON, TALMAGE WADE 117
HANBACK, ALVIN LEE 117
HANBACK, ARLIE C. 117
Hanback, Arlie Craiton 117
Hanback, Cora Stowe 117
HANBACK, DUMONT 117
Hanback, Dumont 6
Hanback, Etta 195
HANBACK, EVERETTE DALTON 117
Hanback, Grady E. 266
HANBACK, JAMES B. 118
Hanback, James Bomount 117
HANBACK, MARVIN 118
Hanback, Myrtle 38
Hanback, Opal 210
Hanback, Ruth Smith 235
Hanback, Sue Andrews 33
Hanback, Thuna Etta (Holt) 118
Hanback, Vernon 266
Hanback, Vina Drucilla Montgomery 117
Harbell, Mary Elizabeth 220
Harbin, Lee Ellis 266
HARBIN, PRICE 118
Harbor, Earmon 62
Harbour, Frank 122
Hardin, Burnice 118
HARDIN, CHARLES 118
Hardin, David 118
Hardin, Della 47
HARDIN, FRANK GIPSON 118
Hardin, Freddy Lee 191
Hardin, Gladys Culp 76
Hardin, Grace 159
HARDIN, JAMES 118
Hardin, James 193
Hardin, James (Jim) 118
HARDIN, JAMES L. 118
HARDIN, JOHN EDWARD 118
Hardin, Kathryn 96
Hardin, Katie 118
Hardin, Lane 118
Hardin, Lorene 191
Hardin, Lula Stutts 118
Hardin, Margie 99
Hardin, Mary Lou 38
Hardin, Mildred 47
HARDIN, WALTER WOODROW 118
HARKEY, ALLEN B. 118
Harkey, Mary Len Moore 173, 174
Harkey, Rose Mary 53
Harmon, Thelma 65
Harner, Elizabeth Nelle Prater 200
HARPER, CHESLEY CLYDE 119
HARPER, EVERETT G. 119
HARPER, EVERETT SANFORD 119
Harper, Everett Sanford 119
Harper, Julia (Stidham) 119
Harper, Luther Franklin 119
Harper, Nola Brewer 119
Harper, Sarah Ayers 34
HARPER, WARREN G. 119
Harris, Anna 126
Harris, Cecil R. 266
HARRIS, DANIEL R. 119
Harris, Daniel Richard 6
Harris, David 96
HARRIS, EDD A. 119
Harris, Ellen 110
HARRIS, HERMAN 119
Harris, Jeannette 251
Harris, Phillip Ray 106
Harris, Reginia 139
Harrison, Ada Christine 129
Harrison, Violet 65

Hart, Joan 42
HARTUP, JAMES HUGO, Jr. 120
Hartwell, Marietta Russ 172
Harvey, T. A. 164
Harville, Jimmie W. 266
Harville, Odell 266
Harville, Thelma 162
Harwell, Lela Wilton 63
Hassel, Martha Adeline 27
Hassell, Alice Hicks 120
HASSELL, BOB ADKINS 120
HASSELL, HOWARD 120
Hassell, Joel Adkins 120
Hassell, Lily Irene (Hartley) 120
Hassell, Margie 120
Hassell, Martha Adeline (Old) 186
Hassell, Ora Maude (Brown) 120
HASSELL, RICHARD FRANK 120
Hassell, Robert Edward 120
Hassell, Thomas Jerrold 120
Hassell, William Amos 120
Hasting, Ginger 67
Hastings, Emma 133
Hatchett, Katie Mae 142
Hawkins, Willie Shannon 27
Hawks, Houston D. 266
Hayes, Beulah Elizabeth Fowler 121
HAYES, CECIL ARTHUR 120
Hayes, Charla Mae Holt 121
Hayes, Danny Michael 121
HAYES, ERNEST L. 120
Hayes, J. D. 121
HAYES, JAMES HIRAM 121
HAYES, JOHN LOUIS 121
Hayes, Lillie (Moser) 121
Hayes, Mary Elizabeth 96
Hayes, May 173
Hayes, Nettie 264
Hayes, Pauline 12
Hayes, Ray 121
HAYES, ROBERT FIELDER 121
Hayes, Thomas 121
Hays, Hattie 260
Hays, Judy Elaine Stults 243
Hays, Marie 258
Hays, Mary Cathleen Berry 42
Hays, Mauveline 226
Hazel Ayers 61
Heard, Ada 43
Heard, Birdie 250
HEARD, CLARENCE EDWARD 121
Heard, Clarence Edward 6
Heard, Eunice 12
Heard, Henry 121
HEARD, JAMES ROSS 121
Heard, Lester Paul 107
Heard, Ora 87
HEARD, REUBEN 121
Heard, Vivian 12
Hearlston, Ava Jean 253, 254
Heimendinger, Martha Ann 92
Held, Margaret 187
Helton, Bettie 121
Helton, Delia Culp 171
HELTON, HAROLD 121
HELTON, JAMES CATON 121
Helton, John A. 12
Helton, Johnny 108
Helton, Katie Duren 121
HELTON, LEON 12
Helton, Lucy Flippo 12, 122
Helton, Mary Elizabeth 171
Helton, Sallie 182
HELTON, TOLBERT MAXEY 122
Helton, Tolbert Maxey 12
HELTON, TOM 122
HENDRIX, CLYDE 12
Hendrix, Della (Keeton) 123
Hendrix, Della Keeton 13
HENDRIX, J.T. 122
HENDRIX, JACK WILLIAM "BILLY" 122
HENDRIX, LESTER 123
Hendrix, Lisa 123
Hendrix, Lydia O'Mally 123
Hendrix, Mattie Keeton 122
Hendrix, Nona 36, 122
HENDRIX, ORVAL 123
Hendrix, Oval 122
Hendrix, Parthenia Clementine Maples 155
Hendrix, Roland V. (R.V.) 13
HENDRIX, ROLLAND V. 123
Hendrix, Roxie Butler 122
Hendrix, Sallie Pitts 196
Hendrix, Shirley 123

Hendrix, Thelma Jean 101
Hendrix, Vernon 13
Hendrixs, Marjorie 259
Hendrixs, Nona Edwards 259
Henearling, Billie Jean 61
Henry, Alexander Dan 36
HENRY, JAMES "JIM" MELVIN 123
Henry, Janice Balentine 36
Henry, Rheba A. 123
HENSLEY, BILLY L. 123
Hensley, Martha Nell 213
Henson, Frank 266
Henson, George, Jr. 266
Henson, Oliver M. 266
Henson, Pugh 6
HENSON, VIRGIL L. 123
Herbert, Stacie Keeton 142
Herndershot, Vivian 126
Hickerson, Addie (Treadwell) 159
Hickerson, Elsie Thelma Culp 124
Hickerson, Florence (Denton) 124
Hickerson, Flossie 209
Hickerson, Gracie 60
Hickerson, Janis Denton 124
Hickerson, Kenneth 125
HICKERSON, KENNETH REECE 124
Hickerson, Mandy (Jones) 125
Hickerson, Mattie Vivian 124
Hickerson, Robbie June Joines 124
HICKERSON, WALTON F. 124
HICKERSON, WILLIAM THIRL 124
HICKERSON, WILLIE FLOYD 124
Hickman, Glenda Jane Rainey 17
Hickman, Kimberly 17
HICKS, BROYLES T. 125
Hicks, Gearldean K. 65
Hicks, Helene Gallaher 101
Higgins, Nanne 169
Higgins, Rebecca 260
Higgins, Sarah Dean 256
Higgins, Willard D. 266
HILL, ANDREW 125
Hill, Bonnie 126
Hill, Brenda Ray 209
Hill, Burnes 126
Hill, Charles Douglas 126
HILL, CHESLEY BROWN 125
HILL, CLAYBORN B. 125
HILL, CLAYTON H. 125
Hill, Edward Wendal 266
HILL, EVERETT LEE 126
HILL, GARLAND 126
Hill, James 126
Hill, Jennie (Reeves) 126
Hill, Jimmy Lee 126
Hill, Kenneth W. 126
HILL, MARVIN 126
Hill, Miles Brison 125
Hill, Monetta 9
Hill, Oda Bell 126
Hill, Patsy D. 234
Hill, Roxie Staggs 125
Hill, Stella 253, 254
Hill, Virgie 126
Hill, Virgie Griffin 126
Hill, Virgie Jones 126
HILL, WAYNE D. 126
HILL, WILLIAM ARTHER 126
Hime, Delia 106
Hime, Lucille Allen 30
Hime, Ruth Allen 30
Hines, Earline 122
Hinson, Ann 73
Hinson, Lillian 36
Hinton, Cecil Elbert 266
Hinton, Earline 226
HINTON, FLOYD GLEN 126
Hinton, Sallie Fraley 126
Hoarz, Jim 56
Hoarz, Madeline 56
Hoataja, Helia 36
Hobbs, Clara Edith 69
HOBBS, HEWEY 20
Hobbs, Mildred 21
Hobbs, Virginia 96
Hodges, Jane Gallaher 101
HODGES, JASPER "JIMMY" E. 126
Hodges, Nannie E. 126
HOGAN, CHARLES L. 127
HOGAN, JOHN RALPH 127
HOGAN, LEAMON G. 127
Holcomb, Gwen 213
Holder, Bessie Sally 131, 246
Holder, Betty Turnbo 238

HOLDER, CLINT 127
HOLDER, HOLLIS HERMAN 127
Holder, Hugh Betty Turnbo 127
HOLDER, JESSE BROWN 127
Holder, Laura C. Pulley 127
Holder, Mary Jose Lineberry 127
Holder, Ruthie 131
Holder, Ruthie H. 130, 132, 133
HOLDER, WINFRED BROMLEY 127
HOLLANDER, DONALD J. 128
Hollander, Eurlene 248
Hollander, Joe 128
Hollis, A. N., Jr. 128
Hollis, A. N., Sr. 128
HOLLIS, A.N., JR. 128
Hollis, Allan Ray, Jr. 128
HOLLIS, ALLAN RAY, Sr. 128
Hollis, Annie Nelson 128
HOLLIS, COLEMAN FRAZIER, Sr. 128
Hollis, Cynthia 128
Hollis, David Franklin 129
HOLLIS, EDWIN CARNELL 128
Hollis, Ethel McKennon 128
HOLLIS, FRED T. "TOM" 128
Hollis, Herbert 128
Hollis, James Herman 130
HOLLIS, JAMES OLIVER PERRY 129
Hollis, James Perry 129
Hollis, James Perry, Jr. 129
Hollis, Jo Bell 260
HOLLIS, JOHN HERMAN 129
Hollis, Joseph Johnson 128
HOLLIS, LAWRENCE 129
HOLLIS, LEE ROY 129
Hollis, Louise Shaver 128
Hollis, Lydle J. 129
HOLLIS, LYTLE J. 129
Hollis, Mamie Lee Ella (Robertson) 129
Hollis, Maude Shutt 128
Hollis, Nona Ann (Lee) 128, 129
Hollis, Paul J. 128
HOLLIS, PAUL JUDSON "P. J." 130
Hollis, Rachel Johnson 128
Hollis, Ruthanna 128
Hollis Sr., A. N. 128, 130
Hollis, Tom 128
Hollis, Virginia 84
HOLLIS, WILLIAM PRATER "BILL" 130
Holly, Wayne 179
HOLT, ALBERT FRANKLIN 130
HOLT, ALTON CHARLIE 130
Holt, Angie B. 264
Holt, Ann 93
Holt, Annie 42
Holt, Annie Blanche 195
Holt, Ardilla Leona 80
Holt, Arlie Warren 6
Holt, Barbara 131, 132, 162
Holt, Bessie Sally Holder 131
Holt, Betty Jean 34
Holt, Bud H. 131
HOLT, CHARLES WILLIAM 130
Holt, Chrystal 106, 108
Holt, Coral 131
Holt, Dean 132
Holt, Ed 248
Holt, Edsel A 131
Holt, Edwin B. 266
Holt, Harvey Dixon 131, 246
Holt, Herbert H. 266
HOLT, HOLLIS ANDREW 130
Holt, Homer 143
HOLT, HOMER L. 130
Holt, Jacqueline 214
HOLT, JAMES F. 131
Holt, Jewel 250
Holt, Jewell Tinin 130
Holt, Joe M. 99
HOLT, JOE SILAS 131
HOLT, JOHN CALVIN 131
Holt, John Emerald 131
Holt, John Henry 130, 131, 132, 133
Holt, Kathleen 226
Holt, Kathryn 131
Holt, Kenneth Ray 130
Holt, Larry Rayborn 131
Holt, Lela 122, 123
Holt, Lois Moore 212
HOLT, LOUIS W. 131
Holt, Mae Edith 246
Holt, Margaret 131

Holt, Marvin Leland 13
HOLT, MELTON JOHNNY 131
HOLT, MERRELL ODOUS, Jr. 131
Holt, Merrell Odous, Sr. 131
HOLT, MOUNTIE ARK. 132
Holt, Myrtle 99
Holt, Nancy Elizabeth 13
Holt, Norris L. 131
Holt, Paul 131
Holt, Perlee Parthanie (Davis) 130
HOLT, PRESTON M. 132
Holt, Price 131
HOLT, PRICE C. 132
HOLT, RALPH E. 132
Holt, Robert 132
Holt, Robert Hightower 132
HOLT, ROBERT HIGHTOWER, Jr. 132
HOLT, ROY BURL 132
Holt, Sarah Emmajean 131
Holt, Sussie Halford 130
HOLT, TAYLOR 132
Holt, Teresa Darlene 132
HOLT, THURMAN C. 132
Holt, Timothy Wayne 130
HOLT, VERNIE L. 132
Holt, Virgil Garfield 130
HOLT, WILLIAM D. 133
HOLT, WILLIAM HAROLD 13
Holt, William Robert 132
HOLT, WILLIS 133
Hood, Ola Mae Staggs 23
Hooper, Sue Beckham 39
Horn, Louise Woods 263
Horton, Bessie 238
Horton, Catherine 133
HORTON, CLARENCE W. 133
Horton, Clyde C. 266
HORTON, EDWARD 133
Horton, Edward 133
HORTON, FRED ALOMZO 13
Horton, Gail Chambers 62
Horton, Genevive 213
Horton, Guinda 151
Horton, Herman H. 266
HORTON, HOMER F. 133
Horton, Isaac 239
HORTON, JAMES PAULK 133
Horton, James Paulk 134
HORTON, JOHN E. 133
Horton, John E. 133
Horton, Josie Evelyn Reeves 133
Horton, Leona 133, 134
Horton, Leona Barnett 37
Horton, Marie 177
Horton, Melissa (Southerland) 134
Horton, Melissa Southerland 13
Horton, Mollie 202
Horton, Nell 58
Horton, Paul 13
HORTON, RAYMOND E. 133
Horton, Sallie 133
Horton, Sarah Jane King 133
HORTON, WAYNE E. 133
HORTON, WILLIAM H. 134
Horton, William H. 133
Hoskins, Cassie Elizabeth Turnbo 134
Hoskins, Robert Holland (Bobby) 134
HOSKINS, TOM FRANK 134
House, Floyd 11
House, William Glynn 11
Houser, Karen 143
HOUSTON, LEAROY 134
Howard, Beverly 172
HOWE, EDDIE 134
Howe, Elsie 134
HOWE, NORMAN 134
Howe, Norman 134
Howe, Roxie (Rose) 134
Howell, A. B. 161
HOWELL, ALBERT B. 134
Howell, Helen 253
Howell, James 135
HOWELL, JESSIE ELLIS "BABE" 135
Howell, Johnny H. 266
Howell, Kathleen 161
Howell, Loyd 135
Howell, Myrtle 256, 257
Huckaba, Anne 103
Hudson, Catherine 76
Hudson, Veda Pebble 56
Huff, Nancy L. 242
HUGHES, BOYD, Pfc. 135

Hughes, Sidney T 135
Hughes, Vada 134
Hunt, Arnold 135
Hunt, Arnold Ray 135
Hunt, Cindy 135
HUNT, CRAIG VAUGHN 135
Hunt, David 135
Hunt, David Leon 135
Hunt, Davis 266
Hunt, Edsel 135
HUNT, FREEMAN S. 135
Hunt, Helen Harveston 135
Hunt, Irene 135
Hunt, Jack R., Jr. 135
HUNT, JACK ROCKY 135
Hunt, Janice Gail 133
Hunt, Josie (Pounders) 135
Hunt, Kathy Elizabeth 135
Hunt, Linda Gayle 99
Hunt, Mary Louise 135
Hunt, Stinson 135
Hunt, Zada Nutt 135
Hurley, Ermadine 96
HURST, JAMES STERLING 135
Hurst, James N. 136
Hurst, Rachel 136
Hurst, Robert Welch 266
HURST, WADE B. 136

I
INMAN, JOHN WILLIAM 136
Inman, Lockie Bell 99
Inman, Mary Ann 247
Inman, Nannie Lee 209
INMAN, SAMUEL CURTIS 136
Inman, Stella (Holder) 136
Inman, Stella Holder 136
Innanen, Naoma Hollis 128
IRWIN, CHARLIE BURT 136
Irwin, Cora 136
Irwin, Hannah (Martin) 136
IRWIN, LEIGHTON BUNDRANT 136
Irwin, Robert Smith "Bobby" 136
Irwin, Sherman 136
IRWIN, WALTER G. 136

J
Jackson, Artue 187
Jackson, Charlie 137
JACKSON, CHESTER 136
JACKSON, CLARENCE BAKER, "C.B." 136
Jackson, Deborah 105
Jackson, Dorris Lee 49
Jackson, Goldie (Baker) 137
Jackson, Ima 99
JACKSON IRA L. 137
Jackson, Iva Mae 109
Jackson, James O. 266
Jackson, Janice Creecy 74
Jackson, Lawrence 13, 137
JACKSON, LAWRENCE A. 13
Jackson, Lester 136
Jackson, Lizzie 136
Jackson, Lola J. 13, 137
Jackson, Mary Ann 137
Jackson, Mary M. Thompson 248
JACKSON, REX 137
JACKSON, SAMUEL 137
Jackson, Sandy 174
JACKSON, ULIS MOORE 137
James, Amanda Meredith 170
James D. Pratt, III 124
James, Dennis 170
James, Lester Ayers 34
Jarrett, Georgie 159
Jaske, Connie 137
JASKE, DONALD LEE 137
Jaske, Donald Lynn 138
Jaske, Emma Bennet 137
Jenkins, Gordon 6
Jeter, Carl 138
Jeter, Dola Jean 60
Jeter, Edd 32
Jeter, Ermin (Benham) 138, 139
Jeter, Ida 200
Jeter, Ida Prater 138
Jeter, John Edd 266
Jeter, John Lawrence 138
Jeter, John Thomas 138
Jeter, Mary Jane (Molly) Pevahouse 138, 200
Jeter, Mollie Jane (Pevahouse) 138
Jeter, Neal T. 138
JETER, PAUL 138

Jeter, Ralph 139
Jeter, Robert Harris 138
JETER, ROBERT WOODROW 138
Jeter, Vernon 193
JETER, VERNON J. 138
JETER, W.J. 138
JETER, WILLIAM H., "Bill" 139
Jobe, Will T. 266
Johnson, Auburn Diane Kelly 143
Johnson, Bettie Collins 252
Johnson, Bonnie 170
Johnson, C. B. 139
Johnson, Carolyn 49
JOHNSON, DALTON D. 139
Johnson, David 106
Johnson, Ellis 111
Johnson, Elsie 257
Johnson, Ira 266
JOHNSON, JAMES EDWIN 139
Johnson, James G. 266
Johnson, Kelly 139
JOHNSON, KERRY PAULK 139
Johnson, Lena (Reeves) 139
Johnson, Mahulda Sims 107, 108
Johnson, Marvin Hoyt 40
Johnson, Millie 261, 262
Johnson, Nona Louise 252
Johnson, Pebble 165
Johnson, Teresa 187
JOHNSON, THOMAS I. 139
Johnson, Wanda Elaine Berry 42
Jones, Ann 173
Jones, Arland 141, 142
Jones, Betty Jo (Helton) 140
Jones, Bobby 139
Jones, Darrin Blake 140
Jones, Emma Frances 136
Jones, Flora (Copeland) 140
Jones, Flora Copeland 42
JONES, GEORGE D. 139
Jones, George Donald 6
Jones, Gertie Staggs 23
Jones, Hughie (Flippo) 139
JONES, J.P. 140
Jones, Jimmie Juanita 211
Jones, Joe 234
JONES, JOSEPH WARREN 140
Jones, Linda 94
Jones, Lynell B. 48
Jones, Margaret Ann 170
Jones, Mary Elsie 139
Jones, Michael Roy 140
Jones, Moses 253
Jones, Pearl 140
JONES, RALPH B. 140
JONES, ROY LEE 140
Jones, Thomas F. 266
JONES, WILLIAM A. 140
Jones, Willie Lee 140
JORDAN, JAMES H. 140
Jordon, Antha Kea 141
Judith Y., Ferrell 265

K
Kannegieter, Joann 177
Kea, Ruth 141
KEA, WILLIAM RAYMO 141
Keanam, Clara 145
Keene, Alma 48
Keeton, Carter 141
KEETON, CLIFFORD 141
Keeton, Clifford 143
Keeton, Ella Ann (Brewer) 141, 142
Keeton, George 141
KEETON, GEORGE Z., Jr. 141
Keeton, Grace 91
KEETON, HENRY CLAYBORN 141
KEETON, HERBERT 141
KEETON, JAMES A. 141
Keeton, John Isaac 141
KEETON, JOHN I. 141
Keeton, Lady Ruth 213
Keeton, Louise 231
Keeton, Maggie Lou Ellen 42
Keeton, Magnolia 102
Keeton, Martha Naomi 188
KEETON, NELSON 142
Keeton, Pearl (Risner) 231
Keeton, Ruby Irwin 235
Keeton, William Alfred 141
KEETON, WILLIAM CARTER 142
KELLEY, ALBERT FRANKLIN 142
KELLEY, ALFRED STANLEY 142
Kelley, Carolyn Sue Eaton 90
KELLEY, CLYDE TALMAGE 143
Kelley, Dee 185

Kelley, DeWitt 143
Kelley, Dick 144
Kelley, Dorothy Frances 196
Kelley, Eddie Gerald 142
KELLEY, EMERL H. 143
Kelley, Ennie 189
Kelley, Eula 239
Kelley, Gary Gene 142
KELLEY, GUY HUGHES 143
Kelley, Hazel Holt 213
Kelley, Horace, Jr. 266
Kelley, Inez Isabell (Montgomery) 143
KELLEY, J.D. 143
Kelley, James Clamon 266
Kelley, Joanie 153
Kelley, Junaga 30
Kelley, Lessie (Copeland) 142, 143
Kelley, Lillie 184
Kelley, Louise 156
KELLEY, NOLAN 143
Kelley, Nona Bell 156
Kelley, Nona Belle (Kelley) 143
Kelley, Peggy 214
KELLEY, RALPH J. 144
KELLEY, RAY F. 144
Kelley, Ray F. 266
Kelley, Roy 143
Kelley, Thomas S,. Jr. 266
Kelley, Tina 187
KELLEY, VIRGIL 144
KELLEY, WILLIE V. 144
KELLY, BILL 143
Kelly, C. F. 13
Kelly, Deborah 111
Kelly, Emily Carrington 13
Kelly, Erma Lee 215
Kelly, Frank 145
KELLY, FREELAN 13
Kelly, Hattie Mae Hollis 144
Kelly, Jerry 144
Kelly, Jonell 29
Kelly, Lorene 55
KELLY, MACK 143
Kelly, Mamie (Gallaher) 143
KELLY, ORBIE OKLEY 145
KELLY, PAUL H. 143
Kelly, Pauline (Rich) 212
Kelly, Theo 17
KELLY, THOMAS S. 144
Kelly, Woodrow 143
KELSO, JOE BETHEL 145
KELSO, JOHN D. 13
Kelso, Lazelle 77
Kelso, Mabel (Brewer) 145
Kelso, Mable Minnie Belle Clayton 13
Kelso, Maxine 34
Kennedy, Nellie Louise Maples 156
Kephart, Alice Izora Spann 145
Kephart, Cindy 240
Kephart, Dicie 14, 158
KEPHART, JAMES RICHARD 145
Kephart, Jimmy 145
Kerns, Mavis 265
Kerr, Ila 67
KEYMON, CLAUDE A. 145
Kiddy, Elsie Adams 9
Kiddy, Frank 145
KIDDY, J.C. 145
Kiddy, Martha Vina Conway 145
Kilburn, Albert N. 266
KILBURN, CECIL 13
Kilburn, Clemon K. 266
Kilburn, Cora E. 111
KILBURN, EDGAR BERRY 145
Kilburn, Emma (Berry) 145
Kilburn, Janie Copeland 111
Kilburn, John Dewey 266
Kilburn, Kathryn 37
Kilburn, Leota 145
KILBURN, MARVIN 145
Kilburn, Nell 218
KILBURN, NIEL 145
Kilburn, Nina B. Dixon 11
Kilburn, Ollie 74, 75
Kilburn, Pauline 253, 254
Kilburn, Roy 266
Kilburn, Ruby 82
KILBURN, WAFORD H. 145
KILBURN, WALTER N. 145
KILPATRICK, OLLIE K. 146
Kimbrell, A.J. 266

FAMILY NOTES

FAMILY NOTES

FAMILY NOTES

FAMILY NOTES

FAMILY NOTES

Warren H. Smith spent 15 months aboard the USS LST 284. It was an ammunition supply ship during the Okinawa Campaign and the Philippines. After the war ended the ship was used to transport occupation troops to Yokohoma, Japan.